FREE Test Taking Tips DVD Offer

To help us better serve you, we have developed a Test Taking Tips DVD that we would like to give you for FREE. **This DVD covers world-class test taking tips that you can use to be even more successful when you are taking your test.**

All that we ask is that you email us your feedback about your study guide. Please let us know what you thought about it – whether that is good, bad or indifferent.

To get your **FREE Test Taking Tips DVD**, email freedvd@studyguideteam.com with "FREE DVD" in the subject line and the following information in the body of the email:

a. The title of your study guide.

b. Your product rating on a scale of 1-5, with 5 being the highest rating.

c. Your feedback about the study guide. What did you think of it?

d. Your full name and shipping address to send your free DVD.

If you have any questions or concerns, please don't hesitate to contact us at freedvd@studyguideteam.com.

Thanks again!

Officer Candidate Tests

Officer Candidate Guide for Your Officer Candidate School Test (AFOQT, ASVAB, ASTB, OAR)

Test Prep Books Military Exam Team

Table of Contents

Quick Overview

As you draw closer to taking your exam, effective preparation becomes more and more important. Thankfully, you have this study guide to help you get ready. Use this guide to help keep your studying on track and refer to it often.

This study guide contains several key sections that will help you be successful on your exam. The guide contains tips for what you should do the night before and the day of the test. Also included are test-taking tips. Knowing the right information is not always enough. Many well-prepared test takers struggle with exams. These tips will help equip you to accurately read, assess, and answer test questions.

A large part of the guide is devoted to showing you what content to expect on the exam and to helping you better understand that content. In this guide are practice test questions so that you can see how well you have grasped the content. Then, answer explanations are provided so that you can understand why you missed certain questions.

Don't try to cram the night before you take your exam. This is not a wise strategy for a few reasons. First, your retention of the information will be low. Your time would be better used by reviewing information you already know rather than trying to learn a lot of new information. Second, you will likely become stressed as you try to gain a large amount of knowledge in a short amount of time. Third, you will be depriving yourself of sleep. So be sure to go to bed at a reasonable time the night before. Being well-rested helps you focus and remain calm.

Be sure to eat a substantial breakfast the morning of the exam. If you are taking the exam in the afternoon, be sure to have a good lunch as well. Being hungry is distracting and can make it difficult to focus. You have hopefully spent lots of time preparing for the exam. Don't let an empty stomach get in the way of success!

When travelling to the testing center, leave earlier than needed. That way, you have a buffer in case you experience any delays. This will help you remain calm and will keep you from missing your appointment time at the testing center.

Be sure to pace yourself during the exam. Don't try to rush through the exam. There is no need to risk performing poorly on the exam just so you can leave the testing center early. Allow yourself to use all of the allotted time if needed.

Remain positive while taking the exam even if you feel like you are performing poorly. Thinking about the content you should have mastered will not help you perform better on the exam.

Once the exam is complete, take some time to relax. Even if you feel that you need to take the exam again, you will be well served by some down time before you begin studying again. It's often easier to convince yourself to study if you know that it will come with a reward!

Test-Taking Strategies

1. Predicting the Answer

When you feel confident in your preparation for a multiple-choice test, try predicting the answer before reading the answer choices. This is especially useful on questions that test objective factual knowledge. By predicting the answer before reading the available choices, you eliminate the possibility that you will be distracted or led astray by an incorrect answer choice. You will feel more confident in your selection if you read the question, predict the answer, and then find your prediction among the answer choices. After using this strategy, be sure to still read all of the answer choices carefully and completely. If you feel unprepared, you should not attempt to predict the answers. This would be a waste of time and an opportunity for your mind to wander in the wrong direction.

2. Reading the Whole Question

Too often, test takers scan a multiple-choice question, recognize a few familiar words, and immediately jump to the answer choices. Test authors are aware of this common impatience, and they will sometimes prey upon it. For instance, a test author might subtly turn the question into a negative, or he or she might redirect the focus of the question right at the end. The only way to avoid falling into these traps is to read the entirety of the question carefully before reading the answer choices.

3. Looking for Wrong Answers

Long and complicated multiple-choice questions can be intimidating. One way to simplify a difficult multiple-choice question is to eliminate all of the answer choices that are clearly wrong. In most sets of answers, there will be at least one selection that can be dismissed right away. If the test is administered on paper, the test taker could draw a line through it to indicate that it may be ignored; otherwise, the test taker will have to perform this operation mentally or on scratch paper. In either case, once the obviously incorrect answers have been eliminated, the remaining choices may be considered. Sometimes identifying the clearly wrong answers will give the test taker some information about the correct answer. For instance, if one of the remaining answer choices is a direct opposite of one of the eliminated answer choices, it may well be the correct answer. The opposite of obviously wrong is obviously right! Of course, this is not always the case. Some answers are obviously incorrect simply because they are irrelevant to the question being asked. Still, identifying and eliminating some incorrect answer choices is a good way to simplify a multiple-choice question.

4. Don't Overanalyze

Anxious test takers often overanalyze questions. When you are nervous, your brain will often run wild, causing you to make associations and discover clues that don't actually exist. If you feel that this may be a problem for you, do whatever you can to slow down during the test. Try taking a deep breath or counting to ten. As you read and consider the question, restrict yourself to the particular words used by the author. Avoid thought tangents about what the author *really* meant, or what he or she was *trying* to say. The only things that matter on a multiple-choice test are the words that are actually in the question. You must avoid reading too much into a multiple-choice question, or supposing that the writer meant something other than what he or she wrote.

5. No Need for Panic

It is wise to learn as many strategies as possible before taking a multiple-choice test, but it is likely that you will come across a few questions for which you simply don't know the answer. In this situation, avoid panicking. Because most multiple-choice tests include dozens of questions, the relative value of a single wrong answer is small. As much as possible, you should compartmentalize each question on a multiple-choice test. In other words, you should not allow your feelings about one question to affect your success on the others. When you find a question that you either don't understand or don't know how to answer, just take a deep breath and do your best. Read the entire question slowly and carefully. Try rephrasing the question a couple of different ways. Then, read all of the answer choices carefully. After eliminating obviously wrong answers, make a selection and move on to the next question.

6. Confusing Answer Choices

When working on a difficult multiple-choice question, there may be a tendency to focus on the answer choices that are the easiest to understand. Many people, whether consciously or not, gravitate to the answer choices that require the least concentration, knowledge, and memory. This is a mistake. When you come across an answer choice that is confusing, you should give it extra attention. A question might be confusing because you do not know the subject matter to which it refers. If this is the case, don't eliminate the answer before you have affirmatively settled on another. When you come across an answer choice of this type, set it aside as you look at the remaining choices. If you can confidently assert that one of the other choices is correct, you can leave the confusing answer aside. Otherwise, you will need to take a moment to try to better understand the confusing answer choice. Rephrasing is one way to tease out the sense of a confusing answer choice.

7. Your First Instinct

Many people struggle with multiple-choice tests because they overthink the questions. If you have studied sufficiently for the test, you should be prepared to trust your first instinct once you have carefully and completely read the question and all of the answer choices. There is a great deal of research suggesting that the mind can come to the correct conclusion very quickly once it has obtained all of the relevant information. At times, it may seem to you as if your intuition is working faster even than your reasoning mind. This may in fact be true. The knowledge you obtain while studying may be retrieved from your subconscious before you have a chance to work out the associations that support it. Verify your instinct by working out the reasons that it should be trusted.

8. Key Words

Many test takers struggle with multiple-choice questions because they have poor reading comprehension skills. Quickly reading and understanding a multiple-choice question requires a mixture of skill and experience. To help with this, try jotting down a few key words and phrases on a piece of scrap paper. Doing this concentrates the process of reading and forces the mind to weigh the relative importance of the question's parts. In selecting words and phrases to write down, the test taker thinks about the question more deeply and carefully. This is especially true for multiple-choice questions that are preceded by a long prompt.

9. Subtle Negatives

One of the oldest tricks in the multiple-choice test writer's book is to subtly reverse the meaning of a question with a word like *not* or *except*. If you are not paying attention to each word in the question, you can easily be led astray by this trick. For instance, a common question format is, "Which of the following is...?" Obviously, if the question instead is, "Which of the following is not...?," then the answer will be quite different. Even worse, the test makers are aware of the potential for this mistake and will include one answer choice that would be correct if the question were not negated or reversed. A test taker who misses the reversal will find what he or she believes to be a correct answer and will be so confident that he or she will fail to reread the question and discover the original error. The only way to avoid this is to practice a wide variety of multiple-choice questions and to pay close attention to each and every word.

10. Reading Every Answer Choice

It may seem obvious, but you should always read every one of the answer choices! Too many test takers fall into the habit of scanning the question and assuming that they understand the question because they recognize a few key words. From there, they pick the first answer choice that answers the question they believe they have read. Test takers who read all of the answer choices might discover that one of the latter answer choices is actually *more* correct. Moreover, reading all of the answer choices can remind you of facts related to the question that can help you arrive at the correct answer. Sometimes, a misstatement or incorrect detail in one of the latter answer choices will trigger your memory of the subject and will enable you to find the right answer. Failing to read all of the answer choices is like not reading all of the items on a restaurant menu: you might miss out on the perfect choice.

11. Spot the Hedges

One of the keys to success on multiple-choice tests is paying close attention to every word. This is never truer than with words like almost, most, some, and sometimes. These words are called "hedges" because they indicate that a statement is not totally true or not true in every place and time. An absolute statement will contain no hedges, but in many subjects, the answers are not always straightforward or absolute. There are always exceptions to the rules in these subjects. For this reason, you should favor those multiple-choice questions that contain hedging language. The presence of qualifying words indicates that the author is taking special care with his or her words, which is certainly important when composing the right answer. After all, there are many ways to be wrong, but there is only one way to be right! For this reason, it is wise to avoid answers that are absolute when taking a multiple-choice test. An absolute answer is one that says things are either all one way or all another. They often include words like *every*, *always*, *best*, and *never*. If you are taking a multiple-choice test in a subject that doesn't lend itself to absolute answers, be on your guard if you see any of these words.

12. Long Answers

In many subject areas, the answers are not simple. As already mentioned, the right answer often requires hedges. Another common feature of the answers to a complex or subjective question are qualifying clauses, which are groups of words that subtly modify the meaning of the sentence. If the question or answer choice describes a rule to which there are exceptions or the subject matter is complicated, ambiguous, or confusing, the correct answer will require many words in order to be expressed clearly and accurately. In essence, you should not be deterred by answer choices that seem excessively long. Oftentimes, the author of the text will not be able to write the correct answer without offering some qualifications and modifications. Your job is to read the answer choices thoroughly and completely and to select the one that most accurately and precisely answers the question.

13. Restating to Understand

Sometimes, a question on a multiple-choice test is difficult not because of what it asks but because of how it is written. If this is the case, restate the question or answer choice in different words. This process serves a couple of important purposes. First, it forces you to concentrate on the core of the question. In order to rephrase the question accurately, you have to understand it well. Rephrasing the question will concentrate your mind on the key words and ideas. Second, it will present the information to your mind in a fresh way. This process may trigger your memory and render some useful scrap of information picked up while studying.

14. True Statements

Sometimes an answer choice will be true in itself, but it does not answer the question. This is one of the main reasons why it is essential to read the question carefully and completely before proceeding to the answer choices. Too often, test takers skip ahead to the answer choices and look for true statements. Having found one of these, they are content to select it without reference to the question above. Obviously, this provides an easy way for test makers to play tricks. The savvy test taker will always read the entire question before turning to the answer choices. Then, having settled on a correct answer choice, he or she will refer to the original question and ensure that the selected answer is relevant. The mistake of choosing a correct-but-irrelevant answer choice is especially common on questions related to specific pieces of objective knowledge. A prepared test taker will have a wealth of factual knowledge at his or her disposal, and should not be careless in its application.

15. No Patterns

One of the more dangerous ideas that circulates about multiple-choice tests is that the correct answers tend to fall into patterns. These erroneous ideas range from a belief that B and C are the most common right answers, to the idea that an unprepared test-taker should answer "A-B-A-C-A-D-A-B-A." It cannot be emphasized enough that pattern-seeking of this type is exactly the WRONG way to approach a multiple-choice test. To begin with, it is highly unlikely that the test maker will plot the correct answers according to some predetermined pattern. The questions are scrambled and delivered in a random order. Furthermore, even if the test maker was following a pattern in the assignation of correct answers, there is no reason why the test taker would know which pattern he or she was using. Any attempt to discern a pattern in the answer choices is a waste of time and a distraction from the real work of taking the test. A test taker would be much better served by extra preparation before the test than by reliance on a pattern in the answers.

FREE DVD OFFER

Don't forget that doing well on your exam includes both understanding the test content and understanding how to use what you know to do well on the test. We offer a completely FREE Test Taking Tips DVD that covers world class test taking tips that you can use to be even more successful when you are taking your test.

All that we ask is that you email us your feedback about your study guide. To get your **FREE Test Taking Tips DVD**, email freedvd@studyguideteam.com with "FREE DVD" in the subject line and the following information in the body of the email:

- The title of your study guide.
- Your product rating on a scale of 1-5, with 5 being the highest rating.
- Your feedback about the study guide. What did you think of it?
- Your full name and shipping address to send your free DVD.

Becoming an Officer

Military Officer Occupations

There are a variety of officer occupations in the military, each of which involves being a manager, leader, and problem solver. Different branches of the military offer certain career opportunities, so not all of the following occupations are necessarily applicable to every branch. However, in general, the following non-exhaustive list provides a brief description of common military officer occupations to aspire to:

- Combat Specialty Officers: These leaders direct and supervise missions and military operations. They lead their units in combat and may specialize in certain weapon systems or types of missions or units.

- Engineering, Science, and Technical Officers: This broad class of officers includes those who may work in a wide variety of roles. Such officers may help design and build structures like bridges and living quarters near to the area of combat, design and develop weapon systems or aircrafts used in combat, or create computer programs to aid in communication or location services.

- Healthcare Officers: These officers must hold the same certifications and perform the same duties as civilian doctors, nurses, physical therapists, dentists, psychologists, etc., but in some sort of military context.

- Legal Services Officers: These attorneys and paralegals work in the Judge Advocate General's (JAG) Corps on any legal needs of the military at large or military personnel.

- Executive, Managerial, and Administrative Officers: These leaders manage departments and staff, coordinate activities and budgets, implement policies, etc. to help military operations run smoothly and efficiently.

- Protective Service Officers: Military police officers focus on law enforcement and ensuring safety, while emergency management officers help plan, prevent, and respond to emergencies.

- Human Resource Officers: These officers help recruit, train, and manage all service members.

- Media and Public Affairs Officers: Connecting the public and military is the primary goal of these officers, who develop advertising and recruiting materials, training videos, and news reports for the civilian population, etc.

- Transportation Officers: These officers operate modes of transportation to ensure the safe, accurate, and prompt arrival and delivery of personnel, supplies, equipment, etc.

- Support Services Officers: Military personnel and their families have their various physical, emotional, and social needs met largely in part to these officers. Roles involve preparing meals, offering worship services, and assisting communication with loved ones, among others.

Military Rank

The hierarchical structure of military ranks helps define authority, roles and responsibilities, and establishes the chain of command. Each of the five branches of the U. S. military—the Army, the Navy, the Air Force, the Marines, and the Coast Guard—have their own established U.S. Military Ranks. Rank is also associated with pay grade.

The armed services have three basic groups: enlisted personnel, warrant officers, and commissioned officers. Enlisted personnel have the least authority, while commissioned officers have the most. Warrant officers typically have technical experience that allows them to be promoted over enlisted personnel by "warrant." Government documentation "commissions" commission officers to their leadership posts.

The following chart delineates the names of the different ranks in each branch of the U.S. Military:

Enlisted Personnel				
Pay Grade	**Army**	**Navy/Coast Guard**	**Air Force**	**Marine Corps**
E-1	Private	Seaman Recruit	Recruit	Private
E-2	Private First Class	Seaman Apprentice	Airman	Private First Class
E-3	Private	Seaman	Airman First Class	Lance Corporal
E-4	Corporal	Petty Officer, Third Class	Senior Airman	Corporal
E-5	Sergeant	Petty Officer, Second Class	Staff Sergeant	Sergeant
E-6	Staff Sergeant	Petty Officer, First Class	Technical Sergeant	Staff Sergeant
E-7	Sergeant First Class	Chief Petty Officer	Master Sergeant	Gunnery Sergeant
E-8	Master Sergeant	Senior Chief Petty Officer	Senior Master Sergeant	Master Gunnery Sergeant or Sergeant Major
E-9	Sergeant Major of the Army	Master Chief Petty Officer	Sergeant Major of the Marine Corps	Sergeant Major
Warrant Officers				
Pay Grade	**Army**	**Navy/Coast Guard**	**Air Force**	**Marine Corps**
W-1	Warrant Officer	None at this level	No Warrant Officers	Warrant Officer
W-2	Chief Warrant Officer Two	Chief Warrant Officer Two		Chief Warrant Officer Two
W-3	Chief Warrant Officer Three	Chief Warrant Officer Three		Chief Warrant Officer Three
W-4	Chief Warrant Officer Four	Chief Warrant Officer Four		Chief Warrant Officer Four
W-5	Master Chief Warrant Officer Five	Master Chief Warrant Officer Five		Master Chief Warrant Officer Five
Commissioned Officers				
Pay Grade	**Army**	**Navy/Coast Guard**	**Air Force**	**Marine Corps**
O-1	Second Lieutenant	Ensign	Second Lieutenant	Second Lieutenant
O-2	First Lieutenant	Lieutenant Junior Grade	First Lieutenant	First Lieutenant
O-3	Captain	Lieutenant	Captain	Captain
O-4	Major	Lieutenant Commander	Major	Major
O-5	Lieutenant Colonel	Commander	Lieutenant Colonel	Lieutenant Colonel
O-6	Colonel	Captain	Colonel	Colonel
O-7	Brigadier General	Rear Admiral (Lower Half)	Brigadier General	Brigadier General
O-8	Major General	Rear Admiral (Upper Half)	Major General	Major General
O-9	Lieutenant General	Vice Admiral	Lieutenant General	Lieutenant General
O-10	General	Admiral	General	General

How to Become an Officer

There are four basic paths to becoming an officer in one of the branches of the U. S. Military.

1. Attend and graduate from a military academy

2. Graduate from college where a concurrent Reserve Officers' Training Corps (ROTC) program was also completed

3. Satisfy all training in Officer Candidate School or Officer Training School

4. Obtain a direct commission to become an officer (This route is rare; only about 10% of officers obtained their position via direct appointment.)

Additionally, candidates must meet age requirements, be U.S. citizens, have obtained a four-year college degree, have no criminal record, and pass designated physical health and fitness requirements.

What to Expect for Each Test Type

ASVAB

Function of the Armed Services Vocational Aptitude Battery (ASVAB) Test

The **Armed Services Vocational Aptitude Battery** (ASVAB) measures developed abilities and helps to predict academic and occupational success in the military. The ASVAB was first introduced in 1968, and over 40 million individuals have taken the exam since its introduction. Once a military applicant takes the ASVAB, military personnel use the score to assign an appropriate job in the military. The test also assesses whether an applicant is qualified to enlist in the military.

The test can be administered via paper and pencil (P&P-ASVAB) or via computer. The computer version – known as the CAT-ASVAB – was implemented after twenty years of evaluation and research. This was the first adaptive test battery to be administered as a high-stakes test. An adaptive test means the test adapts to an individual's ability level based on the answer to the previous question. A harder question will be administered if the previous question was answered correctly, and an easier question will be administered if the previous question was answered incorrectly. There is no entrance exam for the ASVAB.

Test Administration

The ASVAB is administered annually and is taken by over one million military applicants. Most applicants are high school or post-secondary students. Testing is conducted at a Military Entrance Processing Station (MEPS), or if this site is not available, the ASVAB can be taken at a satellite location known as a Military Entrance Test (MET) site. The ASVAB is computer-based at the MEPS but paper-based at most MET sites. The computer-based test takes about one-and-a-half hours for an average person to complete, while the paper and pencil version takes about three hours to complete. If a test taker needs to retake the test, he or she must wait at least a month before retaking. After the second retest, a test taker must wait six months to retest again. Scores may be used for enlistment purposes for up to two years after the date of testing.

Test Format

The paper and pencil test has 225 questions that are broken up into sections with time limits equaling a total of 149 minutes. There is no penalty for guessing on the P&P- ASVAB, and in fact, unanswered questions are marked as incorrect. Because the CAT-ASVAB is an adaptive test, the time limit may vary, but the computer-based version is usually shorter than the paper and pencil administration. There is a penalty for incorrect answers on the CAT-ASVAB, so it is ideal for a tester to answer as much as they can without randomly guessing. Unanswered questions also receive a penalty, which is found by calculating the score that would have been achieved had the test taker randomly guessed on unanswered questions. Both versions of the exam contain four domains: Verbal, Math, Science and Technical, and Spatial. Below is a chart listing the content tests on the ASVAB and the domain they fall under.

The chart lists the tests in the order in which they appear on the exam.

Test	Domain
General Science (GS)	Science/Technical
Arithmetic Reasoning (AR)	Math
Word Knowledge (WK)	Verbal
Paragraph Comprehension (PC)	Verbal
Mathematics Knowledge (MK)	Math
Electronics Information (EI)	Science/Technical
Auto Information (AI)	Science/Technical
Shop Information (SI)	Science/Technical
Mechanical Comprehension (MC)	Science/Technical
Assembling Objects (AO)	Spatial

Scoring

ASVAB scores are determined using an **Item Response Theory** (IRT) model, which tailors the test questions to the ability level of the test taker and enables scores to be presented on the same scale, even though there is variability in the questions attempted by each test taker. The model behind IRT is called 3PL, which represents difficulty, discrimination, and guessing, and is based on the likelihood that a test taker will provide a correct response for each specific question, given his or her performance on other questions. After the final ability estimate is measured, a standardized score is reached. Test takers receive standardized subtest scores and a composite score for the entire exam. Through a process called equating, scores on both versions of the ASVAB can be statistically and fairly compared.

AFOQT

Function of the Test

The Air Force Officer Qualifying Test (AFOQT) is a standardized test given by the United States Air Force. The exam evaluates a test taker's verbal and mathematical proficiency as well as his or her aptitude in certain areas specific to those necessary for potential Air Force career paths. The test is used as part of the admissions process to officer training programs, such as Officer Training School ROTC. Within the Air Force, it is used to qualify candidates for Pilot, Combat Systems Officer (CSO), and Air Battle Manager (ABM) training and is part of the Pilot Candidate Selection Method (PCSM) score. The AFOQT is required for all students receiving a scholarship as well as those in the Professional Officer Course (POC).

The test is taken nationwide by current and potential members of the United States Air Force. In the Air Force ROTC program, it is taken by sophomores prior to field training in the summer after their sophomore year.

Test Administration

The AFOQT is offered through Air Force ROTC programs on college campuses and through military recruiters at Military Entrance Processing facilities. There is no cost to take the AFOQT; instead, individuals wishing to take the test must make arrangements through their ROTC program, recruiter, or commanding officer, as appropriate. Rules for retesting depend on the purpose or program for which the test taker is seeking to use the results, but some ROTC programs permit one retest, with the most recent score counting.

Test Format

The test lasts almost five hours, including three hours and 36.5 minutes of testing time and a little over an hour in breaks and test administration time. It is taken with pencil and scored by machine. It consists of twelve subtests: verbal analogies, arithmetic reasoning, word knowledge, math knowledge, reading comprehension, situational judgment, self-description inventory, physical science, table reading, instrument comprehension, block counting, and aviation information. All of the subtests have multiple-choice questions with four or five possible answers.

Scoring

Scores are based only on the number of correct answers. There is no penalty for guessing incorrectly, aside from the missed opportunity to achieve points from a greater number of correct answers. Scores from the various subtests are used to calculate composite scores, which are reported to the test taker and the Air Force. For example, the "Pilot" composite score is based on the results from the arithmetic reasoning, math knowledge, instrument comprehension, table reading, and aviation information subtests. Other composite scores include Academic Aptitude, Verbal, Quantitative, Combat Systems Officer, Air Battle Manager, and Situational Judgment. Test takers receive a percentile score from 1 to 99 in each of the five composite categories.

There is no set passing score. Instead, the scores needed vary widely depending on the intended job or program for which a test taker is seeking entry. For instance, a candidate seeking to become an officer may be able to do so with a relatively low percentile score (in other words, by only outperforming a small number of other test takers), while an officer seeking to become a pilot may need much higher scores overall, particularly in the Pilot composite category.

Recent/Future Developments

The AFOQT is revised from time to time, based on feedback from the general needs of the Air Force and its officer training programs. The current subtests and content therein are in AFOQT Form T, which took effect on August 1, 2014.

A summary of the number of items on and the time allowed (not including administration time or breaks) for each subtest is as follows:

Subtest	**Items**	**Time (min.)**
Verbal Analogies	25	8
Arithmetic Reasoning	25	29
Word Knowledge	25	5
Math Knowledge	25	22
Reading Comprehension	25	38
Situational Judgment	50	35
Self-Description Inventory	240	45
Physical Science	20	10
Table Reading	40	7
Instrument Comprehension	25	5
Block Counting	30	4.5
Aviation Information	20	8
TOTAL	**550**	**3 hours, 36.5 minutes**

ASTB & OAR

Function of the Test

The Aviation Standard Test Battery (**ASTB** or **ASTB-E**) is used by the United States Navy to select individuals for flight and pilot officer training programs offered by the U.S. Coast Guard, the U.S. Marine Corps, and the U.S. Navy. Any persons interested in becoming an officer are required to take the ASTB so that it can be determined whether or not they meet the standards for officer training or other military occupations.

The Officer Aptitude Rating (**OAR**) test is used by the United States Navy to determine how individuals will perform while in Naval Officer Candidate School (non-aviation). **This test is part of the larger ASTB**, which is used to select individuals for flight and pilot officer training programs offered by the U.S. Coast Guard, the U.S. Marine Corps, and the U.S. Navy.

Sections of the ASTB Test – CAT version				
Subject Areas	**Number of Questions (Multiple-Choice)**	**Time Limit**		
Math Skills Test	30	40 minutes		**O**
Reading Comprehension Test	20	30 minutes		**A**
Mechanical Comprehension Test	30	15 minutes	**A**	**R**
Aviation and Nautical Information Test	20 to 30	Unspecified	**S T**	
Naval Aviation Trait Facet Inventory	88	Unspecified	**B**	
Performance Based Measures Battery	20 to 30	Unspecified		
Biographical Inventory with Response Validation	20 to 30	Unspecified		
Total	**228 to 258**	**2 to 3 ¼ hours**		

ASTB

Test Administration

Candidates can take the ASTB test at over 250 registered locations all over the world. These locations include naval officer recruiting stations, military institutes, and NROTC units at major universities. Officer recruiters schedule test dates for exam candidates once examinees prove that they meet the qualifications. The exam is offered as a computer adaptive (online) exam.

Test takers who wish to retake the ASTB test must wait thirty days after the first test in order to do so, and ninety days before their third retake. They can only take the ASTB test a total of three times over the course of their lifetime. It is important to note that a test taker's most recent test score replaces any score on record, even if he or she received a higher score on a previous test. Test scores are valid for life.

Test Format

The Math Skills Test (MST) utilizes both word problems and equations to test examinees on high school math concepts dealing with algebra and geometry. The Reading Comprehension Test (RCT) incorporates text passages to test examinees on their ability to extract information and make conclusions from what they have read. Finally, the Mechanical Comprehension Test (MCT) is comprised of questions involving high school physics concepts, as well as simple machine mechanics.

The Aviation and Nautical Information Test (ANIT) tests one's knowledge over aviation history, aviation-related concepts, and nautical terminology and procedures. The Naval Aviation Trait Facet Inventory (NATFI) consists of 44 statement pairs that ask how you think, feel, and act regarding different situations. This subsection measures personality traits. The Performance Based Measures Battery (PBM) is a subtest that measures manual dexterity, processing speed, spatial orientation, and divided-attention-driven assessments. Finally, the Biographical Inventory with Response Verification (BI-RV) asks you to identify your experience and background related to aviation.

The following table contains a breakdown of the number of questions and the corresponding time limits for the sections on the ASTB.

Note that individuals can take the Biographical Inventory with Response Validation (BI-RV) portion of the exam on any web-based computer outside of the testing area.

Scoring

The first three sections of the exam use a 1-point increment rating scored between a 20 and 80. For the rest of the categories (besides the BI-RV), the Standard Nine (or stanine) system is used. The Academic Qualifications Rating (AQR), the Pilot Flight Aptitude Rating (PFAR), and the Flight Officer Aptitude Rating (FOFAR) are all scores based on the ASTB subtests using the stanine system. Scores will be shown immediately once all 7 subtests are finished. Blind guessing on the ASTB is discouraged, as these points will count against you.

OAR

The Math Skills Test (MST) utilizes both word problems and equations to test examinees on high school math concepts dealing with algebra and geometry. The Reading Comprehension Test (RCT) incorporates text passages to test examinees on their ability to extract information and make conclusions from what they have read. Finally, the Mechanical Comprehension Test (MCT) is comprised of questions involving high school physics concepts, as well simple machine mechanics.

The following table contains a breakdown of the number of questions and the corresponding time limits for the various subtests of the OAR exam for examinees that choose to take the paper version:

For test takers who choose to take the online version of the exam, the test can ninety minutes to two hours to complete. There are between twenty and thirty multiple-choice questions within each subtest.

Individuals taking the paper version of the OAR test are penalized for leaving questions unanswered, and thus, they are best served by making educated guesses when time is running out or the answer is unknown. In contrast, individuals who are taking the online version of the OAR will not benefit from guessing. It is more important to work accurately and quickly on this version of the exam.

The OAR test is scored on a scale of 20-80 in increments of one point, and a minimum score of 35 is needed to pass. However, most individuals who take the exam receive scores between 40-60. There has been no real difference in passing rates between test takers who take the paper version of the exam versus those who take the online version.

Test takers who attempt the online version of the exam receive their scores immediately upon completion of the exam, while those who take the paper version must send their completed tests into Navy Medicine Operational Training Center (NMOTC) to be scored.

Word Knowledge

Word Origins and Roots

A **word** is a group of letters joined to form a single meaning. On their own, letters represent single sounds, but when placed together in a certain order, letters represent a specific image in the reader's mind in a way that provides meaning. Words can be *nouns, verbs, adjectives,* and *adverbs*, among others. Words also represent a verb tense of *past, present*, or *future*. Words allow for effective communication for commerce, social progress, technical advances, and much more. Simply put, words allow people to understand one another and create meaning in a complex world.

Throughout history, English words were shaped by other cultures and languages, such as Greek, Latin, French, Spanish, German, and others. They were borne from inventions, discoveries, and literary works, such as plays or science fiction novels. Others formed by shortening words that were already in existence. Some words evolved from the use of acronyms, such as *radar* (Radio Detection and Ranging) and *scuba* (Self-Contained Underwater Breathing Apparatus). The English language will continue to evolve as the needs and values of its speakers evolve.

Studying a foreign language in school, particularly Latin or any of the romance languages (Latin-influenced), is advantageous. The roots of much of the English vocabulary have Latin origins; these roots can bind many words together and often allude to a shared definition. Here's an example:

Fervent

a. Lame
b. Joyful
c. Thorough
d. Boiling
e. Cunning

Fervent descends from the Latin word, *fervere*, which means "to boil or glow" and figuratively means "impassioned." The Latin root present in the word is *ferv*, which is what gives fervent the definition: showing great warmth and spirit or spirited, hot, glowing. This provides a link to boiling (D) just by root word association, but there's more to analyze. Among the other choices, none relate to fervent. The word lame (A) means crippled, disabled, weak, or inadequate. None of these match with fervent. While being fervent can reflect joy, joyful (B) directly describes "a great state of happiness," while fervent is simply expressing the idea of having very strong feelings—not necessarily joy. Thorough (C) means complete, perfect, painstaking, or with mastery; while something can be done thoroughly and fervently, none of these words match fervent as closely as boiling does. Cunning (E) means crafty, deceiving or with ingenuity or dexterity. Doing something fervently does not necessarily mean it is done with dexterity. Not only does boiling connect in a linguistic way, but also in the way it is used in our language. While boiling can express being physically hot and undergoing a change, boiling is also used to reflect emotional states. People say they are "boiling over" when in heighted emotional states; "boiling mad" is another expression. Boiling, like fervent, also embodies a sense of heightened intensity. This makes boiling the best choice!

The Latin root *ferv* is seen in other words such as fervor, fervid, and even ferment. All of them are connected to and can be described by boil or glow, whether it is in a physical sense or in a metaphorical one. Such a pattern can be seen in other word sets! Here's another example:

Gracious

a. Fruitful
b. Angry
c. Grateful
d. Understood
e. Overheard

This one's a little easier; the answer is grateful (C), because both words mean thankful! Even if the meanings of both words are known, there's a connection found by looking at the beginnings of both words: *gra/grat*. Once again, there is a root that stretches back to classical language. Both terms come from the Latin, *gratis*, which literally means "thanks."

Understanding root words can help identify the meaning in a lot of word choices, and help the test taker grasp the nature of the given word. Many dictionaries, both in book form and online, offer information on the origins of words, which highlight these roots. When studying for the test, it helps to look up an unfamiliar word for its definition and then check to see if it has a root that can be connected to any of the other terms.

Word Formation

How do English words form? They can be single root words, such as *love, hate, boy*, or *girl*. A **root word** is a word in its most basic form that carries a clear and distinct meaning. Complex English words combine affixes with root words. Some words have no root word, but are instead formed by combining various affixes, such as reject: *re-* is defined as repeating an action or actions, and *-ject* means throw or thrown. Therefore, **reject** is defined as the act of being thrown back. Words consisting of affixes alone are not the norm. Most words consist of either root words on their own or with the addition of affixes. To **affix** is to attach to something. Therefore, affixes in linguistic study are groups of letters that attach themselves to the beginning, middle, or end of root words to enhance or alter the word's meaning. Affixes added to verbs can change the word's tense, and affixes added to nouns can change the word's part of speech from noun to adjective, verb, or adverb.

<u>Roots and Root Words</u>
Words that exist on their own, without affixes, are root words. **Root words** are words written in their most basic form, and they carry a clear and distinct meaning. Consider the word *safe*. The root word, *safe*, acts as both a noun and adjective, and stands on its own, carrying a clear and distinct meaning.

The root of a word however, is not necessarily a part of the word that can stand on its own, although it does carry meaning. Since many English words come from Latin and Greek roots, it's helpful to have a general understanding of roots. Here is a list of common Greek and Latin roots used in the English language:

Root	**Definition**	**Example**
ami	love	amiable
ethno	race	ethnological
infra	beneath or below	infrastructure
lun	moon	Lunar
max	greatest	maximum
pent/penta	five	pentagon
sol	sun	Solar
vac	empty	Vacant

Affixes

Affixes are groups of letters that when added to the beginning or ending of root words, or are attachments within a root or root word itself, can:

- Intensify the word's meaning
- Create a new meaning
- Somewhat alter the existing meaning
- Change the verb tense
- Change the part of speech

There are three types of affixes: prefixes, suffixes, and infixes.

Prefixes

Prefixes are groups of letters attached to the beginning of a root word. *Pre-* refers to coming before, and *fix* refers to attaching to something. Consider the example of the root word *freeze*:

- Freeze: verb – to change from a liquid to solid by lowering the temperature to a freezing state.
- *Anti*freeze: noun – a liquid substance that prevents freezing when added to water, as in a vehicle's radiator.

By adding the prefix *anti-* to the root word *freeze*, the part of speech changed from verb to noun, and completely altered the meaning. *Anti-* as a prefix always creates the opposite in meaning, or the word's antonym.

By having a basic understanding of how prefixes work and what their functions are in a word's meaning, English speakers strengthen their fluency. Here is a list of some common prefixes in the English language, accompanied by their meanings:

Prefix	Definition	Example
ante-	before	antecedent
ex-	out/from	expel
inter-	between/among	intergalactic
multi-	much/many	multitude
post-	after	postscript
sub-	under	submarine
trans-	move between/across	transport
uni-	single/one	universe

Suffixes

Suffixes are groups of letters attached to the ending of a root or root word. Like prefixes, suffixes can:

- Intensify the word's meaning
- Create a new meaning
- Somewhat alter the existing meaning
- Change the verb tense
- Change the part of speech

Consider the example of the root word *fish* when suffixes are added:

- Fish: noun – a cold-blooded animal that lives completely in water and possesses fins and gills.
- Fishing: noun – I love the sport of fishing.
- Fishing: verb – Are you fishing today?

With the addition of the suffix *-ing*, the meaning of root word *fish* is altered, as is the part of speech.

A verb tense shift is made with the addition of the suffix *-ed*:

- Jump: present tense of to jump as in "I jump."
- Jumped: past tense of to jump as in "I jumped."
- Climb: present tense of to climb as in "We climb."
- Climbed: past tense of to climb as in "We climbed."

Here are a few common suffixes in the English language, along with their meanings:

Suffix	Meaning	Example
-ed	past tense	cooked
-ing	materials, present action	clothing
-ly	in a specific manner	lovely
-ness	a state or quality	brightness
-ment	action	enjoyment
-script	to write	transcript
-ee	receiver/performer	nominee
-ation/-ion	action or process	obligation

Infixes

Infixes are letters that attach themselves inside the root or root words. They generally appear in the middle of the word and are rare in the English language. Easily recognizable infixes include parent*s*-in-law, passer*s*-by, or cup*s*ful. Notice the *-s* is added inside the root word, making the word plural.

Special types of infixes, called **tmesis** words, are made from inserting an existing word into the middle of another word or between a compound word, creating a new word. Tmesis words are generally used in casual dialogue and slang speech. They add emphasis to the word's overall meaning and to evoke emotion on the part of the reader. Examples are fan-*bloody*-tastic and un-*freaking*-believable.

Tmesis words have been in existence since Shakespeare's time, as in this phrase from *Romeo and Juliet*, "...he is some *other*where." Shakespeare split up the compound word *somewhere* by inserting the word *other* between the two root words.

Compound Words

A **compound word** is created with the combination of two shorter words. To be a true compound word, two shorter words are combined, and the meaning of the longer word retains the meaning of the two shorter words. Compound words enhance the overall meaning, giving a broader description. There are three types of compound words: closed, hyphenated, and open.

<u>Closed Compound Words</u>

There was a time when closed compound words were not considered legitimate words. Over time and with continued, persistent use, they found a place in the English language. A **closed compound word** refers to a word that shows no separation between the two shorter words from which it is composed. Some examples of closed compound words are:

Closed Compound Word	**Individual Words**	**Meaning**
bookshelf	book/shelf	a shelf that holds books
doorstop	door/stop	an object to hold a door open
bedroom	bed/room	a room where one sleeps
bathroom	bath/room	a room where one bathes
backyard	back/yard	a yard in the back of a building
nightstand	night/stand	a small table beside one's bed

Hyphenated Compound Words

As the name suggests, **hyphenated compound words** include a hyphen that separates the two shorter words within the longer word. Some examples of hyphenated compound words are:

Hyphenated Compound Words	**Individual Words**	**Meaning**
self-service	self/serve	the act of serving one's self
color-blind	color/blind	incapable of accurately distinguishing colors
check-in	check/in	the act of registering as in attendance
year-round	year/round	any affair that takes place throughout the year
toll-free	toll/free	no application of toll/no charge
sugar-coated	sugar/coated	anything sweetened or coated with sugar

Open Compound Words

Open compound words appear as individual words but are they dependent on their partners to form the complete meaning of the compound word. Individually, the words may have meanings that are different than that of the pair together (the open compound word). For example, in *real estate, real* and *estate* have their own meanings that are different than the unique meaning of the compound word. Open compound words are separated from each other by a single space and do not require a hyphen. Some examples of open compound words are:

Open Compound Words	**Meaning**
polka dot	a repeated circular dot that forms a pattern
sleeping bag	a special bag used to sleep in (usually when camping)
solar system	the collection of planets that orbit around the sun
tape recorder	magnetic tape used to record sound
middle class	social group that is considered above lower class and below upper class
family room	a specific room for relaxation and entertainment used by all family members

Parts of Speech

Also referred to as word classes, **parts of speech** refer to the various categories in which words are placed. Words can be placed in any one or a combination of the following categories:

- Nouns
- Determiners
- Pronouns
- Verbs
- Adjectives
- Adverbs
- Prepositions
- Conjunctions

Understanding the various parts of speech used in the English language helps readers to better understand the written language.

Nouns

A **noun** is defined as any word that represents a person, place, animal, object, or idea. Nouns can identify a person's title or name, a person's gender, and a person's nationality, such as banker, commander-in-chief, female, male, or an American.

With animals, nouns identify the kingdom, phylum, class, etc. For example: the animal is an *elephant*, the phylum is *chordata*, and the class is *mammalia*. It should be noted that the words *animal, phylum,* and *class* in the previous sentence are also nouns.

When identifying places, nouns refer to a physical location, a general vicinity, or the proper name of a city, state, or country. Some examples include the *desert*, the *East*, *Phoenix*, the *bathroom*, *Arizona*, an *office*, or the *United States*.

There are eight types of nouns: common, proper, countable, uncountable, concrete, abstract, compound, and collective.

Common nouns are used in general terms, without specific identification. Examples include *girl, boy, country*, or *school*. Proper nouns refer to the specific proper name given to people, places, animals, or entities, such as *Melissa, Martin, Italy*, or *Harvard*.

Countable nouns can be counted: *one car, two cars*, or *three cars*. **Uncountable nouns** cannot be counted, such as *air, liquid*, or *gas*.

To be abstract is to exist, but only in thought or as an idea. An **abstract noun** cannot be physically touched, seen, smelled, heard, or tasted. Examples include *chivalry, day, fear, thought, truth, friendship*, or *freedom*.

To be **concrete** is to be seen, touched, tasted, heard, and/or smelled. Examples include *pie, snow, tree, bird, desk, hair*, or *dog*.

A **compound noun** is another term for an open compound word. Any noun that is written as two nouns that together form a specific meaning is a compound noun. For example, *post office, ice cream*, or *swimming pool*.

A **collective noun** refers to groups or collection of things that together form the whole. The members of the group are often people or individuals. Examples include *orchestra, squad, committee*, or the *majority*. It should be noted that the nouns in these examples are singular, but the word itself refers to a group containing more than one individual.

<u>Determiners</u>

Determiners modify a noun and usually refer to something specific. Determiners fall into one of four categories: *articles, demonstratives, quantifiers*, or *possessive determiners*.

Articles can be both definite articles, as in *the*, and indefinite as in *a, an, some,* or *any*:

> *The* man with *the* red hat.
>
> *A* flower growing in *the* yard.
>
> *Any* person who visits *the* store.

There are four different types of demonstratives: *this, that, these,* and *those*.

True demonstrative words will not directly precede the noun of the sentence but will be the noun. Some examples:

> *This* is the one.
>
> *That* is the place.
>
> *Those* are the files.

Once a demonstrative is placed directly in front of the noun, it becomes a demonstrative pronoun:

This one is perfect.

That place is lovely.

Those boys are annoying.

Quantifiers proceed nouns to give additional information to the noun about how much or how many is referred to. They can be used with countable and uncountable nouns:

She bought *plenty* of apples.

Few visitors came.

I got a *little* change.

Possessive determiners, sometimes called **possessive adjectives**, indicate possession. They are the possessive forms of personal pronouns, such as *for my, your, hers, his, its, their*, or *our*:

That is *my* car.

Tom rode *his* bike today.

Those papers are *hers.*

Pronouns

Pronouns are words that stand in place of nouns. There are three different types of pronouns: **subjective pronouns** (*I, you, he, she, it, we, they*), **objective pronouns** (*me, you, him, her it, us, them*), and **possessive pronouns** (*mine, yours, his, hers, ours, theirs*).

Note that some words are found in more than one pronoun category. See examples and clarifications are below:

You are going to the movies.

In the previous sentence, *you* is a subjective pronoun; it is the subject of the sentence and is performing the action.

I threw the ball to *you.*

Here, *you* is an objective pronoun; it is receiving the action and is the object of the sentence.

We saw *her* at the movies.

Her is an objective pronoun; it is receiving the action and is the object of the sentence.

The house across the street from the park is *hers.*

In this example, *hers* is a possessive pronoun; it shows possession of the house.

Verbs

Verbs are words in a sentence that show action or state. A sentence must contain a subject and a verb. Without a verb, a sentence is incomplete. Verbs may be in the present, past, or future tenses. To form auxiliary, or helping, verbs are required for some tenses in the future and in the past.

> I *see* the neighbors across the street.

See is an action.

> We *were eating* at the picnic.

Eating is the main action, and the verb *were* is the past tense of the verb *to be*, and is the helping or auxiliary verb that places the sentence in the past tense.

> You *will turn* 20 years of age next month.

Turn is the main verb, but *will* is the helping verb to show future tense of the verb *to be*.

Adjectives

Adjectives are a special group of words used to modify or describe a noun. Adjectives provide more information about the noun they modify. For example:

> The boy went to school. (There is no adjective.)

Rewriting the sentence, adding an adjective to further describe the boy and/or the school yields:

> The *young* boy went to the *old* school. (The adjective *young* describes the boy, and the adjective *old* describes the school.)

Adverbs

Adverb can play one of two roles: to modify the adjective or to modify the verb. For example:

> The young boy went to the old school.

We can further describe the adjectives *young* and *old* with adverbs placed directly in front of the adjectives:

> The *very* young boy went to the *very* old school. (The adverb *very* further describes the adjectives *young* and *old*.)

Other examples of using adverbs to further describe verbs include:

> The boy *slowly* went to school.

> The boy *happily* went to school.

The adverbs *slowly* and *happily* further modify the verbs.

Prepositions

Prepositions are special words that generally precede a noun. Prepositions clarify the relationship between the subject and another word or element in the sentence. They clarify time, place, and the positioning of the subjects and objects in a sentence. Common prepositions in the English language include: *near, far, under, over, on, in, between, beside, of, at, until, behind, across, after, before, for, from, to, by*, and *with*.

Conjunctions

Conjunctions are a group of unique words that connect clauses or sentences. They also work to coordinate words in the same clause. It is important to choose an appropriate conjunction based on the meaning of the sentence. Consider these sentences:

I really like the flowers, *however* the smell is atrocious.

I really like the flowers, *besides* the smell is atrocious.

The conjunctions *however* and *besides* act as conjunctions, connecting the two ideas: *I really like the flowers,* and, *the smell is atrocious*. In the second sentence, the conjunction *besides* makes no sense and would confuse the reader. Conjunctions must be chosen that clearly state the intended message without ambiguity.

Some conjunctions introduce an opposing opinion, thought, or fact. They can also reinforce an opinion, introduce an explanation, reinforce cause and effect, or indicate time. For example:

Opposition: She wishes to go to the movies, *but* she doesn't have the money.

Cause and effect: The professor became ill, *so* the class was postponed.

Time: They visited Europe *before* winter came.

Each conjunction serves a specific purpose in uniting two separate ideas. Below are common conjunctions in the English language:

Opposition	Cause & Effect	Reinforcement	Time	Explanation
however	Therefore	besides	afterward	for example
nevertheless	as a result	anyway	before	in other words
but	because of this	after all	firstly	for instance
although	Consequently	furthermore	next	such as

Synonyms

Synonyms are words that mean the same or nearly the same thing in the same language. When presented with several words and asked to choose the synonym, more than one word may be similar to the original. However, one word is generally the strongest match. Synonyms should always share the same part of speech. For instance, *shy* and *timid* are both adjectives and hold similar meanings. The words *shy* and *loner* are similar, but *shy* is an adjective while *loner* is a noun. Another way to test for the best synonym is to reread the sentence with each possible word and determine which one makes the most sense. Consider the following sentence: *He will love you forever.*

Now consider the words: *adore, sweet, kind*, and *nice*. They seem similar, but when used in the following applications with the initial sentence, not all of them are synonyms for *love.*

> He will *adore* you forever.
>
> He will *sweet* you forever.
>
> He will *kind* you forever.
>
> He will *nice* you forever.

In the first sentence, the word *love* is used as a verb. The best synonym from the list that shares the same part of speech is *adore*. *Adore* is a verb, and when substituted in the sentence, it is the only substitution that makes grammatical and semantic sense.

Synonyms can be found for nouns, adjectives, verbs, adverbs, and prepositions. Here are some examples of synonyms from different parts of speech:

- **Nouns**: clothes, wardrobe, attire, apparel
- **Verbs**: run, sprint, dash
- **Adjectives**: fast, quick, rapid, swift
- **Adverbs**: slowly, nonchalantly, leisurely
- **Prepositions**: near, proximal, neighboring, close

Here are several more examples of synonyms in the English language:

Word	Synonym	Meaning
smart	intelligent	having or showing a high level of intelligence
exact	specific	clearly identified
almost	nearly	not quite but very close
to annoy	to bother	to irritate
to answer	to reply	to form a written or verbal response
building	edifice	a structure that stands on its own with a roof and four walls
business	commerce	the act of purchasing, negotiating, trading, and selling
defective	faulty	when a device is not working or not working well

Antonyms

Antonyms are words that are complete opposites. As with synonyms, there may be several words that represent the opposite meaning of the word in question. When choosing an antonym, one should choose the word that represents as close to the exact opposite in meaning as the given word, and ensure it shares the same part of speech. Here are some examples of antonyms:

- Nouns: predator – prey
- Verbs: love – hate
- Adjectives: good – bad
- Adverbs: slowly – swiftly
- Prepositions: above – below

Homonyms

Homonyms are words that sound alike but carry different meanings. There are two different types of homonyms: homophones and homographs.

Homophones

Homophones are words that sound alike but carry different meanings and spellings. In the English language, there are several examples of homophones. Consider the following list:

Word	Meaning	Homophone	Meaning
I'll	I + will	aisle	a specific lane between seats
allowed	past tense of the verb, 'to allow'	aloud	to utter a sound out loud
eye	a part of the body used for seeing	I	first-person singular
ate	the past tense of the verb, 'to eat'	eight	the number preceding the number nine
peace	the opposite of war	piece	part of a whole
seas	large bodies of natural water	seize	to take ahold of/to capture

Homographs

Homographs are words that share the same spelling but carry different meanings and different pronunciations. Consider the following list:

Word	**Meaning**	**Homograph**	**Meaning**
bass	fish	bass	musical instrument
bow	a weapon used to fire arrows	bow	to bend
Polish	of or from Poland	polish	a type of shine (n); to shine (v)
desert	dry, arid land	desert	to abandon

Tips for Synonyms Word Knowledge Questions

This portion of the exam is specifically constructed to test vocabulary skills and the ability to discern the best answer that matches the provided word. Unlike verbal analogies, which will test communication skills and problem-solving abilities along with vocabulary, these questions chiefly test vocabulary knowledge by asking test takers to select the best synonym for the provided word. While logic and reasoning come into play in this section, they are not as heavily emphasized as with the analogies. A prior knowledge of what the words mean is helpful in order to answer correctly. If the meaning of the words is unknown, that's fine, too. Strategies should be used to rule out false answers and choose the correct ones. Here are some study strategies for an optimum performance.

Format of the Questions

The synonyms questions are very simple in construction. Instead of a comparison of words with an underlying connection, like the verbal analogies, the prompt is just a single word. There are no special directions, alternate meanings, or analogies to work with. The objective is to analyze the given word and then choose the answer that means the same thing or is closest in meaning to the given word. Note the example below:

Blustery

a. Hard
b. Windy
c. Mythical
d. Stoney
e. Corresponding

The synonyms questions on the Word Knowledge portion of the exam will usually appear like the above sample. This is generally the standard layout throughout other exams, so some test takers may already be familiar with the structure. The principle remains the same. At the top of the section, clear directions will be given to choose the answer that most precisely defines the given word. In this case, the answer is windy (B), since windy and blustery are synonymous.

Preparation

In truth, there is no set way to prepare for this portion of the exam that will guarantee a perfect score. This is simply because the words used on the test are unpredictable. There is no set list provided to study from. The definition of the provided word needs to be determined on the spot. This sounds challenging, but there are still ways to prepare mentally for the test. It may help to expand your vocabulary a little each day. Several resources are available, in books and online, that collect words and definitions that tend to show up frequently on standardized tests. Knowledge of words can increase the strength of your vocabulary.

Mindset is key. The meanings of challenging words can often be found by relying on the past experiences of the test taker to help deduce the correct answer. How? Well, test takers have been talking their entire lives—knowing words and how words work. It helps to have a positive mindset from the start. It's unlikely that all definitions of words will be known immediately, but the answer can still be found. There are aspects of words that are recognizable to help discern the correct answers and eliminate the incorrect ones. Here are some of the factors that contribute to word meanings!

Pay Attention to Prefixes

As mentioned, the prefix of a word can actually reveal a lot about its definition. Many prefixes are actually Greco-Roman roots as well—but these are more familiar and a lot easier to recognize! When encountering any unfamiliar words, try looking at prefixes to discern the definition and then compare that with the choices. The prefix should be determined to help find the word's meaning. Here's an example question:

Premeditate

a. Sporadic
b. Calculated
c. Interfere
d. Determined
e. Noble

With premeditate, there's the common prefix *pre*. This helps draw connections to other words like prepare or preassemble. *Pre* refers to "before, already being, or having already." Meditate means to think or plan. Premeditate means to think or plan beforehand with intent. Therefore, a term that deals with thinking or planning should be found, but also something done in preparation. Among the word choices, noble (E) and determined (D) are both adjectives with no hint of being related to something done before or in preparation. These choices are incorrect. Sporadic (A) refers to events happening in irregular patterns, so this is quite the opposite of premeditated. Interfere (C) also has nothing to do with premeditate; it goes counter to premeditate in a way similar to sporadic. Calculated (B), however, fits! A route and the cost of starting a plan can be calculated. Calculated refers to acting with a full awareness of consequences, so inherently planning is involved. In fact, calculated is synonymous with premeditated, thus making it the correct choice. Just by paying attention to a prefix, the doors to a meaning can open to help easily figure out which word would be the best choice. Here's another example.

Regain

a. Erupt
b. Ponder
c. Seek
d. Recoup
e. Enamor

Recoup (D) is the right answer. The prefix *re* often appears in front of words to give them the meaning of occurring again. Regain means to repossess something that was lost. Recoup, which also has the *re* prefix, literally means to regain. In this example, both the given word and the answer share the *re* prefix, which makes the pair easy to connect. However, don't rely only on prefixes to choose an answer. Make sure to analyze all options before marking an answer. Going through the other words in this sample, none of them come close to meaning regain except recoup. After checking to make sure that recoup is the best matching word, then mark it!

Positive Versus Negative Sounding Words

Another tool for the mental toolbox is simply distinguishing whether a word has a positive or negative connotation. Like electrical wires, words carry energy; they are crafted to draw certain attention and to have certain strength to them. Words can be described as positive and uplifting (a stronger word) or they can be negative and scathing (a stronger word). Sometimes they are neutral—having no particular connotation. Distinguishing how a word is supposed to be interpreted will not only help learn its definition, but also draw parallels with word choices. While it's true that words must usually be taken in the context of how they are used, word definitions have inherent meanings as well. So, they have a distinct vibe to pick up on. Here is an example.

Excellent

a. Fair
b. Optimum
c. Reasonable
d. Negative
e. Agitation

As you know, excellent is a very positive word. It refers to something being better than good, above average. In this sample, negative (D) and agitation (E) can easily be eliminated because these are both words with negative connotations. Reasonable (C) is more or less a neutral word: it's not bad but it doesn't communicate the higher quality that excellent represents. It's just, well, reasonable. This leaves the possible choices of fair (A) and optimum (B). Or does it? Fair *is* a positive word; it's used to describe things that are good, even beautiful. But in the modern context, fair is defined as good, but somewhat average or just decent: "You did a fairly good job." or, "That was fair." On the other hand, optimum is positive and is a stronger word. Optimum describes the most favorable outcome. This makes optimum the best word choice that matches excellent in both strength and connotation. Not only are the two words positive, but they also express the same level of positivity! Here's another example:

Repulse

a. Draw
b. Encumber
c. Force
d. Disgust
e. Magnify

Repulse sounds negative when said. It is commonly used in the context of something being repulsive, disgusting, or that which is distasteful. It's also defined as an attack that drives people away. This tells us we need a word that also carries a negative meaning. Magnify (E) is positive, while draw (A) and force (C) are both neutral. Encumber (B) and disgust (D) are negative. Disgust is a stronger negative than encumber. Of all the words given, only disgust directly defines a feeling of distaste and aversion that is synonymous with repulse, and matches in both negativity and strength.

Parts of Speech

It is often very helpful to determine the part of speech of a word. Is it an adjective, adverb, noun, or verb, etc.? Often the correct answer will also be the same part of speech as the given word. Isolate the part of speech and what it describes and look for an answer choice that also describes the same part of speech. For example: if the given word is an adverb describing an action word, then look for another adverb describing an action word.

Swiftly

a. Fast
b. Quietly
c. Angry
d. Sudden
e. Quickly

Swiftly is an adverb that describes the speed of an action. Angry (C), fast (A), and sudden (D) can be eliminated because they are not adverbs, and quietly (B) can be eliminated because it does not describe speed. This leaves quickly (E), which is the correct answer. Fast and sudden may throw off some test takers because they both describe speed, but quickly matches more closely because it is an adverb, and swiftly is also an adverb.

Place the Word in a Sentence

Often it is easier to discern the meaning of a word if it is used in a sentence. If the given word can be used in a sentence, then try replacing it with some of the answer choices to see which words seem to make sense in the same sentence. Here's an example.

Remarkable

a. Often
b. Capable
c. Outstanding
d. Shining
e. Excluding

A sentence can be formed with the word remarkable. "My grade point average is remarkable." None of the examples make sense when replacing the word remarkable in the sentence other than the word outstanding (C), so outstanding is the obvious answer. Shining (D) is also a word with a positive connotation, but outstanding fits better in the sentence.

Pick the Closest Answer

As the answer choices are reviewed, two scenarios might stand out. An exact definition match might not be found for the given word among the choices, or there are several word choices that can be considered synonymous to the given word. This is intentionally done to test the ability to draw parallels between the words to produce an answer that best fits the prompt word. Again, the closest fitting word will be the answer. Even when facing these two circumstances, finding the one word that fits best is the proper strategy. Here's an example:

Insubordination

a. Cooperative
b. Disciplined
c. Rebel
d. Contagious
e. Wild

Insubordination refers to a defiance or utter refusal of authority. Looking over the choices, none of these terms provide definite matches to insubordination like insolence, mutiny, or misconduct would. This is fine; the answer doesn't have to be a perfect synonym. The choices don't reflect insubordination in any way, except rebel (C). After all, when rebel is used as a verb, it means to act against authority. It's also used as a noun: someone who goes against authority. Therefore, rebel is the best choice.

As with the verbal analogies section, being a detective is a good course to take. Two or even three choices might be encountered that could be the answer. However, the answer that most perfectly fits the prompt word's meaning is the best answer. Choices should be narrowed one word at a time. The least-connected word should be eliminated first and then proceed until one word is left that is the closest synonym.

Sequence

a. List
b. Range
c. Series
d. Replicate
e. Iconic

A sequence reflects a particular order in which events or objects follow. The two closest options are list (A) and series (C). Both involve grouping things together, but which fits better? Consider each word more carefully. A list is comprised of items that fit in the same category, but that's really it. A list doesn't have to follow any particular order; it's just a list. On the other hand, a series is defined by events happening in a set order. A series relies on sequence, and a sequence can be described as a series. Thus, series is the correct answer!

Types of Sentences

The English language constructs three types of sentences: simple sentences, compound sentences, and complex sentences.

Simple Sentences

Simple sentences are sentences where one idea or action is expressed. Simple sentences can contain conjunctions joining two or more subjects, or two or more objects. However, a simple sentence contains only one verb or action. There is only one complete thought.

In the examples below, there is a simple subject, a simple object, and one verb.

I see the cat.

The cat sees me.

The cat doesn't see me.

In contrast, the use of the conjunction *and* creates a compound subject:

Mary and I see the cat.

Mary and I acts as the compound subject—two or more subjects connected by the conjunction *and*. This is still a simple sentence that has one compound subject, one verb, and one complete thought.

Below is an example of a simple sentence with a compound object joined by the conjunction *and.*

The cat sees *Mary and me.*

While there is a compound object, it is a simple sentence because it contains one subject, one verb, and forms a complete thought.

<u>Compound Sentences</u>

Compound sentences are sentences where two **independent clauses** (complete sentences that can stand on their own) are connected with a coordinating conjunction. For example:

I see the cat, *and* the cat sees me.

I see the cat, *but* the cat doesn't see me.

The independent clauses can be broken apart and written independently as simple sentences:

I see the cat. The cat sees me.

I see the cat. The cat doesn't see me.

<u>Complex Sentences</u>

When a sentence contains one independent clause and one or more dependent clauses, it is a **complex sentence**. A dependent clause is a part of a sentence that will not make semantic or grammatical sense on its own. For example:

I watched the cat while it slept.

The first part of sentence has an independent clause that can stand on its own: *I watched the cat.*

The second part of the sentence contains a dependent clause that, on its own, is nonsensical and an incomplete sentence: *While it slept.*

It is important to choose the appropriate conjunction for a given sentence, as each conjunction holds a distinct meaning. Consider the following sentences and determine which makes more sense:

> I watched the cat *although* it slept.
>
> I watched the cat *while* it slept.

The second sentence employs the more appropriate conjunction. The use of the conjunction, *although*, in the first sentence, creates a nonsensical sentence.

Denotation and Connotation

Connotation is when an author chooses words or phrases that invoke ideas or feelings other than their literal meaning. An example of the use of connotation is the word *cheap*, which suggests something is poor in value or negatively describes a person as reluctant to spend money. When something or someone is described this way, the reader is more inclined to have a particular image or feeling about it or him/her. Thus, connotation can be a very effective language tool in creating emotion and swaying opinion. However, connotations are sometimes hard to pin down because varying emotions can be associated with a word. Generally, though, connotative meanings tend to be fairly consistent within a specific cultural group.

Denotation refers to words or phrases that mean exactly what they say. It is helpful when a writer wants to present hard facts or vocabulary terms with which readers may be unfamiliar. Some examples of denotation are the words *inexpensive* and *frugal*. *Inexpensive* refers to the cost of something, not its value, and *frugal* indicates that a person is conscientiously watching his or her spending. These terms do not elicit the same emotions that *cheap* does.

Authors sometimes choose to use both, but what they choose and when they use it is what critical readers need to differentiate. One method isn't inherently better than the other; however, one may create a better effect, depending upon an author's intent. If, for example, an author's purpose is to inform, to instruct, and to familiarize readers with a difficult subject, his or her use of connotation may be helpful. However, it may also undermine credibility and confuse readers. An author who wants to create a credible, scholarly effect in his or her text would most likely use denotation, which emphasizes literal, factual meaning and examples.

Verbal Analogies

Verbal analogies test the candidate's ability to analyze words carefully and find connections in definition and/or context. The test taker must compare a selected set of words with answer choices and select the ideal word to complete the sequence. While these exercises draw upon knowledge of vocabulary, this is also a test of critical thinking and reasoning abilities. Naturally, such skills are critical for building a career. Mastering verbal analogies will help people think objectively, discern critical details, and communicate more efficiently.

Usually, two words are paired together that provide a frame for the analogy, and then there is a third word that must be found as a match in kind. It may help to think of it like this: A is to B as C is to D. Examine the breakdown below:

Apple (A) is to fruit (B) as carrot (C) is to vegetable (D).

As shown above, there are four words: the first three are given and the fourth word is the answer that must be found. The first two words are given to set up the kind of analogy that is to be replicated for the next pair. We see that apple is paired with fruit. In the first pair, a specific food item, apple, is paired to the food group category it corresponds with, which is fruit. When presented with the third word in the verbal analogy, carrot, a word must be found that best matches carrot in the way that fruit matched with apple. Again, carrot is a specific food item, so a match should be found with the appropriate food group: vegetable! Here's a sample prompt:

Morbid is to dead as jovial is to

a. Hate.
b. Fear.
c. Disgust.
d. Happiness.
e. Desperation.

As with the apple and carrot example, here is an analogy frame in the first two words: morbid and dead. Again, this will dictate how the next two words will correlate with one another. The definition of morbid is: described as or appealing to an abnormal and unhealthy interest in disturbing and unpleasant subjects, particularly death and disease. In other words, morbid can mean ghastly or death-like, which is why the word dead is paired with it. Dead relates to morbid because it describes morbid. With this in mind, jovial becomes the focus. Jovial means joyful, so out of all the choices given, the closest answer describing jovial is happiness (D).

Prompts on the exam will be structured just like the one above. "A is to B as C is to ?" will be given, where the answer completes the second pair. Or sometimes, "A is to B as ? is to ?" is given, where the second pair of words must be found that replicate the relationship between the first pair. The only things that will change are the words and the relationships between the words provided.

While it wouldn't hurt in test preparation to expand vocabulary, verbal analogies are all about delving into the words themselves and finding the right connection, the right word that will fit an analogy. People preparing for the test shouldn't think of themselves as human dictionaries, but rather as detectives. Remember, how the first two words are connected dictates the second pair. From there, picking the correct answer or simply eliminating the ones that aren't correct is the best strategy.

Just like a detective, a test taker needs to carefully examine the first two words of the analogy for clues. It's good to get in the habit of asking the questions: What do the two words have in common? What makes them related or unrelated? How can a similar relationship be replicated with the word I'm given and the answer choices? Here's another example:

Pillage is to steal as meander is to

a. Stroll.
b. Burgle.
c. Cascade.
d. Accelerate.
e. Pinnacle.

Why is pillage paired with steal? In this example, pillage and steal are synonymous: they both refer to the act of stealing. This means that the answer is a word that means the same as meander, which is stroll. In this case, the defining relationship in the whole analogy was a similar definition.

What if test takers don't know what stroll or meander mean, though? Using logic helps to eliminate choices and pick the correct answer. Looking closer into the contexts of the words pillage and steal, here are a few facts: these are things that humans do; and while they are actions, these are not necessarily types of movement. Again, pick a word that will not only match the given word, but best completes the relationship. It wouldn't make sense that burgle (B) would be the correct choice because meander doesn't have anything to do with stealing, so that eliminates burgle. Pinnacle (E) also can be eliminated because this is not an action at all but a position or point of reference. Cascade (C) refers to pouring or falling, usually in the context of a waterfall and not in reference to people, which means we can eliminate cascade as well. While people do accelerate when they move, they usually do so under additional circumstances: they accelerate while running or driving a car. All three of the words we see in the analogy are actions that can be done independently of other factors. Therefore, accelerate (D) can be eliminated, and stroll (A) should be chosen. Stroll and meander both refer to walking or wandering, so this fits perfectly.

The *process of elimination* will help rule out wrong answers. However, the best way to find the correct answer is simply to differentiate the correct answer from the other choices. For this, test takers should go back to asking questions, starting with the chief question: What's the connection? There are actually many ways that connections can be found between words. The trick is to look for the answer that is consistent with the relationship between the words given. What is the prevailing connection? Here are a few different ways verbal analogies can be formed.

Finding Connections in Word Analogies

<u>Connections in Categories</u>
One of the easiest ways to choose the correct answer in word analogies is simply to group words together. Ask if the words can be compartmentalized into *distinct categories*. Here are some examples:

Terrier is to dog as mystery is to
  a. Thriller.
  b. Murder.
  c. Detective.
  d. Novel.
  e. Investigation.

This one might have been a little confusing, but when looking at the first two words in the analogy, this is clearly one in which a category is the prevailing theme. Think about it: a terrier is a type of dog. While there are several breeds of dogs that can be categorized as a terrier, in the end, all terriers are still dogs. Therefore, mystery needs to be grouped into a category. Murders, detectives, and investigations can all be involved in a mystery plot, but a murder (B), a detective (C), or an investigation (E) is not necessarily a mystery. A thriller (A) is a purely fictional concept, a kind of story or film, just like a mystery. A thriller can describe a mystery, but the same issue appears as the other choices. What about novel (D)? For one thing, it's distinct from all the other terms. A novel isn't a component of a mystery, but a mystery can be a type of novel. The relationship fits: a terrier is a type of dog, just like a mystery is a type of novel.

<u>Synonym/Antonym</u>
Some analogies are based on words meaning the same thing or expressing the same idea. Sometimes it's the complete opposite!

Marauder is to brigand as

a. King is to peasant.
b. Juice is to orange.
c. Soldier is to warrior.
d. Engine is to engineer.
e. Paper is to photocopier.

Here, soldier is to warrior (C) is the correct answer. Marauders and brigands are both thieves. They are synonyms. The only pair of words that fits this analogy is soldier and warrior because both terms describe combatants who fight.

Cap is to shoe as jacket is to

a. Ring.
b. T-shirt.
c. Vest.
d. Glasses.
e. Pants.

Opposites are at play here because a cap is worn on the head/top of the person, while a shoe is worn on the foot/bottom. A jacket is worn on top of the body too, so the opposite of jacket would be pants (E) because these are worn on the bottom of the body. Often the prompts on the test provide a synonym or antonym relationship. Just consider if the sets in the prompt reflect similarity or stark difference.

<u>Parts of a Whole</u>

Another thing to consider when first looking at an analogy prompt is whether the words presented come together in some way. Do they express parts of the same item? Does one word complete the other? Are they connected by process or function?

Tire is to car as

a. Wing is to bird.
b. Oar is to boat.
c. Box is to shelf.
d. Hat is to head.
e. Knife is to sheath.

We know that the tire fits onto the car's wheels and this is what enables the car to drive on roads. The tire is part of the car. This is the same relationship as oar is to boat (B). The oars are attached onto a boat and enable a person to move and navigate the boat on water. At first glance, wing is to bird (A) seems to fit too, since a wing is a part of a bird that enables it to move through the air. However, since a tire and car are not alive and transport people, oar and boat fit better because they are also not alive and they transport people. Subtle differences between answer choices should be found.

<u>Other Relationships</u>

There are a number of other relationships to look for when solving verbal analogies. Some relationships focus on one word being a *characteristic/NOT a characteristic* of the other word. Sometimes the first word is *the source/comprised of* the second word. Still, other words are related by their *location*. Some analogies have *sequential* relationships, and some are *cause/effect* relationships. There are analogies that show *creator/provider* relationships with the *creation/provision*. Another relationship might compare an *object* with its *function* or a *user* with his or her *tool*. An analogy may focus on a *change of grammar* or a *translation of language*. Finally, one word of an analogy may have a relationship to the other word in its *intensity.* The type of relationship between the first two words of the analogy should be determined before continuing to analyze the second set of words. One effective method of determining a relationship between two words is to form a comprehensible sentence using both words and then to plug the answer choices into the same sentence. For example, consider the following analogy: *Bicycle is to handlebars as car is to steering wheel.* A sentence could be formed that says: A bicycle navigates using its handlebars; therefore, a car navigates using its steering wheel. If the second sentence makes sense, then the correct relationship has likely been found. A sentence may be more complex depending on the relationship between the first two words in the analogy. An example of this may be: *food is to dishwasher as dirt is to carwash.* The formed sentence may be: A dishwasher cleans food off of dishes in the same way that a carwash cleans dirt off of a car.

Dealing with Multiple Connections

There are many other ways to draw connections between word sets. Several word choices might form an analogy that would fit the word set in your prompt. When this occurs, the analogy must be explored from multiple angles as, on occasion, multiple answer choices may appear to be correct. When this occurs, ask yourself: which one is an even closer match than the others? The framing word pair is another important point to consider. Can one or both words be interpreted as actions or ideas, or are they purely objects? Here's a question where words could have alternate meanings:

Hammer is to nail as saw is to

a. Electric.
b. Hack.
c. Cut.
d. Machete.
e. Groove.

Looking at the question above, it becomes clear that the topic of the analogy involves construction tools. Hammers and nails are used in concert, since the hammer is used to pound the nail. The logical first thing to do is to look for an object that a saw would be used on. Seeing that there is no such object among the answer choices, a test taker might begin to worry. After all, that seems to be the choice that would complete the analogy—but that doesn't mean it's the only choice that may fit. Encountering questions like this test one's ability to see multiple connections between words—don't get stuck thinking that words can only be connected in a single way. The first two words given can be verbs instead of just objects. To hammer means to hit or beat; oftentimes it refers to beating something into place. This is also what nail means when it is used as a verb. Here are the word choices that reveal the answer.

First, it's known that a saw, well, saws. It uses a steady motion to cut an object, and indeed to saw means to cut! Cut (C) is one of our answer choices, but the other options should be reviewed. While some tools are electric (a), the use of power in the tools listed in the analogy isn't a factor. Again, it's been established that these word choices are not tools in this context. Therefore, machete (D) is also ruled out because machete is also not a verb. Another important thing to consider is that while a machete is a tool that accomplishes a similar purpose as a saw, the machete is used in a slicing motion rather than a sawing/cutting motion. The verb that describes machete is hack (B), another choice that can be ruled out. A machete is used to hack at foliage. However, a saw does not hack. Groove (E) is just a term that has nothing to do with the other words, so this choice can be eliminated easily. This leaves cut (C), which confirms that this is the word needed to complete the analogy.

Reading/Paragraph Comprehension

Reading Strategies and Being an Active Reader

Reading comprehension is the ability to read, process, and understand information. Reading comprehension skills such as **decoding** (the ability to use letter sound(s) to form and understand a word(s)), **fluency** (the pace at which one reads), **vocabulary knowledge** (the understanding of words one reads), and **background knowledge** (the use of familiarinformation to decipher unfamiliar texts) are basic building blocks effective readers use. Not only should effective readers utilize the basic comprehension building blocks, they should also use a variety of strategies to become better readers.

Good readers practice these comprehension skills before, during, and after reading. Before readers go through a text or passage, they should ask the following questions: "What do I already know about this subject?" and "What will the book be about?" While reading the text or passage, readers should visualize the text, use new information to make predictions, and continue to self-question. Furthermore, readers should also make connections to a personal experience or another event that occurred within other texts. After reading a text or passage, readers should be able to summarize and process what the main idea of the text or passage was about. Good readers are able to retell the story in their own words.

The chart on the following page shows the six common types of comprehension strategies: question, connect, infer, visualize, what's important, and synthesize.

Question

Monitor reading by asking questions before, during, and after reading a text. "What if?," "I don't understand why," or "Maybe when" are all examples of how to utilize questioning while reading.

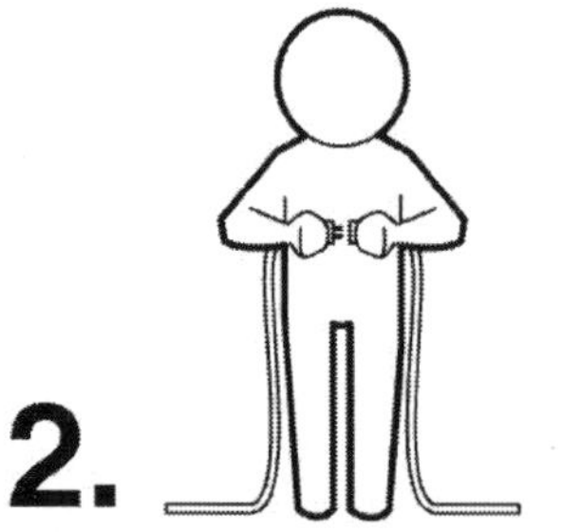

Connect

Use knowledge to help with understanding text. Connecting with other texts or experiences is a way to help with text comprehension." This reminds me of... because" and "When I heard..., it reminds me of" are both examples of how to connect with texts.

Infer

When authors do not give a clear answer, it is often necessary to infer what happens in the text. Inferring helps with making predictions, drawing conclusions, and reflecting on text. "I think," "Maybe," and "Perhaps" are all examples of ways to infer while reading.

Visualize

Create pictures in the mind about the text. "I see," "It must have smelled like," and "I can imagine" are all examples of how to visualize while reading.

What's important

Determine the author's main idea. "The main idea is," "This section is primarily about," and "It is important to remember" are all examples of how to determine what is important while reading.

Synthesize

Combine current knowledge with new information to help with text understanding. "After reviewing," "At first I thought," and "Now I think" are all examples of how to synthesize information while reading.

Topic Versus Main Idea

It is very important to know the difference between the topic and the main idea of the text. Even though these two are similar because they both present the central point of a text, they have distinctive differences. A **topic** is the subject of the text; it can usually be described in a one- to two-word phrase and appears in the simplest form. On the other hand, the **main idea** is more detailed and provides the author's central point of the text. It can be expressed through a complete sentence and is often found in the beginning, middle, or end of a paragraph. In most nonfiction books, the first sentence of the passage usually (but not always) states the main idea. Review the passage below to explore the topic versus the main idea.

> Cheetahs are one of the fastest mammals on the land, reaching up to 70 miles an hour over short distances. Even though cheetahs can run as fast as 70 miles an hour, they usually only have to run half that speed to catch up with their choice of prey. Cheetahs cannot maintain a fast pace over long periods of time because their bodies will overheat. After a chase, cheetahs need to rest for approximately 30 minutes prior to eating or returning to any other activity.

In the example above, the topic of the passage is "Cheetahs" simply because that is the subject of the text. The main idea of the text is "Cheetahs are one of the fastest mammals on the land but can only maintain a fast pace for shorter distances." While it covers the topic, it is more detailed and refers to the text in its entirety. The text continues to provide additional details called supporting details, which will be discussed in the next section.

Supporting Details

Supporting details help readers better develop and understand the main idea. Supporting details answer questions like *who, what, where, when, why,* and *how.* Different types of supporting details include examples, facts and statistics, anecdotes, and sensory details.

Persuasive and informative texts often use supporting details. In persuasive texts, authors attempt to make readers agree with their points of view, and supporting details are often used as "selling points." If authors make a statement, they need to support the statement with evidence in order to adequately persuade readers. Informative texts use supporting details such as examples and facts to inform readers. Review the previous "Cheetahs" passage to find examples of supporting details.

> Cheetahs are one of the fastest mammals on the land, reaching up to 70 miles an hour over short distances. Even though cheetahs can run as fast as 70 miles an hour, they usually only have to run half that speed to catch up with their choice of prey. Cheetahs cannot maintain a fast pace over long periods of time because their bodies will overheat. After a chase, cheetahs need to rest for approximately 30 minutes prior to eating or returning to any other activity.

In the example, supporting details include:

- Cheetahs reach up to 70 miles per hour over short distances.
- They usually only have to run half that speed to catch up with their prey.
- Cheetahs will overheat if they exert a high speed over longer distances.
- Cheetahs need to rest for 30 minutes after a chase.

Look at the diagram below (applying the cheetah example) to help determine the hierarchy of topic, main idea, and supporting details.

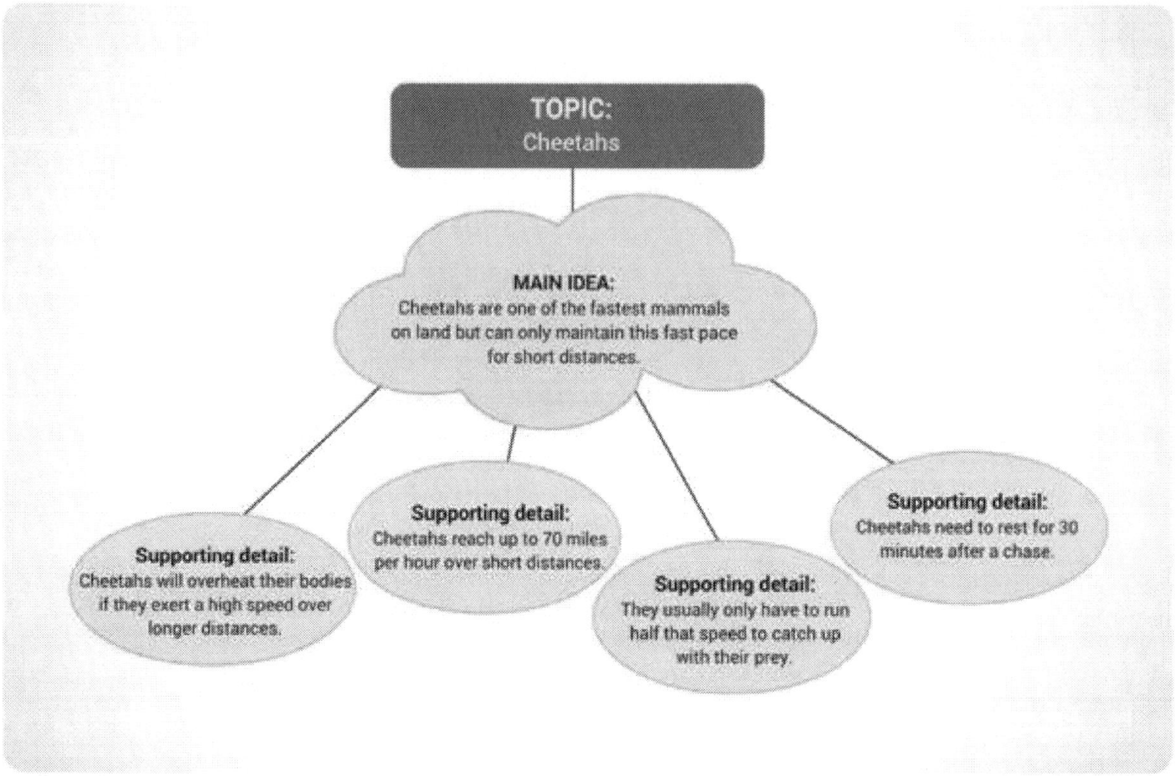

Theme

The **theme** of a text is the central message of the story. The theme can be about a moral or lesson that the author wants to share with the audience. Although authors do not directly state the theme of a story, it is the "big picture" that they intend readers to walk away with. For example, the fairy tale *The Boy Who Cried Wolf* features the tale of a little boy who continued to lie about seeing a wolf. When the little boy actually saw a wolf, no one believed him because of all of the previous lies. The author of this fairy tale does not directly tell readers, "Don't lie because people will question the credibility of the story." The author simply portrays the story of the little boy and presents the moral through the tale.

The theme of a text can center around varying subjects such as courage, friendship, love, bravery, facing challenges, or adversity. It often leaves readers with more questions than answers. Authors tend to insinuate certain themes in texts; however, readers are left to interpret the true meaning of the story.

Point of View and Purpose Questions

Every story has a **narrator,** or someone who tells the story. This is sometimes also referred to as the story's **point of view.** Don't make the mistake of assuming that the narrator and the author are the same person—on the contrary, they may have completely different opinions and personalities. There are also several types of narrators commonly found in fiction, and each type serves a different purpose.

The first type of narrator is a first-person narrator who tells the story from an "I" perspective. A first-person narrator is almost always a character in the story. They might be a main protagonist (like Jane

Eyre in the novel of the same name) or a side character (such as Nelly in *Wuthering Heights*). Also, first-person narrator has an immediate response to the events of the story. However, keep in mind that they are reporting the story through their own perspective, so this narrator may not be totally objective or reliable. Pay attention to language that shows the narrator's tone and consider how the events of the story might be interpreted differently by another character.

Another type of narrator is a second-person narrator who tells the story from a "you" perspective. Readers probably won't encounter this type of narrator often, although it's becoming slightly more common in modern literature. A second-person narrator forces the reader to insert themselves into the story and consider how they would respond to the action themselves.

Much more common is a third-person narrator. This type of narrator is further divided into two subtypes: third-person limited and third-person omniscient. In both cases, the story is told from an outside perspective ("he," "she," and "they," rather than "I," "me," or "you"). In this way, a third-person narrator is more distanced and objective than a first-person narrator. A third-person limited narrator tends to follow one main character in the story, reporting only that character's thoughts and only events that directly involve that character (think of the Harry Potter books, which are told by a third-person narrator but primarily limited to Harry's thoughts and experiences). A third-person omniscient narrator isn't limited to one character, but instead reports freely on the thoughts, actions, and events of all characters and situations in the story (omniscient means "all knowing"). Third-person omniscient is generally the most flexible and objective type of narrator. Readers can find this narrator in the novels of writers like Charles Dickens and Alexandre Dumas, whose stories are spread across dozens of different characters and locations.

By identifying the type of narrator, readers can assess a narrator's objectivity as well as how the narrator's perspective is limited to a single character's experience. When a narrator is unbiased, readers can take their account of events at face value; when a narrator is less objective, readers have to consider how the narrator's personal perspective influences the reader's understanding.

In addition to the point of view, another important factor to consider is the writer's *purpose*. This answers the question, "Why did the author write this?" Three of the most common purposes are to persuade, to inform, or to entertain. Of course, it's possible for these purposes to overlap.

Generally, literary texts are written to **entertain.** That is, the reader is simply supposed to enjoy the story! The romantic, dramatic, and adventurous elements are all designed to get readers involved with the fates of the characters. When the primary purpose of a text is to entertain, the focus is on the plot elements, the characters' thoughts and emotions, and descriptions of places, events, and characters. Examples of texts that entertain include novels, plays, poetry, and memoirs. Within the more general purpose of entertaining, literary texts might include passages to convey emotion or to describe a character's thoughts or feelings.

Another common writing purpose is to **inform.** Informative writing intends to teach the reader about a particular topic. Generally, this type of writing is objective and unbiased. Informative writing may also be descriptive. However, instead of describing thoughts and emotions, informative writing tends to describe concrete facts. After reading an informative text, the reader should be more knowledgeable about the text's subject. Examples of informative writing include textbooks, research articles, and texts about academic topics like science and history. Sometimes, informative writing is also described as writing that intends to teach or give information about a subject.

The third common writing purpose is to **persuade.** Unlike the objective writing found in informative texts, persuasive texts are more subjective. Rather than being neutral, the author expresses an opinion about the subject and tries to convince readers to agree. As with informative texts, persuasive texts often include facts and statistics—however, these are used to support the writer's perspective. Examples of persuasive writing include newspaper editorials and texts about controversial topics like politics or social issues. Sometimes, persuasive writing is also described as writing that intends to convince, argue, or express an opinion about a subject.

In order to determine the purpose of a text, readers can keep the following questions in mind:

- What type of details are included (facts, emotions, imagery, etc.)?
- Facts and statistics tend to indicate informative or persuasive writing, while emotions or imagery point to writing that entertains.
- Is the author neutral or opinionated?
- An opinionated or biased author is probably writing to persuade, while a neutral author writes to inform.
- Is this passage teaching information?
- If readers gained a lot of new knowledge about a subject after reading a text, the primary purpose was probably to inform.

Opinions, Facts, Assumptions, Observations, and Conclusions

Readers must be able to tell the difference between facts and opinions. A **fact** doesn't simply refer to something that is true. Rather, it refers to anything that can be objectively measured and can be *proven* true or false. On the other hand, an opinion is a statement based on subjective observation. There is no measurable way to determine whether an opinion is correct—it simply depends on the perspective of the writer. Consider the following examples:

> Napoleon Bonaparte was the emperor of France from 1804 until 1814, and again in 1815.

This statement is a fact because it contains information that can be proven. By referencing historical documents and records from the nineteenth century, historians are able to objectively establish the dates of Napoleon's reign.

> Napoleon was the most charismatic ruler France has ever had.

This statement is an **opinion** because it contains information that cannot be proven. First, there is no clear way to measure someone's charisma and compare it to that of other leaders. Even if an opinion is based on popular consensus, if it cannot be objectively proven, then it's not a fact.

Consider one more example:

> a. *Beauty and the Beast* is the most important Disney movie.
>
> b. According to a recent survey of Americans aged twenty to forty, the majority of respondents chose *Beauty and the Beast* as "the Disney movie that had the strongest impact on your life."

Sentence *A* is an opinion because it's based on a concept ("important") rather than something measurable. There is no agreed-upon definition of what "important" means, and no way of standardizing people's interpretation of the term. However, sentence *B* is a fact because it presents the statistical results of research. Anybody could look over the research results to confirm whether this statement is true, or they could even attempt to recreate the results themselves.

Remember that informative writing should contain purely factual statements without any biased opinions. Persuasive writing may combine facts and opinions, such as opinions that are supported by facts.

Three other types of statements are observations, assumptions, and conclusions. An **observation** states something the writer has noticed based on things they have seen or experienced. It's a descriptive statement that tends to be objective and unemotional. An **assumption** is something the author may not have observed, but is generally believed to be true. Finally, a **conclusion** is when the writer draws together observations and assumptions in order to make a final statement about them. For example:

a. The dining hall has started offering a new discounted lunch special for students. The dining hall has become much more crowded during lunch hours.

b. Students are usually on a budget and were probably attracted by the discounted prices.

c. The lunch special discount has been a successful way to gain diners.

Statement *A* contains observations because it describes things that can be seen—like the number of customers, or a sign advertising discounted lunch—by anyone who visits the dining hall. Statement *B* is an assumption. Without directly interviewing every student about their finances and their reasons for eating in the dining hall, it's impossible to know whether they're all looking for a low-budget meal. However, it's reasonable to believe this statement could be true based on what the author knows about student life. Finally, statement *C* is a conclusion because it combines all the information in the observations and assumptions to make a statement about the situation as a whole.

Style, Structure, Mood, and Tone

Readers should be able to identify and analyze the components of a writer's **style.** Think about someone's fashion style—a person might dress casually or formally; they might wear trendy clothes or classic clothes; they might prefer simple looks or flashy ones. And the way a person styles their fashion often determines the impression they give to other people. Similarly, writers combine elements of structure, diction, and figurative and connotative language to create their own style.

Structure refers to how a writer organizes ideas. Depending on what the author is attempting to accomplish, certain formats or text structures work better than others. For example, a sequence structure might work for narration but not when identifying similarities and differences between dissimilar concepts. Similarly, a comparison-contrast structure is not useful for narration. It's the author's job to put the right information in the correct format.

Readers should be familiar with the five main literary structures:

1. **Sequence** structure (sometimes referred to as the order structure) is when the order of events proceed in a predictable order. In many cases, this means the text goes through the plot elements: exposition, rising action, climax, falling action, and resolution. Readers are introduced to characters, setting, and conflict in the exposition. In the rising action, there's an increase in

tension and suspense. The climax is the height of tension and the point of no return. Tension decreases during the falling action. In the resolution, any conflicts presented in the exposition are solved, and the story concludes. An informative text that is structured sequentially will often go in order from one step to the next.

2. In the **problem-solution** structure, authors identify a potential problem and suggest a solution. This form of writing is usually divided into two paragraphs and can be found in informational texts. For example, cell phone, cable and satellite providers use this structure in manuals to help customers troubleshoot or identify problems with services or products.

3. When authors want to discuss similarities and differences between separate concepts, they arrange thoughts in a **comparison-contrast** paragraph structure. Venn diagrams are an effective graphic organizer for comparison-contrast structures, because they feature two overlapping circles that can be used to organize similarities and differences. A comparison-contrast essay organizes one paragraph based on similarities and another based on differences. A comparison-contrast essay can also be arranged with the similarities and differences of individual traits addressed within individual paragraphs. Words such as *however*, *but*, and *nevertheless* help signal a contrast in ideas.

4. **Descriptive** writing structure is designed to appeal to your senses. Much like an artist who constructs a painting, good descriptive writing builds an image in the reader's mind by appealing to the five senses: sight, hearing, taste, touch, and smell. However, overly descriptive writing can become tedious; sparse descriptions can make settings and characters seem flat. Good authors strike a balance by applying descriptions only to passages, characters, and settings that are integral to the plot.

5. Passages that use the **cause and effect** structure are simply asking *why* by demonstrating some type of connection between ideas. Words such as *if*, *since*, *because*, *then*, or *consequently* indicate relationship. By switching the order of a complex sentence, the writer can rearrange the emphasis on different clauses. Saying *If Sheryl is late, we'll miss the dance* is different from saying *We'll miss the dance if Sheryl is late*. One emphasizes Sheryl's tardiness while the other emphasizes missing the dance. Paragraphs can also be arranged in a cause and effect format. Since the format—before and after—is sequential, it is useful when authors wish to discuss the impact of choices. Researchers often apply this paragraph structure to the scientific method.

An author's style can also come from **diction,** or word choice. Just like a person's fashion style can be casual or formal depending on the event, an author's writing style can be anywhere from conversational to academic, elevated to colloquial, reflecting the audience and subject matter. For example, a chemistry textbook is going to contain more academic language and scientific terminology than a newspaper article, which is likely to contain common expressions and easier vocabulary. **Colloquial language** refers to the informal language of normal speech, and may include elements of non-standard pronunciation or grammar (words like "y'all," for example). Colloquialisms can often be found in "local color" pieces where the writer wants the reader to feel directly involved in the everyday lives and conversations of people or characters in the text.

Diction also contributes to the *tone* of the text. Keys to recognizing an author's tone include paying attention to any connotative or emotional language as well as what types of details and information are included (or if any important information seems to be missing). If an article about a proposal to build a new highway only includes information about how the highway will increase traffic congestion and negatively impact the environment, readers can feel the author's critical tone towards the subject. On the other hand, if the article also mentions research about how the highway could direct more customers to local businesses and boost the town's economy, the author's tone will probably seem more balanced.

A text's **mood** is the general feeling or atmosphere created by the author's descriptions and imagery (and, again, it relies on diction and selection of details). *Imagery* refers to all of the details in a text that appeal to any of the five senses; it's how the author helps draw a picture in the reader's mind. Imagine a story that starts with, "It was a dark and stormy night..." and includes descriptions of the howling wind outside, the dim flicker of candlelight, the mysterious creak of unknown footsteps coming upstairs. All of this imagery comes together to create a mood of creepiness and mystery.

Making Inferences, Predictions, and Drawing Conclusions

Inferences from the Text

Readers should be able to make **inferences.** Making an inference requires the reader to read between the lines and look for what's *implied* rather than what's directly stated. Using information that is known from the text, the reader is able to make a logical assumption about information that isn't directly stated but is probably true. Read the following passage:

> "Hey, do you wanna meet my new puppy?" Jonathan asked.
>
> "Oh, I'm sorry but please don't—" Jacinta began to protest, but before she could finish Jonathan had already open the passenger side door of his car and a perfectly white ball of fur came bouncing towards Jacinta.
>
> "Isn't he the cutest?" beamed Jonathan.
>
> "Yes—achoo!—he's pretty—aaaachooo!!—adora—aaa—aaaachoo!" Jacinta managed to say in between sneezes. "But if you don't mind, I—I—achoo!—need to go inside."

Which of the following can be inferred from Jacinta's reaction to the puppy?

a. She hates animals.
b. She is allergic to dogs.
c. She prefers cats to dogs.
d. She is angry at Jonathan.

In order to make an inference, the reader must first consider the information presented and then form an idea about what is probably true. Based on the details in the passage, what's the best answer? Important details include the tone of Jacinta's dialogue, which is polite and apologetic, as well as her reaction itself, which is a long string of sneezes. Choices *A* and *D* both express strong emotions ("hates" and "angry") that aren't evident in Jacinta's speech or actions. Choice *C* mentions cats, but there isn't anything in the passage to indicate Jacinta's feelings about those animals. Choice *B* is the most logical choice. As she began sneezing as soon as the dog approached her, it makes sense to guess that Jacinta might be allergic to dogs. So even though Jacinta never directly states, "Sorry, I'm allergic to dogs!" using the clues in the passage, it's still reasonable to guess this is true.

Making inferences is crucial for readers because literary texts often avoid presenting complete and direct information about characters' thoughts or feelings, leaving the reader to interpret clues in the text. In order to make inferences, readers should ask:

- What details are presented in the text?
- Is there any important information that seems to be missing?
- Based on the information that the author does include, what else is probably true?
- Is this inference reasonable based on what is already known?

Inferences are useful in gaining a deeper understanding of characters in a narrative. Readers can use the same strategies outlined above—paying attention to details and using them to make reasonable guesses about the text—to read between the lines and get a more complete picture of how (and why) characters are thinking, feeling, and acting. Read the following passage from O. Henry's story "The Gift of the Magi":

> One dollar and eighty-seven cents. That was all. And sixty cents of it was in pennies. Pennies saved one and two at a time by bulldozing the grocer and the vegetable man and the butcher until one's cheeks burned with the silent imputation of parsimony that such close dealing implied. Three times Della counted it. One dollar and eighty-seven cents. And the next day would be Christmas.
>
> There was clearly nothing to do but flop down on the shabby little couch and howl. So Della did it.

These paragraphs introduce the reader to the character Della. Even though the author doesn't include a direct description of Della, the reader can already form a general impression of her personality and emotions. One detail that should stick out to the reader is repetition: "one dollar and eighty-seven cents." This amount is repeated twice in the first paragraph, along with other descriptions of money: "sixty cents of it was in pennies," "pennies saved one and two at a time." The story's preoccupation with money parallels how Della herself is constantly thinking about her finances—"three times Della counted" her meager savings. Already the reader can guess that Della is having money problems. Next, think about her emotions. The first paragraph describes haggling over groceries "until one's cheeks burned"—another way to describe blushing. People tend to blush when they are embarrassed or ashamed, so readers can infer that Della is ashamed by her financial situation. This inference is also supported by the second paragraph, when she flops down and howls on her "shabby little couch." Clearly, she's in distress. Without saying, "Della has no money and is embarrassed to be poor," O. Henry is able to communicate the same impression to readers through his careful inclusion of details.

A character's *motive* is their reason for acting a certain way. Usually, characters are motivated by something that they want. In the passage above, why is Della upset about not having enough money? There's an important detail at the end of the first paragraph: "the next day would be Christmas." Why is money especially important around Christmas? Christmas is a holiday when people exchange gifts. If Della is struggling with money, she's probably also struggling to buy gifts. So a shrewd reader should be able to guess that Della's motivation is wanting to buy a gift for someone—but she's currently unable to afford it, leading to feelings of shame and frustration.

In order to understand characters in a text, readers should keep the following questions in mind:

- What words does the author use to describe the character? Are these words related to any specific emotions or personality traits (for example, characteristics like rude, friendly, unapproachable, or innocent)?
- What does the character say? Does their dialogue seem to be straightforward, or are they hiding some thoughts or emotions?
- What actions can be observed from this character? How do their actions reflect their feelings?
- What does the character want? What do they do to get it?

Making Predictions

When readers make **predictions,** they try to anticipate what will happen next in the text. Think about how weather forecasters make predictions for future weather conditions. It's not purely guesswork. Rather, they gather a wide variety of relevant data, analyze the information they've collected, and also compare it with previous weather patterns. Finally, they're able to make a well-researched prediction with a high rate of probability. Readers must do the same when making predictions in a text—rather than simply guessing, they draw information from earlier in the text and use preexisting knowledge to form a prediction that's reasonably likely to be true.

In literary texts, authors tend to give clues that guide readers through the narrative. One method is *foreshadowing*, where the author hints at what will happen next in the story. Consider this line from *Romeo and Juliet* in which Juliet desires to learn more about Romeo. She says to her nurse:

> Go ask his name.—If he be married.
>
> My grave is like to be my wedding bed.

At this point in the play, Juliet's lines simply mean that she would be sorely disappointed to learn that Romeo was already attached to another woman. However, for readers who already know how the play ends, this sentence carries another level of meaning—Juliet's marital choices will go hand in hand with her death. In this way, Shakespeare foreshadows the tragic end of Juliet's love story at the very moment it begins.

Of course, authors sometimes give false hints that lead readers to dead ends. This type of misdirection is especially commonplace in genres like mystery and suspense, where the author wants to keep the reader guessing until the very end. A distracting hint that turns out to be false is known as a *red herring.* However, if readers are aware that certain genres are likely to contain red herrings, then readers can be more cautious in evaluating hints. If a clue seems too obvious, it might be a red herring! In a roundabout way, then, red herrings can actually *help* readers make predictions by forcing them to look beyond the most obvious details.

In addition to clues sprinkled throughout the text, readers can also make predictions by considering the tone and mood of a text. For example, if a story has an overall gloomy mood or its diction creates a tone that is melancholy and foreboding, readers will expect that dark or depressing events will follow. On the other hand, if the tone is playful and lighthearted, readers are less likely to expect tragedy and might instead predict a comic or happy outcome. If the outcome of the story is vastly different from what either readers or the story's characters themselves are expecting, the author is probably using irony.

It's also possible to make predictions in non-literary texts. Consider a persuasive article that opens with the following thesis statement:

> There are countless reasons why closing down the city's only public dog park is a bad idea for local citizens.

Readers can expect that the rest of the essay will contain evidence that supports the author's opinion. The same is also true of informative texts. Imagine a scientific article that contains this sentence:

> Surprising new evidence challenges long-held beliefs about the cognitive capabilities of non-human animals.

In the paragraphs that follow, readers might expect to find any of the following: background on previously accepted theories of animal cognition, description of new scientific research or experimentation, and interpretation and discussion of the experiment's results. By making these predictions whenever they encounter a new text, readers will be more prepared to understand new information and opinions. Also, making predictions about information is especially useful when readers have a limited amount of time to read a text for relevant details. By reading either the thesis statement of the article or the topic sentences of each paragraph, readers can then make logical predictions about what information might be discussed later without having to read the entire text first.

<u>Drawing Conclusions Not Explicitly Present in the Text</u>

It's also useful to infer meaning from informative texts. Scientists and researchers make inferences every day in order to develop new theories based on facts and observations. Readers of informative texts should also understand how inferences are applied in academic research. Generally speaking, there are two main types of reasoning—deductive and inductive. An inference based on deductive reasoning considers a principle that is generally believed to be true and then applies it to a specific situation ("All English majors love reading. Annabelle is an English major. Therefore, I can infer that Annabelle loves reading."). Inductive reasoning makes an inference by using specific evidence to make a general inference ("Trina, Arnold, and Uchenna are all from Florida. Trina, Arnold, and Uchenna all love to swim. Therefore, I can infer that people from Florida usually love swimming."). Both deductive and inductive reasoning use what is *known* to be true to make a logical guess about what is *probably* true.

As readers are presented with new information, they should organize it, make sense of it, and reflect on what they learned from the text. Readers draw conclusions at the end of a text by bringing together all of the details, descriptions, facts, and/or opinions presented by the author and asking, "What did I gain from reading this text? How have my ideas or emotions changed? What was the author's overall purpose for writing?" In this case, a **conclusion** is a unifying idea or final thought about the text that the reader can form after they are done reading. As discussed, sometimes writers are very explicit in stating what conclusions should be drawn from a text and what readers are meant to have learned. However, more often than not, writers simply present descriptions or information and then leave it up to readers to draw their own conclusions. As with making inferences, though, readers always need to base their conclusions on textual evidence rather than simply guessing or making random statements.

> When the school district's uniform policy was first introduced fifteen years ago, parents and students alike were incredibly enthusiastic about it. Some of the most appealing arguments in favor of enforcing school uniforms was to create an equal learning environment for all students, to eliminate the focus on fashion and appearance, and to simplify students' morning routine by removing the need to pick a different outfit every day. However, despite this promising beginning, the uniform policy has steadily lost favor over the years. First of all, schools did not

> notice a significant drop in examples of bullying at school, and students continue to report that they feel judged on their appearance based on things like weight and hairstyle. This seems to indicate that uniforms have not been particularly effective at removing the social pressure that teens feel to appear a certain way in front of their peers. Also, many parents have complained that the school's required uniform pieces like jackets, sweaters, and neckties can only be purchased from one specific clothing shop. Because this retailer has cornered the market on school uniforms, they are operating under a total monopoly, and disgruntled parents feel that they are being grossly overcharged for school clothing for their children. The uniform policy is set to be debated at the upcoming school board meeting, and many expect it to be overturned.

After reading this article, a reader might conclude any of the following: that ideas that start with popular support might become unpopular over time; or that there are several compelling counterarguments to the benefits of school uniforms; or that this school district is open to new ideas but also open to criticism. While each conclusion is slightly different, they are all based on information and evidence from the article, and therefore all are plausible. Each conclusion sums up what the reader learned from the passage and what overall idea the writer seems to be communicating.

Another way for readers to make sense of information in a text is to make *generalizations*. This is somewhat related to the concept of inductive reasoning, by which readers move from specific evidence to a more general idea. When readers generalize, they take the specific content of a text and apply it to a larger context or to a different situation. Let's make a generalization from the topic, the bystander effect:

> A bystander is simply a person who watches something happen. Paradoxically, the more people who witness an accident happen, the less likely each individual is to actually intervene and offer assistance. This is known as the bystander effect. Psychologists attribute the bystander effect to something called "diffusion of responsibility." If one individual witnesses an accident, that single person feels the whole burden of responsibility to respond to the accident. However, if there are many witnesses, each person feels that responsibility has been divided amongst many people, so their individual sense of responsibility is much lower and they are less likely to offer help.

This article describes one very specific psychological phenomenon known as the "bystander effect." However, based on this specific information, a reader could form a more general psychological statement such as, "Humans sometimes behave differently when they are alone and when they are in a group."

It's also possible to make generalizations from literary texts. This is a particularly useful reading skill when evaluating the collective works of a particular writer or when forming a general characterization of texts from a particular genre or time period. For example, after reading a handful of novels by Jane Austen, all of which feature clever female protagonists and contain several examples of cynical or unflattering depictions of marriage, a reader can form a general impression of Jane Austen's thoughts on women's social roles. An overarching generalization from these novels might be that, "Education is just as important for women as marriage," or "Marriage isn't a guarantee of happiness or satisfaction." Being able to form generalizations is an important step in drawing connections and establishing relationships between texts.

Understanding Arguments

In nonfiction writing, authors employ argumentative techniques to present their opinion to readers in the most convincing way. First of all, persuasive writing usually includes at least one type of appeal: an appeal to logic (**logos**), emotion (**pathos**), or credibility and trustworthiness (**ethos**). When a writer appeals to logic, they are asking readers to agree with them based on research, evidence, and an established line of reasoning. An author's argument might also appeal to readers' emotions, perhaps by including personal stories and anecdotes (a short narrative of a specific event). A final type of appeal—appeal to authority—asks the reader to agree with the author's argument on the basis of their expertise or credentials. Consider three different approaches to arguing the same opinion:

Logic (Logos)
Below is an example of an appeal to logic. The author uses evidence to disprove the logic of the school's rule (the rule was supposed to reduce discipline problems; the number of problems has not been reduced; therefore, the rule is not working) and he or she calls for its repeal.

> Our school should abolish its current ban on cell phone use on campus. This rule was adopted last year as an attempt to reduce class disruptions and help students focus more on their lessons. However, since the rule was enacted, there has been no change in the number of disciplinary problems in class. Therefore, the rule is ineffective and should be done away with.

Emotion (Pathos)
An author's argument might also appeal to readers' emotions, perhaps by including personal stories and anecdotes. The next example presents an appeal to emotion. By sharing the personal anecdote of one student and speaking about emotional topics like family relationships, the author invokes the reader's empathy in asking them to reconsider the school rule.

> Our school should abolish its current ban on cell phone use on campus. If they aren't able to use their phones during the school day, many students feel isolated from their loved ones. For example, last semester, one student's grandmother had a heart attack in the morning. However, because he couldn't use his cell phone, the student didn't know about his grandmother's condition until the end of the day—when she had already passed away and it was too late to say goodbye. By preventing students from contacting their friends and family, our school is placing undue stress and anxiety on students.

Credibility (Ethos)
Finally, an appeal to authority includes a statement from a relevant expert. In this case, the author uses a doctor in the field of education to support the argument. All three examples begin from the same opinion—the school's phone ban needs to change—but rely on different argumentative styles to persuade the reader.

> Our school should abolish its current ban on cell phone use on campus. According to Dr. Bartholomew Everett, a leading educational expert, "Research studies show that cell phone usage has no real impact on student attentiveness. Rather, phones provide a valuable technological resource for learning. Schools need to learn how to integrate this new technology into their curriculum." Rather than banning phones altogether, our school should follow the advice of experts and allow students to use phones as part of their learning.

Rhetorical Questions

Another commonly used argumentative technique is asking **rhetorical questions**, questions that do not actually require an answer but that push the reader to consider the topic further.

> I wholly disagree with the proposal to ban restaurants from serving foods with high sugar and sodium contents. Do we really want to live in a world where the government can control what we eat? I prefer to make my own food choices.

Here, the author's rhetorical question prompts readers to put themselves in a hypothetical situation and imagine how they would feel about it.

Fallacies

A **fallacy** is a mistaken belief or faulty reasoning, otherwise known as a **logical fallacy**. It is important for readers to recognize logical fallacies because they discredit the author's message. Readers should continuously self-question as they go through a text to identify logical fallacies. Readers cannot simply complacently take information at face value. There are six common types of logical fallacies:

- False analogy
- Circular reasoning
- False dichotomy
- Overgeneralization
- Slippery slope
- Hasty generalization

Each of the six logical fallacies are reviewed individually.

False Analogy

A **false analogy** is when the author assumes two objects or events are alike in all aspects despite the fact that they may be vastly different. Authors intend on making unfamiliar objects relatable to convince readers of something. For example, the letters *A* and *E* are both vowels; therefore, *A* = *E*. Readers cannot assume that because *A* and *E* are both vowels that they perform the same function in words or independently. If authors tell readers, *A* = *E*, then that is a false analogy. While this is a simple example, other false analogies may be less obvious.

Circular Reasoning

Circular reasoning is when the reasoning is decided based upon the outcome or conclusion and then vice versa. Basically, those who use circular reasoning start out with the argument and then use false logic to try to prove it, and then, in turn, the reasoning supports the conclusion in one big circular pattern. For example, consider the two thoughts, "I don't have time to get organized" and "My disorganization is costing me time." Which is the argument? What is the conclusion? If there is not time to get organized, will more time be spent later trying to find whatever is needed? In turn, if so much time is spent looking for things, there is not time to get organized. The cycle keeps going in an endless series. One problem affects the other; therefore, there is a circular pattern of reasoning.

False Dichotomy

A **false dichotomy**, also known as a false dilemma, is when the author tries to make readers believe that there are only two options to choose from when, in fact, there are more. The author creates a false sense of the situation because he or she wants the readers to believe that his or her claim is the most logical choice. If the author does not present the readers with options, then the author is purposefully limiting what readers may believe. In turn, the author hopes that readers will believe that his or her point of view is the most sensible choice. For example, in the statement: *you either love running, or you are lazy*, the fallacy lies in the options of loving to run or being lazy. Even though both statements do not necessarily have to be true, the author tries to make one option seem more appealing than the other.

Overgeneralization
An **overgeneralization** is a logical fallacy that occurs when authors write something so extreme that it cannot be proved or disproved. Words like *all, never, most,* and *few* are commonly used when an overgeneralization is being made. For example,

> All kids are crazy when they eat sugar; therefore, my son will not have a cupcake at the birthday party.

Not *all* kids are crazy when they eat sugar, but the extreme statement can influence the readers' points of view on the subject. Readers need to be wary of overgeneralizations in texts because authors may try to sneak them in to sway the readers' opinions.

Slippery Slope
A **slippery slope** is when an author implies that something will inevitably happen as a result of another action. A slippery slope may or may not be true, even though the order of events or gradations may seem logical. For example, in the children's book *If You Give a Mouse a Cookie*, the author goes off on tangents such as "If you give a mouse a cookie, he will ask for some milk. When you give him the milk, he'll probably ask you for a straw." The mouse in the story follows a series of logical events as a result of a previous action. The slippery slope continues on and on throughout the story. Even though the mouse made logical decisions, it very well could have made a different choice, changing the direction of the story.

Hasty Generalization
A **hasty generalization** is when the reader comes to a conclusion without reviewing or analyzing all the evidence. It is never a good idea to make a decision without all the information, which is why hasty generalizations are considered fallacies. For example, if two friends go to a hairdresser and give the hairdresser a positive recommendation, that does not necessarily mean that a new client will have the same experience. Two referrals is not quite enough information to form an educated and well-formed conclusion.

Overall, readers should carefully review and analyze authors' arguments to identify logical fallacies and come to sensible conclusions.

Figurative Language and Rhetorical Devices

Figurative Language
It's important to be able to recognize and interpret **figurative,** or non-literal, language. Literal statements rely directly on the denotations of words and express exactly what's happening in reality. Figurative language uses non-literal expressions to present information in a creative way. Consider the following sentences:

a. His pillow was very soft and he fell asleep quickly.

b. His pillow was a fluffy cloud and he floated away on it to the dream world.

Sentence *A* is literal, employing only the real meanings of each word. Sentence *B* is figurative. It employs a metaphor by stating that his pillow was a cloud. Of course, he isn't actually sleeping on a cloud, but the reader can draw on images of clouds as light, soft, fluffy, and relaxing to get a sense of how the character felt as he fell asleep. Also, in sentence *B*, the pillow becomes a vehicle that transports him to a magical dream world. The character isn't literally floating through the air—he's simply falling asleep! But by utilizing figurative language, the author creates a scene of peace, comfort, and relaxation that conveys stronger emotions and more creative imagery than the purely literal sentence. While there are countless types of figurative language, there are a few common ones that any reader should recognize.

Simile and **metaphor** are comparisons between two things, but their formats differ slightly. A simile says that two things are *similar* and makes a comparison using "like" or "as"—*A* is like *B*, or *A* is as [some characteristic] as *B*—whereas a metaphor states that two things are exactly the same—*A* is *B*. In both cases, simile and metaphor invite the reader to think more deeply about the characteristics of the two subjects and consider where they overlap. An example of metaphor can be found in the above sentence about the sleeper ("His pillow was a fluffy cloud"). For an example of simile, look at the first line of Robert Burns' famous poem:

> My love is like a red, red rose

This is comparison using "like," and the two things being compared are love and a rose. Some characteristics of a rose are that it's fragrant, beautiful, blossoming, colorful, vibrant—by comparing his love to a rose, Burns asks the reader to apply these qualities to his love. In this way, he implies that his love is also fresh, blossoming, and brilliant.

Similes can also compare things that appear dissimilar. Here's a song lyric from Florence and the Machine:

> Happiness hit her like a bullet in the back

"Happiness" has a very positive connotation, but getting "a bullet in the back" seems violent and aggressive, not at all related to happiness. By using an unexpected comparison, the writer forces readers to think more deeply about the comparison and ask themselves how could getting shot be similar to feeling happy. "A bullet in the back" is something that she doesn't see coming; it's sudden and forceful; and presumably, it has a strong impact on her life. So, in this way, the author seems to be saying that unexpected happiness made a sudden and powerful change in her life.

Another common form of figurative language is **personification,** when a non-human object is given human characteristics. William Blake uses personification here:

> . . . the stars threw down their spears,
>
> And watered heaven with their tears

He imagines the stars as combatants in a heavenly battle, giving them both action (throwing down their spears) and emotion (the sadness and disappointment of their tears). Personification helps to add emotion or develop relationships between characters and non-human objects. In fact, most people use personification in their everyday lives:

> My alarm clock betrayed me! It didn't go off this morning!
>
> The last piece of chocolate cake was staring at me from the refrigerator.

Next is **hyperbole,** a type of figurative language that uses extreme exaggeration. Sentences like, "I love you to the moon and back," or "I will love you for a million years," are examples of hyperbole. They aren't literally true—unfortunately, people cannot jump to outer space or live for a million years—but they're creative expressions that communicate the depth of feeling of the author.

Another way that writers add deeper meaning to their work is through **allusions.** An allusion is a reference to something from history, literature, or another cultural source. When the text is from a different culture or a time period, readers may not be familiar with every allusion. However, allusions tend to be well-known because the author wants the reader to make a connection between what's happening in the text and what's being referenced.

> I can't believe my best friend told our professor that I was skipping class to finish my final project! What a Judas!

This sentence contains a Biblical allusion to Judas, a friend and follower of Jesus who betrayed Jesus to the Romans. In this case, the allusion to Judas is used to give a deeper impression of betrayal and disloyalty from a trusted friend. Commonly used allusions in Western texts may come from the Bible, Greek or Roman mythology, or well-known literature such as Shakespeare. By familiarizing themselves with these touchstones of history and culture, readers can be more prepared to recognize allusions.

<u>Rhetorical Devices</u>

A **rhetorical device** is the phrasing and presentation of an idea that reinforces and emphasizes a point in an argument. A rhetorical device is often quite memorable. One of the more famous uses of a rhetorical device is in John F. Kennedy's 1961 inaugural address: "Ask not what your country can do for you, ask what you can do for your country." The contrast of ideas presented in the phrasing is an example of the rhetorical device of antimetabole. Some other common examples are provided below, but test takers should be aware that this is not a complete list.

Device	**Definition**	**Example**
Allusion	A reference to a famous person, event, or significant literary text as a form of significant comparison	"We are apt to shut our eyes against a painful truth, and listen to the song of that siren till she transforms us into beasts." Patrick Henry
Anaphora	The repetition of the same words at the beginning of successive words, phrases, or clauses, designed to emphasize an idea	"We shall not flag or fail. We shall go on to the end. We shall fight in France, we shall fight on the seas and oceans, we shall fight with growing confidence ... we shall fight in the fields and in the streets, we shall fight in the hills. We shall never surrender." Winston Churchill

Understatement	A statement meant to portray a situation as less important than it actually is to create an ironic effect	"The war in the Pacific has not necessarily developed in Japan's favor." Emperor Hirohito, surrendering Japan in World War II
Parallelism	A syntactical similarity in a structure or series of structures used for impact of an idea, making it memorable	"A penny saved is a penny earned." Ben Franklin
Rhetorical question	A question posed that is not answered by the writer though there is a desired response, most often designed to emphasize a point	"Can anyone look at our reduced standing in the world today and say, 'Let's have four more years of this?'" Ronald Reagan

Paraphrasing

One of the most essential reading skills is the ability to understand paraphrases. A **paraphrase** is restating information using different words to convey the same meaning. The ability to paraphrase, or to identify a good paraphrase, shows that the reader fully comprehends the reading material and is able to express that same information in a new way.

There are a few keys to mastering paraphrasing. The first is knowledge of **synonyms** (words with the same meaning) and **antonyms** (words with the opposite meaning). As paraphrasing depends on rewording information, readers should be familiar with a range of words with related meanings. Consider the following sentences:

> Scientists have yet to find any conclusive explanation for the sudden decrease in bee populations.
>
> Researchers don't have definitive answers for why the number of bees has suddenly dropped.

Both statements offer the same information, but they rely on synonyms (for example, "conclusive" and "definitive" or "decrease" and "drop") to present the facts in a different way. Same meaning, different words!

Another important paraphrasing tip is to be wary of any paraphrases that are *too strong* or *more extreme* than the source information. Remember, a paraphrase shouldn't significantly change the original facts—including the degree of emphasis. Let's look at another example:

> According to a recent survey, over 50 percent of students confessed to cheating on an exam within the past six months.

Which would be a better paraphrase of that statement?

a. One study found that the majority of students admitted to cheating on a test at least once over the last six months.

b. Recently, all students have been cheating on their exams, and schools need to crack down on this epidemic.

The original statement mentions "over 50 percent of students," and Choice *A* replaces that with an appropriate synonym: "the majority of students." However, Choice *B* exaggerates that claim to include "all students." For this reason, *A* is a better paraphrase of the original sentence. Also, *B* inserts an opinion (schools need to take action against cheating) that isn't present in the original sentence. A paraphrase should neither add new information nor remove essential facts that change the meaning of the source.

Another closely related comprehension tool is summarizing. A **summary** takes a long passage and condenses it into a much shorter one. The key to a good summary is to emphasize the main idea and not change the focus of the original information by getting distracted by smaller details. However, important details or supportive evidence should also be accurately reported in the summary. If writers provide irrelevant details in the summary, it may cloud the greater meaning of the text or passage. When summarizing, writers should not include their opinions, quotes, or what they thought the author should have said. A clear summary provides clarity of the text or passage to the readers.

The following checklist lists items that writers should include in a summary:

Summary Checklist

- Title of the story
- Someone: Who is or are the main character(s)?
- Wanted: What did the character(s) want?
- But: What was the problem?
- So: How did the character(s) solve the problem?
- Then: How did the story end? What was the resolution?

Understanding Vocabulary in Context

A useful vocabulary skill for reading comprehension is being able to understand meaning in context. A word's **context** refers to other words and information surrounding it, which can have a big impact on how readers interpret that word's meaning. Of course, many words have more than one definition. For example, consider the meaning of the word "engaged." The first definition that comes to mind might be "promised to be married," but consider the following sentences:

a. The two armies engaged in a conflict that lasted all night.

b. The three-hour lecture flew by because students were so engaged in the material.

c. The busy executive engaged a new assistant to help with his workload.

Were any of those sentences related to marriage? In fact, "engaged" has a variety of other meanings. In these sentences, respectively, it can mean: "battled," "interested or involved," and "appointed or employed." Readers may wonder how to decide which definition to apply. The appropriate meaning is prioritized based on context. For example, sentence *C* mentions "executive," "assistant," and "workload," so readers can assume that "engaged" has something to do with work—in which case, "appointed or employed" is the best definition for this context. Context clues can also be found in sentence *A*. Words like "armies" and "conflicts" show that this sentence is about a military situation, so in this context, "engaged" is closest in meaning to "battled." By using context clues—the surrounding words in the sentence—readers can easily select the most appropriate definition.

Context clues can also help readers when they don't know *any* meanings for a certain word. Test writers will deliberately ask about unfamiliar vocabulary to measure your ability to use context to make an educated guess about a word's meaning.

Which of the following is the closest in meaning to the word "loquacious" in the following sentence?

The *loquacious* professor was notorious for always taking too long to finish his lectures.

a. knowledgeable
b. enthusiastic
c. approachable
d. talkative

Even if the word "loquacious" seems completely new, it's possible to utilize context to make a good guess about the word's meaning. Grammatically, it's apparent that "loquacious" is an adjective that modifies the noun "professor"—so "loquacious" must be some kind of quality or characteristic. A clue in this sentence is "taking too long to finish his lectures." Readers should then consider qualities that might cause a professor's lectures to run long. Perhaps he's "disorganized," "slow," or "talkative"—all words that might still make sense in this sentence. Choice *D*, therefore, is a logical choice for this sentence—the professor talks too much, so his lectures run late. In fact, "loquacious" means "talkative or wordy."

One way to use context clues is to think of potential replacement words before considering the answer choices. You can also turn to the answer choices first and try to replace each of them in the sentence to see if the sentence is logical and retains the same meaning.

Another way to use context clues is to consider clues in the word itself. Most students are familiar with prefixes, suffixes, and root words—the building blocks of many English words. A little knowledge goes a long way when it comes to these components of English vocabulary, and these words can point readers in the right direction when they need help finding an appropriate definition.

Specific Word Choices on Meaning and Tone

Just as one word may have different meanings, the same meaning can be conveyed by different words or synonyms. However, there are very few synonyms that have *exactly* the same definition. Rather, there are slight nuances in usage and meaning. In this case, a writer's *diction*, or word choice, is important to the meaning meant to be conveyed.

Many words have a surface *denotation* and a deeper *connotation*. A word's *denotation* is the literal definition of a word that can be found in any dictionary (an easy way to remember this is that "denotation" and "dictionary definition" all begin with the letter "D"). For example, if someone looked up the word "snake" in the dictionary, they'd learn that a snake is a common reptile with scales, a long body, and no limbs.

A word's *connotation* refers to its emotional and cultural associations, beyond its literal definition. Some connotations are universal, some are common within a particular cultural group, and some are more personal. Let's go back to the word "snake." A reader probably already knows its denotation—a slithering animal—but readers should also take a moment to consider its possible connotations. For readers from a Judeo-Christian culture, they might associate a snake with the serpent from the Garden of Eden who tempts Adam and Eve into eating the forbidden fruit. In this case, a snake's connotations might include deceit, danger, and sneakiness.

Consider the following character description:

> He slithered into the room like a snake.

Does this sound like a character who can be trusted? It's the connotation of the word "snake" that implies untrustworthiness. Connotative language, then, helps writers to communicate a deeper, more emotional meaning.

Read the following excerpt from "The Lamb," a poem by William Blake.

> Little lamb, who made thee?
> Dost thou know who made thee,
> Gave thee life, and bid thee feed
> By the stream and o'er the mead;
> Gave thee clothing of delight,
> Softest clothing, woolly, bright;
> Gave thee such a tender voice,
> Making all the vales rejoice?
> Little lamb, who made thee?
> Dost thou know who made thee?

Think about the connotations of a "lamb." Whereas a snake might make readers think of something dangerous and dishonest, a lamb tends to carry a different connotation: innocence and purity. Blake's poem contains other emotional language—"delight," "softest," "tender," "rejoice"—to support this impression.

Some words have similar denotations but very different connotations. "Weird" and "unique" can both describe something distinctive and unlike the norm. But they convey different emotions:

> You have such a weird fashion sense!

> You have such a unique fashion sense!

Which sentence is a compliment? Which sentence is an insult? "Weird" generally has more negative connotations, whereas "unique" is more positive. In this way, connotative language is a powerful way for writers to evoke emotion.

A writer's diction also informs their tone. *Tone* refers to the author's attitude toward their subject. A writer's tone might be critical, curious, respectful, dismissive, or any other possible attitude. The key to understanding tone is focusing not just on *what* is said, but on *how* it's said.

> a. Although the latest drug trial did not produce a successful vaccine, medical researchers are one step further on the path to eradicating this deadly virus.
>
> b. Doctors faced yet another disappointing setback in their losing battle against the killer virus; their most recent drug trial has proved as unsuccessful as the last.

Both sentences report the same information: the latest drug trial was a failure. However, each sentence presents this information in a different way, revealing the writer's tone. The first sentence has a more hopeful and confident tone, downplaying the doctors' failure ("although" it failed) and emphasizing their progress ("one step further"). The second sentence has a decidedly more pessimistic and defeatist tone, using phrases like "disappointing setback" and "losing battle." The details a writer chooses to include can also help readers to identify their attitude towards their subject matter.

Identifying emotional or connotative language can be useful in determining the tone of a text. Readers can also consider questions such as, "Who is the speaker?" or "Who is their audience?" (Remember, particularly in fiction, that the speaker or narrator may not be the same person as the author.) For example, in an article about military conflict written by a notable anti-war activist, readers might expect their tone to be critical, harsh, or cynical. If they are presented with a poem written between newlyweds, readers might expect the tone to be loving, sensitive, or infatuated. If the tone seems wildly different from what's expected, consider if the writer is using *irony*. When a writer uses irony, they say one thing but imply the opposite meaning.

Math Knowledge

Basic Math, Number Sense, and Arithmetic

Basic Operations of Arithmetic

There are four different basic operations used with numbers: addition, subtraction, multiplication, and division.

- Addition takes two numbers and combines them into a total called the **sum.** The sum is the total when combining two collections into one. If there are 5 things in one collection and 3 in another, then after combining them, there is a total of $5 + 3 = 8$. Note the order does not matter when adding numbers. For example, $3 + 5 = 8$.

- Subtraction is the opposite (or "inverse") operation to addition. Whereas addition combines two quantities together, subtraction takes one quantity away from another. For example, if there are 20 gallons of fuel and 5 are removed, that gives $20 - 5 = 15$ gallons remaining. Note that for subtraction, the order does matter because it makes a difference which quantity is being removed from which.

- Multiplication is repeated addition. 3×4 can be thought of as putting together 3 sets of items, each set containing 4 items. The total is 12 items. Another way to think of this is to think of each number as the length of one side of a rectangle. If a rectangle is covered in tiles with 3 columns of 4 tiles each, then there are 12 tiles in total. From this, one can see that the answer is the same if the rectangle has 4 rows of 3 tiles each: $4 \times 3 = 12$. By expanding this reasoning, the order the numbers are multiplied does not matter.

- Division is the opposite of multiplication. It means taking one quantity and dividing it into sets the size of the second quantity. If there are 16 sandwiches to be distributed to 4 people, then each person gets $16 \div 4 = 4$ sandwiches. As with subtraction, the order in which the numbers appear does matter for division.

<u>Addition</u>

Addition is the combination of two numbers so their quantities are added together cumulatively. The sign for an addition operation is the + symbol. For example, 9 + 6 = 15. The 9 and 6 combine to achieve a cumulative value, called a **sum**.

Addition holds the **commutative property**, which means that numbers in an addition equation can be switched without altering the result. The formula for the commutative property is a + b = b + a. Let's look at a few examples to see how the commutative property works:

$$7 = 3 + 4 = 4 + 3 = 7$$

$$20 = 12 + 8 = 8 + 12 = 20$$

Addition also holds the **associative property**, which means that the grouping of numbers doesn't matter in an addition problem. In other words, the presence or absence of parentheses is irrelevant. The formula for the associative property is $(a + b) + c = a + (b + c)$. Here are some examples of the associative property at work:

$$30 = (6 + 14) + 10 = 6 + (14 + 10) = 30$$

$$35 = 8 + (2 + 25) = (8 + 2) + 25 = 35$$

<u>Subtraction</u>
Subtraction is taking away one number from another, so their quantities are reduced. The sign designating a subtraction operation is the – symbol, and the result is called the **difference**. For example, $9 - 6 = 3$. The number *6* detracts from the number *9* to reach the difference *3*.

Unlike addition, subtraction follows neither the commutative nor associative properties. The order and grouping in subtraction impact the result.

$$15 = 22 - 7 \neq 7 - 22 = -15$$

$$3 = (10 - 5) - 2 \neq 10 - (5 - 2) = 7$$

When working through subtraction problems involving larger numbers, it's necessary to regroup the numbers. Let's work through a practice problem using regrouping:

$$\begin{array}{r} 3\;2\;5 \\ -\;\;7\;7 \\ \hline \end{array}$$

Here, it is clear that the ones and tens columns for 77 are greater than the ones and tens columns for 325. To subtract this number, borrow from the tens and hundreds columns. When borrowing from a column, subtracting 1 from the lender column will add 10 to the borrower column:

$$\begin{array}{rrr} 3\text{-}1 & 10\text{+}2\text{-}1 & 10\text{+}5 \\ - & 7 & 7 \\ \hline \end{array} = \begin{array}{rrr} 2 & 11 & 15 \\ - & 7 & 7 \\ \hline 2 & 4 & 8 \end{array}$$

After ensuring that each digit in the top row is greater than the digit in the corresponding bottom row, subtraction can proceed as normal, and the answer is found to be 248.

<u>Multiplication</u>
Multiplication involves adding together multiple copies of a number. It is indicated by an $\times$ symbol or a number immediately outside of a parentheses, e.g. $5(8 - 2)$. The two numbers being multiplied

together are called **factors**, and their result is called a **product**. For example, $9 \times 6 = 54$. This can be shown alternatively by expansion of either the 9 or the 6:

$$9 \times 6 = 9 + 9 + 9 + 9 + 9 + 9 = 54$$

$$9 \times 6 = 6 + 6 + 6 + 6 + 6 + 6 + 6 + 6 + 6 = 54$$

Like addition, multiplication holds the commutative and associative properties:

$$115 = 23 \times 5 = 5 \times 23 = 115$$

$$84 = 3 \times (7 \times 4) = (3 \times 7) \times 4 = 84$$

Multiplication also follows the distributive property, which allows the multiplication to be distributed through parentheses. The formula for distribution is $a \times (b + c) = ab + ac$. This is clear after the examples:

$$45 = 5 \times 9 = 5(3 + 6) = \ (5 \times 3) + (5 \times 6) = 15 + 30 = 45$$

$$20 = 4 \times 5 = 4(10 - 5) = (4 \times 10) - (4 \times 5) = 40 - 20 = 20$$

Multiplication becomes slightly more complicated when multiplying numbers with decimals. The easiest way to answer these problems is to ignore the decimals and multiply as if they were whole numbers. After multiplying the factors, place a decimal in the product. The placement of the decimal is determined by taking the cumulative number of decimal places in the factors.

For example:

0.7	2.6	1.5
x 3	x 4.2	x 6.4
2.1	10.92	9.60

Let's tackle the first example. First, ignore the decimal and multiply the numbers as though they were whole numbers to arrive at a product: 21. Second, count the number of digits that follow a decimal (one). Finally, move the decimal place that many positions to the left, as the factors have only one decimal place. The second example works the same way, except that there are two total decimal places in the factors, so the product's decimal is moved two places over. In the third example, the decimal should be moved over two digits, but the digit zero is no longer needed, so it is erased and the final answer is 9.6.

<u>Division</u>

Division and multiplication are inverses of each other in the same way that addition and subtraction are opposites. The signs designating a division operation are the ÷ and / symbols. In division, the second number divides into the first.

The number before the division sign is called the **dividend** or, if expressed as a fraction, the **numerator**. For example, in $a \div b$, a is the dividend, while in $\frac{a}{b}$, a is the numerator.

The number after the division sign is called the **divisor** or, if expressed as a fraction, the **denominator**. For example, in $a \div b$, b is the divisor, while in $\frac{a}{b}$, b is the denominator.

Like subtraction, division doesn't follow the commutative property, as it matters which number comes before the division sign, and division doesn't follow the associative or distributive properties for the same reason. For example:

$$\frac{3}{2} = 9 \div 6 \neq 6 \div 9 = \frac{2}{3}$$

$$2 = 10 \div 5 = (30 \div 3) \div 5 \neq 30 \div (3 \div 5) = 30 \div \frac{3}{5} = 50$$

$$25 = 20 + 5 = (40 \div 2) + (40 \div 8) \neq 40 \div (2 + 8) = 40 \div 10 = 4$$

If a divisor doesn't divide into a dividend an integer number of times, whatever is left over is termed the **remainder**. The remainder can be further divided out into decimal form by using long division; however, this doesn't always give a quotient with a finite number of decimal places, so the remainder can also be expressed as a fraction over the original divisor.

Division with decimals is similar to multiplication with decimals in that when dividing a decimal by a whole number, ignore the decimal and divide as if it were a whole number.

Upon finding the answer, or quotient, place the decimal at the decimal place equal to that in the dividend.

$$15.75 \div 3 = 5.25$$

When the divisor is a decimal number, multiply both the divisor and dividend by 10. Repeat this until the divisor is a whole number, then complete the division operation as described above.

$$17.5 \div 2.5 = 175 \div 25 = 7$$

Order of Operations

When working with complicated expressions, parentheses are used to indicate in which order to perform operations. However, to avoid having too many parentheses in an expression, here are some basic rules concerning the proper order to perform operations when not otherwise specified.

1. Parentheses: always perform operations inside parentheses first, regardless of what those operations are
2. Exponents
3. Multiplication and Division
4. Addition and Subtraction

For #3 & #4, work these from left to right. So, if there a subtraction problem and then an addition problem, the subtraction problem will be worked first.

Note that multiplication and division are performed from left to right as they appear in the expression or equation. Addition and subtraction also are performed from left to right as they appear.

As an aid to memorizing this, some students like to use the mnemonic PEMDAS. Furthermore, this acronym can be associated with a mnemonic phrase such as "Pirates Eat Many Donuts At Sea."

Evaluate the following two problems to understand the Order of Operations:

1) $4 + (3 \times 2)^2 \div 4$

First, solve the operation within the parentheses: $4 + 6^2 \div 4$.
Second, solve the exponent: $4 + 36 \div 4$.
Third, solve the division operation: $4 + 9$.
Fourth, finish the operation with addition for the answer, 13.

2) $2 \times (6 + 3) \div (2 + 1)^2$

$2 \times 9 \div (3)^2$
$2 \times 9 \div 9$
$18 \div 9$
2

Properties of Operations

Properties of operations exist that make calculations easier and solve problems for missing values. The following table summarizes commonly used properties of real numbers.

Property	Addition	Multiplication
Commutative	$a + b = b + a$	$a \times b = b \times a$
Associative	$(a + b) + c = a + (b + c)$	$(a \times b) \times c = a \times (bc)$
Identity	$a + 0 = a;\ 0 + a = a$	$a \times 1 = a;\ 1 \times a = a$
Inverse	$a + (-a) = 0$	$a \times \frac{1}{a} = 1;\ a \neq 0$
Distributive	$a(b + c) = ab + ac$	

The cumulative property of addition states that the order in which numbers are added does not change the sum. Similarly, the commutative property of multiplication states that the order in which numbers are multiplied does not change the product. The associative property of addition and multiplication state that the grouping of numbers being added or multiplied does not change the sum or product, respectively. The commutative and associative properties are useful for performing calculations. For example, $(47 + 25) + 3$ is equivalent to $(47 + 3) + 25$, which is easier to calculate.

The identity property of addition states that adding zero to any number does not change its value. The identity property of multiplication states that multiplying a number by 1 does not change its value. The inverse property of addition states that the sum of a number and its opposite equals zero. Opposites are numbers that are the same with different signs (ex. 5 and -5; $-\frac{1}{2}$ and $\frac{1}{2}$). The inverse property of multiplication states that the product of a number (other than 0) and its reciprocal equals 1. Reciprocal numbers have numerators and denominators that are inverted (ex. $\frac{2}{5}$ and $\frac{5}{2}$). Inverse properties are useful for canceling quantities to find missing values (see algebra content). For example, $a + 7 = 12$ is solved by adding the inverse of 7(-7) to both sides in order to isolate a.

The distributive property states that multiplying a sum (or difference) by a number produces the same result as multiplying each value in the sum (or difference) by the number and adding (or subtracting) the products. Consider the following scenario: You are buying three tickets for a baseball game. Each ticket costs $18. You are also charged a fee of $2 per ticket for purchasing the tickets online. The cost is calculated: $3 \times 18 + 3 \times 2$. Using the distributive property, the cost can also be calculated $3(18 + 2)$.

Basic Concepts of Number Theory

<u>Prime and Composite Numbers</u>

Whole numbers are classified as either prime or composite. A prime number can only be divided evenly by itself and one. For example, the number 11 can only be divided evenly by 11 and one; therefore, 11 is a prime number. A helpful way to visualize a prime number is to use concrete objects and try to divide them into equal piles. If dividing 11 coins, the only way to divide them into equal piles is to create 1 pile of 11 coins or to create 11 piles of 1 coin each. Other examples of prime numbers include 2, 3, 5, 7, 13, 17, and 19.

A composite number is any whole number that is not a prime number. A composite number is a number that can be divided evenly by one or more numbers other than itself and one. For example, the number 6 can be divided evenly by 2 and 3. Therefore, 6 is a composite number. If dividing 6 coins into equal piles, the possibilities are 1 pile of 6 coins, 2 piles of 3 coins, 3 piles of 2 coins, or 6 piles of 1 coin. Other examples of composite numbers include 4, 8, 9, 10, 12, 14, 15, 16, 18, and 20.

To determine if a number is a prime or composite number, the number is divided by every whole number greater than one and less than its own value. If it divides evenly by any of these numbers, then the number is composite. If it does not divide evenly by any of these numbers, then the number is prime. For example, when attempting to divide the number 5 by 2, 3, and 4, none of these numbers divide evenly. Therefore, 5 must be a prime number.

<u>Odd and Even Numbers</u>

Even numbers are all divisible by the number 2. **Odd numbers** are not divisible by 2, and an odd quantity of items cannot be paired up into groups of 2 without having 1 item leftover. Examples of even numbers are 2, 4, 6, 20, 100, 242, etc. Examples of odd numbers are 1, 3, 5, 27, 99, 333, etc.

<u>Factors, Multiples, and Divisibility</u>

The **Fundamental Theorem of Arithmetic** states that any integer greater than 1 is either a prime number or can be written as a unique product of prime numbers. Factors can be used to find the combination of numbers to multiply to produce an integer that is not prime. The factors of a number are all integers that can be multiplied by another integer to produce the given number. For example, 2 is multiplied by 3 to produce 6. Therefore, 2 and 3 are both factors of 6. Similarly, $1 \times 6 = 6$ and $2 \times 3 = 6$, so 1, 2, 3, and 6 are all factors of 6. Another way to explain a factor is to say that a given number divides evenly by each of its factors to produce an integer. For example, 6 does not divide evenly by 5. Therefore, 5 is not a factor of 6.

Essentially, **factors** are the numbers multiplied to achieve a product. Thus, every product in a multiplication equation has, at minimum, two factors. Of course, some products will have more than two factors. For the sake of most discussions, assume that factors are positive integers.

To find a number's factors, start with 1 and the number itself. Then divide the number by 2, 3, 4, and so on, seeing if any divisors can divide the number without a remainder, keeping a list of those that do. Stop upon reaching either the number itself or another factor.

Let's find the factors of 45. Start with 1 and 45. Then try to divide 45 by 2, which fails. Now divide 45 by 3. The answer is 15, so 3 and 15 are now factors. Dividing by 4 doesn't work, and dividing by 5 leaves 9. Lastly, dividing 45 by 6, 7, and 8 all don't work. The next integer to try is 9, but this is already known to be a factor, so the factorization is complete. The factors of 45 are 1, 3, 5, 9, 15 and 45.

A **common factor** is a factor shared by two numbers. Let's take 45 and 30 and find the common factors:

> The factors of 45 are: 1, 3, 5, 9, 15, and 45.
> The factors of 30 are: 1, 2, 3, 5, 6, 10, 15, and 30.
> The common factors are 1, 3, 5, and 15.

The **greatest common factor** is the largest number among the shared, common factors. From the factors of 45 and 30, the common factors are 3, 5, and 15. Thus, 15 is the greatest common factor, as it's the largest number.

Multiples of a given number are found by taking that number and multiplying it by any other whole number. For example, 3 is a factor of 6, 9, and 12. Therefore, 6, 9, and 12 are multiples of 3. The multiples of any number are an infinite list. For example, the multiples of 5 are 5, 10, 15, 20, and so on. This list continues without end. A list of multiples is used in finding the **least common multiple**, or **LCM,** for fractions when a common denominator is needed. The denominators are written down and their multiples listed until a common number is found in both lists. This common number is the LCM.

If two numbers share no factors besides 1 in common, then their least common multiple will be simply their product. If two numbers have common factors, then their least common multiple will be their product divided by their greatest common factor. This can be visualized by the formula $LCM = \frac{x \times y}{GCF}$, where *x* and *y* are some integers and LCM and GCF are their least common multiple and greatest common factor, respectively.

Prime factorization breaks down each factor of a whole number until only prime numbers remain. All composite numbers can be factored into prime numbers. For example, the prime factors of 12 are 2, 2, and 3 ($2 \times 2 \times 3 = 12$). To produce the prime factors of a number, the number is factored and any composite numbers are continuously factored until the result is the product of prime factors only. A factor tree, such as the one below, is helpful when exploring this concept.

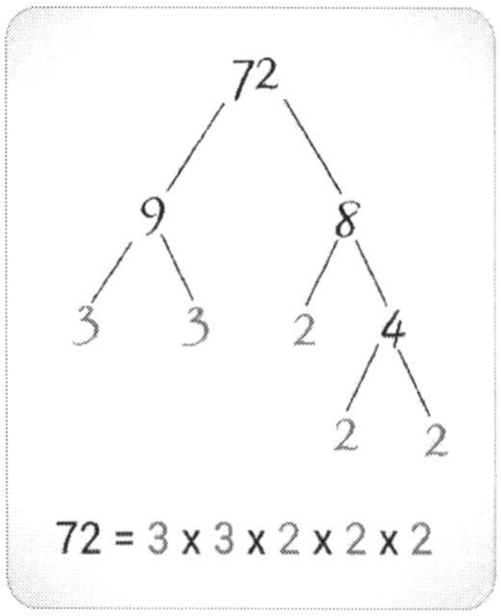

Let's break 129 down into its prime factors. First, the factors are 3 and 43. Both 3 and 43 are prime numbers, so we're done. But if 43 was not a prime number, then it would also need to be factorized until all of the factors are expressed as prime numbers.

Comparing, Classifying, and Ordering Real Numbers

Rational numbers are any number that can be written as a fraction or ratio. Within the set of rational numbers, several subsets exist that are referenced throughout the mathematics topics. **Counting numbers** are the first numbers learned as a child. Counting numbers consist of 1,2,3,4, and so on. **Whole numbers** include all counting numbers and zero (0,1,2,3,4,...). **Integers** include counting numbers, their opposites, and zero (...,-3,-2,-1,0,1,2,3,...). **Rational numbers** are inclusive of integers, fractions, and decimals that terminate, or end (1.7, 0.04213) or repeat ($0.136\overline{5}$).

A **number line** typically consists of integers (...3,2,1,0,-1,-2,-3...), and is used to visually represent the value of a rational number. Each rational number has a distinct position on the line determined by comparing its value with the displayed values on the line. For example, if plotting -1.5 on the number line below, it is necessary to recognize that the value of -1.5 is .5 less than -1 and .5 greater than -2. Therefore, -1.5 is plotted halfway between -1 and -2.

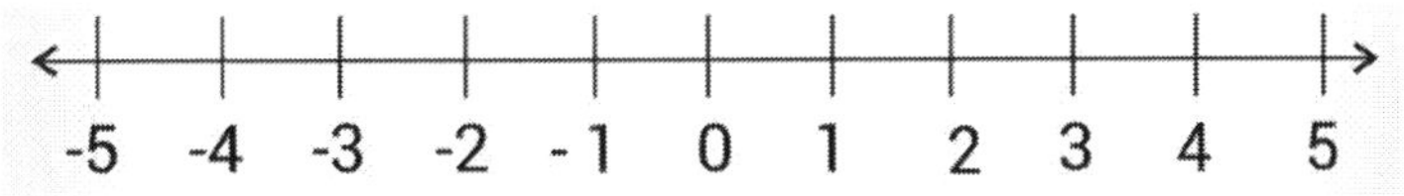

The number system that is used consists of only ten different digits or characters. However, this system is used to represent an infinite number of values. The **place value system** makes this infinite number of values possible. The position in which a digit is written corresponds to a given value. Starting from the decimal point (which is implied, if not physically present), each subsequent place value to the left represents a value greater than the one before it. Conversely, starting from the decimal point, each subsequent place value to the right represents a value less than the one before it.

The names for the place values to the left of the decimal point are as follows:

...	Billions	Hundred-Millions	Ten-Millions	Millions	Hundred-Thousands	Ten-Thousands	Thousands	Hundreds	Tens	Ones

*Note that this table can be extended infinitely further to the left.

The names for the place values to the right of the decimal point are as follows:

Decimal Point (.)	Tenths	Hundredths	Thousandths	Ten-Thousandths	...

*Note that this table can be extended infinitely further to the right.

When given a multi-digit number, the value of each digit depends on its place value. Consider the number 682,174.953. Referring to the chart above, it can be determined that the digit 8 is in the ten-thousands place. It is in the fifth place to the left of the decimal point. Its value is 8 ten-thousands or 80,000. The digit 5 is two places to the right of the decimal point. Therefore, the digit 5 is in the hundredths place. Its value is 5 hundredths or $\frac{5}{100}$ (equivalent to .05).

In accordance with the **base-10 system**, the value of a digit increases by a factor of ten each place it moves to the left. For example, consider the number 7. Moving the digit one place to the left (70), increases its value by a factor of 10 ($7 \times 10 = 70$). Moving the digit two places to the left (700) increases its value by a factor of 10 twice ($7 \times 10 \times 10 = 700$). Moving the digit three places to the left (7,000) increases its value by a factor of 10 three times ($7 \times 10 \times 10 \times 10 = 7{,}000$), and so on.

Conversely, the value of a digit decreases by a factor of ten each place it moves to the right. (Note that multiplying by $\frac{1}{10}$ is equivalent to dividing by 10). For example, consider the number 40. Moving the digit one place to the right (4) decreases its value by a factor of 10 ($40 \div 10 = 4$). Moving the digit two places to the right (0.4), decreases its value by a factor of 10 twice ($40 \div 10 \div 10 = 0.4$) or ($40 \times \frac{1}{10} \times \frac{1}{10} = 0.4$). Moving the digit three places to the right (0.04) decreases its value by a factor of 10 three times ($40 \div 10 \div 10 \div 10 = 0.04$) or ($40 \times \frac{1}{10} \times \frac{1}{10} \times \frac{1}{10} = 0.04$), and so on.

Ordering Numbers

A common question type asks to order rational numbers from least to greatest or greatest to least. The numbers will come in a variety of formats, including decimals, percentages, roots, fractions, and whole numbers. These questions test for knowledge of different types of numbers and the ability to determine their respective values.

Before discussing ordering all numbers, let's start with decimals.

To compare decimals and order them by their value, utilize a method similar to that of ordering large numbers.

The main difference is where the comparison will start. Assuming that any numbers to left of the decimal point are equal, the next numbers to be compared are those immediately to the right of the decimal point. If those are equal, then move on to compare the values in the next decimal place to the right.

For example:

Which number is greater, 12.35 or 12.38?

Check that the values to the left of the decimal point are equal:

12 = 12

Next, compare the values of the decimal place to the right of the decimal:

12.3 = 12.3

Those are also equal in value.

Finally, compare the value of the numbers in the next decimal place to the right on both numbers:

12.3**5** and 12.3**8**

Here the 5 is less than the 8, so the final way to express this inequality is:

$12.35 < 12.38$

Comparing decimals is regularly exemplified with money because the "cents" portion of money ends in the hundredths place. When paying for gasoline or meals in restaurants, and even in bank accounts, if enough errors are made when calculating numbers to the hundredths place, they can add up to dollars and larger amounts of money over time.

Now that decimal ordering has been explained, let's expand and consider all real numbers. Whether the question asks to order the numbers from greatest to least or least to greatest, the crux of the question is the same—convert the numbers into a common format. Generally, it's easiest to write the numbers as whole numbers and decimals so they can be placed on a number line. Follow these examples to understand this strategy.

1) Order the following rational numbers from greatest to least:

$$\sqrt{36}, 0.65, 78\%, \frac{3}{4}, 7, 90\%, \frac{5}{2}$$

Of the seven numbers, the whole number (7) and decimal (0.65) are already in an accessible form, so concentrate on the other five.

First, the square root of 36 equals 6. (If the test asks for the root of a non-perfect root, determine which two whole numbers the root lies between.) Next, convert the percentages to decimals. A percentage means "per hundred," so this conversion requires moving the decimal point two places to the left, leaving 0.78 and 0.9. Lastly, evaluate the fractions:

$$\frac{3}{4} = \frac{75}{100} = 0.75\,; \frac{5}{2} = 2\frac{1}{2} = 2.5$$

Now, the only step left is to list the numbers in the request order:

$$7, \sqrt{36}, \frac{5}{2}, 90\%, 78\%, \frac{3}{4}, 0.65$$

2) Order the following rational numbers from least to greatest:

$$2.5, \sqrt{9}, -10.5, 0.853, 175\%, \sqrt{4}, \frac{4}{5}$$

$$\sqrt{9} = 3$$

$$175\% = 1.75$$

$$\sqrt{4} = 2$$

$$\frac{4}{5} = 0.8$$

From least to greatest, the answer is:

$$-10.5, \frac{4}{5}, 0.853, 175\%, \sqrt{4}, 2.5, \sqrt{9}$$

Performing Operations Involving Exponents

Exponents are used in mathematics to express a number or variable multiplied by itself a certain number of times. For example, x^3 means *x* is multiplied by itself three times. In this expression, x is called the **base**, and 3 is the **exponent.** Exponents can be used in more complex problems when they contain fractions and negative numbers.

Fractional exponents can be explained by looking first at the inverse of exponents, which are **roots.** Given the expression x^2, the square root can be taken, $\sqrt{x^2}$, cancelling out the 2 and leaving *x* by itself, if *x* is positive. Cancellation occurs because $\sqrt{x}$ can be written with exponents, instead of roots, as $x^{\frac{1}{2}}$. The numerator of 1 is the exponent, and the denominator of 2 is called the **root** (which is why it's referred to as a **square root**). Taking the square root of x^2 is the same as raising it to the $\frac{1}{2}$ power. Written out in mathematical form, it takes the following progression:

$$\sqrt{x^2} = (x^2)^{\frac{1}{2}} = x$$

From properties of exponents, $2 \times \frac{1}{2} = 1$ is the actual exponent of *x*. Another example can be seen with $x^{\frac{4}{7}}$. The variable *x,* raised to four-sevenths, is equal to the seventh root of *x* to the fourth power: $\sqrt[7]{x^4}$. In general,

$$x^{\frac{1}{n}} = \sqrt[n]{x}$$

and

$$x^{\frac{m}{n}} = \sqrt[n]{x^m}$$

Negative exponents also involve fractions. Whereas y^3 can also be rewritten as $\frac{y^3}{1}$, y^{-3} can be rewritten as $\frac{1}{y^3}$. A negative exponent means the exponential expression must be moved to the opposite spot in a fraction to make the exponent positive. If the negative appears in the numerator, it moves to the denominator. If the negative appears in the denominator, it is moved to the numerator. In general, $a^{-n} = \frac{1}{a^n}$, and a^{-n} and a^n are reciprocals.

Take, for example, the following expression:

$$\frac{a^{-4}b^2}{c^{-5}}$$

Since *a* is raised to the negative fourth power, it can be moved to the denominator. Since *c* is raised to the negative fifth power, it can be moved to the numerator. The *b* variable is raised to the positive second power, so it does not move.

The simplified expression is as follows:

$$\frac{b^2c^5}{a^4}$$

In mathematical expressions containing exponents and other operations, the order of operations must be followed. **PEMDAS** states that exponents are calculated after any parenthesis and grouping symbols, but before any multiplication, division, addition, and subtraction.

Simplifying and Approximating Radicals

The **square root symbol** is expressed as $\sqrt{\ }$ and is commonly known as the **radical.** Taking the root of a number is the inverse operation of multiplying that number by itself some amount of times. For example, squaring the number 7 is equal to 7×7, or 49. Finding the square root is the opposite of finding an exponent, as the operation seeks a number that when multiplied by itself equals the number in the square root symbol.

For example, $\sqrt{36}$ = 6 because 6 multiplied by 6 equals 36. Note, the square root of 36 is also -6 since -6 x -6 = 36. This can be indicated using a plus/minus symbol like this: ±6. However, square roots are often just expressed as a positive number for simplicity with it being understood that the true value can be either positive or negative.

Perfect squares are numbers with whole number–square roots. The list of perfect squares begins with 0, 1, 4, 9, 16, 25, 36, 49, 64, 81, and 100.

Determining the square root of imperfect squares requires a calculator to reach an exact figure. It's possible, however, to approximate the answer by finding the two perfect squares that the number fits between. For example, the square root of 40 is between 6 and 7 since the squares of those numbers are 36 and 49, respectively.

Square roots are the most common root operation. If the radical doesn't have a number to the upper left of the symbol $\sqrt{}$, then it's a square root. Sometimes a radical includes a number in the upper left, like $\sqrt[3]{27}$, as in the other common root type—the cube root. Complicated roots like the cube root often require a calculator.

Fractions

A **fraction** is an equation that represents a part of a whole, but can also be used to present ratios or division problems. An example of a fraction is $\frac{x}{y}$. In this example, x is called the **numerator,** while y is the **denominator**. The numerator represents the number of parts, and the denominator is the total number of parts. They are separated by a line or slash, known as a fraction bar.. In simple fractions, the numerator and denominator can be nearly any integer. However, the denominator of a fraction can never be zero, because dividing by zero is a function which is undefined.

Imagine that an apple pie has been baked for a holiday party, and the full pie has eight slices. After the party, there are five slices left. How could the amount of the pie that remains be expressed as a fraction? The numerator is 5 since there are 5 pieces left, and the denominator is 8 since there were eight total slices in the whole pie. Thus, expressed as a fraction, the leftover pie totals $\frac{5}{8}$ of the original amount.

Fractions come in three different varieties: proper fractions, improper fractions, and mixed numbers. **Proper fractions** have a numerator less than the denominator, such as $\frac{3}{8}$, but **improper fractions** have a numerator greater than the denominator, such as $\frac{15}{8}$. **Mixed numbers** combine a whole number with a proper fraction, such as $3\frac{1}{2}$. Any mixed number can be written as an improper fraction by multiplying the integer by the denominator, adding the product to the value of the numerator, and dividing the sum by the original denominator. For example, $3\frac{1}{2} = \frac{3 \times 2 + 1}{2} = \frac{7}{2}$. Whole numbers can also be converted into fractions by placing the whole number as the numerator and making the denominator 1. For example, $3 = \frac{3}{1}$.

One of the most fundamental concepts of fractions is their ability to be manipulated by multiplication or division. This is possible since $\frac{n}{n}$ = 1 for any non-zero integer. As a result, multiplying or dividing by $\frac{n}{n}$ will not alter the original fraction since any number multiplied or divided by 1 doesn't change the value of that number. Fractions of the same value are known as equivalent fractions. For example, $\frac{2}{4}, \frac{4}{8}, \frac{50}{100}$, and $\frac{75}{150}$ are equivalent, as they all equal $\frac{1}{2}$.

Although many equivalent fractions exist, they are easier to compare and interpret when reduced or simplified. The numerator and denominator of a simple fraction will have no factors in common other than 1. When reducing or simplifying fractions, divide the numerator and denominator by the greatest common factor. A simple strategy is to divide the numerator and denominator by low numbers, like 2, 3, or 5 until arriving at a simple fraction, but the same thing could be achieved by determining the greatest common factor for both the numerator and denominator and dividing each by it. Using the first method is preferable when both the numerator and denominator are even, end in 5, or are obviously a multiple of another number. However, if no numbers seem to work, it will be necessary to factor the numerator and denominator to find the GCF. Let's look at examples:

1) Simplify the fraction $\frac{6}{8}$:

Dividing the numerator and denominator by 2 results in $\frac{3}{4}$, which is a simple fraction.

2) Simplify the fraction $\frac{12}{36}$:

Dividing the numerator and denominator by 2 leaves $\frac{6}{18}$. This isn't a simple fraction, as both the numerator and denominator have factors in common. Diving each by 3 results in $\frac{2}{6}$, but this can be further simplified by dividing by 2 to get $\frac{1}{3}$. This is the simplest fraction, as the numerator is 1. In cases like this, multiple division operations can be avoided by determining the greatest common factor between the numerator and denominator.

3) Simplify the fraction $\frac{18}{54}$ by dividing by the greatest common factor:

First, determine the factors for the numerator and denominator. The factors of 18 are 1, 2, 3, 6, 9, and 18. The factors of 54 are 1, 2, 3, 6, 9, 18, 27, and 54. Thus, the greatest common factor is 18. Dividing $\frac{18}{54}$ by 18 leaves $\frac{1}{3}$, which is the simplest fraction. This method takes slightly more work, but it definitively arrives at the simplest fraction.

Of the four basic operations that can be performed on fractions, the one which involves the least amount of work is multiplication. To multiply two fractions, simply multiply the numerators, multiply the denominators, and place the products as a fraction. Whole numbers and mixed numbers can also be expressed as a fraction, as described above, to multiply with a fraction. Let's work through a couple of examples.

1) $\frac{2}{5} \times \frac{3}{4} = \frac{6}{20} = \frac{3}{10}$

2) $\frac{4}{9} \times \frac{7}{11} = \frac{28}{99}$

Dividing fractions is similar to multiplication with one key difference. To divide fractions, flip the numerator and denominator of the second fraction, and then proceed as if it were a multiplication problem:

$$1)\ \frac{7}{8} \div \frac{4}{5} = \frac{7}{8} \times \frac{5}{4} = \frac{35}{32}$$

$$2)\ \frac{5}{9} \div \frac{1}{3} = \frac{5}{9} \times \frac{3}{1} = \frac{15}{9} = \frac{5}{3}$$

Addition and subtraction require more steps than multiplication and division, as these operations require the fractions to have the same denominator, also called a common denominator. It is always possible to find a common denominator by multiplying the denominators. However, when the denominators are large numbers, this method is unwieldy, especially if the answer must be provided in its simplest form. Thus, it's beneficial to find the least common denominator of the fractions—the least common denominator is incidentally also the least common multiple.

Once equivalent fractions have been found with common denominators, simply add or subtract the numerators to arrive at the answer:

$$1)\ \frac{1}{2} + \frac{3}{4} = \frac{2}{4} + \frac{3}{4} = \frac{5}{4}$$

$$2)\ \frac{3}{12} + \frac{11}{20} = \frac{15}{60} + \frac{33}{60} = \frac{48}{60} = \frac{4}{5}$$

$$3)\ \frac{7}{9} - \frac{4}{15} = \frac{35}{45} - \frac{12}{45} = \frac{23}{45}$$

$$4)\ \frac{5}{6} - \frac{7}{18} = \frac{15}{18} - \frac{7}{18} = \frac{8}{18} = \frac{4}{9}$$

Decimals

The **decimal system** is a way of writing out numbers that uses ten different numerals: 0, 1, 2, 3, 4, 5, 6, 7, 8, and 9. This is also called a "base ten" or "base 10" system. Other bases are also used. For example, computers work with a base of 2. This means they only use the numerals 0 and 1.

The **decimal place** denotes how far to the right of the decimal point a numeral is. The first digit to the right of the decimal point is in the *tenths* place. The next is the **hundredths**. The third is the **thousandths**.

So, 3.142 has a 1 in the tenths place, a 4 in the hundredths place, and a 2 in the thousandths place.

The **decimal point** is a period used to separate the **ones** place from the **tenths** place when writing out a number as a decimal.

A **decimal number** is a number written out with a decimal point instead of as a fraction, for example, 1.25 instead of $\frac{5}{4}$. Depending on the situation, it can sometimes be easier to work with fractions and sometimes easier to work with decimal numbers.

A decimal number is **terminating** if it stops at some point. It is called **repeating** if it never stops, but repeats a pattern over and over. It is important to note that every rational number can be written as a terminating decimal or as a repeating decimal.

Addition with Decimals

To add decimal numbers, each number in columns needs to be lined up by the decimal point. For each number being added, the zeros to the right of the last number need to be filled in so that each of the numbers has the same number of places to the right of the decimal. Then, the columns can be added together. Here is an example of 2.45 + 1.3 + 8.891 written in column form:

$$\begin{array}{r} 2.450 \\ 1.300 \\ \underline{+\ 8.891} \end{array}$$

Zeros have been added in the columns so that each number has the same number of places to the right of the decimal.

Added together, the correct answer is 12.641:

$$\begin{array}{r} 2.450 \\ 1.300 \\ \underline{+\ 8.891} \\ 12.641 \end{array}$$

Subtraction with Decimals

Subtracting decimal numbers is the same process as adding decimals. Here is 7.89 – 4.235 written in column form:

$$\begin{array}{r} 7.890 \\ -\ \underline{4.235} \\ 3.655 \end{array}$$

A zero has been added in the column so that each number has the same number of places to the right of the decimal.

Multiplication with Decimals

Decimals can be multiplied as if there were no decimal points in the problem. For example, 0.5 x 1.25 can be rewritten and multiplied as 5 x 125, which equals 625.

The final answer will have the same number of decimal *points* as the total number of decimal *places* in the problem. The first number has one decimal place, and the second number has two decimal places. Therefore, the final answer will contain three decimal places:

$$0.5 \times 1.25 = 0.625$$

Division with Decimals

Dividing a decimal by a whole number entails using long division first by ignoring the decimal point. Then, the decimal point is moved the number of places given in the problem.

For example, $6.8 \div 4$ can be rewritten as $68 \div 4$, which is 17. There is one non-zero integer to the right of the decimal point, so the final solution would have one decimal place to the right of the solution. In this case, the solution is 1.7.

Dividing a decimal by another decimal requires changing the divisor to a whole number by moving its decimal point. The decimal place of the dividend should be moved by the same number of places as the divisor. Then, the problem is the same as dividing a decimal by a whole number.

For example, $5.72 \div 1.1$ has a divisor with one decimal point in the denominator. The expression can be rewritten as $57.2 \div 11$ by moving each number one decimal place to the right to eliminate the decimal. The long division can be completed as $572 \div 11$ with a result of 52. Since there is one non-zero integer to the right of the decimal point in the problem, the final solution is 5.2.

In another example, $8 \div 0.16$ has a divisor with two decimal points in the denominator. The expression can be rewritten as $800 \div 16$ by moving each number two decimal places to the right to eliminate the decimal in the divisor. The long division can be completed with a result of 50.

Percentages

Think of percentages as fractions with a denominator of 100. In fact, percentage means "per hundred." Problems often require converting numbers from percentages, fractions, and decimals.

The basic percent equation is the following:

$$\frac{is}{of} = \frac{\%}{100}$$

The placement of numbers in the equation depends on what the question asks.

Example 1
Find 40% of 80.

Basically, the problem is asking, "What is 40% of 80?" The 40% is the percent, and 80 is the number to find the percent "of." The equation is:

$$\frac{x}{80} = \frac{40}{100}$$

Solving the equation by cross-multiplication, the problem becomes 100x = 80(40). Solving for x gives the answer: x = 32.

Example 2
What percent of 100 is 20?

The 20 fills in the "is" portion, while 100 fills in the "of." The question asks for the percent, so that will be x, the unknown. The following equation is set up:

$$\frac{20}{100} = \frac{x}{100}$$

Cross-multiplying yields the equation 100x = 20(100). Solving for x gives the answer of 20%.

Example 3
30% of what number is 30?

The following equation uses the clues and numbers in the problem:

$$\frac{30}{x} = \frac{30}{100}$$

Cross-multiplying results in the equation 30(100) = 30x. Solving for x gives the answer x = 100.

Converting Between Fractions, Decimals, and Percents

Decimals and Percentages
Since a percentage is based on "per hundred," decimals and percentages can be converted by multiplying or dividing by 100. Practically speaking, this always amounts to moving the decimal point two places to the right or left, depending on the conversion. To convert a percentage to a decimal, move the decimal point two places to the left and remove the % sign. To convert a decimal to a percentage, move the decimal point two places to the right and add a "%" sign. Here are some examples:

65% = 0.65
0.33 = 33%
0.215 = 21.5%
99.99% = 0.9999
500% = 5.00
7.55 = 755%

Fractions and Percentages
Remember that a percentage is a number per one hundred. So a percentage can be converted to a fraction by making the number in the percentage the numerator and putting 100 as the denominator:

$$43\% = \frac{43}{100}$$

$$97\% = \frac{97}{100}$$

Note that the percent symbol (%) kind of looks like a 0, a 1, and another 0. So think of a percentage like 54% as 54 over 100.

To convert a fraction to a percent, follow the same logic. If the fraction happens to have 100 in the denominator, you're in luck. Just take the numerator and add a percent symbol:

$$\frac{28}{100} = 28\%$$

Otherwise, divide the numerator by the denominator to get a decimal:

$$\frac{9}{12} = 0.75$$

Then convert the decimal to a percentage:

$$0.75 = 75\%$$

Another option is to make the denominator equal to 100. Be sure to multiply the numerator by the same number as the denominator. For example:

$$\frac{3}{20} \times \frac{5}{5} = \frac{15}{100}$$

$$\frac{15}{100} = 15\%$$

Changing Fractions to Decimals

To change a fraction into a decimal, divide the denominator into the numerator until there are no remainders. There may be repeating decimals, so rounding is often acceptable. A straight line above the repeating portion denotes that the decimal repeats.

Example: Express 4/5 as a decimal.

Set up the division problem.

$$5\overline{)4}$$

5 does not go into 4, so place the decimal and add a zero.

$$5\overline{)4.0}$$

5 goes into 40 eight times. There is no remainder.

$$\begin{array}{r} 0.8 \\ 5\overline{)4.0} \\ -\underline{4.0} \\ 0 \end{array}$$

The solution is 0.8.

Example: Express 33 1/3 as a decimal.

Since the whole portion of the number is known, set it aside to calculate the decimal from the fraction portion.

Set up the division problem.

$$3\overline{)1}$$

3 does not go into 1, so place the decimal and add zeros. 3 goes into 10 three times.

$$\begin{array}{r} 0.333 \\ 3\overline{)1.000} \end{array}$$

This will repeat with a remainder of 3, so place a line over the 3 denotes the repetition.

$$\begin{array}{r} 0.333 \\ 3\overline{\big)1.000} \\ -9 \\ \hline 10 \\ -9 \\ \hline 10 \end{array}$$

The solution is $0.\overline{3}$

Changing Decimals to Fractions

To change decimals to fractions, place the decimal portion of the number, the numerator, over the respective place value, the denominator, then reduce, if possible.

Example: Express 0.25 as a fraction.

This is read as twenty-five hundredths, so put 25 over 100. Then reduce to find the solution.

$$\frac{25}{100} = \frac{1}{4}$$

Example: Express 0.455 as a fraction

This is read as four hundred fifty-five thousandths, so put 455 over 1000. Then reduce to find the solution.

$$\frac{455}{1000} = \frac{91}{200}$$

There are two types of problems that commonly involve percentages. The first is to calculate some percentage of a given quantity, where you convert the percentage to a decimal, and multiply the quantity by that decimal. Secondly, you are given a quantity and told it is a fixed percent of an unknown quantity. In this case, convert to a decimal, then divide the given quantity by that decimal.

Example: What is 30% of 760?

Convert the percent into a useable number. "Of" means to multiply.

$$30\% = 0.30$$

Set up the problem based on the givens, and solve.

$$0.30 \times 760 = 228$$

Example: 8.4 is 20% of what number?

Convert the percent into a useable number.

$$20\% = 0.20$$

The given number is a percent of the answer needed, so divide the given number by this decimal rather than multiplying it.

$$\frac{8.4}{0.20} = 42$$

Ratios and Unit Rates

Using Ratios to Describe a Relationship Between Two Quantities
Ratios are used to show the relationship between two quantities. The ratio of oranges to apples in the grocery store may be 3 to 2. That means that for every 3 oranges, there are 2 apples. This comparison can be expanded to represent the actual number of oranges and apples. Another example may be the number of boys to girls in a math class. If the ration of boys to girls is given as 2 to 5, that means there are 2 boys to every 5 girls in the class. Ratios can also be compared if the units in each ratio are the same. The ratio of boys to girls in the math class can be compared to the ratio of boys to girls in a science class by stating which ratio is higher and which is lower.

Rates are used to compare two quantities with different units. **Unit rates** are the simplest form of rate. With unit rates, the denominator in the comparison of two units is one. For example, if someone can type at a rate of 1000 words in 5 minutes, then his or her unit rate for typing is $\frac{1000}{5} = 200$ words in one minute or 200 words per minute. Any rate can be converted into a unit rate by dividing to make the denominator one. 1000 words in 5 minutes has been converted into the unit rate of 200 words per minute.

Computing Unit Rates
Unit rate word problems will ask to calculate the rate or quantity of something in a different value. For example, a problem might say that a car drove a certain number of miles in a certain number of minutes and then ask how many miles per hour the car was traveling. These questions involve solving proportions. Consider the following examples:

1) Alexandra made $96 during the first 3 hours of her shift as a temporary worker at a law office. She will continue to earn money at this rate until she finishes in 5 more hours. How much does Alexandra make per hour? How much will Alexandra have made at the end of the day?

This problem can be solved in two ways. The first is to set up a proportion, as the rate of pay is constant. The second is to determine her hourly rate, multiply the 5 hours by that rate, and then add the $96.

To set up a proportion, put the money already earned over the hours already worked on one side of an equation. The other side has x over 8 hours (the total hours worked in the day). It looks like this: $\frac{96}{3} = \frac{x}{8}$. Now, cross-multiply to get $768 = 3x$. To get x, divide by 3, which leaves $x = 256$. Alternatively, as x is the numerator of one of the proportions, multiplying by its denominator will reduce the solution by one step. Thus, Alexandra will make $256 at the end of the day. To calculate her hourly rate, divide the total by 8, giving $32 per hour.

Alternatively, it is possible to figure out the hourly rate by dividing $96 by 3 hours to get $32 per hour. Now her total pay can be figured by multiplying $32 per hour by 8 hours, which comes out to $256.

2) Jonathan is reading a novel. So far, he has read 215 of the 335 total pages. It takes Jonathan 25 minutes to read 10 pages, and the rate is constant. How long does it take Jonathan to read one page? How much longer will it take him to finish the novel? Express the answer in time.

To calculate how long it takes Jonathan to read one page, divide the 25 minutes by 10 pages to determine the page per minute rate. Thus, it takes 2.5 minutes to read one page.

Jonathan must read 120 more pages to complete the novel. (This is calculated by subtracting the pages already read from the total.) Now, multiply his rate per page by the number of pages. Thus, $120 \div 2.5 = 300$. Expressed in time, 300 minutes is equal to 5 hours.

3) At a hotel, $\frac{4}{5}$ of the 120 rooms are booked for Saturday. On Sunday, $\frac{3}{4}$ of the rooms are booked. On which day are more of the rooms booked, and by how many more?

The first step is to calculate the number of rooms booked for each day. Do this by multiplying the fraction of the rooms booked by the total number of rooms.

Saturday: $\frac{4}{5} \times 120 = \frac{4}{5} \times \frac{120}{1} = \frac{480}{5} = 96$ rooms

Sunday: $\frac{3}{4} \times 120 = \frac{3}{4} \times \frac{120}{1} = \frac{360}{4} = 90$ rooms

Thus, more rooms were booked on Saturday by 6 rooms.

4) In a veterinary hospital, the veterinarian-to-pet ratio is 1:9. The ratio is always constant. If there are 45 pets in the hospital, how many veterinarians are currently in the veterinary hospital?

Set up a proportion to solve for the number of veterinarians: $\frac{1}{9} = \frac{x}{45}$

Cross-multiplying results in $9x = 45$, which works out to 5 veterinarians.

Alternatively, as there are always 9 times as many pets as veterinarians, is it possible to divide the number of pets (45) by 9. This also arrives at the correct answer of 5 veterinarians.

5) At a general practice law firm, 30% of the lawyers work solely on tort cases. If 9 lawyers work solely on tort cases, how many lawyers work at the firm?

First, solve for the total number of lawyers working at the firm, which will be represented here with x. The problem states that 9 lawyers work solely on torts cases, and they make up 30% of the total lawyers at the firm. Thus, 30% multiplied by the total, x, will equal 9. Written as equation, this is: $30\% \times x = 9$.

It's easier to deal with the equation after converting the percentage to a decimal, leaving $0.3x = 9$. Thus, $x = \frac{9}{0.3} = 30$ lawyers working at the firm.

6) Xavier was hospitalized with pneumonia. He was originally given 35mg of antibiotics. Later, after his condition continued to worsen, Xavier's dosage was increased to 60mg. What was the percent increase of the antibiotics? Round the percentage to the nearest tenth.

An increase or decrease in percentage can be calculated by dividing the difference in amounts by the original amount and multiplying by 100. Written as an equation, the formula is:

$$\frac{new\ quantity - old\ quantity}{old\ quantity} \times 100$$

Here, the question states that the dosage was increased from 35mg to 60mg, so these are plugged into the formula to find the percentage increase.

$$\frac{60\ -\ 35}{35} \times\ 100\ = \frac{25}{35} \times 100 = .7142\ \times 100\ = 71.4\%$$

Using Ratio Reasoning to Convert Rates

Ratios and rates can be used together to convert rates into different units. For example, if someone is driving 50 kilometers per hour, that rate can be converted into miles per hour by using a ratio known as the **conversion factor**. Since the given value contains kilometers and the final answer needs to be in miles, the ratio relating miles to kilometers needs to be used. There are 0.62 miles in 1 kilometer. This, written as a ratio and in fraction form, is $\frac{0.62\ miles}{1\ km}$. To convert 50km/hour into miles per hour, the following conversion needs to be set up: $\frac{50\ km}{hou} \times \frac{0.62\ miles}{1\ km} = 31\ miles\ per\ hour.$

Solving Problems Involving Scale Factors

The ratio between two similar geometric figures is called the **scale factor**. For example, a problem may depict two similar triangles, A and B. The scale factor from the smaller triangle A to the larger triangle B is given as 2 because the length of the corresponding side of the larger triangle, 16, is twice the corresponding side on the smaller triangle, 8. This scale factor can also be used to find the value of a missing side, x, in triangle A. Since the scale factor from the smaller triangle (A) to larger one (B) is 2, the larger corresponding side in triangle B (given as 25), can be divided by 2 to find the missing side in A (x = 12.5). The scale factor can also be represented in the equation $2A = B$ because two times the lengths of A gives the corresponding lengths of B. This is the idea behind similar triangles.

Using Proportional Relationships to Solve Real-World Problems

Proportional Relationships

Much like a scale factor can be written using an equation like $2A = B$, a **relationship** is represented by the equation $Y = kX$. X and Y are **proportional** because as values of X increase, the values of Y also increase. A relationship that is **inversely proportional** can be represented by the equation $Y = \frac{k}{X}$, where the value of Y decreases as the value of x increases and vice versa.

Proportional reasoning can be used to solve problems involving ratios, percentages, and averages. Ratios can be used in setting up proportions and solving them to find unknowns. For example, if a student completes an average of 10 pages of math homework in 3 nights, how long would it take the student to complete 22 pages? Both ratios can be written as fractions. The second ratio would contain the unknown.

The following proportion represents this problem, where x is the unknown number of nights:

$$\frac{10\ pages}{3\ nights} = \frac{22\ pages}{x\ nights}$$

Solving this proportion entails cross-multiplying and results in the following equation: $10x = 22 \times 3$. Simplifying and solving for x results in the exact solution: $x = 6.6\ nights$. The result would be rounded up to 7 because the homework would actually be completed on the 7th night.

The following problem uses ratios involving percentages:

If 20% of the class is girls and 30 students are in the class, how many girls are in the class?

To set up this problem, it is helpful to use the common proportion: $\frac{\%}{100} = \frac{is}{of}$. Within the proportion, % is the percentage of girls, 100 is the total percentage of the class, *is* is the number of girls, and *of* is the total number of students in the class. Most percentage problems can be written using this language. To solve this problem, the proportion should be set up as $\frac{20}{100} = \frac{x}{30}$, and then solved for x. Cross-multiplying results in the equation $20 \times 30 = 100x$, which results in the solution $x = 6$. There are 6 girls in the class.

Problems involving volume, length, and other units can also be solved using ratios. For example, a problem may ask for the volume of a cone to be found that has a radius, $r = 7m$ and a height, $h = 16m$. Referring to the formulas provid1ed on the test, the volume of a cone is given as: $V = \pi r^2 \frac{h}{3}$, where r is the radius, and h is the height. Plugging $r = 7$ and $h = 16$ into the formula, the following is obtained: $V = \pi(7^2)\frac{16}{3}$. Therefore, volume of the cone is found to be approximately 821m^3. Sometimes, answers in different units are sought. If this problem wanted the answer in liters, 821m^3 would need to be converted. Using the equivalence statement 1m^3 = 1000L, the following ratio would be used to solve for liters: $821\text{m}^3 \times \frac{1000L}{1m^3}$. Cubic meters in the numerator and denominator cancel each other out, and the answer is converted to 821,000 liters, or 8.21×10^5 L.

Other conversions can also be made between different given and final units. If the temperature in a pool is 30°C, what is the temperature of the pool in degrees Fahrenheit? To convert these units, an equation is used relating Celsius to Fahrenheit. The following equation is used:

$$T_{°F} = 1.8T_{°C} + 32$$

Plugging in the given temperature and solving the equation for T yields the result:

$$T_{°F} = 1.8(30) + 32 = 86°F$$

Both units in the metric system and U.S. customary system are widely used.

Here are some more examples of how to solve for proportions:

1) $\frac{75\%}{90\%} = \frac{25\%}{x}$

To solve for x, the fractions must be cross multiplied: $(75\%x = 90\% \times 25\%)$. To make things easier, let's convert the percentages to decimals: $(0.9 \times 0.25 = 0.225 = 0.75x)$. To get rid of x's co-efficient, each side must be divided by that same coefficient to get the answer $x = 0.3$. The question could ask for the answer as a percentage or fraction in lowest terms, which are 30% and $\frac{3}{10}$, respectively.

2) $\frac{x}{12} = \frac{30}{96}$

Cross-multiply: $96x = 30 \times 12$

Multiply: $96x$ = 360

Divide: x = $360 \div 96$

Answer: $x = 3.75$

3) $\frac{0.5}{3} = \frac{x}{6}$

Cross-multiply: $3x = 0.5 \times 6$

Multiply: $3x = 3$

Divide: $x = 3 \div 3$

Answer: $x = 1$

You may have noticed there's a faster way to arrive at the answer. If there is an obvious operation being performed on the proportion, the same operation can be used on the other side of the proportion to solve for x. For example, in the first practice problem, 75% became 25% when divided by 3, and upon doing the same to 90%, the correct answer of 30% would have been found with much less legwork. However, these questions aren't always so intuitive, so it's a good idea to work through the steps, even if the answer seems apparent from the outset.

<u>Solving Ratio and Percent Problems</u>

Questions dealing with percentages can be difficult when they are phrased as word problems. These word problems almost always come in three varieties. The first type will ask to find what percentage of some number will equal another number. The second asks to determine what number is some percentage of another given number. The third will ask what number another number is a given percentage of.

One of the most important parts of correctly answering percentage word problems is to identify the numerator and the denominator. This fraction can then be converted into a percentage, as described above.

The following word problem shows how to make this conversion:

A department store carries several different types of footwear. The store is currently selling 8 athletic shoes, 7 dress shoes, and 5 sandals. What percentage of the store's footwear are sandals?

First, calculate what serves as the 'whole', as this will be the denominator. How many total pieces of footwear does the store sell? The store sells 20 different types (8 athletic + 7 dress + 5 sandals).

Second, what footwear type is the question specifically asking about? Sandals. Thus, 5 is the numerator.

Third, the resultant fraction must be expressed as a percentage. The first two steps indicate that $\frac{5}{20}$ of the footwear pieces are sandals. This fraction must now be converted into a percentage:

$$\frac{5}{20} \times \frac{5}{5} = \frac{25}{100} = 25\%$$

Basic Algebra

Algebraic Expressions

An algebraic expression is a statement about an unknown quantity expressed in mathematical symbols. A variable is used to represent the unknown quantity, usually denoted by a letter. An equation is a statement in which two expressions (at least one containing a variable) are equal to each other. An algebraic expression can be thought of as a mathematical phrase and an equation can be thought of as a mathematical sentence.

Algebraic expressions and equations both contain numbers, variables, and mathematical operations. The following are examples of algebraic expressions: $5x + 3, 7xy - 8(x^2 + y)$, and $\sqrt{a^2 + b^2}$. An expression can be simplified or evaluated for given values of variables. The following are examples of equations: $2x + 3 = 7$, $a^2 + b^2 = c^2$, and $2x + 5 = 3x - 2$. An equation contains two sides separated by an equal sign. Equations can be solved to determine the value(s) of the variable for which the statement is true.

<u>Adding and Subtracting Linear Algebraic Expressions</u>

An algebraic expression is simplified by combining like terms. A term is a number, variable, or product of a number, and variables separated by addition and subtraction. For the algebraic expression $3x^2 - 4x + 5 - 5x^2 + x - 3$, the terms are $3x^2$, -4x, 5, -5x^2, x, and -3. Like terms have the same variables raised to the same powers (exponents). The like terms for the previous example are $3x^2$ and -5x^2, -4x and x, 5 and -3. To combine like terms, the coefficients (numerical factor of the term including sign) are added and the variables and their powers are kept the same. Note that if a coefficient is not written, it is an implied coefficient of 1 ($x = 1x$). The previous example will simplify to $-2x^2 - 3x + 2$.

When adding or subtracting algebraic expressions, each expression is written in parenthesis. The negative sign is distributed when necessary, and like terms are combined. Consider the following: add $2a + 5b - 2$ to $a - 2b + 8c - 4$. The sum is set as follows: $(a - 2b + 8c - 4) + (2a + 5b - 2)$. In front of each set of parentheses is an implied positive one, which, when distributed, does not change any of the terms. Therefore, the parentheses are dropped and like terms are combined:

$$a - 2b + 8c - 4 + 2a + 5b - 2$$

$$3a + 3b + 8c - 6$$

Consider the following problem: Subtract $2a + 5b - 2$ from $a - 2b + 8c - 4$. The difference is set as follows:

$$(a - 2b + 8c - 4) - \ (2a + 5b - 2)$$

The implied one in front of the first set of parentheses will not change those four terms. However, distributing the implied -1 in front of the second set of parentheses will change the sign of each of those three terms:

$$a - 2b + 8c - 4 - 2a - 5b + 2$$

Combining like terms yields the simplified expression $-a - 7b + 8c - 2$.

Distributive Property

The distributive property states that multiplying a sum (or difference) by a number produces the same result as multiplying each value in the sum (or difference) by the number and adding (or subtracting) the products. Using mathematical symbols, the distributive property states $a(b + c) = ab + ac$. The expression $4(3 + 2)$ is simplified using the order of operations. Simplifying inside the parenthesis first produces 4×5, which equals 20. The expression $4(3 + 2)$ can also be simplified using the distributive property:

$$4(3 + 2) = 4 \times 3 + 4 \times 2$$

$$12 + 8 = 20$$

Consider the following example: $4(3x - 2)$. The expression cannot be simplified inside the parenthesis because 3*x* and -2 are not like terms, and therefore cannot be combined. However, the expression can be simplified by using the distributive property and multiplying each term inside of the parenthesis by the term outside of the parenthesis: $12x - 8$. The resulting equivalent expression contains no like terms, so it cannot be further simplified.

Consider the expression $(3x + 2y + 1) - (5x - 3) + 2(3y + 4)$. Again, there are no like terms, but the distributive property is used to simplify the expression. Note there is an implied one in front of the first set of parentheses and an implied -1 in front of the second set of parentheses. Distributing the one, -1, and 2 produces:

$$1(3x) + 1(2y) + 1(1) - 1(5x) - 1(-3) + 2(3y) + 2(4)$$

$$3x + 2y + 1 - 5x + 3 + 6y + 8$$

This expression contains like terms that are combined to produce the simplified expression:

$$-2x + 8y + 12$$

Algebraic expressions are tested to be equivalent by choosing values for the variables and evaluating both expressions (see 2.A.4). For example, $4(3x - 2)$ and $12x - 8$ are tested by substituting 3 for the variable *x* and calculating to determine if equivalent values result.

Simple Expressions for Given Values

An algebraic expression is a statement written in mathematical symbols, typically including one or more unknown values represented by variables. For example, the expression $2x + 3$ states that an unknown number (*x*) is multiplied by 2 and added to 3. If given a value for the unknown number, or variable, the value of the expression is determined. For example, if the value of the variable *x* is 4, the value of the expression 4 is multiplied by 2, and 3 is added. This results in a value of 11 for the expression.

When given an algebraic expression and values for the variable(s), the expression is evaluated to determine its numerical value. To evaluate the expression, the given values for the variables are substituted (or replaced) and the expression is simplified using the order of operations. Parenthesis should be used when substituting. Consider the following: Evaluate $a - 2b + ab$ for $a = 3$ and $b = -1$. To evaluate, any variable *a* is replaced with 3 and any variable *b* with -1, producing:

$$3 - 2(-1) + (3)(-1)$$

Next, the order of operations is used to calculate the value of the expression, which is 2.

Parts of Expressions

Algebraic expressions consist of variables, numbers, and operations. A term of an expression is any combination of numbers and/or variables, and terms are separated by addition and subtraction. For example, the expression $5x^2 - 3xy + 4 - 2$ consists of 4 terms: $5x^2$, -3*xy*, 4*y*, and -2. Note that each term includes its given sign (+ or −). The variable part of a term is a letter that represents an unknown quantity. The coefficient of a term is the number by which the variable is multiplied. For the term 4*y*, the variable is *y* and the coefficient is 4. Terms are identified by the power (or exponent) of its variable.

A number without a variable is referred to as a constant. If the variable is to the first power (x^1 or simply *x*), it is referred to as a linear term. A term with a variable to the second power (x^2) is quadratic and a term to the third power (x^3) is cubic. Consider the expression $x^3 + 3x - 1$. The constant is -1. The linear term is 3*x*. There is no quadratic term. The cubic term is x^3.

An algebraic expression can also be classified by how many terms exist in the expression. Any like terms should be combined before classifying. A monomial is an expression consisting of only one term. Examples of monomials are: 17, 2*x*, and $-5ab^2$. A binomial is an expression consisting of two terms separated by addition or subtraction. Examples include $2x - 4$ and $-3y^2 + 2y$. A trinomial consists of 3 terms. For example, $5x^2 - 2x + 1$ is a trinomial.

Verbal Statements and Algebraic Expressions

An algebraic expression is a statement about unknown quantities expressed in mathematical symbols. The statement *five times a number added to forty* is expressed as $5x + 40$. An equation is a statement in which two expressions (with at least one containing a variable) are equal to one another. The statement *five times a number added to forty is equal to ten* is expressed as $5x + 40 = 10$.

Real world scenarios can also be expressed mathematically. Suppose a job pays its employees $300 per week and $40 for each sale made. The weekly pay is represented by the expression $40x + 300$ where *x* is the number of sales made during the week.

Consider the following scenario: Bob had $20 and Tom had $4. After selling 4 ice cream cones to Bob, Tom has as much money as Bob. The cost of an ice cream cone is an unknown quantity and can be represented by a variable (*x*). The amount of money Bob has after his purchase is four times the cost of an ice cream cone subtracted from his original $\$20 \rightarrow 20 - 4x$. The amount of money Tom has after his sale is four times the cost of an ice cream cone added to his original $\$4 \rightarrow 4x + 4$. After the sale, the amount of money that Bob and Tom have are equal:

$$20 - 4x = 4x + 4$$

When expressing a verbal or written statement mathematically, it is vital to understand words or phrases that can be represented with symbols. The following are examples:

Symbol	Phrase
+	Added to; increased by; sum of; more than
−	Decreased by; difference between; less than; take away
×	Multiplied by; 3(4,5...) times as large; product of
÷	Divided by; quotient of; half (third, etc.) of
=	Is; the same as; results in; as much as; equal to
x,t,n, etc.	A number; unknown quantity; value of; variable

Linear Equations

An equation is called **linear** if it can take the form of the equation $y = ax + b$, for any two numbers a and b. A linear equation forms a straight line when graphed on the coordinate plane. An example of a linear equation is shown below on the graph.

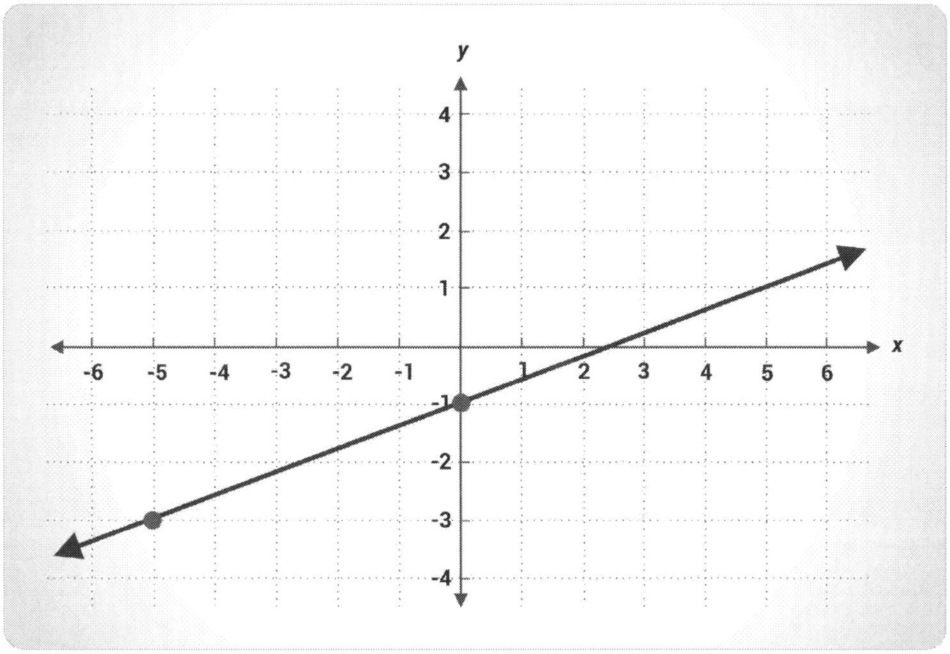

This is a graph of the following equation: $y = \frac{2}{5}x - 1$. A table of values that satisfies this equation is shown below.

x	y
-5	-3
0	-1
5	1
10	3

These points can be found on the graph using the form (x,y).

When graphing a linear equaton, note that the ratio of the change of the *y* coordinate to the change in the *x* coordinate is constant between any two points on the resulting line, no matter which two points are chosen. In other words, in a pair of points on a line, (x_1, y_1) and (x_2, y_2), with $x_1 \neq x_2$ so that the two points are distinct, then the ratio $\frac{y_2 - y_1}{x_2 - x_1}$ will be the same, regardless of which particular pair of points are chosen. This ratio, $\frac{y_2 - y_1}{x_2 - x_1}$, is called the **slope** of the line and is frequently denoted with the letter m. If slope m is positive, then the line goes upward when moving to the right, while if slope m is negative, then the line goes downward when moving to the right. If the slope is 0, then the line is called **horizontal,** and the y coordinate is constant along the entire line. In lines where the x coordinate is constant along the entire line, y is not actually a function of x. For such lines, the slope is not defined. These lines are called **vertical** lines.

Linear equations may take forms other than $y = ax + b$. The most common forms of linear equations are explained below:

1. Standard Form: $Ax + By = C$, in which the slope is given by $m = \frac{-A}{B}$, and the y-intercept is given by $\frac{C}{B}$.

2. Slope-Intercept Form: $y = mx + b$, where the slope is m and the y intercept is b.

3. Point-Slope Form: $y - y_1 = m(x - x_1)$, where the slope is m and (x_1, y_1) is any point on the chosen line.

4. Two-Point Form: $\frac{y-y_1}{x-x_1} = \frac{y_2-y_1}{x_2-x_1}$, where (x_1, y_1) and (x_2, y_2) are any two distinct points on the chosen line. Note that the slope is given by $m = \frac{y_2-y_1}{x_2-x_1}$.

5. Intercept Form: $\frac{x}{x_1} + \frac{y}{y_1} = 1$, in which x_1 is the x-intercept and y_1 is the y-intercept.

These five ways to write linear equations are all useful in different circumstances. Depending on the given information, it may be easier to write one of the forms over another.

If $y = mx$, y is directly proportional to x. In this case, changing x by a factor changes y by that same factor. If $y = \frac{m}{x}$, y is inversely proportional to x. For example, if x is increased by a factor of 3, then y will be decreased by the same factor, 3.

The Slope of a Linear Function

Rate of change for any line calculates the steepness of the line over a given interval. Rate of change is also known as the **slope** or rise/run. The slope of a linear function is given by the change in y divided by the change in x. So the formula looks like this:

$$slope = \frac{y_2 - y_1}{x_2 - x_1}$$

In the graph below, two points are plotted. The first has the coordinates of (0,1) and the second point is (2,3). Remember that the x coordinate is always placed first in coordinate pairs. Work from left to right when identifying coordinates. Thus, the point on the left is point 1 (0,1) and the point on the right is point 2 (2,3).

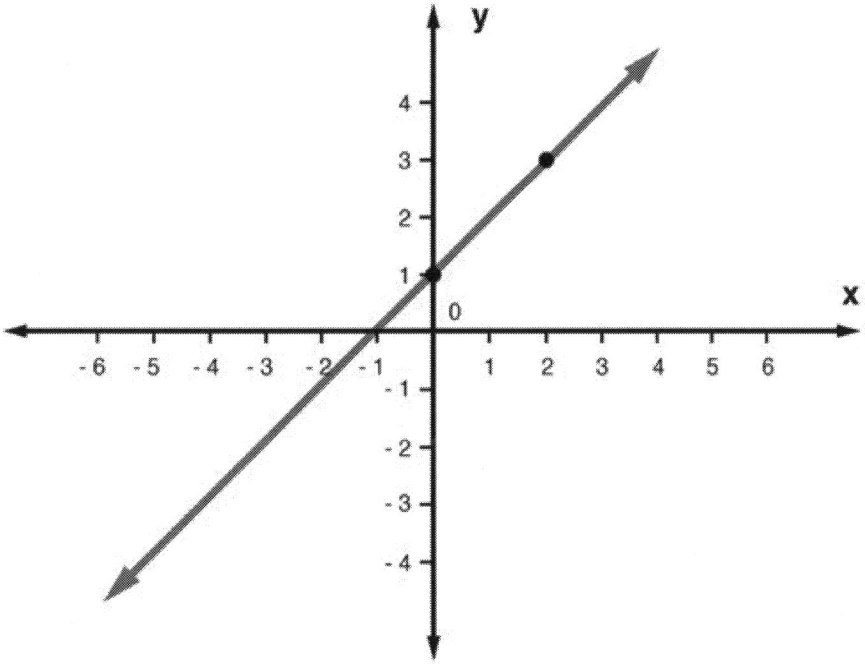

Now we need to just plug those numbers into the equation:

$$slope = \frac{3-1}{2-0}$$

$$slope = \frac{2}{2}$$

$$slope = 1$$

This means that for every increase of 1 for x, y also increased by 1. You can see this in the line. When x equalled 0, y equalled 1, and when x was increased to 1, y equalled 2.

Slope can be thought of as determining the rise over run:

$$slope = \frac{rise}{run}$$

The rise being the change vertically on the y axis and the run being the change horizontally on the x axis.

Solving Equations Using Reasoning

Solving equations in one variable is the process of isolating that variable on one side of the equation. The letters in an equation and any numbers attached to them are the variables as they stand for unknown quantities that you are trying to solve for. *X* is commonly used as a variable, though any letter can be used. For example, in $3x - 7 = 20$, the variable is $3x$, and it needs to be isolated. The numbers (also called constants) are -7 and 20. That means $3x$ needs to be on one side of the equals sign (either side is fine), and all the numbers need to be on the other side of the equals sign.

To accomplish this, the equation must be manipulated by performing opposite operations of what already exists. Remember that addition and subtraction are opposites and that multiplication and division are opposites. Any action taken to one side of the equation must be taken on the other side to maintain equality.

So, since the 7 is being subtracted, it can be moved to the right side of the equation by adding seven to both sides:

$$3x - 7 = 20$$

$$3x - 7 + 7 = 20 + 7$$

$$3x = 27$$

Now that the variable $3x$ is on one side and the constants (now combined into one constant) are on the other side, the 3 needs to be moved to the right side. 3 and x are being multiplied together, so 3 then needs to be divided from each side.

$$\frac{3x}{3} = \frac{27}{3}$$

$$x = 9$$

Now x has been completely isolated, and thus we know its value.

The solution is found to be $x = 9$. This solution can be checked for accuracy by plugging $x = 9$ in the original equation. After simplifying the equation, $20 = 20$ is found, which is a true statement:

$$3 \times 9 - 7 = 20$$

$$27 - 7 = 20$$

$$20 = 20$$

Equations that require solving for a variable (**algebraic equations**) come in many forms. Here are some more examples:

No number attached to the variable:

$$x + 8 = 20$$

$$x + 8 - 8 = 20 - 8$$

$$x = 12$$

Fraction in the variable:

$$\frac{1}{2}z + 24 = 36$$

$$\frac{1}{2}z + 24 - 24 = 36 - 24$$

$$\frac{1}{2}z = 12$$

Now we multiply the variable by its inverse:

$$\frac{2}{1} \times \frac{1}{2}z = 12 \times \frac{2}{1}$$

$$z = 24$$

Multiple instances of x:

$$14x + x - 4 = 3x + 2$$

All instances of x can be combined.

$$15x - 4 = 3x + 2$$

$$15x - 4 + 4 = 3x + 2 + 4$$

$$15x = 3x + 6$$

$$15x - 3x = 3x + 6 - 3x$$

$$12x = 6$$

$$\frac{12x}{12} = \frac{6}{12}$$

$$x = \frac{1}{2}$$

Linear Inequalities

Linear equations and linear inequalities are both comparisons of two algebraic expressions. However, unlike equations in which the expressions are equal, linear inequalities compare expressions that may be unequal. Linear equations typically have one value for the variable that makes the statement true. Linear inequalities generally have an infinite number of values that make the statement true.

When solving a linear equation, the desired result requires determining a numerical value for the unknown variable. If given a linear equation involving addition, subtraction, multiplication, or division, working backwards isolates the variable. Addition and subtraction are inverse operations, as are multiplication and division. Therefore, they can be used to cancel each other out.

The first steps to solving linear equations are distributing, if necessary, and combining any like terms on the same side of the equation. Sides of an equation are separated by an **equal** sign. Next, the equation is manipulated to show the variable on one side. Whatever is done to one side of the equation must be done to the other side of the equation to remain equal. Inverse operations are then used to isolate the variable and undo the order of operations backwards. Addition and subtraction are undone, then multiplication and division are undone.

For example, solve $4(t-2)+2t-4=2(9-2t)$

Distributing: $4t-8+2t-4=18-4t$

Combining like terms: $6t-12=18-4t$

Adding $4t$ to each side to move the variable: $10t-12=18$

Adding 12 to each side to isolate the variable: $10t=30$

Dividing each side by 10 to isolate the variable: $t=3$

The answer can be checked by substituting the value for the variable into the original equation, ensuring that both sides calculate to be equal.

Linear inequalities express the relationship between unequal values. More specifically, they describe in what way the values are unequal. A value can be greater than (>), less than (<), greater than or equal to (≥), or less than or equal to (≤) another value. $5x+40>65$ is read as *five times a number added to forty is greater than sixty-five.*

When solving a linear inequality, the solution is the set of all numbers that make the statement true. The inequality $x+2\geq 6$ has a solution set of 4 and every number greater than 4 (4.01; 5; 12; 107; etc.). Adding 2 to 4 or any number greater than 4 results in a value that is greater than or equal to 6. Therefore, $x\geq 4$ is the solution set.

To algebraically solve a linear inequality, follow the same steps as those for solving a linear equation. The inequality symbol stays the same for all operations *except* when multiplying or dividing by a negative number. If multiplying or dividing by a negative number while solving an inequality, the relationship reverses (the sign flips). In other words, > switches to < and vice versa. Multiplying or dividing by a positive number does not change the relationship, so the sign stays the same. An example is shown below.

Solve $-2x-8\leq 22$

Add 8 to both sides: $-2x\leq 30$

Divide both sides by -2: $x\geq -15$

Solutions of a linear equation or a linear inequality are the values of the variable that make a statement true. In the case of a linear equation, the solution set (list of all possible solutions) typically consists of a single numerical value. To find the solution, the equation is solved by isolating the variable. For example, solving the equation $3x-7=-13$ produces the solution $x=-2$. The only value for x which produces a true statement is -2. This can be checked by substituting -2 into the original equation to check that both sides are equal. In this case, $3(-2)-7=-13\rightarrow -13=-13$; therefore, -2 is a solution.

Although linear equations generally have one solution, this is not always the case. If there is no value for the variable that makes the statement true, there is no solution to the equation. Consider the equation

$x + 3 = x - 1$. There is no value for *x* in which adding 3 to the value produces the same result as subtracting one from the value. Conversely, if any value for the variable makes a true statement, the equation has an infinite number of solutions. Consider the equation $3x + 6 = 3(x + 2)$. Any number substituted for *x* will result in a true statement (both sides of the equation are equal).

By manipulating equations like the two above, the variable of the equation will cancel out completely. If the remaining constants express a true statement (ex. $6 = 6$), then all real numbers are solutions to the equation. If the constants left express a false statement (ex. $3 = -1$), then no solution exists for the equation.

Solving a linear inequality requires all values that make the statement true to be determined. For example, solving $3x - 7 \geq -13$ produces the solution $x \geq -2$. This means that -2 and any number greater than -2 produces a true statement. Solution sets for linear inequalities will often be displayed using a number line. If a value is included in the set (≥ or ≤), a shaded dot is placed on that value and an arrow extending in the direction of the solutions. For a variable > or ≥ a number, the arrow will point right on a number line, the direction where the numbers increase. If a variable is < or ≤ a number, the arrow will point left on a number line, which is the direction where the numbers decrease. If the value is not included in the set (> or <), an open (unshaded) circle on that value is used with an arrow in the appropriate direction.

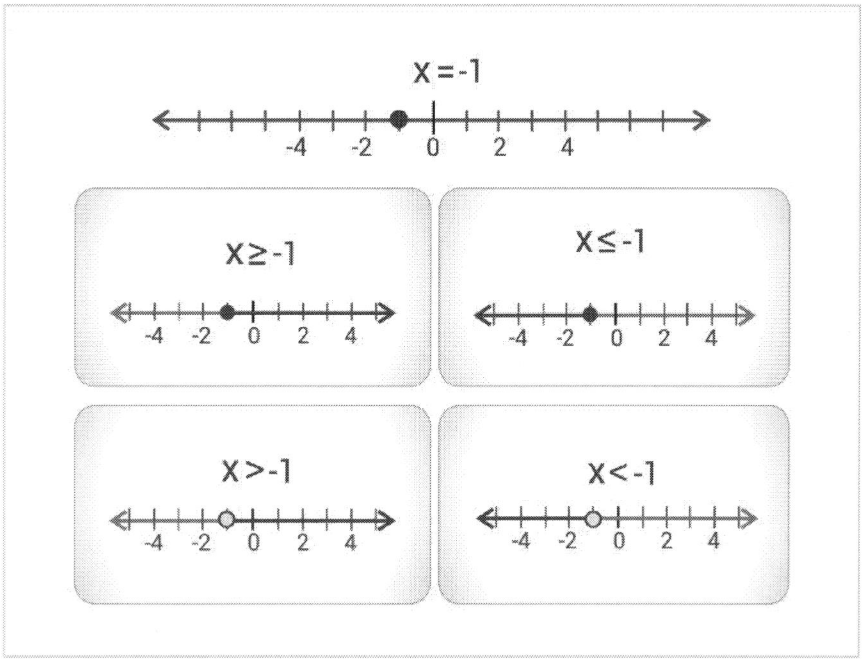

Similar to linear equations, a linear inequality may have a solution set consisting of all real numbers or can contain no solution. When solved algebraically, a linear inequality in which the variable cancels out and results in a true statement (ex. $7 \geq 2$) has a solution set of all real numbers. A linear inequality in which the variable cancels out and results in a false statement (ex. $7 \leq 2$) has no solution.

<u>Linear Inequalities in One Variable</u>

Linear inequalities and linear equations are both comparisons of two algebraic expressions. However, unlike equations in which the expressions are equal to each other, linear inequalities compare expressions that are unequal. Linear equations typically have one value for the variable that makes the statement true. Linear inequalities generally have an infinite number of values that make the statement true. Exceptions to these last two statements are covered in Section 6.

Writing Linear Inequalities

Linear inequalities are a concise mathematical way to express the relationship between unequal values. More specifically, they describe in what way the values are unequal. A value could be greater than ($>$); less than ($<$); greater than or equal to ($\geq$); or less than or equal to ($\leq$) another value. The statement "five times a number added to forty is more than sixty-five" can be expressed as $5x + 40 > 65$. Common words and phrases that express inequalities are:

Symbol	Phrase
$<$	is under, is below, smaller than, beneath
$>$	is above, is over, bigger than, exceeds
$\leq$	no more than, at most, maximum
$\geq$	no less than, at least, minimum

Solving Linear Inequalities

When solving a linear inequality, the solution is the set of all numbers that makes the statement true. The inequality $x + 2 \geq 6$ has a solution set of 4 and every number greater than 4 (4.0001, 5, 12, 107, etc.). Adding 2 to 4 or any number greater than 4 would result in a value that is greater than or equal to 6. Therefore, $x \geq 4$ would be the solution set.

Solution sets for linear inequalities often will be displayed using a number line. If a value is included in the set ($\geq$ or $\leq$), there is a shaded dot placed on that value and an arrow extending in the direction of the solutions. For a variable $>$ or $\geq$ a number, the arrow would point right on the number line (the direction where the numbers increase); and if a variable is $<$ or $\leq$ a number, the arrow would point left (where the numbers decrease). If the value is not included in the set ($>$ or $<$), an open circle on that value would be used with an arrow in the appropriate direction.

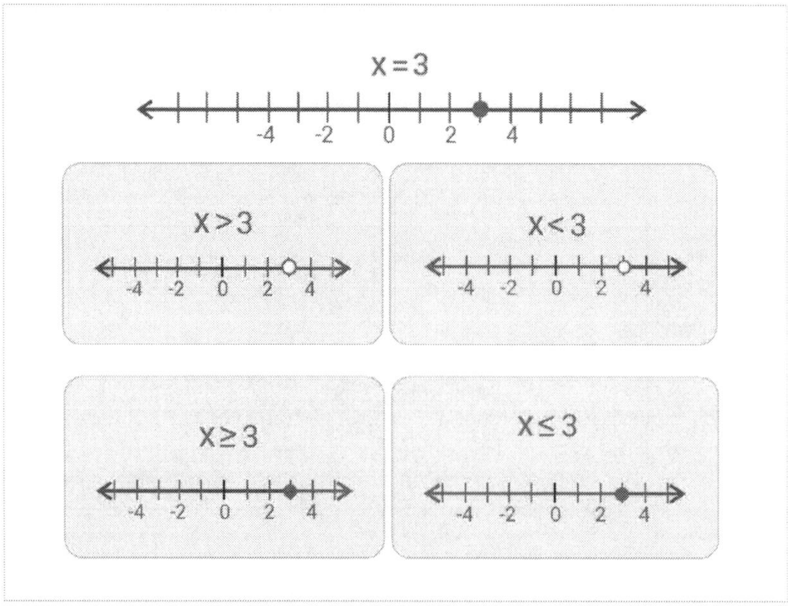

Students may be asked to write a linear inequality given a graph of its solution set. To do so, they should identify whether the value is included (shaded dot or open circle) and the direction in which the arrow is pointing.

In order to algebraically solve a linear inequality, the same steps should be followed as in solving a linear equation (see section on *Solving Linear Equations*). The inequality symbol stays the same for all operations EXCEPT when dividing by a negative number. If dividing by a negative number while solving an inequality, the relationship reverses (the sign flips). Dividing by a positive does not change the relationship, so the sign stays the same. In other words, $>$ switches to $<$ and vice versa. An example is shown below.

Solve $-2(x+4) \leq 22$

Distribute: $-2x - 8 \leq 22$

Add 8 to both sides: $-2x \leq 30$

Divide both sides by -2: $x \geq 15$

Polynomials

Algebraic expressions are built out of monomials. A **monomial** is a variable raised to some power multiplied by a constant: ax^n, where *a* is any constant and *n* is a whole number. A constant is also a monomial.

A **polynomial** is a sum of monomials. Examples of polynomials include $3x^4 + 2x^2 - x - 3$ and $\frac{4}{5}x^3$. The latter is also a monomial. If the highest power of *x* is 1, the polynomial is called **linear**. If the highest power of *x* is 2, it is called **quadratic**.

Factoring

Factors for polynomials are similar to factors for integers—they are numbers, variables, or polynomials that, when multiplied together, give a product equal to the polynomial in question. One polynomial is a factor of a second polynomial if the second polynomial can be obtained from the first by multiplying by a third polynomial.

$6x^6 + 13x^4 + 6x^2$ can be obtained by multiplying together $(3x^4 + 2x^2)(2x^2 + 3)$. This means $2x^2 + 3$ and $3x^4 + 2x^2$ are factors of $6x^6 + 13x^4 + 6x^2$.

In general, finding the factors of a polynomial can be tricky. However, there are a few types of polynomials that can be factored in a straightforward way.

If a certain monomial divides each term of a polynomial, it can be factored out:

$$x^2 + 2xy + y^2 = (x+y)^2$$

$$x^2 - 2xy + y^2 = (x-y)^2$$

$$x^2 - y^2 = (x+y)(x-y)$$

$$x^3 + y^3 = (x+y)(x^2 - xy + y^2)$$

$$x^3 - y^3 = (x-y)(x^2 + xy + y^2)$$

$$x^3 + 3x^2y + 3xy^2 + y^3 = (x + y)^3$$

$$x^3 - 3x^2y + 3xy^2 - y^3 = (x - y)^3$$

These rules can be used in many combinations with one another. For example, the expression $3x^3 - 24$ factors to $3(x^3 - 8) = 3(x - 2)(x^2 + 2x + 4)$.

When factoring polynomials, a good strategy is to multiply the factors to check the result.

Expanding Polynomials

Some polynomials may need to be expanded to identify the final solution—*polynomial expansion* means that parenthetical polynomials are multiplied out so that the parentheses no longer exist. The polynomials will be in the form $(a + b)^n$ where n is a whole number greater than 2. The expression can be simplified using the *distributive property*, which states that a number, variable, or polynomial that is multiplied by a polynomial in parentheses should be multiplied by each item in the parenthetical polynomial. Here's one example:

$$(a + b)^2 = (a + b)(a + b)$$

$$a^2 + ab + ab + b^2$$
$$a^2 + 2ab + b^2$$

Here's another example to consider:

$$(a + b)^3 = (a + b)(a + b)(a + b)$$

$$(a^2 + ab + ab + b^2)(a + b)$$

$$(a^2 + 2ab + b^2)(a + b)$$

$$a^3 + 2a^2b + ab^2 + a^2b + 2ab^2 + b^3$$

$$a^3 + 3a^2b + 3ab^2 + b^3$$

Performing Arithmetic Operations on Polynomials

An expression of the form ax^n, where *n* is a non-negative integer, is called a **monomial** because it contains one term. A sum of monomials is called a **polynomial**. For example, $-4x^3 + x$ is a polynomial, while $5x^7$ is a monomial. A function equal to a polynomial is called a **polynomial function**.

The monomials in a polynomial are also called the **terms** of the polynomial.

The constants that precede the variables are called **coefficients**.

The highest value of the exponent of *x* in a polynomial is called the **degree** of the polynomial. So, $-4x^3 + x$ has a degree of 3, while $-2x^5 + x^3 + 4x + 1$ has a degree of 5. When multiplying polynomials, the degree of the result will be the sum of the degrees of the two polynomials being multiplied.

Addition and subtraction operations can be performed on polynomials with like terms. **Like terms** refers to terms that have the same variable and exponent. The two following polynomials can be added together by collecting like terms:

$$(x^2 + 3x - 4) + (4x^2 - 7x + 8)$$

The x^2 terms can be added as $x^2+4x^2 = 5x^2$. The x terms can be added as $3x + -7x = -4x$, and the constants can be added as $-4 + 8 = 4$. The following expression is the result of the addition:

$$5x^2 - 4x + 4$$

When subtracting polynomials, the same steps are followed, only subtracting like terms together.

Multiplication of polynomials can also be performed. Given the two polynomials, $(y^3 - 4)$ and $(x^2 + 8x - 7)$, each term in the first polynomial must be multiplied by each term in the second polynomial. The steps to multiply each term in the given example are as follows:

$$(y^3 \times x^2) + (y^3 \times 8x) + (y^3 \times -7) + (-4 \times x^2) + (-4 \times 8x) + (-4 \times -7)$$

Simplifying each multiplied part, yields:

$$x^2y^3 + 8xy^3 - 7y^3 - 4x^2 - 32x + 28$$

None of the terms can be combined because there are no like terms in the final expression. Any polynomials can be multiplied by each other by following the same set of steps, then collecting like terms at the end.

Quadratic Functions

A **quadratic function** can be written in the form $y = ax^2 + bx + c$. The u-shaped graph of a quadratic function is called a **parabola**. The graph can either open up or open down (upside down u). The graph is symmetric about a vertical line, called the **axis of symmetry**. Corresponding points on the parabola are directly across from each other (same *y*-value) and are the same distance from the axis of symmetry (on either side). The axis of symmetry intersects the parabola at its **vertex**. The *y*-value of the vertex represents the minimum or maximum value of the function. If the graph opens up, the value of *a* in its equation is positive and the vertex represents the minimum of the function. If the graph opens down, the value of *a* in its equation is negative and the vertex represents the maximum of the function.

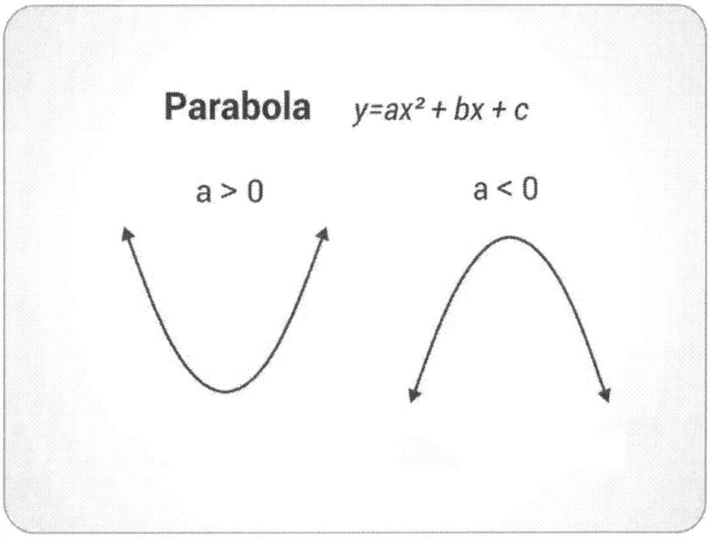

A quadratic function can be written in the standard form: $y = ax^2 + bx + c$. It can be represented by a u-shaped graph called a parabola. For a quadratic function where the value of *a* is positive, as the inputs increase, the outputs increase until a certain value (maximum of the function) is reached. As inputs increase past the value that corresponds with the maximum output, the relationship reverses and the outputs decrease. For a quadratic function where *a* is negative, as the inputs increase, the outputs (1) decrease, (2) reach a maximum, and (3) then increase.

Consider a ball thrown straight up into the air. As time passes, the height of the ball increases until it reaches its maximum height. After reaching the maximum height, as time increases, the height of the ball decreases (it is falling toward the ground). This relationship can be expressed as a quadratic function where time is the input (*x*) and the height of the ball is the output (*y*).

Equations with one variable (linear equations) can be solved using the addition principle and multiplication principle. If $a = b$, then $a + c = b + c$, and $ac = bc$. Given the equation $2x - 3 = 5x + 7$, the first step is to combine the variable terms and the constant terms. Using the principles, expressions can be added and subtracted onto and off both sides of the equals sign, so the equation turns into $-10 = 3x$. Dividing by 3 on both sides through the multiplication principle with $c = \frac{1}{3}$ results in the final answer of $x = \frac{-10}{3}$.

However, this same process cannot be used to solve nonlinear equations, including quadratic equations. Quadratic equations have a higher degree than linear ones (2 versus 1) and are not solved by simply using opposite operations. When an equation has a degree of 2, completing the square is an option. For example, the quadratic equation $x^2 - 6x + 2 = 0$ can be rewritten by completing the square. The goal of completing the square is to get the equation into the form $(x - p)^2 = q$. Using the example, the constant term 2 first needs to be moved over to the opposite side by subtracting. Then, the square can be completed by adding 9 to both sides, which is the square of half of the coefficient of the middle term $-6x$. The current equation is $x^2 - 6x + 9 = 7$. The left side can be factored into a square of a binomial, resulting in $(x - 3)^2 = 7$. To solve for x, the square root of both sides should be taken, resulting in $(x - 3) = \pm\sqrt{7}$, and $x = 3 \pm \sqrt{7}$.

Other ways of solving quadratic equations include graphing, factoring, and using the quadratic formula. The equation $y = x^2 - 4x + 3$ can be graphed on the coordinate plane, and the solutions can be observed where it crosses the x-axis. The graph will be a parabola that opens up with two solutions at 1 and 3.

If quadratic equations take the form $ax^2 - b = 0$, then the equation can be solved by adding *b* to both sides and dividing by *a* to get $x^2 = \frac{b}{a}$ or $x = \pm\sqrt{\frac{b}{a}}$. Note that this is actually two separate solutions, unless *b* happens to be 0.

If a quadratic equation has no constant—so that it takes the form $ax^2 + bx = 0$—then the *x* can be factored out to get $x(ax + b) = 0$. Then, the solutions are $x = 0$, together with the solutions to $ax + b = 0$. Both factors x *and* $(ax + b)$ can be set equal to zero to solve for x because one of those values must be zero for their product to equal zero. For an equation $ab = 0$ to be true, either $a = 0$, or $b = 0$.

A given quadratic equation $x^2 + bx + c$ can be factored into $(x + A)(x + B)$, where $A + B = b$, and $AB = c$. Finding the values of A and B can take time, but such a pair of numbers can be found by guessing and checking. Looking at the positive and negative factors for *c* offers a good starting point.

For example, in $x^2 - 5x + 6$, the factors of 6 are 1, 2, and 3. Now,$(-2)(-3) = 6$, and $-2 - 3 = -5$. In general, however, this may not work, in which case another approach may need to be used.

A quadratic equation of the form $x^2 + 2xb + b^2 = 0$ can be factored into $(x + b)^2 = 0$. Similarly, $x^2 - 2xy + y^2 = 0$ factors into $(x - y)^2 = 0$.

The first method of completing the square can be used in finding the second method, the quadratic formula. It can be used to solve any quadratic equation. This formula may be the longest method for solving quadratic equations and is commonly used as a last resort after other methods are ruled out.

It can be helpful in memorizing the formula to see where it comes from, so here are the steps involved.

The most general form for a quadratic equation is $ax^2 + bx + c = 0$.

First, dividing both sides by *a* leaves us with:

$$x^2 + \frac{b}{a}x + \frac{c}{a} = 0$$

To complete the square on the left-hand side, c/a can be subtracted on both sides to get:

$$x^2 + \frac{b}{a}x = -\frac{c}{a}$$

$(\frac{b}{2a})^2$ is then added to both sides.

This gives:

$$x^2 + \frac{b}{a}x + (\frac{b}{2a})^2 = (\frac{b}{2a})^2 - \frac{c}{a}$$

The left can now be factored and the right-hand side simplified to give:

$$(x + \frac{b}{2a})^2 = \frac{b^2 - 4ac}{4a}$$

Taking the square roots gives:

$$x + \frac{b}{2a} = \pm\frac{\sqrt{b^2 - 4ac}}{2a}$$

Solving for x yields the quadratic formula:

$$x = \frac{-b \pm \sqrt{b^2 - 4ac}}{2a}$$

It isn't necessary to remember how to get this formula, but memorizing the formula itself is the goal.

If an equation involves taking a root, then the first step is to move the root to one side of the equation and everything else to the other side. That way, both sides can be raised to the index of the radical in order to remove it, and solving the equation can continue.

Exponential Functions

The general form for an **exponential function** is $y = ab^x$ where *b* must be a positive number and cannot equal 1. When the value of *b* is greater than 1, the function models exponential **growth** (as *x* increases, *y* increases). When the value of *b* is less than 1, the function models exponential **decay** (as *x* increases, *y* decreases). If *a* is positive, the graph consists of points above the *x*-axis; and if *a* is negative, the graph consists of points below the *x*-axis. An asymptote is a line that a graph approaches.

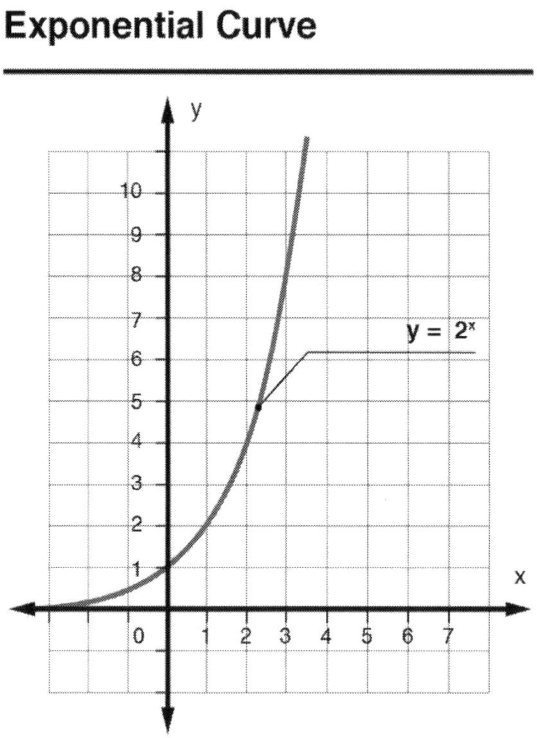

To solve an equation involving exponential expressions, the goal is to isolate the exponential expression. Once this process is completed, the logarithm—with the base equaling the base of the exponent of both sides—needs to be taken to get an expression for the variable. If the base is e, the natural log of both sides needs to be taken.

To solve an equation with logarithms, the given equation needs to be written in exponential form, using the fact that $\log_b y = x$ means $b^x = y$, and then solved for the given variable. Lastly, properties of logarithms can be used to simplify more than one logarithmic expression into one.

When working with logarithmic functions, it is important to remember the following properties. Each one can be derived from the definition of the logarithm as the inverse to an exponential function:

$$\log_b 1 = 0$$

$$\log_b b = 1$$

$$\log_b b^p = p$$

$$\log_b MN = \log_b M + \log_b N$$

$$\log_b \frac{M}{N} = \log_b M - \log_b N$$

$$\log_b M^p = p \log_b M$$

When solving equations involving exponentials and logarithms, the following fact should be used:

If f is a one-to-one function, $a = b$ is equivalent to $f(a) = f(b)$.

Using this, together with the fact that logarithms and exponentials are inverses, allows manipulations of the equations to isolate the variable.

Example:

Solve $4 = \ln(x - 4)$.

Using the definition of a logarithm, the equation can be changed to $e^4 = e^{\ln(x-4)}$.

The functions on the right side cancel with a result of $e^4 = x - 4$.

This then gives $x = 4 + e^4$.

Systems of Equations and Inequalities

A **system of equations** is a group of equations that have the same variables or unknowns. These equations can be linear, but they are not always so. Finding a solution to a system of equations means finding the values of the variables that satisfy each equation. For a linear system of two equations and two variables, there could be a single solution, no solution, or infinitely many solutions.

A single solution occurs when there is one value for x and y that satisfies the system. This would be shown on the graph where the lines cross at exactly one point. When there is no solution, the lines are parallel and do not ever cross. With infinitely many solutions, the equations may look different, but they are the same line. One equation will be a multiple of the other, and on the graph, they lie on top of each other.

The process of elimination can be used to solve a system of equations. For example, the following equations make up a system:

$$x + 3y = 10 \text{ and } 2x - 5y = 9$$

Immediately adding these equations does not eliminate a variable, but it is possible to change the first equation by multiplying the whole equation by -2. This changes the first equation to

$$-2x - 6y = -20$$

The equations can be then added to obtain $-11y = -11$. Solving for y yields $y = 1$. To find the rest of the solution, 1 can be substituted in for y in either original equation to find the value of $x = 7$. The solution to the system is (7, 1) because it makes both equations true, and it is the point in which the lines intersect. If the system is **dependent**—having infinitely many solutions—then both variables will cancel out when the elimination method is used, resulting in an equation that is true for many values of *x* and *y*. Since the system is dependent, both equations can be simplified to the same equation or line.

A system can also be solved using **substitution.** This involves solving one equation for a variable and then plugging that solved equation into the other equation in the system. This equation can be solved for one variable, which can then be plugged in to either original equation and solved for the other variable. For example, $x - y = -2$ and $3x + 2y = 9$ can be solved using substitution. The first equation can be solved for x, where $x = -2 + y$. Then it can be plugged into the other equation:

$$3(-2 + y) + 2y = 9$$

Solving for y yields:

$$-6 + 3y + 2y = 9$$

That shows that $y = 3$. If $y = 3$, then $x = 1$.

This solution can be checked by plugging in these values for the variables in each equation to see if it makes a true statement.

Finally, a solution to a system of equations can be found graphically. The solution to a linear system is the point or points where the lines cross. The values of x and y represent the coordinates (x, y) where the lines intersect. Using the same system of equation as above, they can be solved for y to put them in slope-intercept form, $y = mx + b$. These equations become $y = x + 2$ and $y = -\frac{3}{2}x + 4.5$. The slope is the coefficient of x, and the y-intercept is the constant value.

This system with the solution is shown below:

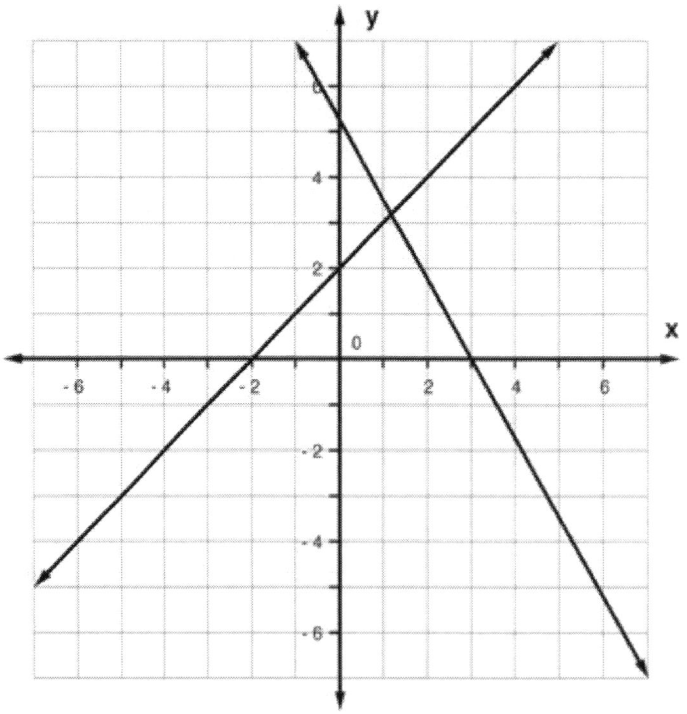

A solution for a system of equations is an ordered pair that makes both equations true. Graphing both lines on a coordinate plane can help find the solution to the system. If the lines intersect, the point of intersection is the solution to the system. Every point on a line represents an ordered pair that makes its equation true. The ordered pair represented by this point of intersection lies on both lines and therefore makes both equations true. This ordered pair should be checked by substituting its values into both of the original equations of the system. Note that given a system of equations and an ordered pair, the ordered pair can be determined to be a solution or not by checking it in both equations.

If, when graphed, the lines representing the equations of a system do not intersect, then the two lines are parallel to each other or they are the same exact line. Parallel lines extend in the same direction without ever meeting. A system consisting of parallel lines has no solution. If the equations for a system represent the same exact line, then every point on the line is a solution to the system. In this case, there would be an infinite number of solutions. A system consisting of intersecting lines is referred to as independent; a system consisting of parallel lines is referred to as inconsistent; and a system consisting of coinciding lines is referred to as dependent.

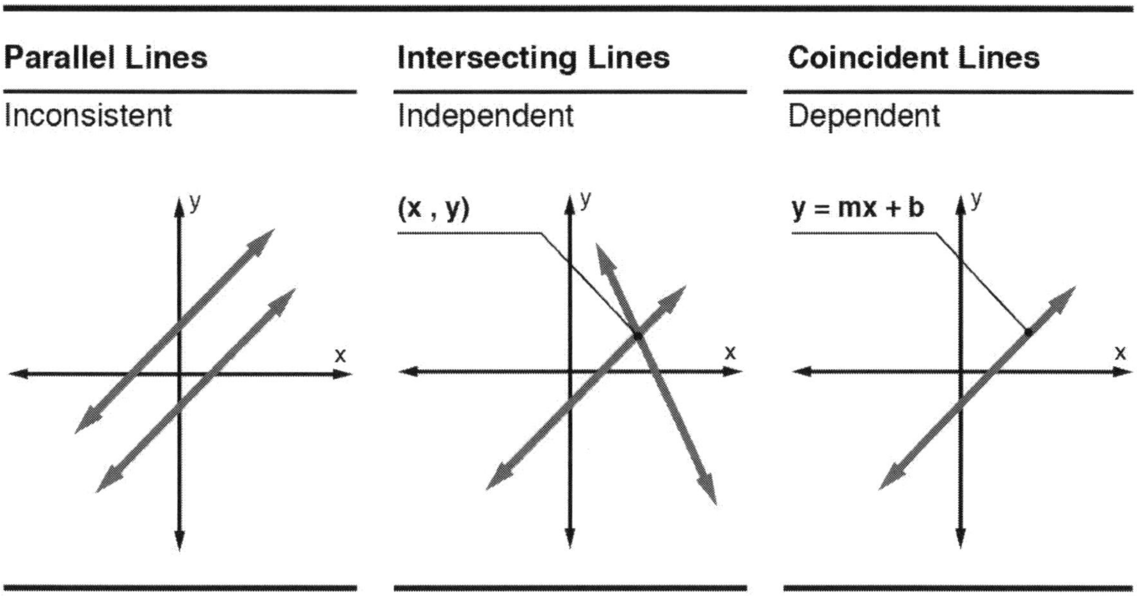

Systems of linear inequalities are like systems of equations, but the solutions are different. Since inequalities have infinitely many solutions, their systems also have infinitely many solutions. Finding the solutions of inequalities involves graphs. A system of two equations and two inequalities is linear; thus, the lines can be graphed using slope-intercept form. If the inequality has an equals sign, the line is solid. If the inequality only has a greater than or less than symbol, the line on the graph is dotted. Dashed lines indicate that points lying on the line are not included in the solution. After the lines are graphed, a region is shaded on one side of the line. This side is found by determining if a point—known as a **test point**—lying on one side of the line produces a true inequality. If it does, that side of the graph is shaded. If the point produces a false inequality, the line is shaded on the opposite side from the point. The graph of a system of inequalities involves shading the intersection of the two shaded regions.

A system of linear inequalities consists of two linear inequalities making comparisons between two variables. Students may be given a scenario and asked to express it as a system of inequalities:

> A consumer study calls for at least 60 adult participants. It cannot use more than 25 men. Express these constraints as a system of inequalities.

This can be modeled by the system: $x + y \geq 60; x \leq 25$, where *x* represents the number of men and *y* represents the number of women. A solution to the system is an ordered pair that makes both inequalities true when substituting the values for *x* and *y*.

The solution set for a system of inequalities is the region of a graph consisting of ordered pairs that make both inequalities true. To graph the solution set, each linear inequality should first be graphed with appropriate shading. The region of the graph should be identified where the shading for the two inequalities overlaps. This region contains the solution set for the system.

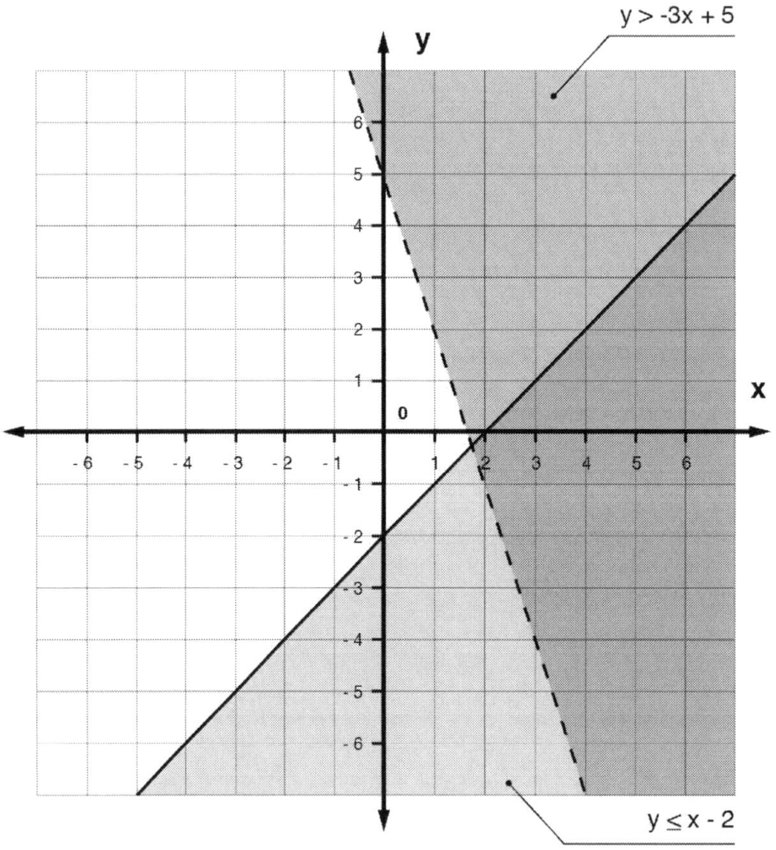

An ordered pair from the region of solutions can be selected to test in the system of inequalities.

Just as with manipulating linear inequalities in one variable, if dividing by a negative number in working with a linear inequality in two variables, the relationship reverses and the inequality sign should be flipped.

Recognizing and Representing Simple Sequences or Patterns

Evaluating, Extending, or Algebraically Representing Rules that Involve Number Patterns
Patterns are an important part of mathematics. When mathematical calculations are completed repeatedly, patterns can be recognized. Recognizing patterns is an integral part of mathematics because it helps you understand relationships between different ideas. For example, a sequence of numbers can be given, and being able to recognize the relationship between the given numbers can help in completing the sequence.

For instance, given the sequence of numbers 7, 14, 21, 28, 35, ..., the next number in the sequence would be 42. This is because the sequence lists all multiples of 7, starting at 7. Sequences can also be built from addition, subtraction, and division. Being able to recognize the relationship between the values that are given is the key to finding out the next number in the sequence.

Patterns within a sequence can come in 2 distinct forms. The items either repeat in a constant order, or the items change from one step to another in some consistent way. The **core** is the smallest unit, or number of items, that repeats in a repeating pattern. For example, the pattern oo▲oo▲o... has a core that is oo▲. Knowing only the core, the pattern can be extended. Knowing the number of steps in the core allows the identification of an item in each step without drawing/writing the entire pattern out. For example, suppose you must find the tenth item in the previous pattern. Because the core consists of three items (oo▲), the core repeats in multiples of 3. In other words, steps 3, 6, 9, 12, etc. will be ▲ completing the core with the core starting over on the next step. For the above example, the 9th step will be ▲ and the 10th will be o.

The most common patterns where each item changes from one step to the next are arithmetic and geometric sequences. In an **arithmetic sequence**, the items increase or decrease by a constant difference. In other words, the same thing is added or subtracted to each item or step to produce the next. To determine if a sequence is arithmetic, see what must be added or subtracted to step one to produce step two. Then, check if the same thing is added/subtracted to step two to produce step three. The same thing must be added/subtracted to step three to produce step four, and so on. Consider the pattern 13, 10, 7, 4, ... To get from step one (13) to step two (10) by adding or subtracting requires subtracting by 3. The next step is checking if subtracting 3 from step two (10) will produce step three (7), and subtracting 3 from step three (7) will produce step four (4). In this case, the pattern holds true. Therefore, this is an arithmetic sequence in which each step is produced by subtracting 3 from the previous step. To extend the sequence, 3 is subtracted from the last step to produce the next. The next three numbers in the sequence are 1, -2, -5.

A **geometric sequence** is one in which each step is produced by multiplying or dividing the previous step by the same number. To see if a sequence is geometric, decide what step one must be multiplied or divided by to produce step two. Then check if multiplying or dividing step two by the same number produces step three, and so on. Consider the pattern 2, 8, 32, 128, ... To get from step one (2) to step two (8) requires multiplication by 4. The next step determines if multiplying step two (8) by 4 produces step three (32), and multiplying step three (32) by 4 produces step four (128). In this case, the pattern holds true. Therefore, this is a geometric sequence in which each step is found by multiplying the previous step by 4. To extend the sequence, the last step is multiplied by 4 and repeated. The next three numbers in the sequence are 512; 2,048; 8,192.

Patterns Involving Shapes or Figures

Arithmetic and geometric sequences can also be represented by shapes. For example, an arithmetic sequence could consist of shapes with three sides, four sides, and five sides. A geometric sequence could consist of eight blocks, four blocks, and two blocks (each step is produced by dividing the number of blocks in the previous step by 2).

Using Patterns to Make Conjectures, Predictions, or Generalizations

Patterns can be used to make conjectures, predictions, or generalizations. One of the most common question types test takers will encounter is to identify what number or shape will come next, which involves making a prediction based on understanding the presented pattern.

When given two number patterns, the corresponding terms should be examined to determine if a relationship exists between them. Corresponding terms between patterns are the pairs of numbers which appear in the same step of the two sequences. Consider the following patterns 1, 2, 3, 4,... and 3, 6, 9, 12, ... The corresponding terms are: 1 and 3; 2 and 6; 3 and 9; and 4 and 12. To identify the relationship, each pair of corresponding terms is examined. You can also examine the possibilities of performing an operation (+, −, ×, ÷) to each sequence. In this case:

$1 + 2 = 3$ or $1 \times 3 = 3$

$2 + 4 = 6$ or $2 \times 3 = 6$

$3 + 6 = 9$ or $3 \times 3 = 9$

$4 + 8 = 12$ or $4 \times 3 = 12$

The pattern is that the number from the first sequence multiplied by 3 equals the number in the second sequence. By assigning each sequence a label (input and output) or variable (*x* and *y*), the relationship can be written as an equation. The first sequence represents the inputs, or *x*, and the second sequence represents the outputs, or *y*. So, the relationship can be expressed as: $y = 3x$.

Consider the following sets of numbers:

a	2	4	6	8
b	6	8	10	12

To write a rule for the relationship between the values for *a* and the values for *b*, the corresponding terms (2 and 6; 4 and 8; 6 and 10; 8 and 12) are examined. The possibilities for producing *b* from *a* are:

$2 + 4 = 6$ or $2 \times 3 = 6$

$4 + 4 = 8$ or $4 \times 2 = 8$

$6 + 4 = 10$

$8 + 4 = 12$ or $8 \times 1.5 = 12$

The pattern is that adding 4 to the value of *a* produces the value of *b*. The relationship can be written as the equation $a + 4 = b$.

Geometry

Lines

The basic unit of geometry is a point. A **point** represents an exact location on a plane, or flat surface. The position of a point is indicated with a dot and usually named with a single uppercase letter, such as point

A or point *T*. A point is a place, not a thing, and therefore has no dimensions or size. A set of points that lies on the same line is called **collinear**. A set of points that lies on the same plane is called **coplanar**.

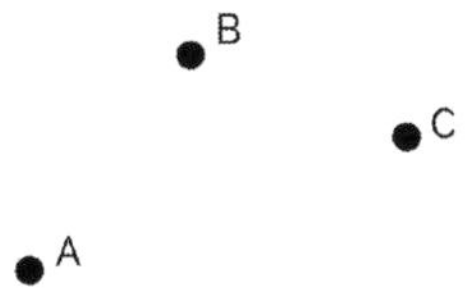

The image above displays point *A*, point *B*, and point *C*.

A **line** is as series of points that extends in both directions without ending. It consists of an infinite number of points and is drawn with arrows on both ends to indicate it extends infinitely. Lines can be named by two points on the line or with a single, cursive, lower case letter. The two lines below could be named line *AB* or line *BA* or $\overleftrightarrow{AB}$ or $\overleftrightarrow{BA}$; and line *m*.

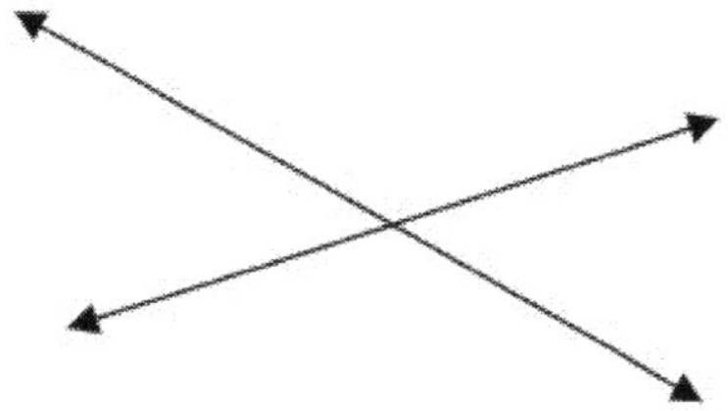

Two lines are considered parallel to each other if, while extending infinitely, they will never intersect (or meet). **Parallel** lines point in the same direction and are always the same distance apart. Two lines are considered **perpendicular** if they intersect to form right angles. Right angles are 90°. Typically, a small box is drawn at the intersection point to indicate the right angle.

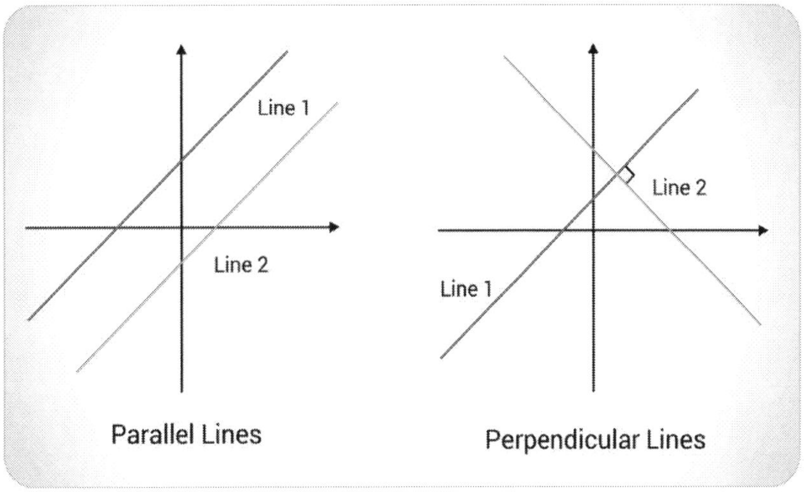

Line 1 is parallel to line 2 in the left image and is written as line 1 || line 2. Line 1 is perpendicular to line 2 in the right image and is written as line 1 ⊥ line 2.

A **ray** has a specific starting point and extends in one direction without ending. The endpoint of a ray is its starting point. Rays are named using the endpoint first, and any other point on the ray. The following ray can be named ray *AB* and written $\overrightarrow{AB}$.

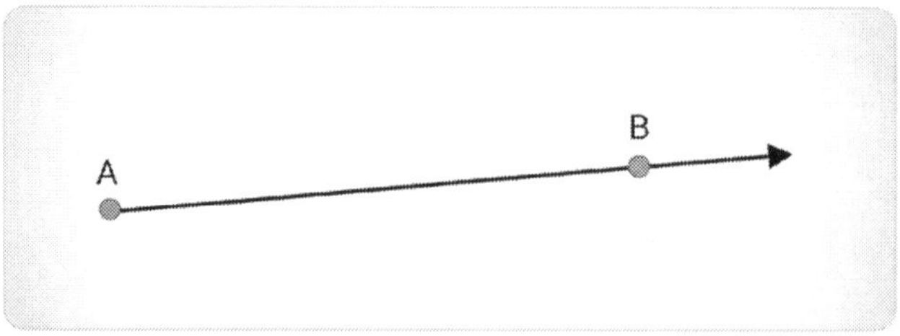

A **line segment** has specific starting and ending points. A line segment consists of two endpoints and all the points in between. Line segments are named by the two endpoints. The example below is named segment *KL* or segment *LK*, written $\overline{KL}$ or $\overline{LK}$.

Parallel, Perpendicular, and Intersecting Lines

Two lines are parallel if they have the same slope and different intercept. Two lines are **perpendicular** if the product of their slope equals -1. Parallel lines never intersect unless they are the same line, and perpendicular lines intersect at a right angle. If two lines aren't parallel, they must intersect at one point. If lines do cross, they're labeled as **intersecting lines** because they "intersect" at one point. If they intersect at more than one point, they're the same line. Determining equations of lines based on properties of parallel and perpendicular lines appears in word problems. To find an equation of a line, both the slope and a point the line goes through are necessary. Therefore, if an equation of a line is needed that's parallel to a given line and runs through a specified point, the slope of the given line and the point are plugged into the point-slope form of an equation of a line. Secondly, if an equation of a line is needed that's perpendicular to a given line running through a specified point, the negative reciprocal of the slope of the given line and the point are plugged into the **point-slope form**. Also, if the point of intersection of two lines is known, that point will be used to solve the set of equations. Therefore, to solve a system of equations, the point of intersection must be found. If a set of two equations with two unknown variables has no solution, the lines are parallel.

The **Parallel Postulate** states that if two parallel lines are cut by a transversal, then the corresponding angles are equal. Here is a picture that highlights this postulate:

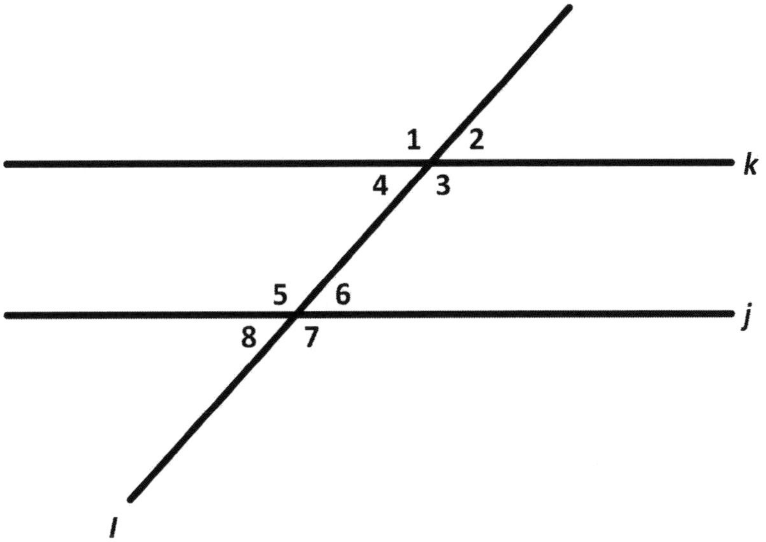

Because lines *k* and *i* are parallel, when cut by transversal *l,* angles 1 and 5 are equal, angles 2 and 6 are equal, angles 4 and 8 are equal, and angles 3 and 7 are equal. Note that angles 1 and 2, 3 and 4, 5 and 6, and 7 and 8 add up to 180 degrees.

This statement is equivalent to the **Alternate Interior Angle Theorem**, which states that when two parallel lines are cut by a transversal, the resultant interior angles are congruent. In the picture above, angles 3 and 5 are congruent, and angles 4 and 6 are congruent.

The Parallel Postulate or the Alternate Interior Angle Theorem can be used to find the missing angles in the following picture:

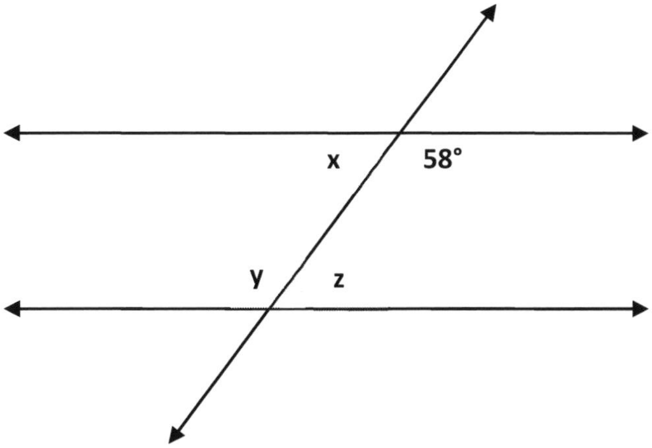

Assuming that the lines are parallel, angle x is found to be 122 degrees. Angle x and the 58-degree angle add up to 180 degrees. The Alternate Interior Angle Theorem states that angle y is equal to 58 degrees. Also, angles y and z add up to 180 degrees, so angle z is 122 degrees. Note that angles x and z are also alternate interior angles, so their equivalence can be used to find angle z as well.

An equivalent statement to the Parallel Postulate is that the sum of all angles in a triangle is 180 degrees. Therefore, given any triangle, if two angles are known, the third can be found accordingly.

Angles

An **angle** can be visualized as a corner. It is defined as the formation of two rays connecting at a vertex that extend indefinitely.

An angle consists of two rays that have a common endpoint. This common endpoint is called the **vertex** of the angle. The two rays can be called sides of the angle. The angle below has a vertex at point *B* and the sides consist of ray *BA* and ray *BC*. An angle can be named in three ways:

1. Using the vertex and a point from each side, with the vertex letter in the middle.
2. Using only the vertex. This can only be used if it is the only angle with that vertex.
3. Using a number that is written inside the angle.

The angle below can be written $\angle ABC$ (read angle *ABC*), $\angle CBA$, $\angle B$, or $\angle 1$.

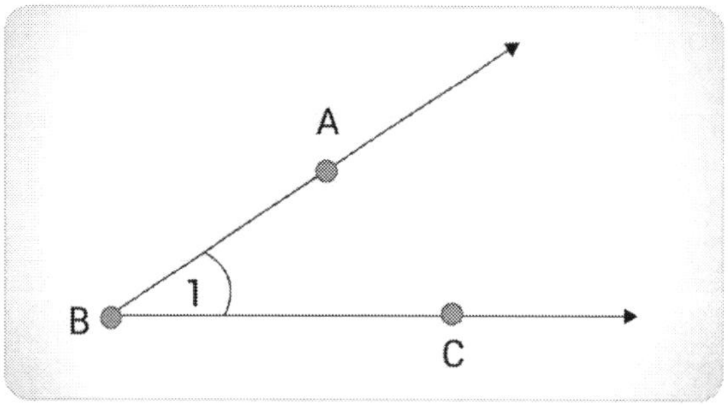

An angle divides a plane, or flat surface, into three parts: the angle itself, the interior (inside) of the angle, and the exterior (outside) of the angle. The figure below shows point *M* on the interior of the angle and point *N* on the exterior of the angle.

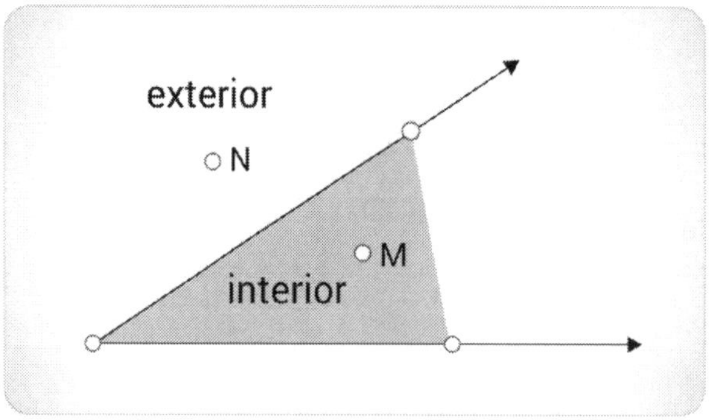

Angles can be measured in units called degrees, with the symbol °. The degree measure of an angle is between 0° and 180°, is a measure of rotation, and can be obtained by using a protractor.

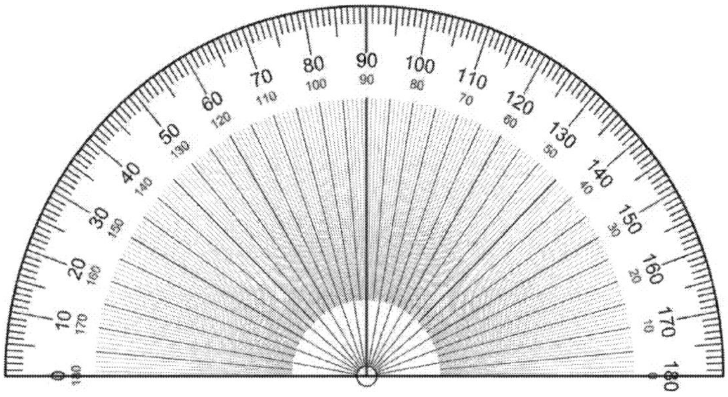

A straight angle (or simply a line) measures exactly 180°. A right angle's sides meet at the vertex to create a square corner. A right angle measures exactly 90° and is typically indicated by a box drawn in the interior of the angle. An acute angle has an interior that is narrower than a right angle. The measure of an acute angle is any value less than 90° and greater than 0°. For example, 89.9°, 47°, 12°, and 1°. An obtuse angle has an interior that is wider than a right angle. The measure of an obtuse angle is any value greater than 90° but less than 180°. For example, 90.1°, 110°, 150°, and 179.9°. Any two angles that sum up to 90 degrees are known as *complementary angles.*

- Acute angles: Less than 90°
- Obtuse angles: Greater than 90°
- Right angles: 90°
- Straight angles: 180°

To determine angle measures for adjacent angles, angles that share a common side and vertex, at least one of the angles must be known. Other information that is necessary to determine such measures include that there are 90^0 in a right angle, and there are 180^0 in a straight line. Therefore, if two adjacent angles form a right angle, they will add up to 90^0, and if two adjacent angles form a straight line, they add up to 180^0.

If the measurement of one of the adjacent angles is known, the other can be found by subtracting the known angle from the total number of degrees.

For example, given the following situation, if angle *a* measures 55^0, find the measure of unknown angle *b*:

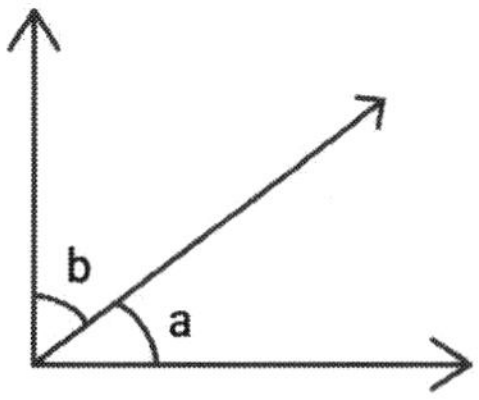

To solve this simply subtract the known angle measure from 90^0.

$$90° - 55° = 35°$$

The measure of $b = 35°$.

Given the following situation, if angle 1 measures 45^0, find the measure of the unknown angle 2:

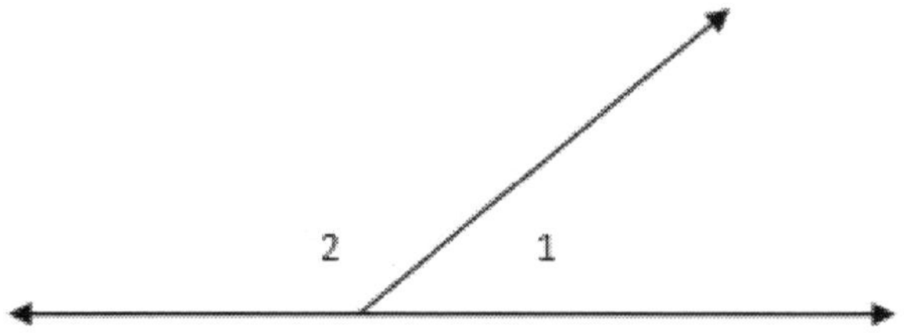

To solve this, simply subtract the known angle measure from 180^0.

$$180° - 45° = 135°$$

The measure of angle 2 = $135°$.

In the case that more than two angles are given, use the same method of subtracting the known angles from the total measure.

For example, given the following situation, if angle $y = 40^0$, and angle $z = 25^0$, find unknown angle x.

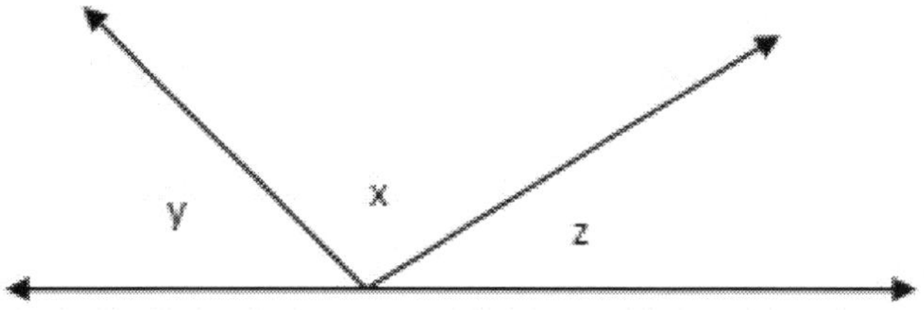

Subtract the known angles from 180^0.

$$180° - 40° - 25° = 115°$$

The measure of angle $x = 115^0$.

Polygons

The vocabulary regarding many two-dimensional shapes is an important part classifying these figures. Flat or two-dimensional shapes include circles, triangles, hexagons, and rectangles, among others. A shape can be classified based on whether it is open like the letter U or closed like the letter O. Further classifications involve counting the number of sides and vertices (corners) on the shapes. This can help to tell the difference between shapes.

A **polygon** is a closed geometric figure in a plane (flat surface) consisting of at least 3 sides formed by line segments.

Polygons can be either convex or concave. A polygon that has interior angles all measuring less than 180° is **convex**. A **concave** polygon has one or more interior angles measuring greater than 180°. Examples are shown below.

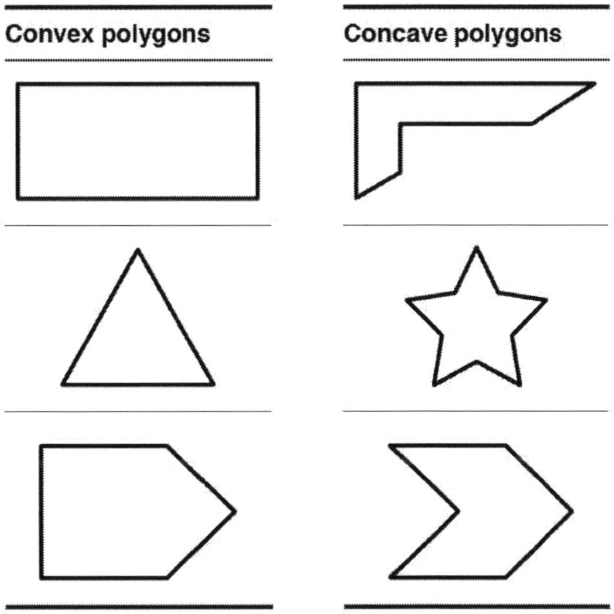

Polygons are often defined as two-dimensional shapes. Common two-dimensional shapes include circles, triangles, squares, rectangles, pentagons, and hexagons. A **circle** is a two-dimensional shape without sides, so it is not a polygon.

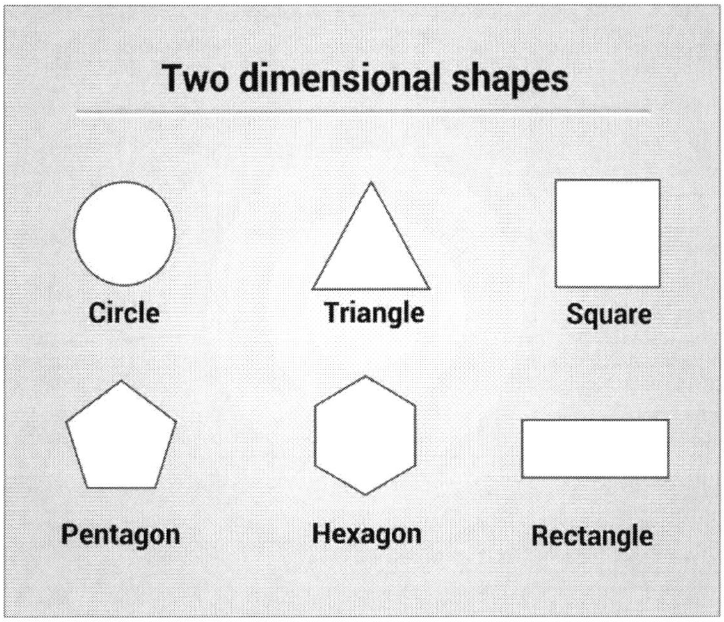

Polygons can be classified by the number of sides (also equal to the number of angles) they have. The following are the names of polygons with a given number of sides or angles:

# of sides	**3**	**4**	**5**	**6**	**7**	**8**	**9**	**10**
Name of polygon	Triangle	Quadrilateral	Pentagon	Hexagon	Septagon (or heptagon)	Octagon	Nonagon	Decagon

Equiangular polygons are polygons in which the measure of every interior angle is the same. The sides of equilateral polygons are always the same length. If a polygon is both equiangular and equilateral, the polygon is defined as a **regular polygon**. Examples are shown below:

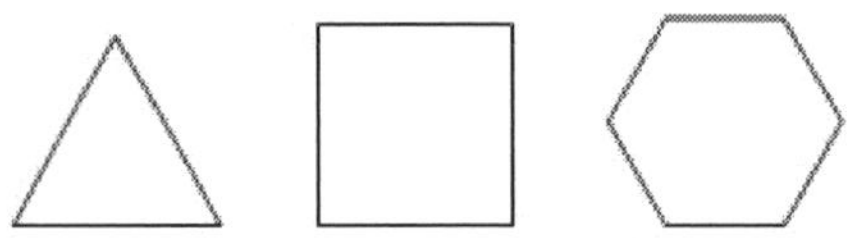

Calculating Area and Perimeter

Perimeter is the measurement of a distance around something or the sum of all sides of a polygon. Think of perimeter as the length of the boundary, like a fence. In contrast, **area** is the space occupied by a defined enclosure, like a field enclosed by a fence.

When thinking about perimeter, think about walking around the outside of something. When thinking about area, think about the amount of space or **surface area** something takes up.

<u>Squares</u>
The perimeter of a square is measured by adding together all of the sides. Since a square has four equal sides, its perimeter can be calculated by multiplying the length of one side by 4. Thus, the formula is $P = 4 \times s$, where s equals one side. For example, the following square has side lengths of 5 meters:

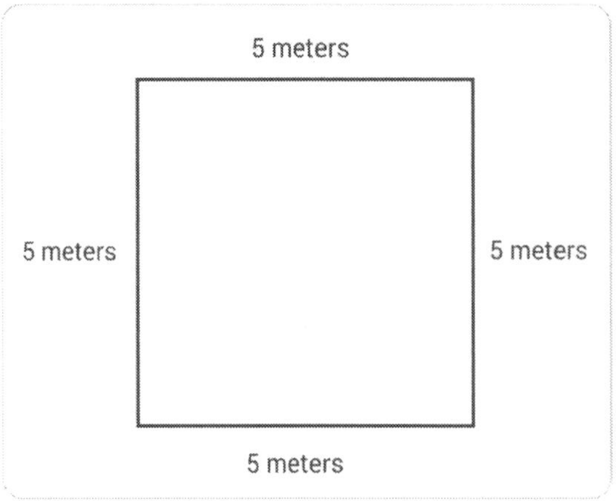

The perimeter is 20 meters because 4 times 5 is 20.

The area of a square is the length of a side squared, and the area of a rectangle is length multiplied by the width. For example, if the length of the square is 7 centimeters, then the area is 49 square centimeters. The formula for this example is $A = s^2 = 7^2 = 49$ square centimeters. An example is if the rectangle has a length of 6 inches and a width of 7 inches, then the area is 42 square inches:

$$A = lw = 6(7) = 42 \text{ square inches}$$

Rectangles

Like a square, a rectangle's perimeter is measured by adding together all of the sides. But as the sides are unequal, the formula is different. A rectangle has equal values for its lengths (long sides) and equal values for its widths (short sides), so the perimeter formula for a rectangle is:

$$P = l + l + w + w = 2l + 2w$$

l equals length
w equals width

The area is found by multiplying the length by the width, so the formula is $A = l \times w$.

For example, if the length of a rectangle is 10 inches and the width 8 inches, then the perimeter is 36 inches because:

$$P = 2l + 2w = 2(10) + 2(8) = 20 + 16 = 36 \text{ inches}$$

Triangles

A triangle's perimeter is measured by adding together the three sides, so the formula is $P = a + b + c$, where a, b, and c are the values of the three sides. The area is the product of one-half the base and height so the formula is:

$$A = \frac{1}{2} \times b \times h$$

It can be simplified to:

$$A = \frac{bh}{2}$$

The base is the bottom of the triangle, and the height is the distance from the base to the peak. If a problem asks to calculate the area of a triangle, it will provide the base and height.

For example, if the base of the triangle is 2 feet and the height 4 feet, then the area is 4 square feet. The following equation shows the formula used to calculate the area of the triangle:

$$A = \frac{1}{2}bh = \frac{1}{2}(2)(4) = 4 \text{ square feet}$$

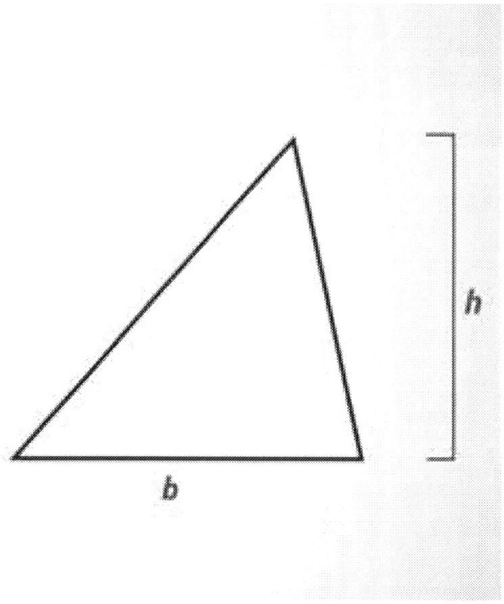

Circles

A circle's perimeter—also known as its circumference—is measured by multiplying the diameter by π.

Diameter is the straight line measured from one end to the direct opposite end of the circle.

π is referred to as pi and is equal to 3.14 (with rounding).

So the formula is $\pi \times d$.

This is sometimes expressed by the formula $C = 2 \times \pi \times r$, where r is the radius of the circle. These formulas are equivalent, as the radius equals half of the diameter.

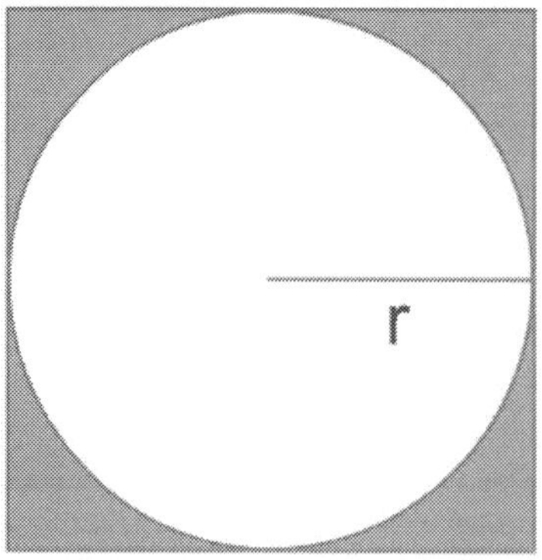

The area of a circle is calculated through the formula $A = \pi \times r^2$. The test will indicate either to leave the answer with π attached or to calculate to the nearest decimal place, which means multiplying by 3.14 for π.

Irregular Shapes

The perimeter of an irregular polygon is found by adding the lengths of all of the sides. In cases where all of the sides are given, this will be very straightforward, as it will simply involve finding the sum of the provided lengths. Other times, a side length may be missing and must be determined before the perimeter can be calculated. Consider the example below:

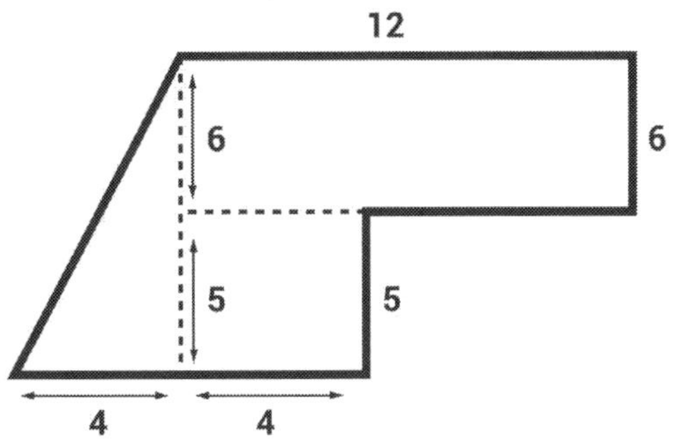

All of the side lengths are provided except for the angled side on the left. Test takers should notice that this is the hypotenuse of a right triangle. The other two sides of the triangle are provided (the base is 4 and the height is 6 + 5 = 11). The Pythagorean Theorem can be used to find the length of the hypotenuse, remembering that $a^2 + b^2 = c^2$.

Substituting the side values provided yields $(4)^2 + (11)^2 = c^2$.

Therefore, $c = \sqrt{16 + 121} = 11.7$

Finally, the perimeter can be found by adding this new side length with the other provided lengths to get the total length around the figure: 4+4+5+8+6+12+11.7=50.7. Although units are not provided in this figure, remember that reporting units with a measurement is important.

The area of an irregular polygon is found by decomposing, or breaking apart, the figure into smaller shapes. When the area of the smaller shapes is determined, these areas are added together to produce the total area of the area of the original figure. Consider the same example provided before:

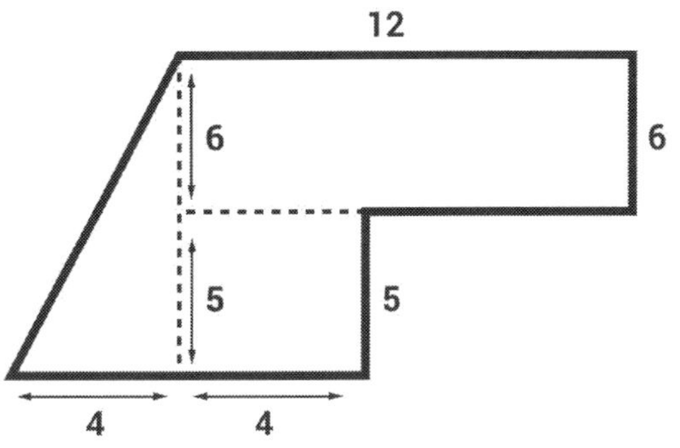

The irregular polygon is decomposed into two rectangles and a triangle. The area of the large rectangles ($A = l \times w \rightarrow A = 12 \times 6$) is 72 square units. The area of the small rectangle is 20 square units ($A = 4 \times 5$). The area of the triangle ($A = \frac{1}{2} \times b \times h \rightarrow A = \frac{1}{2} \times 4 \times 11$) is 22 square units. The sum of the areas of these figures produces the total area of the original polygon:$A = 72 + 20 + 22 \rightarrow A$ = 114 square units.

Circles

<u>Arc</u>

The **arc of a circle** is the distance between two points on the circle. The length of the arc of a circle in terms of **degrees** is easily determined if the value of the central angle is known. The length of the arc is simply the value of the central angle. In this example, the length of the arc of the circle in degrees is 75°.

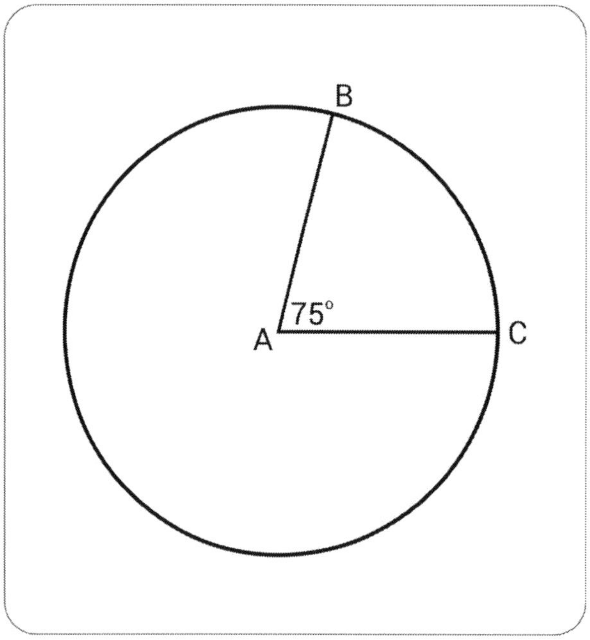

To determine the length of the arc of a circle in **distance**, the student will need to know the values for both the central angle and the radius. This formula is:

$$\frac{central\ angle}{360°} = \frac{arc\ length}{2\pi r}$$

The equation is simplified by cross-multiplying to solve for the arc length.

In the following example, the student should substitute the values of the central angle (75°) and the radius (10 inches) into the equation above to solve for the arc length.

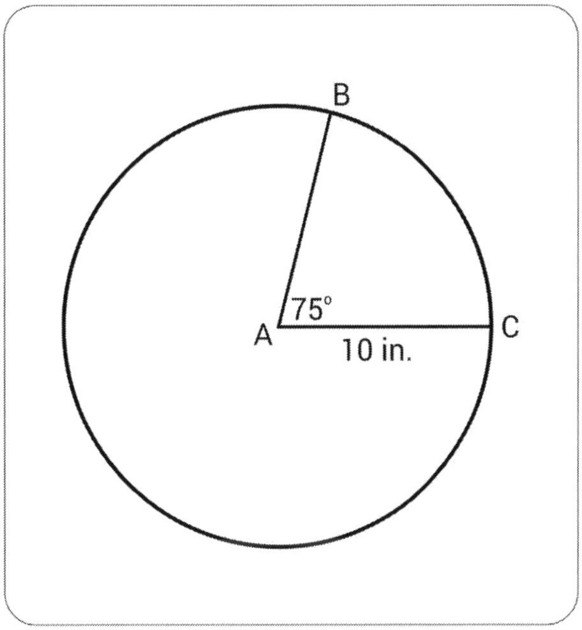

$$\frac{75°}{360°} = \frac{\text{arc length}}{2(3.14)(10\text{in.})}$$

To solve the equation, first cross-multiply: 4710 = 360(arc length). Next, divide each side of the equation by 360. The result of the formula is that the arc length is 13.1 (rounded).

Triangles

Triangles can be further classified by their sides and angles. A triangle with its largest angle measuring 90° is a **right triangle**. A 90° angle, also called a **right angle,** is formed from two perpendicular lines. It looks like a hard corner, like that in a square. The little square draw into the angle is the symbol used to denote that that angle is indeed a right angle. Any time that symbol is used, it denotes the measure of the angle is 90°. Below is a picture of a right angle, and below that, a right triangle.

A right angle:

Here is a right triangle, which is a triangle that contains a right angle:

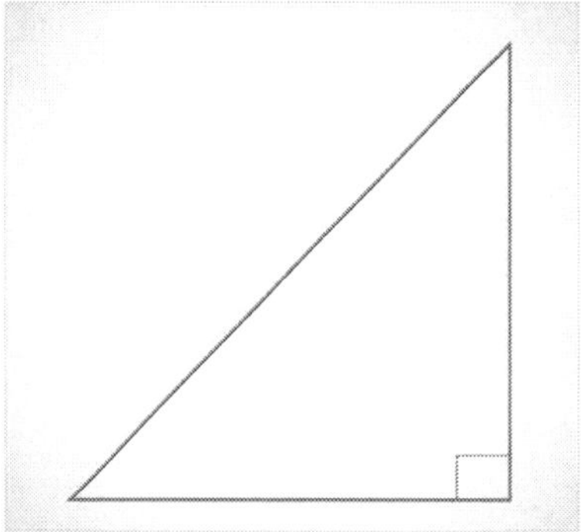

A triangle with the largest angle less than 90° is an acute triangle. A triangle with the largest angle greater than 90° is an obtuse triangle.

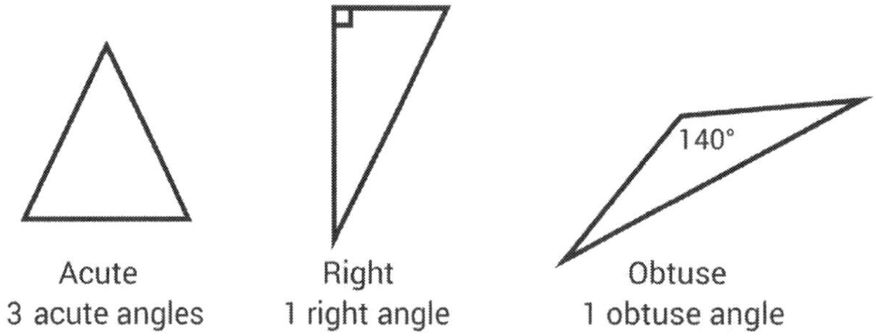

A triangle consisting of two equal sides and two equal angles is an isosceles triangle. A triangle with three equal sides and three equal angles is an equilateral triangle. A triangle with no equal sides or angles is a scalene triangle.

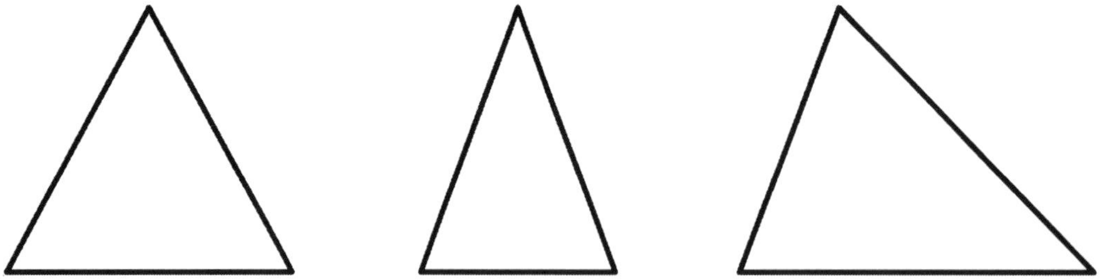

Equilateral Triangle **Isosceles Triangle** **Scalene Triangle**

Relationships Between Sides and Angles

The **Exterior Angle Theorem** states that the measure of an exterior angle of a triangle is equal to the sum of the measures of the two non-adjacent interior angles inside the triangle. It can be shown here:

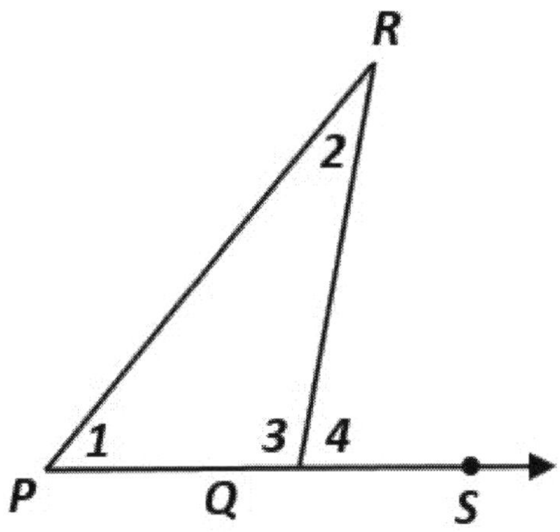

The measure of angle 4 is equal to the sum of the measures of angles 1 and 2. Also, the Triangle Inequality Theorem states that for any triangle, the sum of the lengths of two sides is greater than or equal to the length of the third side. For example, in the picture above, $PQ + QR \geq PR$.

Within similar triangles, corresponding sides are proportional, and angles are congruent. In addition, within similar triangles, the ratio of the side lengths is the same. This property is true even if side lengths are different. Within right triangles, trigonometric ratios can be defined for the acute angle within the triangle. The functions are defined through ratios in a right triangle. **Sine** of acute angle, A, is opposite over hypotenuse, **cosine** is adjacent over hypotenuse, and **tangent** is opposite over adjacent. Note that expanding or shrinking the triangle won't change the ratios. However, changing the angle measurements will alter the calculations.

Within a right triangle, two complementary angles exist because the third angle is always 90 degrees. In this scenario, the *sine* of one of the complementary angles is equal to the cosine of the other angle. The opposite is also true. This relationship exists because sine and cosine will be calculated as the ratios of the same side lengths.

Medians, Midpoints, and Altitudes

A **median** of a triangle is the line drawn from a vertex to the midpoint on the opposite side. A triangle has three medians, and their point of intersection is known as the **centroid**. An **altitude** is a line drawn from a vertex perpendicular to the opposite side. A triangle has three altitudes, and their point of intersection is known as the **orthocenter**. An altitude can actually exist outside, inside, or on the triangle depending on the placement of the vertex. Many problems involve these definitions. For example, given one endpoint of a line segment and the midpoint, the other endpoint can be determined by using the midpoint formula. In addition, area problems heavily depend on these definitions. For example, it can be proven that the median of a triangle divides it into two regions of equal areas. The actual formula for the area of a triangle depends on its altitude.

Special Triangles

An **isosceles triangle** contains at least two equal sides. Therefore, it must also contain two equal angles and, subsequently, contain two medians of the same length. An isosceles triangle can also be labelled as an **equilateral triangle** (which contains three equal sides and three equal angles) when it meets these conditions. In an equilateral triangle, the measure of each angle is always 60 degrees. Also within an equilateral triangle, the medians are of the same length. A **scalene triangle** can never be an equilateral or an isosceles triangle because it contains no equal sides and no equal angles. Also, medians in a scalene triangle can't have the same length. However, a **right triangle**, which is a triangle containing a 90-degree angle, can be a scalene triangle. There are two types of special right triangles. The **30-60-90 right triangle** has angle measurements of 30 degrees, 60 degrees, and 90 degrees. Because of the nature of this triangle, and through the use of the Pythagorean theorem, the side lengths have a special relationship. If *x* is the length opposite the 30-degree angle, the length opposite the 60-degree angle is $\sqrt{3}x$, and the hypotenuse has length $2x$. The **45-45-90 right triangle** is also special as it contains two angle measurements of 45 degrees. It can be proven that, if x is the length of the two equal sides, the hypotenuse is $x\sqrt{2}$. The properties of all of these special triangles are extremely useful in determining both side lengths and angle measurements in problems where some of these quantities are given and some are not.

The Pythagorean Theorem

The Pythagorean theorem is an important result in geometry. It states that for right triangles, the sum of the squares of the two shorter sides will be equal to the square of the longest side (also called the **hypotenuse**). The longest side will always be the side opposite to the 90° angle. If this side is called *c*, and the other two sides are *a* and *b*, then the Pythagorean theorem states that $c^2 = a^2 + b^2$. Since lengths are always positive, this also can be written as $c = \sqrt{a^2 + b^2}$.

A diagram to show the parts of a triangle using the Pythagorean theorem is below.

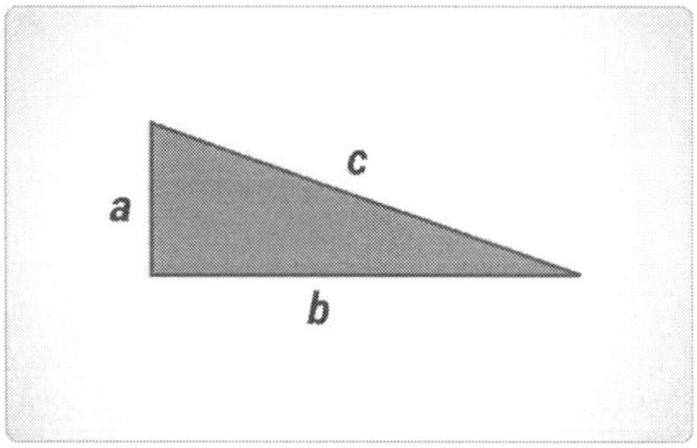

As an example of the theorem, suppose that Shirley has a rectangular field that is 5 feet wide and 12 feet long, and she wants to split it in half using a fence that goes from one corner to the opposite corner. How long will this fence need to be? To figure this out, note that this makes the field into two right triangles, whose hypotenuse will be the fence dividing it in half. Therefore, the fence length will be given by $\sqrt{5^2 + 12^2} = \sqrt{169} = 13$ feet long.

Quadrilaterals

Many four-sided figures can also be identified using properties of angles and lines. A **quadrilateral** is a closed shape with four sides. A **parallelogram** is a specific type of quadrilateral that has two sets of parallel lines that have the same length. A **trapezoid** is a quadrilateral having only one set of parallel sides. A **rectangle** is a parallelogram that has four right angles. A **rhombus** is a parallelogram with two acute angles, two obtuse angles, and four equal sides. The acute angles are of equal measure, and the obtuse angles are of equal measure. Finally, a **square** is a rhombus consisting of four right angles. It is important to note that some of these shapes share common attributes. For instance, all four-sided shapes are quadrilaterals. All squares are rectangles, but not all rectangles are squares.

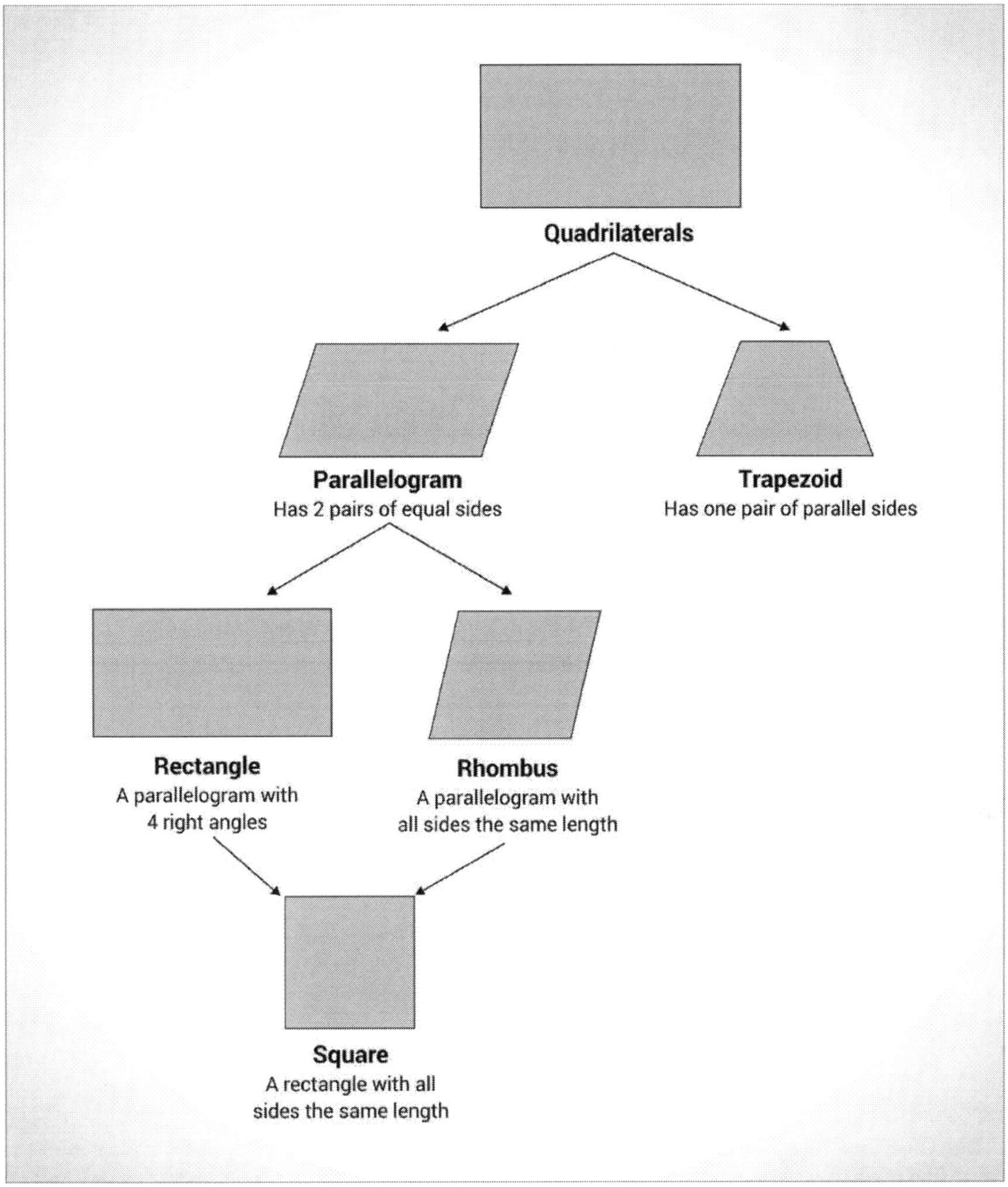

Volume

Volume is the measurement of how much space an object occupies, like how much space is in the cube. Volume is useful in determining the space within a certain three-dimensional object. Volume can be calculated for a cube, rectangular prism, cylinder, pyramid, cone, and sphere. By knowing specific dimensions of the objects, the volume of the object is computed with these figures. The units for the volumes of solids can include cubic centimeters, cubic meters, cubic inches, and cubic feet.

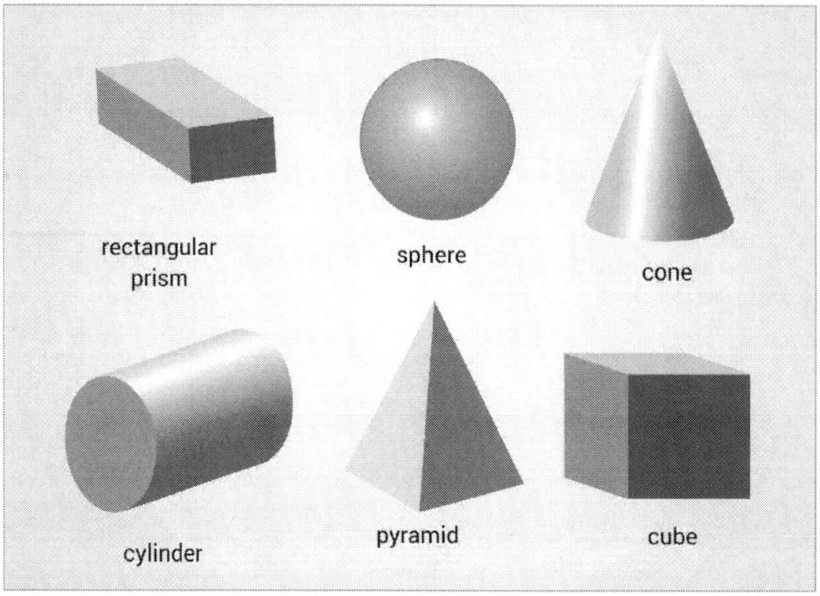

<u>Cube</u>
The cube is the simplest figure for which volume can be determined because all dimensions in a cube are equal. In the following figure, the length, width, and height of the cube are all represented by the variable *a* because these measurements are equal lengths.

The volume of any rectangular, three-dimensional object is found by multiplying its length by its width by its height. In the case of a cube, the length, width, and height are all equal lengths, represented by the variable *a*. Therefore, the equation used to calculate the volume is $(a \times a \times a)$ or a^3. In a real-world example of this situation, if the length of a side of the cube is 3 centimeters, the volume is calculated by utilizing the formula $(3 \times 3 \times 3) = 9$ cm^3.

<u>Rectangular Prism</u>
The dimensions of a rectangular prism are not necessarily equal as those of a cube. Therefore, the formula for a rectangular prism recognizes that the dimensions vary and use different variables to represent these lengths. The length, width, and height of a rectangular prism are represented with the variables *a, b*, and *c*.

The equation used to calculate volume is length times width times height. Using the variables in the diagram above, this means $a \times b \times c$. In a real-world application of this situation, if *a*=2 cm, *b*=3 cm, and *c*=4 cm, the volume is calculated by utilizing the formula $3 \times 4 \times 5 =$ 60 cm^3.

Cylinder

Discovering a cylinder's volume requires the measurement of the cylinder's base, length of the radius, and height. The height of the cylinder can be represented with variable *h*, and the radius can be represented with variable *r*.

The formula to find the volume of a cylinder is $\pi r^2 h$. Notice that πr^2 is the formula for the area of a circle. This is because the base of the cylinder is a circle. To calculate the volume of a cylinder, the slices of circles needed to build the entire height of the cylinder are added together. For example, if the radius is 5 feet and the height of the cylinder is 10 feet, the cylinder's volume is calculated by using the following equation: $\pi 5^2 \times 10$. Substituting 3.14 for π, the volume is 785.4 ft^3.

Pyramid

To calculate the volume of a pyramid, the area of the base of the pyramid is multiplied by the pyramid's height by $\frac{1}{3}$. The area of the base of the pyramid is found by multiplying the base length by the base width.

Therefore, the formula to calculate a pyramid's volume is $(L \times W \times H) \div 3$.

Cone

The formula to calculate the volume of a circular cone is similar to the formula for the volume of a pyramid. The primary difference in determining the area of a cone is that a circle serves as the base of a cone. Therefore, the area of a circle is used for the cone's base.

The variable *r* represents the radius, and the variable *h* represents the height of the cone. The formula used to calculate the volume of a cone is $\frac{1}{3}\pi r^2 h$. Essentially, the area of the base of the cone is multiplied by the cone's height. In a real-life example where the radius of a cone is 2 meters and the height of a cone is 5 meters, the volume of the cone is calculated by utilizing the formula $\frac{1}{3}\pi 2^2 \times 5 = 21$. After substituting 3.14 for π, the volume is 785.4 ft^3.

Sphere

The volume of a sphere uses π due to its circular shape.

The length of the radius, *r*, is the only variable needed to determine the sphere's volume. The formula to calculate the volume of a sphere is $\frac{4}{3}\pi r^3$. Therefore, if the radius of a sphere is 8 centimeters, the volume of the sphere is calculated by utilizing the formula:

$$\frac{4}{3}\pi(8)^3 = 2{,}143\ cm^3$$

Probability, Statistics, and Data Interpretation

Counting Techniques

There are many counting techniques that can help solve problems involving counting possibilities. For example, the **Addition Principle** states that if there are m choices from Group 1 and n choices from Group 2, then $n + m$ is the total number of choices possible from Groups 1 and 2. For this to be true, the groups can't have any choices in common. The **Multiplication Principle** states that if Process 1 can be completed n ways and Process 2 can be completed m ways, the total number of ways to complete both Process 1 and Process 2 is $n \times m$. For this rule to be used, both processes must be independent of each other. Counting techniques also involve permutations. A **permutation** is an arrangement of elements in a set for which order must be considered. For example, if three letters from the alphabet are chosen, ABC and BAC are two different permutations. The multiplication rule can be used to determine the total number of possibilities. If each letter can't be selected twice, the total number of possibilities is $26 \times 25 \times 24 = 15{,}600$. A formula can also be used to calculate this total. In general, the notation $P(n, r)$ represents the number of ways to arrange r objects from a set of n and, the formula is:

$$P(n,r) = \frac{n!}{(n-r)!}$$

In the previous example:

$$P(26,3) = \frac{26!}{23!} = 15{,}600$$

Contrasting permutations, a **combination** is an arrangement of elements in which order doesn't matter. In this case, ABC and BAC are the same combination. In the previous scenario, there are six permutations that represent each single combination. Therefore, the total number of possible combinations is $15{,}600 \div 6 = 2{,}600$. In general, $C(n, r)$ represents the total number of combinations of n items selected r at a time where order doesn't matter, and the formula is:

$$C(n,r) = \frac{n!}{(n-r)!\; r!}$$

Therefore, the following relationship exists between permutations and combinations:

$$C(n,r) = \frac{P(n,r)}{n!} = \frac{P(n,r)}{P(r,r)}$$

<u>Fundamental Counting Principle</u>
The **fundamental counting principle** states that if there are *m* possible ways for an event to occur, and *n* possible ways for a second event to occur, there are $m \cdot n$ possible ways for both events to occur. For example, there are two events that can occur after flipping a coin and six events that can occur after rolling a die, so there are $2 \times 6 = 12$ total possible event scenarios if both are done simultaneously. This principle can be used to find probabilities involving finite sample spaces and independent trials because it calculates the total number of possible outcomes. For this principle to work, the events must be independent of each other.

Probability of Simple and Compound Events

<u>Independence and Conditional Probability</u>
Sample Subsets
A sample can be broken up into subsets that are smaller parts of the whole. For example, consider a sample population of females. The sample can be divided into smaller subsets based on the characteristics of each female. There can be a group of females with brown hair and a group of females that wear glasses. There also can be a group of females that have brown hair *and* wear glasses. This "and" relates to the **intersection** of the two separate groups of brunettes and those with glasses. Every female in that intersection group has both characteristics. Similarly, there also can be a group of females that either have brown hair *or* wear glasses. The "or" relates to the union of the two separate groups of brunettes and glasses. Every female in this group has at least one of the characteristics. Finally, the

group of females who do not wear glasses can be discussed. This "not" relates to the **complement** of the glass-wearing group. No one in the complement has glasses. **Venn diagrams** are useful in highlighting these ideas. When discussing statistical experiments, this idea can also relate to events instead of characteristics.

Verifying Independent Events

Two events aren't always independent. For example, females with glasses and brown hair aren't independent characteristics. There definitely can be overlap because females with brown hair can wear glasses. Also, two events that exist at the same time don't have to have a relationship. For example, even if all females in a given sample are wearing glasses, the characteristics aren't related. In this case, the probability of a brunette wearing glasses is equal to the probability of a female being a brunette multiplied by the probability of a female wearing glasses. This mathematical test of $P(A \cap B) = P(A)P(B)$ verifies that two events are independent.

Conditional Probability

Conditional probability is the probability that event A will happen given that event B has already occurred. An example of this is calculating the probability that a person will eat dessert once they have eaten dinner. This is different than calculating the probability of a person just eating dessert. The formula for the conditional probability of event A occurring given B is $P(A|B) = \frac{P\,(A \text{ and } B)}{P(B)}$, and it's defined to be the probability of both A and B occurring divided by the probability of event B occurring. If A and B are independent, then the probability of both A and B occurring is equal to $P(A)P(B)$, so $P(A|B)$ reduces to just $P(A)$. This means that A and B have no relationship, and the probability of A occurring is the same as the conditional probability of A occurring given B. Similarly:

$$P(B|A) = \frac{P\,(B \text{ and A})}{P(A)} = P(B) \text{ if A and B are independent}$$

Independent Versus Related Events

To summarize, conditional probability is the probability that an event occurs given that another event has happened. If the two events are related, the probability that the second event will occur changes if the other event has happened. However, if the two events aren't related and are therefore independent, the first event to occur won't impact the probability of the second event occurring.

Measuring Probabilities with Two-Way Frequency Tables

When measuring event probabilities, two-way frequency tables can be used to report the raw data and then used to calculate probabilities. If the frequency tables are translated into relative frequency tables, the probabilities presented in the table can be plugged directly into the formulas for conditional probabilities. By plugging in the correct frequencies, the data from the table can be used to determine if events are independent or dependent.

Differing Probabilities

The probability that event A occurs differs from the probability that event A occurs given B. When working within a given model, it's important to note the difference. $P(A|B)$ is determined using the formula $P(A|B) = \frac{P\,(A \text{ and } B)}{P(B)}$ and represents the total number of A's outcomes left that could occur after B occurs. $P(A)$ can be calculated without any regard for B. For example, the probability of a student finding a parking spot on a busy campus is different once class is in session.

The Addition Rule

The probability of event A or B occurring isn't equal to the sum of each individual probability. The probability that both events can occur at the same time must be subtracted from this total. This idea is shown in the **addition rule**: $P(A \text{ or } B) = P(A) + P(B) - P(A \text{ and } B)$. The addition rule is another way to determine the probability of compound events that aren't mutually exclusive. If the events are mutually exclusive, the probability of both A and B occurring at the same time is 0.

<u>Simple and Compound Events</u>

A **simple event** consists of only one outcome. The most popular simple event is flipping a coin, which results in either heads or tails. A **compound event** results in more than one outcome and consists of more than one simple event. An example of a compound event is flipping a coin while tossing a die. The result is either heads or tails on the coin and a number from one to six on the die. The probability of a simple event is calculated by dividing the number of possible outcomes by the total number of outcomes. Therefore, the probability of obtaining heads on a coin is $1/_2$, and the probability of rolling a 6 on a die is $1/_6$. The probability of compound events is calculated using the basic idea of the probability of simple events. If the two events are independent, the probability of one outcome is equal to the product of the probabilities of each simple event. For example, the probability of obtaining heads on a coin and rolling a 6 is equal to: $\frac{1}{2} \times \frac{1}{6} = \frac{1}{12}$. The probability of either A or B occurring is equal to the sum of the probabilities minus the probability that both A and B will occur. Therefore, the probability of obtaining either heads on a coin or rolling a 6 on a die is:

$$\frac{1}{2} \times \frac{1}{6} - \frac{1}{12} = \frac{7}{12}$$

The two events aren't mutually exclusive because they can happen at the same time. If two events are mutually exclusive, and the probability of both events occurring at the same time is zero, the probability of event A or B occurring equals the sum of both probabilities. An example of calculating the probability of two mutually exclusive events is determining the probability of pulling a king or a queen from a deck of cards. The two events cannot occur at the same time.

Basic Statistics

The field of statistics describes relationships between quantities that are related, but not necessarily in a deterministic manner. For example, a graduating student's salary will often be higher when the student graduates with a higher GPA, but this is not always the case. Likewise, people who smoke tobacco are more likely to develop lung cancer, but, in fact, it is possible for non-smokers to develop the disease as well. **Statistics** describes these kinds of situations, where the likelihood of some outcome depends on the starting data.

Descriptive statistics involves analyzing a collection of data to describe its broad properties such average (or mean), what percent of the data falls within a given range, and other such properties. An example of this would be taking all of the test scores from a given class and calculating the average test score. **Inferential statistics** attempts to use data about a subset of some population to make inferences about the rest of the population. An example of this would be taking a collection of students who received tutoring and comparing their results to a collection of students who did not receive tutoring, then using that comparison to try to predict whether the tutoring program in question is beneficial.

To be sure that inferences have a high probability of being true for the whole population, the subset that is analyzed needs to resemble a miniature version of the population as closely as possible. For this reason, statisticians like to choose random samples from the population to study, rather than picking a specific group of people based on some similarity. For example, studying the incomes of people who live in Portland does not tell anything useful about the incomes of people who live in Tallahassee.

A statistical question is answered by collecting data with variability. Data consists of facts and/or statistics (numbers), and variability refers to a tendency to shift or change. Data is a broad term, inclusive of things like height, favorite color, name, salary, temperature, gas mileage, and language. Questions requiring data as an answer are not necessarily statistical questions. If there is no variability in the data, then the question is not statistical in nature. Consider the following examples: what is Mary's favorite color? How much money does your mother make? What was the highest temperature last week? How many miles did your car get on its last tank of gas? How much taller than Bob is Ed?

None of the above are statistical questions because each case lacks variability in the data needed to answer the question. The questions on favorite color, salary, and gas mileage each require a single piece of data, whether a fact or statistic. Therefore, variability is absent. Although the temperature question requires multiple pieces of data (the high temperature for each day), a single, distinct number is the answer. The height question requires two pieces of data, Bob's height and Ed's height, but no difference in variability exists between those two values. Therefore, this is not a statistical question. Statistical questions typically require calculations with data.

Consider the following statistical questions:

How many miles per gallon of gas does the 2016 Honda Civic get? To answer this question, data must be collected. This data should include miles driven and gallons used. Different cars, different drivers, and different driving conditions will produce different results. Therefore, variability exists in the data. To answer the question, the mean (average) value could be determined.

Are American men taller than Chinese men? To answer this question, data must be collected. This data should include the heights of American men and the heights of Chinese men. All American men are not the same height and all Chinese men are not the same height. Some American men are taller than some Chinese men and some Chinese men are taller than some American men. Therefore, variability exists in the data. To answer the question, the median values for each group could be determined and compared.

The following are more examples of statistical questions: What proportion of 4th graders have a favorite color of blue? How much money do teachers make? Is it colder in Boston or Chicago?

Describing Distributions

Mean, Median, and Mode

The center of a set of data (statistical values) can be represented by its mean, median, or mode. These are sometimes referred to as measures of central tendency.

Mean

The first property that can be defined for this set of data is the **mean**. This is the same as average. To find the mean, add up all the data points, then divide by the total number of data points. For example, suppose that in a class of 10 students, the scores on a test were 50, 60, 65, 65, 75, 80, 85, 85, 90, 100.

Therefore, the average test score will be:

$$\frac{50+60+65+65+75+80+85+85+90+100}{10}=75.5$$

The mean is a useful number if the distribution of data is normal (more on this later), which roughly means that the frequency of different outcomes has a single peak and is roughly equally distributed on both sides of that peak. However, it is less useful in some cases where the data might be split or where there are some outliers. **Outliers** are data points that are far from the rest of the data. For example, suppose there are 10 executives and 90 employees at a company. The executives make $1000 per hour, and the employees make $10 per hour.

Therefore, the average pay rate will be:

$$\frac{\$1000 \times 11+\$10 \times 90}{100}=\$119 \, per \; hour$$

In this case, this average is not very descriptive since it's not close to the actual pay of the executives *or* the employees.

Median

Another useful measurement is the **median**. In a data set, the median is the point in the middle. The middle refers to the point where half the data comes before it and half comes after, when the data is recorded in numerical order. For instance, these are the speeds of the fastball of a pitcher during the last inning that he pitched (in order from least to greatest):

90, 92, 93, 93, 95, 96, 97, 97, 97

There are nine total numbers, so the middle or *median* number in the 5th one, which is 95.

In cases where the number of data points is an even number, then the average of the two middle points is taken. In the previous example of test scores, the two middle points are 75 and 80. Since there is no single point, the average of these two scores needs to be found. The average is:

$$\frac{75+80}{2}=77.5$$

The median is generally a good value to use if there are a few outliers in the data. It prevents those outliers from affecting the "middle" value as much as when using the mean.

Since an outlier is a data point that is far from most of the other data points in a data set, this means an outlier also is any point that is far from the median of the data set. The outliers can have a substantial effect on the mean of a data set, but usually do not change the median or mode, or do not change them by a large quantity. For example, consider the data set (3, 5, 6, 6, 6, 8). This has a median of 6 and a mode of 6, with a mean of $\frac{34}{6} \approx 5.67$. Now, suppose a new data point of 1000 is added so that the data set is now (3, 5, 6, 6, 6, 8, 1000). This does not change the median or mode, which are both still 6. However, the average is now $\frac{1034}{7}$, which is approximately 147.7. In this case, the median and mode will be better descriptions for most of the data points.

The reason for outliers in a given data set is a complicated problem. It is sometimes the result of an error by the experimenter, but often they are perfectly valid data points that must be taken into consideration.

Mode
One additional measure to define for *X* is the **mode**. This is the data point that appears most frequently. If two or more data points all tie for the most frequent appearance, then each of them is considered a mode. In the case of the test scores, where the numbers were 50, 60, 65, 65, 75, 80, 85, 85, 90, 100, there are two modes: 65 and 85.

Quartiles and Percentiles
The **first quartile** of a set of data *X* refers to the largest value from the first ¼ of the data points. In practice, there are sometimes slightly different definitions that can be used, such as the median of the first half of the data points (excluding the median itself if there are an odd number of data points). The term also has a slightly different use: when it is said that a data point lies *in the first quartile*, it means it is less than or equal to the median of the first half of the data points. Conversely, if it lies *at* the first quartile, then it is equal to the first quartile.

When it is said that a data point lies in the **second quartile**, it means it is between the first quartile and the median.

The **third quartile** refers to data that lies between ½ and ¾ of the way through the data set. Again, there are various methods for defining this precisely, but the simplest way is to include all of the data that lie between the median and the median of the top half of the data.

Data that lies in the **fourth quartile** refers to all of the data above the third quartile.

Percentiles may be defined in a similar manner to quartiles. Generally, this is defined in the following manner:

If a data point lies **in the n-th percentile**, this means it lies in the range of the first *n*% of the data.

If a data point lies **at the n-th percentile**, then it means that *n*% of the data lies below this data point.

Standard Deviation
Given a data set *X* consisting of data points $(x_1, x_2, x_3, \dots x_n)$, the **variance** of *X* is defined to be:

$$\frac{\sum_{i=1}^{n}(x_i - \bar{X})^2}{n}$$

This means that the variance of *X* is the average of the squares of the differences between each data point and the mean of *X*.

Given a data set *X* consisting of data points $(x_1, x_2, x_3, \dots x_n)$, the **standard deviation** of *X* is defined to be:

$$s_x = \sqrt{\frac{\sum_{i=1}^{n}(x_i - \bar{X})^2}{n}}$$

In other words, the standard deviation is the square root of the variance.

Both the variance and the standard deviation are measures of how much the data tend to be spread out. When the standard deviation is low, the data points are mostly clustered around the mean. When the standard deviation is high, this generally indicates that the data are quite spread out, or else that there are a few substantial outliers.

As a simple example, compute the standard deviation for the data set (1, 3, 3, 5). First, compute the mean, which will be $\frac{1+3+3+5}{4} = \frac{12}{4} = 3$.

Now, find the variance of *X* with the formula:

$$\sum_{i=1}^{4}(x_i - \bar{X})^2 = (1-3)^2 + (3-3)^2 + (5-3)^2$$

$$-2^2 + 0^2 + 0^2 + 2^2 = 8$$

Therefore, the variance is $\frac{8}{4} = 2$. Taking the square root, the standard deviation will be $\sqrt{2}$.

Note that the standard deviation only depends upon the mean, not upon the median or mode(s). Generally, if there are multiple modes that are far apart from one another, the standard deviation will be high. A high standard deviation does not always mean there are multiple modes, however.

<u>Describing a Set of Data</u>

A set of data can be described in terms of its center, spread, shape and any unusual features. The center of a data set can be measured by its mean, median, or mode. The spread of a data set refers to how far the data points are from the center (mean or median). A data set with data points clustered around the center will have a small spread. A data set covering a wide range will have a large spread.

When a data set is displayed as a graph like the one below, the shape indicates if a sample is normally distributed, symmetrical, or has measures of skewness. When graphed, a data set with a normal distribution will resemble a bell curve.

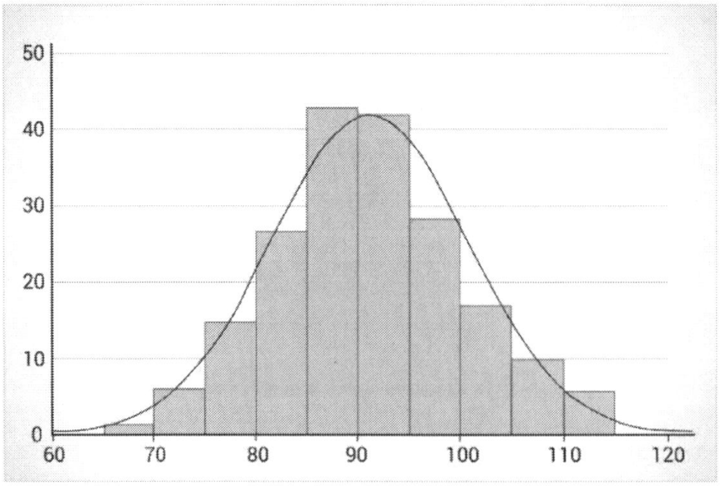

If the data set is symmetrical, each half of the graph when divided at the center is a mirror image of the other. If the graph has fewer data points to the right, the data is skewed right. If it has fewer data points to the left, the data is skewed left.

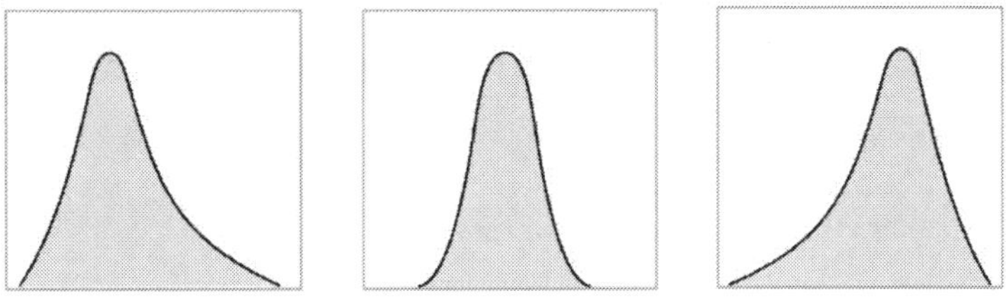

Right-Skewed Symmetric Left-Skewed

A description of a data set should include any unusual features such as gaps or outliers. A gap is a span within the range of the data set containing no data points. An outlier is a data point with a value either extremely large or extremely small when compared to the other values in the set.

The graphs above can be referred to as **unimodal** since they all have a single peak. This is contrast to **bimodal** graph that have multiple peaks.

Comparing Data

Comparing data sets within statistics can mean many things. The first way to compare data sets is by looking at the center and spread of each set. The center of a data set can mean two things: median or mean. The **median** is the value that's halfway into each data set, and it splits the data into two intervals. The **mean** is the average value of the data within a set. It's calculated by adding up all of the data in the set and dividing the total by the number of data points. Outliers can significantly impact the mean. Additionally, two completely different data sets can have the same mean. For example, a data set with values ranging from 0 to 100 and a data set with values ranging from 44 to 56 can both have means of 50. The first data set has a much wider range, which is known as the **spread** of the data. This measures how varied the data is within each set.

Reading and Interpreting Graphs

Various graphs can be used to visually represent a given set of data. Each type of graph requires a different method of arranging data points and different calculations of the data. To construct a histogram, the range of the data points is divided into equal intervals. The frequency for each interval is then determined, which reveals how many points fall into each interval. A graph is constructed with the vertical axis representing the frequency and the horizontal axis representing the intervals. The lower value of each interval should be labeled along the horizontal axis. Finally, for each interval, a bar is drawn from the lower value of each interval to the lower value of the next interval with a height equal to the frequency of the interval. Because of the intervals, histograms do not have any gaps between bars along the horizontal axis.

To construct a box (or box-and-whisker) plot, the five number summary for the data set is calculated as follows: the **second quartile (Q_2)** is the median of the set. The **first quartile (Q_1)** is the median of the values below Q_2. The **third quartile (Q_3)** is the median of the values above Q_2. The **upper extreme** is the highest value in the data set if it is not an **outlier** (greater than 1.5 times the interquartile range Q_3 - Q_1). The lower extreme is the least value in the data set if it is not an outlier (more than 1.5 times lower than the interquartile range). To construct the box-and-whisker plot, each value is plotted on a number line, along with any outliers. The **box** consists of Q_1 and Q_3 as its *top* and *bottom* and Q_2 as the dividing line inside the box. The **whiskers** extend from the lower extreme to Q_1 and from Q_3 to the upper extreme.

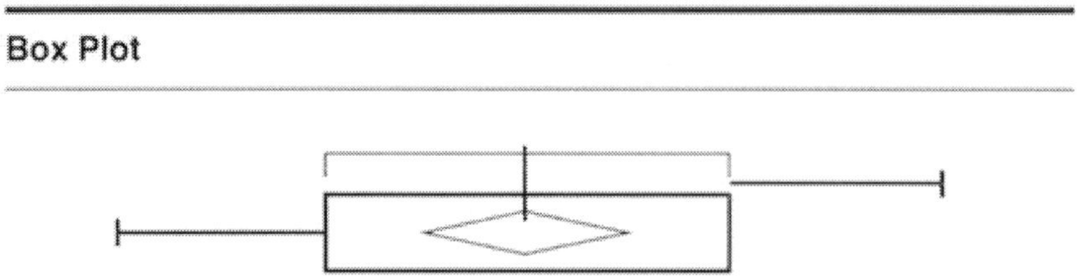

A scatter plot displays the relationship between two variables. Values for the independent variable, typically denoted by *x*, are paired with values for the dependent variable, typically denoted by *y*. Each set of corresponding values are written as an ordered pair (*x*, *y*). To construct the graph, a coordinate grid is labeled with the *x*-axis representing the independent variable and the *y*-axis representing the dependent variable. Each ordered pair is graphed.

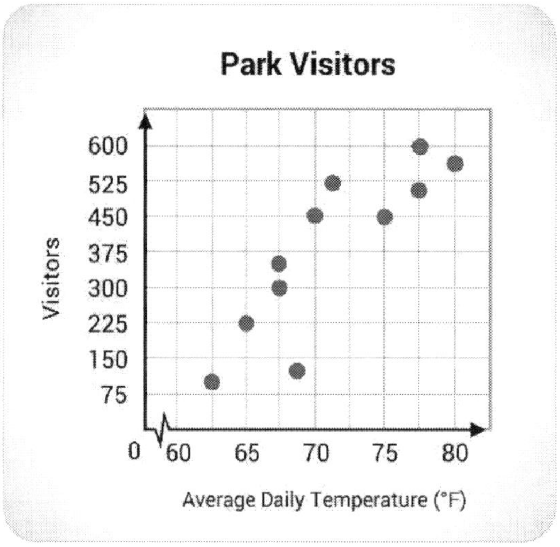

Like a scatter plot, a **line graph** compares variables that change continuously, typically over time. Paired data values (ordered pair) are plotted on a coordinate grid with the *x*- and *y*-axis representing the variables. A line is drawn from each point to the next, going from left to right. The line graph below displays cell phone use for given years (two variables) for men, women, and both sexes (three data sets).

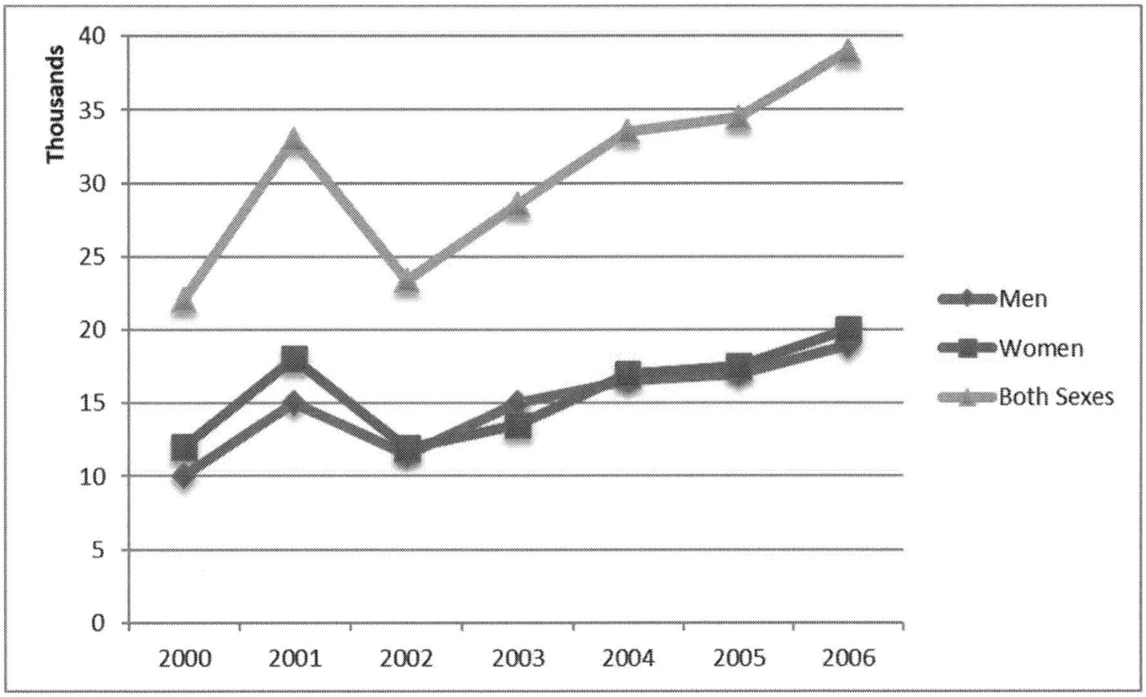

A **line plot**, also called **dot plot**, displays the frequency of data (numerical values) on a number line. To construct a line plot, a number line is used that includes all unique data values. It is marked with x's or dots above the value the number of times that the value occurs in the data set.

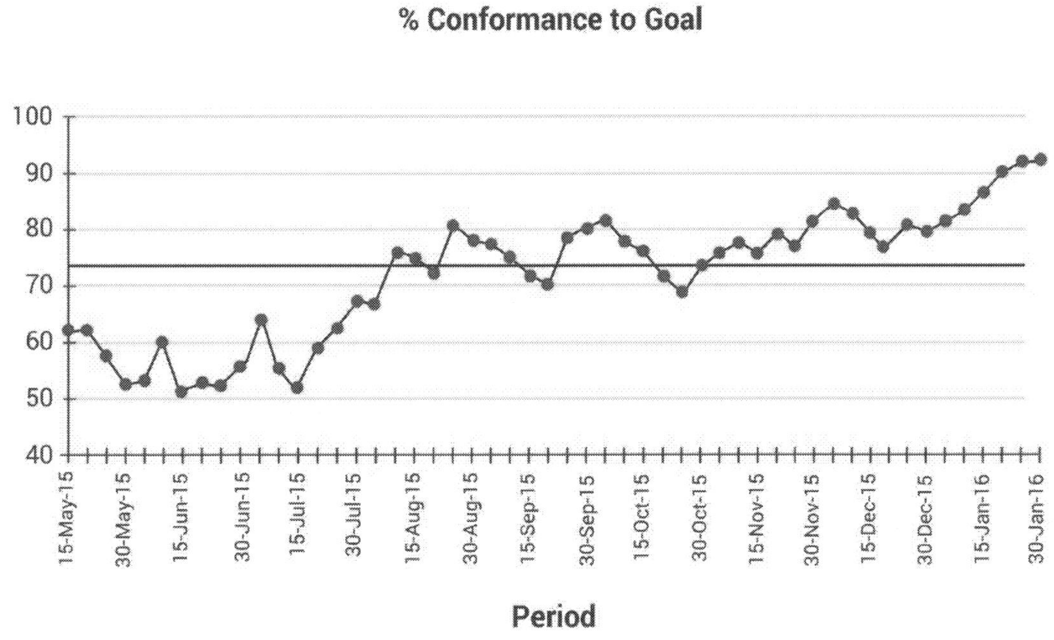

A **picture graph** is a diagram that shows pictorial representation of data being discussed. The symbols utilized can represent the quantity of the objects being discussed. By using the key, it should be determined that each fruit symbol in the following graph represents a count of two fruits. One drawback of picture graphs is that they can be less accurate if each symbol represents a large number.

For example, if each banana symbol represented ten bananas, and students consumed 22 bananas, it may be challenging to draw and interpret two and one-fifth bananas as a frequency count of 22.

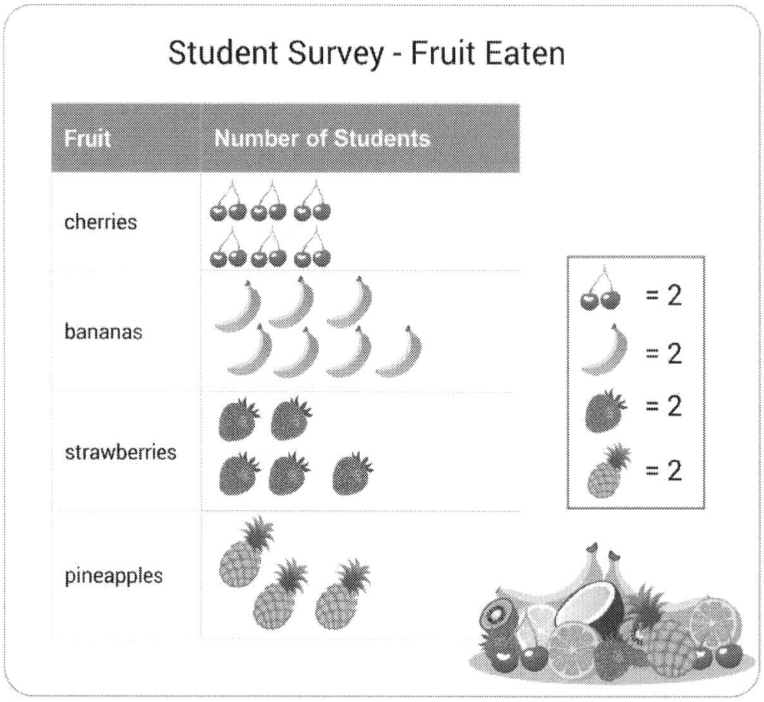

A **stem-and-leaf plot** is a method of displaying sets of data by organizing the numbers by their stems (usually the tens digit) and the different leaf values (usually the ones digit).

For example, to organize a number of movie critic's ratings, as listed below, a stem and leaf plot could be utilized to display the information in a more condensed manner.

Movie critic scores: 47, 52, 56, 59, 61, 64, 66, 68, 68, 70, 73, 75, 79, 81, 83, 85, 86, 88, 88, 89, 90, 90, 91, 93, 94, 96, 96, 99.

	Movie Ratings
4	7
5	2 6 9
6	1 4 6 8 8
7	0 3 5 9
8	1 3 5 6 8 8 9
9	0 0 1 3 4 6 6 9
Key	6 | 1 represents 61

Looking at this stem and leaf plot, it is easy to ascertain key features of the data set. For example, what is the range of the data in the stem-and-leaf plot?

Using this method, it is easier to visualize the distribution of the scores and answer the question pertaining to the range of scores, which is $99 - 47 = 52$.

A **tally chart** is a diagram in which tally marks are utilized to represent data. Tally marks are a means of showing a quantity of objects within a specific classification. Here is an example of a tally chart:

Number of days with rain	Number of weeks
0	𝍷𝍷
1	𝍸
2	𝍸
3	𝍸
4	𝍸 𝍸 𝍸 𝍷𝍷𝍷𝍷
5	𝍸 𝍷
6	𝍸 𝍷
7	𝍷𝍷𝍷𝍷

Data is often recorded using fractions, such as half a mile, and understanding fractions is critical because of their popular use in real-world applications. Also, it is extremely important to label values with their units when using data. For example, regarding length, the number 2 is meaningless unless it is attached to a unit. Writing 2 cm shows that the number refers to the length of an object.

Another way to represent data is with a **frequency table**. Like a tally chart, these can display the number of times specific answers are given, in order to provide a clearer overall picture of information. The following is the data representing the scores gathered on a patient satisfaction survey, visualized on a frequency dot table.

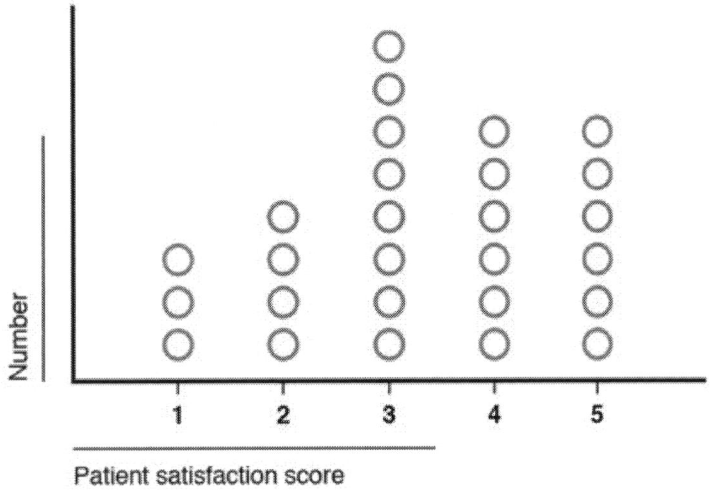

It is clear that the majority of the scores are in the middle, and higher at 2.0 and 2.5.

A **bar graph** is a diagram in which the quantity of items within a specific classification is represented by the height of a rectangle. Each type of classification is represented by a rectangle of equal width. Here is an example of a bar graph:

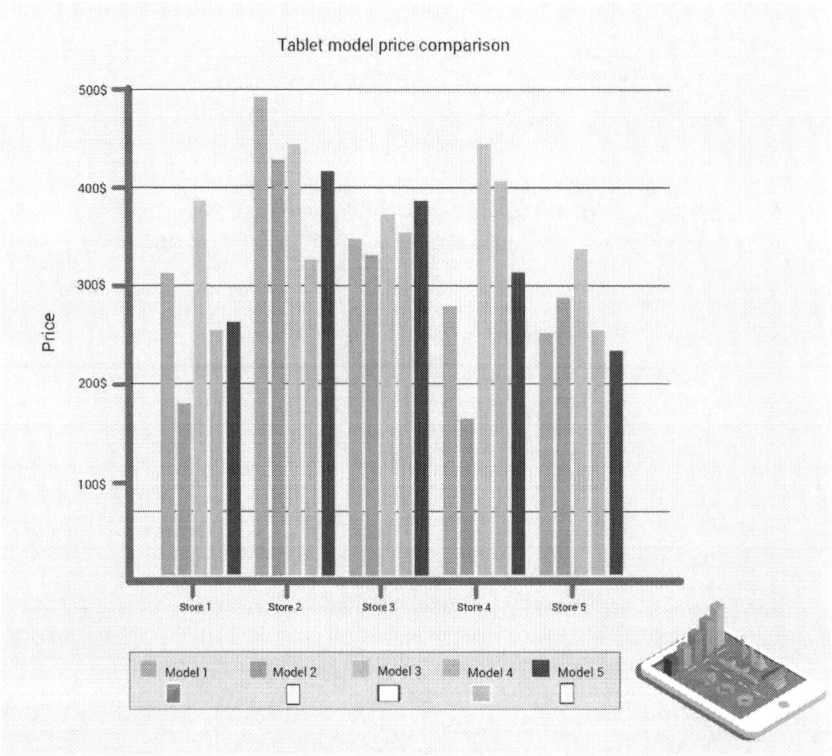

A **circle graph**, also called a **pie chart**, shows categorical data with each category representing a percentage of the whole data set. To make a circle graph, the percent of the data set for each category must be determined. To do so, the frequency of the category is divided by the total number of data points and converted to a percent. For example, if 80 people were asked what their favorite sport is and 20 responded basketball, basketball makes up 25% of the data ($\frac{20}{80}$ =.25=25%). Each category in a data set is represented by a slice of the circle proportionate to its percentage of the whole.

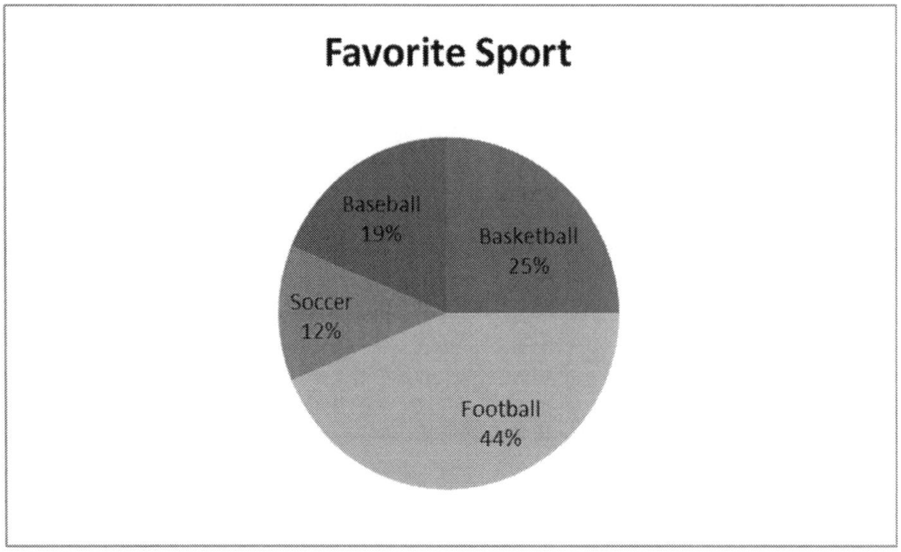

Arithmetic Reasoning and Word Problems

Using Variables to Construct and Solve Equations in Real-World Contexts

An algebraic expression is a statement about an unknown quantity expressed in mathematical symbols. A **variable** is used to represent the unknown quantity, usually denoted by a letter. An equation is a statement in which two expressions (at least one containing a variable) are equal to each other. An algebraic expression can be thought of as a mathematical phrase and an equation can be thought of as a mathematical sentence.

Algebraic expressions and equations both contain numbers, variables, and mathematical operations. The following are examples of algebraic expressions: $5x + 3, 7xy - 8(x^2 + y)$, and $\sqrt{a^2 + b^2}$. An expression can be simplified or evaluated for given values of variables. The following are examples of equations: $2x + 3 = 7$, $a^2 + b^2 = c^2$, and $2x + 5 = 3x - 2$. An equation contains two sides separated by an equal sign. Equations can be solved to determine the value(s) of the variable for which the statement is true.

An algebraic expression is a statement about unknown quantities expressed in mathematical symbols. The statement *five times a number added to forty* is expressed as $5x + 40$. An equation is a statement in which two expressions (with at least one containing a variable) are equal to one another. The statement *five times a number added to forty is equal to ten* is expressed as $5x + 40 = 10$.

Real world scenarios can also be expressed mathematically. Suppose a job pays its employees $300 per week and $40 for each sale made. The weekly pay is represented by the expression $40x + 300$ where *x* is the number of sales made during the week.

Consider the following scenario: Bob had $20 and Tom had $4. After selling 4 ice cream cones to Bob, Tom has as much money as Bob. The cost of an ice cream cone is an unknown quantity and can be represented by a variable (*x*). The amount of money Bob has after his purchase is four times the cost of an ice cream cone subtracted from his original $\$20 \rightarrow 20 - 4x$. The amount of money Tom has after his sale is four times the cost of an ice cream cone added to his original $\$4 \rightarrow 4x + 4$. After the sale, the amount of money that Bob and Tom have are equal $\rightarrow 20 - 4x = 4x + 4$.

Translating Verbal Relationships into Algebraic Equations or Expressions

When expressing a verbal or written statement mathematically, it is vital to understand words or phrases that can be represented with symbols. The following are examples:

Symbol	Phrase
+	Added to; increased by; sum of; more than
−	Decreased by; difference between; less than; take away
×	Multiplied by; 3(4,5…) times as large; product of
÷	Divided by; quotient of; half (third, etc.) of
=	Is; the same as; results in; as much as; equal to
x,t,n, etc.	A number; unknown quantity; value of; variable

Addition and subtraction are **inverse operations**. Adding a number and then subtracting the same number will cancel each other out, resulting in the original number, and vice versa. For example, $8 + 7 - 7 = 8$ and $137 - 100 + 100 = 137$. Similarly, multiplication and division are inverse operations.

Therefore, multiplying by a number and then dividing by the same number results in the original number, and vice versa. For example, $8 \times 2 \div 2 = 8$ and $12 \div 4 \times 4 = 12$. Inverse operations are used to work backwards to solve problems. In the case that 7 and a number add to 18, the inverse operation of subtraction is used to find the unknown value ($18 - 7 = 11$). If a school's entire 4th grade was divided evenly into 3 classes each with 22 students, the inverse operation of multiplication is used to determine the total students in the grade ($22 \times 3 = 66$). Additional scenarios involving inverse operations are included in the tables below.

There are a variety of real-world situations in which one or more of the operators is used to solve a problem. The tables below display the most common scenarios.

Addition & Subtraction

	Unknown Result	**Unknown Change**	**Unknown Start**
Adding to	5 students were in class. 4 more students arrived. How many students are in class? $5 + 4 = ?$	8 students were in class. More students arrived late. There are now 18 students in class. How many students arrived late? $8 + ? = 18$ Solved by inverse operations $18 - 8 = ?$	Some students were in class early. 11 more students arrived. There are now 17 students in class. How many students were in class early? $? + 11 = 17$ Solved by inverse operations $17 - 11 = ?$
Taking from	15 students were in class. 5 students left class. How many students are in class now? $15 - 5 = ?$	12 students were in class. Some students left class. There are now 8 students in class. How many students left class? $12 - ? = 8$ Solved by inverse operations $8 + ? = 12 \rightarrow 12 - 8 = ?$	Some students were in class. 3 students left class. Then there were 13 students in class. How many students were in class before? $? - 3 = 13$ Solved by inverse operations $13 + 3 = ?$

	Unknown Total	Unknown Addends (Both)	Unknown Addends (One)
Putting together/ taking apart	The homework assignment is 10 addition problems and 8 subtraction problems. How many problems are in the homework assignment? $10 + 8 = ?$	Bobby has $9. How much can Bobby spend on candy and how much can Bobby spend on toys? $9 = ? + ?$	Bobby has 12 pairs of pants. 5 pairs of pants are shorts, and the rest are long. How many pairs of long pants does he have? $12 = 5 + ?$ Solved by inverse operations $12 - 5 = ?$

	Unknown Difference	Unknown Larger Value	Unknown Smaller Value
Comparing	Bobby has 5 toys. Tommy has 8 toys. How many more toys does Tommy have than Bobby? $5 + ? = 8$ Solved by inverse operations $8 - 5 = ?$ Bobby has $6. Tommy has $10. How many fewer dollars does Bobby have than Tommy? $10 - 6 = ?$	Tommy has 2 more toys than Bobby. Bobby has 4 toys. How many toys does Tommy have? $2 + 4 = ?$ Bobby has 3 fewer dollars than Tommy. Bobby has $8. How many dollars does Tommy have? $? - 3 = 8$ Solved by inverse operations $8 + 3 = ?$	Tommy has 6 more toys than Bobby. Tommy has 10 toys. How many toys does Bobby have? $? + 6 = 10$ Solved by inverse operations $10 - 6 = ?$ Bobby has $5 less than Tommy. Tommy has $9. How many dollars does Bobby have? $9 - 5 = ?$

Multiplication and Division

	Unknown Product	**Unknown Group Size**	**Unknown Number of Groups**
Equal groups	There are 5 students, and each student has 4 pieces of candy. How many pieces of candy are there in all? $5 \times 4 =?$	14 pieces of candy are shared equally by 7 students. How many pieces of candy does each student have? $7 \times ? = 14$ Solved by inverse operations $14 \div 7 =?$	If 18 pieces of candy are to be given out 3 to each student, how many students will get candy? $? \times 3 = 18$ Solved by inverse operations $18 \div 3 =?$

	Unknown Product	**Unknown Factor**	**Unknown Factor**
Arrays	There are 5 rows of students with 3 students in each row. How many students are there? $5 \times 3 =?$	If 16 students are arranged into 4 equal rows, how many students will be in each row? $4 \times ? = 16$ Solved by inverse operations $16 \div 4 =?$	If 24 students are arranged into an array with 6 columns, how many rows are there? $? \times 6 = 24$ Solved by inverse operations $24 \div 6 =?$

	Larger Unknown	**Smaller Unknown**	**Multiplier Unknown**
Comparing	A small popcorn costs $1.50. A large popcorn costs 3 times as much as a small popcorn. How much does a large popcorn cost? $1.50 \times 3 =?$	A large soda costs $6 and that is 2 times as much as a small soda costs. How much does a small soda cost? $2 \times ? = 6$ Solved by inverse operations $6 \div 2 =?$	A large pretzel costs $3 and a small pretzel costs $2. How many times as much does the large pretzel cost as the small pretzel? $? \times 2 = 3$ Solved by inverse operations $3 \div 2 =?$

Work word problems are examples of people working together in a situation that uses fractions.

Example

One painter can paint a designated room in 6 hours, and a second painter can paint the same room in 5 hours. How long will it take them to paint the room if they work together?

The first painter paints $\frac{1}{6}$of the room in an hour, and the second painter paints $\frac{1}{5}$of the room in an hour.

Together, they can paint $\frac{1}{x}$ of the room in an hour. The equation is the sum of the painters rate equal to the total job or $\frac{1}{6} + \frac{1}{5} = \frac{1}{x}$.

The equation can be solved by multiplying all terms by a common denominator of 30x with a result of $5x + 6x = 30$.

The left side can be added together to get 11x, and then divide by 11 for a solution of $\frac{30}{11}$ or about 2.73 hours.

Solving Verbal Problems Presented in an Algebraic Context

There is a four-step process in problem-solving that can be used as a guide:

1. Understand the problem and determine the unknown information.
2. Translate the verbal problem into an algebraic equation.
3. Solve the equation by using inverse operations.
4. Check the work and answer the given question.

Example
Three times the sum of a number plus 4 equals the number plus 8. What is the number?

The first step is to determine the unknown, which is the number, or x.

The second step is to translate the problem into the equation, which is $3(x + 4) = x + 8$.

The equation can be solved as follows:

$3x + 12 = x + 8$	Apply the distributive property
$3x = x - 4$	Subtract 12 from both sides of the equation
$2x = -4$	Subtract x from both sides of the equation
$x = -2$	Divide both sides of the equation by 2

The final step is checking the solution. Plugging the value for x back into the equation yields the following problem: $3(-2) + 12 = -2 + 8$. Using the order of operations shows that a true statement is made: $6 = 6$

Solving Word Problems

Overall, the problem-solving process in mathematics involves a step-by-step procedure that one must follow when deciding what approach to take. First, one must understand the problem by deciding what is being sought, then if enough information is given, and what units are necessary in the solution. This is a crucial, but sometimes difficult step. It involves carefully reading the entire problem, identifying (perhaps even underlining) the facts or information that *is* known, and then deciphering the question words to determine what the problem is asking. In this way, math problems require students to be detectives, evaluating the "clues" or facts given in the problem, deciding what the problem is looking for, and evaluating whether sufficient information or "clues" are presented in the problem to solve the posed question.

In general, when solving word problems (also called story problems), it's important to understand what is being asked and to properly set up the initial equation. Always read the entire problem through, and then separate out what information is given in the statement. Decide what you are being asked to find and label each quantity with a variable or constant. Then write an equation to determine the unknown variable. Remember to label answers; sometimes knowing what the answers' units can help eliminate other possible solutions.

When trying to solve any word problem, look for a series of key words indicating addition, subtraction, multiplication, or division to help you determine how to set up the problem:

Addition: add, altogether, together, plus, increased by, more than, in all, sum, and total

Subtraction: minus, less than, difference, decreased by, fewer than, remain, and take away

Multiplication: *times*, *twice*, *of*, *double*, and *triple*

Division: divided by, cut up, half, quotient of, split, and shared equally

If a question asks to give words to a mathematical expression and says "equals," then an = sign must be included in the answer. Similarly, "less than or equal to" is expressed by the inequality symbol ≤, and "greater than or equal" to is expressed as ≥. Furthermore, "less than" is represented by <, and "greater than" is expressed by >.

These strategies are applicable to other question types. For example, calculating salary after deductions, balancing a checkbook, and calculating a dinner bill are common word problems similar to business planning. Just remember to use the correct operations. When a balance is increased, use addition. When a balance is decreased, use subtraction. Common sense and organization are your greatest assets when answering word problems.

For example, suppose the following word problem is encountered:

Walter's Coffee Shop sells a variety of drinks and breakfast treats.

Price List	
Hot Coffee	$2.00
Slow-Drip Iced Coffee	$3.00
Latte	$4.00
Muffin	$2.00
Crepe	$4.00
Egg Sandwich	$5.00

Costs	
Hot Coffee	$0.25
Slow-Drip Iced Coffee	$0.75
Latte	$1.00
Muffin	$1.00
Crepe	$2.00
Egg Sandwich	$3.00

Walter's utilities, rent, and labor costs him $500 per day. Today, Walter sold 200 hot coffees, 100 slow-drip iced coffees, 50 lattes, 75 muffins, 45 crepes, and 60 egg sandwiches. What was Walter's total profit today?

First, it is necessary to establish what is known (the "facts"), what one wants to know, (the question), how to determine the answer (the process), and if there is enough information to solve (sufficient "clues"). The problem clearly asks: "what was Walter's total profit today," so to accurately answer this type of question, the total cost of making his drinks and treats must be calculated, then the total revenue he earned from selling those products must be determined. After arriving at these two totals, the profit is measured found by deducting the total cost from the total revenue.

Now that the question and steps are identified, the provided facts are evaluated. Walter's costs for today:

Item	Quantity	Cost Per Unit	Total Cost
Hot Coffee	200	\$0.25	\$50
Slow-Drip Iced Coffee	100	\$0.75	\$75
Latte	50	\$1.00	\$50
Muffin	75	\$1.00	\$75
Crepe	45	\$2.00	\$90
Egg Sandwich	60	\$3.00	\$180
Utilities, rent, and labor			\$500
Total Costs			\$1,020

Walter's revenue for today:

Item	Quantity	Revenue Per Unit	Total Revenue
Hot Coffee	200	\$2.00	\$400
Slow-Drip Iced Coffee	100	\$3.00	\$300
Latte	50	\$4.00	\$200
Muffin	75	\$2.00	\$150
Crepe	45	\$4.00	\$180
Egg Sandwich	60	\$5.00	\$300
Total Revenue			\$1,530

Walter's Profit = *Revenue* – *Costs* = \$1,530 – \$1,020 = \$510

In this case, enough information was given in the problem to adequately solve it. If, however, the number of sandwiches and drinks were not provided, or Walter's cost per unit sold, insufficient information would prevent one from arriving at the answer.

Determining Distance, Rate, and Time

In word problems, multiple quantities are often provided with a request to find some kind of relation between them. This often will mean that one variable (the dependent variable whose value needs to be found) can be written as a function of another variable (the independent variable whose value can be figured from the given information). The usual procedure for solving these problems is to start by giving each quantity in the problem a variable, and then figuring the relationship between these variables.

For example, suppose a car gets 25 miles per gallon. How far will the car travel if it uses 2.4 gallons of fuel? In this case, y would be the distance the car has traveled in miles, and x would be the amount of fuel burned in gallons (2.4). Then the relationship between these variables can be written as an algebraic equation, $y = 25x$. In this case, the equation is $y = 25 \times 2.4 = 60$, so the car has traveled 60 miles.

Some word problems require more than just one simple equation to be written and solved. Consider the following situations and the linear equations used to model them.

Suppose Margaret is 2 miles to the east of John at noon. Margaret walks to the east at 3 miles per hour. How far apart will they be at 3 p.m.? To solve this, *x* would represent the time in hours past noon, and *y* would represent the distance between Margaret and John. Now, noon corresponds to the equation where *x* is 0, so the *y* intercept is going to be 2. It's also known that the slope will be the rate at which the distance is changing, which is 3 miles per hour. This means that the slope will be 3 (be careful at this point: if units were used, other than miles and hours, for *x* and *y* variables, a conversion of the given information to the appropriate units would be required first). The simplest way to write an equation given the *y*-intercept, and the slope is the Slope-Intercept form, is $y = mx + b$. Recall that *m* here is the slope and *b* is the *y* intercept. So, $m = 3$ and $b = 2$. Therefore, the equation will be $y = 3x + 2$. The word problem asks how far to the east Margaret will be from John at 3 p.m., which means when *x* is 3. So, substitute $x = 3$ into this equation to obtain $y = 3 \times 3 + 2 = 9 + 2 = 11$. Therefore, she will be 11 miles to the east of him at 3 p.m.

For another example, suppose that a box with 4 cans in it weighs 6 lbs., while a box with 8 cans in it weighs 12 lbs. Find out how much a single can weighs. To do this, let *x* denote the number of cans in the box, and *y* denote the weight of the box with the cans in lbs. This line touches two pairs: $(4, 6)$ and (8, 12). A formula for this relation could be written using the two-point form, with $x_1 = 4, y_1 = 6, x_2 = 8, y_2 = 12$. This would yield $\frac{y-6}{x-4} = \frac{12-6}{8-4}$, or $\frac{y-6}{x-4} = \frac{6}{4} = \frac{3}{2}$. However, only the slope is needed to solve this problem, since the slope will be the weight of a single can. From the computation, the slope is $\frac{3}{2}$. Therefore, each can weighs $\frac{3}{2}$ lb.

Determining Tax, Tip, and Interest

Determining the tax and tip on a bill involves calculating a proportion. For example, a standard tip on a restaurant bill is 20%. This can be calculated using mental math by shifting the decimal place for the bill amount one place to the left (to calculate 10%) and then doubling that amount. Consider the following:

A bill for dinner is $68.24. What will be a 20% tip on the bill?

Step one: Take $68.24 and shift the decimal point one place to the left: $6.82

This is 10% of the bill.

Step two: Double the amount in step one: $6.82 $\times$ $2 = \$13.64$.

This is the 20% tip.

Computations can be taken one step further by adding the tip to the bill to find the total:

$68.24 + $13.64 = $81.88

One exponential formula that is commonly used is the *interest formula*: $A = Pe^{rt}$. In this formula, interest is compounded continuously. A is the value of the investment after the time, t, in years. P is the initial amount of the investment, r is the interest rate, and e is the constant equal to approximately 2.718. Given an initial amount of $200 and a time of 3 years, if interest is compounded continuously at a rate of 6%, the total investment value can be found by plugging each value into the formula. The invested value at the end is $239.44. In more complex problems, the final investment may be given, and the rate may be the unknown. In this case, the formula becomes $239.44 = 200e^{r3}$.

Solving for r requires isolating the exponential expression on one side by dividing by 200, yielding the equation $1.20 = e^{r3}$. Taking the natural log of both sides results in $\ln(1.2) = r3$. Using a calculator to evaluate the logarithmic expression, $r = 0.06 = 6\%$.

Determining Discounts and Depreciation

Discounts and the amount something depreciates in value also involve calculating percentages and then subtracting the calculated amounts from the initial value. For example, consider the following problem and the two proposed methods to arrive at the answer:

A store is having a spring sale, where everything is 70% off. You have $45.00 to spend. A jacket is regularly priced at $80.00. Do you have enough to buy the jacket and a pair of gloves, regularly priced at $20.00?

There are two ways to approach this.

Method 1:

Set up the equations to find the sale prices: the original price minus the amount discounted.
$80.00 - ($80.00 (0.70)) = sale cost of the jacket.
$20.00 – ($20.00 (0.70)) = sale cost of the gloves.
Solve for the sale cost.
$24.00 = sale cost of the jacket.
$6.00 = sale cost of the gloves.
Determine if you have enough money for both.
$24.00 + $6.00 = total sale cost.
$30.00 is less than $45.00, so you can afford to purchase both.

Method 2:

Determine the percent of the original price that you will pay.
100% – 70% = 30%
Set up the equations to find the sale prices.
$80.00 (0.30) = cost of the jacket.
$20.00 (0.30) = cost of the gloves.
Solve.
$24.00 = cost of the jacket.
$6.00 = cost of the gloves.
Determine if you have enough money for both.
$24.00 + $6.00 = total sale cost.
$30.00 is less than $45.00, so you can afford to purchase both.

General Science

The Basics

Common Units of Measurement

There are two primary systems of measurement: the metric system and the English system. The metric system is a system of decimals, and the English system is composed of arbitrary measurements.

The Metric System

The Metric System was developed in France during the French Revolution in 1799, in order to distinguish itself from the British Empire and also to create a universal system of measurement. Almost every country, except three, has adopted it as their official measuring system. The physical quantities of the metric system are length, mass, volume, and time, and each has a basic unit of measurement: the meter (m), the gram (g), the liter (L), and the second (s), respectively.

Physical Quantity	**Basic Unit of Measurement**	**Symbol**
Length	meter	M
Mass	gram	G
Volume	liter	L
Time	second	S

Conversions within these measurements are easily made by multiplying or dividing by factors of ten and are indicated by the prefix attached to the unit. The most common units are listed below:

Prefix	Symbol	Factor	Power	Examples
kilo-	K	1,000	10^3	kilometer, kilogram, kiloliter, kilosecond
hecto-	H	100	10^2	hectometer, hectogram, hectoliter, hectosecond
deca-	Da	10	10^1	decameter, decagram, decaliter, decasecond
None	None	1	10^0	meter, gram, liter, second
deci-	D	0.1	10^{-1}	decimeter, decigram, deciliter, decisecond
centi-	C	0.01	10^{-2}	centimeter, centigram, centimeter, centisecond
milli-	M	0.001	10^{-3}	millimeter, milligram, milliliter, millisecond

Conversions within the Metric System

The wonderful thing about the metric system is it's incredibly easy to convert within the same unit of measurement—simply multiply or divide by ten!

Suppose a scientist wants to convert 23 meters to kilometers. The first method is to simply move the decimal point to the right or left depending on the prefix.

	LEFT				*RIGHT*	
kilo-	*hecto-*	*deca-*	*UNIT*	*deci-*	*centi-*	*milli-*
3	*2*	*1*		*1*	*2*	*3*

A decimal point for whole numbers always follows the ones unit—in this case, after the 3. To remember where the decimal is placed, imagine the number instead as 23.0.

After the decimal has been located, move it in accordance with the prefix. As shown above, *kilo* is *three* places to the *left* of the unit (meters, in this case). Therefore, the decimal is moved three units to the left:

$$23.0m \rightarrow \overset{\downarrow}{.}\underset{3\,2\,1}{\underbrace{023}}0 \rightarrow 0.023km$$

Thus, 23 meters is equivalent to 0.023 kilometers.

Another method of conversion relies on forming an equation. To demonstrate, one should follow the steps below:

1. Write down the problem.

$$23m = ?\,km$$

2. Identify the conversion.

$$1km = 1{,}000m$$

3. Write down the conversion as a fraction.

$$\frac{1km}{1{,}000m}$$

4. Write the original unit and conversion fraction as a multiplication problem.

$$23m \times \frac{1km}{1{,}000m}$$

5. Cancel units that appear on the top and bottom.

$$23\cancel{m} \times \frac{1km}{1{,}000\cancel{m}}$$

6. Solve the equation.

$$23\cancel{m} \times \frac{1km}{1{,}000\cancel{m}} = 0.023km$$

Again, 23 meters is equivalent to 0.023 kilometers.

The English System

The English system of measurement was developed centuries ago using the human body as well as familiar objects. The inch, for example, was the distance between King Henry I's second and third knuckle, and the foot was distance between his heel and toes. The common units of the English system are listed below:

Length	**Mass**	**Volume**
1 foot (ft.) = 12 inches (in) 3 feet (ft.) = 1 yard (yd.) 5,280 feet (ft.) = 1 mile (mi)	16 ounces (oz.) = 1 pound (lb.) 2,000 pounds (lb.) = 1 ton	16 fluid oz. (fly oz.) = 1 pint 2 pints = 1 quart 4 quarts = 1 gallon

Conversion within the English System

Due to the arbitrary nature of the English system, one cannot simply convert one unit to another by moving decimals. The best way to convert is to use the second method—equations—listed above.

Say, for example, a scientist wanted to convert 3.6 miles into feet. The second method for this problem could be condensed into the following:

$$3.6\,\cancel{mi} \times \frac{5{,}280ft}{1\cancel{mi}} = 19{,}008ft$$

Conversions Between Systems

Converting units between systems can be tricky because they follow different rules. The best way is to look up an English to Metric system conversion factor and then use the second method to solve the problem. The below table lists the common conversion values:

English System	**Metric System**
1 inch	2.54 cm
1 foot	0.3048 m
1 yard	0.914 m
1 mile	1.609 km
1 ounce	28.35 g
1 pound	0.454 kg
1 fluid ounce	29.574 mL
1 quart	0.946 L
1 gallon	3.785 L

Suppose a scientist wanted to convert 3.6 miles to meters. The second method for this problem could be condensed into the following:

$$3.6\cancel{mi} \times \frac{1.609\cancel{km}}{1\cancel{mi}} \times \frac{1{,}000m}{1\cancel{km}} = 5{,}792m$$

Scientific Notation

Scientific Notation is used to represent numbers that are either very small or very large. For example, the distance to the Sun is approximately 150,000,000,000 meters. Instead of writing this number with so many zeros, it can be written in scientific notation as 1.5×10^{11}meters. The same is true for very small numbers, but the exponent becomes negative. If the mass of a human cell is 0.000000000001 kilograms, that measurement can be easily represented by 1.0×10^{-12} kilograms. In both situations, scientific notation makes the measurement easier to read and understand. Each number is translated to an expression with one digit in the tens place multiplied by an expression corresponding to the zeros.

When two measurements are given and both involve scientific notation, it is important to know how these interact with each other:

- In addition and subtraction, the exponent on the ten must be the same before any operations are performed on the numbers. For example, $(1.3 \times 10^4) + (3.0 \times 10^3)$ cannot be added until one of the exponents on the ten is changed. The 3.0×10^3 can be changed to 0.3×10^4, then the 1.3 and 0.3 can be added. The answer comes out to be 1.6×10^4.

- For multiplication, the first numbers can be multiplied and then the exponents on the tens can be added. Once an answer is formed, it may have to be converted into scientific notation again depending on the change that occurred.

- The following is an example of multiplication with scientific notation:

$$(4.5 \times 10^3) \times (3.0 \times 10^{-5}) = 13.5 \times 10^{-2}$$

- Since this answer is not in scientific notation, the decimal is moved over to the left one unit, and 1 is added to the ten's exponent. This results in the final answer: 1.35×10^{-1}.

- For division, the first numbers are divided, and the exponents on the tens are subtracted. Again, the answer may need to be converted into scientific notation form, depending on the type of changes that occurred during the problem.

- **Order of magnitude** relates to scientific notation and is the total count of powers of 10 in a number. For example, there are 6 orders of magnitude in 1,000,000. If a number is raised by an order of magnitude, it is multiplied by 10. Order of magnitude can be helpful in estimating results using very large or small numbers. An answer should make sense in terms of its order of magnitude.

- For example, if area is calculated using two dimensions with 6 orders of magnitude, because area involves multiplication, the answer should have around 12 orders of magnitude. Also, answers can be estimated by rounding to the largest place value in each number. For example, 5,493,302 ×2,523,100 can be estimated by 5 × 3 = 15 with 6 orders of magnitude.

The Scientific Method

Human beings are, by nature, very curious. Long before the scientific method was established, people have been making observations and predicting outcomes, manipulating the physical world to create extraordinary things—from the first man-made fire in 6000 B.C.E. to the satellite that orbited Pluto in 2016. Although the history of the scientific method is sporadic and attributed to many different people, it remains the most reliable way to obtain and utilize knowledge about the observable universe.

The scientific method consists of the following steps:

- Make an observation
- Create a question
- Form a hypothesis
- Conduct an experiment
- Collect and analyze data
- Form a conclusion

The first step is to identify a problem based on an observation—the who, what, when, where, why, and how. An **observation** is the analysis of information using basic human senses: sight, sound, touch, taste, and smell. Observations can be two different types—qualitative or quantitative. A qualitative observation describes what is being observed, such as the color of a house or the smell of a flower. Quantitative observations measure what is being observed, such as the number of windows on a house or the intensity of a flower's smell on a scale of 1-5.

Observations lead to the identification of a problem, also called an **inference**. For example, if a fire truck is barreling down a busy street, the inferences could be:

- There's a fire.
- Someone is hurt.
- Some kid pulled the fire alarm at a local school.

Inferences are logical predictions based on experience or education that lead to the formation of a hypothesis.

A **hypothesis** is a testable explanation of an observed scenario and is presented in the form of a statement. It's an attempt to answer a question based on an observation, and it allows a scientist to predict an outcome. A hypothesis makes assumptions on the relationship between two different variables, and answers the question: "If I do this, what happens to that?"

In order to form a hypothesis, there must be an independent variable and a dependent variable that can be measured. The **independent variable** is the variable that is manipulated, and the **dependent variable** is the result of the change.

For example, suppose a student wants to know how light affects plant growth. Based upon what he or she already knows, the student proposes (hypothesizes) that the more light to which a plant is exposed, the faster it will grow.

- Observation: Plants exposed to lots of light seem to grow taller.
- Question: Will plants grow faster if there's more light available?
- Hypothesis: The more light the plant has, the faster it will grow.
- Independent variable: The amount of time exposed to light (able to be manipulated)
- Dependent variable: Plant growth (the result of the manipulation)

Once a hypothesis has been formed, it must be tested to determine whether it's true or false. (How to test a hypothesis is described in a subsequent section.) After it has been tested and validated as true over and over, then a hypothesis can develop into a theory, model, or law.

Development of Theories, Models, and Laws

Theories, models, and laws have one thing in common: they develop on the basis of scientific evidence that has been tested and verified by multiple researchers on many different occasions. Listed below are their exact definitions:

- **Theory:** An explanation of natural patterns or occurrences—i.e., the theory of relativity, the kinetic theory of gases, etc.

- **Model:** A representation of a natural pattern or occurrence that's difficult or impossible to experience directly, usually in the form of a picture or 3-D representation—i.e., Bohr's atomic model, the double-helix model of DNA, etc.

- **Law:** A mathematical or concise description of a pattern or occurrence in the observable universe—i.e., Newton's law of gravity, the laws of thermodynamics, etc.

The terms *theory, model,* and *law* are often used interchangeably in the sciences, although there's an essential difference: theories and models are used to explain *how and why* something happens, while laws describe exactly *what* happens. A common misconception is that theories develop into laws. But theories and models never become laws because they inherently describe different things.

Type	**Function**	**Examples**
Theory	To explain how and why something happens	Einstein's Theory of Special Relativity The Big Bang Theory
Model	To represent how and why something happens	A graphical model or drawing of an atom
Laws	To describe exactly what happens	$E = mc^2$ $F = ma$ $PV = nRT$

In order to ensure that scientific theories are consistent, scientists continually gather information and evidence on existing theories to improve their accuracy.

Earth Science

Types and Basic Characteristics of Rocks and Minerals and Their Formation Processes

Geology is the study of the nature and composition of the rocks and materials that make up the Earth, how they were formed, and the physical and chemical processes that have changed Earth over time.

Characteristics of Rocks and Their Formation Processes

Earth can be imagined as a giant construction of billions of Lego blocks, and that these blocks represent different minerals. A **mineral** is a naturally occurring inorganic solid composed of certain chemical elements (or atoms) in a defined crystalline structure. When minerals are aggregated together with other minerals, **organic compounds** (carbon-containing remains of decomposed plant or animal matter), and/or **mineraloids** (minerals that lack a defined crystalline structure), rocks are formed. Rock types are classified based on their mechanism of formation and the materials of their compositions. The three fundamental classifications of rocks include:

- Sedimentary
- Igneous
- Metamorphic

Sedimentary rocks form at the Earth's surface (on land and in bodies of water) through deposition and cementation of fragments of other rocks, organic matter, and minerals. These materials, called sediment, are deposited and accumulate in layers called strata, which get pressed into a solid over time when more sediment settles on top. Sedimentary rocks are further classified as either clastic/detrital, biochemical, chemical, or other. **Clastic** or **detrital** rocks are composed of other inorganic rocks or organic particles, respectively. **Biochemical** rocks have an organic component, like coal, which is composed of decayed plant matter. **Chemical** rocks form from a solution containing dissolved materials that became supersaturated and minerals precipitate out of solution. Halite, or rock salt, is an example of a chemical sedimentary rock. Sedimentary rocks that do not fit into these types are categorized as "other." These rocks are from fragments formed by asteroid or comet impacts or from fragments of volcanic lava.

Igneous rocks are composed of molten material beneath the Earth's surface called **magma** and are classified based on where the magma cooled and solidified. They can be intrusive/plutonic, extrusive/volcanic, or hypabyssal. **Intrusive** or **plutonic** rocks, such as granite, form when magma cools slowly within or beneath the Earth's surface. Because they solidify slowly, these rocks tend to have a coarse grain, larger crystalline structure of their mineral constituents, and rough appearance. By contrast, extrusive/volcanic form from rapid cooling as magma escapes the Earth's surface as lava and have a smooth or fine-grained appearance, with tiny crystals or ones that are too small to see. A common example of an extrusive igneous rock is glassy obsidian. **Hypabyssal** rocks are formed at levels between intrusive and extrusive (just below the surface); they aren't nearly as common.

Metamorphic rocks form from the transformation of other rocks via a process called metamorphism. This transformation happens when existing rocks—sedimentary, igneous, or other metamorphic rocks—are subjected to significant heat and pressure, which causes physical and/or chemical changes. Based on their appearance, metamorphic rocks are classified as either foliated or non-foliated. **Foliated** rocks are layered or folded, which means they form from compression in one direction and result in visible layers or banding within the rock. Examples include gneiss or slate. **Non-foliated** rocks, such as marble, receive equal pressure from all directions and thus have a homogenous appearance.

It should be noted that classification is not always completely clear, and some rocks don't quite fit the criteria for one of these three categories, so they are sometimes lumped together in a category called "other rocks." A classic example is a fossil. A **fossil** is a rock formed from the remains or impression of dead plants or animals, but it doesn't fit into any biochemical class of rocks because fossils themselves are wholly composed of organic material and only formed under strict conditions, although they are commonly found within sedimentary rock.

<u>The Rock Cycle</u>

Although it may not always be apparent, rocks are constantly being destroyed while new ones are created in a process called the *rock cycle*. This cycle is driven by plate tectonics and the water cycle, which are discussed in detail later. The rock cycle starts with **magma,** the molten rock found deep within the Earth. As magma moves toward the Earth's surface, it hardens and transforms into igneous rock.

Then, over time, igneous rock is broken down into tiny pieces called **sediment** that are eventually deposited all over the surface. As more and more sediment accumulates, the weight of the newer sediment compresses the older sediment underneath and creates sedimentary rock. As sedimentary rock is pushed deeper below the surface, the high pressure and temperature transform it into metamorphic rock. This metamorphic rock can either rise to the surface again or sink even deeper and melt back into magma, thus starting the cycle again.

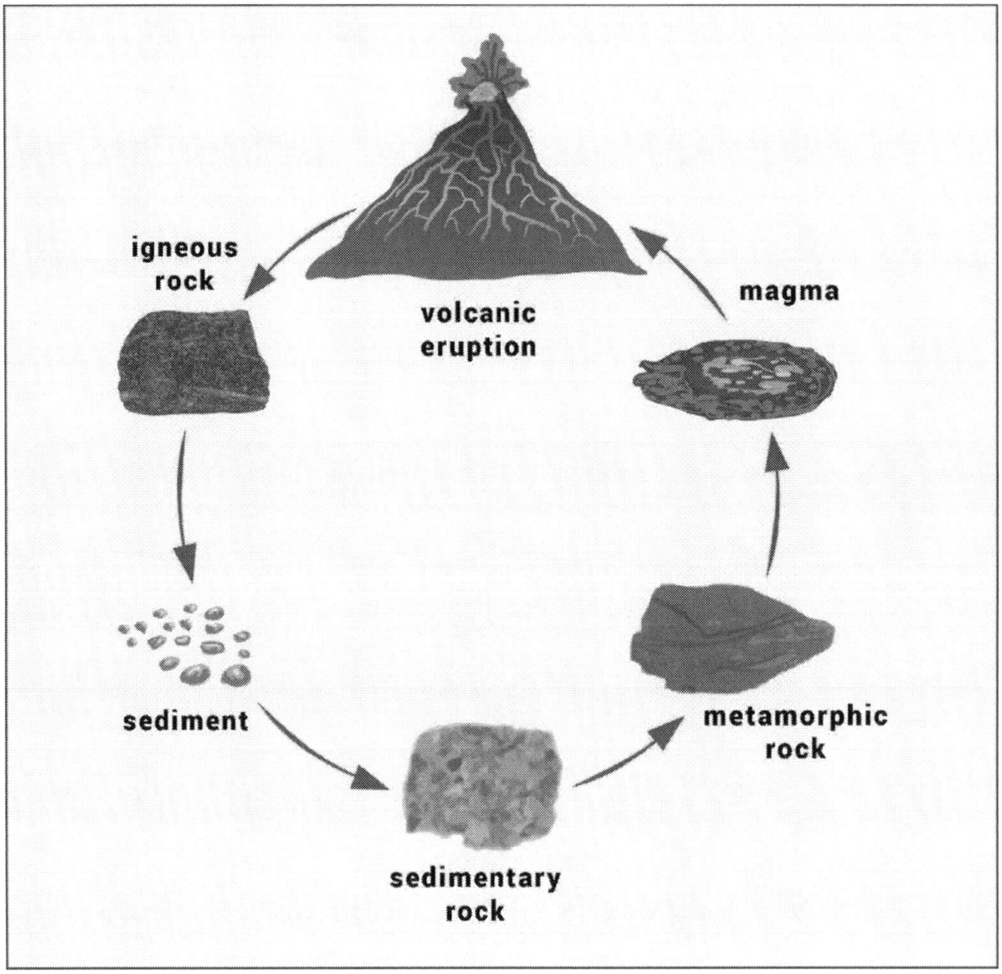

Characteristics of Minerals and Their Formation Processes

A **mineral,** such as gold, is a naturally occurring inorganic solid composed of one type of molecule or element that's organized into a crystalline structure. Rocks are aggregates of different types of minerals. Depending on their composition, minerals can be mainly classified into one of the following eight groups:

- Carbonates: formed from molecules that have either a carbon, nitrogen, or boron atom at the center.
- Elements: formed from single elements that occur naturally; includes metals such as gold and nickel, as well as metallic alloys like brass.
- Halides: formed from molecules that have halogens; halite, which is table salt, is a classic example.

- Oxides: formed from molecules that contain oxygen or hydroxide and are held together with ionic bonds; encompasses the phosphates, silicates, and sulfates.

- Phosphates: formed from molecules that contain phosphates; the apatite group minerals are in this class.

- Silicates: formed from molecules that contain silicon, silicates are the largest class and usually the most complex minerals; topaz is an example of a silicate.

- Sulfates: formed from molecules that contain either sulfur, chromium, tungsten, selenium, tellurium, and/or molybdenum.

- Sulfides: formed from molecules that contain sulfide (S^{2-}); includes many of the important metal ores, such as lead and silver.

One important physical characteristic of a mineral is its **hardness,** which is defined as its resistance to scratching. When two crystals are struck together, the harder crystal will scratch the softer crystal. The most common measure of hardness is the Mohs Hardness Scale, which ranges from 1 to 10, with 10 being the hardest. Diamonds are rated 10 on the Mohs Hardness Scale, and talc, which was once used to make baby powder, is rated 1. Other important characteristics of minerals include **luster** or shine, **color,** and **cleavage,** which is the natural plane of weakness at which a specific crystal breaks.

Plate Tectonics

The theory of plate tectonics states that the Earth's superficial layer (the crust and upper mantle, together called the **lithosphere**) is a collection of variably-sized plates that move and interact with each other on top of the more molten **asthenosphere** in the mantle below. It is estimated that there are between 9 and 15 major plates and up to 40 minor plates. Some of these plates are **oceanic**, which means they contain an ocean basin, while others are **continental** and carry a landmass. The line formed by the meeting of two plates is called a **fault**. A well-known example is the San Andreas Fault, where the Pacific and North American plates meet. These faults are classified as **convergent** (plates colliding into each other) or **divergent** (plates moving away from each other). **Transform boundaries** occur when two plates slide past each other in opposite directions horizontally.

The larger plates are:

- North American plate
- Eurasian plate
- Pacific plate
- Australian plate
- Antarctic plate

- South American plate
- African plate
- Indian plate

Major plates of the lithosphere

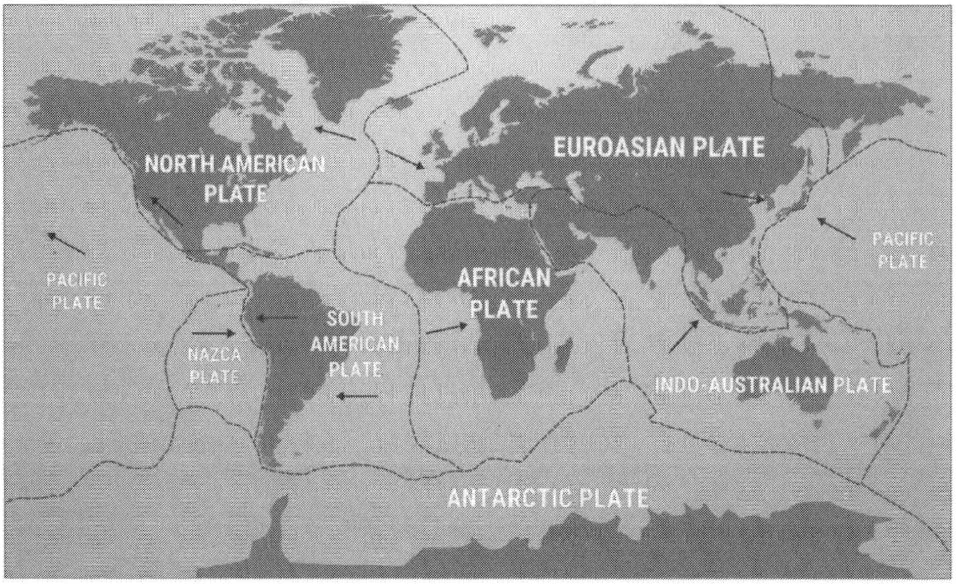

For the most part, these plates contain the countries/continents for which they are named. Scientists theorize that these plates were once part of a supercontinent, called **Pangea**, that existed over 175 million years ago. Evidence for Pangea's existence comes from geological findings, corresponding shapes of adjacent but currently independent landmasses, and fossils of identical species found in areas that used to be joined but have since separated.

Planet Earth is not a perfect sphere; it's actually slightly ellipsoid or oblong (like a football), and it's divided into three main layers from surface to center: the crust, mantle, and core. The crust and core are solid, while the mantle possesses a more fluid quality. In plate tectonics, the plates are considered to be the Earth's **lithosphere**, which is the crust and uppermost solid portion of mantle. One can visualize the plates as flat planks of wood covering the surface of a pool bobbing up and down and bumping, sliding, or moving away from each other. These different plate interactions create Earth's landscape.

At convergent boundaries, the collision of two plates can give rise to mountain ranges. Another possibility is that one plate slides atop another and pushes it down, creating magma and volcanoes, a process called **subduction**. This frequently happens when an oceanic and continental plate converge, and the denser oceanic plate sinks below under the continental plate. Volcanic activity also occurs at divergent boundaries—when the two plates separate—and magma escapes to the surface and solidifies. This is how new land is formed. Faults are not the only places a volcano may appear; plates may contain areas called **hot spots**, and when these hot spots reach the surface, a volcano forms. Earthquakes are another consequence of plate tectonics, occurring as a result of sliding or colliding plates. Friction energy created between two plates can become an earthquake.

Earth's Layers

Earth has three major layers: a thin solid outer surface or **crust,** a dense **core,** and a **mantle** between them that contains most of the Earth's matter. This layout resembles an egg, where the eggshell is the crust, the mantle is the egg white, and the core is the yolk. The outer crust of the Earth consists of igneous or sedimentary rocks over metamorphic rocks. Together with the upper portion of the mantle, it forms the **lithosphere**, which is broken into tectonic plates.

The mantle can be divided into three zones. The **upper mantle** is adjacent to the crust and composed of solid rock. Below the upper mantle is the **transition zone**. The **lower mantle** below the transition zone is a layer of completely solid rock. Underneath the mantle is the molten **outer core** followed by the compact, solid **inner core.** The inner and outer cores contain the densest elements, consisting of mostly iron and nickel.

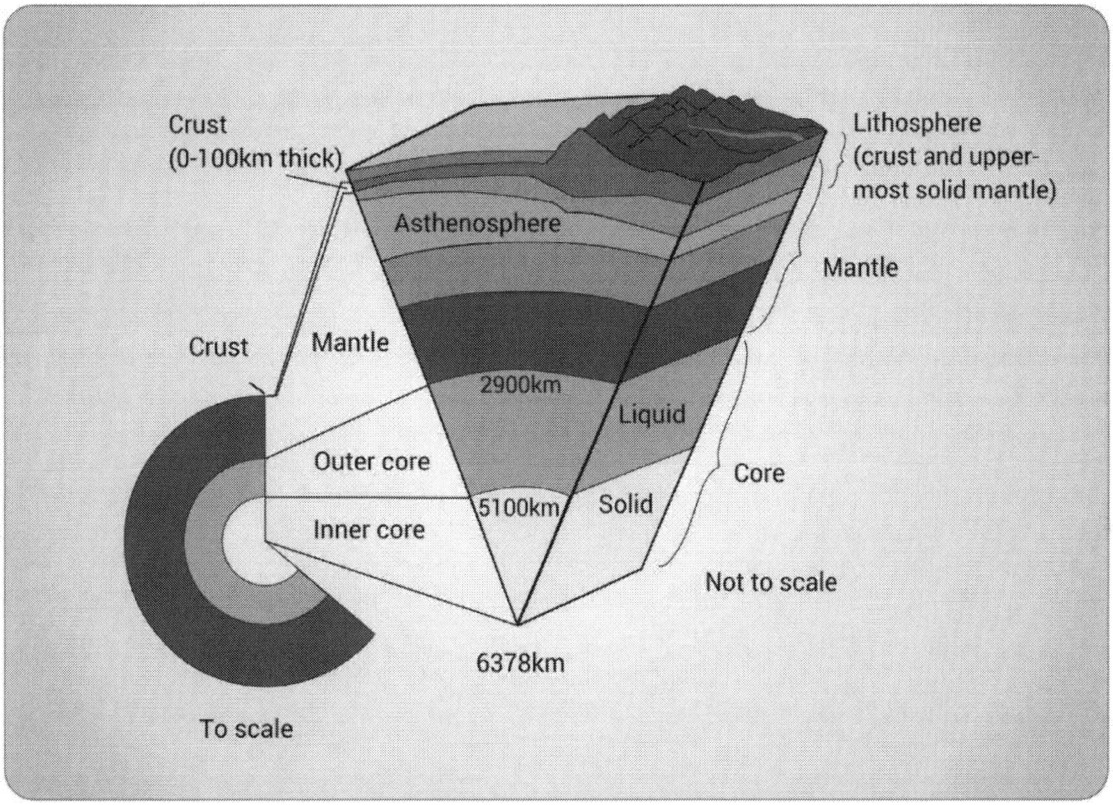

Geography

Geography is the study of the Earth's layout and features. There are imaginary lines that circle the globe and divide it into sections that help people track time and navigate. These lines run both vertically and horizontally from pole to pole. Vertical lines, also called **meridians**, measure east/west distance and are described as **longitudinal**. They are 15 degrees apart from each other, and the first line or point of zero, designated the Prime Meridian, serves as the reference line. Horizontal lines measure north/south distance and are described as **latitudinal**. The central latitude line is the **equator**—the line between the Northern and Southern Hemispheres. Each degree between these lines is further divided into sixty intervals called **minutes**, and each minute is divided into sixty intervals called **seconds**. For latitudinal lines, degree count increases as one moves away from the equator toward either pole. Using these lines and the coordinate system, any location on the planet can be precisely described; the advent of GPS technology has made this process much more user-friendly.

Aside from the equator, the Earth has four other latitudinal lines with specific names:

- Tropic of Cancer
- Tropic of Capricorn
- Arctic Circle
- Antarctic Circle

The Tropic of Cancer, or Northern Tropic, is the northernmost latitudinal line. It lies directly beneath the Sun during the June solstice (the specific date in June can vary each year). It is also called the northern solstice or summer solstice (in the Northern hemisphere) because it is when the Northern Hemisphere is most tilted toward the Sun and marks the beginning of summer for the Northern Hemisphere.

The **Tropic of Capricorn,** or Southern Tropic, is the southernmost latitudinal line. During the December or southern solstice, the Northern Hemisphere is tilted away from the Sun, while the Southern Hemisphere is tilted towards it. This date marks the beginning of winter for the Northern Hemisphere and summer for the Southern Hemisphere.

The **Arctic Circle** is the northernmost major circle of latitude. When the Northern Tropic receives light from directly overhead on the June solstice, the Sun doesn't fall below the horizon at or above the Arctic Circle, so that 24 hours of daylight are experienced.

The **Antarctic Circle** is the southern counterpart of the Arctic Circle. On the December solstice, people at, or below, the Antarctic Circle see that the Sun stays above the horizon for 24 hours. On the same date on the opposite pole (above the Arctic Circle), the Sun does not rise during the full day.

A good way to think about the major circles of latitude is remembering they are based upon how much direct sunlight (solar radiation) they receive at certain times of the year. Earth rotates on an axis that is tilted 23.5 degrees while it revolves around the Sun. This tilt causes the seasons experienced on Earth. Earth can be imagined as a spinning top that is teetering side to side; when the top leans toward the Sun, it gets more light, and the bottom is hidden. Then when it leans away from the Sun, the bottom gets more light, and the top is hidden. Throughout this motion, the equator remains almost directly under the Sun all year and doesn't experience four different seasons. That's why areas close to the equator are warm all year round.

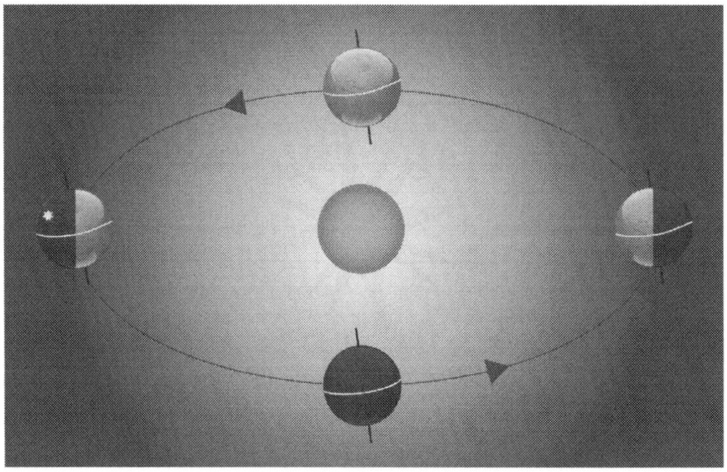

The Earth is also divided into different biomes or ecosystems. The simplest classification dictates that there are five different ecosystems:

- **Aquatic**: Contains marine and freshwater systems and found at all latitudes
- **Desert**: Areas of low precipitation and usually windy; can be found at nearly all latitudes
- **Forest**: Tropical, temperate, or boreal; types of trees depend on latitude
- **Grassland**: Prairies, savannahs, steppes; can exist in tropical, temperate, and cold climates
- **Tundra**: Found far from the equator toward either pole; receives the least amount of total annual sunlight

Weather, Atmosphere, and the Water Cycle

The study of the Earth's weather, atmosphere, and water cycle is called **meteorology**. The weather experienced in an area at a given time is a product of Earth's atmosphere above that location. The different atmospheric layers are defined by their temperature but are thought of by their distance above sea level (listed from lowest to highest):

- **Troposphere**: Sea level to 11 miles above sea level
- **Stratosphere**: 11 miles to 31 miles above sea level
- **Mesosphere**: 31 miles to 50 miles above sea level
- **Ionosphere**: 50 miles to 400 miles above sea level
- **Exosphere**: 400 miles to 800 miles above sea level

Above the exosphere is outer space. Together, the ionosphere and exosphere are considered the **thermosphere**. The ozone layer lies within the stratosphere, while the troposphere is where the conditions that lead to the observable weather on Earth originates. The manner in which the temperature changes is different in each of these layers. In the troposphere, it gets colder as the layer gets further from sea level, while the stratosphere gets warmer, the mesosphere gets colder, and the thermosphere gets warmer in this same direction.

The **atmosphere** is a layer of gas particles floating in space. The atmospheric levels are created by gravity and its pull on those particles. The Earth's atmosphere is mostly comprised of nitrogen and oxygen (78% and 21%, respectively) along with significantly lower amounts of other gases including 1% argon and 0.039% carbon dioxide. Gas particles have mass, and pressure is higher at the bottom (at the surface of Earth) because of all that mass in the layers above. Therefore, the farther away one gets from Earth's surface, the air gets thinner, as there are fewer air molecules compressing lower particles together. That's why breathing becomes more difficult when a person climbs to higher altitudes. To visualize this, one can imagine that when a person takes a breath, he or she is breathing in a cup of air. At higher altitudes, that cup is still the same size; it just holds fewer particles of gas.

Weather is a state of the atmosphere at a given place and time based on conditions such as air pressure, temperature, and moisture. Weather includes conditions like clouds, storms, temperature, tornadoes, hurricanes, and blizzards. In a given location on Earth, the weather experienced varies day-to-day, based on atmospheric conditions. The average weather for a particular area over a long period (usually over 30 years) is defined as that area's **climate**. The main force driving weather is the atmospheric variations between different areas on Earth. The major circles of latitude experience these differences because of the Sun. When there's a large difference in temperature between two areas, a jet stream forms. Pressure differences occur when there are temperature differences caused by surface variations (like mountains and valleys).

The **water cycle** is another factor that drives weather. It is the movement of water above, within, and on the surface of the Earth. During any phase of the cycle, water can exist in any of its three phases: liquid, ice, and vapor.

The processes that drive the cycle are:

- **Precipitation**: Rain, snow, hail, and sleet
- **Canopy interception**: Precipitation that falls on trees and doesn't hit the ground, eventually evaporating back into the atmosphere
- **Snowmelt**: Runoff from melting snow
- **Runoff**: Water moving across land that either seeps into the ground, evaporates, gets stored as lakes, or gets extracted by living organisms. It also includes surface and channel runoff.
- **Infiltration**: Water that moves from ground surface into the ground
- **Subsurface flow**: Moving water underground
- **Transpiration**: Release of vapor into the atmosphere from plants and soil
- **Percolation**: Water that flows down through soil and rocks
- **Evaporation**: Transformation from liquid water to gaseous vapor driven primarily by solar radiation
- **Sublimation**: Transformation of ice to gaseous vapor, never becoming a liquid
- **Deposition**: Transformation of vapor to solid ice
- **Condensation**: Transformation of vapor to liquid water

Water in the atmosphere exists as clouds, which are visible masses made of water droplets, tiny crystals of ice, dust, and various chemicals. The study of clouds, called **nephology**, is a subspecialty of meteorology. There are many types of clouds, and they can be classified based on the altitude at which they occur. It's important to note that clouds primarily occur in the troposphere. The classes of clouds are:

- **High clouds**: Occurring between 5,000 and 13,000 meters above sea level
  - **Cirrus**: Thin and wispy "mare's tail" appearance
  - **Cirrocumulus**: Rows of small puffs
  - **Cirrostratus**: Thin sheets that cover the sky
- **Middle clouds**: Occurring between 2,000 and 7,000 meters above sea level
  - **Altocumulus**: Gray and white and made up of water droplets
  - **Altostratus**: Grayish or bluish gray clouds
- **Low clouds**: Occurring below 2,000 meters above sea level
  - **Stratus**: Gray and cover the sky
  - **Stratocumulus**: Gray and lumpy low-lying clouds
  - **Nimbostratus**: Dark gray with uneven bases that occur with rain or snow

Here are some examples of different types of clouds:

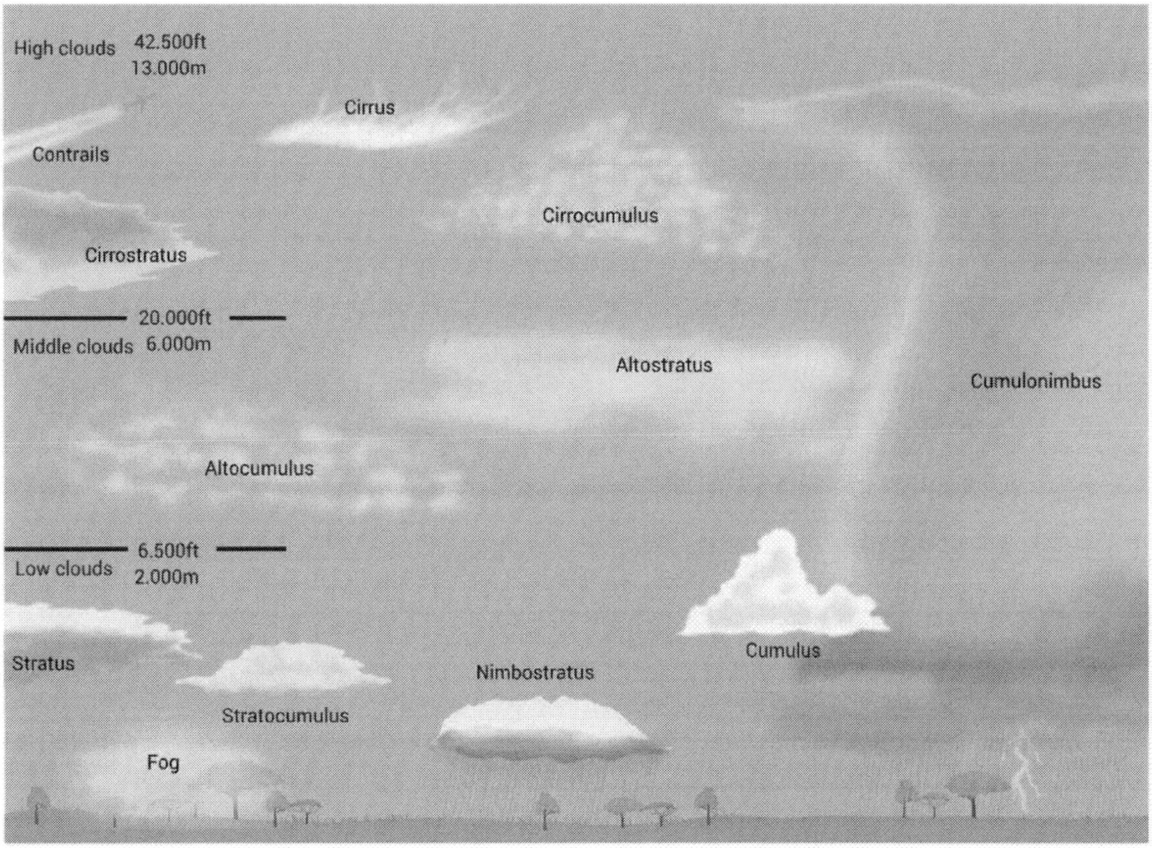

The vast majority of water on Earth is found in its oceans, which contain salt water, unlike lakes and other bodies, which contain freshwater. Salt water has a higher density than freshwater due to the dissolved salt. The total mass of all oceanic water is estimated to be 1.4 x 10^{24} grams, covering approximately 70% of the Earth's surface (361,254,000 km^2). The deepest part of the ocean is an area called the Challenger Deep in the Mariana Trench where the ocean floor is nearly 11,000 meters below sea level. The major oceans are the Pacific, Atlantic, and Indian Oceans. The Arctic and Southern Oceans are near each pole and are smaller.

Astronomy

Astronomy is the study of celestial bodies, or objects in space, and how they interact with each other. It is one of the oldest sciences; people have always looked up at the night sky with curiosity and amazement. Earth is a celestial body; others include the Sun, moon, other planets, black holes, satellites, asteroids, meteors, comets, stars, and galaxies. Information about celestial bodies and processes is obtained from observation via visible light and radiation throughout the universe. These observations are used in a field called **theoretical astronomy**, where scientists create theoretical models to explain or predict celestial processes or events.

From what astronomers have observed, the size of the universe is believed to be 91 billion light years. That means that if a person stood at the edge of the universe and flipped a switch to turn on a light at the opposite edge of the universe, it would take 91 billion years for the light to reach the person. And it's believed that the universe is constantly enlarging. A popular theory is that the universe was born 13 billion years ago, after an explosion called the **Big Bang**, and that the debris from that explosion (planets and stars) has been floating away from the epicenter ever since. It is also believed that the Universe is mainly made up of dark energy (about 73%) along with 23% dark matter and 4% regular matter, including stars, planets, and living organisms. The space between planets, stars, and galaxies is **interstellar space**, which is filled with **interstellar medium** (gas and dust).

Objects in the universe, including the Earth, are clumps of matter. Consistent with the laws of physics and gravity, these clumps form clusters. These clusters are solar systems, galaxies, galaxy clusters, superclusters, and something astronomers call the Great Wall of Galaxies.

Galaxies are clusters of stars, rocks, ice, and space dust. Like everything else in space, the exact number of galaxies is unknown, but there could be as many as a hundred billion. There are three types of galaxies: spiral, elliptical, and irregular. Most galaxies are **spiral galaxies**; they have a large, central galactic bulge made up of a cluster of older stars. They look like a disk with spinning arms. **Elliptical galaxies** are groups of stars with no pattern of rotation. They can be spherical or extremely elongated, and they don't have arms. **Irregular galaxies** vary significantly in size and shape.

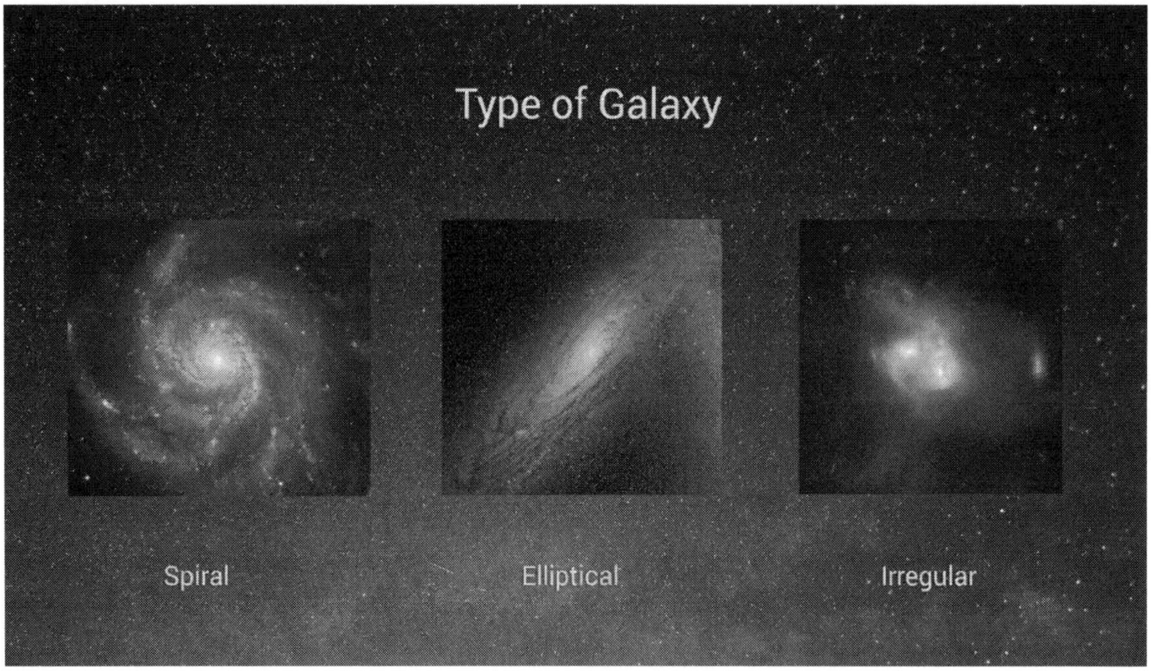

To say that galaxies are large is an understatement. Most galaxies are 1,000 to 100,000 parsecs in diameter, with one **parsec** equal to about 19 trillion miles. The Milky Way is the galaxy that contains Earth's Solar System. It's one of the smaller galaxies that has been studied. The diameter of the Milky Way is estimated to be between 31,000 to 55,000 parsecs.

Earth's solar system is a planetary system on an ecliptic plane with a large sun in the center that provides gravitational pull. The Sun is primarily made of hydrogen and helium—metals comprise only 2% of its mass. It's 1.3 million kilometers wide, weighs 1.989×10^{30} kilograms, and has temperatures of 5,800 Kelvin (9980 degrees Fahrenheit) on the surface (also called the photosphere) and 15,600,000 Kelvin (28 million degrees Fahrenheit) in its core. It is the Sun's huge size and mass that give it so much gravity—enough to compress the hydrogen and helium (which exist as gas on Earth) into liquid form. The **Sun** is basically a series of giant explosions creating light and heat, and it's that huge gravitational force that pulls in those explosions and maintains the Sun's structure. The pressure at the Sun's core is 250 billion atmospheres, making it over 150 times denser than Earth's water!

Astronomers used to think there were nine total planets in the Solar System, but Pluto is now considered a dwarf planet, along with Ceres, Haumea, Makemake, and Eris. The eight planets can be divided into four inner (terrestrial) and four outer (Jovian) planets. Generally, the terrestrial planets are small, and the Jovian planets are larger and less dense with rings and moons. Listed in order of closest to the Sun to furthest, the planets are:

- **Mercury**: The smallest planet in the system and the one that is closest to the Sun. Because it's so close, it only takes about 88 days for Mercury to completely orbit the Sun. It has a large iron core and the surface has craters like Earth's moon. There's no atmosphere, and it doesn't have any orbiting moons/satellites. From Earth, Mercury looks bright.

- **Venus**: The second planet is bright and has about the same size, composition, and gravity as Earth. It orbits the Sun every 225 days. Its atmosphere creates clouds of sulfuric acid, and there's even thunder and lightning.

- **Earth**: The third planet orbits the Sun every year (about 365 days). Scientists believe it's the only planet in this system that's capable of supporting life.

- **Mars**: The Red Planet looks red because there's iron oxide on the surface. It also takes around 687 days to complete its orbit around the Sun. Interestingly, a day on Mars (one rotation about its axis), is very similar to the 24-hour day on Earth. Mars has a thin atmosphere as well as the largest mountain, canyon, and crater that astronomers have ever been able to see. Volcanoes, valleys, deserts, and polar ice caps like those on Earth have also been seen on its surface.

- **Jupiter**: The largest planet in the solar system is comprised mainly of hydrogen and helium (helium makes up 25% of its mass). The atmosphere on Jupiter has band-like clouds made of ammonia crystals that create tremendous storms and turbulence on the surface. Winds blow at around 100 meters per second, or over 220 miles per hour!

- **Saturn**: The second-largest planet is comprised mainly of hydrogen and helium along with other trace elements. The core is believed to be rock and ice. Saturn has a layer of metallic hydrogen. Winds are even stronger than those on Jupiter, reaching up to 1,100 miles per hour. Saturn has 61 moons, but the planet is most famous for its beautiful rings. There's no definitive explanation for how the rings formed, but two popular theories say they could be remnants from when Saturn itself formed, or they were moons that were destroyed in the past.

- **Uranus**: This planet has the coldest atmosphere of any in the Solar System, with a temperature that reaches -224.2 degrees Celsius (-371.56 °F). It's also mainly made of hydrogen and helium, but it has water, ammonia, methane, and even some hydrocarbons (the material humans are made of). A solid surface has yet to be observed through the thick layer of gas covering the planet. Uranus has 27 known moons.

- **Neptune**: The furthest planet is the third-largest by mass, and the second-coldest. It has 12 orbiting moons, an atmosphere like Uranus', a Great Dark Spot, and the strongest recorded winds of any planet in the system (reaching speeds of 2,100 kilometers per hour).

The image below shows each planet in relation to the others.

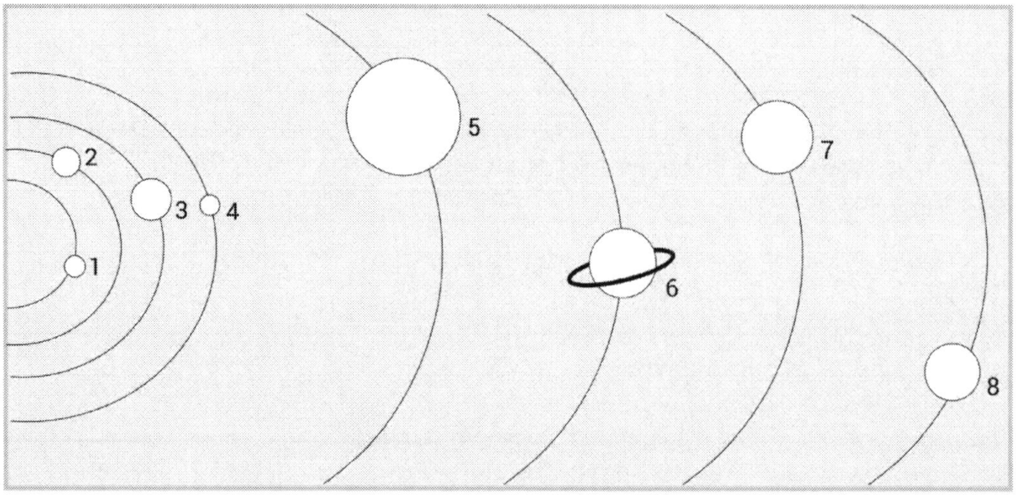

The nearest star to Earth's solar system is Proxima Centauri, which is about 270,000 Astronomical Units away. The closest object to Earth is the Moon, which is about 384,401 kilometers or 238,910 miles away. The Moon has two phases as it revolves around Earth—the waxing phase and the waning phase—which each last about two weeks. During the **waxing** phase, the Moon goes from new (black) to full moon; then it **wanes**, going from full to black. The Moon appears white because it's illuminated by the Sun. The edge of the shadow on the Moon is called the **lunar terminator**. The phases of waxing and waning in the Northern Hemisphere are:

- Waxing: The right side of the Moon is illuminated
    - **New moon** (dark): The Moon rises and sets with the Sun
    - **Crescent**: Tiny sliver illuminated on the right side
    - **First quarter**: The right half is illuminated; its phase is due south on the meridian
    - **Gibbous**: More than half is illuminated on the right side
    - **Full moon**: Rises at sunset and sets at sunrise
- Waning: The left side of the Moon is illuminated
    - **Gibbous**: More than half is illuminated on the left side
    - **Last quarter**: Half-illuminated on the left side; rises at midnight and sets at noon
    - **Crescent**: Tiny sliver illuminated on the left
    - **New moon** (dark): Rises and sets with the Sun again

Eclipses occur when the Earth, the Sun, and the Moon are all in line. If the three bodies are perfectly aligned, a total eclipse occurs; otherwise, it's only a partial eclipse. A solar eclipse occurs when the Moon is between the Earth and the Sun, blocking sunlight from reaching the Earth. A lunar eclipse occurs when the Earth interferes with the Sun's light reflecting off the full moon. The Earth casts a shadow on the Moon, but the particles of the Earth's atmosphere refract the light, so some light reaches the Moon, causing it to look yellow, brown, or red.

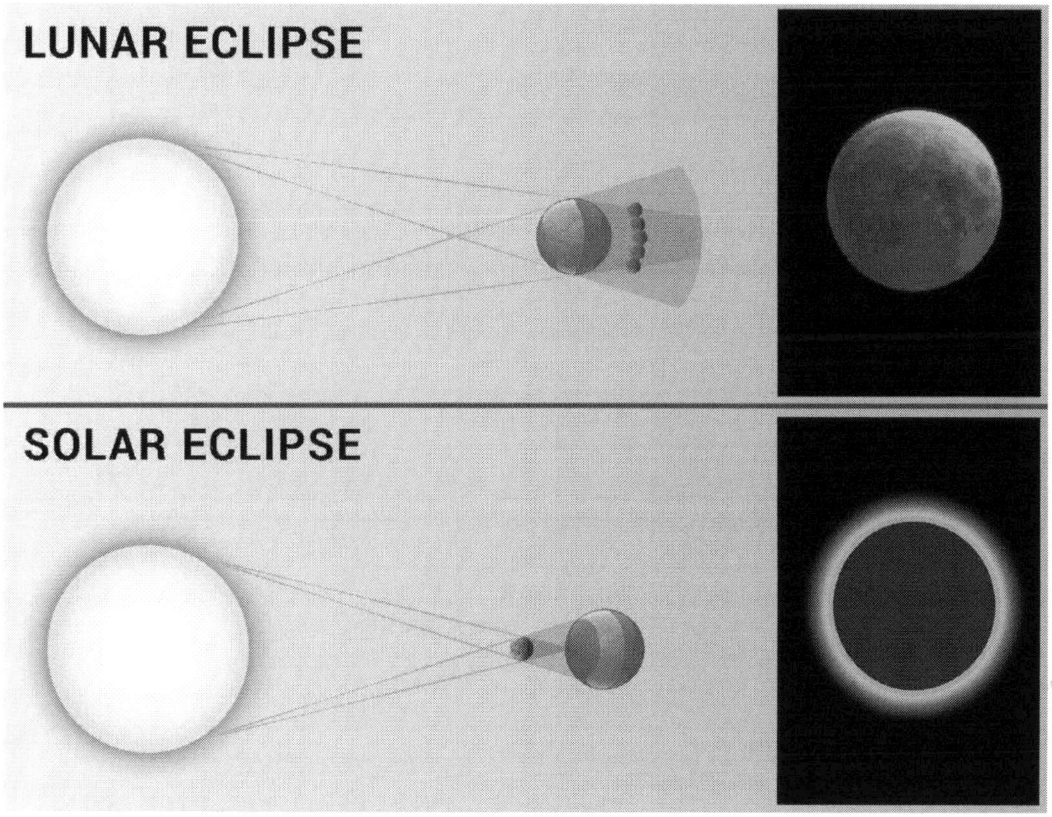

Life Science

Biology is the study of living organisms—it's the study of life. It encompasses many different areas of science, all of which fall under the category of biology or biological science, several of which are addressed in this section.

Cells

Every living thing on this planet is made of cells, either as a single cell (**unicellular**) or as a conglomerate of millions of cells (**multicellular**). In general, cells are quite similar, but they can be split into two categories: prokaryotic and eukaryotic. **Prokaryotic** cells are comparatively quite small and do not have a nucleus. **Eukaryotic** cells contain a nucleus as well as other membrane-bound organelles, which essentially have different functions within the cell and compartmentalize the cell's materials. It's generally believed that unicellular organisms can either be prokaryotic or eukaryotic, but multicellular organisms are always eukaryotic.

Prokaryotic cells include these structures:

- **Plasmids**: Small, circular pieces of DNA usually found in bacteria
- **Nucleoids**: Larger bundles of DNA
- **Ribosomes**: Protein builders (the construction workers of a cell)
- **Cytoplasm**: Thick gel-like solution that fills a cell
- **Cytoskeleton**: Filament-like skeleton that helps a cell maintain its shape
- **Plasma membrane**: The wall of the cell
- **Flagella**: Tails that whip around and help a cell move

Most of these structures are also found in eukaryotic cells and, depending on the type of eukaryotic cell, the following structures, called **organelles**, may also be present:

- **Nucleus**: Holds most a cell's DNA

- **Endoplasmic reticulum**: Tubular organelle attached to the nucleus and may have ribosomes attached to its walls. It functions like a big factory, producing proteins and lipids.

- **Golgi apparatus**: Similar to an endoplasmic reticulum, but not attached to a nucleus. Its role in a cell is to pack and transport materials in the cell.

- **Vacuoles**: Storage bubbles inside a cell

- **Mitochondria**: Small organelles that use oxidative energy to produce adenosine triphosphate (ATP), which is the energy molecule for the cell

- **Chloroplasts**: Organelles found in plants that produce ATP through the process of photosynthesis

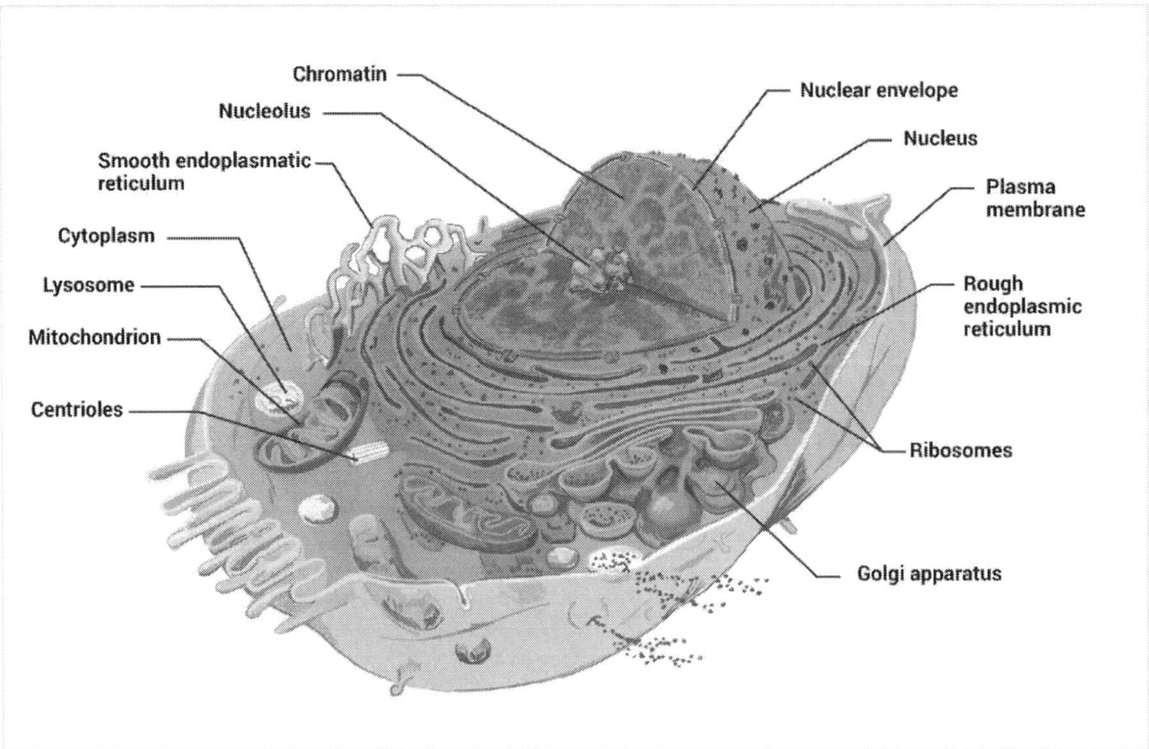

All cells contain genetic material in the form of **DNA** (deoxyribonucleic acid), and all DNA is made of the same material, although the specific arrangement of the DNA sequence can code for different genes and proteins. This is like how all books written in English have the same letters, but they can tell different stories. Prokaryotic cells hold their DNA in their cytoplasm in the form of a nucleoid. Eukaryotic cells contain most their DNA in a nucleus, and the rest can be found in either mitochondria or chloroplasts, depending on the type of cell. DNA exists inside the cell in the form of **chromosomes**, tightly wound bundles of DNA. Each species has a specific number of chromosomes that, all together, provide the blueprints that a cell requires to function, live, and reproduce. The number of chromosomes inside a cell usually dictates how it reproduces. When a cell has only one set of chromosomes, it's considered to be **haploid** and reproduces through **binary fission**. If it has two sets of chromosomes (one from each parent), it's a **diploid** and goes through **mitosis**.

Cellular Reproduction and Mitosis

All cells reproduce by division: one cell splits and becomes two, then two to four, and so on. There are two methods of cell division: binary fission and mitosis. Prokaryotic cells can do either but usually divide via binary fission; eukaryotic cells only divide through mitosis. Binary fission is simple—as the cell is haploid, it just makes a copy of its DNA and splits in two. That's why bacteria can divide so rapidly. Mitosis is more complicated because eukaryotic cells are more complex than prokaryotes. Mitosis is divided into four different phases and, when combined with interphase and cytokinesis, forms the cell cycle (a cell's life):

- **Interphase**: The longest phase of the cell cycle, it occurs when the cell is living and functioning. Interphase is further divided into phases: G1, S, and G2
    - **G1**: First gap. The cell grows and functions.
    - **S**: Synthesis. The cell continues to grow, and it begins duplicating its DNA.
    - **G2**: Second gap. The cell is still growing and starts preparing for mitosis.
    - **G0**: Some cells (like neurons) enter a phase called G0. This means that the cell leaves the cell cycle and stops dividing. But, remembering that there's never a *never* in science, some cells can leave G0 and re-enter the cell cycle at G1.
- **Mitosis**: Cellular reproduction
    - **Prophase**: DNA begins to condense into chromosomes, the nuclear envelope starts to disintegrate, and two centrosomes start to move to opposite ends of the cell and form a mitotic spindle. Centrosomes are made of centrioles and microtubules, and they coordinate microtubule placement and use them to move things around inside the cell.
    - **Metaphase**: The mitotic spindle moves to the center of the cell, and pairs of chromosomes line up along the central spindle.

- **Anaphase**: The pairs of chromosomes (sisters) start to pull apart. A cleavage furrow (groove) starts to form on the membrane/wall down the middle of the cell.

- **Telophase**: The groove gets deeper until the membrane/wall is pinched, forming two cells containing one identical copy of each chromosome. The mitotic spindle disappears, the nuclear membrane reforms, and the chromosomes unpack to make chromatin.

- **Cytokinesis**: The actual splitting of the cell and all its contents to make two cells. It's not really a phase, but rather a process that starts during and finishes at the end mitosis.

Meiosis

Meiosis, or sexual division, happens only in specialized sex cells and produces four cells called gametes. In humans, sex cells are found in the ovaries and in the testes, and are in contrast to somatic cells which constitute the rest of the body of the organism. Each gamete contains half the number of chromosomes of a normal cell, and each is said to be **haploid (n)** rather than **diploid (2n)**. In humans, a gamete has 23 chromosomes instead of the 46 which are typically found in somatic cells. The female gamete is called an *egg* and the male gamete is called a **sperm**.

Preceding meiosis, the DNA is synthesized, and the chromatin coalesces into chromosomes, as in mitosis. However, the pairs of sister chromatids that are homologous combine together, joining their centromeres into a single **chiasma** and forming a **tetrad.** At this point, sections of the different chromatids may break off and rejoin, possibly in another place. Half of a leg of one chromatid may swap with that of another chromatid; the chromatids essentially exchange some of their genes with one another. This process, called **crossing over** or *genetic* **recombination**, happens in prophase I and leads to greater genetic diversity.

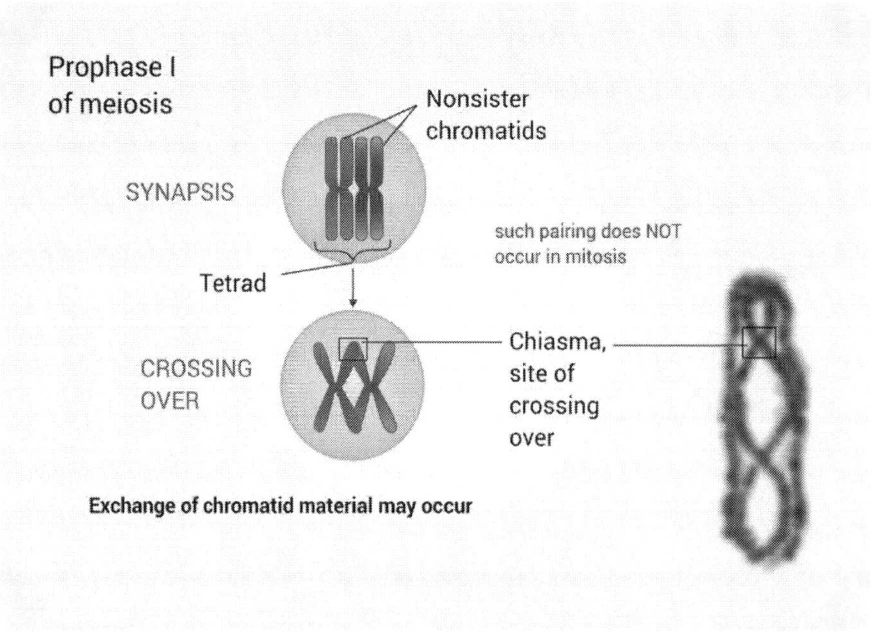

Like mitosis, meiosis is divided into stages of prophase, metaphase, anaphase, telophase, and cytokinesis. However, as the end products have half the genetic material as the end products of mitosis, another round of division, so meiosis is first partitioned into meiosis I and meiosis II, each round similar in scope to mitosis. During meiosis I, homologous chromosome pairs are separated into two daughter cells. Each daughter cell is haploid (n) because, although each cell at the end of meiosis I has 46 chromatids, half of them are duplicates of the other and not considered unique genetic material.

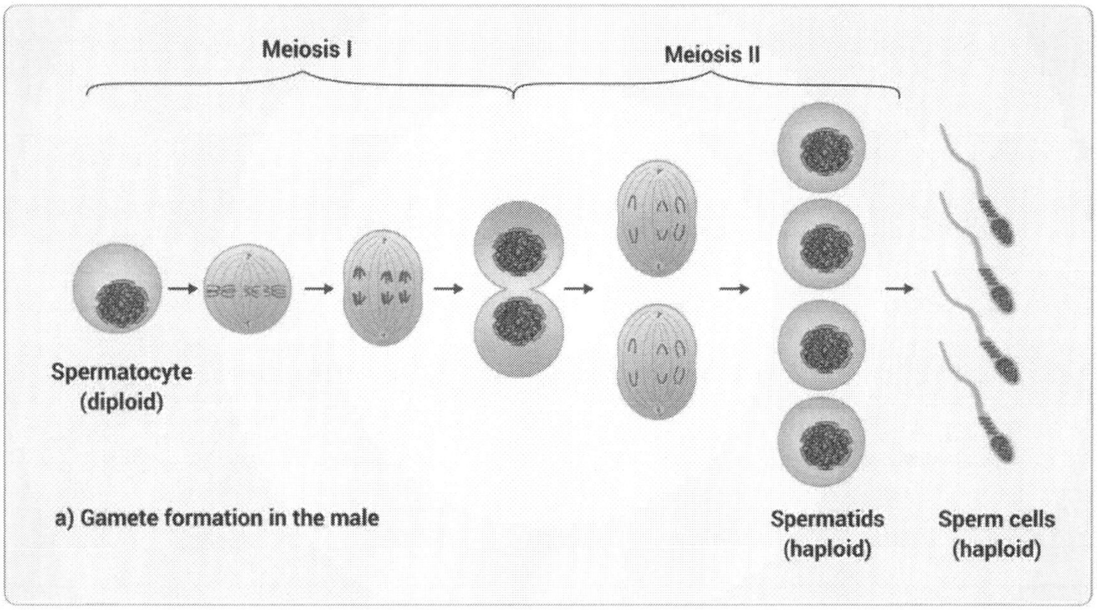

After cytokinesis I, the daughter cells immediately enter prophase II, rather than duplicating DNA or entering interphase. The nucleus disintegrates, the centrioles migrate to the ends of the cell, and the next round of divisions begins. This results in four haploid (n) daughter cells, the gametes of egg and sperm referenced earlier.

A common problem that arises in both meiosis and mitosis but is especially noticeable in meiosis is that of **nondisjunction**. Nondisjunction is the failure of homologous chromosomes or sister chromatids to separate during anaphase. This causes the daughter cells to have one more or one fewer chromosomes than usual and can ultimately result in genetic conditions like Down's syndrome when a meiotic egg with nondisjunction is fertilized.

The Cell Cycle
Here's what the cycles look like:

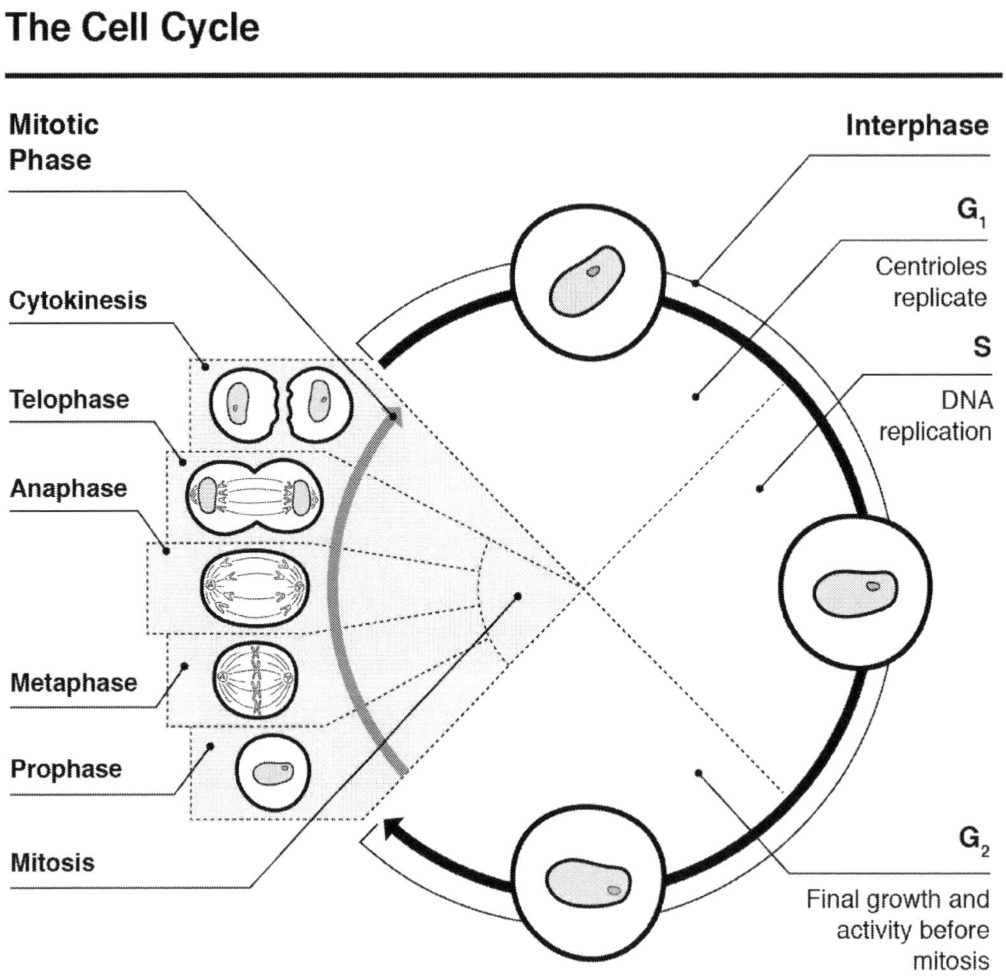

Cells of eukaryotic organisms used for sexual reproduction go through a process called meiosis. **Meiosis** only occurs in the **gametic** (sexually reproductive) cells and results in the production of sperm and oocytes (eggs). Meiosis is divided into two phases: Meiosis I and Meiosis II. Here is a timeline of meiosis in the cell cycle:

- **Interphase**: Like all other cells, contains the S-phase in which a cell duplicates its DNA.
- **Meiosis I**: Deals with homologous chromosomes (a pair containing a chromosome from each mother and father). It's further divided into phases:
    - **Prophase I**: The longest phase of meiosis
        - **Leptotene**: Chromosomes start to look like the letter "X" and consist of two sister chromatids (a chromatid is one side of the X).

  - **Zygotene**: Homologous chromosomes line up.

  - **Pachytene**: Chromosome crossover begins. This process accounts for genetic recombination, wherein fragments of the mother's and father's genes are exchanged and allows an offspring to be a thorough mix of its parents, which increases genetic diversity.

  - **Diplotene**: Homologous chromosomes start to separate from each other.

  - **Diakinesis**: The chromosomes condense further.

  - **Synchronous processes**: The two centrosomes appear and migrate to opposite sides of the cell.

- **Metaphase I**: Paired homologous chromosomes line up in the middle of the cell.
- **Anaphase I**: The pairs start to separate from one another.
- **Telophase I**: The completely separated pairs decondense, and the cell splits into two haploid cells.

- **Interkinesis or interphase II**: Rest period

- **Meiosis II**: Equational segregation, which is the splitting of sister chromatids
  - **Prophase II**: The nuclear envelope disappears, chromatids condense, and centrosomes appear.
  - **Metaphase II**: Sister chromatids line up in the middle of the cell.
  - **Anaphase II**: Sister chromatids start to separate.
  - **Telophase II**: Chromosomes are completely separated, they decondense, and the cells split (resulting in a total of four haploid cells).

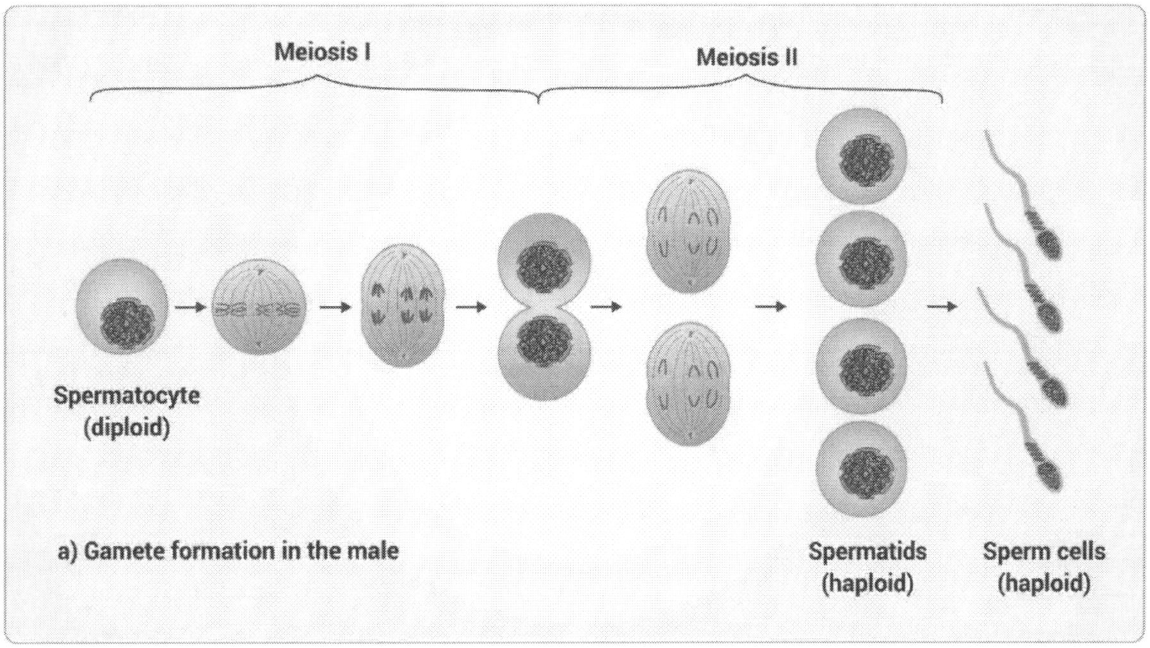

a) Gamete formation in the male

Plant and Animal Cells

The two main classes of eukaryotes are plants and animals. Although a human is noticeably different from a carrot, cells in these organisms have only a few differences. The main differences are the cell structure, appearance, and method of energy production.

Plant cells have a **cell wall** made of cellulose—a strong, fibrous material that adds bulk to stool because it's so hard to break down. This material must be strong in order to prevent the cell from bursting when water enters and increases the intracellular pressure. Animal cells don't have a cell wall. Instead, they have a **cell membrane** composed of several materials (which differ depending on cell type) embedded in a phospholipid bilayer. This bilayer is exactly what it sounds like: two layers of phospholipids stacked tail-to-tail. A **phospholipid** is a molecule with a glycerol (phosphate) head and two fatty acid (lipid) tails. This membrane is much weaker compared a plant's cellulose wall, so animal cells are much more susceptible to bursting from water pressure. And herein lies an important characteristic of the phospholipid bilayer: the tails inside the layer are actually **hydrophobic** (water-repellent) so they are able to prevent too much water from entering and killing the cell.

The shapes and sizes of plant and animal cells are also quite different. Plant cells have a consistent rectangular shape and are generally much larger, ranging from 10–100 micrometers. Animal cells vary in shape and are around 10–30 micrometers. Human liver cells (which are round) look completely different from nerve cells (which have a large cell body and long projections outward). The vacuoles are also different; plant cells tend to have just one large vacuole, while animal cells have several tiny ones.

The most important difference between plants and animals is how they create energy. Animals must consume energy from other living organisms. Plants have the amazing ability to use energy from the sun to power their growth and survival. The little organelles that make this possible are the **chloroplasts** in plants and **mitochondria** in animals. Both use carbon, oxygen, and water. Through photosynthesis, a chloroplast is able to extract carbon from the carbon dioxide (CO_2) in the air and combine it with water (H_2O) to make glucose ($C_6H_{12}O_6$) and oxygen (O_2). Glucose provides energy for animal cells. In the body, mitochondria use the energy embedded inside glucose molecules and combine them with oxygen to create carbon dioxide, water, and ATP (a form of useable energy for physiological processes). This process is called cellular respiration. Memorizing the chemical equations for these reactions may help with understanding these processes:

- **Photosynthesis**: $6\ H_2O + 6\ CO_2 + \text{sunlight} \rightarrow C_6H_{12}O_6 + 6\ O_2$
    - Six molecules of water and six of carbon dioxide make one glucose molecule and six molecules of oxygen.
- **Cellular respiration**: $C_6H_{12}O_6 + 6\ O_2 \rightarrow 6\ H_2O + 6\ CO_2 + \text{heat (energy)}$
    - Note that this is basically the reverse of photosynthesis.

Bacterial cells are a completely different story. There are a huge variety of bacteria, and they can actually share characteristics with both plant and animal cells. Some can utilize photosynthesis, some can only perform cellular respiration, and some can even do both or neither!

Photosynthesis

Photosynthesis refers to the process used by plants, some algae, and some bacteria to convert sunlight into chemical energy. It combines water and carbon dioxide using light energy to produce the sugar glucose and oxygen. Glucose is converted to adenosine triphosphate (ATP) through cellular respiration.

ATP is the molecule that provides energy for all cellular activities and can be thought of as a sort of energy currency.

Photosynthesis is the most prolific process to create useable energy for life on Earth. In plants, photosynthesis takes place in chloroplasts, organelles containing photosynthetic structures and chemicals. **Thylakoids,** the structural units of photosynthesis, are found within chloroplasts and use **chlorophyll,** a green pigment, to harness sunlight in photosynthesis.

Photosynthesis has two types of reactions: light-dependent and light-independent. Light-dependent reactions produce ATP and release oxygen into the atmosphere. Light-independent reactions utilize ATP to produce glucose.

In photosynthesis, solar energy is used to fix carbon dioxide into glucose, oxidizing water to oxygen.

$$6CO_2 + 6H_2O + Energy \rightarrow C_6H_{12}O_6 + 6O_2$$

In aerobic respiration, the opposite happens, and glucose and oxygen are broken down into carbon dioxide and water to liberate energy in the form of ATP.

$$C_6H_{12}O_6 + 6O_2 \rightarrow 6CO_2 + 6H_2O + Energy$$

Heterotrophs are organisms that eat other living things to obtain organic compounds. This is usually simplified as the thought of eating other animals for food to gain energy, as most animals are unable to produce their own food. As a result, heterotrophs are completely dependent on autotrophs and other heterotrophs as food sources. All animals are considered heterotrophs.

Autotrophs are able to fix carbon dioxide into useable organic compounds. Most of them produce their own food by harnessing the power of sunlight and employing photosynthesis. As a result, autotrophs are not dependent on other organisms for sources of carbon. All plants are considered autotrophs.

Cellular Respiration

Cellular respiration is the pathway used by cells to release energy stored in food molecules. It culminates in the production of ATP (adenosine triphosphate), which is the energy currency for all cellular activities.

The two types of cellular respiration are aerobic respiration and anaerobic respiration. Aerobic respiration requires oxygen while anaerobic respiration does not, but aerobic respiration produces significantly more ATP and is the principal mode of respiration carried out by human cells.

In aerobic respiration, a molecule of glucose is broken down in the cytoplasm into pyruvate during **glycolysis** before further being broken down to a pair of carbon atoms called an **acetyl group**. This acetyl group is ferried by acetyl coenzyme A to the mitochondria where it enters the **Krebs cycle** (also known as the **tricaboxylic acid cycle** and the **TCA cycle**). In the Krebs cycle, the acetyl group is further broken down into carbon dioxide ($C_2 \rightarrow CO_2$) while the energy of its bonds are translated into molecules of NADH (reduced nicotinamide adenine dinucleotide).

These molecules of NADH are the source of electrons and hydrogen ions that are used in the last phase of aerobic respiration to generate ATP so that the energy from the sugar can actually be used. The electrons and hydrogens from the NADH enter the **electron transport chain** (also called the ETC or

oxidative phosphorylation) where many complicated reactions occur before finally reducing oxygen to water ($O_2 \rightarrow H_2O$).

If no oxygen is available, aerobic respiration can't continue to completion. The cell stops aerobic respiration after the glucose is broken down to pyruvate, and instead converts it to lactate (or lactic acid). This is **fermentation,** and it generates ATP, but it does so only at a much lower rate than aerobic respiration. Because it doesn't use oxygen, fermentation is a type of anaerobic respiration. Many types of bacteria use it as their primary source of energy, but it is also a last defense for human cells when deprived of oxygen for long periods of time.

Genetics

Genetics is the study of how living organisms pass down traits to their offspring and future generations. It all starts with **DNA**—the universal language of genetic information. An organism's physical features and cellular instructions are written as **genes**, which are single units of genetic information that are stored in every cell as a set of chromosomes.

The discovery of DNA is usually credited to two scientists, Francis Crick and James Watson. However, before them, in 1869 at the University of Tübingen, Friedrich Miescher became the first person to ever identify and isolate DNA from a cell; at that time, he called it **nuclein**. In 1952, a doctoral student named Raymond Gosling was able to take an x-ray diffraction image of DNA known as **photograph 51**, famous for inspiring Watson and Crick. From that photograph, they were able to deduce the information needed to develop their model of DNA. In 1953, they correctly postulated that DNA has a double-helical structure and that it carried the genetic information. Watson and Crick won the Nobel Prize in Physiology or Medicine in 1962.

A **double helix** looks like a twisted ladder; it is twisted to save space. When looking at DNA, the side rails of the ladder are considered the backbones, and the rungs are pairs of nitrogenous bases. Each backbone is a string of sugars and phosphates covalently bonded together. By contrast, the bonds between paired bases is quite weak—they are attached via hydrogen bonds. If DNA is broken down into its building blocks, a pile of nucleotides is acquired. A single **nucleotide** contains one five-carbon sugar (pentose) and one phosphate group (backbone components) attached to a nitrogenous base (one half of a rung). So, if all the pieces of DNA look so similar, how can it vary enough to provide all the information needed to create a living organism?

The answer comes from the **nitrogenous bases**; the order in which the bases are placed in a DNA strand provides specific information. Here's the unbelievable part: There are only four different bases for DNA. That means a person's entire genetic code, along with every other single organism that has ever lived, is written with just four letters! It's important to note that human DNA is a combination of about 3 billion bases, and different species can have different DNA lengths.

The two types of nitrogenous bases—the **purines** and the **pyrimidines** (along with an easy mnemonic to memorize which base belongs to each group) —are as follows:

- **Purine** – PURe *A*s *G*old
  - Adenine (A)
  - Guanine (G)
- **Pyrimidines – Sharp PYRamids *CUT***
  - Cytosine (C)
  - Thymine (T)
  - Uracil (U) doesn't contribute to DNA—it's the fifth base found only in RNA

When double-stranded DNA forms, the unique order of bases is preserved because each purine can only form a hydrogen bond with a specific pyrimidine. When looking at the paired bases in each rung of the ladder, the only two pairs are A – T and G – C.

Here's a simplified example of a short segment of double-stranded DNA (dsDNA):

`5′- ATCGTTTGAGCACTAGCG -3′` (strand #1)

`3′- TAGCAAACTCGTGATCGC -5′` (strand #2)

Note how As are always present across Ts and Gs across Cs. Before DNA gets replicated, the two strands have to separate, creating this:

`5′- ATCGTTTGAGCACTAGCG -3′` (strand #1) + `3′- TAGCAAACTCGTGATCGC -5′` (strand #2)

Replication involves grabbing unattached nucleotide bases and pairing them appropriately, creating this:

`5′- ATCGTTTGAGCTCTAGCG -3′` (strand #1)   `3′- TAGCAAACTCGTGATCGC -5′` (strand #2)

`3′- TAGCAAACTCGAGATCGC -5′` (new strand) + `5′- ATCGTTTGAGCACTAGCG -3′` (new strand)

The two products are completely identical to the original (the one on the right just needs to be flipped so that the new strand is on top). The designations 5′ and 3′ provide a sense of direction when dealing with DNA. In organic chemistry, the nucleotide sugar ring's carbon atoms are numbered. When looking at strand #1 above, 5′ on the left and 3′ on the right means the sugars of that strand are connected with the 5th carbons on the left and the 3rd carbons are on the right. Moving toward the 5′ end is called upstream and going toward the 3′ is downstream. All of this is important because when cells replicate DNA, the new strand is created in a 5′ to 3′ direction (the 5′ carbon has a phosphate group that provides the energy to form a covalent bond with the hydroxyl group on the 3′ carbon). The 5′ end is considered the "head" and the 3′ end is the "tail" of the strand.

Remember:

- **Upstream**: Move from 3′ to 5′ (going up in #).
- **Downstream**: Move from 5′ to 3′ (going down in #).
- **Replication**: Read upstream, create downstream.

The collection of genes within an individual organism is called the **genotype**. Not all genes are expressed (recessive genes can be overpowered by dominant ones), and the physical manifestation of those genes is called a **phenotype**. The variations of genes are called **alleles**. The specific location of a gene sequence is referred to as a gene's **locus**.

An easy example for these terms is eye color. Everybody possesses a gene that dictates eye color. Each color is a different allele. If a boy received one blue eye allele and one brown eye allele from his mother and father, and the boy has brown eyes, that means he is phenotypically brown-eyed. It doesn't mean he doesn't have the allele for blue eyes; the blue-eye allele just isn't physically manifested. In this fictitious example, the gene for brown eyes is dominant while that for blue eyes is recessive, so brown eyes get expressed.

Humans have 23 pairs of chromosomes, one set from a father and one from a mother, giving each person pairs of the same allele or gene trait. That's called Mendel's first law of segregation. When studying genetics, an allele is represented by uppercase or lowercase letter depending on which trait is being studied. An uppercase letter means that allele is dominant, and a lowercase letter represents a recessive trait. In the eye color example, "B" represents brown eyes and "b" is blue eyes (because it's recessive). If, for simplicity, these are the only two alleles available, then the only possible pairs are BB, Bb, and bb. When a brown-eyed father (he happens to be Bb) and a blue-eyed mother (as blue eyes are recessive, she must be bb) have a child, they each give one of their two alleles. Mendel's second law of independent assortment dictates that each parent has a 50% chance of passing down either allele. The only exception to this law is if two genes are linked, which means that they are inherited together and don't follow proper segregation rules.

A Punnett square can be used to illustrate the possible combinations:

	Mom b	**Mom b**
Dad B	Bb	Bb
Dad b	bb	bb

The top row has the mother's alleles and the left column has the father's. The shaded squares represent the possible combinations offspring can be born with. If the child ended up getting a "b" from both parents, giving it bb, it is a **homozygous** pair. In this case, it would be recessive (blue eyes). If the child received Bb, its genotype would be considered **heterozygous**, and the child would have brown eyes because the brown-eyed gene (B) would dominate the blue-eyed gene (b).

Organism Classification

Biological classification, or taxonomy, is the science of grouping organisms based on common characteristics. The father of modern taxonomy is the Swedish botanist Carl Linnaeus. There are eight levels of organization in the biological classification system including:

- Domain: Domains classify organisms by common characteristics such as cellular chemistry and structure. The concept of domains was introduced by Carl Woese in the late 1970s, but not widely adopted by biologists until 1990. The three domains are Bacteria, Eukarya, and Archaea.
- Kingdom: Kingdoms group organisms according to nutritional strategies and developmental features. Most scientists recognize five kingdoms: *Animalia*, *Plantae*, *Monera*, *Protista*, and *Fungi*. However, since the two divisions of *Monera* (*Bacteria* and *Archaea*) are treated as their own domains, this organizational scheme is under fire. Additionally, scientists have recently begun debates over the inclusion of viruses as a separate domain.
- Phylum: Within the animal kingdom, phyla of note include *Chordata*, *Mollusca*, *Cnidaria* (jellyfish), *Porifera* (sponges), and *Arthropoda* (insects).
- Class: Within the phylum *Chordata*, classes of note include *Chondrichthyes* (bony fish), *Amphibia*, *Reptilia*, *Aves*, and *Mammalia*. These classes also fall in the subphylum *Vertebrata*, which is distinguished by its unique notochord, dorsal hollow nerve cord, pharyngeal slits, and post-anal tail.
- Order: Within the class *Mammalia*, orders of note include *Lagomorpha* (rabbits), *Rodentia*, *Carnivora*, *Chiroptera* (bats), and *Primates*. It also includes the monotremes (like platypi and echidnas) and the marsupials (like opossums and kangaroos). This class is specially known for its teeth's enamel coating and the presence of a middle ear to sense sound.
- Family: Within the order *Primates*, the most commonly known family is *Hominidae*, to which the great apes and humans belong. This order is typically divided into the prosimians and anthropoids, and it includes monkeys, lemurs, and gibbons.
- Genus: Within the family *Hominidae*, there are four genera which encompass orangutans, gorillas, chimpanzees, and humans. Humans belong to the genus *Homo*.
- Species: Finally, within the genus *Homo*, humans are recognized by the species *sapiens*, but modern humans are further specified by the subspecies *sapiens* again. By conventional reference, modern humans are classified as *Homo sapiens sapiens*.

Moving down the list, each subsequent level becomes more specific. Each organism receives a scientific two-part name, referred to as binomial nomenclature. The first part of the name is the genus and the first letter is capitalized, while the second part of the name is the species and the first letter is lowercased. By convention, the name must be Latin and italicized. The two-part name may also be abbreviated by shortening the genus to its first letter with a period coming after. For example, the scientific two-part name for humans is *Homo sapiens* (abbreviated *H. sapiens*). Biological classification has been practiced for more than 300 years and is constantly evolving.

Anatomy

Anatomy is the science of the structure and parts of organisms. This guide focuses on human anatomy. Although people have studied the human body for hundreds of years, doctors and scientists are still trying to answer many questions. How exactly does the brain work? Why are cancer cells more likely to appear in specific populations? What makes a cell decide to be a liver cell instead of a neuron during development?

While the human body and a car look nothing alike, they are actually somewhat similar. A person is basically a machine. They both have systems or components that, when put together, can consume fuel and perform work or movement. The human body can be divided into ten different systems:

Cardiovascular/Circulatory System

The **cardiovascular/circulatory system** consists of the heart, blood (which carries nutrients and waste), and blood vessels. The heart's job is to pump oxygenated blood to the rest of the body through blood vessels called arteries. **Exchange** (delivering nutrients and extracting waste) at the tissues occurs in capillaries, which are the smallest blood vessels. When the body has used the oxygenated blood, it returns to the heart via vessels called veins. The heart can then circulate it through the lungs to be re-oxygenated. There are four special chambers of the heart, and each has its own role. They are:

- **Right atrium**: Collects de-oxygenated blood returning from the body and holds it until the right ventricle is ready.
- **Right ventricle**: Receives blood from the right atrium and pumps it into the lungs to re-oxygenate it.
- **Left atrium**: Collects oxygenated blood from the lungs and holds it until the left ventricle is ready.
- **Left ventricle**: The most powerful chamber of the heart, the left ventricle receives blood from the left atrium and pumps it around the body. It must be strong in order to achieve the high pressure needed to circulate blood throughout the body.

Along with oxygen, blood (which consists of plasma, red blood cells, white blood cells, and platelets) carries nutrients and waste products through the body. The average adult has around five liters of blood in the body and, in a healthy individual at rest, that volume can be circulated through the body every minute! There are two special systems within the circulatory system called the hepatic and hypophyseal portal systems. They are special in that they are veins that carry deoxygenated blood to an organ other than the heart. The **hepatic portal** carries highly nutritional blood from the digestive system to the liver for processing before returning to the heart. The **hypophyseal portal** carries specific hormones between the hypothalamus and pituitary within the brain, so that these hormones don't need to travel through the rest of the body before reaching their destination.

Digestive System

The **digestive system** manages food consumption and processing, from chewing to nutrient absorption and defecation. Although the digestive system is inside the body, it is considered to be an open system because it's technically exposed to the outside (an uncut string can be seen from mouth to anus if a person swallowed it). This system consists of the mouth, throat, esophagus, stomach, small and large intestines, and anus. The mouth roughly chews or breaks down food with the teeth, tongue, and saliva so that it can move to the stomach via the esophagus. The stomach's job is to further break down the food so the intestines can absorb it. The small intestines are (from stomach to large intestine) the duodenum, jejunum, and ileum. Most nutrients are absorbed in the small intestine. The large intestine—consisting of the colon, rectum, and anus—absorbs any remaining nutrients and eliminates waste.

Endocrine System

The **endocrine system** is the hormonal or glandular system of the body. Organ systems communicate with each another via hormones that travel in the bloodstream. This system is vital for maintaining homeostasis (equilibrium of the body). Like the circulatory system, it is intimately involved with all other systems of the body. The endocrine system consists of the hypothalamus, pancreas, ovaries, testes, gastrointestinal tract, and the adrenal, parathyroid, pineal, pituitary, and thyroid glands. These organs are all endocrine glands (they secrete into the blood), which differ from exocrine glands, which secrete outside the body (such as sweat and salivary glands). An example of a vital hormone is epinephrine or adrenaline, which is excreted by the adrenal glands atop the kidneys. When people feel danger, increased adrenaline can aid chances of survival by making them alert and increasing blood flow to muscles for quick actions.

Integumentary System

The **integumentary system** is the skin and all things contained within it (hair, nails, sensory receptors, and sweat and oil glands). The skin is the largest organ of the human body, and its main function is to protect everything inside, much like the chassis of a car protects its passengers. Skin also cushions the body, excretes waste, and regulates body temperature. It is composed of the epidermis (the outer layer), dermis, and hypodermis. The epidermis is composed of cells called keratinocytes (making it waterproof) and melanocytes (the cells that give a person a tan or dark color). At the base of the epidermis is a layer of basal cells, which replicate to form the epidermis. The dermis, or middle layer, is composed of connective tissue and holds the sweat and oil glands, touch and temperature sensors, and hair follicles. The hypodermis, also known as the subcutaneous layer, provides cushioning and contains fat, nerves, and blood vessels.

Immune/Lymphatic System

The **immune** and **lymphatic system** work together to fight off and clean out elements that are potentially harmful to the body; they consist of white blood cells, lymph nodes, lymphatic vessels, and select organs such as the spleen. Lymphatic vessels are similar to veins, but instead of carrying blood, they carry waste fluid from the body. Along these vessels are lymph nodes that hold white blood cells, which protect the body from foreign invaders. There are five types of white blood cells: monocytes, neutrophils, lymphocytes (includes B-cells and T-cells), eosinophils, and basophils. Monocytes and neutrophils eat and destroy invaders like bacteria and viruses. Lymphocytes (B-cells) produce antibodies to protect the body from infections.

Musculoskeletal System

The **musculoskeletal system** contains the muscles, skeleton, cartilage, tendons, and ligaments. In addition to enabling movement, it protects vital organs, such as the heart and lungs inside the ribcage and the brain inside the skull. An adult skeleton has 206 bones, which are classified as long, short, flat, irregular, or sesamoid (small and sesame seed-like) bones. Bones are connected at joints like the elbow or knee. The connective tissue joining bone to bone is called a ligament. A tendon is connective tissue that links muscle to bone. Cartilage is a material that lines a joint to provide cushioning and reduces friction during movement; it also forms structural components of certain tissues like the eyes. Other vital roles of the skeletal system are storing calcium for the body and holding marrow, where red and white blood cells are produced.

Nervous System

The **nervous system** is the body's brain and nerves, similar to a modern car's onboard computer. It's split into two parts: the **central nervous system** (CNS) and **peripheral nervous system** (PNS). The CNS consists of the brain and spinal cord. The brain allows for thought, memory, and emotion. It also provides the electrical impulses that tell the rest of the body what to do. It sends and receives these electrical signals to the body via the PNS. The nervous system is also divided into the **somatic** (voluntary) and **autonomic** (involuntary) divisions based on function. The somatic nervous system contains the nerves and parts of the brain that control voluntary movement. The autonomic system consists of the sympathetic and parasympathetic nervous systems, the "fight or flight" and "rest and digest" systems, respectively.

Renal/Urinary System

The **renal/urinary system** consists of the kidneys, ureters, bladder, and urethra. The kidneys filter excess water and waste—such as ammonia—from the blood to make urine, which travels to the bladder through a tube called the ureter. From the bladder, urine is excreted from the body via the urethra. Although people are normally born with two kidneys, it is possible to survive with just one.

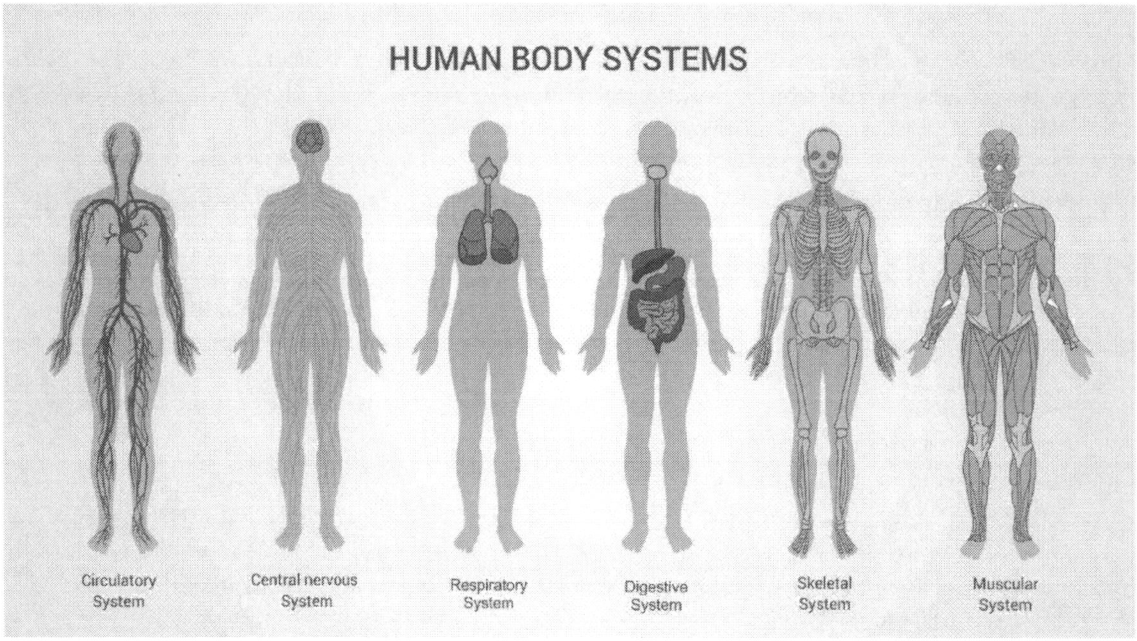

Reproductive System

Consisting of the sex organs, the **reproductive system** is the only system that differs in males and females. Males have a penis, prostate, and scrotum containing the testes. Females have a vagina, cervix, uterus, ovaries, fallopian tubes, and mammary glands (in the breasts). Aside from producing and protecting sperm and oocytes (eggs) for reproduction, testes and ovaries make the hormones (testosterone and estrogen) essential for the development of male and female secondary sexual characteristics, such as the Adam's apple and breasts. Sex cells replicate via meiosis, creating haploid cells. When a sperm cell fertilizes an oocyte, the two haploid sets of chromosomes create a diploid set, which develops into a baby.

Pulmonary/Respiratory System

Comprised of the nose, mouth, throat, trachea, lungs, and diaphragm, the **pulmonary/respiratory system** facilitates the exchange of gases—mainly carbon dioxide and oxygen—in a process called

respiration. Oxygen-rich air enters the nose and mouth and travels down the trachea to the lungs. Structures within the lungs called alveoli (air sacs) allow red blood cells to exchange the carbon dioxide produced by the body with oxygen through diffusion. By themselves, the lungs are unable to actively expand or contract to pull in and expel air (ventilate). The actual work is done by the diaphragm, a layer of muscle that makes up the floor of the chest cavity that holds the heart and lungs. When a person inhales, the diaphragm contracts and straightens, which creates negative pressure inside the pleural cavity and pulls the lungs open to draw in air from the environment. During exhalation, the diaphragm relaxes and moves up into the chest cavity, which releases the negative pleural pressure and allows the lungs to expel air. Breathing is an involuntary process, meaning that it is controlled by the autonomic nervous system—specifically an area of the brain called the brain stem.

Biological Relationships

The study of biological relationships is called **ecology**, which explores how organisms affect one another. These relationships can be defined as either **intraspecific** (within the same species) or **interspecific** (between different species) interactions. For example, a man being friendly to his neighbor can be considered an intraspecific interaction, while a man interacting with a dog is an interspecific interaction. These can also be categorized in terms of the effects they have on participating organisms:

- **Competition**: This is the basis for natural selection or survival of the fittest. Competition occurs when the organisms' interactions are mutually harmful, as they compete with one another in order to benefit themselves.
- **Amensalism**: Occurs when an organism harms another, but the organism inflicting harm does not benefit from the interaction.
- **Antagonism**: One individual or species hunts another (inflicting harm) for the benefit of food. The harmed species is not working toward the same goal, differentiating amensalism from competition. Classic examples of antagonism are predation and parasitism.
- **Neutralism**: Occurs when different individuals or species interact with one another and neither species is harmed or benefits from the relationship.
- **Facilitation**: Describes interactions in which one participant benefits without harming the other.
    - **Commensalism**: Occurs when only one participant receives benefit from the interaction.
    - **Mutualism**: Occurs when both parties benefit from the interaction.
- **Symbiosis**: A close mutualistic relationship between organisms of different species. A popular example is the relationship between a clown fish and a sea anemone. The clown fish cleans the sea anemone, and in return, it is protected from predators by the anemone's stinging arms.

Another large area of ecological studies is the **food chain**—the network of links between organisms. Producer organisms like grass or algae make up the bottom of the chain, while the top is comprised of apex predators such as lions and tigers. The food chain is useful for depicting the flow of energy, or nutrition, from bottom to top.

Terms commonly used while discussing the food chain include:

- **Autotroph**: A producer in the food chain with the ability to produce organic compounds from the environment. Photosynthetic plants are examples of autotrophs.
- **Heterotroph**: A consumer in the food chain that must consume organic materials to thrive. Humans are examples of heterotrophs.
- **Lithotroph**: An organism with the ability to use inorganic material to survive. Lithotrophs are exclusively microbes, such as those that survive deep underwater, where they utilize inorganic sulfur that escapes from volcanic vents.

Biological Concepts

Biological concepts include all the terms discussed in earlier sections concerning biology, as well as:

- **Territoriality**: The behavior of an organism that claims a specific sociographical area/location and defends it, usually because its food or sexual mates are in that area.
- **Community**: A collection of individual organisms living and interacting within a specific area.
- **Niche**: The role of a species in a community.
- **Dominance**: Refers to the most prevalent species in a community.
- **Altruism**: A biological interaction in which one individual or species provides benefit to another at a cost to itself. A wealthy man is considered altruistic when he donates money to the poor.
- **Threat display**: Behavior of an organism with the intent to scare other individuals.
- **Competitive exclusion**: Also called Gause's Law, which dictates that when two species within the same community are competing for the same resource, they cannot stably coexist. In other words, one will dominate the other.
- **Species diversity**: Refers to the number of different species in a community.
- **Biotic**: Living organisms in a community, such as other species.
- **Abiotic**: Non-living factors such as terrain and weather.
- **Ecosystem**: Encompasses a community and all its environmental factors.
- **Biomass**: Mass of organic matter within an ecosystem.
- **Mimicry**: An organism that adapts the appearance or actions of a different species in order to avoid predators or harm.

Chemistry

Atomic Structure

Atoms are made up of three subatomic particles: protons, neutrons, and electrons. The **protons** have a positive charge and are located in the nucleus of the atom. **Neutrons** have a neutral charge and are also located in the nucleus. **Electrons** have a negative charge, are the smallest of the three particles, and are located in orbitals that surround the nucleus in a cloud. An atom is neutral if it has an equal number of electrons and protons. If an atom does not have an equal number of electrons and protons, it is an **ion**. When there are fewer electrons than protons, leaving it with a positive charge, it is termed a **cation**. When there are more electrons than protons, leaving a negative charge, it is an **anion**.

There are many levels of orbitals that surround the nucleus and house electrons. Each orbital has a distinct shape and three quantum numbers that characterize it: n, l, and m_l. The n is the principal quantum number and is always a positive integer, or whole number. As n increases, the size of the orbital increases, and the electrons are less tightly bound to the nucleus because they are further away. The angular momentum quantum number is represented by l and defines the shape of the orbital. There are four numerical values of l that correspond to four letter representations of the orbital: 0 or s, 1 or p, 2 or d, and 3 or f. Lastly, m_l represents the magnetic quantum number and describes the orientation of the orbital in space. It has a value in between -1 and 1, including zero.

Electrons exist outside the nucleus in energy levels, and with each increasing period, there is an additional energy level. Hydrogen and helium are the only elements that have only one energy level, which is an s orbital, which can only hold two electrons. Their relative electron configurations are $1s^1$ and $1s^2$. Each orbital holds two electrons with opposite spins.

Energy level two can hold a total of eight electrons: two in the s orbital, and six in the p orbital, of which there are three, since electrons pair up: $p_xp_yp_z$. All alkali metals and alkali Earth metals have an electron configuration that ends in either s^1 or s^2. For example, magnesium ends in $3s^s$ and cesium ends in $6s^1$. Groups 3A to 8A all end in the Xp^y configuration, with X representing the energy level and y representing how for inland it is. For example, oxygen is $2p^4$. The third energy level has s, p, and d orbitals, and together can hold 18 electrons, since d can hold 10. D orbitals start with the transition metals, and even though it appears that they are in the fourth energy level, they actually are on the third. The energy level for the whole d block is actually the period number minus one. For example:

Mn: $1s^22s^22p^63s^23p^64s^23d^5$

The f block, which can hold 14 electrons, has a similar pattern for its period number, except two is subtracted from the period number instead of one.

Periodic Table

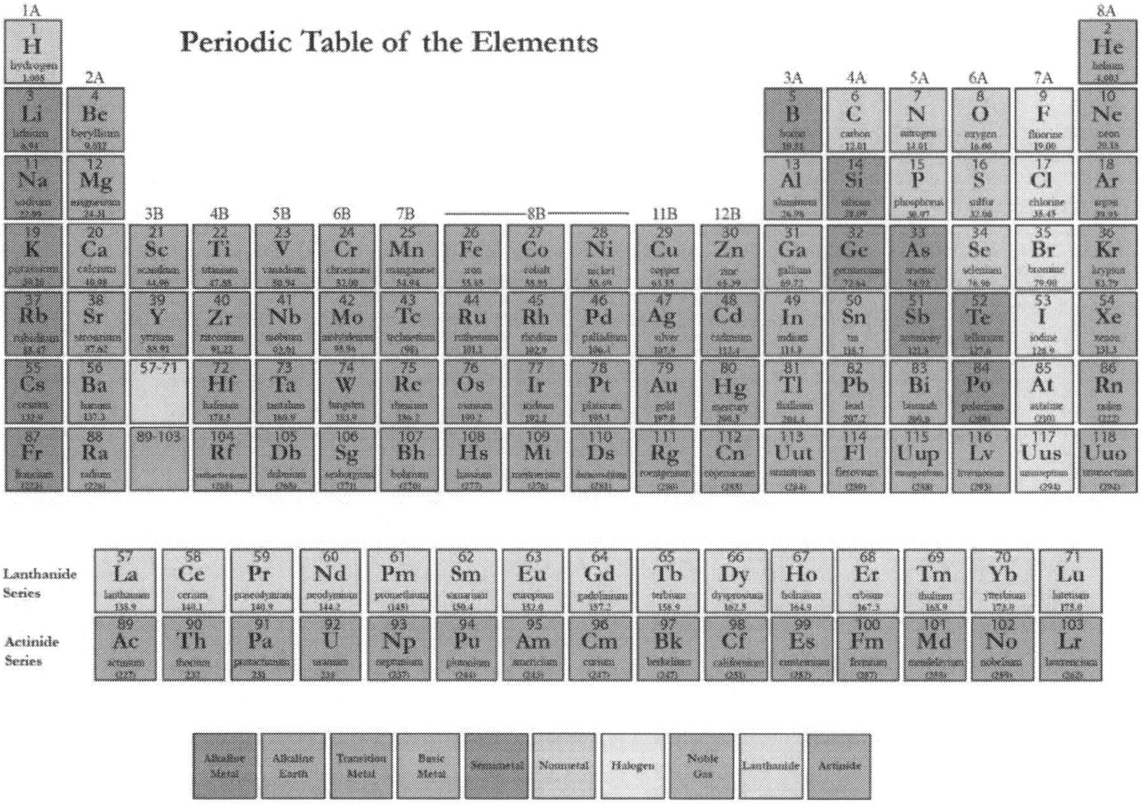

The **periodic table** is a chart of all 118 known elements. The elements are organized according to their quantity of protons (also known as their atomic number), their electron configurations, and their chemical properties. The rows are called periods, and the columns are called groups. Elements in a given group have similar chemical behaviors. For example, Group 8A is the noble gases, and because their outer electron shell is full, they are non-reactive. The closer the element is to having a full set of valence electrons, the more reactive it is. Group 1, the alkali metals, and Group 7, the halogens, are both highly reactive for that reason. The alkali metals form **cations** and lose their lone electron while halogens pick up an electron and become **anions**.

In each box in the period table, an element's symbol is the abbreviation in the center, and its full name is located directly below that. The number in the top left corner is the atomic number, and the atomic mass of the element is the number underneath the name. The atomic mass of the element is noted in atomic mass units, or amu, which represents the number of protons and neutrons combined. The number of protons defines the element, but the mass number can be different due to the existence of elements with a varying number of neutrons, which are called isotopes. The amu shown on the periodic table is a weighted mass (based on abundance) of all known isotopes of a particular element.

Chemical Bonds Between Atoms

Chemical bonds refer to the manner in which atoms are attached to one another. Atoms may be held together with three fundamental types of chemical bonds—ionic, covalent, or hydrogen.

Ionic Bonding

In an **ionic bond,** an atom loses one or more electrons to another who gains them. The atoms do this so that they can achieve a full outermost shell of electrons, which is the configuration with the lowest amount of energy, and these are typically the strongest types of bonds. Ionic bonds typically occur in metals and nonmetals to form salts like $MgCl_2$ and BF_3. When an atom has a different number of electrons than its number of protons, it is termed an **ion.** A positively charged ion is referred to as a **cation,** while a negatively charged ion is referred to as an **anion.** For example, a sodium cation (Na^{+1}) can form an ionic bond to a chlorine anion (Cl^{-1}) to form sodium chloride (NaCl), which is also known as table salt. The majority of the molecules formed with ionic bonds such as this have a crystalline structure.

Covalent Bonding

In a **covalent bond**, two or more atoms share one or more electrons. Covalent bonds are the most plentiful type of bond making up the human body. They are typically found in molecules containing carbon. Only six elements typically form covalent bonds: carbon (C), nitrogen (N), phosphorus (P), oxygen (O), sulfur (S), and hydrogen (H). Covalent bonds are a crucial source of energy for living organisms. Covalent bonds are comparable in strength to ionic bonds, but stronger than hydrogen bonds, and are typically used to bind the basic macromolecules—carbohydrates, lipids, nucleic acids, and proteins—together.

Hydrogen Bonding

Hydrogen bonds are temporary and weak. They typically occur between two partial, opposite electrical charges. For example, hydrogen bonds form when a hydrogen (H) atom in the vicinity of nitrogen (N), fluorine (F), or oxygen (O) atoms. These partial electrical charges are called **dipoles,** and are caused by the unequal sharing of electrons between covalent bonds. Water is the most prevalent molecule that forms hydrogen bonds.

Hydrogen bonds contribute to the adhesiveness and cohesiveness properties of molecules like water. Adhesiveness confers glue-like properties to molecules which ensure they stick or connect more easily with other molecules, similar to wetting a suction cup before sticking it to a surface. Cohesiveness refers to a molecule's ability to form hydrogen bonds with itself. For example, the cohesiveness of water is the reason why it has a high boiling point, which is a physical property.

Acids and Bases

Acids and bases are defined in many different ways. An **acid** can be described as a substance that increases the concentration of H^+ ions when it is dissolved in water, as a proton donor in a chemical equation, or as an electron-pair acceptor. A **base** can be a substance that increases the concentration of OH^- ions when it is dissolved in water, accepts a proton in a chemical reaction, or is an electron-pair donor.

Autoionization of Water

Water can act as either an acid or a base. When mixed with an acid, water can accept a proton and become an H_3O^+ ion. When mixed with a base, water can donate a proton and become an OH^- ion. Sometimes water molecules donate and accept protons from each other; this process is called **autoionization**. The chemical equation is written as follows: $H_2O + H_2O \rightarrow OH^- + H_3O^+$.

PH Scale

The **pH scale** is a numeric scale that determines whether a solution is acidic, basic, or neutral. The pH of a solution is equal to the inverse base 10 logarithm of its activity of H^+ ions ($pH = \log_{10}(1/(H^+ \text{ activity}))$).

Solutions with a pH value greater than seven are considered basic and those with a pH value less than seven are considered acidic. Pure water is neutral and has a pH of 7.0.

Strength of Acids and Bases

Acids and bases are characterized as strong, weak, or somewhere in between. Strong acids and bases completely or almost completely ionize in an aqueous solution. The chemical reaction is driven completely forward, to the right side of the equation, where the acidic or basic ions are formed. Weak acids and bases do not completely disassociate in an aqueous solution. They only partially ionize and the solution becomes a mixture of the acid or base, water, and the acidic or basic ions. Strong acids are complemented by weak bases, and vice versa. A conjugate acid is an ion that forms when its base pair gains a proton. For example, the conjugate acid NH_4^+ is formed from the base NH_3. The conjugate base that pairs with an acid is the ion that is formed when an acid loses a proton. NO_2^- is the conjugate base of the acid HNO_2.

Chemical Reactions

Types of Chemical Reactions

Chemical reactions are characterized by a chemical change in which the starting substances, or **reactants**, differ from the substances formed, or **products**. Chemical reactions may involve a change in color, the production of gas, the formation of a precipitate, or changes in heat content. The following are the five basic types of chemical reactions:

- **Decomposition Reactions**: A compound is broken down into smaller elements. For example, $2H_2O \rightarrow 2H_2 + O_2$. This is read as, "2 molecules of water decompose into 2 molecules of hydrogen and 1 molecule of oxygen."

- **Synthesis Reactions**: Two or more elements or compounds are joined together. For example, $2H_2 + O_2 \rightarrow 2H_2O$. This is read as, "2 molecules of hydrogen react with 1 molecule of oxygen to produce 2 molecules of water."

- **Single Displacement Reactions**: A single element or ion takes the place of another element in a compound. It is also known as a substitution reaction. For example, $Zn + 2\ HCl \rightarrow ZnCl_2 + H_2$. This is read as, "zinc reacts with 2 molecules of hydrochloric acid to produce one molecule of zinc chloride and one molecule of hydrogen." In other words, zinc replaces the hydrogen in hydrochloric acid.

- **Double Displacement Reactions**: Two elements or ions exchange a single element to form two different compounds, resulting in different combinations of cations and anions in the final compounds. It is also known as a metathesis reaction. For example, H_2SO_4 + 2 NaOH → $Na_2\ SO_4$ + 2 H_2O
    - Special types of double displacement reactions include:
        - **Oxidation-Reduction (or Redox) Reactions**: Elements undergo a change in oxidation number. For example, 2 $S_2O_3^{2-}$ (aq) + I_2 (aq) → $S_4O_6^{2-}$ (aq) + 2 I^- (aq).
        - **Acid-Base Reactions**: Involves a reaction between an acid and a base, which produces a salt and water. For example, HBr + NaOH → NaBr + H_2O.
        - **Combustion Reactions**: A hydrocarbon (a compound composed of only hydrogen and carbon) reacts with oxygen (O_2) to form carbon dioxide (CO_2) and water (H_2O). For example, CH_4 + $2O_2$ → CO_2 + $2H_2O$.

Balancing Chemical Reactions

Chemical reactions are conveyed using chemical equations. **Chemical equations** must be balanced with equivalent numbers of atoms for each type of element on each side of the equation. Antoine Lavoisier, a French chemist, was the first to propose the **Law of Conservation of Mass** for the purpose of balancing a chemical equation. The law states, "Matter is neither created nor destroyed during a chemical reaction."

The **reactants** are located on the left side of the arrow, while the **products** are located on the right side of the arrow. **Coefficients** are the numbers in front of the chemical formulas. **Subscripts** are the numbers to the lower right of chemical symbols in a formula. To tally atoms, one should multiply the formula's coefficient by the subscript of each chemical symbol. For example, the chemical equation 2 H_2 + O_2 → $2H_2O$ is balanced. For H, the coefficient of 2 multiplied by the subscript 2 = 4 hydrogen atoms. For O, the coefficient of 1 multiplied by the subscript 2 = 2 oxygen atoms. Coefficients and subscripts of 1 are understood and never written. When known, the form of the substance is noted with (g) for gas, (s) for solid, (l) for liquid, or (aq) for aqueous.

Stoichiometry

Stoichiometry investigates the quantities of chemicals that are consumed and produced in chemical reactions. Chemical equations are made up of reactants and products; stoichiometry helps elucidate how the changes from reactants to products occur, as well as how to ensure the equation is balanced.

Limiting Reactants

Chemical reactions are limited by the amount of starting material—or reactants—available to drive the process forward. The reactant that is present in the smallest quantity in a reaction is called the **limiting reactant**. The limiting reactant is completely consumed by the end of the reaction. The other reactants are called **excess reactants**. For example, gasoline is used in a combustion reaction to make a car move and is the limiting reactant of the reaction. If the gasoline runs out, the combustion reaction can no longer take place, and the car stops.

Reaction Yield

The quantity of product that should be produced after using up all of the limiting reactant can be calculated and is called the **theoretical yield** of the reaction. Since the reactants do not always act as they should, the actual amount of resulting product is called the **actual yield.** The actual yield is divided by the theoretical yield and then multiplied by 100 to find the percent yield for the reaction.

Solution Stoichiometry

Solution stoichiometry deals with quantities of solutes in chemical reactions that occur in solutions. The quantity of a solute in a solution can be calculated by multiplying the molarity of the solution by the volume. Similar to chemical equations involving simple elements, the number of moles of the elements that make up the solute should be equivalent on both sides of the equation.

When the concentration of a particular solute in a solution is unknown, a titration is used to determine that concentration. In a titration, the solution with the unknown solute is combined with a standard solution, which is a solution with a known solute concentration. The point at which the unknown solute has completely reacted with the known solute is called the equivalence point. Using the known information about the standard solution, including the concentration and volume, and the volume of the unknown solution, the concentration of the unknown solute is determined in a balanced equation. For example, in the case of combining acids and bases, the equivalence point is reached when the resulting solution is neutral. HCl, an acid, combines with NaOH, a base, to form water, which is neutral, and a solution of Cl^- ions and Na^+ ions. Before the equivalence point, there are an unequal number of cations and anions and the solution is not neutral.

Reaction Rates and Equilibrium

Reaction Rates

The **rate of a reaction** is the measure of the change in concentration of the reactants or products over a certain period of time. Many factors affect how quickly or slowly a reaction occurs, such as concentration, pressure, or temperature. As the concentration of a reactant increases, the rate of the reaction also increases, because the frequency of collisions between elements increases. High-pressure situations for reactants that are gases cause the gas to compress and increase the frequency of gas molecule collisions, similar to solutions with higher concentrations. Reactions rates are then increased with the higher frequency of gas molecule collisions. Higher temperatures usually increase the rate of the reaction, adding more energy to the system with heat, and increasing the frequency of molecular collisions.

Equilibrium

Equilibrium is described as the state of a system when no net changes occur. Chemical equilibrium occurs when opposing reactions occur at equal rates. In other words, the rate of reactants forming products is equal to the rate of the products breaking down into the reactants — the concentration of reactants and products in the system does not change. Although the concentrations are not changing, the forward and reverse reactions are likely still occurring. This type of equilibrium is called a **dynamic equilibrium**. In situations where all reactions have ceased, a static equilibrium is reached. Chemical equilibriums are also described as homogeneous or heterogeneous. **Homogeneous equilibrium** involves substances that are all in the same phase, while **heterogeneous equilibrium** means the substances are in different phases when equilibrium is reached.

When a reaction reaches equilibrium, the conditions of the equilibrium are described by the following equation, based on the chemical equation aA + bB $\leftrightarrow$ cC + dD:

$$K_c = \frac{[C]^c[D]^d}{[A]^a[B]^b}$$

This equation describes the law of mass action. It explains how the reactants and products react during dynamic equilibrium. K_c is the equilibrium constant, and it is obtained when molarity values are put into the equation for the reactants and products. It is important to note that K_c is only dependent on the stoichiometry of the equation. If K_c is greater than 1, the equilibrium occurs when there are more products generated; the equilibrium lies to the right. If K_c is less than 1, the equilibrium occurs when there are more reactants generated and the equilibrium is to the left.

Similar to finding K_c, the quantity of reactants and products, as well as the direction of the reaction, can be determined at any point of time by finding Q, the reaction quotient. Q_c is substituted for the K_c in the equation above. If Q is less than K, the concentration of the reactants is too large, and the concentration of the products is too small, so the reaction must move from left to right to achieve equilibrium. If Q is equal to K, the system is at equilibrium. If Q is greater than K, the concentration of the products is too large, and the concentration of the reactants is too small; the reaction must move from right to left to reach equilibrium.

Oxidation-Reduction Reactions

Oxidation-reduction reactions, or **redox reactions**, are chemical reactions in which electrons are transferred from one compound to another. A helpful mnemonic device to remember the basic properties of redox reactions is "LEO the lion says GER", in which "LEO" means Lose Electrons Oxidation and "GER" stands for Gain Electrons Reduction. A **reducing agent** is an electron donor, and an **oxidizing agent** is an electron acceptor.

An example of an oxidation-reduction reaction is the **electrochemical cell**, which is the basis for batteries. The electrochemical cell comprises two different cells, each equipped with a separate conductor, and a salt bridge. The **salt bridge** isolates reactants but maintains the electric current. The **cathode** is the electrode that is reduced, and the **anode** is the electrode that is oxidized. **Anions** and **cations** carry electrical current within the cell, and electrons carry current within the electrodes. The voltmeter in the picture below shows the difference in potential between the two cells. As this redox reaction moves toward equilibrium, the potential will decrease and approach 0.000V. In this example, silver is reduced while copper is oxidized.

An Electrochemical Cell

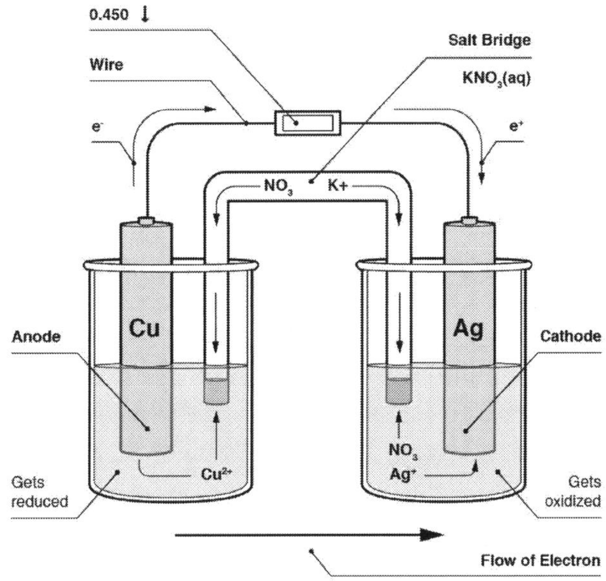

Properties of Water

Water is the most abundant substance on Earth. It is a compound composed of hydrogen and oxygen with the chemical formula H_2O. Water is also **polar,** which means it is negatively charged at one end and positively charged at the other end. The oxygen is more **electronegative** than the hydrogens, meaning that its protons pull in more of the electrons than do the hydrogens. This leaves the oxygen with a partial negative charge and the hydrogens with a partial positive charge.

Water is **amphoteric** and **self-ionizable** in that it tends to dissociate, or split, into hydrogen ions (H^+) and hydroxyl ions (OH^-) randomly. No other substance on Earth may be found naturally in all three states of matter—liquid, solid, and gas. Water is also unique due to its liquid state being more dense than its solid state (ice), which is why ice floats in liquid water. Water is colorless, odorless, and tasteless. It freezes at 32 ^{0}F and boils at 212 ^{0}F. Pure water has a pH of 7, which makes it neutral. Water is considered the universal solvent because it can dissolve many substances.

Many of the properties of water are due to its polarity and hydrogen bonding. Water has the following properties:

- Cohesiveness: Refers to the force of attraction between molecules of identical substances. Cohesiveness is mainly the result of hydrogen bonding in water.
- Adhesiveness: Refers to the force of attraction between molecules of different substances, like water and glass. Adhesiveness is mainly the result of hydrogen bonding in water.
- High specific heat: Refers to the amount of heat required to raise the temperature of water by one degree Celsius. Water's high specific heat is a consequence of hydrogen bonding. As a result, water can store a great deal of heat energy.
- High surface tension: The cohesiveness of water molecules is responsible for its high surface tension. The strong cohesion of its molecules makes water sticky and elastic.
- High heat of vaporization: Refers to the energy required to transform a given amount of water from a liquid to a gas at a given pressure. Water's high heat of vaporization is due to hydrogen bonding.

Solubility

Solubility is defined as the ability of a particular solute to dissolve in a solvent. It is usually measured in grams or moles of solute per a known volume of solution. Solubility of gases in a solution is influenced by pressure. Henry's Law states the amount of dissolved gas in a solution is directly proportional to the pressure of the solution. Solubility is also influenced by temperature; increasing temperature will speed up the rate at which most solids dissolve. When a solution reaches the point where no more solute is dissolving—often indicated by the precipitation of solid—it is called a **saturated solution**. In the case of gas solubility, a temperature increase will decrease gas solubility in water. Solubility of solids may also be impacted by common ion effects. Two compounds housing the same dissociating cation, combined in solution, will often significantly reduce the solubility of the material being evaluated. Physical agitation—such as stirring, sonication, or mixing—may speed up the dissolving process by increasing the molecular interactions of solute and solvent.

Precipitation Titrations

A titration in which the end point is determined by formation of a precipitate is called a **precipitation titration**. The most common precipitation titrations are argentometric (*Argentum* means silver in Latin), which involves a silver ion, with silver nitrate ($AgNO_3$) being the titrant. Silver nitrate is a very useful titrant because it reacts very quickly. All products in these titrimetric precipitations are silver salts. A very simple argentometric precipitation titration is often performed to determine the amount of chlorine in seawater, as the chlorine anion is present most abundantly. The reaction is as follows:

$$AgNO_3\,(aq) + NaCl\,(aq) \rightarrow AgCl\,(s) + NaNO_3\,(aq)$$

Silver chloride is almost completely insoluble in water, so it precipitates out of solution. A selective indicator, potassium chromate (K_2CrO_4), is added to determine when the reaction is complete. When all of the chloride ions from the sample have precipitated, silver ions then react with chromate ions to form Ag_2CrO_4, which is orange in color. The volume of the sample, amount of titrant required to complete the precipitation, molar mass of the reacting species, and the density of the sample are sufficient information to calculate the concentration of chloride ions.

Titration curves are useful in providing a graphical account of what occurs before, during, and after the equivalence point. Argentometric titration curves are sigmoidal when the concentration function is plotted on the y-axis and the reagent volume is plotted on the x-axis. An example is shown below:

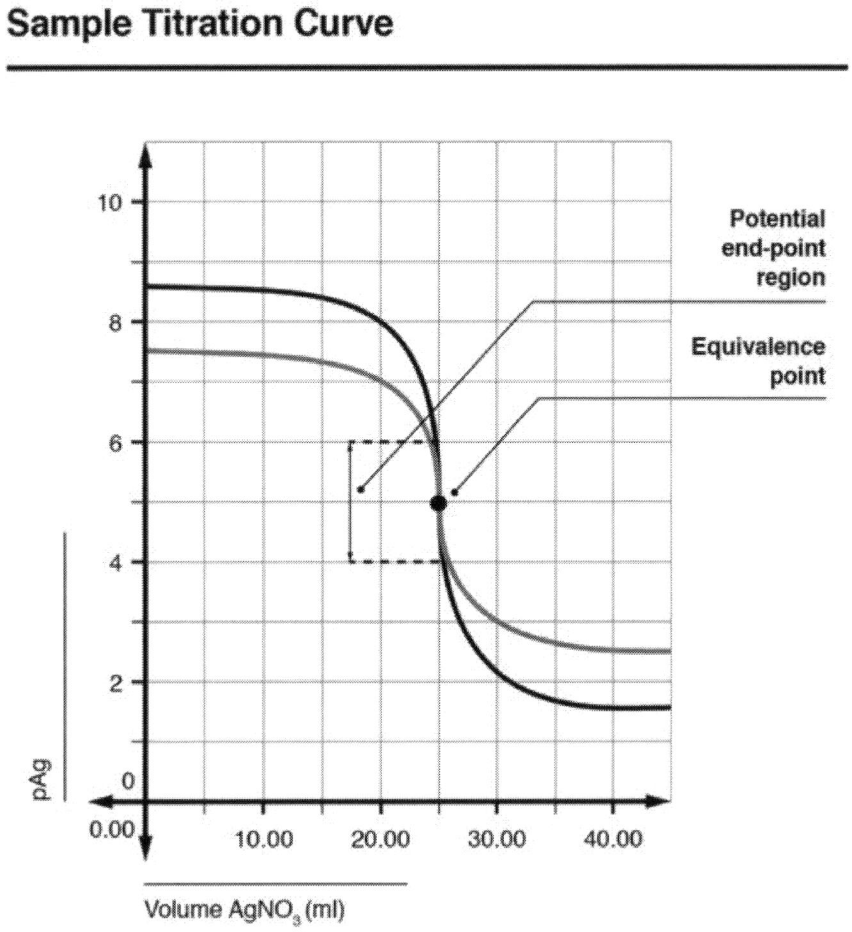

Note that at the equivalence point, there is a sharp drop in reagent concentration, and then beyond the equivalence point, the concentration decreases gradually. Around the equivalence point, small volumes of titrant added cause dramatic changes in the concentration of analyte and reagent. At equivalence, the molar concentrations of sample cation/titrant anion and sample anion/titrant cation are equal.

Valence Bonds, Hybridization, and Molecular Orbitals

Valence Bond Theory

In **valence bond theory**, electrons are treated in a quantum mechanics fashion. Valence bond theory is good for describing the shapes of covalent compounds. Instead of electrons being pinpointed to an exact location, it's possible to map out a region of space—known as **atomic orbitals**—that the electron may inhabit. In valence bond theory, electrons are treated as excitations of the **electron field**, which exist everywhere. When energy is given to an electron field, electrons are said to exist inside a **wave function**—a mathematical function describing the probability that an electron is in a certain place at any given time. Standing waves are created when energy is given to a wave function. Electrons function as standing waves around a nucleus.

There are two things to consider in valence bond theory: the overlapping of the orbitals and the potential energy changes in a molecule as the atoms get closer or further apart. For example, the Lewis structure of H_2 is H – H, but this doesn't describe the strength of the bond. The electron cloud in the nucleus of one atom is interacting with the cloud of electrons in the nucleus of another atom. If the potential energy is mapped out as a function of distance between the two atoms, something like this is obtained:

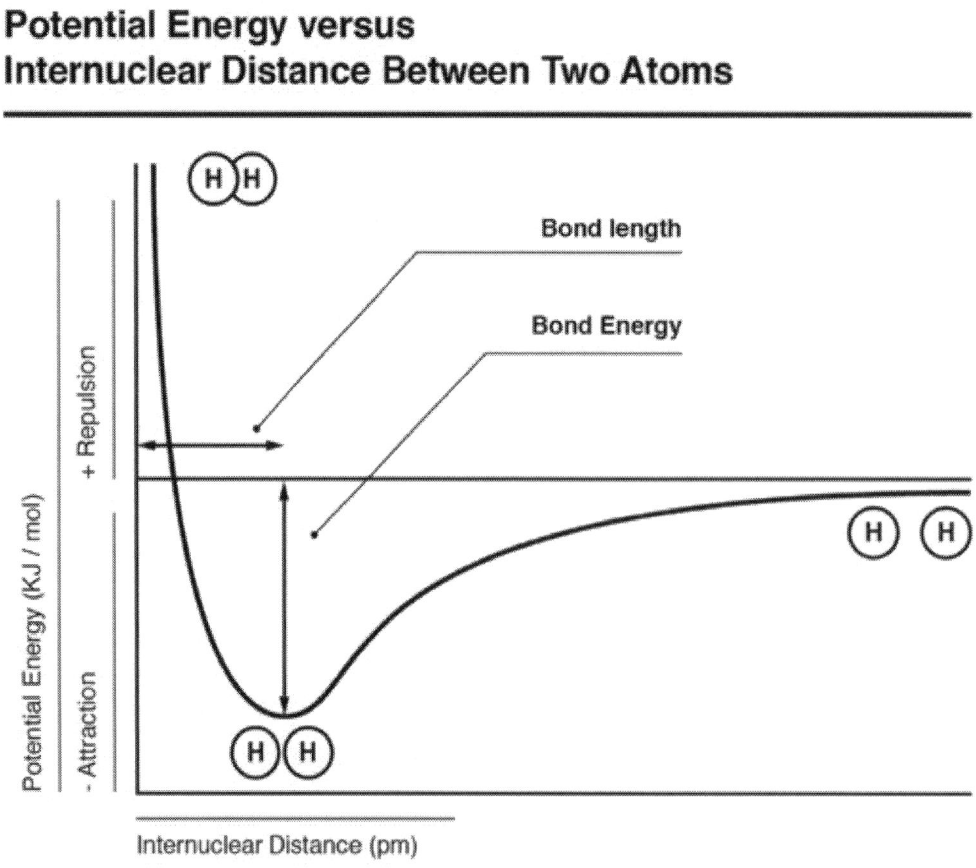

The atoms approach this minimum value at a distance known as the **bond energy.** The link that corresponds to this is the equilibrium bond length—a happy medium corresponding to a minimum in potential energy. This minimum of energy is achieved when the atomic orbitals are overlapping and so contain two **spin-paired electrons**—when the two atoms' orbitals are overlapping each other. A greater amount of energy is needed to separate those two atoms when they are overlapped.

Molecular Orbitals

Atomic orbitals explain the behavior of a single electron or pairs of electrons in an atom. They are regions of space in which the electrons are more likely to spend their time. Every orbital can contain two electrons and is at its lowest energy when it has two electrons. One electron spins up, and one spins down. As mentioned, the standard atomic orbitals are known as *s, p, d,* and *f* orbitals.

- The simplest of the orbitals is the **s orbital**—the inner orbital of any atom or the outer orbital for light molecules, such as hydrogen and helium. The s orbital is spherical in shape and can contain two electrons.

- After the first and second s orbitals are filled, the **p orbitals** are filled. There are three p orbitals, one on each of the x, y, and z axes. Each p orbital can contain two electrons for a total of six electrons.

- After the p orbitals are filled, the **d orbitals** are filled next. There are five d orbitals, for a total of ten electrons.

- The **f orbitals** are next; there are seven f orbitals, which can contain a total of fourteen electrons.

Each shell/energy level has an increasing number of subshells available to it:

- The first shell only has the 1s subshell, so it has two electrons.
- The second shell has the 2s and 2p subshells, so it has (2 + 6) eight electrons.
- The third shell has the 3s, 3p and 3d subshells, so it has (2 + 6 + 10) 18 electrons.
- The fourth shell has the 4s, 4p, 4d and 4f subshells, so it has (2 + 6 + 10 + 14) 32 electrons.

To find the maximum number of electrons per shell, the formula $2n^2$ is used, where n is the shell number. For example, elements in the third period have three subshells—space for up to 18 electrons—but will only have up to eight valence electrons. This is because the *3d* orbitals are not filled—i.e., the elements from the third period do not completely fill their third shell.

Any element in the periodic table can be written in terms of its electron configuration. For instance, Calcium (Ca), which is in the fourth period on the periodic table and has an atomic number of 20, can be written as $1s^2 2s^2 2p^6 3s^2 3p^6 4s^2$. However, it's important to remember that the transition metals do not follow this rule. This is because quantum energy level rules allow for some of their shells to remain unfilled. For example, the transition metal scandium (Sc), which has an atomic number of 21, has the electron configuration $1s^2 2s^2 2p^6 3s^2 3p^6 3d^1 4s^2$, and the *d* subshell is not filled.

In **molecular orbital theory**, the assumption is that bonding, non-bonding, and anti-bonding orbitals, which have different energies, are formed when atoms are brought together. For N atomic orbitals in a molecule, the assumed result would be N molecular orbitals, which can be described by wave functions.

For example, for a molecule that has two atomic orbitals, two molecular orbitals must be formed: one bonding and one anti-bonding. The molecular orbitals would be separated by a certain energy. A molecule that has three atomic orbitals would form one bonding, one non-bonding, and one anti-bonding molecular orbital. A molecule that has ten atoms would form five anti-bonding and five bonding molecular orbitals.

Sigma bonds (σ bonds) are formed by direct overlapping of atomic orbitals, and they are the strongest type of covalent bond. Sigma bonds are symmetrical around the bond axis. Common sigma bonds—where z is the axis of the bond—are s+s, p_z+p_z, $s+p_z$, and $d_z{}^2+d_z{}^2$.

In contrast, **pi bonds (π bonds)** are usually weaker than sigma bonds and are a type of covalent bond where two ends of one p-orbital overlap the two ends of another p-orbital. D-orbitals can also form pi bonds.

Generally, **single bonds** are sigma bonds, and multiple bonds consist of one sigma bond plus one pi bond. A **double bond** is one sigma bond plus one pi bond. A **triple bond** consists of one sigma bond and two pi bonds. For example, ethylene has **delta bonds (δ bonds)** that are formed from four ends of one atomic orbital overlapping with four ends of another atomic orbital.

Hybridization

Sometimes, the *s*, *p*, *d*, and *f* orbitals do not fully explain where an electron will be at any given time. This is where hybrid orbitals come in. **Hybrid orbitals** are combinations of the standard atomic orbitals. For instance, if the *s* and *p* orbitals hybridize, instead of being two different kinds of orbitals, they become four identical orbitals. When the *s* orbital hybridizes with all three *p* orbitals, it's called sp^3 hybridization, and it forms a tetrahedral shape. This is the type of hybridization that occurs in H_2O. The description used depends on the properties of the compound, including its numbers of lone pairs of electrons.

Bond Energies

The **bond energy** can be described as the amount of energy required to break apart one mole of covalently-bonded gases. Bond energies are measured in kilojoules per mole of bonds (kJ/mol). The **mole** is a unit of measurement that is commonly used in chemistry. One mole of something is equal to Avogadro's number: $6.02214078 \times 10^{23}$. To calculate the number of moles of something, some simple formulas can be used:

$$\text{Moles} = \text{mass (g)} / \text{Relative mass (grams per mole)}.$$

Example: How many moles are there in 30 grams of helium?

On the periodic table, Helium's relative mass is approximately two. Using this information and the formula yields:

$$\text{Moles} = 30 / 2 = 15 \text{ moles}$$

During a chemical reaction, some bonds are broken, and some are formed. Bonds do not break or form spontaneously—they require energy to be added or released. The energy needed to break a bond is the **bond energy**. As mentioned, generally, the shorter the bond length, the greater the bond energy.

When atoms combine to make bonds and form a compound, energy is always released, normally as heat. Certain types of bonds have similar bond energies, despite each molecule being different. For example, all C-H bonds will have a value of roughly 413 kJ/mol. There are reference lists available with average bond energies that have been calculated for various atoms bonded together.

Using bond energies, it is possible to calculate the **enthalpy change** within a system. When a chemical reaction occurs, there will always be an accompanying change in energy. Energy is released to make bonds; conversely, energy is required to break bonds.

- Some reactions are **exothermic**—where energy is released during the reaction, usually in the form of heat—because the energy of the products is lower than the energy of the reactants. In exothermic reactions, energy can be thought of as a **product**.

- Some reactions are **endothermic**—where energy is absorbed from the surroundings because the energy of the reactants is lower than the energy of the products. In endothermic reactions, energy can be thought of as a **reactant**.

It is possible to look at the two sides of a chemical reaction and work out whether energy is gained or lost during the formation of the products, thus determining whether the reaction is exothermic or endothermic. Here is an example:

Two moles of water forming two moles of hydrogen and one mole of oxygen:

$$2H_2O(g) \rightarrow 2H_2 + O_2(g)$$

The sum on the reactant's side (2 moles of water) is equal to four sets of H-O bonds, which is 4 x 460 kJ/mol = 1840 kJ/mol. This is the input.

The sum on the product's side is equal to 2 moles of H-H bonds and 1 mole of O=O bonds, which is 2 x 436.4 kJ/mol and 1 x 498.7 kJ/mol = 1371.5 kJ/mol. This is the output.

The total energy difference is 1840 – 1371.5 = +468.5 kJ/mol.

The energy difference is positive, which means that the reaction is endothermic, and the reaction will require energy (i.e., heat) to be carried out.

Covalent and van der Waals Radii

The **covalent radius (rcov)** is the length of one half of the bond length when two atoms of the same kind are bonded through a single bond in a neutral molecule. The sum of two covalent radii from atoms that are covalently bonded should, theoretically, be equal to the covalent bond length:

$$rcov(AB) = r(A) + r(B)$$

The van der Waals radius, rv, can be defined as half the distance between the nuclei of two non-bonded atoms of the same element when they are as close as possible to each other without being in the same molecule or being covalently bonded.

The covalent radii changes depending on the environment that an atom is in and whether it is single, double, or triple bonded, but average values exist for use in calculations, for example.

The van der Waals radii also changes based on the intermolecular forces present, but average values also exist. These values are useful for determining how closely molecules can pack into a solid.

Physics

Energy

Energy may be defined as the capacity to do work. It can be transferred between objects, comes in a multitude of forms, and can be converted from one form to another. The **Law of Conservation of Energy** states, "Energy can neither be created nor be destroyed."

Kinetic Energy and Potential Energy

The two primary forms of energy are kinetic energy and potential energy. **Kinetic energy** involves the energy of motion. Kinetic energy can be calculated using the equation: $KE = 0.5mv^2$, where m is the mass and v is the velocity of the object.

Potential energy represents the energy possessed by an object by virtue of its position. Potential energy may be calculated using the equation: $PE = mgh$, where m is the mass, g is the acceleration of gravity, and h is the height of the object.

Other Forms of Energy

The following are forms of kinetic energy:

- **Radiant energy**: Represents electromagnetic energy, which usually travels in waves or particles. Examples of radiant energy include visible light, gamma rays, X-rays, and solar energy.
- **Thermal energy**: Refers to the vibration and movement of molecules and atoms within a substance. It is also known as heat. When an object is heated, its molecules and atoms move and collide with each other more quickly. Examples of thermal energy include geothermal energy from the Earth, heated swimming pools, baking in an oven, and the warmth of a campfire on a person's skin.
- **Sound energy**: Represents the movement of energy through a substance, such as water or air, in waves. Vibrations cause sound energy. Examples of sound energy include a person's voice, clapping, singing, and musical instruments.
- **Electrical energy**: Utilizes charged particles called electrons moving through a wire. Some examples of electrical energy include lightning, batteries, alternating current (AC), direct current (DC), and static electricity.
- **Mechanical energy**: Represents the energy derived from the movement of objects. It is also called motion energy. Examples of mechanical energy include wind, flight of an airplane, electrons orbiting an atom's nucleus, and running.

The following are forms of potential energy:

- **Chemical energy**: Represents the energy stored in the bonds of molecules and atoms. Chemical energy usually undergoes conversion to thermal energy. Examples of chemical energy include petroleum, coal, and natural gas.

- **Elastic energy**: Represents the energy stored in an object as its volume or shape is distorted. It is also known as stored mechanical energy. Examples of elastic energy include stretched rubber bands and coiled springs.

- **Gravitational energy**: Refers to the energy stored as a result of an object's place or position. Increases in height and mass translate into increased gravitational energy. Examples of systems using gravitational energy include rollercoasters and hydroelectric power.

- **Nuclear energy**: Refers to the energy stored in an atom's nucleus. Vast amounts of energy can be released through the combination or splitting of nuclei. An example of nuclear energy is the nucleus of the element uranium.

Mechanics

<u>Description of Motion in One and Two Dimensions</u>
The description of motion is known as **kinetics**, and the causes of motion are known as **dynamics**. Motion in one dimension is a **scalar** quantity. It consists of one measurement such as length (length/distance is also known as **displacement**), speed, or time. Motion in two dimensions is a **vector** quantity. This is a speed with a direction, or **velocity**.

Velocity is the measure of the change in distance over the change in time. All vector quantities have a direction that can be relayed through the sign of an answer, such as -5.0 m/s or +5.0 m/s. The objects registering these velocities would be traveling in opposite directions, where the change in distance is denoted by Δx and the change in time is denoted by Δt:

$$v = \frac{\Delta x}{\Delta t}$$

Acceleration is the measure of the change in an object's velocity over a change in time, where the change in velocity, $v_2 - v_1$, is denoted by Δv and the change in time, $t_1 - t_2$, is denoted by Δt:

$$a = \frac{\Delta v}{\Delta t}$$

The **linear momentum,** p, of an object is the result of the object's mass, m, multiplied by its velocity, v, and is described by the equation:

$$p = mv$$

This aspect becomes important when one object hits another object. For example, the linear momentum of a small sports car will be much smaller than the linear momentum of a large semi-truck. Thus, the semi-truck will cause more damage to the car than the car to the truck.

Newton's Three Laws of Motion

Newton's Three Laws of Motion

Sir Isaac Newton summarized his observations and calculations relating to motion into three concise laws:

First Law of Motion: Inertia

This law states that an object in motion tends to stay in motion or an object at rest tends to stay at rest unless the object is acted upon by an outside force.

For example, a rock sitting on the ground will remain in the same place, unless it is pushed or lifted from its place.

This law also includes the relation of weight to gravity and force between objects relative to the distance separating them.

$$Weight = G\frac{Mm}{r^2}$$

Where G is the gravitational constant, M and m are the masses of the two objects, and r is the distance separating the two objects.

Second Law of Motion: F = ma

This law states that the force on a given body is the result of the object's mass multiplied by the acceleration acting upon the object. For objects falling on Earth, acceleration is caused by gravitational force (9.8 m/s^2).

Third Law of Motion: Action-Reaction

This law states that for every action there is an equal and opposite reaction. For example, if a person punches a wall, the wall exerts a force back on the person's hand equal and opposite to his or her punching force. Since the wall has more mass, it absorbs the impact of the punch better than the person's hand.

Mass, Weight, and Gravity

Mass is a measure of how much of a substance exists, or how much inertia an object has. The mass of an object does not change based on the object's location, but the weight of an object does vary with its location.

For example, a 15-kg mass has a weight that is determined by acceleration from the force of gravity here on Earth. However, if that same 15 kg mass was weighed on the moon, it would weigh much less, since the acceleration force from the moon's gravitational force is approximately one-sixth of that on Earth.

Weight = mass × acceleration of gravity

$$W_{Earth} = 15 \text{ kg} \times 9.8 \text{ m/s}^2 > W_{Moon} = 15 \text{ kg} \times 1.62 \text{ m/s}^2$$

$$W_{Earth} = 147\text{N} > W_{Moon} = 24.3\text{N}$$

Analysis of Motion and Forces

Projectile motion describes the path of an object in the air. Generally, it is described by two-dimensional movement, such as a stone thrown through the air. This activity takes the shape of a parabolic curve. However, the definition of projectile motion also applies to free fall, or the non-arced motion of an object in a path straight up and/or straight down. When an object is thrown horizontally, it is subject to the same influence of gravity as an object that is dropped straight down. The farther the projectile motion, the farther the distance of the object's flight.

Friction is a force that opposes motion. It can be caused by several materials; there are even frictions caused by air or water. Whenever two differing materials touch, rub, or pass by each other, this can create friction, or an oppositional force. To move an object across a floor, the force exerted on the object must overcome the frictional force keeping the object in place. Friction is also why people can walk on surfaces. Without the oppositional force of friction to a shoe pressing on the floor, a person would not be able to grip the floor to walk—similar to the challenges of walking on ice. Without friction, shoes slip and are unable to help people push forward and walk.

When calculating the effects of objects colliding with each other, several things are important to remember. One of these is the definition of **momentum**: the mass of an object multiplied by the object's velocity. It is expressed by the following equation:

$$p = mv$$

Here, p is equal to an object's momentum, m is equal to the object's mass, and v is equal to the object's velocity.

Another important thing to remember is the principal of the **conservation of linear momentum**. The total momentum for objects in a situation will be the same before and after a collision. There are two primary types of collisions: **elastic** and **inelastic**. In an elastic collision, the objects collide and then travel in different directions. During an inelastic collision, the objects collide and then stick together in their final direction of travel. The total momentum in an elastic collision is calculated by using the following formula:

$$m_1v_1 + m_2v_2 = m_1v_1 + m_2v_2$$

Here, m_1 and m_2 are the masses of two separate objects, and v_1 and v_2 are their velocities, respectively.

The total momentum in an inelastic collision is calculated by using the following formula:

$$m_1v_1 + m_2v_2 = (m_1 + m_2)v_f$$

Here, v_f is the final velocity of the two masses after they stick together post-collision.

Example:

> If two bumper cars are speeding toward each other and collide head-on, they are designed to bounce off of each other and head in different directions. This would be an elastic collision.
>
> If real cars were speeding toward each other and collided head-on, there is a good chance their bumpers might get caught together and their subsequent direction of travel would be in the same direction together.

Circular motion takes place around an **axis,** which is an invisible line around which an object can rotate. This type of motion can be observed in the movements of a toy top. There is actually a point (or rod) through the center of a toy top on which the top can be observed as the spinning point for the top. This rod is called the axis.

When objects move in a circle by spinning on their own axis, or from being tethered around a central point (also an axis), they exhibit **circular motion**. In many ways, circular motion is similar to linear (straight line) motion. One difference is, when spinning an object on or around an axis, a force is created that feels like it is pushing out from the center of the circle. In reality, the force is actually pulling into the center of the circle, and the reactionary force is what is creating the feeling of pushing out. The inward force is the real force and is called **centripetal** force. The outward, or reactionary, force is called **centrifugal** force. The reactionary force is not the real force—it just feels like it is there. This has also been referred to as a **fictional** force. The true force is the one pulling inward, or the centripetal force. The terms *centripetal* and *centrifugal* are often mistakenly interchanged.

Example:

> A traditional upright-style washing machine spins a load of laundry to remove the water from the load. The machine spins a barrel with holes in a circle at a high rate of speed. A force is pulling in toward the center of the circle (centripetal force). At the same time, the force reactionary to the centripetal force is pressing the laundry up against the outer sides of the barrel, thus pushing the water through the small holes that line the outer wall of the barrel.

An object moving in a circular motion also has momentum. In a circular motion, this is called **angular momentum**. It is determined by rotational inertia, rotational velocity, and the distance of the mass from the axis of rotation, or center of rotation.

Objects exhibiting circular motion also demonstrate the conservation of angular momentum. This means that the angular momentum of a system is always constant, regardless of the placement of the mass. Rotational inertia can be affected by how far the mass of the object is placed with respect to the center of rotation (axis of rotation). The farther the mass is from the center of rotation, the slower the rotational velocity. Conversely, if the mass is closer to the center of rotation, the rotational velocity increases. A change in one affects the other, thus conserving the angular momentum. This holds true as long as no external forces act on the system.

Example:

> When ice skaters are spinning on one ice skate, they can extend their arms to slow their rotational velocity. However, when skaters bring their arms in close to their bodies (or shorten the distance between the mass and the center of rotation), their rotational velocity increases, and they will spin much faster. Some skaters extend their arms straight above their heads, which causes an extension of the axis of rotation, thus removing any distance between the mass and the center of rotation and maximizing their rotational velocity. In other words, they spin extremely fast.

The center of mass is the point that provides the average location for the total mass of a system. The word "system" can apply to just one object/particle or to many. The center of mass for a system can be calculated by finding the average of the mass of each object and multiplied by its distance from an origin point using the following formula:

$$x_{center\ of\ mass} = \frac{m_1 x_1 + m_2 x_2}{m_1 + m_2}$$

In this case, *x* is the distance from the point of origin for the center of mass and each respective object, and *m* is the mass of each object.

To calculate for more than one object, the pattern can be continued by adding additional masses and their respective distances from the origin point.

Simple Machines

A **simple machine** is a mechanical device that changes the direction or magnitude of a force. There are six basic types of simple machines: lever, wedge, screw, inclined plane, wheel and axle, and pulley.

Here is how each type works and an example:

- A **lever** helps lift heavy items higher with less force, such as a crowbar lifting a large cast iron lid.
- A **wedge** helps apply force to a specific area by focusing the pressure, such as an axe splitting a tree.
- An **inclined plane** helps move heavy items up vertical distances with less force, such as a loading dock ramp.
- A **screw** is an inclined plane wrapped around an axis and allows more force to be applied by extending the distance of the plane, such as a screw being turned into a piece of wood rather than hitting a nail into the wood.
- A **wheel and axle** allows the use of rotational force around an axis to assist with applying force, such as a wheelbarrow making it easier to haul large loads by employing a wheel and axle at the front.
- A **pulley** is an application of a wheel and axle with the addition of cords or ropes and helps move objects vertically, such as pulling a bucket out of a well is easier with a pulley and ropes.

Here's some visual representations:

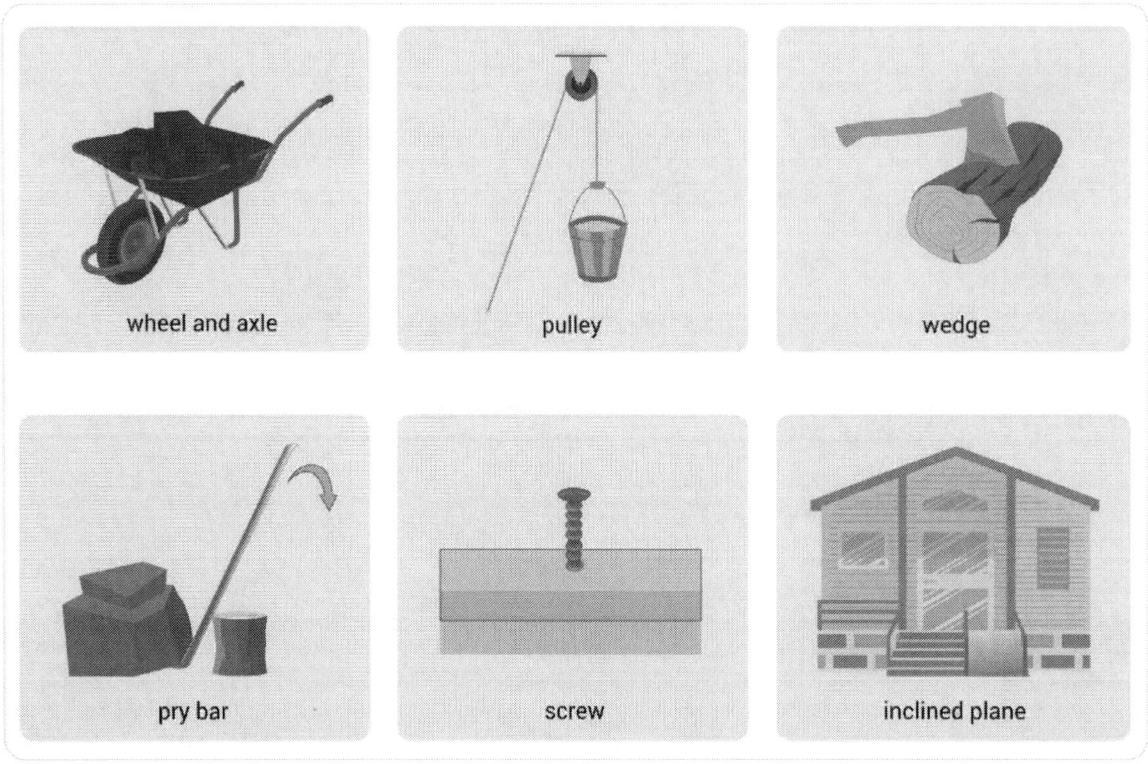

Using a simple machine employs an advantage to the user. This is referred to as the **mechanical advantage**. It can be calculated by comparing the force input by the user to the simple machine with the force output from the use of the machine (also displayed as a ratio).

$$Mechanical\ Advantage\ = \frac{output\ force}{input\ force}$$

$$MA\ = \frac{F_{out}}{F_{in}}$$

When using a lever, it can be helpful to calculate the torque, or circular force, necessary to move something. This is also employed when using a wrench to loosen a bolt.

$$Torque\ =\ F\ \times\ distance\ of\ lever\ arm\ from\ the\ axis\ of\ rotation$$

$$T\ =\ F\ \times\ d$$

Electricity and Magnetism

<u>Electrical Nature of Common Materials</u>
Generally, an atom carries no net charge because the positive charges of the protons in the nucleus balance the negative charges of the electrons in the outer shells of the atom. This is considered to be electrically neutral. However, electrons are the only portion of the atom known to have the freedom to "move," and this can cause an object to become electrically charged. This happens either through a gain or a loss of electrons. Electrons have a negative charge, so a gain creates a negative charge for the object. On the contrary, a loss of electrons creates a positive charge for the object. This charge can also

be focused on specific areas of an object, causing a notable interaction between charged objects. For example, if a person rubs a balloon on a carpet, the balloon transfers some of its electrons to the carpet. So, if a person were to hold the balloon near his or her hair, the electrons in the "neutral" hair would make the hair stand on end. This is due to the electrons wanting to fill the deficit of electrons on the balloon. Unless electrically forced into a charged state, most natural objects in nature tend toward reestablishing and maintaining a neutral charge.

When dealing with charges, it is easiest to remember that **like charges *repel*** each other and **opposite charges attract** each other. Therefore, negatives and positives attract, while two positives or two negatives repel each other. Similarly, when two charges come near each other, they exert a force on one another. This is described through **Coulomb's Law**:

$$F = k\frac{q_1 q_2}{r^2}$$

Where F is equal to the force exerted by the interaction, k is a constant ($k = 8.99 \times 10^9$ N m^2/C^2), q_1 and q_2 are the measure of the two charges, and r is the distance between the two charges.

When materials readily transfer electricity or electrons, or can easily accept or lose electrons, they are considered to be good conductors. The transferring of electricity is called **conductivity**. If a material does not readily accept the transfer of electrons or readily loses electrons, it is considered to be an insulator. For example, copper wire easily transfers electricity because copper is a good conductor. However, plastic does not transfer electricity because it is not a good conductor. In fact, plastic is an insulator.

Basic Electrical Concepts

In an electrical circuit, the flow from a power source, or the voltage, is "drawn" across the components in the circuit from the positive end to the negative end. This flow of charge creates an electric current (I), which is the time (t) rate of flow of net charge (q). It is measured with the formula:

$$I = \frac{q}{t}$$

Current is measured in **amperes** (amps). There are two main types of currents: (1) **direct current** (DC) — a one directional flow of charges through a circuit; and (2) **alternating current** (AC) — a circuit with a changing directional flow of charges or magnitude.

Every circuit will show a loss in voltage across its conducting material. This loss of voltage is from resistance within the circuit and can be caused by multiple factors, including resistance from wiring and components such as light bulbs and switches. To measure the resistance in a given circuit, **Ohm's law** is used:

$$Resistance = \frac{Voltage}{current}$$

$$R = \frac{V}{I}$$

Resistance (R) is measured in **Ohms** (Ω).

Components in a circuit can be wired **in series** or **in parallel**. If the components are wired in series, a single wire connects each component to the next in line. If the components are wired in parallel, two wires connect each component to the next. The main difference is that the voltage across those in series is directly related from one component to the next. Therefore, if the first component in the series becomes inoperable, no voltage can get to the other components. Conversely, the components in parallel share the voltage across each other and are not dependent on the component wired prior to the next to allow the voltage across the wire.

To calculate the resistance of circuit components wired in series or parallel, the following equations are used:

Resistance in series:

$$\mathrm{R_{total}} = R_1 + R_2 + R_3 + \cdots$$

Resistance in parallel:

$$\mathrm{R_{total}} = \frac{1}{R_1} + \frac{1}{R_2} + \frac{1}{R_3} + \cdots$$

To make electrons move so they can carry their charge, a change in voltage must be present. On a small scale, this is demonstrated through the electrons traveling from the light switch to a person's finger. This might happen in a situation where a person runs his or her socks on a carpet, touches a light switch, and receives a small jolt from the electrons that run from the switch to the finger. This minor jolt is due to the deficit of electrons created by rubbing the socks on the carpet, and then the electrons going into the ground. The difference in charge between the switch and the finger caused the electrons to move.

If this situation were to be created on a larger and more sustained scale, the factors would need to be more systematic, predictable, and harnessed. This can be achieved through batteries/cells and generators. Batteries or cells have a chemical reaction that occurs inside, causing energy to be released and charges to be able to move freely. Batteries generally have nodes (one positive and one negative), where items can be hooked up to complete a circuit and allow the charge to travel freely through the item. Generators convert mechanical energy into electric energy using power and movement.

Basic Properties of Magnetic Fields and Forces

Consider two straight rods that are made from magnetic material. They will naturally have a negative end (pole) and a positive end (pole). These charged poles react just like any charged item: opposite charges attract and like charges repel. They will attract each other when arranged positive pole to negative pole. However, if one rod is turned around, the two rods will now repel each other due to the alignment of negative to negative and positive to positive. These types of forces can also be created and amplified by using an electric current. For example, sending an electric current through a stretch of wire creates an electromagnetic force around the wire from the charge of the current. This force exists as long as the flow of electricity is sustained. This magnetic force can also attract and repel other items with magnetic properties. Depending on the strength of the current in the wire, a greater or smaller magnetic force can be generated around the wire. As soon as the current is stopped, the magnetic force also stops.

Optics and Waves

Electromagnetic Spectrum

The movement of light is described like the movement of waves. Light travels with a wave front, has an amplitude (height from the neutral), a cycle or wavelength, a period, and energy. Light travels at approximately 3.00×10^8 m/s and is faster than anything created by humans.

Light is commonly referred to by its measured wavelengths, or the distance between two successive crests or troughs in a wave. Types of light with the longest wavelengths include radio, TV, and micro and infrared waves. The next set of wavelengths are detectable by the human eye and create the **visible spectrum**. The visible spectrum has wavelengths of 10^{-7} m, and the colors seen are red, orange, yellow, green, blue, indigo, and violet. Beyond the visible spectrum are shorter wavelengths, also called the **electromagnetic spectrum**, containing ultraviolet light, X-rays, and gamma rays. The wavelengths outside of the visible light range can be harmful to humans if they are directly exposed or exposed for long periods of time.

Basic Characteristics and Types of Waves

A **mechanical wave** is a type of wave that passes through a medium (solid, liquid, or gas). There are two basic types of mechanical waves: longitudinal and transverse.

A **longitudinal wave** has motion that is parallel to the direction of the wave's travel. It can best be shown by compressing one side of a tethered spring and then releasing that end. The movement travels in a bunching/un-bunching motion across the length of the spring and back.

A **transverse wave** has motion that is perpendicular to the direction of the wave's travel. The particles on a transverse wave do not move across the length of the wave, but instead oscillate up and down to create peaks and troughs.

A wave with a mix of both longitudinal and transverse motion can be seen through the motion of a wave on the ocean—with peaks and troughs, and particles oscillating up and down.

Mechanical waves can carry energy, sound, and light, but they need a medium through which transport can occur. An electromagnetic wave can transmit energy without a medium, or in a vacuum.

A more recent addition in the study of waves is the **gravitational wave**. Its existence has been proven and verified, yet the details surrounding its capabilities are still somewhat under inquiry. They are purported to be ripples that propagate as waves outward from their source and travel in the curvature of space/time. They are thought to carry energy in a form of radiant energy called gravitational radiation.

Basic Wave Phenomena

When a wave crosses a boundary or travels from one medium to another, certain actions occur. If the wave is capable of traveling through one medium into another medium, it experiences **refraction**. This is the bending of the wave from one medium to another due to a change in density and thus the speed of the wave. For example, when a pencil is sitting in half of a glass of water, a side view of the glass makes the pencil appear to be bent at the water level. What the viewer is seeing is the refraction of light waves traveling from the air into the water. Since the wave speed is slowed in water, the change makes the pencil appear bent.

When a wave hits a medium that it cannot penetrate, it is bounced back in an action called **reflection**. For example, when light waves hit a mirror, they are reflected, or bounced, off the mirror. This can cause it to seem like there is more light in the room, since there is "doubling back" of the initial wave. This same phenomenon also causes people to be able to see their reflection in a mirror.

When a wave travels through a slit or around an obstacle, it is known as **diffraction**. A light wave will bend around an obstacle or through a slit and cause what is called a **diffraction pattern**. When the waves bend around an obstacle, it causes the addition of waves and the spreading of light on the other side of the opening.

Dispersion is used to describe the splitting of a single wave by refracting its components into separate parts. For example, if a wave of white light is sent through a dispersion prism, the light appears as its separate rainbow-colored components, due to each colored wavelength being refracted in the prism.

When wavelengths hit boundaries, different things occur. Objects will absorb certain wavelengths of light and reflect others, depending on the boundaries. This becomes important when an object appears to be a certain color. The color of an object is not actually within that object, but rather, in the wavelengths being transmitted by that object. For example, if a table appears to be red, that means the table is absorbing all other wavelengths of visible light except those of the red wavelength. The table is reflecting, or transmitting, the wavelengths associated with red back to the human eye, and so it appears red.

Interference describes when an object affects the path of a wave, or another wave interacts with a wave. Waves interacting with each other can result in either **constructive interference** or **destructive interference**, based on their positions. With constructive interference, the waves are in sync with each other and combine to reinforce each other. In the case of deconstructive interference, the waves are out of sync and reduce the effect of each other to some degree. In **scattering**, the boundary can change the direction or energy of a wave, thus altering the entire wave. **Polarization** changes the oscillations of a wave and can alter its appearance in light waves. For example, polarized sunglasses remove the "glare" from sunlight by altering the oscillation pattern observed by the wearer.

When a wave hits a boundary and is completely reflected, or cannot escape from one medium to another, it is called **total internal reflection**. This effect can be seen in the diamonds with a brilliant cut. The angle cut on the sides of the diamond causes the light hitting the diamond to be completely reflected back inside the gem, making it appear brighter and more colorful than a diamond with different angles cut into its surface.

The **Doppler effect** applies to situations with both light and sound waves. The premise of the Doppler effect is that, based upon the relative position or movement of a source and an observer, waves can seem shorter or longer than they are in actuality. When the Doppler effect is noted with sound, it warps the noise being heard by the observer. This makes the pitch or frequency seem shorter or higher as the source is approaching, and then longer or lower as the source is getting farther away. The frequency/pitch of the source never actually changes, but the sound in respect to the observer makes it seem like the sound has changed. This can be observed when a siren passes by an observer on the road. The siren sounds much higher in pitch as it approaches the observer and then lower after it passes and is getting farther away.

The Doppler effect also applies to situations involving light waves. An observer in space would see light approaching as being shorter wavelengths than the light is in actuality, causing it to seem blue. When the light wave gets farther away, the light would seem red because of the apparent elongation of the wavelength. This is called the **red-blue shift**.

Basic Optics

When reflecting light, a mirror can be used to observe a virtual (not real) image. A **plane mirror** is a piece of glass with a coating in the background to create a reflective surface. An image is what the human eye sees when light is reflected off the mirror in an unmagnified manner. If a **curved mirror** is used for reflection, the image seen will not be a true reflection. Instead, it will either be magnified or made smaller in its image than its actual size. Curved mirrors can also make the object appear closer or farther away than the actual distance the object is from the mirror.

Lenses can be used to refract or bend light to form images. Examples of lenses are the human eye, microscopes, and telescopes. The human eye interprets the refraction of light into images that humans understand to be actual size. **Microscopes** allow objects that are too small for the unaided human eye to be enlarged enough to be seen. **Telescopes** allow objects to be viewed that are too far away to be seen with the unaided eye. **Prisms** are pieces of glass that can have a wavelength of light enter one side and appear to be divided into its component wavelengths on the other side. This is due to the ability of the prism to slow certain wavelengths more than others.

<u>Sound</u>

Sound travels in waves and is the movement of vibrations through a medium. It can travel through air (gas), land, water, etc. For example, the noise a human hears in the air is the vibration of the waves as they reach the ear. The human brain translates the different frequencies (pitches) and intensities of the vibrations to determine what created the noise.

A tuning fork has a predetermined frequency because of the size (length and thickness) of its tines. When struck, it allows vibrations between the two tines to move the air at a specific rate. This creates a specific tone, or note, for that size of tuning fork. The number of vibrations over time is also steady for that tuning fork and can be matched with a frequency (the number of occurrences over time). All frequencies heard by the human ear are categorized by using frequency and are measured in Hertz (cycles per second).

The level of sound in the air is measured with sound level meters with a decibel (dB) scale. These meters respond to changes in air pressure caused by sound waves and measure sound intensity. One decibel is $1/10^{th}$ of a *bel*, named after Alexander Graham Bell, inventor of the telephone. The decibel scale is logarithmic (not linear like a scale on a ruler), so it is measured in factors of 10. This means, for example, that a 10 dB increase with a sound meter is equal to a 10-fold increase in sound intensity.

Mechanical Comprehension

Review of Physics and Mechanical Principles

The proper use of tools and machinery depends on an understanding of basic physics, which includes the study of motion and the interactions of mass, force, and energy. These terms are used every day, but their exact meanings are difficult to define. In fact, they're usually defined in terms of each other.

The matter in the universe (atoms and molecules) is characterized in terms of its **mass**, which is measured in kilograms in the **International System of Units (SI)**. The amount of mass that occupies a given volume of space is termed **density**.

Mass occupies space, but it's also a component that inversely relates to acceleration when a force is applied to it. This **force** is the application of energy to an object with the intent of changing its position (mainly its acceleration).

To understand **acceleration**, it's necessary to relate it to displacement and velocity. The **displacement** of an object is simply the distance it travels. The **velocity** of an object is the distance it travels in a unit of time, such as miles per hour or meters per second:

$$Velocity = \frac{Distance\ Traveled}{Time\ Required}$$

There's often confusion between the words "speed" and "velocity." Velocity includes speed *and* direction. For example, a car traveling east and another traveling west can have the same speed of 30 miles per hour (mph), but their velocities are different. If movement eastward is considered positive, then movement westward is negative. Thus, the eastbound car has a velocity of 30 mph while the westbound car has a velocity of -30 mph.

The fact that velocity has a **magnitude** (speed) and a direction makes it a vector quantity. A **vector** is an arrow pointing in the direction of motion, with its length proportional to its magnitude.

Vectors can be added geometrically as shown below. In this example, a boat is traveling east at 4 knots (nautical miles per hour) and there's a current of 3 knots (thus a slow boat and a very fast current). If the boat travels in the same direction as the current, it gets a "lift" from the current and its speed is 7 knots. If the boat heads *into* the current, it has a forward speed of only 1 knot (4 knots – 3 knots = 1 knot) and makes very little headway. As shown in the figure below, the current is flowing north across the boat's path. Thus, for every 4 miles of progress the boat makes eastward, it drifts 3 miles to the north.

Working with Velocity Vectors

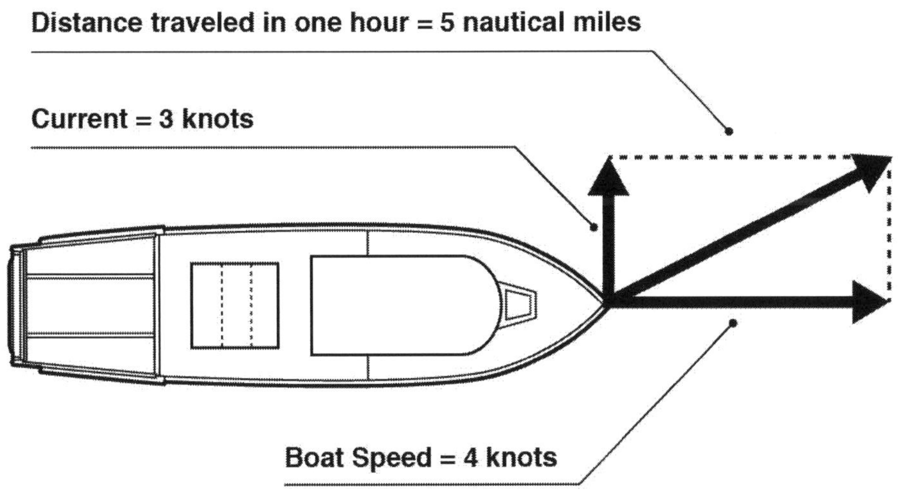

The total distance traveled is calculated using the *Pythagorean Theorem* for a right triangle, which should be memorized as follows:

$$a^2 + b^2 = c^2 \text{ or } c = \sqrt{a^2 + b^2}$$

Of course, the problem above was set up using a Pythagorean triple (3, 4, 5), which made the calculation easy.

Another example where velocity and speed are different is with a car traveling around a bend in the road. The speed is constant along the road, but the direction (and therefore the velocity) changes continuously.

The **acceleration** of an object is the change in its velocity in a given period of time:

$$Acceleration = \frac{Change\ in\ Velocity}{Time\ Required}$$

For example, a car starts at rest and then reaches a velocity of 70 mph in 8 seconds. What's the car's acceleration in feet per second squared? First, the velocity must be converted from miles per hour to feet per second:

$$70\frac{miles}{hour}\times\frac{5{,}280\,feet}{mile}\times\frac{hour}{3600\,seconds}=102.67\,feet/second$$

Starting from rest, the acceleration is:

$$Acceleration=\frac{102.67\dfrac{feet}{second}-0\,\dfrac{feet}{second}}{8\,seconds}=12.8\,feet/second^2$$

Newton's Laws

Isaac Newton's three laws of motion describe how the acceleration of an object is related to its mass and the forces acting on it. The three laws are:

- Unless acted on by a force, a body at rest tends to remain at rest; a body in motion tends to remain in motion with a constant velocity and direction.
- A force that acts on a body accelerates it in the direction of the force. The larger the force, the greater the acceleration; the larger the mass, the greater its inertia (resistance to movement and acceleration).
- Every force acting on a body is resisted by an equal and opposite force.

To understand Newton's laws, it's necessary to understand forces. These forces can push or pull on a mass, and they have a magnitude and a direction. Forces are represented by a vector, which is the arrow lined up along the direction of the force with its tip at the point of application. The magnitude of the force is represented by the length of the vector.

The figure below shows a mass acted on or "pushed" by two equal forces (shown here by vectors of the same length). Both vectors "push" along the same line through the center of the mass, but in opposite directions. What happens?

A Mass Acted on by Equal and Opposite Forces

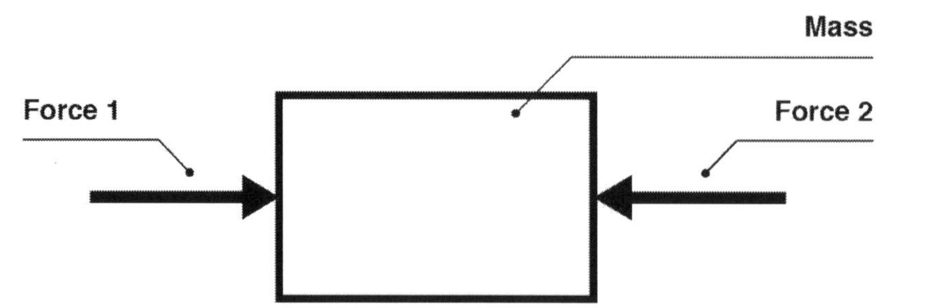

According to Newton's third law, every force on a body is resisted by an equal and opposite force. In the figure above, Force 1 acts on the left side of the mass. The mass pushes back. Force 2 acts on the right side, and the mass pushes back against this force too. The net force on the mass is zero, so according to Newton's first law, there's no change in the **momentum** (the mass times its velocity) of the mass. Therefore, if the mass is at rest before the forces are applied, it remains at rest. If the mass is in motion with a constant velocity, its momentum doesn't change. So, what happens when the net force on the mass isn't zero, as shown in the figure below?

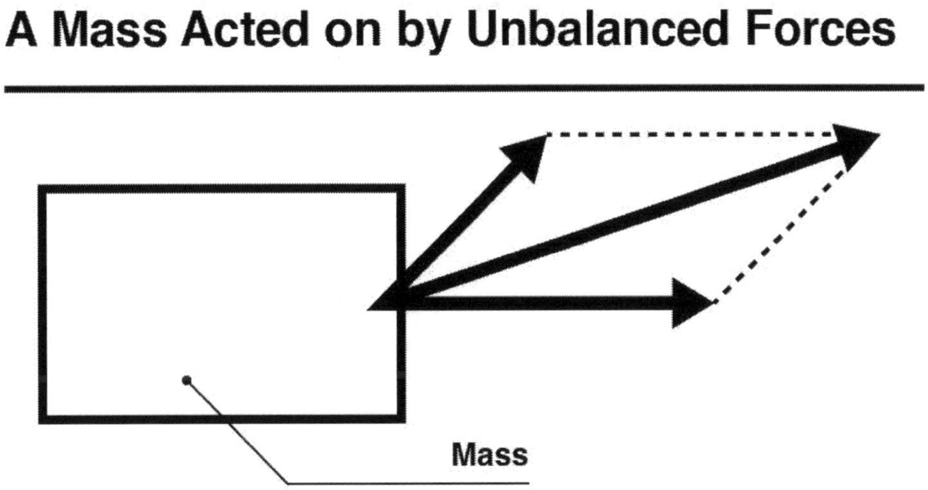

Notice that the forces are vector quantities and are added geometrically the same way that velocity vectors are manipulated.

Here in the figure above, the mass is pulled by two forces acting to the right, so the mass accelerates in the direction of the net force. This is described by Newton's second law:

Force = Mass x Acceleration

The force (measured in *newtons*) is equal to the product of the mass (measured in kilograms) and its acceleration (measured in meters per second squared or meters per second, per second). A better way to look at the equation is dividing through by the mass:

Acceleration = Force/Mass

This form of the equation makes it easier to see that the acceleration of an object varies directly with the net force applied and inversely with the mass. Thus, as the mass increases, the acceleration is reduced for a given force. To better understand, think of how a baseball accelerates when hit by a bat. Now imagine hitting a cannonball with the same bat and the same force. The cannonball is more massive than the baseball, so it won't accelerate very much when hit by the bat.

In addition to forces acting on a body by touching it, gravity acts as a force at a distance and causes all bodies in the universe to attract each other. The **force of gravity** (F_g) is proportional to the masses of the two objects (m and M) and inversely proportional to the square of the distance (r^2) between them (and G is the proportionality constant). This is shown in the following equation:

$$F_g = G\frac{mM}{r^2}$$

The force of gravity is what causes an object to fall to Earth when dropped from an airplane. Understanding gravity helps explain the difference between mass and weight. Mass is a property of an object that remains the same while it's intact, no matter where it's located. A 10-kilogram cannonball has the same mass on Earth as it does on the moon. On Earth, it weighs 98.1 newtons because of the attractive force of gravity, so it accelerates at 9.81 m/s^2. However, on the moon, the same cannonball has a weight of only about 16 newtons. This is because the gravitational attraction on the moon is approximately one-sixth that on Earth. Although Earth still attracts the body on the moon, it's so far away that its force is negligible.

For Americans, there's often confusion when talking about mass because the United States still uses **pounds** as a measurement of weight. In the traditional system used in the United States, the unit of mass is called a **slug**. It's derived by dividing the weight in pounds by the acceleration of gravity (32 feet/s^2); however, it's rarely used today. To avoid future problems, test takers should continue using SI units and remember to express mass in kilograms and weight in Newtons.

Another way to understand Newton's second law is to think of it as an object's change in momentum, which is defined as the product of the object's mass and its velocity:

Momentum = Mass x Velocity

Which of the following has the greater momentum: a pitched baseball, a softball, or a bullet fired from a rifle?

A bullet with a mass of 5 grams (0.005 kilograms) is fired from a rifle with a muzzle velocity of 2200 mph. Its momentum is calculated as:

$$2200\frac{miles}{hour} \times \frac{5{,}280\,feet}{mile} \times \frac{m}{3.28\,feet} \times \frac{hour}{3600\,seconds} \times 0.005kg = 4.92\frac{kg.m}{seconds}$$

A softball has a mass between 177 grams and 198 grams and is thrown by a college pitcher at 50 miles per hour. Taking an average mass of 188 grams (0.188 kilograms), a softball's momentum is calculated as:

$$50\frac{miles}{hour} \times \frac{5280\,feet}{mile} \times \frac{m}{3.28\,ft} \times \frac{hour}{3600\,seconds} \times 0.188kg = 4.19\frac{kg.m}{seconds}$$

That's only slightly less than the momentum of the bullet. Although the speed of the softball is considerably less, its mass is much greater than the bullet's.

A professional baseball pitcher can throw a 145-gram baseball at 100 miles per hour. A similar calculation (try doing it!) shows that the pitched hardball has a momentum of about 6.48 kg.m/seconds. That's more momentum than a speeding bullet!

So why is the bullet more harmful than the hard ball? It's because the force that it applies acts on a much smaller area.

Instead of using acceleration, Newton's second law is expressed here as the change in momentum (with the delta symbol "Δ" meaning "change"):

$$Force = \frac{\Delta\,Momentum}{\Delta\,Time} = \frac{\Delta\,(Mass \times Velocity)}{\Delta\,Time} = Mass \times \frac{\Delta\,Velocity}{\Delta\,Time}$$

The rapid application of force is called **impulse.** Another way of stating Newton's second law is in terms of the impulse, which is the force multiplied by its time of application:

$$Impluse = Force \times \Delta\, Time = Mass \times \Delta\, Velocity$$

In the case of the rifle, the force created by the pressure of the charge's explosion in its shell pushes the bullet, accelerating it until it leaves the barrel of the gun with its **muzzle velocity** (the speed the bullet has when it leaves the muzzle). After leaving the gun, the bullet doesn't accelerate because the gas pressure is exhausted. The bullet travels with a constant velocity in the direction it's fired (ignoring the force exerted against the bullet by friction and drag).

Similarly, the pitcher applies a force to the ball by using their muscles when throwing. Once the ball leaves the pitcher's fingers, it doesn't accelerate and the ball travels toward the batter at a constant speed (again ignoring friction and drag). The speed is constant, but the velocity can change if the ball travels along a curve.

Projectile Motion

According to Newton's first law, if no additional forces act on the bullet or ball, it travels in a straight line. This is also true if the bullet is fired in outer space. However, here on Earth, the force of gravity continues to act so the motion of the bullet or ball is affected.

What happens when a bullet is fired from the top of a hill using a rifle held perfectly horizontal? Ignoring air resistance, its horizontal velocity remains constant at its muzzle velocity. Its vertical velocity (which is zero when it leaves the gun barrel) increases because of gravity's acceleration. Each passing second, the bullet traces out the same distance horizontally while increasing distance vertically (shown in the figure below). In the end, the projectile traces out a **parabolic curve**.

Projectile Path for a Bullet Fired Horizontally from a Hill (Ignoring Air Resistance)

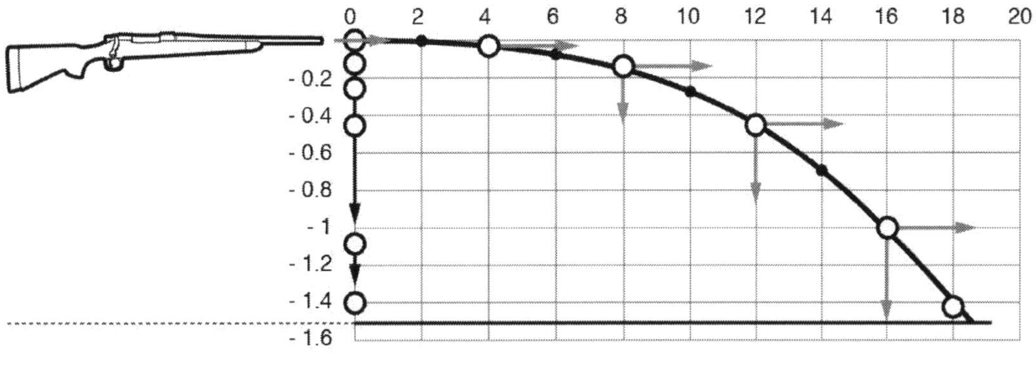

This vertical, downward acceleration is why a pitcher must put an arc on the ball when throwing across home plate. Otherwise the ball will fall at the batter's feet.

It's also interesting to note that if an artillery crew simultaneously drops one cannonball and fires another one horizontally, the two cannonballs will hit the ground at the same time since both balls are accelerating at the same rate and experience the same changes in vertical velocity.

What if air resistance is taken into account? This is best answered by looking at the horizontal and vertical motions separately.

The horizontal velocity is no longer constant because the initial velocity of the projectile is continually reduced by the resistance of the air. This is a complex problem in fluid mechanics, but it's sufficient to note that that the projectile doesn't fly as far before landing as predicted from the simple theory.

The vertical velocity is also reduced by air resistance. However, unlike the horizontal motion where the propelling force is zero after the cannonball is fired, the downward force of gravity acts continuously. The downward velocity increases every second due to the acceleration of gravity. As the velocity increases, the resisting force (called **drag**) increases with the square of the velocity. If the projectile is fired or dropped from a sufficient height, it reaches a terminal velocity such that the upward drag force equals the downward force of gravity. When that occurs, the projectile falls at a constant rate.

This is the same principle that's used for a parachute. Its drag (caused by its shape that scoops up air) is sufficient enough to slow down the fall of the parachutist to a safe velocity, thus avoiding a fatal crash on the ground.

So, what's the bottom line? If the vertical height isn't too great, a real projectile will fall short of the theoretical point of impact. However, if the height of the fall is significant and the drag of the object results in a small terminal fall velocity, then the projectile can go further than the theoretical point of impact.

What if the projectile is launched from a moving platform? In this case, the platform's velocity is added to the projectile's velocity. That's why an object dropped from the mast of a moving ship lands at the base of the mast rather than behind it. However, to an observer on the shore, the object traces out a parabolic arc.

<u>Angular Momentum</u>
In the previous examples, all forces acted through the center of the mass, but what happens if the forces aren't applied through the same line of action, like in the figure below?

A Mass Acted on by Forces Out of Line with Each Other

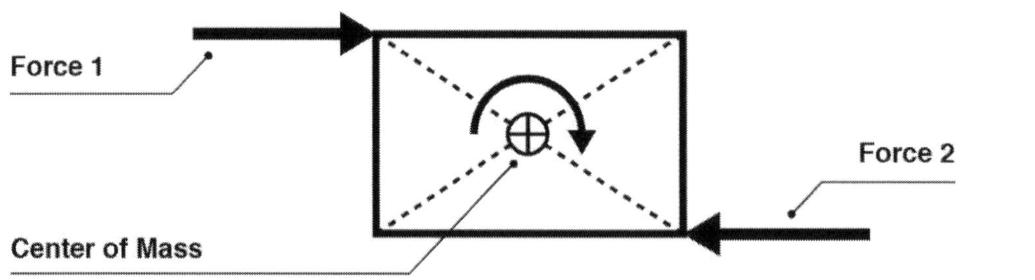

When this happens, the two forces create **torque** and the mass rotates around its center of gravity. In the figure above, the center of gravity is the center of the rectangle (**Center of Mass**), which is determined by the two, intersecting main diagonals. The center of an irregularly shaped object is found by hanging it from two different edges, and the center of gravity is at the intersection of the two "plumb lines."

Newton's second law still applies when the forces form a moment pair, but it must be expressed in terms of angular acceleration and the moment of inertia. The **moment of inertia** is a measure of the body's resistance to rotation, similar to the mass's resistance to linear acceleration. The more compact the body, the less the moment of inertia and the faster it rotates, much like how an ice skater spinning with outstretched arms will speed up as the arms are brought in close to the body.

The concept of torque is important in understanding the use of wrenches and is likely to be on the test. The concept of torque and moment/lever arm will be taken up again below when the physics of simple machines is presented.

<u>Energy and Work</u>
The previous examples of moving boats, cars, bullets, and baseballs are examples of simple systems that are thought of as particles with forces acting through their center of gravity. They all have one property in common: **energy**. The energy of the system results from the forces acting on it and is considered its ability to do work.

Work or the energy required to do work (which are the same) is calculated as the product of force and distance traveled along the line of action of the force. It's measured in **foot-pounds** in the traditional system (which is still used in workshops and factories) and in **newton meters** (*N·m*) in the International System of Units (SI), which is the preferred system of measurement today.

<u>Potential and Kinetic Energy</u>
Energy can neither be created nor destroyed, but it can be converted from one form to another. There are many forms of energy, but it's useful to start with mechanical energy and potential energy.

The **potential energy** of an object is equal to the work that's required to lift it from its original elevation to its current elevation. This is calculated as the weight of the object or its downward force (mass times the acceleration of gravity) multiplied by the distance (y) it is lifted above the reference elevation or "datum." This is written:

$$PE = mgy$$

The mechanical or **kinetic energy** of a system is related to its mass and velocity:

$$KE = \frac{1}{2}mv^2$$

The **total energy** is the sum of the kinetic energy and the potential energy, both of which are measured in foot-pounds or newton meters.

If a weight with a mass of 10 kilograms is raised up a ladder to a height of 10 meters, it has a potential energy of 10m x 10kg x 9.81m/s^2 = 981N·m. This is approximately 1000 newton meters if the acceleration of gravity (9.81 m/s^2) is rounded to 10 m/s^2, which is accurate enough for most earth-bound calculations. It has zero kinetic energy because it's at rest, with zero velocity.

If the weight is dropped from its perch, it accelerates downward so that its velocity and kinetic energy increase as its potential energy is "used up" or, more precisely, converted to kinetic energy.

When the weight reaches the bottom of the ladder, just before it hits the ground, it has a kinetic energy of 981 N·m (ignoring small losses due to air resistance). The velocity can be solved by using the following:

$$981\,N \cdot m = \frac{1}{2} 10\,kg \times v^2 \quad \text{or} \quad v = 14.01\,m/s$$

When the 10-kilogram weight hits the ground, its potential energy (which was measured from the ground) and its velocity are both zero, so its kinetic energy is also zero. What's happened to the energy? It's dissipated into heat, noise, and kicking up some dust. It's important to remember that energy can neither be created nor destroyed, so it can only change from one form to another.

The conversion between potential and kinetic energy works the same way for a pendulum. If it's raised and held at its highest position, it has maximum potential energy but zero kinetic energy.

Potential and Kinetic Energy for a Swinging Pendulum

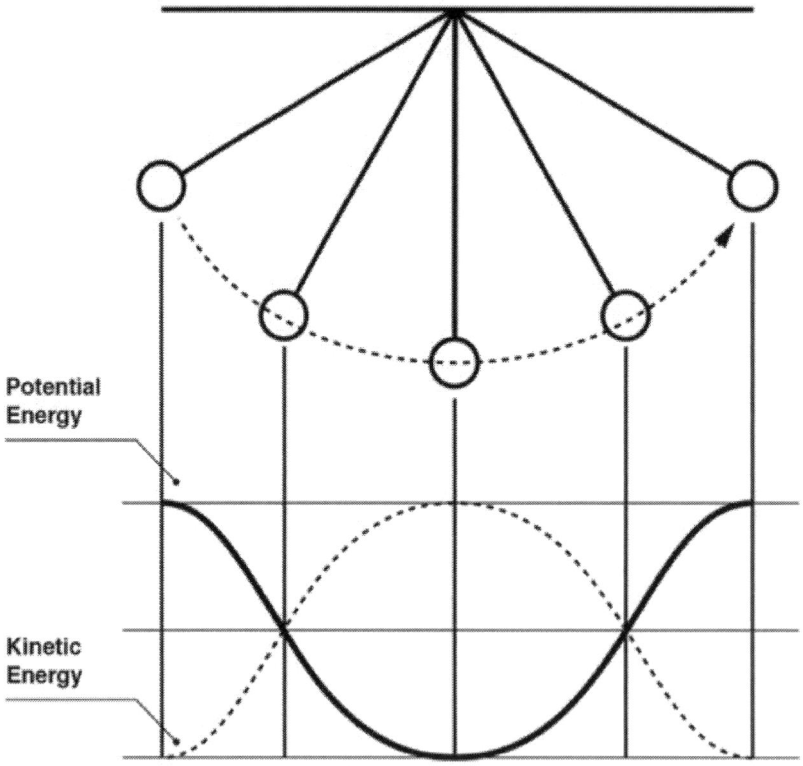

When the pendulum is released from its highest position (see left side of the figure above), it swings down so that its kinetic energy increases as its potential energy decreases. At the bottom of its swing, the pendulum is moving at its maximum velocity with its maximum kinetic energy. As the pendulum swings past the bottom of its path, its velocity slows down as its potential energy increases.

Work
The released potential energy of a system can be used to do **work**.

For instance, most of the energy lost by letting a weight fall freely can be recovered by hooking it up to a pulley to do work by pulling another weight back up (as shown in the figure below).

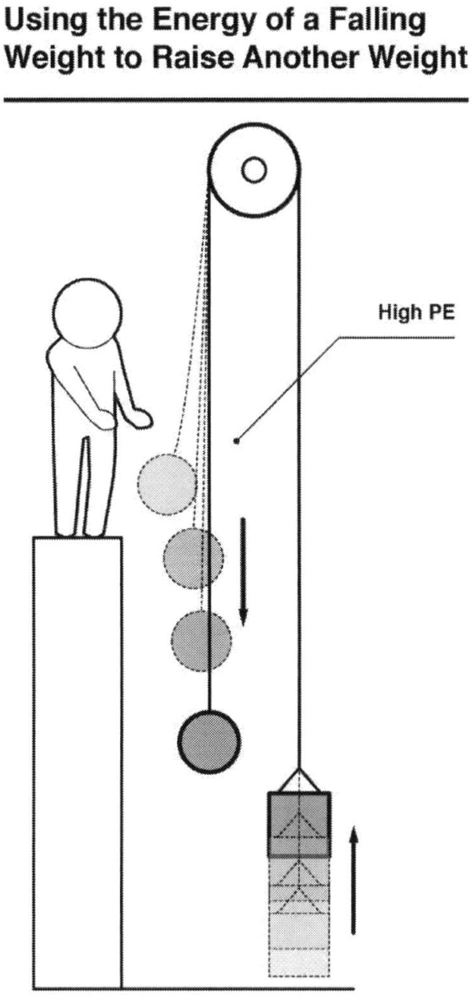

In other words, the potential energy expended to lower the weight is used to do the work of lifting another object. Of course, in a real system, there are losses due to friction. The action of pulleys will be discussed later in this study guide.

Since **energy** is defined as *the capacity to do work*, energy and work are measured in the same units:

$$Energy = Work = Force \times Distance$$

Force is measured in **newtons** (*N*)**.** Distance is measured in meters. The units of work are **newton meters** *(N·m)*. The same is true for kinetic energy and potential energy.

Another way to store energy is to compress a spring. Energy is stored in the spring by stretching or compressing it. The work required to shorten or lengthen the spring is given by the equation:

$$F = k \times d$$

Here, "d" is the length in meters and "k" is the resistance of the spring constant (measured in N·m), which is a constant as long as the spring isn't stretched past its elastic limit. The resistance of the spring is constant, but the force needed to compress the spring increases with each millimeter it's pushed.

The potential energy stored in the spring is equal to the work done to compress it, which is the total force times the change in length. Since the resisting force of the spring increases as its displacement increases, the average force must be used in the calculation:

$$W = PE = F \times d = \frac{1}{2}(F_i + F_f)d \times d = \frac{1}{2}(0 + F_f)d \times d = \frac{1}{2}Fd^2$$

The potential energy in the spring is stored by locking it into place, and the work energy used to compress it is recovered when the spring is unlocked. It's the same when dropping a weight from a height—the energy doesn't have to be wasted. In the case of the spring, the energy is used to propel an object.

Potential and Kinetic Energy of a Spring

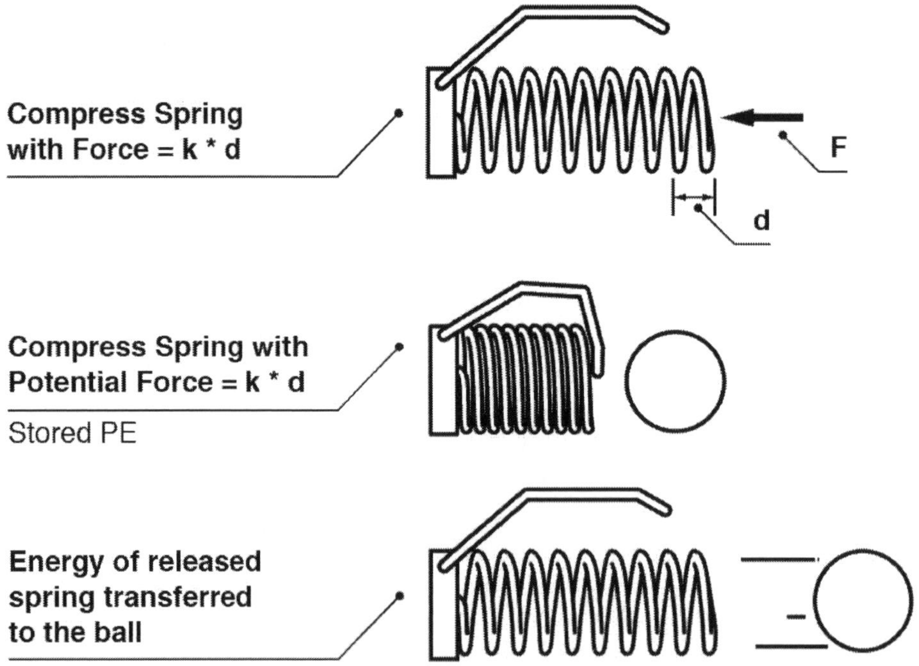

Pushing a block horizontally along a rough surface requires work. In this example, the work needs to overcome the force of friction, which opposes the direction of the motion and equals the weight of the block times a **friction factor** (*f*). The friction factor is greater for rough surfaces than smooth surfaces, and it's usually greater *before* the motion starts than after it has begun to slide. These terms are illustrated in the figure below.

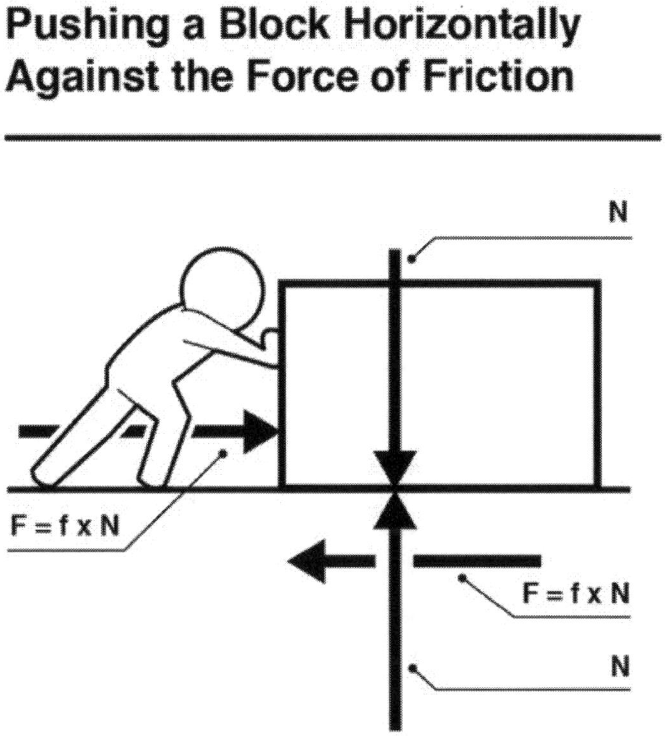

When pushing a block, there's no increase in potential energy since the block's elevation doesn't change. Expending the energy to overcome friction is "wasted" in the generation of heat. Yet, to move a block from point A to point B, an energy cost must be paid. However, friction isn't always a hindrance. In fact, it's the force that makes the motion of a wheel possible.

Heat energy can also be created by burning organic fuels, such as wood, coal, natural gas, and petroleum. All of these are derived from plant matter that's created using solar energy and photosynthesis. The chemical energy or *"heat"* liberated by the combustion of these fuels is used to warm buildings during the winter or even melt metal in a foundry. The heat is also used to generate steam, which can drive engines or turn turbines to generate electric energy.

In fact, work and heat are interchangeable. This fact was first recognized by gun founders when they were boring out cast, brass cannon blanks. The cannon blanks were submerged in a water bath to reduce friction, yet as the boring continued, the water bath boiled away!

Later, the amount of work needed to raise the temperature of water was measured by an English physicist (and brewer) named James Prescott Joule. The way that Joule measured the mechanical equivalent of heat is illustrated in the figure below. This setup is similar to the one in the figure above with the pulley, except instead of lifting another weight, the falling weight's potential energy is converted to the mechanical energy of the rotating vertical shaft. This turns the paddles, which churns the water to increase its temperature. Through a long series of repeated measurements, Joule showed that 4186 N·m of work was necessary to raise the temperature of one kilogram of water by one degree Celsius, no matter how the work was delivered.

Device Measuring the Mechanical Energy Needed to Increase the Temperature of Water

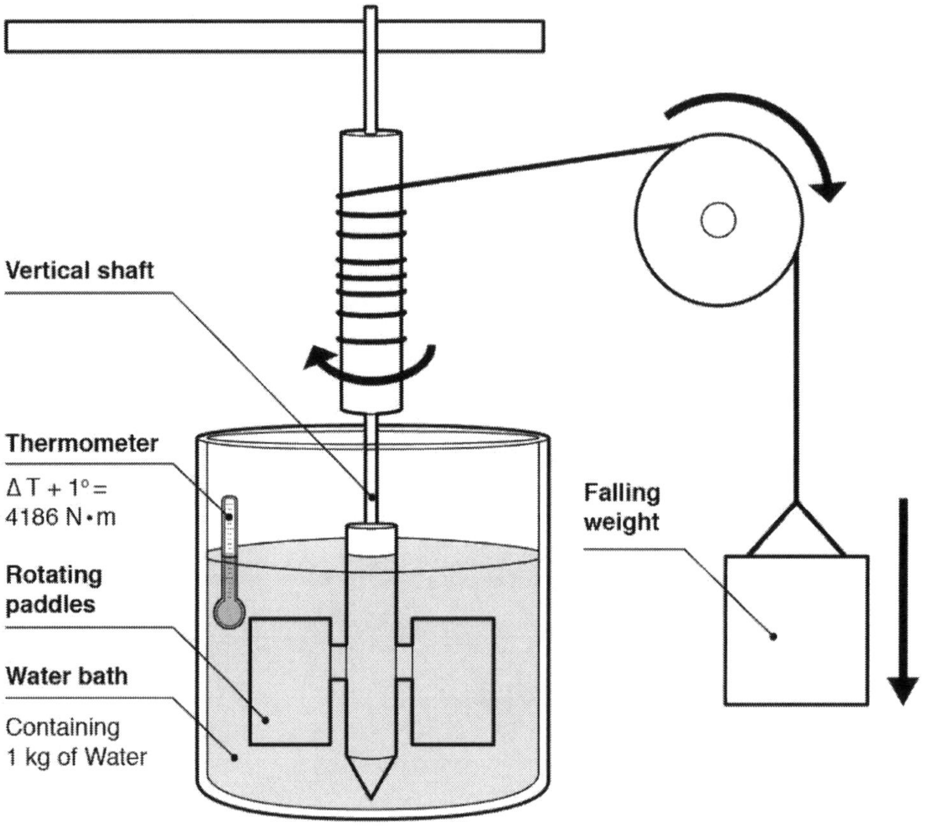

In recognition of this experiment, the newton meter is also called a **joule**. Linking the names for work and heat to the names of two great physicists is truly appropriate because heat and work being interchangeable is of the greatest practical importance. These two men were part of a very small, select group of scientists for whom units of measurement have been named: Marie Curie for radioactivity, Blaise Pascal for pressure, James Watt for power, Andre Ampere for electric current, and only a few others.

Just as mechanical work is converted into heat energy, heat energy is converted into mechanical energy in the reverse process. An example of this is a closely fitting piston supporting a weight and mounted in a cylinder where steam enters from the bottom.

In this example, water is heated into steam in a boiler, and then the steam is drawn off and piped into a cylinder. Steam pressure builds up in the piston, exerting a force in all directions. This is counteracted by the tensile strength of the cylinder; otherwise, it would burst. The pressure also acts on the exposed face of the piston, pushing it upwards against the load (displacing it) and thus doing work.

Work developed from the pressure acting over the area exerts a force on the piston as described in the following equation:

$$Work = Pressure \times Piston\,Area \times Displacement$$

Here, the work is measured in newton meters, the pressure in newtons per square meter or **pascals** (*Pa*), and the piston displacement is measured in meters.

Since the volume enclosed between the cylinder and piston increases with the displacement, the work can also be expressed as:

$$Work = Pressure \times \Delta\,Volume$$

For example, a 10-kilogram weight is set on top of a piston-cylinder assembly with a diameter of 25 centimeters. The area of the cylinder is:

$$Area = \frac{\pi \times d^2}{4} = 0.785 \times 0.25^2 = .049\,m^2$$

If the acceleration due to gravity is approximately 10 m/s^2, and the area is rounded to .05 meters squared, then the pressure needed to counteract the weight of the 10-kilogram weight is estimated as:

$$P = \frac{F}{A} \approx 10\ \times \frac{10}{0.05} = 2000\frac{N}{m^2} = 2000\,Pa = 2\,KPa$$

If steam with a pressure slightly greater than this value is piped into the cylinder, it slowly lifts the load. If steam at a much higher pressure is suddenly admitted to the cylinder, it throws the load into the air. This is the principle used to steam-catapult airplanes off the deck of an aircraft carrier.

Power

Power is defined as the rate at which work is done, or the time it takes to do a given amount of work. In the International System of Units (SI), work is measured in **newton meters** (*N·m*) or **joules** (*J*). Power is measured in joules/second or *watts (W)*.

For example, to raise a 1-kilogram mass one meter off the ground, it takes approximately 10 newton meters of work (approximating the gravitational acceleration of 9.81 m/s^2 as 10 m/s^2). To do the work in 10 seconds, it requires 1 watt of power. Doing it in 1 second requires 10 watts of power. Essentially, *doing it faster means dividing by a smaller number*, and that means greater power.

Although SI units are preferred for technical work throughout the world, the old traditional (or English) unit of measuring power is still used. Introduced by James Watt (the same man for whom the SI unit of power "watt" is named), the unit of **horsepower** (*HP*) rated the power of the steam engines that he and his partner (Matthew Boulton) manufactured and sold to mine operators in 18th century England. The mine operators used these engines to pump water out of flooded facilities in the beginning of the Industrial Revolution.

To provide a measurement that the miners would be familiar with, Watt and Boulton referenced the power of their engines with the "power of a horse."

Watt's measurements showed that, on average, a well-harnessed horse could lift a 330-pound weight 100 feet up a well in one minute (330 pounds is the weight of a 40-gallon barrel filled to the brim).

Remembering that power is expressed in terms of energy or work per unit time, horsepower came to be measured as:

$$1\,HP = \frac{100\,feet\ \times\ 330\,pounds}{1\,minute} \times \frac{1\,minute}{60\,seconds} = 550\,foot\,pounds/second$$

A horse that pulled the weight up faster, or pulled up more weight in the same time, was a more *powerful* horse than Watt's "average horse."

Hundreds of millions of engines of all types have been built since Watt and Boulton started manufacturing their products, and the unit of horsepower has been used throughout the world to this day. Of course, modern technicians and engineers still need to convert horsepower to watts to work with SI units. An approximate conversion is *1 HP = 746 W.*

Take for example a 2016 CTS-V Cadillac rated at 640 HP. If a **megawatt** (*MW*) is one million watts, that means the Cadillac has almost half a megawatt of power as shown by this conversion:

$$640\,HP \times \frac{746\,W}{1\,HP} = 477{,}440\,W = 477.4\,kW$$

The power of the Cadillac is comparable to that of the new Westinghouse AP-1000 Nuclear Power Plant, which is rated at 1100 MW or the equivalent of 2304 Cadillacs (assuming no loss in power). That would need a very big parking lot and a tremendous amount of gasoline!

A question that's often asked is, "How much energy is expended by running an engine for a fixed amount of time?" This is important to know when planning how much fuel is needed to run an engine. For example, how much energy is expended in running the new Cadillac at maximum power for 30 minutes?

In this case, the energy expenditure is approximately 240 kilowatt hours. This must be converted to joules, using the conversion factor that one watt equals one joule per second:

$$240{,}000\,W\,hours \times \frac{3600\,seconds}{1\,hour} = 8.64(10)^8\,joules$$

So how much gasoline is burned? Industrial tests show that a gallon of gasoline is rated to contain about 1.3×10^8 joules of energy. That's 130 million joules per gallon. The gallons of gasoline are obtained by dividing:

$$\frac{8.64(10)^8 J}{1.3(10)^8 J/gallon} = 6.65\,gallons \times \frac{3.8\,liters}{gallon} = 25.3\,liters$$

The calculation has now come full circle. It began with power. Power equals energy divided by time. Power multiplied by time equals the energy needed to run the machine, which came from burning fuel.

Fluids

In addition to the behavior of solid particles acted on by forces, it is important to understand the behavior of fluids. **Fluids** include both liquids and gasses. The best way to understand fluid behavior is to contrast it with the behavior of solids, as shown in the figure below.

First, consider a block of ice, which is solid water. If it is set down inside a large box it will exert a force on the bottom of the box due to its weight as shown on the left, in Part A of the figure. The solid block exerts a pressure on the bottom of the box equal to its total weight divided by the area of its base:

$$Pressure = Weight\ of\ block/Area\ of\ base$$

That pressure acts only in the area directly under the block of ice.

If the same mass of ice is melted, it behaves much differently. It still has the same weight as before because its mass hasn't changed. However, the volume has decreased because liquid water molecules are more tightly packed together than ice molecules, which is why ice floats (it is less dense).

The Behavior of Solids and Liquids Compared

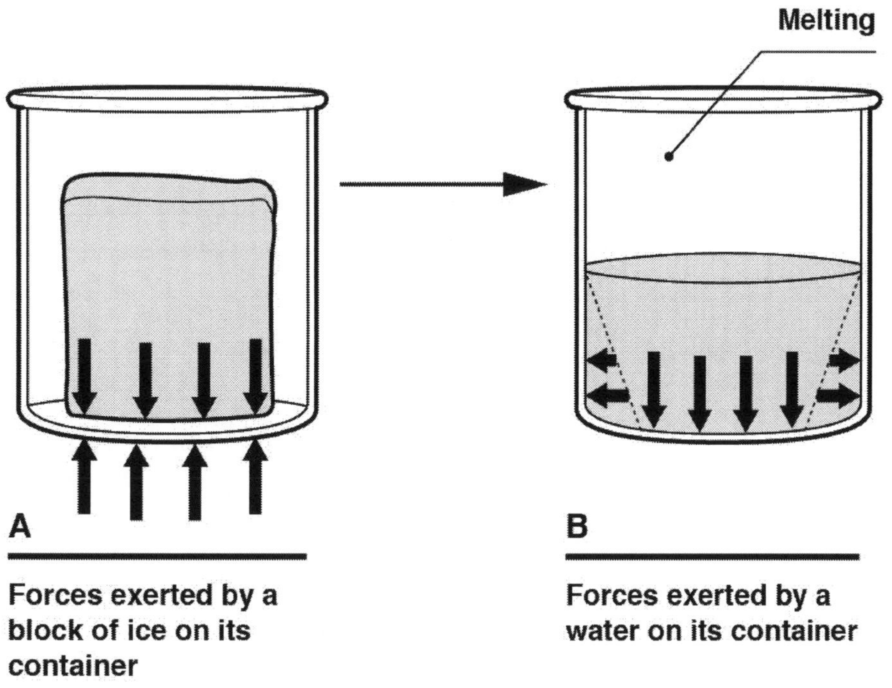

The melted ice (now water) conforms to the shape of the container. This means that the fluid exerts pressure not only on the base, but on the sides of the box at the water line and below. Actually, pressure in a liquid is exerted in all directions, but all the forces in the interior of the fluid cancel each other out, so that a net force is only exerted on the walls. Note also that the pressure on the walls increases with the depth of the water.

The fact that the liquid exerts pressure in all directions is part of the reason some solids float in liquids. Consider the forces acting on a block of wood floating in water, as shown in the figure below.

Floatation of a Block of Wood

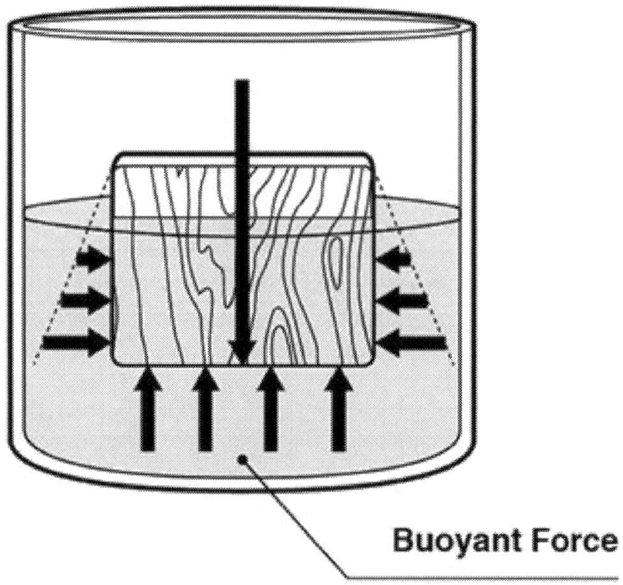

The block of wood is submerged in the water and pressure acts on its bottom and sides as shown. The weight of the block tends to force it down into the water. The force of the pressure on the left side of the block just cancels the force of the pressure on the right side.

There is a net upward force on the bottom of the block due to the pressure of the water acting on that surface. This force, which counteracts the weight of the block, is known as the **buoyant force**.

The block will sink to a depth such that the buoyant force of the water (equal to the weight of the volume displaced) just matches the total weight of the block. This will happen if two conditions are met:

- The body of water is deep enough to float the block
- The density of the block is less than the density of the water

If the body of water is not deep enough, the water pressure on the bottom side of the block won't be enough to develop a buoyant force equal to the block's weight. The block will be "beached" just like a boat caught at low tide.

If the density of the block is greater than the density of the fluid, the buoyant force acting on the bottom of the boat will not be sufficient to counteract the total weight of the block. That's why a solid steel block will sink in water.

If steel is denser than water, how can a steel ship float? The steel ship floats because it's hollow. The volume of water displaced by its steel shell (hull) is heavier than the entire weight of the ship and its contents (which includes a lot of empty space). In fact, there's so much empty space within a steel ship's hull that it can bob out of the water and be unstable at sea if some of the void spaces (called ballast tanks) aren't filled with water. This provides more weight and balance (or "trim") to the vessel.

The discussion of buoyant forces on solids holds for liquids as well. A less dense liquid can float on a denser liquid if they're **immiscible** (do not mix). For instance, oil can float on water because oil isn't as dense as the water. Fresh water can float on salt water for the same reason.

Pascal's law states that a change in pressure, applied to an enclosed fluid, is transmitted undiminished to every portion of the fluid and to the walls of its containing vessel. This principle is used in the design of hydraulic jacks, as shown in the figure below.

A force (F_1) is exerted on a small "driving" piston, which creates pressure on the hydraulic fluid. This pressure is transmitted through the fluid to a large cylinder. While the pressure is the same everywhere in the oil, the pressure action on the area of the larger cylinder creates a much higher upward force (F_2).

Illustration of a Hydraulic Jack Exemplifying Pascal's Law

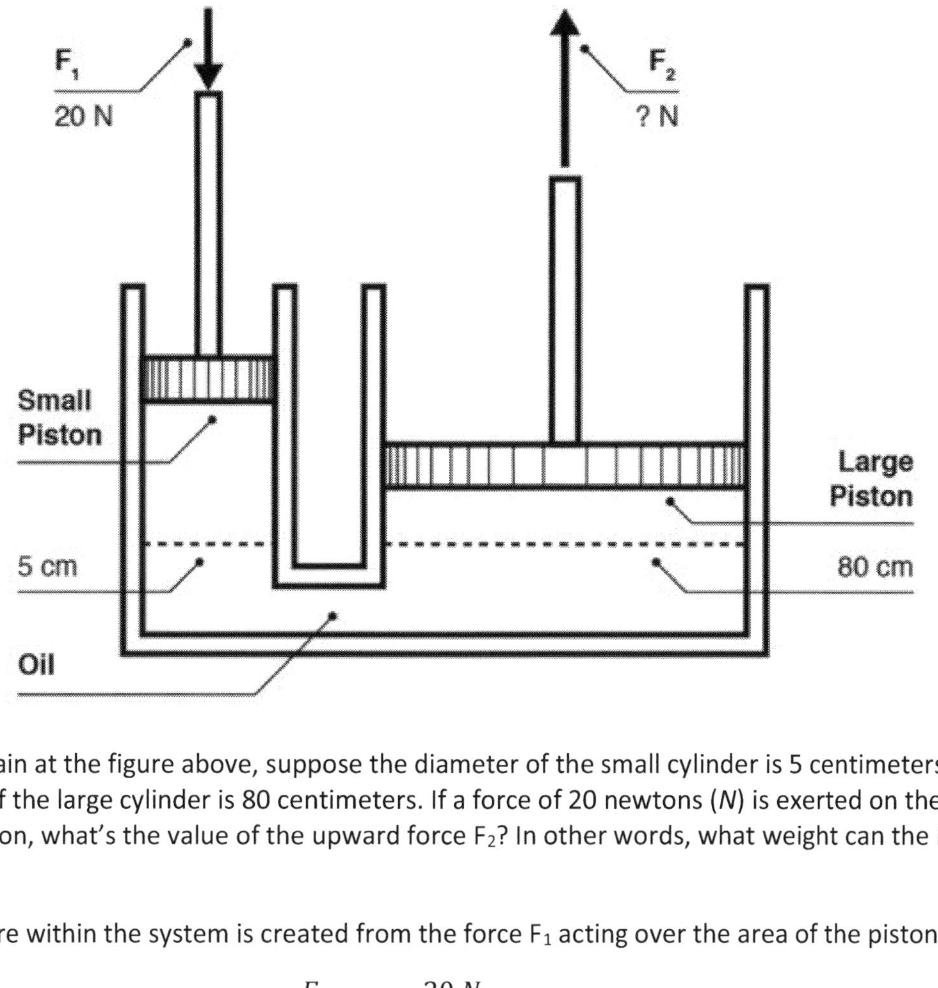

Looking again at the figure above, suppose the diameter of the small cylinder is 5 centimeters and the diameter of the large cylinder is 80 centimeters. If a force of 20 newtons (N) is exerted on the small driving piston, what's the value of the upward force F_2? In other words, what weight can the large piston support?

The pressure within the system is created from the force F_1 acting over the area of the piston:

$$P = \frac{F_1}{A} = \frac{20\ N}{\pi\,(0.05\ m)^2/4} = 10{,}185\ Pa$$

The same pressure acts on the larger piston, creating the upward force, F_2:

$$F_2 = P \times A = 10{,}185\ Pa \times \pi \times (0.8\ m)^2/4 = 5120\ N$$

Because a liquid has no internal shear strength, it can be transported in a pipe or channel between two locations. A fluid's **rate of flow** is the volume of fluid that passes a given location in a given amount of time and is expressed in *m^3/second*. The **flow rate** (*Q*) is determined by measuring the **area of flow** (*A*) in *m^2*, and the **flow velocity** (*v*) in *m/s*:

$$Q = v \times A$$

This equation is called the **Continuity Equation**. It's one of the most important equations in engineering and should be memorized. For example, what is the flow rate for a pipe with an inside diameter of 1200 millimeters running full with a velocity of 1.6 m/s (measured by a **sonic velocity meter**)?

Using the Continuity Equation, the flow is obtained by keeping careful track of units:

$$Q = v \times A = 1.6\frac{m}{s} \times \frac{\pi}{4} \times \left(\frac{1200\ mm}{1000\ mm/m}\right)^2 = 1.81\ m^3/second$$

For more practice, imagine that a pipe is filling a storage tank with a diameter of 100 meters. How long does it take for the water level to rise by 2 meters?

Since the flow rate (*Q*) is expressed in m^3/second, and volume is measured in m^3, then the time in seconds to supply a volume (*V*) is *V/Q*. Here, the volume required is:

$$Volume\ Required = Base\ Area \times Depth = \frac{\pi}{4}100^2 \times 2\ m = 15{,}700\ m^3$$

Thus, the time to fill the tank another 2 meters is 15,700 *m^3* divided by 1.81 *m^3/s* = 8674 seconds or 2.4 hours.

It's important to understand that, for a given flow rate, a smaller pipe requires a higher velocity.

The energy of a flow system is evaluated in terms of potential and kinetic energy, the same way the energy of a falling weight is evaluated. The total energy of a fluid flow system is divided into potential energy of elevation, and pressure and the kinetic energy of velocity. **Bernoulli's Equation** states that, for a constant flow rate, the total energy of the system (divided into components of elevation, pressure, and velocity) remains constant. This is written as:

$$Z + \frac{P}{\rho g} + \frac{v^2}{2g} = Constant$$

Each of the terms in this equation has dimensions of meters. The first term is the **elevation energy**, where *Z* is the elevation in meters. The second term is the **pressure energy**, where *P* is the pressure, ρ is the density, and *g* is the acceleration of gravity. The dimensions of the second term are also in meters. The third term is the **velocity energy**, also expressed in meters.

For a fixed elevation, the equation shows that, as the pressure increases, the velocity decreases. In the other case, as the velocity increases, the pressure decreases.

The use of the Bernoulli Equation is illustrated in the figure below. The total energy is the same at Sections 1 and 2. The area of flow at Section 1 is greater than the area at Section 2. Since the flow rate is the same at each section, the velocity at Point 2 is higher than at Point 1:

$$Q = V_1 \times A_1 = V_2 \times A_2, \qquad V_2 = V_1 \times \frac{A_1}{A_2}$$

Finally, since the total energy is the same at the two sections, the pressure at Point 2 is less than at Point 1. The tubes drawn at Points 1 and 2 would actually have the water levels shown in the figure; the pressure at each point would support a column of water of a height equal to the pressure divided by the unit weight of the water ($h = P/\rho g$).

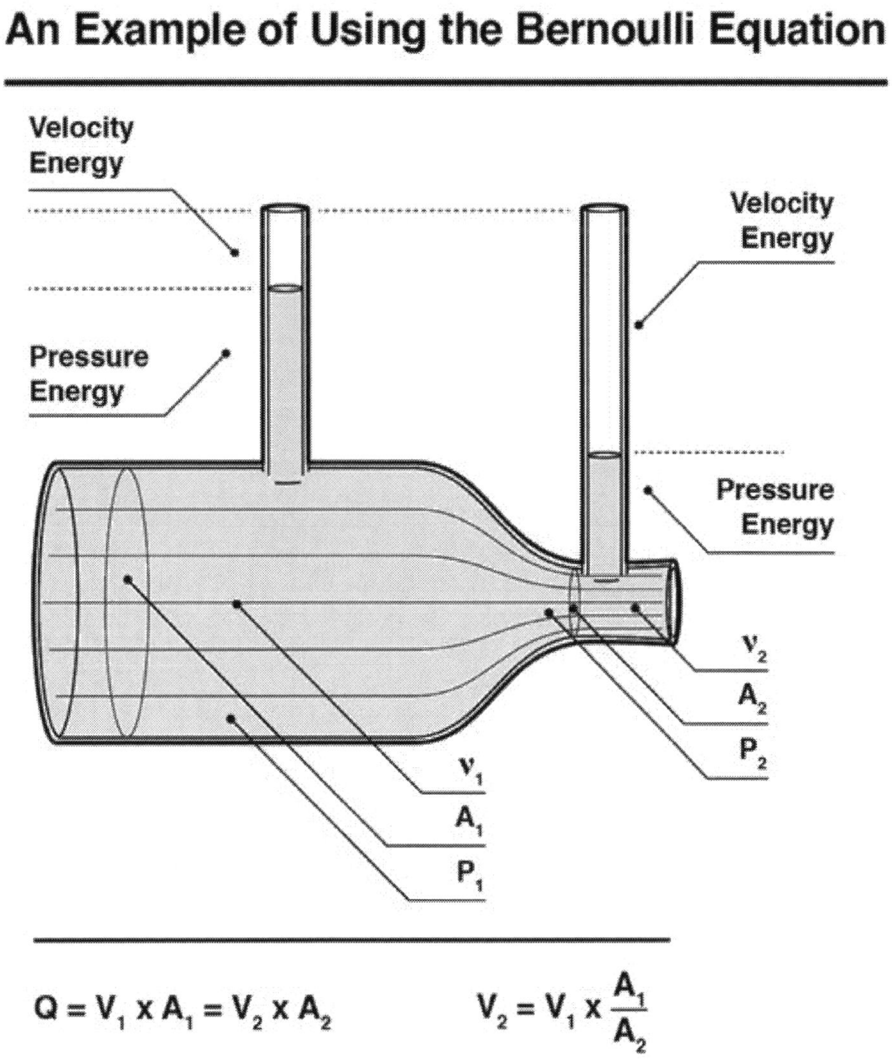

Machines

Now that the basic physics of work and energy have been discussed, the common machines used to do the work can be discussed in more detail.

A **machine** is a device that: transforms energy from one form to another, multiplies the force applied to do work, changes the direction of the resultant force, or increases the speed at which the work is done.

The details of how energy is converted into work by a system are extremely complicated but, no matter how complicated the "linkage" between the components, every system is composed of certain elemental or simple machines. These are discussed briefly in the following sections.

Levers

The simplest machine is a **lever**, which consists of two pieces or components: a **bar** (or beam) and a **fulcrum** (the pivot-point around which motion takes place). As shown below, the **effort** acts at a distance (L_1) from the fulcrum and the **load** acts at a distance (L_2) from the fulcrum.

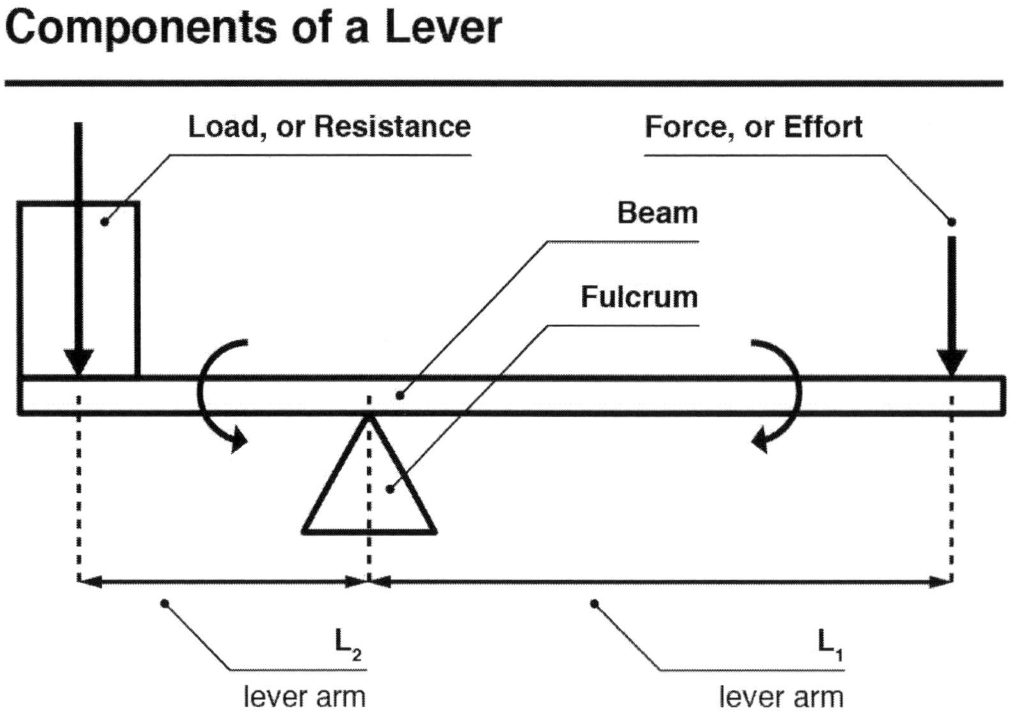

These lengths L_1 and L_2 are called **lever arms**. When the lever is balanced, the load (R) times its lever arm (L_2) equals the effort (F) times its lever arm (L_1). The force needed to lift the load is:

$$F = R \times \frac{L_2}{L_1}$$

This equation shows that as the lever arm L_1 is increased, the force required to lift the resisting load (R) is reduced. This is why Archimedes, one of the leading ancient Greek scientists, said, "Give me a lever long enough, and a place to stand, and I can move the Earth."

The ratio of the moment arms is the so-called "mechanical advantage" of the simple lever; the effort is multiplied by the mechanical advantage. For example, a 100-kilogram mass (a weight of approximately

1000 N) is lifted with a lever like the one in the figure below, with a total length of 3 meters, and the fulcrum situated 50 centimeters from the left end. What's the force needed to balance the load?

$$F = 1000\ N\ \times \frac{0.5\ meters}{2.5\ meters} = 200\ N$$

Depending on the location of the load and effort with respect to the fulcrum, three "classes" of lever are recognized. In each case, the forces can be analyzed as described above.

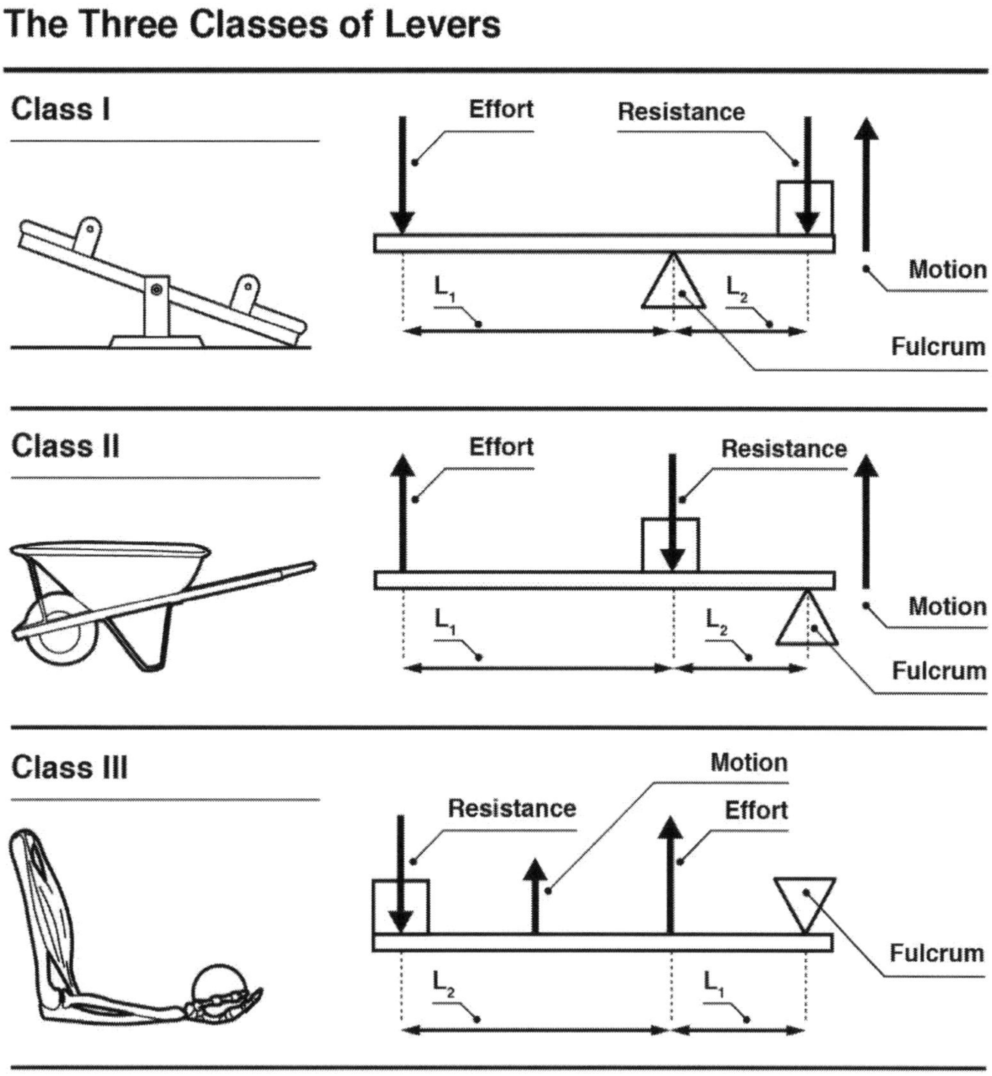

As seen in the figure, a **Class I** lever has the fulcrum positioned between the effort and the load. Examples of Class I levers include see-saws, balance scales, crow bars, and scissors. As explained above, the force needed to balance the load is $F = R \times (L_2/L_1)$, which means that the mechanical advantage is L_2/L_1. The crane boom shown back in the first figure in this section was a Class I lever, where the tower acted as the fulcrum and the counterweight on the left end of the boom provided the effort.

For a **Class II** lever, the load is placed between the fulcrum and the effort. A wheel barrow is a good example of a Class II lever. The mechanical advantage of a Class II lever is $(L_1 + L_2)/L_2$.

For a **Class III** lever, the effort is applied at a point between the fulcrum and the load, which increases the speed at which the load is moved. A human arm is a Class III lever, with the elbow acting as the fulcrum. The mechanical advantage of a Class III lever is $(L_1 + L_2)/L_1$.

Wheels and Axles

The wheel and axle is a special kind of lever. The **axle**, to which the load is applied, is set perpendicular to the **wheel** through its center. Effort is then applied along the rim of the wheel, either with a cable running around the perimeter or with a **crank** set parallel to the axle.

The mechanical advantage of the wheel and axle is provided by the moment arm of the perimeter cable or crank. Using the center of the axle (with a radius of *r*) as the fulcrum, the resistance of the load (*L*) is just balanced by the effort (*F*) times the wheel radius:

$$F \times R = L \times r \quad \text{or} \quad F = L \times \frac{r}{R}$$

This equation shows that increasing the wheel's radius for a given shaft reduces the required effort to carry the load. Of course, the axle must be made of a strong material or it'll be twisted apart by the applied torque. This is why steel axles are used.

Gears, Belts, and Cams

The functioning of a wheel and axle can be modified with the use of gears and belts. **Gears** are used to change the direction or speed of a wheel's motion.

The direction of a wheel's motion can be changed by using **beveled gears**, with the shafts set at right angles to each other, as shown in part *A* in the figure below.

The speed of a wheel can be changed by meshing together **spur gears** with different diameters. A small gear (A) is shown driving a larger gear (B) in the middle section *(B)* in the figure below. The gears rotate in opposite directions; if the driver, Gear A, moves clockwise, then Gear B is driven counter-clockwise. Gear B rotates at half the speed of the driver, Gear A. In general, the change in speed is given by the ratio of the number of teeth in each gear:

$$\frac{Rev_{Gear\ B}}{Rev_{Gear\ A}} = \frac{Number\ of\ Teeth\ in\ A}{Number\ of\ Teeth\ in\ B}$$

Rather than meshing the gears, **belts** are used to connect them as shown in part *(C)*.

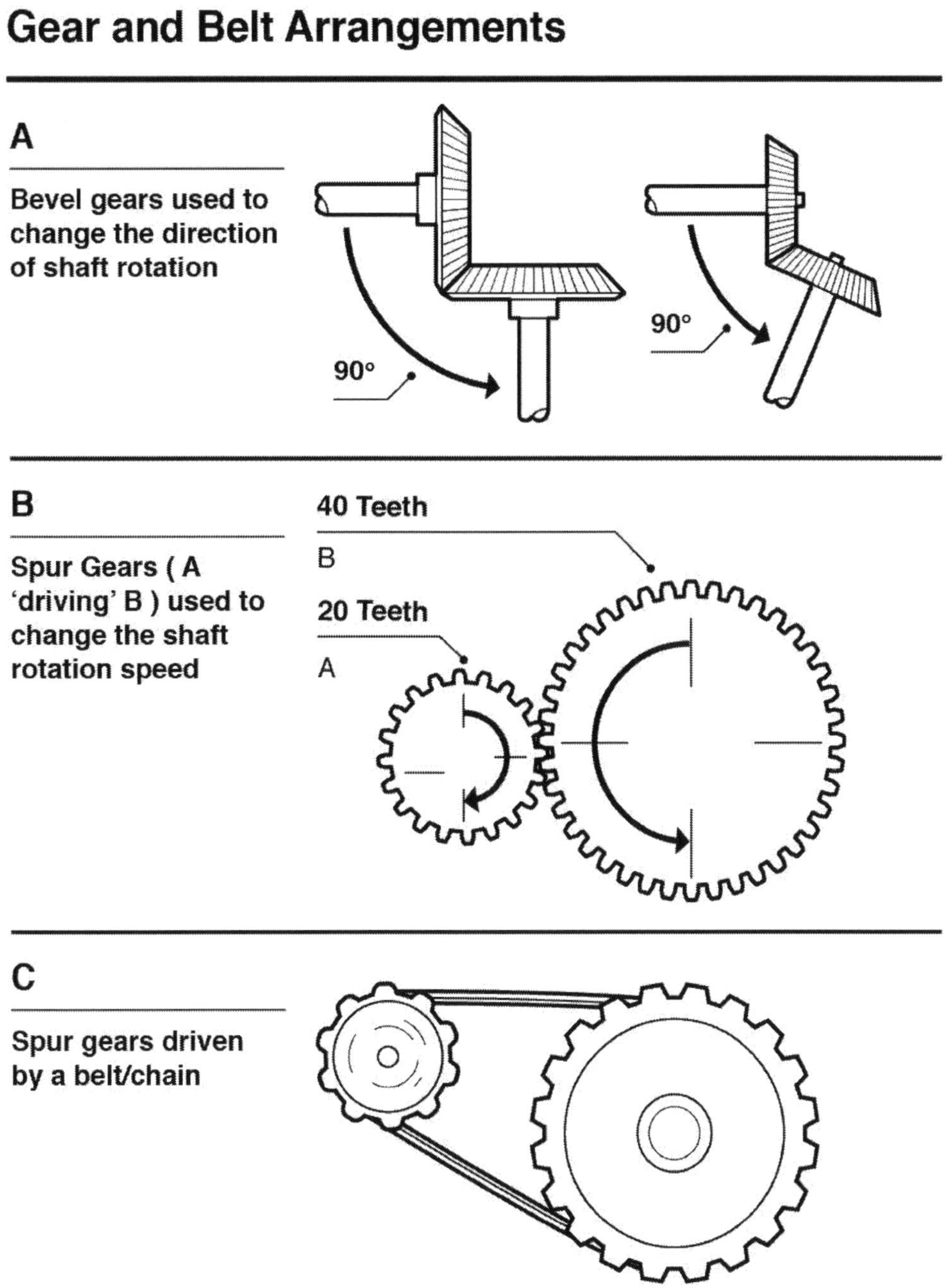

Gears can change the speed and direction of the axle rotation, but the rotary motion is maintained. To convert the rotary motion of a gear train into linear motion, it's necessary to use a **cam** (a type of off-centered wheel shown in the figure below, where rotary shaft motion lifts the valve in a vertical direction.

Conversion of Rotary to Vertical Linear Motion with a Cam

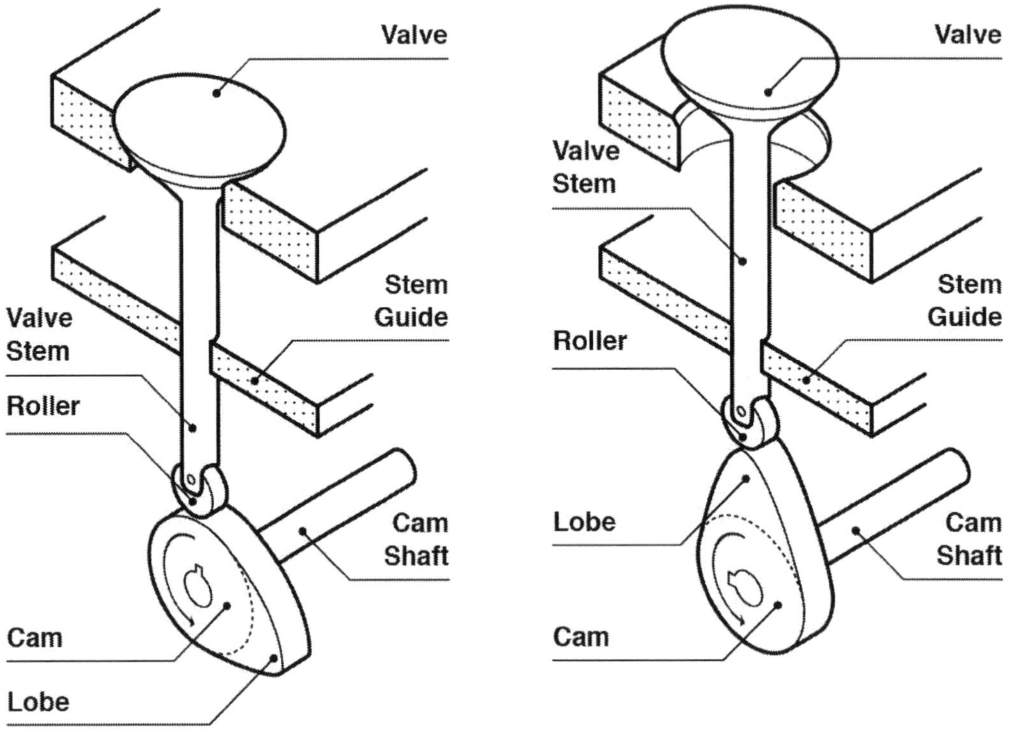

Pulleys

A **pulley** looks like a wheel and axle but provides a mechanical advantage in a different way. A **fixed pulley** was shown previously as a way to capture the potential energy of a falling weight to do useful work by lifting another weight. As shown in part *A* in the figure below, the fixed pulley is used to change the direction of the downward force exerted by the falling weight, but it doesn't provide any mechanical advantage.

The lever arm of the falling weight (A) is the distance between the rim of the fixed pulley and the center of the axle. This is also the length of the lever arm acting on the rising weight (B), so the ratio of the two arms is 1:0, meaning there's no mechanical advantage. In the case of a wheel and axle, the mechanical advantage is the ratio of the wheel radius to the axle radius.

A **moving pulley**, which is really a Class II lever, provides a mechanical advantage of 2:1 as shown below on the right side of the figure *(B)*.

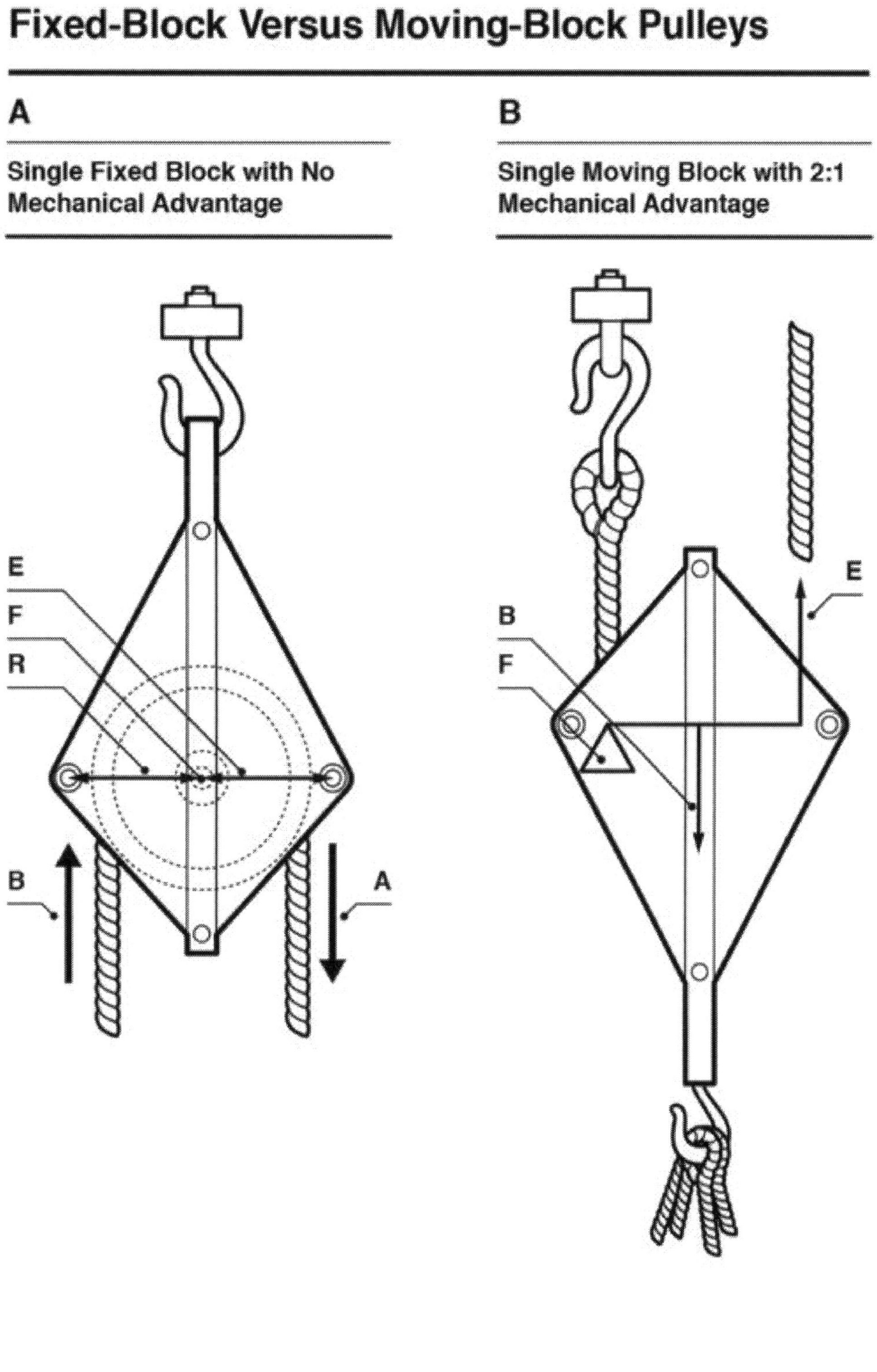

As demonstrated by the rigs in the figure below, using a wider moving block with multiple sheaves can achieve a greater mechanical advantage.

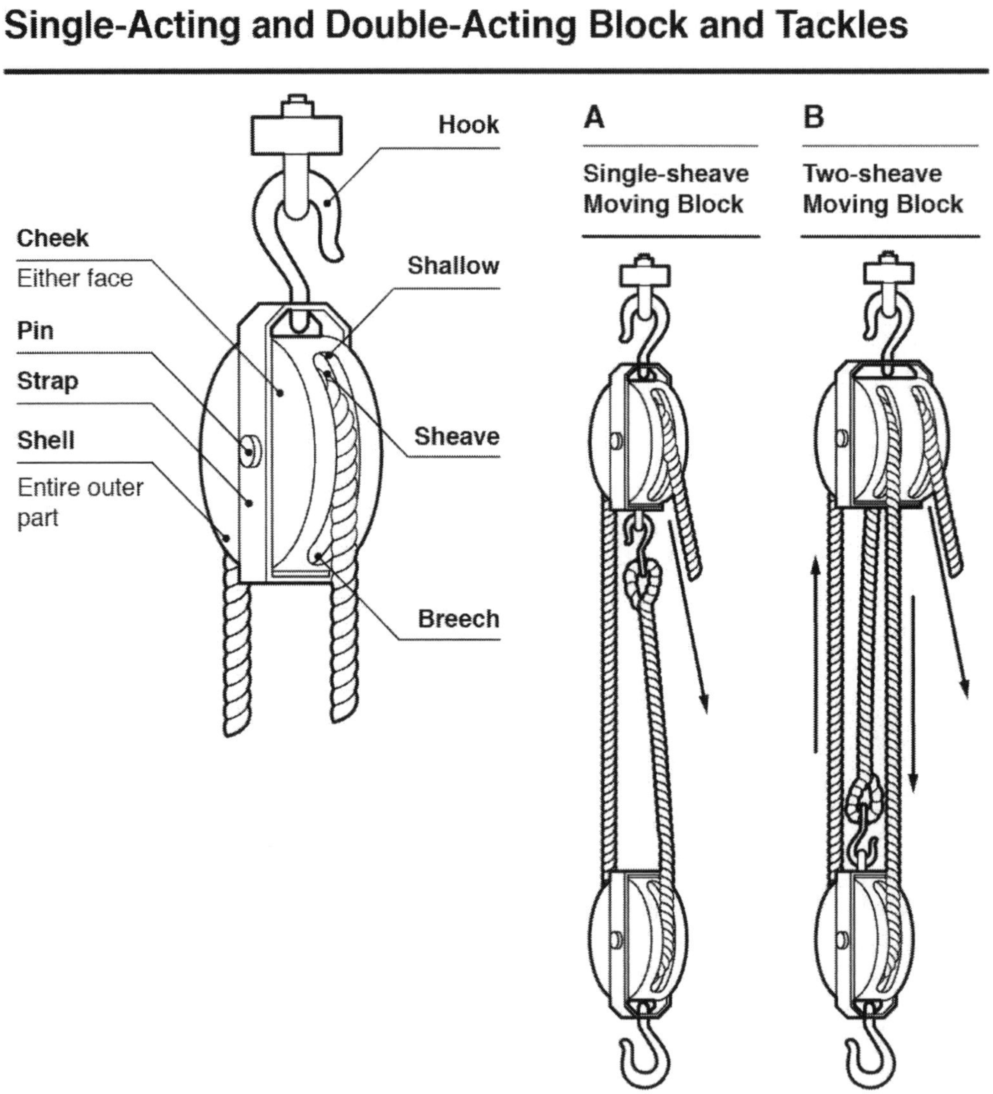

The mechanical advantage of the multiple-sheave block and tackle is approximated by counting the number of ropes going to and from the moving block. For example, there are two ropes connecting the moving block to the fixed block in part *A* of the figure above, so the mechanical advantage is 2:1. There are three ropes connecting the moving and fixed blocks in part *B*, so the mechanical advantage is 3:1. The advantage of using a multiple-sheave block is the increased hauling power obtained, but there's a cost; the weight of the moving block must be overcome, and a multiple-sheave block is significantly heavier than a single-sheave block.

Ramps

The **ramp** (or inclined plane) has been used since ancient times to move massive, extremely heavy objects up to higher positions, such as in the pyramids of the Middle East and Central America.

For example, to lift a barrel straight up to a height (*H*) requires a force equal to its weight (*W*). However, the force needed to lift the barrel is reduced by rolling it up a ramp, as shown below. So, if the ramp is *D* meters long and *H* meters high, the force (*F*) required to roll the weight (*W*) up the ramp is:

$$F = \frac{H}{D} \times W$$

Definition Sketch for a Ramp or Inclined Plane

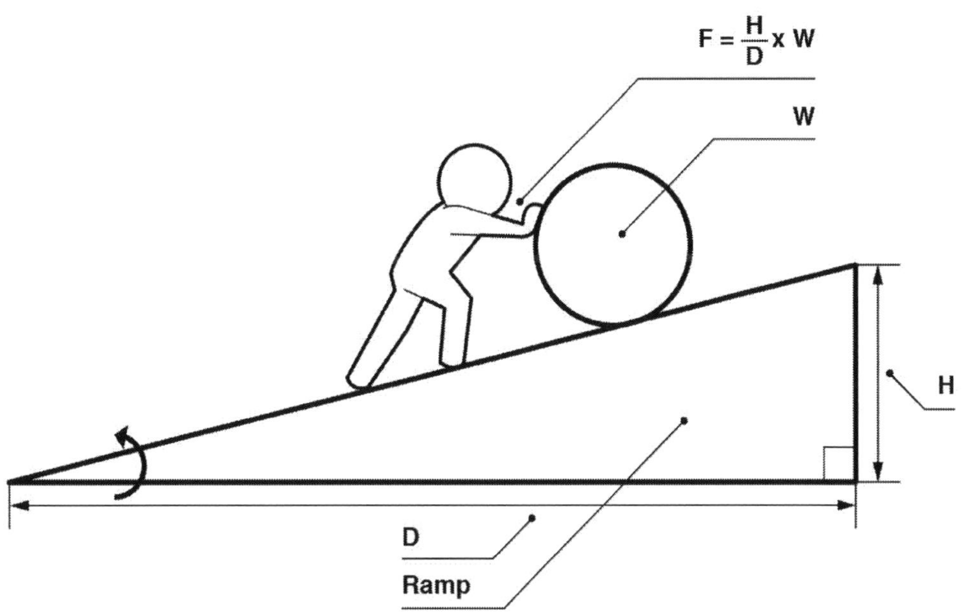

For a fixed height and weight, the longer the ramp, the less force must be applied. Remember, though, that the useful work done (in *N-m*) is the same in either case and is equal to *W* × *H.*

Wedges

If an incline or ramp is imagined as a right triangle like in the figure above, then a **wedge** would be formed by placing two inclines (ramps) back to back (or an isosceles triangle). A wedge is one of the six simple machines and is used to cut or split material. It does this by being driven for its full length into the material being cut. This material is then forced apart by a distance equal to the base of the wedge. Axes, chisels, and knives work on the same principle.

Screws

Screws are used in many applications, including vises and jacks. They are also used to fasten wood and other materials together. A screw is thought of as an inclined plane wrapped around a central cylinder. To visualize this, one can think of a barbershop pole, or cutting the shape of an incline (right triangle) out of a sheet of paper and wrapping it around a pencil (as in part *A* in the figure below). Threads are made from steel by turning round stock on a lathe and slowly advancing a cutting tool (a wedge) along it, as shown in part *B*.

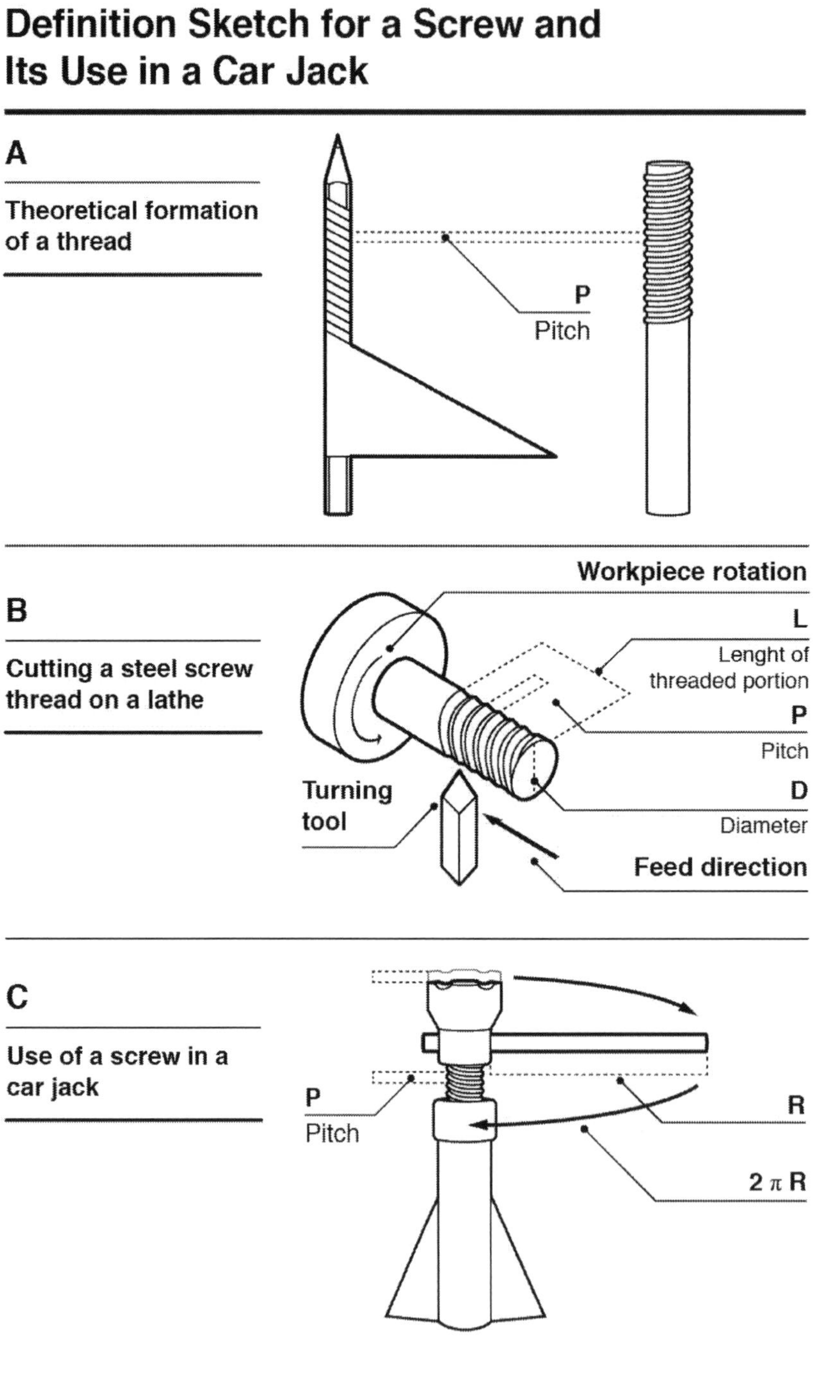

The application of a simple screw in a car jack is shown in part *C* in the figure above. The mechanical advantage of the jack is derived from the pitch of the screw winding. Turning the handle of the jack one revolution raises the screw by a height equal to the **screw pitch** (*p*). If the handle has a length *R*, the distance the handle travels is equal to the circumference of the circle it traces out. The theoretical mechanical advantage of the jack's screw is:

$$MA = \frac{F}{L} = \frac{p}{2\pi R} \text{ so } \quad F = L \times \frac{p}{2\pi R}$$

For example, the theoretical force (*F*) required to lift a car with a mass (*L*) of 5000 kilograms, using a jack with a handle 30 centimeters long and a screw pitch of 0.5 cm, is given as:

$$F \cong 50{,}000\ N \times \frac{0.5\ cm}{6.284 \times 30\ cm} \cong 130\ N$$

The theoretical value of mechanical advantage doesn't account for friction, so the actual force needed to turn the handle is higher than calculated.

Electronics Information

Electric Charge

Electricity is a form of energy, like heat or movement, that can be harnessed to perform useful work. Electrical energy results from the electric force that exists between atoms and molecules with electrical charge, which is associated with the atomic structure of those substances. Atoms contain various subatomic particles. Protons, which are in the nucleus, carry a +1 charge. Electrons, which surround the outer part of an atom in orbitals or clouds, carry a –1 charge. Net charges of atoms or molecules occur when there is an imbalance in the number of electrons and protons. A net positive charge occurs when there are more protons than electrons, while a net negative charge results when there are more electrons than protons.

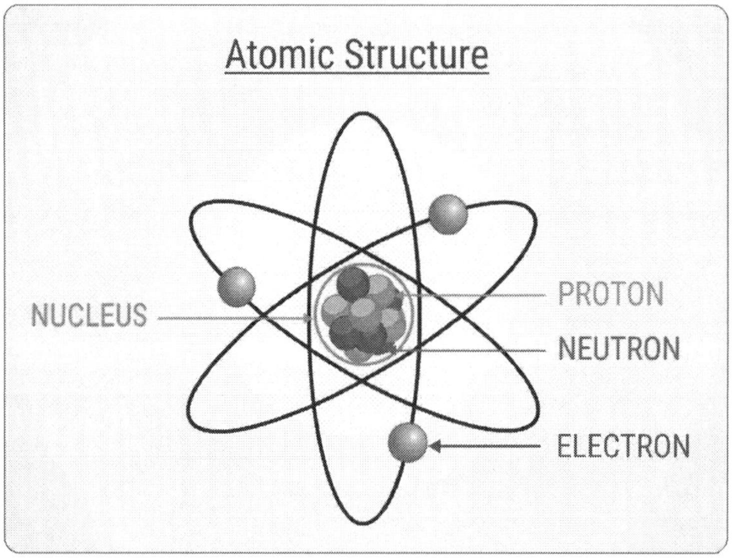

Atoms or molecules with electric charges that are the same experience a force that causes them to repel one another, while those with opposite charges attract each other. Therefore, two positive charges repel one another, two negative charges repel one another, but a positive and a negative charge attract one another. The unit of charge is denoted by C, the coulomb.

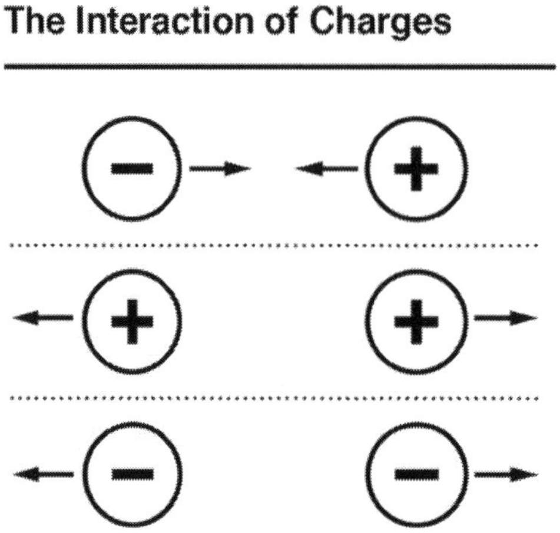

Similar to the Law of Conservation of Energy (which states that energy cannot be created or destroyed, only transferred from one form to another), there is a **conservation of charge** in the universe and in an isolated system. In a given isolated system, individual objects may experience a net loss or gain of charge with the transfer of charge from one object to another from within the system, but the overall charge within the system (or universe) cannot be created or destroyed. Individual positive or negative charges can be created or destroyed, but only in pairs (one positive with one negative), so that the net change in charge is zero.

Current

The properties of any atom vary based on the number and arrangement of electrons in the cloud surrounding the nucleus. For example, electrons in the outer orbitals of metals are relatively free to drift between atoms because they are not pulled in strongly by their atom's own nucleus. These electrons, which carry a negative charge, move through conductive materials, such as other metals, by jumping quickly from atom to atom, creating an electrical flow. This electrical flow is energy that can be harnessed to do work.

The Flow of Electrons Creates Electrical Current

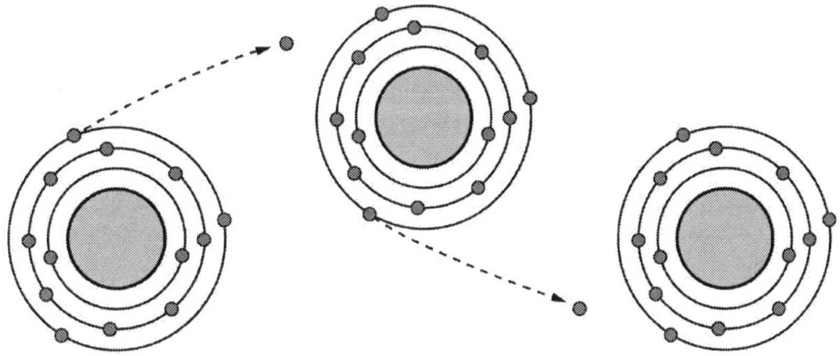

Current is the rate at which the electrical charge—or the number of electrons—flows through a conductive material. It is measured in amperes (A), with each ampere equal to approximately 6.24×10^{18} electrons per second.

Electric current carries energy much like pipes carry water. Water tanks serving an area are often elevated and have various pipes to transport the water down under ground, into each house, and then into smaller pipes leading to each sink, toilet, or shower. The purpose behind elevating the tank is to create pressure in the pipes carrying the water caused by the water above it pushing down. This pressure results in water flow, which can be equated to voltage (akin to pressure) that pushes electrons (the "water") through a circuit. With the water pipes, when the faucet is closed, water does not flow through the pipes, but water flows faster and faster the more the faucet is turned on to allow water in. The rate of water flow is analogous to current—the rate of electron flow through a circuit.

Voltage

As mentioned in the above example with the water tank, **voltage** is the push, or potential, behind electrical work. It is measured in volts (V) and can be thought of as the electromotive potential. Voltage causes current, such that if there is a closed path for electrons and a voltage, current will flow. If there is a suitable path for electrons but no voltage, or voltage in the absence of a viable path, current will cease.

A voltage source is the general term used to describe anything that can be used to generate voltage, such as a battery or generator.

Resistance

Electrical resistance, measured in ohms (Ω), is the amount of pressure inhibiting the flow of electrical current. Like friction, which slows the rate of movement, resistance dissipates energy and reduces the rate of flow or the movement of current. The amount of resistance that a given object contributes to a circuit depends on the properties of the object, particularly the material. Materials that are inherently more resistant inhibit the ease at which the electrons in the material's atoms can be displaced.

Some circuits have resistors built into them, which are specific electrical components designed to contribute a certain resistance to the circuit.

Resistance is inversely related to conductance, such that a highly conductive material has little resistance, and a material with high resistance has little conductance.

Materials vary in resistance because of the ease (or difficulty) with which electrons in the material's atoms can be displaced. The cross-sectional area and length of a given material also affect the resistance in a predictable relationship. The longer a given conductor is, the greater the resistance it provides; the greater the cross-sectional area (larger material), the less resistance there is. This relationship is quantitatively expressed as $R = \rho \cdot LA$, where ρ is the inherent resistivity of the specific conducting material, L is the length of the material, and A is the cross-sectional area.

Basic Circuits

A **circuit** is a closed loop through which current can flow. A simple circuit contains a voltage source and a resistor. The current flows from the positive side of the voltage source through the resistor to the negative side of the voltage source. Note that if the switch is open or there is some other disconnected wire or break in continuity in the circuit, there will be no electromotive force; the circuit must be a closed loop to create a net flow of electrons from the voltage source through the wires and system.

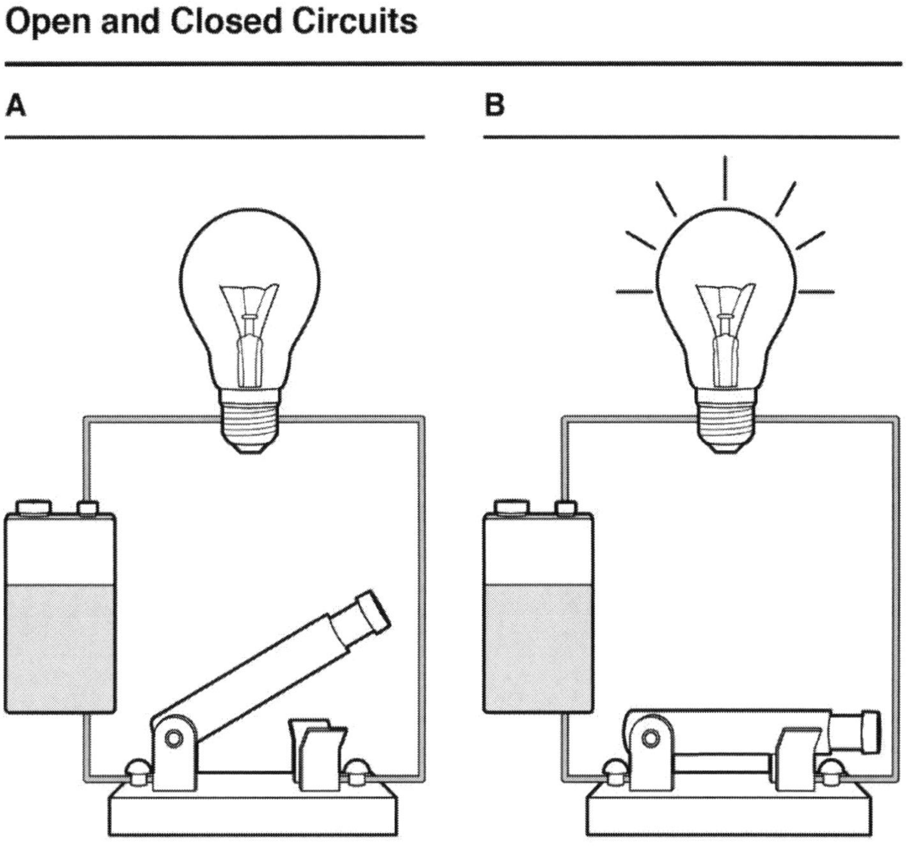

Open Circuit with no electric current

Closed Circuit with electric current flowing

Ohm's Law

Ohm's Law describes the relationship between voltage, current, and resistance, which are criteria used to characterize a given circuit. The difference in electrical potential (or voltage drop) between two different points in a circuit can be calculated by multiplying the current between the two points (*I*) and the total resistance of the electrical devices in the circuit between the two points (*R*).

$\Delta\text{Voltage } (V) = \text{current } (I) \times \text{resistance } (R)$, where *V* is voltage (in volts), *I* is current (in amperes), and *R* is resistance (in ohms).

Mathematically, the above equation can be manipulated to isolate current, which then is found to be directly proportional to the voltage drop (the electric potential difference) and inversely proportional to the total resistance.

$$I = \frac{V}{R} \; or \; R = \frac{V}{I}$$

This means that a greater battery voltage (electric potential difference) yields a greater current in the circuit, while greater resistance decreases current. Essentially, charge flows fastest when the battery voltage increases and resistance decreases.

The relationships in these equations can be understood by examining a simple circuit as a reference and then changing one variable sequentially to examine the outcome.

The Relationships Between Voltage, Resistance, and Current in a Basic Circuit

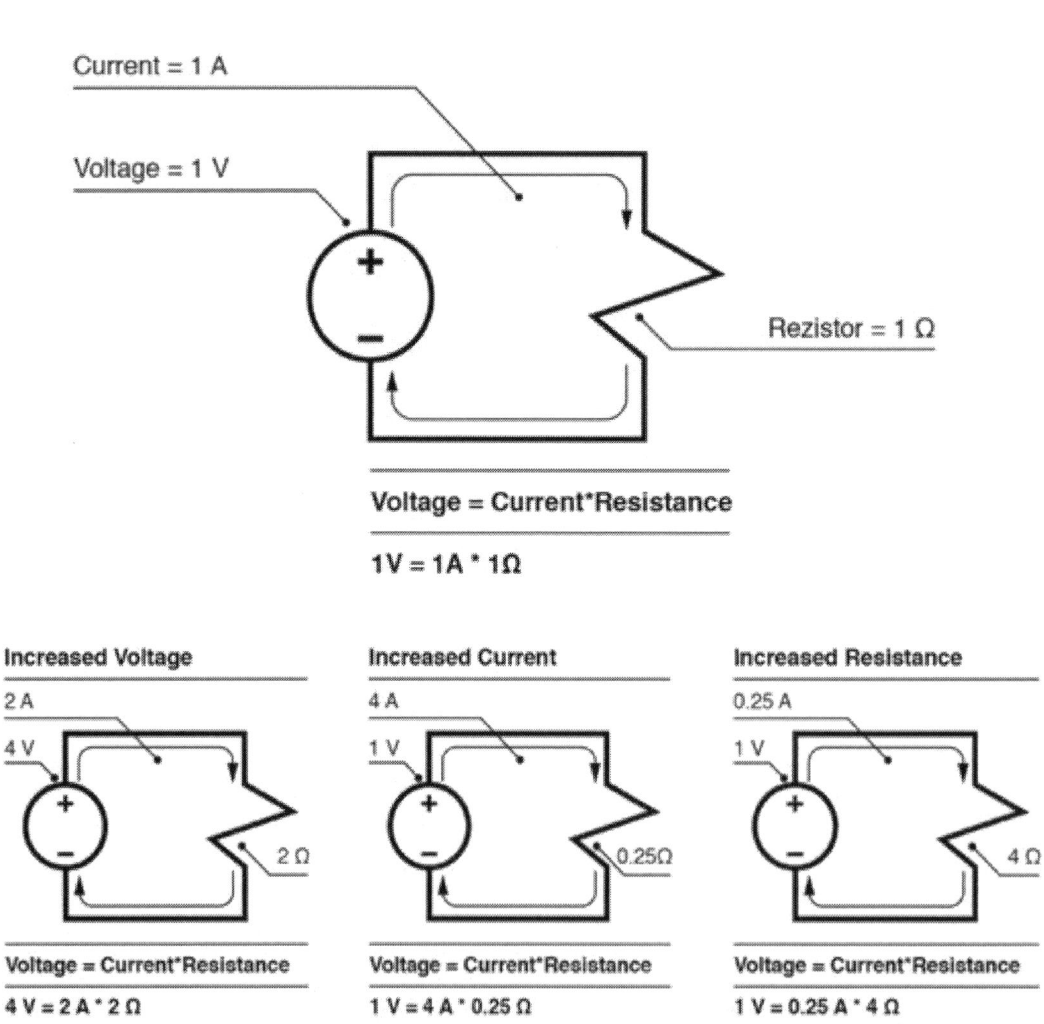

Alternatively, the following "Ohm's Triangle" is a useful tool to memorize the relationships governed by Ohm's Law. Test takers will need to memorize this equation for the ASVAB exam. The triangle serves as a pictorial reminder and method to generate the correct relationships between voltage, current, and resistance.

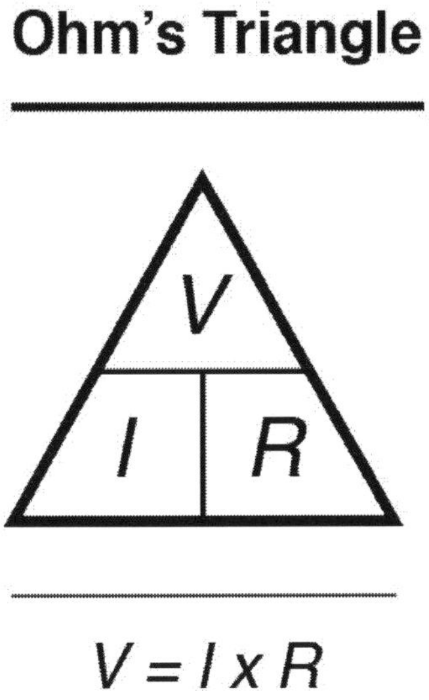

Recalling the standard Ohm's Law that $V = I \times R$ helps set up the basic triangle from which the other two equations can be visually transposed for those who find mathematically manipulating equations difficult.

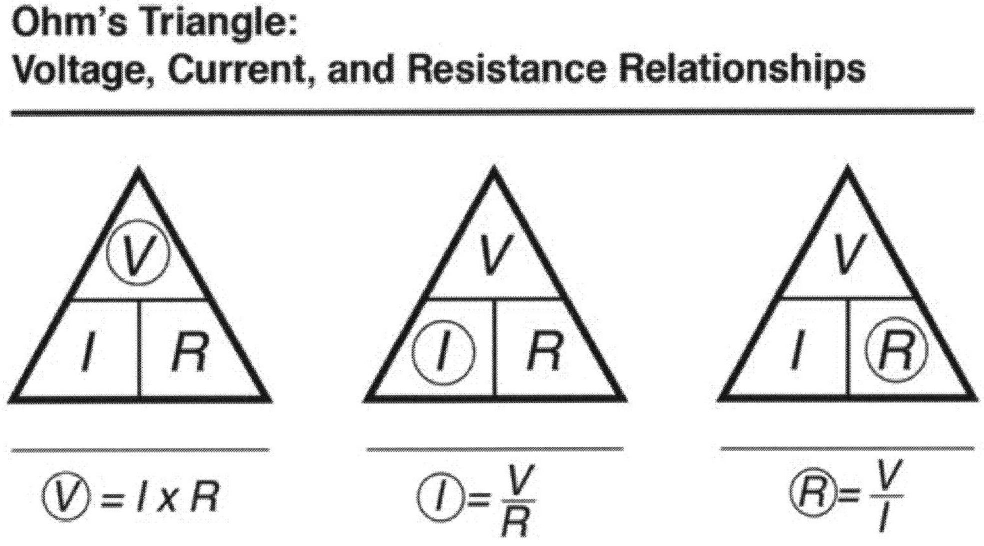

Series and Parallel Circuits

When two or more electrical devices are powered by the same energy source (such as a battery) in a circuit, they can be connected in series or in parallel.

Series Circuits

In a **series circuit**, the electric charge passes consecutively through each device. When in series, charge passes through every light bulb. In a series circuit, there is a single pathway for electric current to flow, and all of the devices are added in succession to the same line. There are no branches coming off of this line, nor are there smaller loops within the circuit. The same electric current runs through each device, but the voltage drops as more devices or resistors are added to the string of connected devices. Essentially, the overall resistance in a series circuit increases with the addition of each resistor. This phenomenon can be observed in a series circuit composed of light bulbs. With the addition of each light bulb in succession, the brightness of each bulb decreases. Also unique to series circuits is the interdependence of the devices connected in the series. Using the example of the light bulbs, if one of the bulbs is unscrewed or defective in some way, all bulbs in the loop (regardless of whether there is an issue with them individually or not) will go out. Simply put, for any device in a series circuit to function, all other devices in the same circuit must also be functioning.

As mentioned, the same current runs through all resistors in the series circuit, and this current must be the same across each resistor. If this was not the case, the electrons would have to build up somewhere, but current cannot be stored; the electrons going into the resistor must all go out so that the "flow in equals flow out."

While current doesn't change, voltage does drop after each resistor in such a way that the total voltage across the circuit is equal to the sum of the voltages across each device or resistor. An equivalent basic circuit or the equivalent total resistance in the circuit can be calculated by adding the specific resistance for each resistor together.

$$R_{equiv} = R_1 + R_2 + R_3 \dots$$

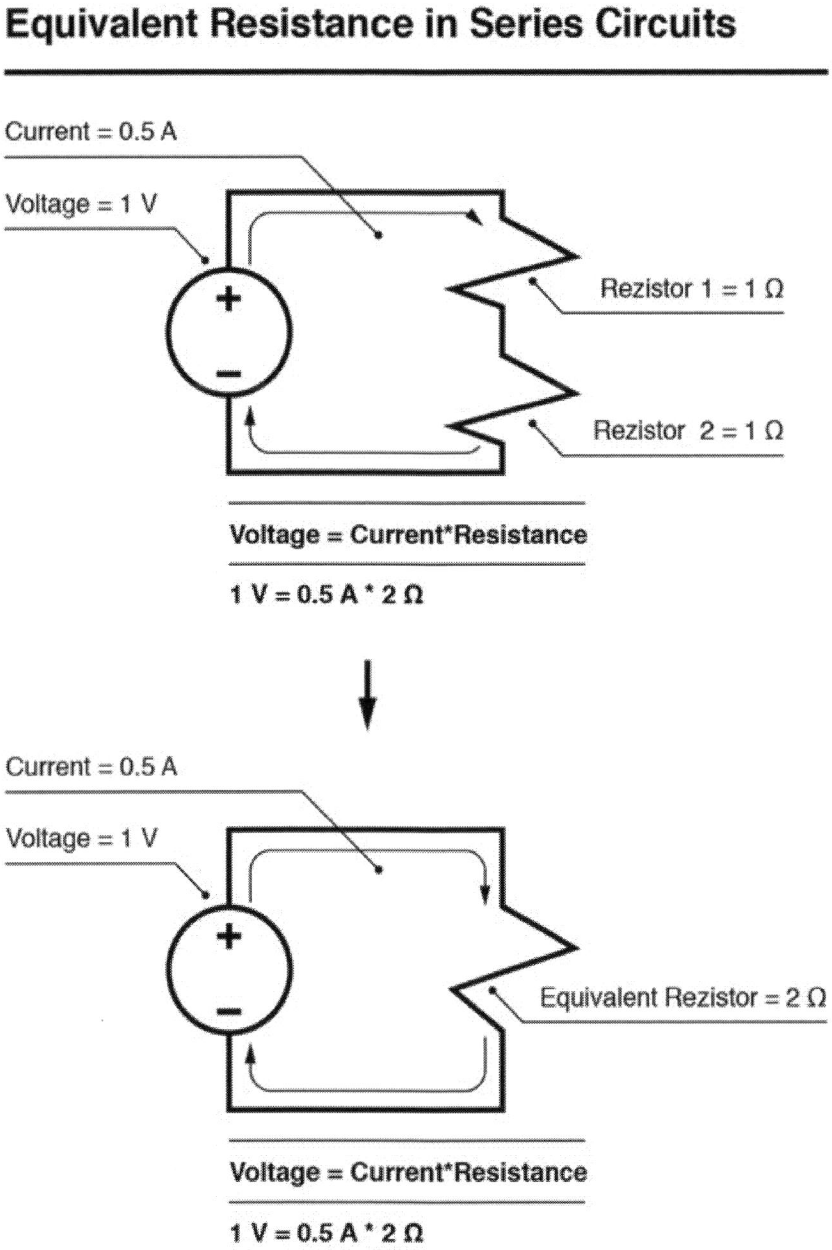

Current is the same at all locations along the circuit, whether measured at the battery, the first resistor, or after the last resistor. There is no accumulation or pileup of charge at any given location, and charge does not decrease or get used up by resistors such that there is any less charge at one point in the path compared to another.

Therefore:

$$I_{battery} = I_{resistor1} = I_{resistor2} = I_{resistor3} \cdots$$

Parallel Circuits

When devices are connected in a **parallel circuit**, the charge passes through the external circuit and will only traverse one of the branches during its path back to the other terminal of the energy source. For example, if there are several light bulbs on separate branches connected in a parallel series, a single charge only passes through one of the light bulbs. Therefore, the voltage is the same across each resistor because each resistor is attached directly to the power source and the ground. In stark contrast to series circuits, as the number of devices or resistors increases in a parallel circuit, the overall current also increases. Somewhat counterintuitively, the addition of more resistors in a separate branch of the circuit actually decreases the overall resistance in the parallel circuit, so the current increases. Another difference between parallel and series circuits is that the removal or malfunctioning of one device in the parallel circuit does not affect the overall current or the current in the other branches. This feature makes parallel circuits advantageous for many applications, such as home wiring, to prevent a total failure of multiple devices and with a defect in a single device. In summary, in series circuits, the current stays the same, but the voltage drops, while in parallel circuits, the current increases, and the voltage stays constant.

A useful analogy to differentiate between series and parallel circuits as well as to understand that adding resistors to a parallel circuit actually increases current is to equate each series to tollbooths on highways. Bottlenecks can occur at points along the highway where cars must pay tolls. The flow rate of the cars is reduced significantly in these areas. Therefore, the tollbooths are analogous to resistors, and the rate of car travel is like the electric current. To remedy the bottlenecks that occur, the transportation authority may decide to add three more tollbooths, which is essentially adding more resistors. If the tollbooths were added in series, each car would have to stop and pay a toll at every tollbooth in a consecutive manner. If the toll was originally $.80, the addition of the three new tollbooths would result in a car stopping at all four tollbooths and paying $.20 per stop. This would have the obvious effect of increasing the jam (total resistance), and traffic flow rate (electric current) would stay the same because still only one car at a time could pass through. Alternatively, if the three additional tollbooths were added in a parallel fashion, each tollbooth would be placed on a separate branch of the road, and cars would select one of the four possible branches and stop at only the one tollbooth in their branch. In contrast to adding tollbooths in series, this arrangement would increase traffic flow and improve the initial bottleneck issue by creating more pathways by which cars (or charge) can flow. Essentially, the electric current increases over baseline in parallel circuits and decreases in series.

Here is an example image:

Altering the Flow Rate on a Tollway

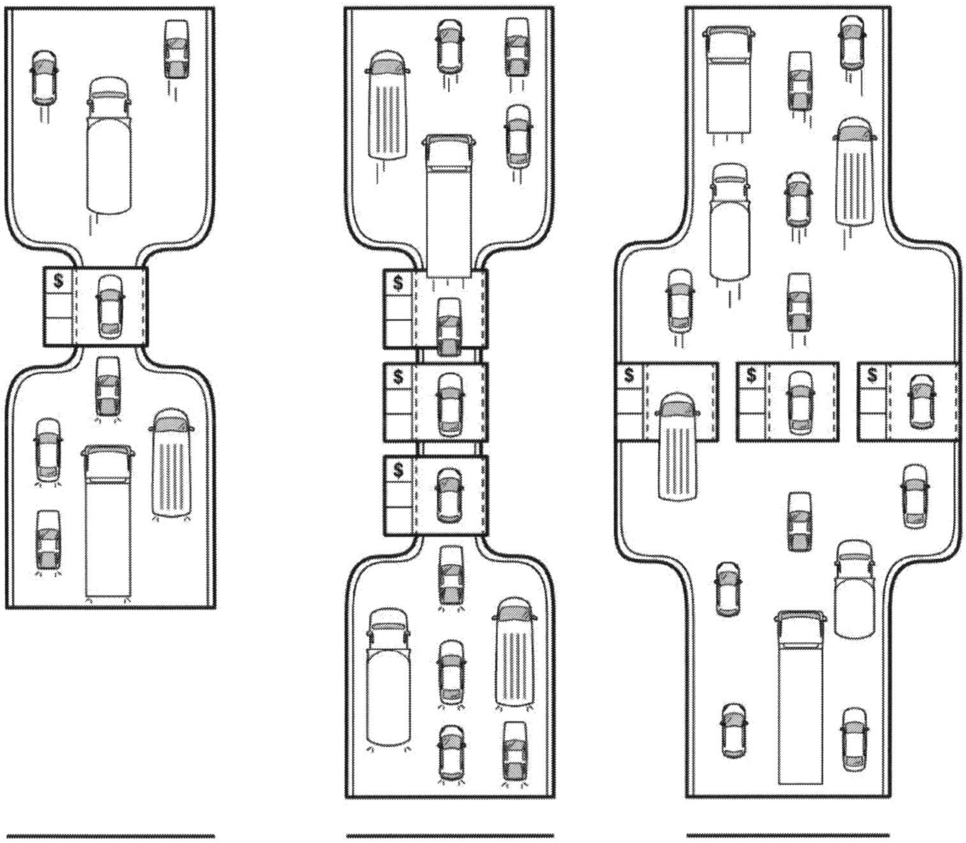

A Single Resistor | **Three Resistors Placed in Series** | **Three Resistors Placed in Parallel**

Like with series circuits, resistors in parallel can also be reduced to an equivalent circuit, but not by simply adding the resistances. The equivalent resistance (R_{eq}) is instead found by solving Ohm's Law for the current through each resistor, setting this value equal to the total current (I_t), and remembering that the voltages are all identical. Essentially, this yields an equation that shows that the inverse of the equivalent resistance of parallel resistors is equal to the sum of the inverses of the resistance of each leg of the parallel circuit.

Mathematically, that means:

$$I_t = \frac{V}{R_{eq}} = \frac{V}{R_1} + \frac{V}{R_2} \text{ or } \frac{1}{R_{eq}} = \frac{1}{R_1} + \frac{1}{R_2} \text{ so } R_{eq} = \frac{1}{\frac{1}{R_1} + \frac{1}{R_2}}$$

Equivalent Resistance in Parallel Circuits

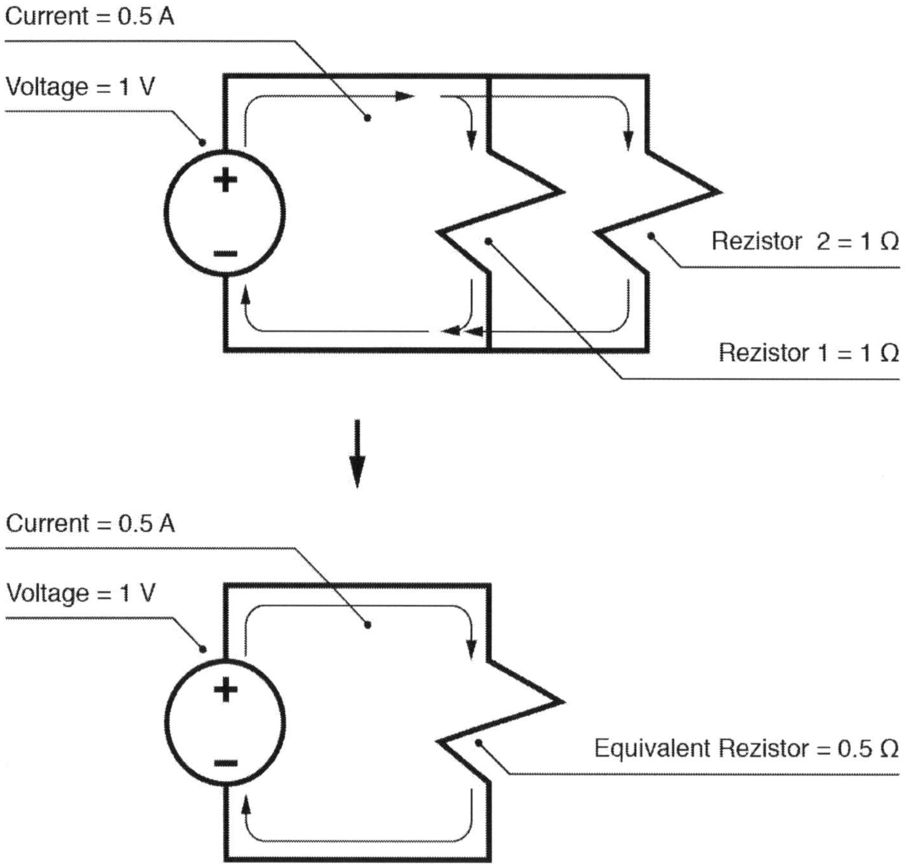

$$R_{equiv} = \frac{1}{\frac{1}{1\,\Omega} + \frac{1}{1\,\Omega}} = 0.5\,\Omega$$

As mentioned, the total resistance decreases as additional resistors are added to the parallel series, and the equivalent resistance is always lower than that of the smallest resistor.

Electrical Power

Electrical power in a circuit refers to the energy produced or absorbed, and it is expressed in watts (W). In a given circuit, certain components such as light bulbs consume electrical power and convert it to light/heat, while other components, for example, the battery, produce power. Power, in watts, is equal to the current from a voltage source in amperes multiplied by the voltage of that source:

$$\text{Power } (W) = \text{current } (I) \times \text{voltage } (V)$$

Using Ohm's Law and substitution, this relation can also be written in the following two ways:

$$W = I^2R$$

$$W = \frac{V^2}{R}$$

Of note, sometimes power ratings (the rate that electric power is converted to a different form of usable energy [such as light or motion]) on electric motors or other devices is expressed in horsepower, or hp, where 1 hp = 746 W.

AC Versus DC

The circuits previously described are **direct current (DC) circuits**, which are circuits wherein the voltage source has a constant value, and the current flows unidirectionally. This type of circuit is usually used for the wiring on ships, airplanes, and electronic devices like cell phones and televisions. Batteries produce DC, and devices called rectifiers convert **alternating current (AC)** to DC. In contrast, voltage alternates over time in AC circuits, and current flow can switch directions. AC electricity is used in most land-based, heavy machinery and powers houses and buildings because large amounts of AC electricity can be transmitted over long distances with significantly less loss of power than with DC electricity. In the United States, AC electricity is generated (via alternators) at a frequency of 60 cycles per second with 120- and 240-volt service available to users via a three-wire distribution system.

Capacitors

Capacitors are devices that store electric charge and resist changes in voltage. They are made from two parallel plates made of conductive surfaces that are separated by a space or an insulating material such as ceramic or Teflon. Capacitors filter signals by blocking DC signals but permitting AC ones.

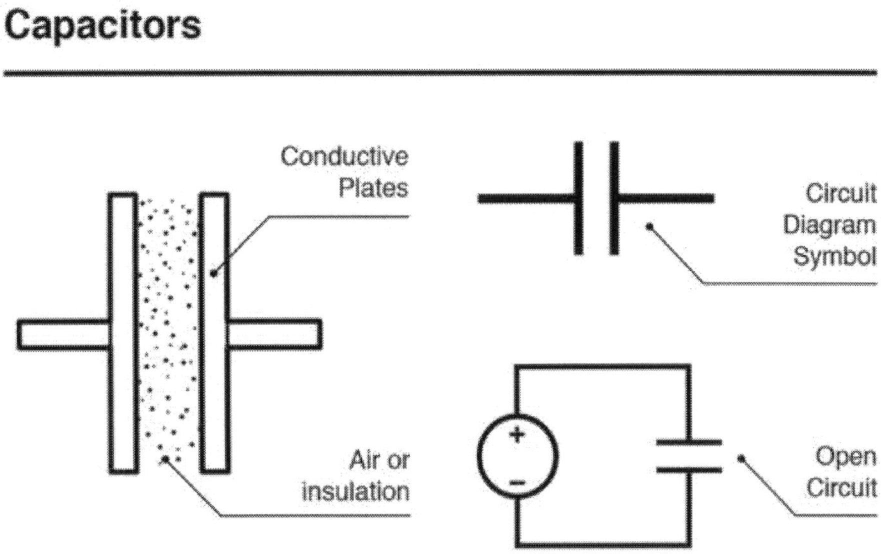

Inductors

Inductors are coils of wire that develop a magnetic field in the presence of electrical flow. This magnetic field resists changes in the magnitude of changes in current in AC circuits. They can function as filters because they block AC signals but not DC, and they can separate signals of varying frequencies.

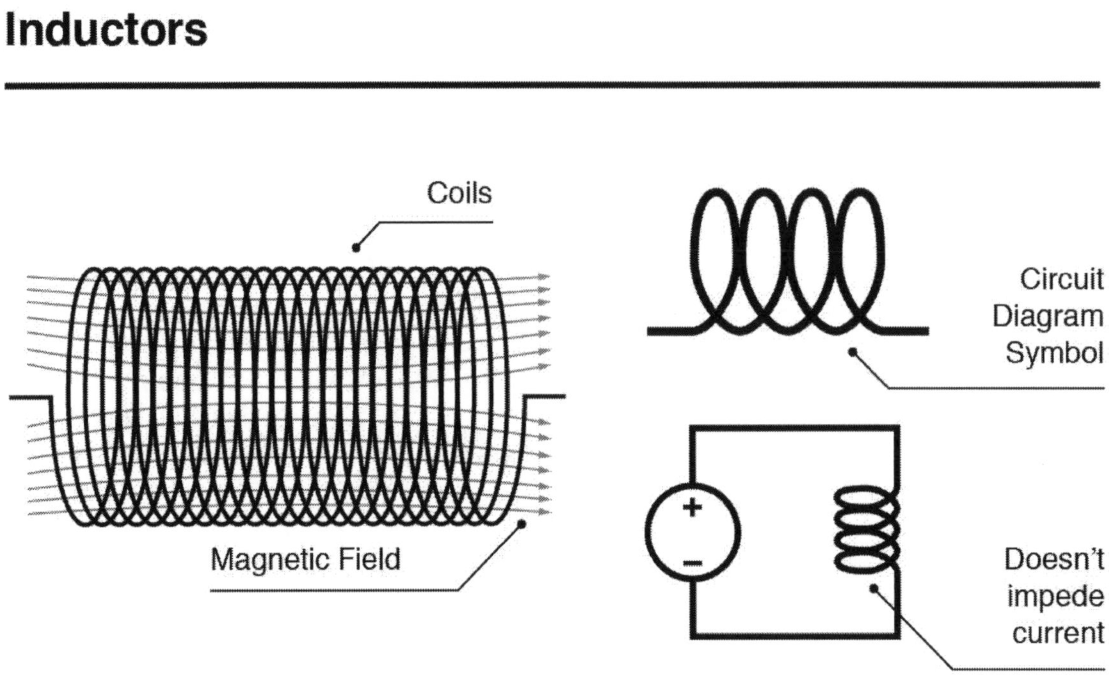

Electrical Diagrams

Test takers should be familiar with reading **block diagrams**, which depict electrical circuits with various symbols. The following figure includes frequently encountered symbols, and basic definitions for the important terms not yet covered are listed below the figure.

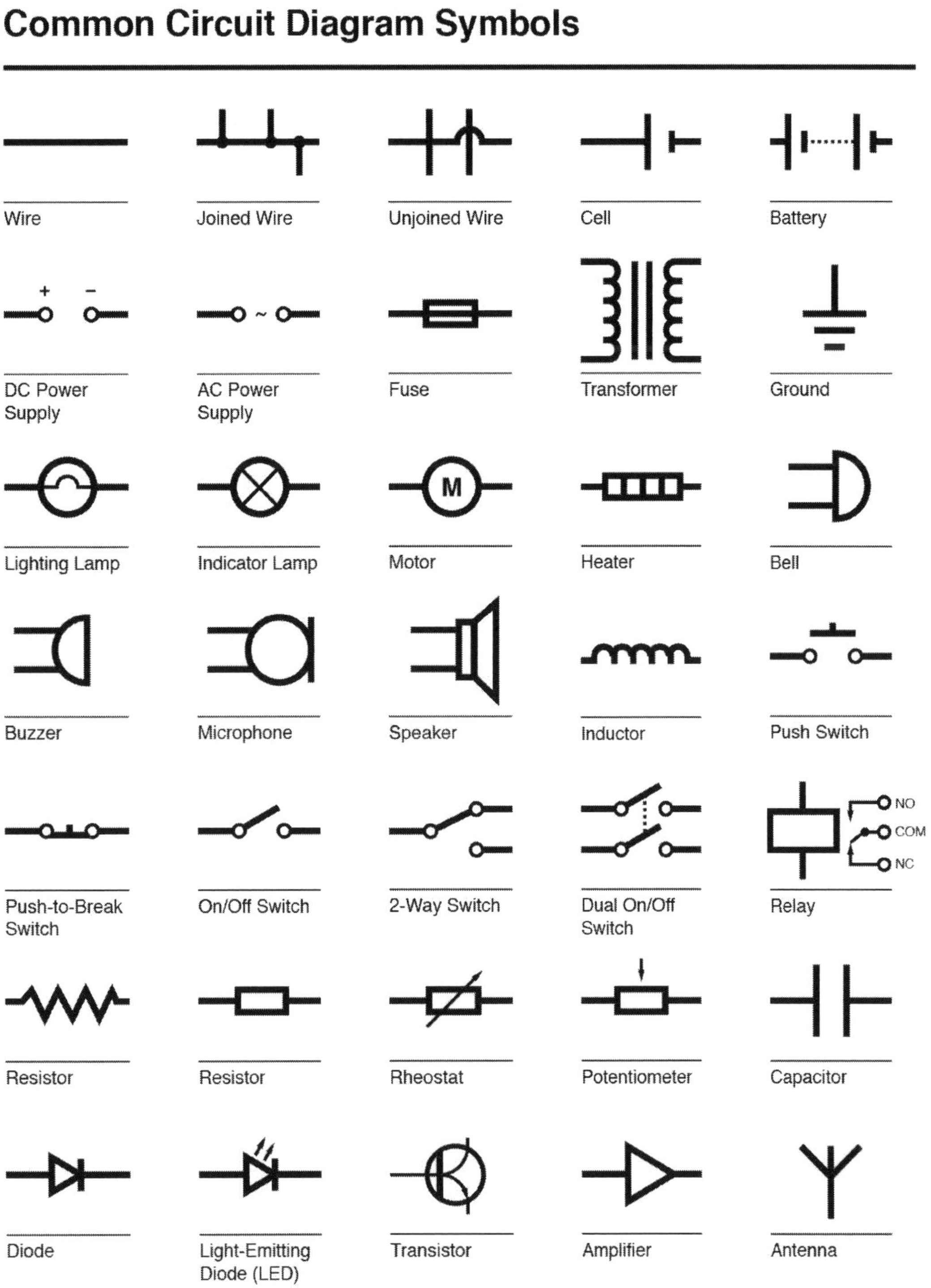

- **Cell**: The electronic unit that supplies current; batteries contain multiple cells.
- **Fuse**: A safety device that protects against current that surpasses a specified value by opening the circuit to prevent current flow.
- **Transformer**: A device that increases or decreases AC voltage by transferring energy via magnetic field induction between two coils of wire that are not electrically connected.
- **Ground**: The electrical connection to the earth, which enables the ground to serve as a zero-point reference for voltage against which other voltages in a circuit can be measured.
- **Transducer**: A device, such as a motor or lamp, that converts energy from one form into a different form.
- **Relay**: A type of switch that can open or close a circuit electromagnetically or electrically.
- **Rheostat**: A two-terminal variable resistor that controls current (such as lamp brightness).
- **Potentiometer**: A three-terminal variable resistor that controls voltage.
- **Diode**: The electrical equivalent of a valve; it permits electricity to flow in only one direction, indicated by the arrow in diagrams. Light-emitting diodes (LEDs) illuminate when current passes through.
- **Transistor**: A type of semiconductor (not quite a conductor yet not fully an insulator) that amplifies or switches electric signals or power.
- **Amplifier**: An electrical circuit contained in a device that increases the voltage, power, or current of a signal.

Aviation and Nautical Information Test (ANIT)

Army Aviation

Aerodynamics

The Nature of Flight

Flight is not a natural state. All objects are affected by *gravity*, which constantly pulls things downwards—unless something else is providing support. A person sitting in a chair is certainly off the ground and, despite the constant pull of gravity, as long as he or she is supported by the chair, that's not likely to change. Even as gravity pulls down on the person, he or she collides with the chair, which then pushes the person up. It may seem rather confusing that an inanimate object has the ability to push up, but that is exactly what the chair does. If it didn't, then the chair would simply collapse under the person's weight, and the person would fall to the ground. Instead, the chair's rigidity keeps the chair intact, and the chair pushes upwards with enough force to maintain its shape and form. The ultimate takeaway message, here, is that in order to overcome the downward force of gravity, there needs to be some source of upward force to cancel it out.

Overcoming the force of gravity presents a unique challenge for an aircraft, as there isn't any chair equivalent that can conveniently lift a helicopter off the ground. Even if there were, this hypothetical object would also be affected by gravity and would, in turn, need to be supported by the ground. Obviously, this force has to come from somewhere. In the case of a helicopter, the force comes in the form of lift generated by an airfoil.

Lift

An *airfoil* (used in virtually all aspects of flight) is a blade; it cuts through the air so that air passes above and below it. Moreover, the air is not treated equally by the airfoil's design. The top of the airfoil is *cambered*, or curved, allowing the air to quickly get past the airfoil and create a low pressure. The air that goes below the airfoil has a shorter distance to travel and is slower, which results in high pressure. *Lift* is the upward force created by the difference in air pressure above and below the blade. It is what allows a helicopter to fly. A good way to visualize why this works is to consider a block between two springs:

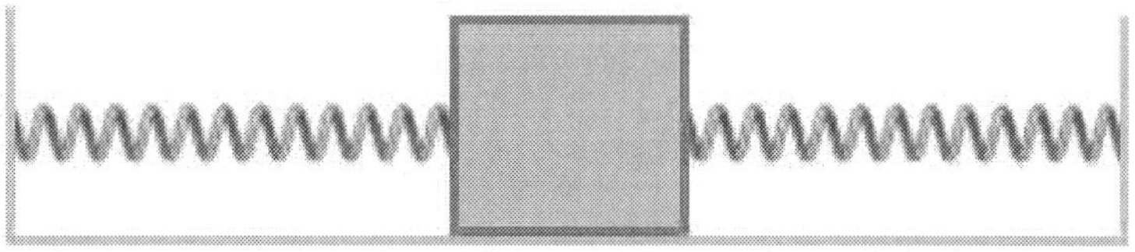

When the block is directly between the two springs, the block doesn't move because the pressure from the springs is equal and opposite, canceling each other out. However, if one spring were to be compressed while the other was stretched, the compressed spring would suddenly be exerting more force, while the stretched spring would exert less. The block will be pushed until the springs are once equal and opposite. Likewise, the reduced pressure above the airfoil pushes *downward* with less force than the increased pressure below pushes *upward*, and lift is created.

The amount of lift created depends on several things, from the material and shape of the airfoil to the density of the air in the vicinity. A pilot can directly influence only two—the angle of incidence (pitch angle) and the angle of attack (AOA):

Pitch Angle

The pitch angle is the angle between the *chord line* (a line drawn between the leading edge and the trailing edge of the airfoil) and the direction of the rotor's spin. The angle can be directly controlled using the collective on the helicopter (to be discussed in further detail, below).

AOA

The *AOA* is the angle between the chord line and the direction of the incoming air. On a windless day, AOA and pitch angle can potentially be the same when hovering as the only relative wind will be that created by the rotation, but knowing the difference is important.

Typically, in order to create lift, a *positive AOA* is needed—the *front* of the blade needs to be raised above the *back*, relative to the wind. If the angle is *zero* (when the two are actually at the same height, relative to the wind), no lift will be generated. *Negative lift* is technically possible by flying at a *negative AOA*. There are exceptions; however, some airfoils (specifically those that are either *cambered* or *nonsymmetrical*) can be designed to generate lift with a zero, or even negative, AOA, though increasing the AOA will still result in more lift.

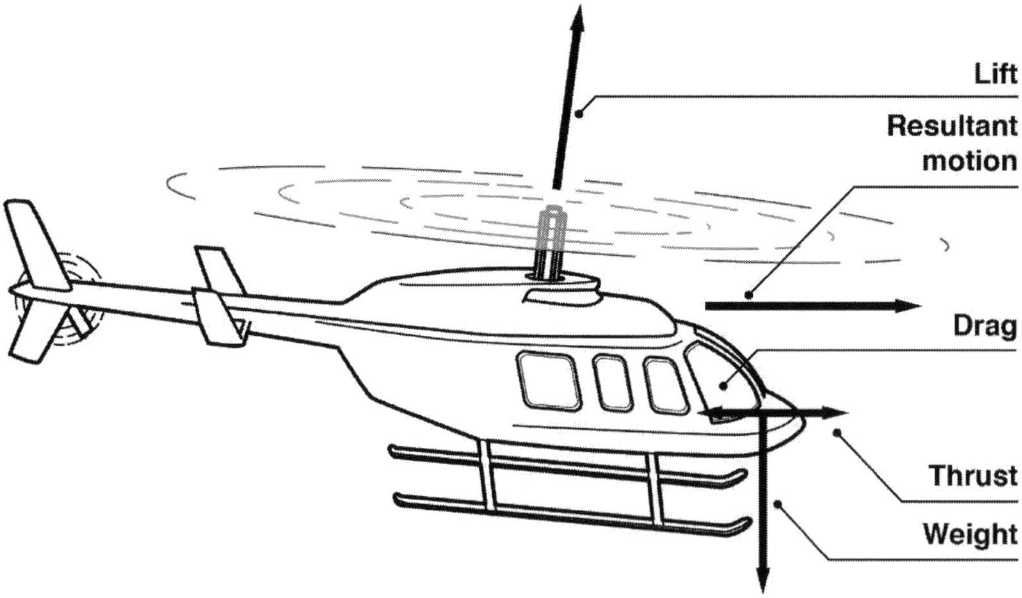

Weight

It's not enough to simply create lift. *Weight* is the force acting on a body due to gravity, and *gravity* is the acceleration acting on a body due to the Earth's mass. The average acceleration upwards must be larger than the average gravity acting on the body, and the total generated lift needs be a larger force than the loaded weight. The *weight of the aircraft* refers to the weight of the helicopter itself, all of its passengers, cargo, fuel, and anything else that would fall to the ground, if they were not supported by the helicopter. The heavier the aircraft, the greater the force needed to move it, thus requiring more lift to get off the ground. Of course, gravity does not stop because the helicopter is off the ground, and the helicopter must continue maintaining at least as much lift or it risks losing altitude.

There are several factors that can potentially increase the weight and ultimately increase the amount of lift needed to stay aloft. To say that the aircraft's *weight* has increased, however, is a bit of a misnomer as the mass of the helicopter does not generally change significantly midflight (other than the burning of fuel). Rather, some factors can either decrease the effectiveness of lift or increase the potency of weight. Either change requires that additional lift is created to compensate as if its weight had actually increased. Strong winds and other adverse weather conditions can cause this, but a more frequently observable example is the simple act of banking the helicopter.

When *banking* the helicopter, the lift is no longer generated directly downwards; rather, some of the vertical lift is redirected into horizontal movement. This results in a descent, unless the total airfoil is increased to produce the appropriate amount of vertical lift once more. While, at small angles, the effect is quite tame, the effect gets exponentially stronger for each increase in banking angle. For example, a bank of 25° would result in a 10% increase in required lift, but increasing the angle by just nine more degrees, to an angle of 34°, the helicopter will have already reached a 20% increase. By the time an angle of 48° is reached, the lift will have increased by half again of what an upright helicopter requires. Were a helicopter to bank all the way to 90°, the airfoils would be generating only horizontal lift, with no vertical lift, and so the helicopter would essentially be free falling.

The added strain created by this effect is often called the *load factor* (or the *G load*) because the strain increases the load, or weight, on the airfoil. The value of the load factor does not give an exact value for this additional weight, but rather is expressed as a percentage of the helicopter's resting weight. This value can be calculated using the following equation:

$$G = \frac{L_1}{L_0}$$

Here, G is the load factor, L_1 is the actual load on the rotor blades, and L_0 is the resting, or normal, load. So, a 1-ton helicopter with a load factor of 3 experiences the same force as a 3-ton helicopter hovering at rest. If the helicopter is not able to generate sufficient lift to offset this increase, the helicopter will begin to lose altitude unless the pilot can adjust for the weight in other ways, such as reducing the banking angle. For that reason, knowing how much lift the helicopter can produce is crucial. Otherwise, the helicopter may become overloaded, which will cause the rotor to droop, and the aircraft will descend.

Thrust

Lift and weight are perhaps the most important forces involved in the helicopter's movement, but if they were the only two, the helicopter would be little more than a glorified elevator capable only of rising and falling. Just as force is needed to lift the helicopter vertically from the ground, force is also needed to move the helicopter horizontally. This force, called *thrust*, can be in any direction, but is almost always measured in horizontal motion. Thrust is primarily created by converting lift via alterations of the pitch angle and AOA. Since horizontal movement does not have to contend with gravity, less effort is required to shift the helicopter horizontally compared to that required vertically. This means that only a small portion of lift needs to be sacrificed to achieve some movement, although more can be sacrificed if faster horizontal movement is desired.

Drag

Just as lift contends with the weight of gravity, thrust also has an opposing force to overcome, called drag. *Drag* is actually a composite force, usually broken up into three subcategories known as profile, parasitic, and induced. All three forces change in varying amounts with the speed of the helicopter and, in most cases, with increasing, comes increasing drag. The faster the helicopter travels, the more thrust force is required to overcome the increased drag. However, there is a narrow but important exception, which will be discussed in more detail below.

Anyone who has ever ridden a bike or stood outside on a windy day has experienced drag. Drag is simply the sensation of the wind exerting force on objects that the wind passes through. The strength of that drag depends only on the relative speed of the wind, such that standing still in 20 MPH winds creates just as much drag as moving 20 MPH in still winds, or even moving 10 MPH into a 10 MPH wind. Regardless of the exact combination, the result is the same—both the object and the air attempt to occupy the same space, and the object must exert force to displace the air, even as the air tries to do the same to the object. The faster the wind is moving relative to the object, the more air that object has to push out of the way and the more air that pushes back on the object. This explains why increasing velocity also increases drag.

Parasitic Drag

Parasitic drag is the simplest of the three subtypes of drag and functions exactly as explained above. It is caused by the non-lifting portions of the helicopter, such as the fuselage, engine cowlings, hub, mast, landing gear, and external loads. Specifically, parasitic drag increases with airspeed and is the dominant type of drag at high airspeeds.

Profile Drag

Profile drag is similar to parasitic drag, but with one critical difference—it only concerns the drag created by the frictional resistance of spinning airfoils. Since the airfoils are much smaller than the rest of the helicopter and designed to be as aerodynamic as possible, profile drag is a lot smaller than the high speeds of the rotor blades might suggest, although the drag is still significant at lower speeds. Drag does increase as velocity increases, but only by a small margin, because relative to the speed at which the rotor blades are spinning, the velocity added by a moving helicopter only represents a small percent increase to its effective speed. Going from 5 MPH to 10 MPH will quadruple parasitic drag, but the rotor's speed is changing from approximately 605 MPH to 610 MPH, which would only increase the rotor's drag by less than one percent. This is not entirely accurate; since the airfoil is rotating, the actual speed of the rotor blade relative to the air changes, based on how far down the blade contact occurs and what direction the blade is currently spinning. However, this example should at least explain why profile drag increases so slowly relative to parasitic drag. When compared to the other two types of drag, profile drag remains midway throughout—neither dominating nor negligible.

Induced Drag

Induced drag is a byproduct of the lift created by the rotor, and its very existence is unique. As the blades spin, they briefly leave a small gap of empty space behind them where they once were, which is quickly filled by the air above and below the blade. Since the air is at a different pressure above and below, the air creates a spiral directly behind the blade, which pushes air in the opposite direction of lift. When the lift the helicopter creates is at an angle (such as is the case while banking), the induced drag is too, which causes some of the normally-downward directed force to instead face rearwards. This rearwards force pushes the helicopter back as the helicopter tries to move forward. The greater the AOA is, the greater the portion of the force that is directed rearwards. Since the angle of attack is usually greatest at lower airspeeds and reduced at higher airspeeds, this is the only drag that typically decreases as airspeed increases. When compared to the other two types of drag, induced drag is the primary force at low speeds, but at higher speeds becomes barely meaningful.

The *total drag* on the helicopter is simply the sum of the three subtypes. The graphic below shows how the individual components of drag add up at different speeds:

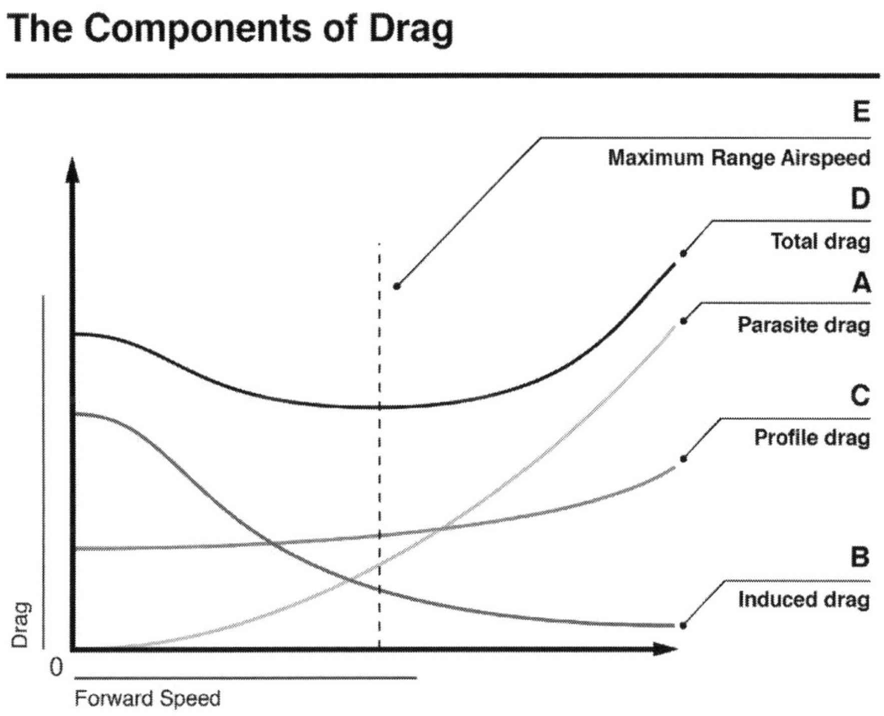

Induced drag generally contributes the most at lower speeds, while parasitic drag dominates at higher velocities. This unique behavior means that most helicopters have an optimal velocity, wherein induced drag has decreased significantly, but parasitic drag has not yet taken over. This speed is important because this value is the point at which the lift to drag ratio is highest, and is often used to determine a helicopter's best rate of climb and other numerical figures. This point is called the *maximum lift/drag ratio*, or $\frac{L}{D_{max}}$. Point E on the drag/airspeed relationship diagram represents the maximum range airspeed. This airspeed will allow the helicopter to fly the furthest distance on a tank of gas.

Weight and Balance

In discussing the forces acting upon the helicopter, it's important to expand upon weight—perhaps the most important force to consider when flying—and how weight relates to another concept: balance.

Weight

The basic concept of weight has already been discussed earlier as it exists principally as the opposing force to lift. This section will focus on the more technical aspects of weight and how weight pertains to helicopters. The heavier something is, the more difficult that object is to move, thus the greater the lift required to get off the ground. Even if the helicopter is theoretically capable of generating the lift needed to do so, the strain of an overloaded helicopter can cause structural damage to the helicopter.

When talking about helicopters, there are several terms that are often used when discussing weight: basic empty weight, maximum gross weight, and weight limitations.

Basic Empty Weight

Basic empty weight, as the name suggests, is the weight of the helicopter once everything directly unattached to the helicopter is removed. More technically, the basic empty weight solely includes the weight of the helicopter itself, any optional equipment, and all the fluids contained within the components themselves, including unusable fuel, transmission oil, hydraulic fluid, etc. As a general rule of thumb, if the helicopter could still function properly without something, that something isn't included in the basic empty weight.

Some helicopters may also have a different value listed called the *licensed empty weight*, which is the basic empty weight with the engine and transmission oil excluded. If this is the case, the oil's weight will need to be accounted for and added manually when determining the actual weight of the helicopter.

Maximum Gross Weight

The *maximum gross weight* is the maximum weight that a helicopter can bear safely. This weight is often broken up into an internal maximum gross weight and external maximum gross weight.

Internal maximum gross weight is the maximum weight within the interior of the helicopter, including the pilot, passengers, and any gear or baggage.

External maximum gross weight is the weight that can be supported externally by the helicopter, including external winches. When properly balanced, the external maximum gross weight can reach tremendous levels.

Weight Limitations

It is very important for a pilot to understand the *weight limitations* on the helicopter. As weight increases, the power required to produce the lift needed to compensate for the additional weight must also increase. By reducing weight, the helicopter is able to safely takeoff or land at a location that would not be possible for heavier aircraft. If sufficient takeoff power is questionable, the takeoff should be delayed until the aircraft is lighter or the density altitude has decreased. If airborne, a landing zone that favors better conditions, or that does not require landing to a hover, would be a safer choice. Also, aircraft operating at higher gross weights are required to produce more torque. The additional torque requires more tail rotor thrust to compensate for the main rotor torque effect. Some helicopters may experience loss of tail rotor thrust during high altitude operations.

If the helicopter is packed too lightly, it can easily become unbalanced with the sole addition of the pilot, which can, in turn, make controlling the helicopter more difficult. This is easily remediated by adding extra weight in the rear of the helicopter to act as ballast. The goal is ultimately to balance the weight, using the center of the rotor disk (for single rotor helicopters) or some space between them (for multi-rotor helicopters). This need for balance connects to the concept of the center of gravity.

<u>Center of Gravity</u>

The *center of gravity* is the point at which the entire weight of the helicopter, including both internal and external attachments, is averaged. It's helpful to visualize an unweighted seesaw to understand how this works.

With no other forces acting on it, the seesaw will be perfectly balanced, and the center of gravity is on the pivot point or the fulcrum. When a ten-pound weight is added to one side, there will be more weight on one side of the pivot; the center of gravity is no longer on the pivot, and the seesaw begins to tip. Putting a second, identical weight opposite of the first would cancel the two out. The weight can also be canceled with a larger weight placed closer to the fulcrum or a smaller weight placed further away.

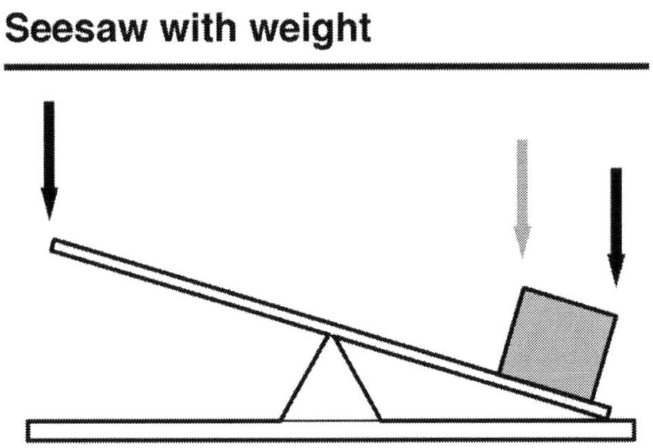

A helicopter acts similarly to a seesaw, with the rotor disk acting as the pivot point. Too much weight on one side will cause the helicopter to tip. Unlike a seesaw, however, a helicopter can adjust the angle of its rotor disk in order to stabilize, but doing so comes at the cost of some lift. This lost lift, in turn, results in reduced performance, and reduced performance makes every other task that much more difficult. Therefore, knowing how to spot and solve center of gravity problems is crucial.

While lateral center of balance problems can occur, they are less frequently a problem when compared to longitudinal center of gravity issues. This is primarily due to the shape of helicopters, which are generally longer than they are wide, so more weight is required to disrupt the helicopter's stable flight. Laterally-imbalanced centers of gravity are occasionally created as some helicopters might dictate which seat to use when flying solo. When using a side mounted winch, or something similar, the weight can quickly place the helicopter outside of the center of gravity limits. However, a front-loaded or aft-loaded center of gravity is much more common.

Front-Loaded Center of Gravity
A *front-loaded center of gravity* can be identified by the fuselage tipping forward, with the nose pointing down towards the ground. This will cause the helicopter to pull forward when hovering and makes slowing down from forward movement more difficult.

This is most often the result of having a heavy pilot at the front, with little-to-no cargo in the rear. A front-loaded center of gravity can also occur midflight, if the fuel tank is located in the rear. As the fuel is consumed, the weight in the rear decreases, and the front begins to tip.

A common solution to a front-loaded center of gravity is to add weight to the back of the helicopter, until the fuselage is once again level. If a longer flight is expected, it may be beneficial to add weight to the rear of the helicopter in anticipation of the fuel tank decreasing in weight.

Aft-Loaded Center of Gravity
An *aft-loaded center of gravity* can be identified by the fuselage tipping backwards, with the nose pointing up towards the sky. This will cause the helicopter to pull backwards when in a neutral hover position and will make accelerating forward more difficult.

An aft-loaded center of gravity, in conjunction with strong winds, can even potentially tilt the helicopter sufficiently that the tail bloom is forced into the rotor disk when attempting to move forwards. This is a fringe case, requiring both a significantly aft-loaded center of gravity and a compromising factor, such as strong winds or poor technique. Pilots should be cognizant of the risk of this condition, even if two of the three conditions are met. An aft-loaded center of gravity is most often the result of having a light pilot with a large amount of cargo in the rear, possibly including a full fuel reserve.

A common solution to an aft-loaded center of gravity is to remove weight from the back of the helicopter and add weight to the front until the fuselage is once again level. Some helicopters have a forward tilt built into the mast to compensate for an aft-loaded center of gravity.

Recognizing a front- or aft-loaded center of gravity is much easier when doing so outside the craft than doing so while within the helicopter. For this reason, using ground personnel to observe the helicopter to spot a displaced center of gravity can be very beneficial, but if that's not possible, the signs of poor center of balance can still be observed from within. If there are no strong winds, a front- or aft-loaded center of gravity can be identified by the helicopter's tendency to pull forward or backwards, respectively. If strong winds are present, separating idle movements caused by the winds and those caused by the center of gravity can be exceedingly difficult. If that is the case, the horizon will need to be used as a level guide as the helicopter lifts off.

Flight Controls

Now that the principles of flight have been covered, the next step is to understand the controls of flight. There are four primary controls that are used to control the helicopter: the collective pitch control, the throttle, the cyclic pitch control, and the anti-torque pedals. Each has a specific function in moving the helicopter through the air, except for the throttle, whose purpose is to control the engine's power output.

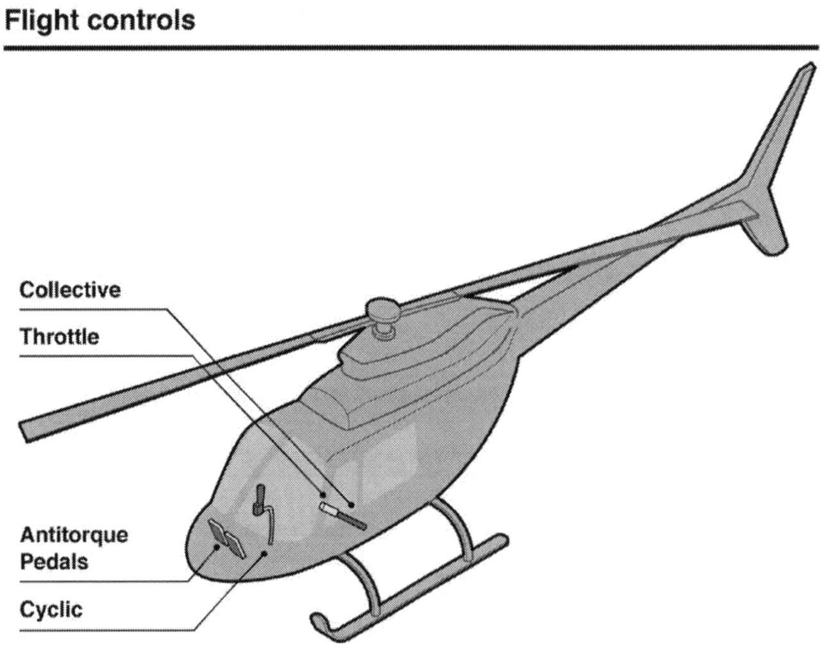

The Collective Pitch Control

The *collective pitch control*, often simply called the *collective*, is primarily used to create lift and control vertical movement. The collective is typically located to the left of the pilot's seat and can be raised or lowered to increase or decrease lift, respectively.

Mechanically, the collective achieves this by altering the pitch of the rotor blades simultaneously (collectively). By increasing the pitch of the blades, the angle of incidence is also increased, and more lift is generated. Conversely, decreasing the pitch of the blades results in a lower angle of incidence and less lift. However, increasing or decreasing lift will also have an identical effect on the drag on the blades. This drag will slow down the rotations per minute (RPM) of the helicopter, unless compensated for by increasing the power to the engine using the throttle.

The Throttle

The *throttle* is used to control the power to the engine. Rotor RPM needs to stay within a certain range to operate the helicopter safely; the throttle is used whenever the RPM drops or rises beyond that value. Using the throttle is much like a motorcycle throttle, with a clockwise turn decreasing power and a counterclockwise turn increasing power.

Since sudden and drastic changes can quickly lead to a destabilized flight, slower and smoother adjustments to the throttle are ideal for maintaining control of the helicopter. Making large, sudden adjustments often leads to over-controlling, where the desired position is passed, and an opposite adjustment is needed to correct the mistake. This is actually excellent advice for all the controls, but is particularly true for the throttle, because the throttle controls the all-important RPM.

Although every helicopter has a throttle, not every helicopter requires manual use of the throttle. Some helicopters are equipped with either a correlator or a governor, which is a tool designed to simplify throttle control. Both are designed to maintain RPM so the pilot does not need to, although they do so in different ways.

A *correlator* is a mechanical tool that links the collective to the throttle, automatically increasing and decreasing the throttle as the collective is used. While effective, the correlator does not account for any other factor that could decrease RPM, so some manual control is still occasionally required.

The *governor* includes an electronic sensor that tracks the current RPM directly, rather than using the position of the collective to guess. If the governor detects that the RPM is out of the desired range, it will automatically adjust the throttle as needed. Since the governor measures the RPM directly, it can account for any variable that might impact RPM. In a properly set-up governor system, the pilot rarely needs to touch the throttle at all.

The Cyclic Pitch Control

The *cyclic pitch control*, or the *cyclic*, is primarily used to generate thrust and control horizontal movement. The cyclic is usually located between the pilot's legs or the two pilot seats and can be pushed in any direction.

Like the collective, the cyclic functions by altering the pitch of the rotor blades. However, unlike the collective, the cyclic does not increase the pitch of all the blades at the same rate, but rather cyclically. In other words, the cyclic alters the pitch of the blade based on where that blade is in the disk. The cyclic might decrease the pitch of the blades as they approach the aft, only to increase the pitch again as the blade nears the front. This results in the lift being generated unequally, which, in turn, causes the disk to tilt. Since generated lift is always perpendicular to the rotor disk, tipping the disk in this way results in a small, horizontal component to the lift, which creates the thrust needed to move.

For example, if forward movement is desired, the pilot pushes the cyclic forward. In a counterclockwise-spinning rotor blade, this causes the blades' pitch to swivel as they rotate, keeping a low pitch as the blade moves over on the right and increasing to a higher pitch as the blade moves by the left. In a clockwise-spinning rotor blade, the pitch is reversed. This results in the rotor blade tipping forward, converting a small portion of the generated lift into forward thrust.

<u>The Anti-Torque Pedals</u>

The *anti-torque pedals* are located at the feet of the pilot, much like the gas and brake pedals of a car. The purpose of this flight control mechanism is to control the pitch of the tail rotor blades.

As the main rotor spins, the rotor creates torque that spins the helicopter in the opposite direction to counteract. The tail rotor does this by creating thrust at the tail of the helicopter. Since this thrust pushes so far away from the center of gravity, rather than simply pushing the helicopter to the side, the anti-torque pedals instead create torque in the opposite direction than that of the main rotor.

The anti-torque pedals themselves allow the pilot to alter the pitch of the tail rotor, which, in turn, increases or decreases the torque the rotor creates. This has two purposes.

The first purpose is to counteract the torque of the main rotor. As the main rotor's pitch increases or decreases, its torque does as well, so the tail rotor must also be able to increase or decrease its opposing torque in order to keep the helicopter's heading constant. The second purpose is by willfully allowing the tail rotor's torque to increase or decrease past the main rotor's torque, a pilot can create a controlled rotation that allows the helicopter to change to a new heading.

The anti-torque pedals are designed so that pushing the left pedal creates more torque in a counterclockwise direction, and pushing the right pedal creates torque in a clockwise direction. In a counterclockwise rotor helicopter, this means that the left pedal increases the pitch of the tail rotor, while the right pedal decreases the pitch. This is because the torque generated by the main rotor is clockwise, so the tail rotor must generate counterclockwise torque to counter the main rotor, and the pitch determines the strength of that counterclockwise torque.

It may help to remember that no net torque is not the same as no torque at all. Even when flying perfectly straight, there are two torques acting on the helicopter: one from the main rotor and one from the tail rotor.

This scenario is not that different from the example used when discussing lift—the block between two springs. The only difference is that now, rather than having one compressed spring and one stretched spring, there are two compressed springs, both attempting to push the block. The anti-torque pedals effectively control the compression of one of the springs. By reducing the compression, the other spring can push the block one way, and by increasing the compression, the controlled spring can overpower the other spring, moving the other way instead, like a game of reverse tug-of-war. Replace compression with torque, and one has the anti-torque pedals.

Some helicopters, rather than having a tail rotor, have multiple main rotors that spin in opposing directions. This allows the counter-rotating main rotor systems' torques to cancel each other out, removing the need for the tail rotor. Such helicopters do still have anti-torque pedals, but they alter the pitch of the main rotors, rather than altering the pitch of tail rotors. Specifically, the right anti-torque pedal increases the pitch of all counterclockwise rotor blades, which increases the clockwise torque, and the left pedal increases the torque of all the clockwise rotor blades, which increases the counterclockwise torque. In this way, the pedals can serve the same function, despite not having a tail rotor.

Trim Control

In-flight variable trim control along the three axes is used to level an aircraft in pitch and roll while eliminating yaw. The trim system serves to counter the aerodynamic forces that affect the balance of the aircraft in flight. The control pressures on an aircraft change as conditions change during a flight. Trim control systems can compensate for the change in weight and center of gravity that occurs in flight as the aircraft burns fuel, as well as compensating for change in wind and atmospheric pressure. Trim can relieve all possible control pressures held after the desired attitude has been reached. Larger and more sophisticated aircraft tend to have a more sophisticated trim system in the pitch, roll, and yaw axes. Smaller aircraft tend to have only pitch control.

The primary flight controls are positioned in-line with the aircraft surfaces during straight-and-level flight. When the flight is not balanced, one or more flight control surfaces will need to be adjusted by continuous control input. This input can be performed through the use of trim tabs; therefore, avoiding the need for constant adjustments by the pilot. The trim systems also prevent the pilot from having to exert strong control force for an extended amount of time—essentially easing the physical workload required to control the aircraft.

Angle of Attack

The angle of attack (AOA) is the angle between the relative wind and the chord line (line between the leading and trailing edge of the airfoil). The AOA can be used to affect the amount of lift on an aircraft. The greater the AOA, the greater the lift generated until the AOA reaches the critical angle of attack. The critical angle of attack induces a stall because the induced drag exceeds the lift. During a stall, the wing is no longer able to create sufficient lift to oppose gravity. Stall angle is usually around 20°. Thus once it's been reached, any subsequent increase in the AOA hurts aerodynamics.

Basic Maneuvers

The Four Fundamentals

There are many different maneuvers, but all can ultimately be broken down into what are known as the four fundamentals of flight—straight-and-level flight, turns, climbs, and descents. Learning any maneuver is just a matter of learning the specific combination required by that maneuver.

Straight-And-Level Flight

Straight-and-level flight is perhaps the simplest maneuver as once a helicopter has reached the desired speed, only minimal control is required to keep moving. Most of the pilot's effort will be directed towards keeping the helicopter level, which means using the various controls to make sure that the heading, airspeed, and altitude remain constant and that the helicopter's course relative to the ground remains in a straight line. An exception is when this fundamental maneuver is combined with another, such as a climb or descent. Even then, care should be taken to ensure that any adjustments that are made to the flight path are done slowly and smoothly.

Turns

Turns are unique among the fundamentals as they have two methods depending on the speed of the helicopter. If the helicopter is flying at low speeds (or even just hovering), turns are performed using the anti-torque pedals, while at higher speeds, the cyclic is used to bank the helicopter. In either case, the goal of the turn is to change the helicopter's heading. A perfect turn would result in no altitude or airspeed change, and the rate of turning would remain constant, aside from the initial acceleration and final deceleration.

The reason for this difference is due to the *laws of motion*, which state that an object in motion will remain in motion. The anti-torque pedals change only the heading of the helicopter, not the velocity, so while in motion, attempting to turn using only the anti-torque pedals will result in the helicopter flying in the same direction, only sideways.

To actually change the direction of flight, the helicopter needs to change the direction of the generated thrust, which is where banking comes in. By tilting the rotor disk to the side, the helicopter creates sideways thrust, which accelerates the helicopter in the new desired direction.

Climbs and Descents

Ascent and *descent* are two sides of the same coin and follow a very similar procedure. During both, the collective will be used to alter the pitch of the main rotor blades, which, in turn, will change altitude either up or down. When the collective is increased in counter-clockwise rotating helicopters, the nose of the helicopter tends to pitch up, and the pilot is required to apply forward cyclic to maintain the same airspeed. In addition, when power is increased, the nose of the helicopter will turn right, due to the torque increase, and the pilot is required to increase left pedal input to maintain the desired heading and trim. When the collective is reduced, the opposite occurs. The nose pitches down and to the left. The pilot has to apply aft cyclic and the right pedal to compensate for these aerodynamic changes.

Hovering

Hovering is perhaps the most common technique employed by helicopter pilots, and the ability to do so is what distinguishes helicopters from many other aircraft. The goal of a hover is to position the helicopter so that the helicopter remains a set distance off the ground (typically just a couple of feet) and then remains stationary. This is, unfortunately, not as easy as it sounds, as a helicopter is anything but stable. The helicopter cannot simply be brought up to a desired height, then parked in the air like a car might be parked in a driveway. Instead, the controls must be constantly fined-tuned to keep the helicopter at a stationary hover.

The collective is usually the easiest to adjust, as the collective acts as a position control. A *position control* is any control that controls position, rather than velocity or acceleration. The handles on a foosball table are an excellent example of a position control, with the figure moving at a rate proportionate to the handles. Due to a phenomenon called *ground effect*, this is similar to how the collective works, in that raising the collective will cause the helicopter to rise a proportionate amount and then stop.

This also makes the collective less susceptible to over-control, as the collective must be raised significantly before the helicopter overcomes the ground effect and begins rising freely. Since the goal of hovering is to get to a certain altitude and then stop, this is ideal behavior, and once the desired altitude is reached, the collective is not likely to need much adjustment.

Ground effect refers to the reduced drag and increased lift that is experienced by an aircraft flying in close proximity to the ground. For a fixed-wing aircraft, it is considered in ground effect when the wing is in close proximity to the ground. A helicopter is considered to be in ground effect when it is within one rotor diameter of the ground. For example, if the rotor diameter of the helicopter is 50 feet, then 50 feet and below is considered to be in ground effect.

The anti-torque pedals, meanwhile, are a *rate control*, which means that the pedals control the rate of change. An example of a rate control is the gas pedal on a car, with the car accelerating faster the harder its pedal is pushed and the car slowing down when the pedal is released. Similarly, pushing the anti-torque pedal causes the helicopter to begin rotating in that direction at a rate determined by the pressure on the pedal. Releasing the pedal causes the rotation to slow to a stop.

It is ideal in a hover to use only minimal pressure on the pedals to keep the helicopter's bearing constant. Otherwise, there is the chance that the pedals might be over-controlled, with the helicopter unable to stop rotating before reaching the desire point. On calm days, the anti-torque pedals might not even be needed to maintain a hover, but on windy days, the thrust generated by the tail rotor can become inconsistent, requiring far more manipulation to steady.

By far the most difficult, however, is the cyclic. Whereas the collective is position-controlled and the anti-torque pedals are rate-controlled, the cyclic is *acceleration-controlled*. Manipulation of the collective results in movement to a particular position, while pressing the anti-torque pedals to continue to spin the helicopter until released. In comparison, use of the cyclic causes the helicopter to speed up as long as the cyclic is held, but upon release, the helicopter will continue to move in that direction at a similar velocity until the cyclic is pushed in the opposite direction to create a negative acceleration and decrease the velocity to zero.

For example, if a horizontal drift is noticed, the cyclic must be pushed gently in the desired direction of movement for a brief moment, released, and then reapplied in the opposite direction as the destination is reached. If the cyclic is only pushed once, the helicopter will continue to move in that direction until drag eventually slows the helicopter to a stop. This makes the cyclic doubly-easy to over-control as there are twice as many opportunities to do so, and acceleration is more difficult to perceive than position or speed. This also means that the helicopter is almost always moving slightly, and controlling the cyclic in such a way that the helicopter's velocity is truly zero is nearly impossible. Even if the helicopter did reach zero velocity, it would only take the slightest of breezes to shift the helicopter slightly and begin the process anew.

<u>Vertical Takeoff to Hover</u>

In a *vertical takeoff to hover*, the objective is to start from a landed position and end with the helicopter hovering just a few feet off the ground. Before beginning this maneuver, there are a few steps that must be done outside the helicopter.

The first task is to make sure that the helicopter has the necessary clearance to take off. The next step is to make sure that the area around the helicopter, particularly above and to the left and right of the aircraft, is free of any obstructions. Once that has been done, takeoff can proceed.

With the collective fully down, the cyclic should be placed in a neutral position, and the collective should be increased smoothly. Pedals should be applied to maintain heading, and the cyclic should be coordinated for a vertical ascent. As the aircraft leaves the ground, the proper control response and aircraft center of gravity (COG) should be checked.

<u>Hovering Turn</u>

In a *hovering turn*, the object is to change the heading of the helicopter while maintaining a constant position relative to the ground. Neither a horizontal nor a vertical position should shift during the maneuver. The anti-torque pedals are the primary controls needed for this maneuver.

To perform the hovering turn, light pressure should be applied on the anti-torque pedals in the direction desired. The helicopter should begin to rotate in that direction. Just like a hover, keeping the helicopter otherwise stationary is important, which means the cyclic and collective may need to be used to prevent the helicopter from drifting. However, doing so should be no more difficult than before.

When the helicopter nears the desired heading, the pedals should be released, and the helicopter's rate of turn should begin to slow and eventually stop. If the pedals have been used lightly, this should take very little time, and the pedals can be released moments before reaching the target heading without fear of overshooting the target heading. If the pedals are pushed with more pressure and the helicopter is allowed to rotate at a faster rate, considerably more space will be required. This is because the helicopter will not only turn further in a set amount of time, but also require more time to stop. Therefore, a slower, steady rate of turn is preferable.

The above all assume a relatively windless day, as strong winds can greatly impact a hovering turn. While turning away from the direction of the wind, the tail turns into the wind, which is more difficult due to the increased drag, so it requires more pressure to maintain turning speed.

When the helicopter reaches a parallel position, the tail tends to *weathervane* and may even be pulled with the wind. If this happens, it may be necessary to switch the pedals to keep the helicopter from turning too swiftly. This switching-over is possibly the hardest part about a hovering turn, as the sudden shift requires an equally swift shift in the pedals.

In addition to the difficulty from trying to find the proper pedal position to keep the helicopter from spinning too quickly, the sudden change in forces often upsets the balance of the other controls, requiring smaller, but still significant, adjustments simultaneously.

The graphic below shows a theoretical 360-degree turn and the necessary adjustments to keep the helicopter moving consistently throughout every 90° increment.

The Necessary Adjustments for a 360° Turn

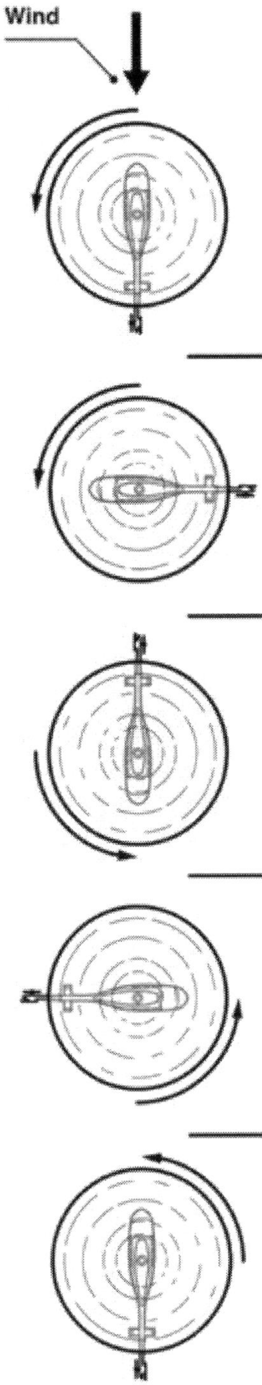

Cyclic - Forward

Pedal	Some left in hover, more left to start turn to left
Collective	Power required to hover at desired height
Throttle	As necessary to maintain r.p.m.

Cyclic - Right

Pedal	Most left pressure in turn
Collective	Most power in turn
Throttle	As necessary to maintain r.p.m.

Cyclic - Rearward

Pedal	Changing from left to right pressure
Collective	Power reducing
Throttle	As necessary to maintain r.p.m.

Cyclic - Left

Pedal	Most right pedal pressure in turn
Collective	Least power in turn
Throttle	As necessary to maintain r.p.m.

Cyclic - Forward

Pedal	Some right to stop turn, then left to maintain heading
Collective	Increasing as left pedal applied
Throttle	As necessary to maintain r.p.m.

Hovering to Forward Flight

In a *hovering to forward flight* maneuver, the helicopter will be leaving a hovering position to move forward. This maneuver is not designed to be a quick flight maneuver and is not to be used for long travel distances. Instead, the purpose of this maneuver is to reposition the helicopter or to travel short distances. Ideally, the helicopter should not exceed the speed of a brisk walk during its execution.

Starting from a hovering position, the first step is to make sure that the intended path is cleared and that the helicopter is properly lined up with the desired target. If not, the pilot can perform a hovering turn to align the helicopter correctly. Once that is done, two points directly between the helicopter and the destination should be mentally identified. These are the *reference points* and will be used to ensure the helicopter does not drift during the maneuver.

To begin, the pilot should apply slight pressure to the cyclic. As previously mentioned, the cyclic is acceleration-controlled, so there is no need for the pressure to be sustained. Continuing to hold the cyclic forward will just cause the helicopter to continuously get faster, while the helicopter will continue to move forward, even if the cyclic is released. Because the cyclic functions by tipping the rotor disk and redirecting some lift to create thrust, the altitude may drop slightly while the cyclic is applied, but as long as the pressure applied to the cyclic is light, the lost altitude should be negligible and return once the cyclic is put back into the neutral position.

Once the helicopter has begun to move, it will continue to do so for quite some time. During this time, the reference points should be frequently checked to make sure that the two points—the destination and the helicopter—still form a straight line. If not, that means that the helicopter has drifted, and use of the cyclic may be necessary to correct the drift. Heading will also need to be maintained; although, barring crosswind conditions, the only time a heading is at risk of changing is whenever the cyclic is applied.

As the target is reached, rearward cyclic pressure should be applied to slow the helicopter down. Releasing and reapplying pressure may be necessary to control the helicopter's airspeed during the approach, with the goal being to slow down to a hover just as the position is reached. The cyclic may be used to increase speed or reverse it, if the destination is under-shot or over-shot respectively, but when making this sort of minor adjustment, the cyclic should be used sparingly in order to maintain control of the helicopter's motion.

Note that even though this is called *forward flight*, the same technique is used when performing *sideward* or *rearward* flight, with only a few modifications. Rather than applying forward cyclic pressure, a sideward or rearward flight requires a sideward or rearward pressure, respectively. Reference points will still be used to watch for signs that the helicopter is drifting from its path, but because of the reduced visibility of the helicopter's side and rear arcs, clearing the area first is especially important, and using ground personnel to assist is highly recommended whenever possible.

Lastly, a problem unique to sideward flight is that the aircraft will attempt to *weathervane*. This is when the helicopter begins to turn due to the helicopter's tail striking the air. In this instance, use of the anti-torque pedals is necessary to counteract the weathervane effect.

<u>Takeoff from Hover</u>

In a normal *takeoff from hover*, the goal is to bring the helicopter from a hovering position to straight and level flight in the air. While similar in principle to forward flight, takeoff differs primarily in the altitude and speed of flight. For safety reasons, certain combinations of velocity and altitude are prohibited, and although the exact range varies depending on the helicopter, a higher velocity generally requires a higher altitude and vice versa. What this means is that while the helicopter is accelerating, it will also need to climb in order to stay within those parameters. Thus, the collective and cyclic must be used in unison. Typically, this maneuver is broken up into five transitional phases, as seen below, starting with a hovering position at phase one and ending with straight and level flight at phase five.

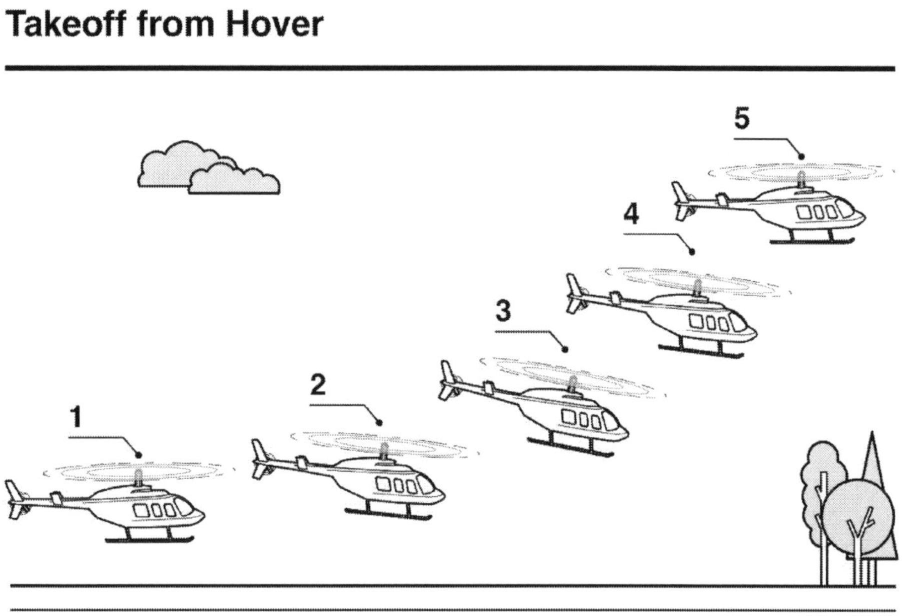

In *phase one*, the helicopter is in hover. Before moving forward with the rest of the maneuver, a *performance check* is advisable—checking the power required to hover against performance planning data. A performance check is used to determine if the aircraft is within the maximum gross weight and if sufficient power is available to perform the mission.

The pilot must ensure that all the controls move freely, that they do not get stuck at any point during their full rotation of movement, and that there is sufficient power available to continue. Just as with forward flight, two reference points should be obtained in between the helicopter and its intended direction of flight, which will be used to ensure the helicopter is kept laterally stable.

The *second phase* begins by applying forward pressure on the cyclic. Because a higher speed is desired, more pressure can be applied to the cyclic than that used when performing forward flight, although the increase should be steady rather than rapid, to ensure the helicopter remains in controlled flight. This greater pressure on the cyclic results in a greater portion of lift being used to create thrust, and while this amount is negligible in forward flight, that is not be the case here.

The collective will need to be raised to keep the helicopter from losing altitude. Raising the collective requires a proportionate increase in power to keep RPM constant, and the increased power from the throttle will create more torque, which needs to be accounted for with the anti-torque pedals. This means that during this phase, *all four controls need to be used simultaneously*. This is the reason why the cyclic should be increased slowly during this phase, to give ample time to adjust the other controls as needed.

In *phase three*, the helicopter has gained enough speed to reach *effective translational lift* (ETL). This typically occurs around speeds of 16 to 24 knots; it is easily recognizable by the helicopter beginning to climb and the nose beginning to rise. At this point, the collective should be increased to begin climbing, and the cyclic must be pushed forward enough to counteract the nose's inclination to rise during this phase.

Again, because the collective is being raised, the pilot should expect to increase the throttle and use the anti-torque pedals to counteract the increased torque and maintain the RPM and heading.

In *phase four*, the helicopter is climbing and accelerating forward simultaneously. Care must be taken to control both, so that the helicopter does not end up in the shaded area of the height-velocity diagram, but otherwise this phase is mostly about maintenance.

A Sample Height Velocity Diagram for Smooth, Level, Firm Surfaces

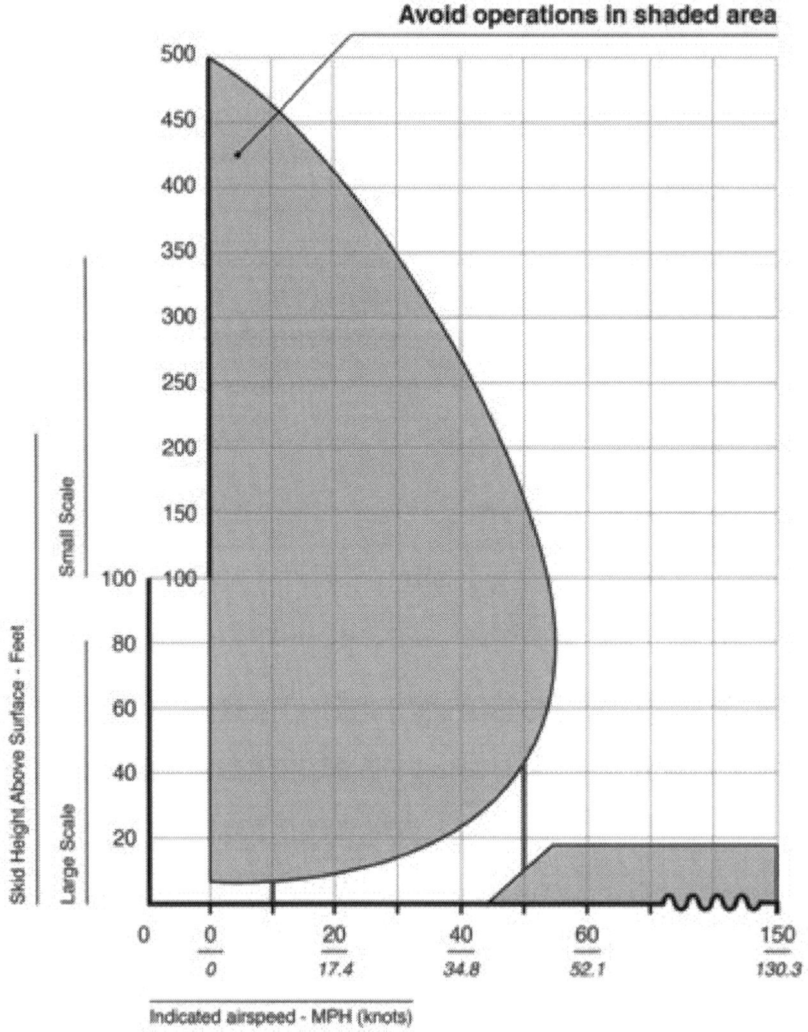

In *phase five*, the helicopter has escaped the curved section of the height-velocity diagram, and the helicopter can now climb or accelerate, mostly at will. The shaded areas must still be avoided, but typically by this phase, enough distance has been put between the shaded areas and the helicopter's height/velocity that such concerns should only be an afterthought—something to be remembered if airspeed or altitude decreases significantly, but otherwise, it's not likely to be relevant in normal flight. At this point, the helicopter has entered straight and level flight.

Takeoff from Surface

A *takeoff from the surface*, sometimes called a *running takeoff*, is similar in many ways to a takeoff from a hover—both involve increasing altitude and airspeed significantly, and both end up in straight and level flight. In fact, after a certain point, the technique for both become identical. However, there are enough differences, particularly early in the maneuver, to warrant a brief discussion.

Typically, this maneuver is used in preference to a takeoff from a hover only when the helicopter lacks sufficient power to hover. This is usually because the helicopter is overweight, but is also sometimes due to environmental conditions, such as high-density altitude.

As the name implies, a takeoff from the surface involves starting from a landed position and ending in a straight and level flight. This maneuver involves sliding across the surface as speed is picked up, so wheeled helicopters perform better than skidded ones. However, special "skid shoes" can be equipped to the helicopter to help.

The maneuver begins with the helicopter on the surface, with the collective and throttle at their lowest respective settings. Since this maneuver involves the helicopter riding across the ground for some distance, it is especially important to clear the area that will be servicing as the runway. The throttle should be increased until the proper RPM is achieved; then, the collective should be raised. The goal is to reach the point where the helicopter is light on its skids. The anti-torque pedals and cyclic are used as needed to ensure that the helicopter is properly turned towards the intended flight path; then, the pilot should begin with slight forward pressure on the cyclic.

The helicopter will begin to slide forward on the ground. As it does so, use of the anti-torque pedals should continue to keep the helicopter's heading constant, and left or right cyclic should be applied if the helicopter starts to drift laterally. As the helicopter accelerates, the rotor will become more effective, and the helicopter will start to become progressively lighter. This will reduce the friction between the wheels (or skids) and the ground, causing the helicopter to accelerate even faster.

Eventually, the helicopter will become light enough to lift off the ground. As it does, the pilot should increase the collective to assist and prepare to increase the cyclic when the helicopter's nose begins to rise due to translational lift. From this point, the technique to finish takeoff is identical to a takeoff from hover (starting from phase three) and the same procedure can be used.

Straight and Level Flight

In *straight and level flight*, the goal is to keep a helicopter in cruising flight on a straight flightpath and prevent any change in altitude, velocity, or heading that the pilot doesn't initiate. A helicopter is anything but stable, so this is often easier said than done. Fortunately, the helicopter is very controllable, so an experienced pilot can often make corrections before the helicopter has even begun to move, relying more on feel than sight.

The airspeed of a helicopter depends primarily on its attitude (or pitch up or down relative to the horizon), which, in turn, is controlled by the cyclic. Increasing the pressure to the cyclic increases the rate at which the attitude changes, but in most cases, there's little need for rapid acceleration. Instead, the cyclic should be applied slowly and in moderation. Although drag dampens the helicopter's acceleration somewhat, the cyclic is still an acceleration control, and too much forward pressure can make maintaining a constant rate difficult.

Additionally, there is a bit of control lag with the cyclic, in that there is a short delay between input through the cyclic and output through the helicopter. One all too common mistake is for a pilot to adjust the cyclic too far. This results in the helicopter moving much faster than intended, a loss of altitude, and many other potential complications that could easily be avoided simply by remembering the delay between input and output.

The same procedure also works in reverse, should the speed need to be decreased. Applying aft pressure to the cyclic raises the helicopter's nose and levels out its attitude. With less thrust being generated, the drag created by the helicopter's movements eventually slows the helicopter down until the thrust and the drag are once again opposite. Additional care must be taken while slowing down, however, so that the helicopter does not end in the shaded area of the velocity-height diagram.

Whenever the cyclic is used, the collective almost certainly needs to be adjusted as well. As mentioned previously, the cyclic functions by changing the angle of the rotor disk, which changes the direction of lift and repurposes some of the lift as thrust. In order to keep the same altitude, lift must remain the same. This can be achieved by increasing or decreasing the collective, while simultaneously adjusting the cyclic, so that the lift lost to thrust is immediately regained by raising the collective. Of course, increasing the collective requires more power, so the throttle also needs to be rotated to keep RPM. More power creates more torque, so the anti-torque pedals need to be used as well.

Banking Turns

There are many parallels between hovering forward flight and straight and level flight. Though each has their own nuances, many of the same principles from one apply to the other as both use a similar mechanism to create and control airspeed. The same cannot be said for hovering turns and banking turns, which share only one commonality—the goal to change the heading of the helicopter.

In a hovering turn, the primary control used to make the turn is the anti-torque pedals. However, when attempting to perform a *banking turn*, the cyclic is used instead. Specifically, the cyclic is pushed laterally to bank the helicopter, which allows the generated thrust to rotate the helicopter in an arc.

The final banking angle, and the rate at which it banks, depends on the duration and force applied to the cyclic. Like always, the control should be applied slowly so that control of the helicopter's turn can be maintained. When the desired turn angle is reached, releasing the cyclic to its neutral position will keep the helicopter banking at that angle.

The greater the angle, the sharper the turn, but this sharpness comes at the cost of the lift generated. Thus, the greater the angle, the more the collective needs to be raised to keep altitude throughout the maneuver and the more power that is needed to keep up the RPM. Care should be taken to ensure that sufficient power is available to complete the turn at the desired angle or else the helicopter will lose altitude.

The anti-torque pedals are still needed during this maneuver, but since the heading is supposed to change during the maneuver, using the helicopter's facing as a guideline for when to apply the pedals will not work. Instead, the pilot should look for signs of slipping or skidding and react appropriately. Both involve a failure of the helicopter's heading and actual direction of movement to match, which result in inefficient flight.

Slipping occurs when the helicopter's banking angle is too great for the rate of turn. In this case, the helicopter's nose will be pointing outwards from the direction of the turn. This results in the helicopter sliding laterally into the turn. This can be corrected by increasing the pressure on the pedal in the direction of the turn or decreasing the pressure on the pedal away from the turn.

Skidding occurs when the helicopter's rate of turn is too great for the angle of bank. In this case, the helicopter's nose will be pointing inwards from the direction of the turn. This results in the helicopter sliding laterally away from the turn. This can be corrected by increasing the pressure on the pedal away from the turn or by decreasing the pressure on the pedal in the direction of the turn.

Once the turn nears the finish, cyclic pressure should be applied in the opposite direction of the turn to level out the helicopter, and the helicopter will stop turning. Reducing the banking angle will restore the lift, so the collective and throttle will need to be decreased. Otherwise, the helicopter might climb. Also, if the cyclic is not applied until the turn is actually reached, the helicopter will end up turning too far as the helicopter requires time to level out. To prevent this, the pilot should begin to apply counter cyclic pressure shortly before arriving at the desired angle.

Normal Climb and Descent

Although technically two separate maneuvers, climbing and descending are very similar in execution, with one being basically the opposite of the other. Both primarily use the collective and the throttle, although both allow for cyclic adjustments to influence the rate of climb and descent at the expense of airspeed.

To perform a climb, the collective must be raised to generate additional thrust. The throttle needs to be raised in tandem to keep RPM consistent, which requires additional application of the anti-torque pedals to keep the helicopter's heading constant. Since this application increases the total thrust generated (irrespective of the angle of the rotor disk), it will also increase the airspeed of the helicopter, if the helicopter has any forward attitude. Minor aft pressure should be applied to the cyclic to raise the helicopter's attitude slightly. This change in attitude will decrease the amount of thrust derived from the lift, but the lost thrust should be replaced as the net lift is increased.

If a faster climb is desired, more aft pressure can be applied to the cyclic, further reducing the amount of generated thrust to increase the amount of generated lift. This results in decreased airspeed, however, so caution must be taken to ensure that the helicopter continues to maintain enough airspeed to stay out of the shaded areas of the velocity-height diagram. However, as altitude increases, the shaded area gets smaller and smaller, allowing progressively lower speeds.

When leveling off a climb, the helicopter's momentum will carry it beyond the desired altitude, so the pilot should begin leveling off a bit before reaching the desired height. Typically, 10% of the helicopter's rate of ascent is ideal, so a 100 FPM climb would only need 10 feet to stop in time, while climbing at 700 FPM would need 70 feet.

The collective should be lowered slowly, adjusting the throttle and anti-torque pedals as needed to keep the RPM and heading consistent throughout the process. As the lift decreases, the thrust decreases. The pilot should apply forward pressure on the cyclic as well to keep airspeed and assist with reducing lift. As the intended height is reached, cyclic pressure should be applied to return to the desired attitude, and any final adjustments to the collective and throttle should be made to stabilize the helicopter's altitude.

A descent functions very much the same, just in reverse. To descend, thrust must be decreased, to allow gravity to pull the helicopter down. To do this, the collective must be lowered, and the throttle must be dialed back. With less lift being generated, thrust and airspeed will also decrease. If a constant airspeed is desired, the cyclic will need to be pushed forward slightly to increase the thrust component of the lift.

Since the greater thrust component comes at the cost of the lift, this also results in the helicopter descending faster.

By applying the same method, the descent can be sped up by increasing the forward pressure on the cyclic further and increasing airspeed, causing the helicopter to descend more rapidly. Just as with a climb, the helicopter must not be allowed to reach the shaded area of the velocity-height diagram.

When leveling off a descent, just as with a climb, a pilot should expect forward momentum to carry the helicopter some distance after beginning to slow down. The same 10% rule applies here. To begin leveling off from a descent, the collective should be raised slowly, controlling throttle and the anti-torque pedals to maintain RPM and heading, just as was done when climbing.

Also, like climbing, leveling off will influence airspeed; in this case, the increasing lift will increase thrust, and aft pressure to the cyclic is needed to keep airspeed constant. Adjustments should continue to be made to the collective and cyclic, until the helicopter has leveled out at the desired airspeed.

Taxiing

Taxiing is less a maneuver and more of a combination of other maneuvers performed with additional limitations. Taxiing is primarily used to move a helicopter a short distance, either to ferry passengers or cargo or simply to reposition the helicopter for some other purpose, such as a cleared runway to allow the helicopter to take off. Taxiing is also unique in that it often involves the use of taxiways or other prescribed routes to follow ahead of time, not unlike a road. There are three types of taxiing, each with its own uses. The three are hover, air, and surface taxiing.

Hover Taxiing

Hover Taxiing involves moving about in a hovering helicopter and employs hovering, forward flight, and hovering turns to move about. Although the exact height of flight varies by taxiway, it is virtually always no more than 25 feet above the ground. Because of the low speed of hover taxiing, this is most often used to reposition a helicopter rather than as a form of transportation.

Air Taxiing

Air taxiing involves higher speeds and altitudes, although generally it does not exceed heights of 100 feet. Since the helicopter is flying both higher and faster, straight and level flight and banking turns are used instead, as well as climbing and descending when necessary.

Additionally, a takeoff is always required to enter an air taxi, whether from a hover or the surface. Otherwise, there is little difference between free flight and a taxiway, though in the latter, the helicopter pilot is expected to avoid flying directly above other vehicles or personnel, whether on the ground or in the sky.

Surface Taxiing

Surface taxiing is the only one that requires any technique that hasn't already been discussed. In a surface taxi, the helicopter is kept on the ground the entire time. To accomplish this, the collective is raised until the helicopter is light on its wheels (or skids), just as if preparing for a surface takeoff. Also, like a surface takeoff, the collective is then used to create forward movement. That, however, is where the similarities end.

When performing a surface taxi, the helicopter should never move faster than a brisk walk, to prevent the lift from having any chance of taking the helicopter off the ground. Additionally, although some cyclic is needed to start the forward movement, the speed of the helicopter is controlled through the collective instead.

Although the friction between the wheels (or skids) and the ground makes the helicopter far more stable than when it is in the sky, yawing still occurs, requiring some anti-torque pedal application to negate. Likewise, any strong winds capable of pushing the helicopter need to be countered by applying cyclic pressure in the direction of the incoming wind.

Fixed-Wing Aircraft

A fixed-wing aircraft is one in which movement of the wings in relation to the aircraft is not used to generate lift, even though technically they flex in flight, as do all wings. In contrast, helicopters generate lift through rotating airfoils.

Fixed-wing aircraft have the following items in common: wings, flight controls, tail assembly, landing gear, fuselage, and an engine or powerplant. Here's an illustration of the parts of a plane:

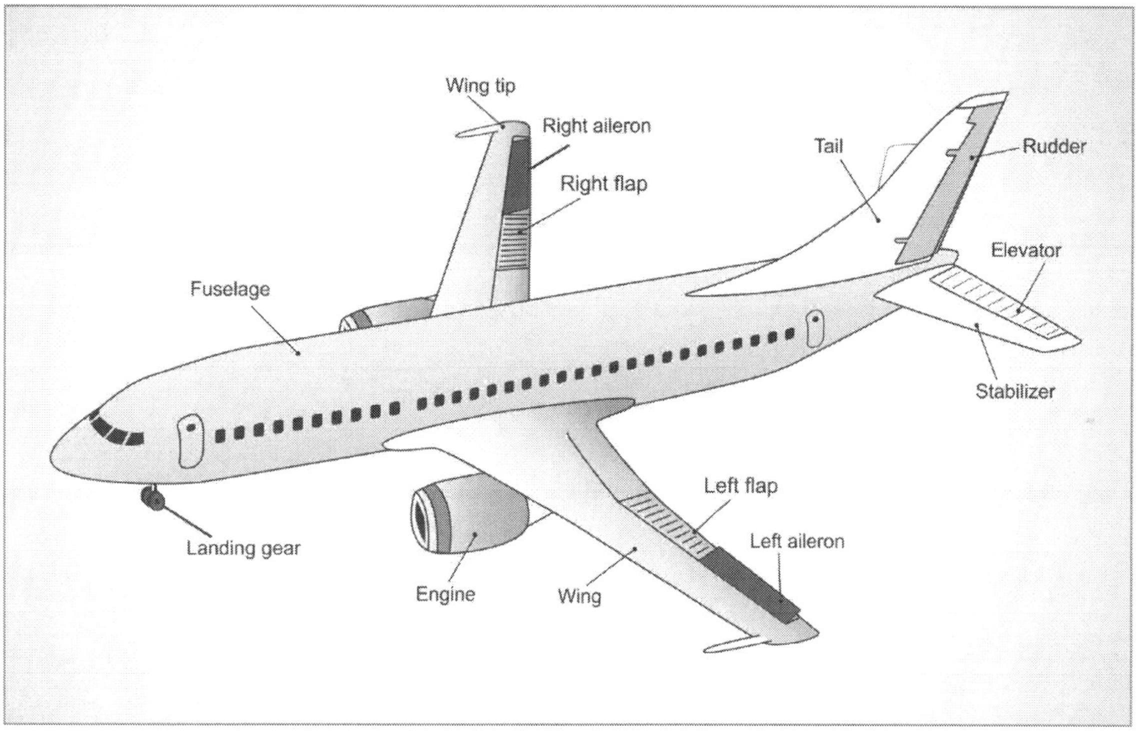

Wings

An airfoil is a surface such as a wing, elevator, or aileron that is designed to help create lift and control of an aircraft by using and manipulating air flow. The standard wing, or airfoil, is mounted to the sides of the fuselage. The outline or cross section of the airfoil is referred to as the "airfoil profile." The standard wing has an upper surface that is curved while the lower surface is relatively flat. The air moves over the curved surface of the wing at a higher speed than it moves under the flat surface. The difference in airflow on the surfaces of the wing creates lift due to the aircraft's forward airspeed, which enables flight.

Many modern aircraft structures use full cantilever wings, meaning no external bracing is required. The strength in this design is from the internal structural members and the fuselage. Semi-cantilever wings use some form of external bracing, whether it be wires or struts.

Aircraft wing designs vary based on the characteristics and type of performance needed for the aircraft. Changing the wing design changes the amount of lift that can be created and the amount of stability and control the aircraft will have at different speeds. Some aircraft have wings that are designed to tilt, sweep, or fold. So long as they do not generate lift, they are still considered fixed-wing aircraft. Wing geometry is related to the shape of the aircraft wings when viewed from the front of the aircraft, or from above.

Flight Controls

Flight controls, like the name implies, are used to direct the forces on an aircraft in flight for the purpose of directional and attitude control. Flight controls vary from simple mechanical (manually operated) systems, to hydro-mechanical systems, to fly-by-wire systems. Fly-by-wire systems send signal via wire to control the plane.

When discussing flight controls, it's important to understand the terms *leading edge* and *trailing edge*. *Leading edge* refers to the front part of the wing that separates air, forcing it to go above or below the wing. *Trailing edge* is the back part of the wing and where the air comes back together.

The flight controls typically are divided into primary and secondary systems.

The primary flight controls are responsible for the movement of the aircraft along its three axes of flight. Primary flight controls on an aircraft are the *elevators*, *ailerons*, and *rudder*. Elevators are mounted on the trailing edges of horizontal stabilizers and are used for controlling aircraft pitch about the lateral axis. The ailerons are mounted on the trailing edges of the wings and are used for controlling aircraft roll about the longitudinal axis. The rudder is mounted on the trailing edge of the vertical fin and is used for controlling rotation (yaw) around the vertical axis. Here's an illustration of pitch, roll, and yaw along the three axes.

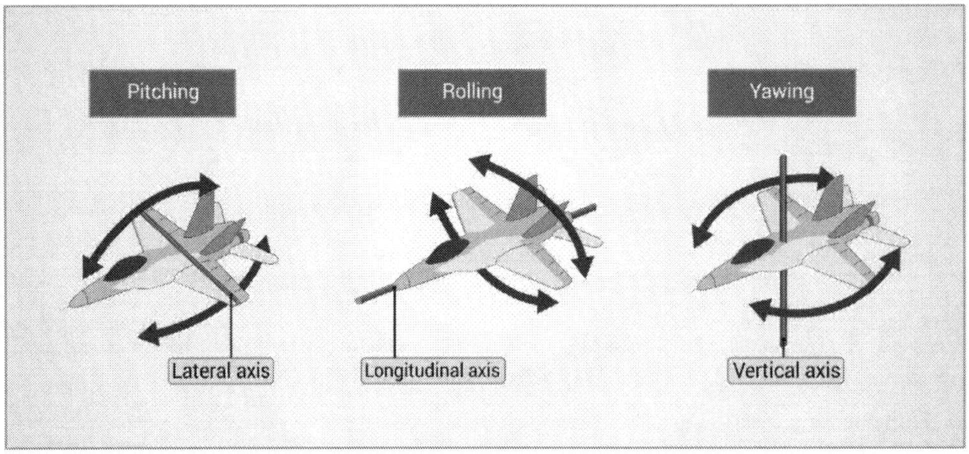

Secondary, or auxiliary, flight controls include (but are not limited to): flaps, slats, spoilers, speed brakes, and the trim system. Flaps are the hinged portion of the wing trailing edge between the ailerons and the fuselage, and sometimes may be located on the leading edge of a wing as well. If used during takeoff, flaps reduce the amount of runway and time needed to takeoff. During landings, flaps increase the drag on the wings slowing the plane down and allowing it to go slower right before it lands, which then reduces the amount of runway needed. Essentially, flaps allow the aircraft to produce more lift at slower airspeeds. Flaps are also utilized on some planes to increase maneuverability. The amount of flap extension and the angle can be adjusted by the flap levers located in the cockpit.

Spoilers are located on the upper, or trailing edge, of the wing and are used to decrease lift. They allow the nose of the aircraft to be pitched down without increasing the airspeed, allowing for a safe landing speed. Slats are located on the middle to outboard portion of the leading edge of the wing. They are used to create additional lift and slower flight by extending the shape of the wing. Flaps and slats are hidden inside the wing and are extended during takeoff and landing.

The trim system is an inexpensive autopilot that eliminates the need for the pilot to constantly maintain pressure on the controls. Most aircraft trim systems contain trim, balance, anti-balance, and servo tabs. These tabs are found on the trailing edge of primary flight control surfaces and are used to counteract hydro-mechanical and aerodynamic forces acting on the aircraft.

Tail Assembly

The tail assembly of an aircraft is commonly referred to as the empennage. The empennage structure typically includes a tail cone, fixed stabilizers (horizontal and vertical), and moveable surfaces to assist in directional control. The moveable surfaces are the rudder, which is attached to the vertical stabilizer, and the elevators attached to the horizontal stabilizers.

Landing Gear

Aircraft require landing gear not only for takeoffs and landings but also to support the aircraft while it is on the ground. The landing gear must be designed to support the entire weight of the aircraft and handle the loads placed on it during landing, as well as be as light as possible. Small aircraft that fly at low-speeds usually have fixed landing gear, which means it is stationary and does not have the ability to retract in flight. Aircraft that fly at higher speeds require retractable landing gear so that the gear is not in the airstream. Retractable landing gear makes the aircraft more aerodynamic by reducing drag, but usually at the cost of additional weight when compared to the fixed landing gear. Also, the landing gear should only be operated (extended or retracted) when the airspeed indicator is at or below the aircraft's maximum landing-gear operating speed, or V_{LO}. Airspeeds above V_{LO} can damage the landing gear operating mechanism. When the gear is down and locked, the aircraft should not be operated above the aircraft's maximum landing-gear extended speed, or V_{LE}. Since landing gear is more stable when all the way down than when being moved, V_{LE} will be higher for an aircraft than V_{LO}. A switch or lever that resembles the shape of a wheel is used to raise and lower the landing gear.

Landing gear is made from a variety of materials, such as magnesium, steel, and aluminum. Most landing gear has some type of shock absorbers and braking system. Not all landing gear uses wheels. Depending on what the aircraft is used for, it may have skis, skids, pontoons, or floats instead of tires for landing on snow, ice, or water.

Landing gear is typically found in two configurations: tricycle gear and conventional gear (also known as tail wheel gear).

Tricycle gear is the most common configuration. Tricycle gear has a single wheel in the front (usually under the nose) and two wheels side-by-side at the center of gravity of the aircraft. Large, heavy aircraft may contain extra wheels in this configuration. Small aircraft equipped with nose landing gear can typically be steered with rudder pedals.

Conventional tail wheel aircraft or "tail draggers" were more common in the early days of aviation. The two main wheels supported the heaviest portion of the aircraft, with the third smaller wheel was near the tail. Having the smaller wheel in the tail allowed the aircraft to rest at an incline on the ground, which provided more clearance for the nose propeller. In some conventional gear, the tail wheel could be steered mechanically with the rudder pedals.

Fuselage

The fuselage is the main structure, or airframe, of an aircraft. The fuselage is where the cockpit, or cabin, of the aircraft is, and where passengers or cargo may be located. It provides attachment points for the main components of the aircraft such as the wings, engines, and empennage. If an aircraft is a single-engine, the fuselage houses the powerplant as well. If the powerplant is a reciprocating engine, it is mounted in the front of the aircraft, while a turbine engine would be mounted in the rear of the aircraft. *Cowling* is the term for the covering of an airplane's engine which is streamlined to maximize aerodynamics.

Aircraft contain a battery that is charged by an alternator or generator. Wiring takes the electric current to where it's needed throughout the plane. Some type of warning system will be in place to warn of inadequate current output. This could be a warning light or an ammeter. If the number showing on an ammeter is positive, it means the battery is charging. If the number is negative, it means that the alternator or generator cannot keep up with the amount of current being used. Some aircraft have a load meter, which shows the amount of current being drawn from the battery.

Fuselage structures are usually classified as truss, monocoque, and semi-monocoque. The truss fuselage is typically made of steel tubing welded together, which enables the structure to handle tension and compression loads. In lighter aircraft, an aluminum alloy may be used along with cross-bracing. A single shell fuselage is referred to as monocoque, which uses a stronger skin to handle the tension and compression loads. There is also a semi-monocoque fuselage, which is basically a combination of the truss and monocoque fuselage, and is the most commonly used.

Powerplant

The powerplant of an aircraft is its engine, which is a component of the propulsion system that generates mechanical power and thrust. Most modern aircraft engines are typically either turbine or piston engines.

Flight Envelope

The flight envelope (also known as the performance envelope or service envelope) refers to the capabilities of an aircraft based on its design in terms of altitude, airspeed, loading factors, and maneuverability. When an aircraft is pushed to the point where it exceeds design limitations for that specific aircraft, it is considered to be operating outside the envelope, which is considered dangerous.

All aircraft have approved flight manuals that contain the flight limitations or parameters. To ensure an aircraft is being operated properly, a pilot needs to be familiar with the aircraft's flight envelope prior to flight. The flight parameters are based on the engine and wing design and include the following: maximum and minimum speed, stall speed, climb rate, glide ratio, maximum altitude, and the maximum amount of gravity forces (g-forces) the aircraft can withstand.

- The *maximum speed* of an aircraft is based on air resistance getting lower at higher altitudes, to a point where increased altitude no longer increases maximum speed due to lack of oxygen to "feed" the engine.
- The *stalling speed* is the minimum speed at which an aircraft can maintain level flight. As the aircraft gains altitude, the stall speed increases (since the aircraft's weight can be better supported through speed).
- The *climb rate* is the vertical speed of an aircraft, which is the increase in altitude in respect to time.
- The *climb gradient* is the ratio of the increase in altitude to the horizontal air distance.
- The *glide ratio* is the ratio of horizontal distance traveled per rate of fall.
- The *maximum altitude* of an aircraft is also referred to as the service ceiling. The ceiling is usually determined by the aircraft performance and the wings, and is where an altitude at a given speed can no longer be increased at level flight.
- The *maximum g-forces* each aircraft can withstand varies but is based on its design and structural strength.

Commercial aircraft are considered to have a small flight envelope, since the range of speed and maneuverability is rather limited, and they are designed to operate efficiently under moderate conditions. The Federal Aviation Administration (FAA) is the controlling body in the United States pertaining to authorized flight envelopes and restrictions for commercial and civilian aircraft. The FAA may reduce a flight envelope for added safety as needed.

Military aircraft, especially fighter jets, have extremely large flight envelopes. By design, these aircraft are very maneuverable and can operate at high speeds as their purpose requires. The term "pushing the envelope" originally referred to military pilots taking an aircraft to the extreme limits of their capabilities, mostly during combat, but also during aircraft flight testing. The term "outside the envelope" is when the aircraft is pushed outside the design specifications and is considered very dangerous. Operating outside the limits of the aircraft can severely degrade the life of components, or even lead to mechanical failure.

Some of the modern fly-by-wire aircraft have built-in flight envelope protection. This protection is built into the control system and helps prevent a pilot from forcing an aircraft into a situation that exceeds its structural and aerodynamic operational limits. This system is beneficial in emergency situations because it prevents the pilots from endangering the aircraft while making split-second decisions.

Helicopters

Helicopters, a type of rotary-wing or rotorcraft, are extremely versatile aircraft that may be used for a wide array of situations where a typical aircraft could not perform. A helicopter differs from other types of aircraft that derive lift from their wings, as it gets its lift and thrust from the rotors. The rotors are basically rotating airfoils; hence the name rotorcraft. The "rotating wing," or main rotor, may have two or more blades whose profiles resemble that of aircraft wings.

Although rotorcraft come in many shapes and sizes, they mostly have the same major components in common. There is a cabin, an airframe, landing gear, a powerplant, a transmission, and an anti-torque system. The cabin of the rotorcraft houses the crew and cargo. The airframe is the fuselage where components are mounted and attached. The landing gear may be made up of wheels, skis, skids, or floats.

Due to its operating characteristics, a helicopter is able to:

- Take off and land vertically (in almost any small, clear area)
- Fly forward, backward, and laterally
- Operate at lower speeds
- Hover for extended periods of time

Common uses for the helicopter include military operations, search and rescue, law enforcement, firefighting, medical transport, news reporting, and tourism.

Helicopters are subjected to the same forces as other aircraft: lift, weight, thrust, and drag. In addition, helicopters also have some unique forces they are subjected to: torque, centrifugal and centripetal force, gyroscopic precession, dissymmetry of lift, effective translational lift, transverse flow effect, and Coriolis effect.

Here are some examples of different helicopter designs:

Torque

Torque from the engine turning the main rotor forces the body of the helicopter in the opposite direction. Most helicopters use a tail rotor, which counters this torque force by pushing or pulling against the tail.

Centrifugal and Centripetal Force

Centrifugal force is the apparent force that causes rotating bodies to move away from the center of rotation. Centripetal force is the force that keeps an object a certain distance from the center of rotation.

Gyroscopic Precession
Gyroscopic precession is when the applied force to a rotating object is shown 90° later than where the force was applied.

Dissymmetry of Lift
Dissymmetry of lift is the difference in lift between the advancing and retreating blades of the rotor system. The difference in lift is due to directional flight. The rotor system compensates for dissymmetry of lift with blade flapping, which allows the blades to twist and lift in order to balance the advancing and retreating blades. The pilot also compensates by cyclic feathering. Together, blade flapping and cyclic feathering eliminate dissymmetry of lift.

Effective Translational Lift
Effective translational lift (ETL) is the improved efficiency that results from directional flight. Efficiency is gained when the helicopter moves forward, as opposed to hovering. The incoming airflow essentially pushes the turbulent air behind the helicopter, which provides a more horizontal airflow for the airfoil to move through. This typically occurs between 16 and 24 knots.

Transverse Flow Effect
Transverse flow effect is the difference in airflow between the forward and aft portions of the rotor disk. During forward flight, there is more downwash in the rear portion of the rotor disk. The downward flow on the rear portion of the disk results in a reduced AOA and produces less lift. The front half of the rotor produces more lift due to an increased AOA. Transverse flow occurs between 10 and 20 knots and can be easily recognized by the increased vibrations during take-off and landing.

Coriolis Effect
The Coriolis Effect is when an object moving in a rotating system experiences an inertial force (Coriolis) acting perpendicular to the direction of motion and the axis of rotation. In a clockwise rotation, the force acts to the left of the motion of an object. If the rotation is counterclockwise, the force acts to the right of the motion of an object.

A typical helicopter is controlled through use of the cyclic control stick, the collective controls lever, and the anti-torque pedals.

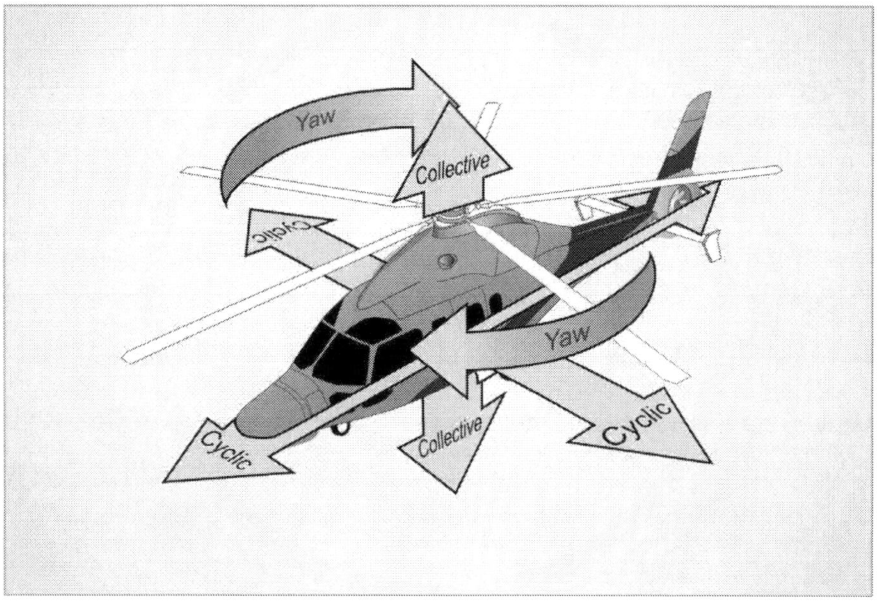

Cyclic Control

The cyclic is the control stick that is used to control the movement of the helicopter forward, backward, or sideways. Simply stated, the cyclic changes the pitch of the rotor blades cyclically in any of 360°. The cyclic stick also contains several buttons that control the trim, intercom, and radio. These will differ slightly depending on each model helicopter.

Collective Controls

The collective control is used to increase the pitch of the main rotor simultaneously at all points of the rotor blade rotation. The collective increases or decreases total rotor thrust; the cyclic changes the direction of rotor thrust. In forward flight, the collective pitch changes the amount of thrust, which in turn can change the speed or altitude based on the use of the cyclic. During hovering, the collective control is used to adjust the altitude of hover.

Anti-Torque Pedals

The anti-torque pedals are used to control yaw on a helicopter. These pedals are located in the same place, and serve a similar purpose, as rudder pedals on an airplane. Application of pressure on a pedal changes the pitch of the tail rotor blade, which will increase or reduce the tail rotor thrust and cause the nose of the helicopter to yaw in the desired direction.

Airport Information

Airports vary in size and complexity, from small dirt or grass strips to a large major airport with miles of paved runways and taxiways. Pilots are required to know the procedures and rules of the specific airports being used and understand pavement markings, lights, and signs that provide takeoff, landing, and taxiway information.

Procedures have been developed for airport traffic patterns and traffic control. These procedures include specific routes or specific runways for takeoffs and landings. Each airport traffic pattern depends on a number of factors, including obstructions and wind conditions.

Terms

- Clearway: A specified area after the runway that is clear of obstacles, at the same or nearly the same altitude as the runway, and specifically for planes to fly over in their initial ascent.
- Decision height (DH): The lowest height (in feet) in which if a pilot cannot see specified visual references, they must stop landing.
- Holding/Flying a Hold: Refers to a plane flying in an oval flight path near the airport while waiting for clearance to land.
- Runway visual range (RVR): The distance away from the airport in which a pilot should be able to see runway markings and/or lights.
- Threshold: The start or end of a runway.
- Taxiway: The paved area that planes travel on between the terminal and runway. The path a plane should follow on a taxiway is marked by a yellow line.
- Taxiway intersections: Where two taxiway routes intersect.

Signs

Here are some common taxiway signs:

Name	**Sign Color**	**Letter Color**	**Function**
no entry	red	white	indicates an area planes should not go into
runway location	black	yellow	displays current runway name
taxiway location	black	yellow	displays current taxiway name
direction/runway exit	yellow	black	displays name of upcoming taxiway that airplane is about to intersect with
runway	red	white	displays name of runway that airplane is about to intersect with

Lighting

These lights are visible to about 3 miles in the daytime and up to 20 miles at night.

- Approach Lighting Systems (ALS): A series of light bars leading up to a runway that assist the pilot in lining up with the runway.
- Runway centerline lights: These are used to facilitate landing at night or under adverse visibility conditions. These lights are embedded into the runway. They begin as white, then alternate between red and white, and then are completely red at the end of the runway.
- Obstructions/aircraft warning lights: *Red* or *white* lights used to mark obstructions (like building and cell towers) both in airports and outside of them.
- Runway edge lights: These are *white* and highlight the boundaries of the runway. These are referred to a high, medium, or low intensity depending on the maximum intensity they can produce.
- Runway end identifier lights (REIL): Many airport runways have these two flashing *red* lights. They provide a warning that the runway is ending.
- Taxiway centerline lights: *Green* lights indicating the middle of a taxiway.
- Taxiway edge lights: *Blue* lights denoting the edge of a taxiway.
- Threshold lights: *Green* lights that indicate the start of the runway

Visual Approach Slope Indicators (VASI)

The visual approach slope indicator (VASI) is a light system of two sets of lights designed to provide visual guidance during approach of a runway. The light indicators are visible 3 to 5 miles away during daylight hours and up to 20 miles away in darkness. The indicators are designed to be used once the aircraft is already visually aligned with the runway. Both sets of lights can appear as white or red. When the front lights appear white and the back lights appear red, it indicates that the plane is at the proper angle. If both lights appear white, it means the pilot is too high, and if both appear red, it means the pilot is too low.

Precision Instrument Runways
Precision instrument runways have operational visual and electronic aids that provide directional guidance. These aides may be the ILS, Precision Approach Radar (PAR), or Microwave Landing System (MLS). Instrument runways have visual aids with a decision height greater than 200 feet and a runway visual range of 2,600 feet. These runways have *runway end lights*, which consist of eight lights (four on each side of the runway) that can appear as green or red—green to approaching planes and red to planes on the runway.

Non-Precision Instrument Runways
Non-precision instrument runways provide horizontal guidance only when there is an approved procedure for a straight-in non-precision instrument approach. The non-precision runways do not have full Instrument Landing System (ILS) capabilities, but they have approved procedures for localizer, Global Positioning System (GPS), Automatic Direction Finder (ADF), and Very High Frequency Omni-Directional Range (VOR) instrument approaches.

Visual Flight Rules Runways (VFR)
Visual flight rules (VFR) runways, also known as visual runways, operate completely under visual approach procedures. The pilot must be able to see the runway to land safely. There are no instrument approach procedures for this type of runway. They are typically found at small airports. Visual runways have centerline, designators, and threshold markings, as well as hold position markings for taxiway intersections.

Localizer Type Directional Aid (LDA)
Directional runways use a Localizer Type Directional Aid (LDA). The LDA provides a localizer-based instrument approach to an airport where, usually due to terrain, the localizer antenna is not in alignment with the runway. The LDA is more of a directional tool to enable the pilot to get close enough to where the runway can be seen.

Nautical Information

Nautical History

The U.S. Navy was founded in the fall of 1775 with a focus on establishing and maintaining peace, safety, and a democratic way of life. The Navy has also been a key player in humanitarian efforts, combatting international aggression and coming to the aid of nations in times of crisis. Although rarely used, the Navy's official motto is *Semper Constans—always constant, always trustworthy*.

1700s – 1800s
Although the first American Navy was established in June of 1775 as the Rhode Island Navy, the Continental Navy was established by the Continental Congress just four months later. From that point on, October 13, 1775 has been recognized as the official beginning of the U.S. Navy.

New to his presidency, Thomas Jefferson ordered the U.S. Navy to combat Tripolian pirates in the Mediterranean. The Navy's resilience, coupled with President Jefferson's negotiation skills, resulted in the successful reopening of safe shipping lanes.

In 1807, the British HMS Leopard was triumphant in capturing the USS Chesapeake in its attempt to locate British Navy deserters, but the Chesapeake reemerged and fought again during the War of 1812.

<u>1900s</u>

In 1900, the Navy received the USS Holland—the first commissioned Navy submarine—and seven years later, the Navy welcomed sixteen battleships known as the *Great White Fleet*. In 1915, The Navy Reserve was born and by August of 1916, the first U.S. Navy reservists were sent to find and destroy German U-boats. In 1917, the USS Fanning and the USS Nicholson were the first to successfully sink the German U-boat known as U-58, and in 1918, the U.S. Navy was successful in sinking yet another U-boat. By September of that same year, the war had ended.

Although the United States had not officially entered World War II until the surprise attack on Pearl Harbor on December 7, 1941, Navy Reservists were readying themselves for battle. Immediately following the attack, the Navy was deployed. Fighting tirelessly against German and Japanese forces of aggression, the Navy was well equipped, fully trained, and focused on its mission. One of the most significant battles was fought on the seas near Midway Island. Due in large part to the Pacific Fleet cryptanalysists who were instrumental in intercepting hundreds of Japanese messages every day and who correctly translated approximately a quarter of these messages, the U.S. Navy was able to ready themselves for the planned attack and in so doing, ultimately succeeded against the Japanese. By June 6, 1944, Operation Overlord (D-Day) was successfully carried out on the shores of Northern France. With the aid of allied forces from both Britain and Canada, the United States forced the surrender of German Nazis. The war was finally over.

During the 1950s, the U.S. Navy was involved in significant operations, from the destruction of Korean torpedo boats in the Battle of Chumanchin Chan, to the launching of the USS Nautilis in 1954—its first nuclear submarine. The U.S. Navy now boasts a submarine fleet with full nuclear power capabilities.

By the early 1960s, the U.S. Navy added the USS Enterprise to its fleet, which was the world's first nuclear-powered aircraft carrier that paved the way for the Navy's present-day super carriers. From 1963 to 1972, the Navy SEALS (Sea, Air, and Land), known as the United States' special operators, played a significant role in the conflict with North Vietnam, earning countless recognitions and awards for their many acts of honor and heroism.

The 1980s saw the invasion of the Gulf of Sidra against the Libyan dictator, Colonel Muammar Gaddafi, as well as the 1988 Operation Praying Mantis, in which the Navy, the SEALS, and the Marines entered into the largest U.S. Naval battle since WWII. This combat mission was also the first to use ship-to-ship missiles. With the invasion of Iraq in the 1990s, the Navy proved invaluable with its Airborne Warning and Control System (AWACS), its Grumman E-2 Hawkeyes, and its satellite communication systems. In 1995, in a response to Bosnian Serb aggression, the Navy employed Tomahawk missiles and fighter bombers, and in the 1999 Kosovo War, the Navy challenged Yugoslavia to heroically combat ethnic cleansing.

On September 11, 2001, the United States endured the worst attack on its civilians in its history. After the attacks on the World Trade Center and the Pentagon, Operation Enduring Freedom led the invasion of Afghanistan with the Navy SEALS as the first ground troops. In 2003, the Navy invaded Iraq and by December of that same year, a joint special operations team captured Saddam Hussein, who was executed in 2006. In 2009, The MV Maersk Alabama, along with its captain, Richard Phillips, was overtaken by Somali pirates. SEAL snipers quickly positioned themselves with the full authority to use deadly force. Three successful targets were hit and killed, and Captain Phillips was rescued.

On the humanitarian front, from 2005 to 2013, the world saw devastating tsunamis, hurricanes, earthquakes, and typhoons. The USNS Mercy and the USNS Comfort set off on countless medical deployments to bring medical personnel and supplies to devastated areas.

Common Nautical Terms

The following terms and accompanying definitions are some of the most commonly used in the U.S. Navy:

- Airedale: Any sailors who work in the air wing
- All Hands: Officers and enlisted personnel in the ship's company
- Barracks: A building where Sailors live when not on active duty on water
- Bomb Farm: Specific location on a ship where bombs are stored
- Bubble Head: Submariners
- Cadillac: A bucket containing wheels and a ringer
- Carry On: An order allowing for one to resume duties
- Chit: Form required when requesting a leave of absence
- Crank: Mess deck worker
- Cumshaw: An exchange of goods or services outside of official procedures and usually void of monetary payment
- First Lieutenant: The officer responsible for the Deck Department and/or Division on the ship
- Galley: The kitchen
- Ground Tackle: Necessary equipment when anchoring a ship
- Head: Bathroom
- Knee-Knockers: Bottom portion of a door's frame
- Leave: Authorized leave of absence
- Lifeline: Safety lines placed around the decks of a ship in order to help prevent personnel from falling over the side
- Marlinspike: A life-sized model ship used for recruits to practice some skills of basic seamanship
- Mess Deck: Dining area for the crew
- Muster: A meeting
- Navy Reserve: A component of the U.S. Navy in which sailors and officers are brought into active duty as needed
- Officers: The Navy's and Navy Reserve's management team
- P-Days: Processing days when recruits arrive at boot camp and are issued equipment, uniforms, and supplies
- Ricky: A recruit
- Scullery: An area to wash dishes
- Scuttlebutt: Water fountain
- Sick Bay: Medical facility
- Snipe: Those who work in the engineering department
- Taps: Time for sleep

Ship Directions, Lights, and Parts of a Vessel

The following section provides an overview of some common terms in the Navy regarding ship directions, vessel lights, and parts of a vessel:

- Aboard: On a ship
- Above: A higher level or deck on a ship
- Ashore: Toward the shore
- Athwartships: Toward a ship's sides
- Below: The ship's lower deck
- Bottom: The lowest portion of a ship's hull
- Bow (Stem): The ship's front
- Port: The left side of the ship
- Starboard: The right side of the ship
- Stern: The rear of the ship
- Underdeck: A ship's lower deck
- Waterline: Where the water surface meets the hull of the ship

Lights

With advanced technology, the Navy now employs the use of signal lights, especially if there is a need to silence radio communications. With sophisticated lighting designed to operate in the infrared spectrum, the Navy is fully capable of nighttime travel. Infrared lighting has the added advantage of being difficult to detect.

Air traffic control towers still use signal lamps; however, these lights are rarely used for any other purpose other than as a backup source of light for instances when an aircraft's radio experiences a complete loss of power. The three dominant colors for lighting are white, red, and green, and although some messages may still be conveyed using lighting, these messages are limited to basic instructions rather than Morse code.

There are four main common navigation lights, namely:

- Sidelights: Red and green lights that are visible to another vessel approaching from the side or head on. Red indicates a vessel's portside and the green indicates its starboard side.

- Stern Lights: Strictly white in color, they are only seen from behind or nearly behind the vessel.

- Masthead Lights: Also white, masthead lights not only shine on both sides of a ship, but they shine forward as well. All power-driven vessels are required to have masthead lights.

- All-Round White Lights: Acting as an anchor light when sidelights are out, all-round white lights are generally used for vessels less than 39.4 feet long. They combine a masthead light and a stern light to form a single white light visible by other vessels from any direction.

Parts of a Vessel

Below the main outside deck, the main body of the ship is referred to as the *hull*. It is comprised of an outside covering known as the *skin,* as well as an inside framework to which the skin is securely fastened. These two parts are generally made of steel and securely welded.

The *keel*, the main centerline of the hull and known as the *backbone* of the ship, runs from the stem at the bow directly to the sternpost. Frames are fastened to the keel and act as the ship's *ribs*, giving the hull a specific shape and strength. To support the decks, deck beams and bulkheads provide additional strength that works to resist water pressure on the hull's sides.

Hull Construction

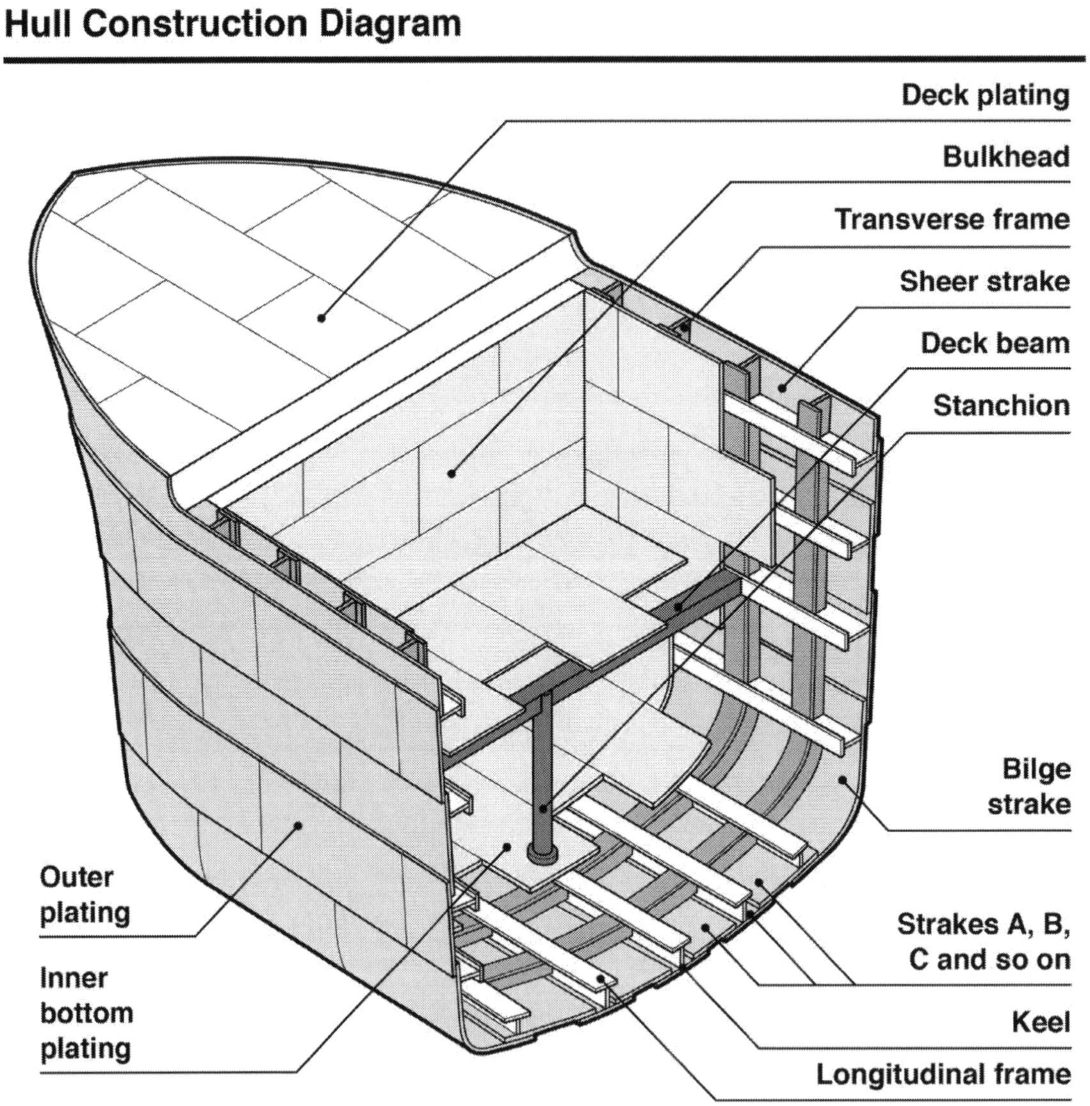

Bulkheads and Decks

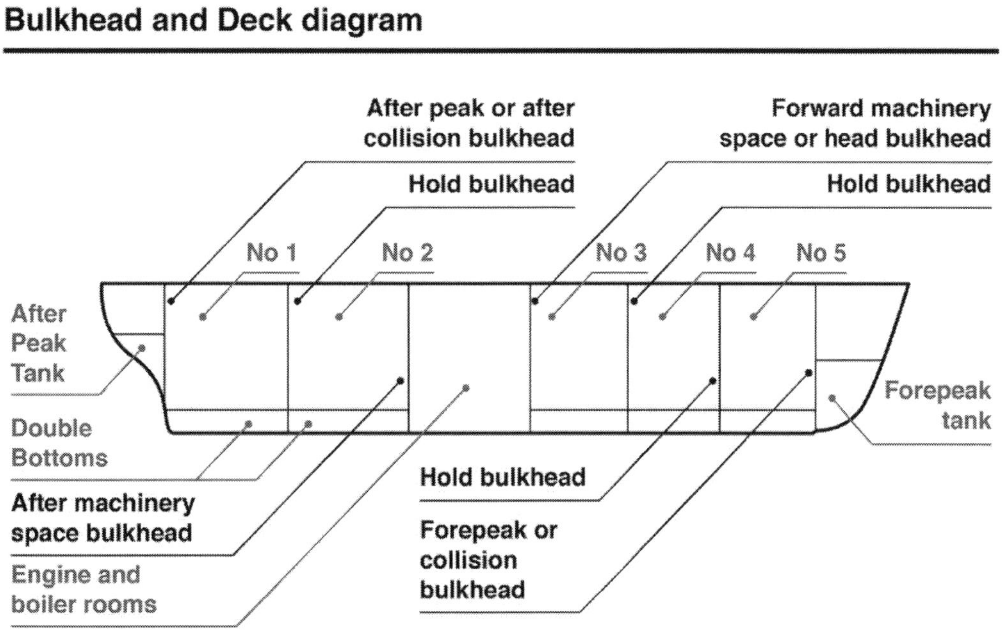

External Parts of a Hull

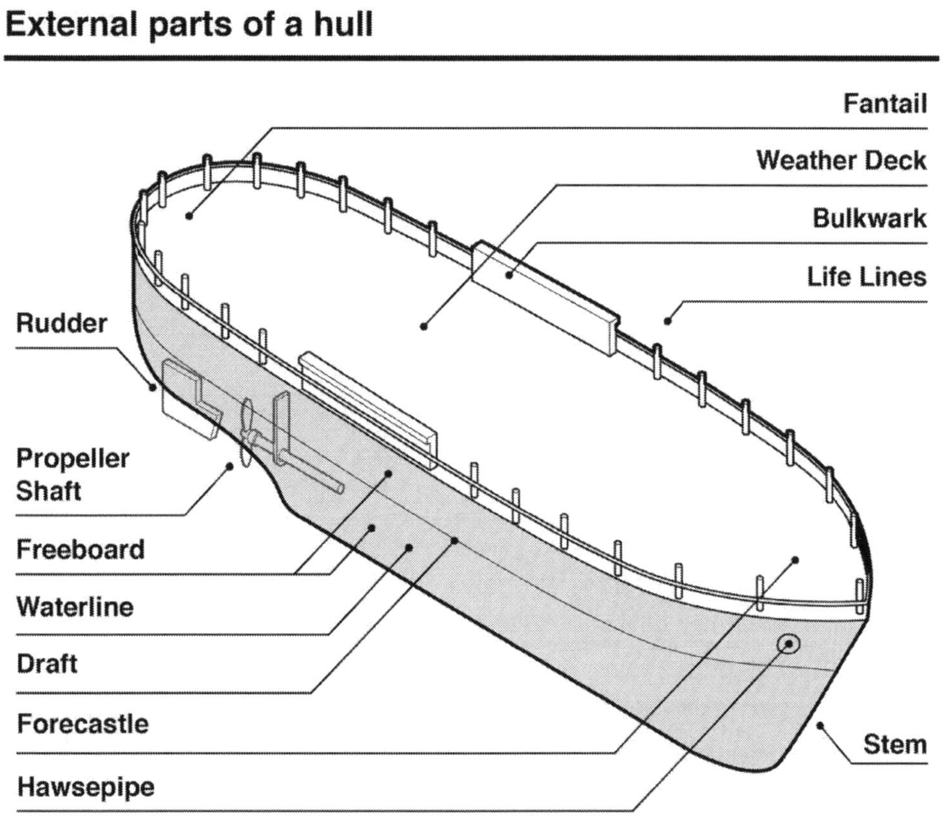

Weather Decks

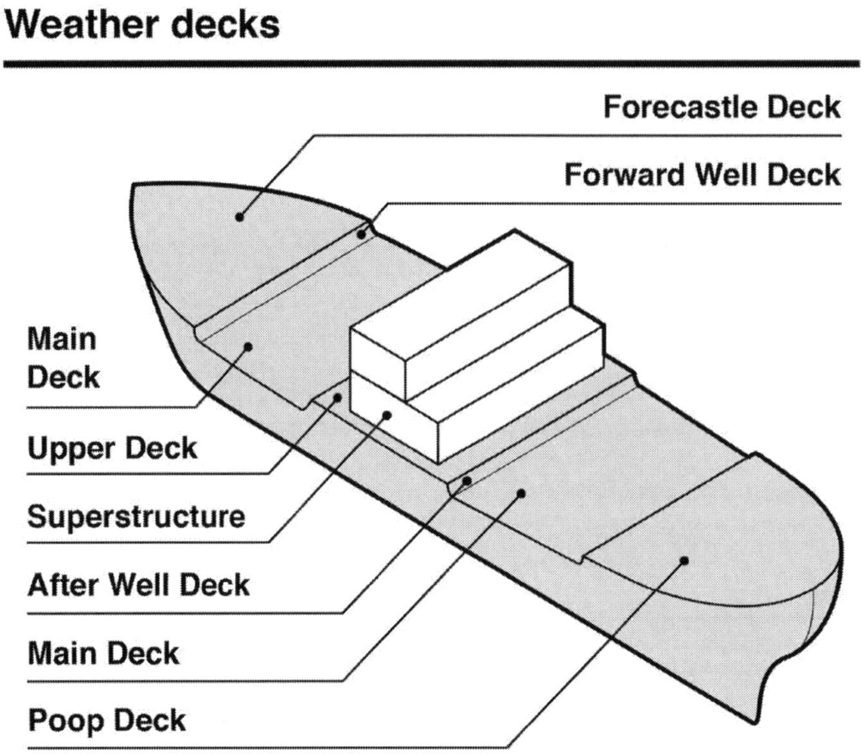

Types of Vessels

The U.S. Navy is arguably one of the most powerful and modern navies in the world. From aircraft carriers and submarines, to multi-mission ships including cruisers, destroyers, frigates, amphibious crafts and more, the U.S. Navy is ready to go at a moment's notice.

- Amphibious War Crafts: These vessels are admired for their swift travel in water and over land, delivering troops and assisting in crisis response, humanitarian operations, and disaster relief.
- Carriers: The largest warships in history, the U.S. Navy's carriers are considered the best in the world, operating in international waters and each acting as a sovereign U.S. territory.
- Cruisers: Known as seaborne platforms with modern guided-missile systems, cruisers are capable of eliminating targets in the air, shore, sea, and beneath the surface of the sea.
- Destroyers: Multi-mission vessels equipped to operate in battle groups or on their own with guided-missiles.
- Hospital Ships: Hospital ships that provide invaluable humanitarian relief and medical care at home and abroad to deployed troops as well as to civilians throughout the globe following a crisis or tragedy.

- Littoral Combat Ships: Littoral Combat Ships meaning *near shore*, operate close to land, and work to detect mines, quiet diesel submarines, as well as fast-surface crafts

- Submarines: Watercrafts capable of independent underwater operation

- Types: Attack, Ballistic Missile, Guided Missile, and Deep Submergence Rescue Vehicles.

- USS New York: An amphibious transport dock intended to bring home Marine Landing Forces

- Vessels: With a primary purpose of retrieving troops, equipment, and supplies, each vessel also provides unique capabilities, and all are equipped with tracked and wheeled, all-terrain vehicles with other amphibious craft and assault vehicles

Instrument History

Early tools and instrumentation by ocean navigators consisted largely of maps, nautical charts, the mariner's compass, astrolabes, sextants, chip logs, and calipers. With significant advancements in naval instrumentation, the modern era has largely replaced these tools with electronic and technological instrumentation such as the following:

- ARPA: An acronym for Automatic Radar Plotting Aid. ARPAs display the position of a ship and other vessels nearby.

- Automatic Tracking Aid: Automatic Tracking Aids display information on tracked targets in order to create a planned layout for a safer, collision-free course.

- Echo Sounder: This measures the water's depth below a ship using sound waves.

- GPS: Introduced in the late 1990s, the global positioning system (GPS) employs the same basic principles of time difference from separate signals as did the LORAN, but its signals come from satellites instead.

- Gyroscopic Compass: Introduced in 1907, the gyroscopic compass has one significant advantage over the magnetic compass—it is not affected by the Earth's (or even the ship's) magnetic field and will always point to the true north.

- Long Range Tracking and Identification System (LRIT): The LRIT is a thorough tracking system for ships around the world.

- Long Range Navigation – LORAN: LORAN was a U.S. navigation system developed in the early 1940s. It employed pulsed radio transmissions in order to determine a ship's position but was decommissioned in 2010.

- Radio Detection and Ranging (RADAR): Radar sends out radio waves and detects any reflections made from distant objects. Installed on ships, radar is still very useful in helping ships locate other ships as well as land when visibility proves difficult.

Weather and Sea Conditions

The United States Naval Meteorology and Oceanography Command (NMOC) provides the military, the scientific community, and civilians with essential information regarding weather and sea conditions, from the depths of the ocean to the far reaches of space.

The various components of the NMOC provide critical weather and sea condition information to the Navy:

- The Naval Oceanography Operations command (NOOC): Known as the *operational arm* of the NMOC, the NOOC advises the U.S. Navy with regard to the impact of ocean and atmospheric conditions that impact U.S. naval operations.

- The U.S. Naval Observatory (USNO): As one of the country's first federal agencies for scientific research, the USNO specializes in the areas of producing, positioning, timing, and navigating. NOOC reports their findings directly to the U.S. Navy and the United States Department of Defense.

- The Joint Typhoon Warning Center (JTWC): Located in Pearl Harbor, Hawaii, the JTWC works in cooperation with the U.S. Navy, as well as with the United States Air Force. Charged with the responsibility of issuing tropical cyclone warnings in the Indian Ocean and the North-West and South Pacific Ocean, the JTWC has been in operation since 1959.

- The Fleet Numerical Meteorology and Oceanography Center (FNMOC): Located in Monterey, California, the FNMOC shares with the U.S. and coalition forces the most current and most reliable global meteorology and oceanographic support.

- The Naval Oceanographic Office (NAVO): Works to share relevant oceanographic knowledge to support U.S. National security and maximize sea power.

Navigation and Travel Controls

Navigation refers to studying, monitoring, and controlling movement from one place to another by way of land, water, sky, or space. To determine as exact a positioning as possible, it is critical that operators of any vessel pay strict attention to a number of indicators:

- Longitude: An angle on the Earth's surface that ranges from 0 degrees at the Equator to 90 degrees at either the North or South Pole.

- Latitude: The imaginary lines that run vertically around the Earth called meridians whose purpose is to measure how far east or west any given object is located.

- Loxodrome (Rhumb Line): An imaginary line that cuts through all meridians at the same angle and is the path taken by a ship or plane that maintains a constant compass direction.

- Dead Reckoning (DR): The method of navigation used by ships and aircraft using the vessel's last known position—the fix.

- Celestial Navigation: Although largely replaced by GPS, this ancient science of position fixing with the use of angular measurements taken between the Sun, Moon, a planet, or a star, is making a comeback in the U.S. Navy with a growing concern that the Navy is relying too heavily on GPS systems, which can be hacked and blocked.

- Radio Navigation: The application of radio frequencies to determine the exact position of an object on the Earth's surface
- Radar Navigation: Transmits microwave signals intended to locate other vessels and objects or to help determine the distance between objects and/or vessels
- Satellite Navigation: The system can determine the exact location of objects by using orbiting satellite signals.

Boating Right of Ways

General Boat-Passing Rules

A vessel trailing behind another is referred to as the *give-way* vessel, as it is charged with the greater burden of responsibility should it decide to pass. The vessel in front is referred to as the *stand-on* vessel, with the advantage over the latter. This vessel's skipper can deny the latter passage if he or she feels the passage would be too dangerous.

Sounding two short sounds from a vessel's horn is the universal signal that a vessel would like to pass another vessel from its portside. If the vessel receives two short sounds in return, this indicates permission to pass. However, if the stand-on vessel sends 5 horn sounds, permission is denied.

If two vessels are on a path that could result in a collision, the stand-on vessel has the right of way, with the privilege to pass in front of the give-way vessel on its portside.

If two vessels are head-on, both vessels should immediately steer to the right in order to safely pass one another portside to portside.

International Regulations

The International Regulations for the Prevention of Collisions at Sea (COLREGS) governs the rules on the oceans. COLREGS also helps to establish the political line dividing inland waterways, which adhere to unique navigation rules as well as coastal waterways that follow international navigation rules. The primary purpose of COLREGS is to help to prevent collision on open waters.

Although the term *right of way* is not used by COLREGS, there are nonetheless specific rules to follow. All COLREG rules are clearly laid out into three main sections:

- Conduct of Vessels in Any Condition of Visibility: This section primarily mainly deals with lookout, safe speed, risk of collision, collision avoidance, narrow channels, and traffic separation schemes.
- Conduct of Vessels in Sight of One Another: Section Two focuses on sailing vessels, overtaking, head-on and crossing situations, actions by give-way and stand-on vessels, and the responsibility between vessels.
- Conduct of Vessels in Restricted Visibility: The final section focuses on lights, shapes, sound and light signals, and exemptions.

Docks

From 1842 to 1966, the Bureau of Yards and Docks was a unique branch of the U.S. Navy charged with building and maintaining the Navy's yards, dry docks, and any other facility directly related to ship construction, maintenance, and repair. As part of the Department of Defense's reorganization efforts, the Bureau was abolished in 1966 and replaced by the Naval Facilities Engineering Command (NAVFAC).

Docks can refer to either *dry docks*, *dock landing ships*, and even, *landing platform docks*, all of which are critical to the Navy's ability to load and unload military personnel, civilians, equipment, and cargo.

Dry docks can refer to either a narrow basin or a vessel that has the capability of being flooded in order to allow a load to be safely floated in. The dock is then drained to allow that same load to be safely secured on the dock floor. Dry docks are also a beneficial platform to construct, maintain, and repair a variety of waterborne vessels.

Dock Landing Ships, also called Landing Ships, Docks, or LSDs for short, are the smallest of the amphibious warships, even though they are the fourth largest ship in the Navy, measuring over 600 feet in length. They carry landing craft and amphibious vehicles and can also carry helicopters. LSDs have well decks that are almost the length of the ship itself. With a helicopter pad above the well deck, LSDs have limited space for troops and equipment. Its main purpose is to serve as a mobile deck for landing craft.

With a shorter well deck, Landing Platform Docks (LPDs) are amphibious warfare vessels that embark, transport, and land elements of a landing force, such as troops, for expeditionary warfare missions. LPDs have the capability of carrying amphibious tractors, but the deck is not used for housing landing craft, although some can be carried. LPDs have the capability of housing hundreds of troops as well as crew members.

Nautical Units and Maps

With unique nautical measurement systems, the U.S. Navy can better determine speed, depth, and wind force of their vessels. The following is a general list of common nautical measurement terms along with their definitions:

- Fathom: The equivalent of 6 six feet which is almost exactly one-thousandth of a nautical mile (6,080 feet).
- Fathom Curves (Bathymetric Lines): A grouping of fathoms—e.g., 20 fathoms (120 feet), 50 fathoms (300 feet), 100 fathoms (600 feet), and so on.
- Nautical Mile: 10 cable lengths or the equivalent of 1.1508 miles. The distance of one nautical mile corresponds to one minute of latitude on a chart.
- Cable Length: The length of a ship's cable—approximately 600 feet
- Knot: The measure of speed on water. 1 knot is equivalent to 1 nautical mile per hour

- Beaufort Scale: Although not used as often any more, the following gives a few of the Beaufort Scale measurements:

  - 0 knots: calm
    22 – 27 knots: strong breeze
    48 – 55 knots: storm
    64 knots and above: hurricane

- Cardinal Directions: Directions are measured on a compass in degrees starting at the North and traveling clockwise. North represents zero degrees, East is 90 degrees, South is 180 degrees, and West is 270 degrees.

Safety

Several years ago, the U.S. Navy recognized the need for centralized management of all safety efforts. Gradually, a single command emerged to deal with all Navy safety concerns both on and off land. Additionally, with the introduction to the Occupational Safety and Health Act (OSHA), the need for increased awareness for safety became a centralized concern for the Navy.

Today, the Commander of the Naval Safety Center is charged with advising and assisting the Chief Naval Operations (CNO) in promoting, monitoring, and evaluating the Department of the Navy safety programs.

Some of the most significant safety concerns for the Navy are listed below:

Personal
IMSAFE (Illness, Medication, Stress, Alcohol, Fatigue, and Emotion) is a personal checklist used as a daily reminder to check for the wellbeing of all those Enlisted.

Electrical
The U.S. Navy offers training for all those who work near electrical systems. All personnel should receive training in basic electrical safety, the requirements for using personal protective equipment (PPE), how to recognize symptoms of electrical shock and electrical shock trauma, and emergency first-aid responder techniques.

Hazards
Hazards are a part of life in virtually every living space, and the U.S. Navy is no exception. After receiving mandatory training, Navy personnel will be expected to:

- Adhere to all safety precautions related to work or duties
- Report unsafe conditions
- Wear issued, protective equipment and clothing
- Wear eye and/or full-face protection
- Report all injuries or illnesses
- Remain alert and look for any possibilities of danger

Auto and Shop Information

The following pages will contain information that informs the reader about the most essential tools and techniques necessary for working on American-made vehicles and American-manufactured combustion engine automobiles. The information contained in this manual is crucial to effectuating important tasks required for servicing automobiles.

All engines and vehicle systems require maintenance; common everyday tools and task-specific tools are required to complete vehicle maintenance. An array of screw drivers, wrenches, hammers, and other task-specific tools must be available in order to successfully fix the various systems of a vehicle.

Types of Automotive Tools

There are several tools that are indispensable to the auto mechanic:

- **Wrenches**: A mechanic cannot do without an assortment of wrenches: The 9/16" and ½" fixed open wrench are among the most common and necessary tools for the vehicle mechanic. Most nuts and bolts in an American-made vehicle have numerous nine-sixteenths and one-half inch nuts and bolts. These wrenches are important for taking apart connections and housings that are located inside the vehicle. A multitude of wrenches of different sizes are required to fix the many different types of vehicles that exist in the world today. Variable wrenches that can adjust in size are useful in cases where the available fixed size wrenches are not of the specific size needed for an oddly-sized nut or bolt.

  A complete ratchet set is also a necessary kit for the mechanic. A ratchet tool has a handle and a right angle circular notched head that fits over the nut. Different sized ratchets attach to the right-angle at the end of the tool's handle.

- **Vice grips**: Medium-sized vice grips lock into place in order to hold onto something, which enables the mechanic to grip items with a grip-locking feature. Vice grips often work as another pair of hands to hold something while the mechanic implements repairs. Various sizes of vice grips are important tools in a mechanic's arsenal because the mechanic can position and hold items with the assistance of the vice grips, which lock the item being held into place.

- **Channel lock pliers**: The jaws on these pliers are positioned at a horizontal right-angle, which enables the mechanic to grab onto a nut or bolt that would be hard to turn without the right-angle jaw feature of the channel lock pliers. Channel lock pliers are also adjustable. The gap between the jaws is variable due to a tongue and groove sizing system that lets the user adjust the jaw gap by the tongue and groove adjustment feature located below the jaws. Every mechanic should have at least one channel pliers. Some channel pliers have rubber handles that protect the mechanic from electrical shock when working near wires that contain a live electric current.

- **Flat head screwdrivers**: One large screwdriver, preferably about 10 inches long, is an important tool that can do double duty as a small pry bar. The large screwdriver is indispensable for turning those larger screws the mechanic will encounter. A smaller flat head screwdriver is good for the more diminutive slotted screws. The 5-inch screwdriver is also useful for prying things up when a smaller tool is required. Various sized flat head screwdrivers round out the mechanic's toolbox so that he or she can perform many different types of vehicle repairs.

- **Phillips-head screwdrivers**: the four slotted "Phillips" screws are encountered throughout a vehicle and various sized Phillips-head screwdrivers are important for the mechanic to have on hand to effectuate repairs.

Automotive Systems

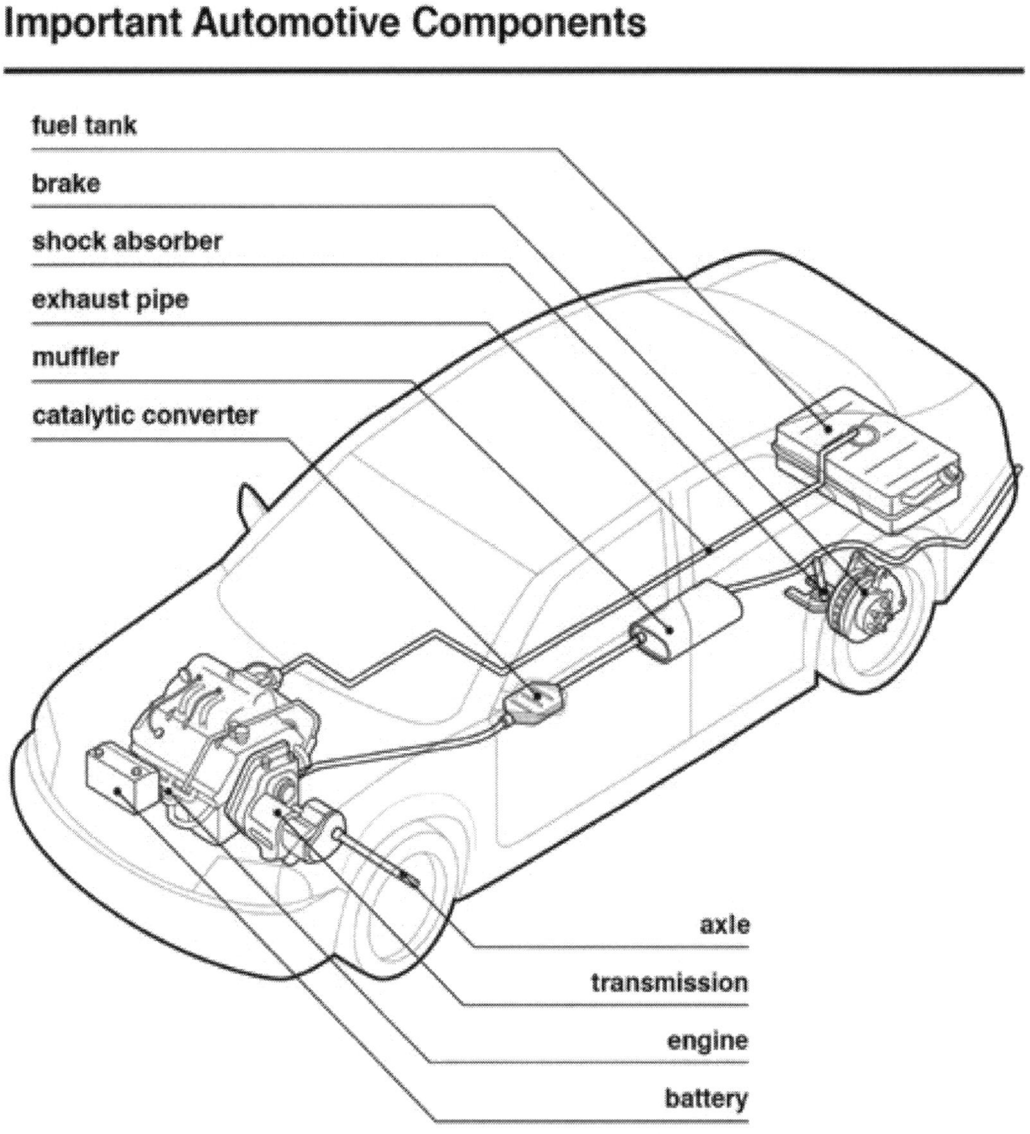

There are many types, makes, and models of vehicles and just as many different companies that manufacture vehicles, but the focus here is on regular gas combustion engine vehicles. Electrically-powered vehicles and self-driving vehicles are starting to become more commonplace, but the electrical and artificial intelligence technology is still in its relative infancy. The main source of power for vehicles around the world is still the gasoline combustion engine.

Primary systems of the vehicle must be maintained and repaired. The primary systems of a vehicle include, but are not limited to:

- Engine System
- Ignition System
- Electrical System
- Drive System
- Lubrication System
- Cooling System
- Exhaust System
- Brake System
- Suspension System
- Steering System

Each system will be reviewed briefly.

Engine Sketch

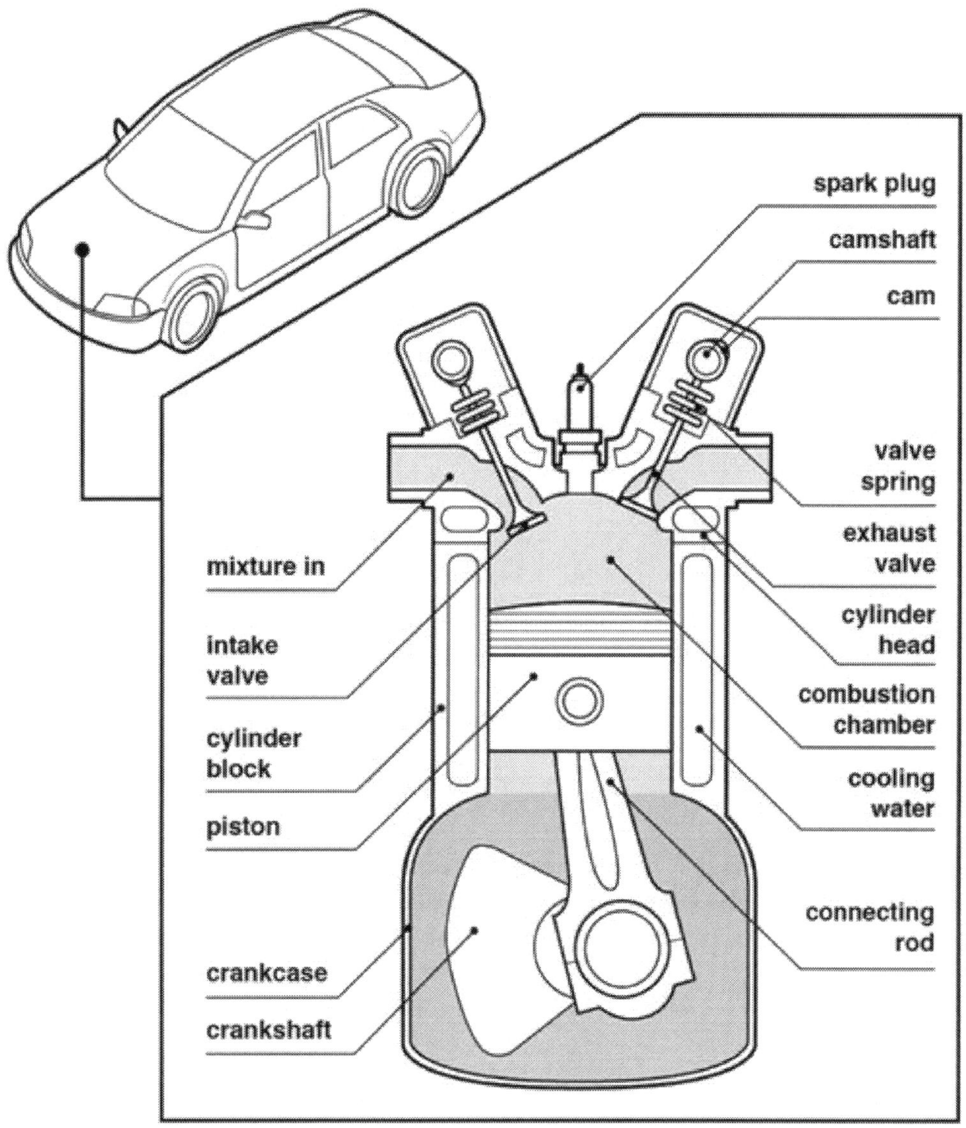

Engine Systems and Components

Primary engine systems for a gasoline combustion-based motor include:

- **Engine block**: the main frame or central structure of the engine upon which every other engine piece rests or functions within the block
- **Pistons**: cylindrical objects that rest like hats on movable metal arms that take in and compress gas within the piston chamber
- **Spark plugs**: electrical components that create a spark that ignites gas within the piston chamber

- **Rocker arms**: a small hinged metal arm that is positioned horizontally over the piston chamber to control the intake valve and exhaust valve of the piston chamber
- **Cams**: steel nodes along the camshaft that are machined to operate the rocker shafts or rocker arms
- **Valves**: an intake valve and an exhaust valve is positioned over every cylinder chamber
- **Fuel injectors**: nozzles that inject fuel into the piston chamber
- **Carburetors**: air intake components that intake air to feed to the engines' combustion process
- **Electrical wires**: numerous and increasingly complex wires that carry electrical current to all auto systems are under the hood of all modern cars
- **Starters**: a starter module and a starter motor starts the combustion process in a gas engine
- **Gaskets**: fitted pieces of thin material, formed to fit exactly over an orifice in order to keep gas or liquid from leaking out

Using the proper tools for repairs is important because all of the engine's components can be repaired or replaced but using the proper tool for the task is essential.

The **power system** of the automobile is the engine. For this reason, it is perhaps the most essential system. The engine is responsible for the operation of many other systems in the vehicle. Without the power of the engine, many systems—such as the drive system or the cooling system—would not operate.

Many different types of repairs to an engine might have to be completed. One common repair that is needed is to fix the valve cover gaskets. A **valve cover gasket** is a rubber-like fitted piece that fits precisely to the dimensions of the valve cover and seals off a section of the engine over the valves to prevent oil from spewing out. The gaskets also prevent air from unintentionally entering the engine. The valves of the pistons are located directly above the pistons. These valves are covered by metal rectangular castings that protect the spark plugs. The heat produced at the top of the engine can degrade the valve cover gaskets or "seals," which causes oil to spurt out from the gaps in the worn gaskets, necessitating replacement. Variable wrenches are helpful to loosen the nuts holding down the valve cover gaskets.

The engine works in concert with many other systems in the vehicle and the engine also provides power to certain other vehicle systems, such as "power steering" and the electrical system. All other systems and components work together with the engine's power; such as braking components, steering components, shocks, exhaust mufflers, and exhaust pipes. There are many job-specific tools made to handle the repairs of these vehicle systems.

<u>The Ignition System</u>

Ignition Systems and Components

The car's **ignition key**, when turned in traditional cars or pushed in some newer vehicles, completes an electrical connection from the car's battery and sends current to the ignition module that controls the electrical ignition motor. The electrical **ignition motor,** or starter motor, turns the crankshaft, which then initiates the up and down motion of the cylinders while the valves above the cylinders inject gas into the piston chambers. The **spark plugs** ignite the gas and create combustion in the cylinders.

The **ignition** is the system that can be the most problematic because so many things must happen simultaneously and in synchronization for the combustion process to start within the piston chambers. Just one wire connected improperly or an insufficiently charged vehicular battery can result in non-ignition.

Combustion inside the engine cylinders is a self-perpetuating power system, as long as gas continually feeds into the cylinders. When the key is turned, it completes an electrical connection between the car's battery and the starter motor. The starter motor is electrically driven by the battery and turns the crankshaft. When the crankshaft turns, the pistons are powered into motion and travel up and down in sealed cylindrical chambers. When the piston rises, it compresses the vaporized gasoline that has been introduced into the piston chamber. When the gas is compressed by the pistons' "up-stroke," a sparkplug "fires" or sparks, and ignites the compressed gas inside the piston chamber. When the gas inside the piston chamber explodes, the resulting explosive force drives the piston downward. This downward piston force is transferred to the crankshaft of the engine, which then transfers that kinetic energy to the transmission system and drive system of the vehicle. The **alternator** is an electrical generator powered by the gas engine; it is an important main unit in the vehicle's electrical system, which produces electricity so the sparkplugs will keep firing for the duration of the vehicle's operation.

If the sparkplugs are fouled, a buildup of carbon occurs between the small gap of metal that makes the spark, which hinders a spark from forming. This carbon buildup between the spark gap located at the end of the sparkplug occurs from extensive engine operation, the residual buildup of carbon from the incendiary action of the spark, and the aftermath of exploding gases. The resulting carbon deposits prevent the sparkplug from "firing" or sparking, which normally enables the cylinder gases to fire. The engine will not work properly or start if the carbon buildup between the sparkplug gap prevents the sparking from taking place. The spark ignites the gases in the engine's piston chamber. Without the gas explosion in the piston chamber, the engine will not "crank" or start. **Sparkplug fowling** is a common malady that affects the ignition system of a vehicle. Thankfully, it is a relatively easy fix for the mechanic with the right tools and knowledge. The first step is to take the sparkplug out by using a specific tool called a sparkplug wrench. This task-specific wrench has a small rubber integral part in the jaws that pulls the sparkplug out of its placement. The mechanic must clean the sparkplug contact with coarse sand paper.

The **coil wire** provides the electricity to the individual sparkplugs. With extensive vehicle operation, the coil can vibrate off and out of place, disconnecting it. The coil wire is one of the few components in a vehicle that can be taken out and replaced by hand.

Two other common repairs to the ignition system are **replacement of the starter module** and **replacement of the starter motor**. The **starter module** is a unit that is connected to the battery and to the starter motor. The starter module controls the voltage that goes into the starter motor. In some vehicles, the starter motor is prone to malfunction. To replace the starter motor, the mechanic must first locate the starter motor's location within the maze of components and wires that surround the engine. Sometimes it is difficult to locate the starter motor because manufacturers often place the starter motor towards the bottom of the engine. Sometimes the gears in the starter motor will lock up, resulting in the vehicle's main combustion motor failing to start. A crow bar is useful to physically strike the starter with a sharp, yet calculated, hit. If this technique does not free up the starter motor, then it must be immediately replaced. To do so, the mechanic must disconnect the battery first, before working near the starter motor. Two bolts hold the starter motor in place and a variable wrench or socket wrench is an essential tool to do so. The all-important screwdrivers—both Phillips-head and flat head—are some of the most useful tools to have on hand to disconnect the wires to the battery. Larger screwdrivers can be used to pry up the contacts from the battery if they have rusted.

The Electrical System

Electrical Systems and Components

The **battery** is the heart of the vehicle's electrical system; it is where the electrical system begins and ends. The start of the electrical system in an automobile is a positive and negative battery cable connection. The flow of electricity from the positive to negative terminals of the battery is the essence of the electrical system. Electricity must complete a closed loop to the battery in order for there to be an electrical flow. Two cables are inherent to the function of the battery—one cable from and one cable to the battery. A negative cable attaches from the battery to the body of the vehicle. The greatest draw on the battery occurs when the ignition system starts.

Another essential part of the electrical system is a unit known as the **alternator**. The alternator is driven by the crankshaft. The spinning of the alternator by the crankshaft produces electricity for the vehicle while the engine is running. The vehicle computer monitors the voltage regulator. The starter's electric motor, which is connected to the battery, engages the combustion motor by starting the combustion process in the piston chambers. The starter electric motor turns the crankshaft, which then moves the pistons and simultaneously the sparkplugs spark, igniting the gas in the piston chambers. A large wire coming from battery to the solenoid is one part of the circuit and a thin wire attached to the vehicle body completes the circuit. The starter electrically grounds to the engine block via a wire.

Wires that comprise the vehicle's electrical system are fastened in many different ways, which is why connection failures can be a common malady with the electrical system. The connection points in a vehicle's electrical systems are the main culprits when problems arise. There are mechanical connectors on the battery that are comprised of clamps and nuts and bolts. In the electrical system, there are also plastic connectors and wiring harnesses that have many different wires within them, like branches on a tree. When the key is turned (or a button pressed), the electrical connection/ignition starts a current that runs from the battery to the starter, which then turns the engine's crankshaft. When the main combustion engine turns on and is operating, the engine powers a pulley with a rubber belt, which then powers the alternator, which charges the battery for the next ignition. The alternator produces electric current that powers the vehicle's accessories. The alternator generates electricity only because it is being powered or turned by the combustion engine.

If the alternator fails, then it must be replaced. A **tensioner** device is used to keep tension on the pulley bands. The rubber bands use a pulley system, so it is important for the mechanic to use a pry bar to get tension on the rubber bands that go over the pulleys.

The Drive System

Drive Systems and Components

While the engine is running, the flywheel turns the crankshaft. This moves the pistons in their respective cylinders. Any components located in the lower end the engine near the block, or components located inside the engine or located just below the engine block, are difficult to repair and require many tools. The use of an auto shop with a vehicle lift and full array of specialized tools is required to effectuate repairs to the lower part of the engine. The car's transmission transmits power produced by the engine to the wheels. The transmission is a complex component that requires special training to carry out needed repairs.

The Lubrication System

Lubrication Systems and Components

The oil contained in an oil pan below the engine is the "life blood" vat of the vehicle's lubrication system. When the pistons move, and the combustion engine starts operating, it starts the mechanical operation of the oil pump, which then circulates oil from the pan located below the engine. The oil moves up to the valves above. The oil coats the pistons then drops back into the oil pan. Lubrication prevents heat damage to the engine due to friction. The oil pump sits inside the oil pan. To replace the oil pump, the mechanic must drop the oil pan down by using different sized wrenches, and then the new oil pump can be reconnected.

Rocker arms are an essential part of the engine near the valves. Rocker arms require a steady, constant dousing of oil to work efficiently. A full pan of fresh oil is essential because old oil can gum up the works of an engine. The use of various wrenches facilitates the removal of the oil pan.

Cooling System

Cooling Systems and Components

An automobile engine commonly runs at an average temperature of 180 degrees Fahrenheit, which is the optimal temperature for the sound operation of most auto engines. The temperature of the engine's interior cylinder walls is 350 degrees Fahrenheit and the top of the cylinder is 600 degrees. The actual combustion fire in the cylinder combustion chamber is 3,000 degrees Fahrenheit.

In order to cool the engine, water circulates in channels throughout the engine. As the engine runs, the engine fan takes in air through the radiator. As the air passes by the fins of the radiator, the flowing water cooled by the air cools the engine. Cooled water flows through the engine jacket.

Hoses from the radiator carry water into the engine channels. Sometimes the hoses break or develop holes and must be replaced. Hose clamps connect the hoses to the engine and to the radiator. The hose clamps can be disconnected by needle nose pliers used on the hose clamp. To drain the coolant from the engine, a wrench is needed to unscrew the cylinder block drain plug. Some cars have bleed screws that must be opened using Allen wrenches with hexagonal nuts.

Engine temperature is sometimes controlled with the use of a unit called a **thermostat**. If the thermostat gets stuck open, the vehicle will overheat. If the thermostat gets stuck closed, it will not generate any heat for the car to use to heat the passenger compartment on cold days.

Cylinder head gasket problems require several tools, including a torque wrench. **Cylinder heads** must be torqued down to a specific pressure. Next, the intake manifold must be taken off and then the head fuel injection must be removed. All of the bolts must be removed and then the cylinder head can be lifted, and the old gasket should be scraped off. Head gaskets are made from a composite material. The head gaskets on a car's engine can be blown if the car overheats.

The Exhaust System

Exhaust Systems and Components

The **exhaust manifold**, also known as a **front pipe**, is designed to take gases and gas byproducts from the engine cylinders and channel them into the exhaust. Then the exhaust gas travels down an exhaust pipe to a catalytic converter, which is a filter designed to reduce harmful pollutant gases. The center section, also known as a **muffler** or **silencer**, is designed to reduce noise. The tailpipe further reduces noise and funnels exhaust gases away from the vehicle.

Exhaust gases produced by combustion in the piston chambers are channeled to the exhaust manifold. Without an exhaust manifold, a vehicle will run very loud and the engine will not function properly because there will not be enough pressure to keep the pistons operating. The exhaust manifold often gets worn out from the hot gases and damaged by vibrations emanating from the engine. Wrenches are necessary to replace the exhaust manifold. There is a gasket for the exhaust manifold known as the **exhaust manifold gasket**. After the exhaust manifold, there are clamps in the front of and to the back of the catalytic converter. The **catalytic converter** filters harmful gases from going into the environment. There is the muffler for the exhaust system that is also held in place by U clamps. A wrench is needed to take the muffler off the U clamps and each has two bolts. On some cars, straps hang the muffler and let the muffler sway with some give. Metal mounts also support most mufflers and extend down from the body, also giving the muffler system some sway and give. The give is advantageous because when the muffler gets hot; it expands and can split in places if totally bolted down. Other vehicles have a welded muffler system, which benefits from the steadfastness of a metallic weld.

Important tools to fix the exhaust system include ratchet sets, open end wrenches, and channel lock pliers. Channel lock pliers are adjustable, so if the mechanic encounters many different sizes of nuts to remove, the width between the jaws of the pliers can be adjusted. The jaws are typically an inch to two inches in length and extend at a right-angle from the two handles. The gap between the jaws is variable, due to a tongue-and-groove sizing system that lets the user adjust the jaw gap. Some channel lock pliers have rubber handles that protect the mechanic from electrical shock when working near wires that contain a live electric current and can be used to remove rubber supports that might be along the exhaust system. Channel wrenches and silicon spray can be used to help remove parts. Two bolts that hold the muffler to the tailpipe might be spring-loaded.

The Brake System

Brake Systems and Components

When the brake is depressed, the brake fluid flows through the master cylinder and then to each wheel's break cylinder. The resulting fluid pressure causes physical pressure, which creates friction. A hydraulic brake system is an extension of Pascal's Law, which states: "Pressure exerted anywhere in a contained incompressible fluid is distributed equally in all direction throughout the fluid."

The most common brake systems in a vehicle are **disc brake systems** and **drum brake systems**. The main components of a disc brake system are the wheel hub assembly, the brake caliper assembly, the disc brake rotor, the wheel, and the lug nuts. The wheel hub assembly holds the wheel and the disc rotor. The bearing inside the wheel hub assembly allows the smooth rotation of the wheel and the disc rotor. The disc rotor is the component that the brake pads squeeze against. This creates friction, which slows the rotation of the wheel. The disc rotor produces a lot of heat due to friction and that is one of the main reasons why brake pads wear out and need to be replaced. The brake caliper assembly uses the hydraulic force from the brake pedal to squeeze the brake pads to the rotor's surface, creating friction and decelerating the wheel. The caliper assembly consists of the caliper bracket, the inner brake pad, the slider pins, the dust boots and rubber bellows, the outer brake pad, and the brake piston. The caliper frame has fittings that hold the hose that contains the fluid that goes to the piston within the caliper frame. When the brake pedal is depressed by the vehicle operator, the fluid flows from the master cylinder to the caliper piston. The fluid pushes the piston, which makes the inner brake pad squeeze against the rotor surface. The piston also exerts force on the caliper frame and outward force is exerted on the caliper slide pins, which enables the outer brake pad to squeeze the rotor at the same time as the inner brake bad. The caliper frame slides along the slider pins.

The **disc break calibers** contain two brake pads. Disc brake pads can get worn by repeated braking of the vehicle. A jack to lift the car is required if a mechanic's garage lift is not available. Wrenches are needed to replace brake pads.

The lack of brake fluid can cause a vehicle's breaks to fail, so it is important to check the brake fluid reservoir in the car. Holes can form in the break pipes and hydraulic system leakage can occur. Brake fluid pipes must be replaced if there is any leakage of brake fluid.

Drum brakes are also used in many vehicles. The drum brakes are often used on the rear wheels of a vehicle. The important components of a drum brake system include:

- **Drum**: a round cast iron metal housing that looks like a bowl
- **Wheel cylinder**: the component that forces the brake shoes out towards the inside walls of the drum
- **Brake shoes**: these components press against the inside of the drum rim
- **Hub**: supports drum brake and wheel
- **Springs**: pull the brake shoes back away from the drum when the brake is released
- **Adjuster**: a small cylindrical part that regulates the distance of the brake shoes from the surface of the inside of the drum. As the shoes get worn, the distance between the shoe and the drum becomes greater and the drum break adjuster component keeps the distance constant. The adjuster has a small wheel that adjusts the distance when the brake is repaired and the shoe distance is set.
- **Strut**: keeps the shoes from compressing too far and keeps the shoes in alignment.
- **Backing plate**: holds the drum in place and also supports the drum brake cylinder.

Drum brakes usually have a short shoe and a long shoe. The short shoe goes in front, towards the front of the vehicle. The long shoe is placed more to the rear of the vehicle.

There are a few specialized tools that need to be used when fixing drum brakes: a multi-spring tool (which looks like large forceps), an adjuster tool, spring removal tools that have special ends that help remove the springs (these tools are important because the springs have a lot of force and could injure the mechanic if they pop off), a screwdriver, and needle nose pliers.

Before servicing the brakes, the mechanic must park the vehicle on a level surface and make sure that the parking brake is not engaged because this will press the brake shoes against the drum and prevent the brake drum from being removed. The mechanic must always place cars with automatic transmissions in park and those with standard transmissions in neutral before working on the rear drum brakes. The first step is to pop open the hood of the vehicle and check the brake fluid reservoir to make sure that there is the proper amount of brake fluid, which should be filled to the "full" line. This is the fluid that goes to the master cylinder and it should appear clear without debris. If the fluid is cloudy or dark, it is recommended that it is replaced. Before taking off the wheel, the lug nuts on the wheel must first be loosened and only then should the vehicle be jacked up. If a lug nut is rusted on or too tight to take off without using great force, then the vehicle should not be jacked up. If great force is applied while the vehicle is jacked up, the vehicle can slip off of its supports. The drum brake contains many parts and they can be difficult to reassemble if there is no reference to their proper positions. The mechanic should take a picture of the drum brake before any disassembly. A rubber mallet can be an essential tool if the drum is stuck and will not come off. A few taps with the rubber mallet should loosen up the drum for removal. Some drums use retaining screws, and a screwdriver must be used before the drums are removed. A brake adjusting tool is essential. The brake adjusting tool resembles a small, hand-size crow bar. The brake adjusting screw is an important component of the drum brake and must be loosened before attempting to remove the brake shoes. A brake spring washer tool is a good addition to the mechanic's arsenal for removing the springs in a drum brake. When replacing the wheel after working on the brake drum, a ratchet and socket tool is beneficial for ensuring that the lug nuts on the wheel are tight, after which a torque wrench is used to achieve optimal lug nut tightness.

Suspension System

Suspension Systems and Components

The **suspension system** of a vehicle helps provide a smooth ride when driving. Vibration can cause a host of maladies within a car and can literally shake a car to pieces if uncontrolled. The less vibration that a vehicle experiences, the fewer the necessary repairs. The other important factors associated with the suspension system is that the system keeps the vehicle upright and supports the vehicle from excessively tilting and swaying when the vehicle is turning, accelerating, and braking.

Suspension systems are comprised of many components. The main components are springs, shock absorbers, and control arms. The control arms are attached to the vehicle's chassis frame. The springs most used in vehicles are coiled springs because their shape permits them to be mounted directly over the shock absorbers. Some vehicles use leaf springs (flattened bands of metal that are stacked) for the rear wheels of the vehicle.

Shock absorbers are also referred to as dampers. Modern shock absorbers look like tubes that are usually gas-filled (older shock absorbers were oil-filled) within the tube and dampen the vibrations of the road. The shock absorber also dampens the oscillations of the springs and offers a positive and negative resistance, in both directions up and down to the springs, yielding a more stable ride.

The **front suspension** components consist of arms that are frequently referred to as wishbones, hence, the term **double wishbone suspension**. The arms of the wishbone usually have one to two ball joints that enable steering and vertical movement. The lower arm of the wishbone supports the spring and shock absorber, while the upper wishbone supports the steering component to the wheel. A comparable suspension system is known as the **MacPherson strut suspension**. The MacPherson system is desirable and offers some advantages. In the MacPherson system, the upper wishbone arm is replaced by a strut (a longer shock absorber body), which enables grouped functions in one unit; the strut also acts as the upright support for the spring and alleviates the need for another wishbone arm. This simpler design adds to passenger comfort.

An **anti-roll bar** attached between the shock absorber components of both front wheels resists the rolling that occurs when turning. The inertia of the turn places force on the outer springs. The anti-roll bar presents a counterforce that maintains stability against the vehicle's sway.

Rear suspension systems in vehicles usually have an independent configuration where each rear wheel can move up and down independently from the other rear wheel. A non-independent rear suspension system has a solid axle connecting both rear wheels. This is not as desirable as an independent configuration because if one wheel hits a bump, the other wheel is also affected, because the sole axle transmits the force of the bump to the other wheel. The key component of the independent rear suspension system is the universal joint. Instead of one solid rear axle, each of the driveshafts extends from the differential (the unit that transmits power from the drive shaft to the axle) into universal joints. The universal joints enable the wheel axles to move up and down while the differential gear casing stays in place.

The Steering System

The Steering System and Components

All vehicles have a **steering wheel** that turns the front wheels of the vehicle. The front end of a vehicle usually has a lot of weight because the engine is located in front. In early vehicles, before the advent of power steering, it was sometimes difficult for the driver to turn the front wheels. With the help of the engine's power, steering has become almost effortless and very responsive. The steering mechanisms are usually powered by an **engine-driven pump** and a **hydraulic system**. With an older rack and pinion steering system, the rotational movement of the steering wheel is transferred to the frame mounted rack and pinion steering assembly. The **rack** and **pinion mechanism** offer precise steering abilities but require more effort to move the wheels. The main steering components consist of a steering wheel, steering shaft, a steering rack or steering box, and arm mechanism. Universal joints are placed throughout the steering shafts so that the steering mechanisms can get around oddly placed components in the vehicle that are attributed to other vehicle systems. Also, the universal joints allow for repositioning of the wheel for the operator's comfort.

The **steering box component** is a gear box designed to make steering easier for the vehicle operator. These units often become loose and consequently result in a lot of unwanted "play" in the steering of the vehicle. The steering will feel loose and the operator may have to compensate by physically steering with increased revolutions. A new replacement steering box is easily installed but the mechanic must have a "stubby" short ratchet in order to access the congested part of the engine compartment. A short-handled ratchet is a tool that can fit where larger tools would be encumbered by limited space. A pry bar is a necessary tool to work surfaces apart. While mostly 34mm and 24mm nut sizes are encountered in the steering systems, mechanics should have an array of different sized ratchets and wrenches to adjust a variety of nuts and bolt sizes.

Automotive Components

There are several essential components of a vehicle that require replacement including:

- **Brake Pads**: One of the most frequently replaced components in a vehicle are the brake pads. The use of a mechanic shop car lift makes the break pad replacement process much easier because the mechanic can stand and work under the vehicle in relative comfort. The first step in replacing the brake pads is to take out the slide pins that the caliper rides on using a socket and wrench to remove nuts that hold the slide pins in place. Once the caliper is removed, the mechanic can keep the caliper away from the brake disc by letting the caliber hang with the use of a piece of wire hanger. Finally, the brake pads that are now visible to the mechanic should easily come off of the caliper. The replacement of brake pads is easy because they fit right over the disc and are supported by small appendages around the disc. The mechanic fits the caliper (the device that produces the pressure around the disc) over the brake pads and proceeds to perform the initial tightening of the caliper around the brake pads and onto the caliper support. The most important step is at the end of the brake pad replacement process: the tightening of the brake caliper using a torque wrench to exact specifications set forth by the vehicle's manufacturer. A torque wrench shows the exact amount of tightening by using a mechanical meter that displays foot pounds. For example, if Ford specified 30-foot pounds of torque was required for one of their car's brake calipers, then it would be most important to adhere to that specification. If the bolt is too tight, the caliper pin may break, or the entire brake system could become damaged. If the torque is insufficient, then the caliper pin might fall out. The mechanic must make certain that all hydraulic brake lines are back in place and then insert the spring clips that go inside the caliper. The spring clips lessen the amount of brake squeal by holding the brake pads in place using tension. The spring clips go inside the caliper and the clips are specific to the vehicle manufacturer.

- **Drum brakes**: The shoes of the drum break often need replacing and a few specialized tools must be employed, such as an "adjuster" tool and a "spring" tool. The complete description of replacing drum brakes is a complex process and beyond the scope of the ASVAB exam.

- **Valve cover gaskets** keep gas and oil from escaping onto the surface of the engine and causing a smoking condition. If replacement is necessary, the valve covers must be unbolted and new gaskets placed along the rim of the valve cover base.

- **Tires**: The wear on a tire depends on the mileage driven on the tire and the type of tire on the car. A softer tire will adhere to the road better but will have a much shorter life than a hard tire with a deep tread. Tires are usually replaced after 25,000 to 60,000 miles of travel.

- **Lights**: Head lights, tail lights, indicator lights, and interior lights of a car must be changed when burnt out or damaged

- **Hoses**: Radiator hoses, transmission hoses, and brake lines must occasionally be replaced. Just three tools are necessary for fixing a broken hose: a flat head screwdriver, a cutter type scissor tool, and channel lock pliers. After the screw holding the hose in place at the source is removed by using the flat head screwdriver, the mechanic has an opportunity to further inspect the hose. If the hose damage permits cutting the damage away and using the remaining length of hose to reconnect the hose, then a new hose might not be required. A complete hose replacement requires loosening the hose band on the other end of the hose and removing the hose. A hose band is a metal ring that goes around the hose and secures the hose to the mouth of where the hose must be placed. The hose ring is tightened with either a slotted screw or small nut.

- **Wires**: Heat sometimes melts the wires in a vehicle. A short in the electrical system of a car can lead to a dangerous fire condition. Wires must be inspected and if worn, must be replaced.

- **Electrical connectors**: Age and heat can rot out an electrical connector. Simple tools are used to replace these components.

Procedures for Automotive Troubleshooting and Repair

The first step to auto troubleshooting is to be aware that there is a problem with the functioning of the vehicle. Sometimes a vehicular problem can be detected just by listening to a sound that is discordant, such as pinging, the grating sound of a worn brake pad against the rotor of the wheel, or a knocking sound when the vehicle's wheel is turned. This latter sound can indicate that the ball joints are loose in the steering mechanism. Another way to ascertain if there is a potential vehicular problem is to keep acute attention on the gauges of the car. If the temperature gauge on the vehicle's dashboard is reading close to a red-hot zone, it can indicate that the vehicle is lacking coolant or perhaps that the pump for the coolant is not operating properly, causing the engine to become hotter than normal.

Puddles of Liquid Under the Vehicle

The vehicle operator and vehicle mechanic must be cognizant of any puddles of liquid that have formed under the vehicle. These puddles are caused by leaks in vehicular systems. The motorist should take note of these puddles as they might spell significant vehicle operation trouble down the road. The type of liquid that has accumulated must be determined first. For example, it may be innocuous rain or condensation from the vehicle's air conditioning system. **Transmission fluid** is a purplish color and the sight of this puddle can indicate a serious problem. The mechanic should touch the fluid with the index finger and thumb. If the fluid is slightly viscous and purple, then it is most likely transmission fluid. An immediate inspection is necessary to determine the source of the transmission leak. The transmission is a very expensive unit and to avoid replacement, the motorist must repair the leak. If a vehicle's transmission fluid becomes too low, then gears within the transmission can grind together and ruin the transmission to the point where it must be replaced.

Leaking brake fluid also necessitates immediate repair. If the brake fluid is too low in the brake fluid reservoir, then the vehicle will not stop, which puts the motorist and others in grave danger. **Brake fluid** is slightly viscous and darker in color. The mechanic must determine from where the brake fluid is leaking and then plug the leak. The master cylinder or one of the many tubes that bring brake fluid to the wheels might be leaking.

Antifreeze is greenish-yellow and has a distinct smell. When a coolant pipe leaks or a vehicle's radiator has sustained a small hole and is leaking antifreeze, the coolant liquid contacts the hot engine. The coolant liquid, commonly known as antifreeze, will smoke when it comes in contact with the hot engine. If an antifreeze leak is suspected, the coolant vat should be checked and if low, there may be a leak. The location of the leak can sometimes be detected by the location of the coolant puddle under the vehicle. Usually the location of the puddle is directly below the leak. From there, the mechanic can use a bright flashlight to locate the exact position of the leak. Various methods of repair can be used to remedy the coolant leak.

A leaking **oil pan** is usually detected when a car moves from a parking spot and there is a significant spot of oil where the car was parked. Specifically, there is an amount of oil detected on the pavement under the car's engine when parked. Any amount of oil detected on the pavement can denote a dangerous and costly condition that must be repaired. Even a small leak over time will deplete the oil pan of oil and consequently leave the engine without essential lubricant. The damage done to the engine can be catastrophic, resulting in an engine seizure. The engine is usually the most expensive part of a car and its loss is costly. Insurance companies will not cover the engine replacement in the case of an oil leak because the damage was perpetrated by the negligence of the car owner. When an oil pan leaks, it has usually been struck by a rock or some other protruding object that the underside of the vehicle has come in contact with. If there is a hole in the oil pan, then it must be replaced. Usually just two or more bolts hold the oil pan in place and these can be loosened with the help of a ratchet tool. When replacing the oil pan component, the mechanic must make sure that the proper gaskets are available. All vehicle systems that use liquids usually have gaskets to prevent the liquid from squirting out through the connections within the systems.

Water condensation from the vehicle's exhaust tailpipes is not a concern. Most vehicles have water drips from the tailpipes when the vehicle is first turned on and operated for the first few minutes. The resulting natural accumulation of water condensation will remain in the tailpipe and cause rust to the entire outer half of the exhaust system. This only becomes problematic if the vehicle is only operated for a few minutes or less. Vehicles that often travel just a few miles at a time will experience a rotting out of the muffler and tailpipes because the condensation does not have ample time to dry out as it does with the extended use of the vehicle. To alleviate the possibility of ruining the exhaust system due to water condensation, a vehicle should be driven more than just a few miles to dry out the watery condensation that has formed in the exhaust system.

The Vehicle Lift

Proper operational knowledge of a car "lift" function is essential for the vehicle mechanic. A **car lift** enables the mechanic to operate under the car without having to lay supine underneath the vehicle. Moreover, the lift permits the removal and installation of larger components under a vehicle. Working under a four-thousand-pound car can be extremely dangerous if the mechanic is not familiar with the safe operation of the car lift. Car lifts usually have adjustable arms that have rubber pads, which rest against the underside of the vehicle at the frame's strongest points. Care must be taken to place the rubber ends of the lift's arms in the proper position at the strongest points of the underside of the car where the weight of the car can be supported without damaging the vehicle. The car is raised to a point where the mechanic feels that he or she can comfortably and safely work under the car and then the lift is locked in place.

An adequately equipped machine shop or vehicle repair shop contains many tools including the following:

- A **Metal Inert Gas** (MIG) welder is useful for bonding metals. MIG welding is a form of electrical welding that requires a safe workspace away from ignitable fuels. The shop welder must wear a welding helmet to protect against hot flying sparks and flames and an air ventilation and exhaust extraction system is necessary when welding indoors. For safety, the MIG welding machine should be of quality design.

- A hand-operated **Sawzall™** (a name that is a trademark of the Milwaukee Electric Tool Company) is an important shop tool. This automatic electric hacksaw or jigsaw can cut many materials, including metal. It is essential for removing unwanted parts and for fabricating parts. The newer Sawzall™ operates by long lasting batteries that remove the need for cumbersome electrical cords.

- A **stout hand drill** with a lot of torque is essential for drilling through steel as well as concrete. A diversified drill set enables the mechanic to work on different types of repairs.

- Assorted **Cobalt wrenches** arranged neatly by size on a wall or in a tool box will facilitate the work of the mechanic. These are strong fixed wrenches that work on many sized nuts.

- **Wire strippers** are necessary for electrical work. An assortment of wires and electrical connectors should be available in the shop.

- A **rubber mallet** should be used when the surface of the object being struck would be damaged with a regular metal hammer.

- A box of **assorted steel nuts, bolts,** and **washers** organized in a tool box.

- A **carbide blade chop saw** enables the shop mechanic to cut metal and wood. A chop saw is a circular bladed saw that is on a hinge. Items are placed under the blade and the operator lowers the circular saw to cut the object.

- A **scrap bin** should be used for disposing of metal shavings and other unwanted material refuse produced from working with materials. Sharp metal pieces lying around the shop floor can cause injury, so they must be removed. A scrap bin made of a heavy gauge metal or plastic is necessary to contain the refuse produced by a machine shop.

- A **multi-drawer tool box** can improve efficiency; time is always an important factor when considering a repair or part fabrication. The tool box enables the mechanic to have instant access to the necessary tools in an organized fashion. Sometimes, tools can become misplaced and unnecessary time might be spent looking for the proper tool. The tool box lets the mechanic sort out the various chisels, sockets, hex keys, wrenches, crescent wrenches, various pliers, and other multiple tools. A well-sorted multi-level, multi-drawer standing tool box enables the mechanic to find the exact tool required and act with it to complete the job at hand. Drawers with smooth ball bearing action let the mechanic open and close the drawer quickly and easily.

- **Metal files** are often important for trimming components. Various grades of roughness give the mechanic options when shaving materials to specific sizes.

- The value of **simple shelving** in the shop space should not be underestimated. Shelves permit the mechanic to see where items are located, improve accessibility to such items, and can support heavy cans of paint and other tools. Shelves help prevent damage to expensive equipment by getting it off the floor or out of messy piles. Metal shelving can easily be constructed and secured against the walls of the mechanic's shop.

- **Dial calipers** make important precise measurements. They are easy to use and are essential for measuring the width of materials to be worked on.

- An **angle grinder** (side grinder or disc grinder) lets the mechanic shape a variety of materials depending on what type of circular brush is used. It can be used for cutting, grinding, and polishing. Some angle grinders are on a stand while other angle grinders are handheld. They are powered by an electric motor, gas engine, or compressed air.

- A **filtration system** to expel bad air is essential for the shop. Fume extraction and oil smoke extraction as well as dust and oil mist must be sucked out of the air by a fume extraction system. These units are essentially big standing vacuums that pull the toxic air away from the mechanic.

- A **Tungsten Inert Gas** (TIG) welder uses a tungsten electrode that delivers the current to the welding arc. The MIG process is easier because it uses a continuously feeding wire whereas TIG uses long welding rods that slowly feed into the weld puddle. TIG welding is used on metals of thinner gauges.

- **Mill drills** are used very frequently in all types of machine shops. A mill drill is a large, electrically-powered vertical drill that drills down vertically with a bit. Milling is a machining process that uses rotary cutters to remove material by feeding in a direction at an angle to the axis tool. Milling is one of the most commonly used processes for machining parts to precise sizes and shapes. The shop's scrap bin should be accessible as this machining process produces a large amount of metal waste.

- A **lathe** is an essential tool that will conform metals to size and shave surfaces to the desired dimensions. It is similar to a mill drill but is based on working with a horizontal axis. The lathe is a machine for shaping material by means of a rotating drive that turns the material piece being worked on against changeable cutting tools. A lathe can be used in the manufacturing of various machine components.

- An **air compressor** is a useful unit to have in a machine shop because some tools operate off of compressed air, such as wheel nut wrenches, which are used to remove tires from the wheel of a car. Air compressors are also useful for inflating tires and blowing out debris and dirt from machinery and small spaces.

Construction Procedures

Concrete is an advancement that has revolutionized the ability to build comfortable residential structures using materials that are fantastically resilient to the elements. The structures built with brick, stone, and concrete can outlive the length of a human life. There are brick structures from 500 years ago that are still standing today, and some stone and concrete built houses can last for thousands of years.

When building a brick or stone building, the concrete mix must be of a perfect consistency, much like peanut butter, and not too loose. A veteran bricklayer will spread the concrete evenly on top of a brick like spreading peanut butter completely over a piece of bread. Bricks are an important exterior material used in different applications all over the world, but the red brick is the predominant type of brick in the United States. When constructing a brick wall, the bricks must be straight and level, so that the force of gravity does not disturb the wall over time.

Constructing Brick Walls

To **construct a brick wall**, the mortar is spread completely over the top of each brick with a trowel or spatula tool. These flat tools are used to smooth out the mortar used between the bricks and to wipe away excess mortar that spills over the sides of the brick. The brick wall should be free of mortar on the sides of the bricks. One layer of bricks should be laid down and each brick should be tapped with the end of the trowel's handle. A "spoon" tool is used to create a concave indentation in the concrete that surrounds each brick. A bubble leveler is a very important tool and should be used consistently through the building of a brick wall.

Balloon frame or "stick built" houses require the use of a circular saw and many two-inch by six-inch boards. When building a house, only 2"x 6" boards are allowed because this size allows enough space for insulation to be installed.

The Roof

A waterproof, weatherproof **roof** on top of a structure is an essential part of the structure that must be resilient. There are just a few important tools and techniques to employ for the construction of a new roof. A hammer, a bucket of nails, a sufficient number of shingles, and tar paper are the main materials that are required. A flat shovel or the front of the spade can be used to get underneath the old shingles of the roof to shovel them off and expose the base roof plywood. Then tar paper is put over the plywood using a staple gun and then shingles are added from the bottom of the roof to the top. Roofing nails with big heads and shafts long enough to go through the tar paper, shingles, and plywood must be used.

Foundation

A poured concrete **foundation** is standard for the first stage in building a structure in locations where temperatures can often go below freezing. **Rebar**—iron/metal rods that extend through the concrete—are used as a reinforcement for the foundation. **Wood frames** can serve as molds for cement walls and are easily built using wooden beams, a circular saw, a hammer, and nails. Cement does not stick to wood, so wood is a good foundation framing material. After the concrete hardens in the frame, then the wood easily comes off away from the concrete. Concrete wall thickness is determined by the size and design of the intended structure but 18" thickness is the norm. The foundation should be at least 46 inches below the ground line. In locations that have temperatures that plummet below freezing, the posts and foundations must be buried below the frost line. In Florida, it is legal to build a house on top of slab; houses can be built on slab anywhere where the temperature does not dip below freezing.

Below 17 degrees Fahrenheit, concrete should not be poured. When temperatures dip down, it is good to add antifreeze to the water. If water freezes, then the concrete will not cure. Tools used for constructing a foundation include a wheel barrow for transporting the cement to the immediate location where it is needed, a shovel to push the concrete into spaces, and a cement "squeegee" to level the cement once it is poured into place.

Portals: Door Frames and Window Frames

Typically, either 2" x 4" or 2" x 6" boards form a window sill. Four boards support the sill; these boards are also referred to as **studs**. Trimmer studs extend vertically from the bottom horizontal stud and these form the sides of the window frame and are nailed into the king stud, which is one of the studs that make up the main frame of the wall. The trimmer studs support the **header assembly**, which is the top of window frame. The header assembly is four different individual pieces of wood and often must conform to building code regulations within the structure's municipality. Two 2" x 6" boards are recommended for the riser part of the header. Between the top of the header and bottom of the upper plate (top horizontal stud), fitted studs—usually three—brace the header against the upper plate. A row of two nails every sixteen inches should secure the trimmer studs to the king stud. If using 2" x 6" framing, then three nails should be used every sixteen inches along the sill support studs next to the trimmer studs. Nails can be used to secure the horizontal sill to the vertical supporting studs. A drilled hole with a bolt can also be installed horizontally through the king stud and the trimmer stud into the vertical sill. The header should have four nails through the king stud into the riser part of the top window frame.

A **door frame** is very similar except that there is no triple support from below because the door goes all the way down to the floor. The trimmer studs on either side of the portal make up the door frame sides. The trimmer studs support the top or header of door. The door header should have rows of three nails every sixteen inches. The header of a door should be strong because it needs to support anything that is above it. It is recommended that a precisely fitting sheet of plywood is used between the header riser boards (the boards that are placed facing forward). A board nailed onto the bottom of the header will lead to a nice flush, flat surface.

Table Reading

This section of the test measures whether you can read a table accurately. The table below shows X- and Y-values in a grid format. The numbers on the horizontal, or top, part of the table are the X-values, and the numbers on the vertical, or side, part of the table are the Y-values. In other words, the X-values correspond to columns, and the Y-values correspond to rows. Each question will provide you with two coordinates, an X and a Y, and you must quickly interpret the table to determine the correct value. Each question will have five possible answers, and you should choose the correct one.

Using the example table below, here are some practice questions and explanations to better help you understand how to use these tables.

	-3	-2	-1	0	+1	+2	+3
+3	14	15	17	19	20	21	22
+2	15	17	19	21	22	23	24
+1	16	18	20	22	24	25	26
0	18	19	21	23	25	26	28
-1	20	22	23	25	27	28	30
-2	21	23	24	26	28	29	31
-3	22	24	25	27	29	30	32

Example Problem 1

X	Y	A	B	C	D	E
0	+1	22	25	20	19	16

The answer to this example question would be A, 22. To answer this problem, first go to the X-axis and find the 0 column. Then follow the 0 column down to the +1 row on the Y-axis. The number at that point is 22. Some corresponding coordinates for the incorrect answers in this example would be:

B = 25: +1, 0

C = 20: +1, +3

D = 19: 0, +3

E = 16: -3, +1

What are some helpful tips for answering these questions correctly?

- Take your time. The easiest way to make mistakes in this section is assuming that the questions are easy and subsequently making simple mistakes.
- Make sure to correctly read the X and Y headings. It is easy to select the second column when you have an X-value of 2, but that wouldn't be the right column.
- Start with the X coordinate and stay within that selected column. Do not mistakenly travel to another column when you are selecting the Y-value.
- After you have the X column selected, go down to the corresponding Y-value row. Remember, don't change columns!
- Use your fingers or a piece of paper to mark the columns and rows as it helps you keep track of where you are and not jump to a neighboring column or row.
- Practice these types of questions until you are comfortable answering them correctly and within a certain window of time. On test day, take the same amount of time as you had been with the practice questions.

Instrument Comprehension

Purpose of Instrument-Comprehension Questions

The purpose of the instrument-comprehension questions is to ensure that vital instruments are understood. There needs to be a familiarity with the instruments and knowledge of their purposes, as well as how to read them.

Presentation of the Instrument-Comprehension Questions

Depending on the types of instruments covered in the test, the comprehension questions will vary in layout. For example, the practice questions in this section pertain to the artificial horizon and the compass. These two instruments are presented with the readings that you would need to be able to translate in order to determine the orientation of the aircraft, were they presented to you in the cockpit.

Reading the Compass and Artificial-Horizon Instruments

The compass on an aircraft is a navigational instrument used to determine the direction of flight, or the "aircraft heading." Compass reading is simple. As most people are aware, the needle reflects the direction being faced. When the aircraft is facing north, the needle will be pointing at the "N." If the aircraft is facing southwest, the needle will point to "SW."

The artificial horizon, also known as the attitude indicator, is an aircraft instrument that shows the aircraft orientation as compared with the Earth's horizon. This instrument indicates the pitch and bank of the aircraft, which is the tilt of the nose and the wings. The artificial horizon becomes relatively easy to read and interpret once you visualize it from the pilot seat.

The artificial horizon utilizes a small airplane or wings and a horizon bar. The aircraft in the instrument is representative of the host aircraft that is being flown. The horizon bar represents the actual horizon of the Earth. Many artificial-horizon instruments are blue in the upper half representing the sky and dark on the lower half, which represents the ground. If the aircraft or wings in the instrument are above the horizon bar, the aircraft is nose up or climbing. If the aircraft is shown below the horizon bar in the instrument, then the aircraft is nose down, or descending in altitude. When the symbolic aircraft is even with the horizon bar, the plane is in level flight.

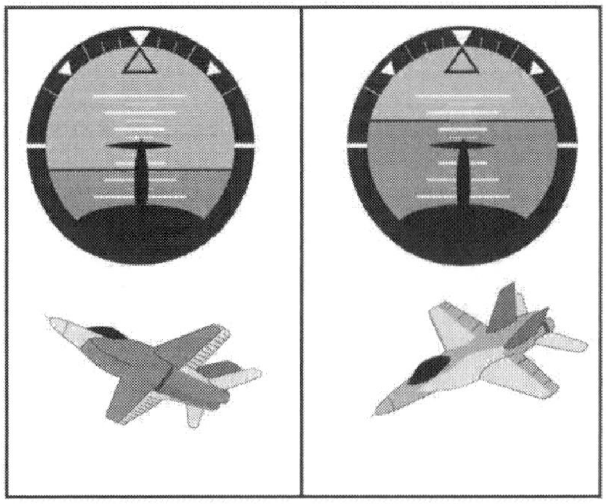

The artificial-horizon instrument typically will have degree marks that indicate the amount of aircraft banking that occurs during turning maneuvers. The horizon bar will tilt opposite of the direction of the wings, which will show the orientation of the aircraft to the horizon during banking.

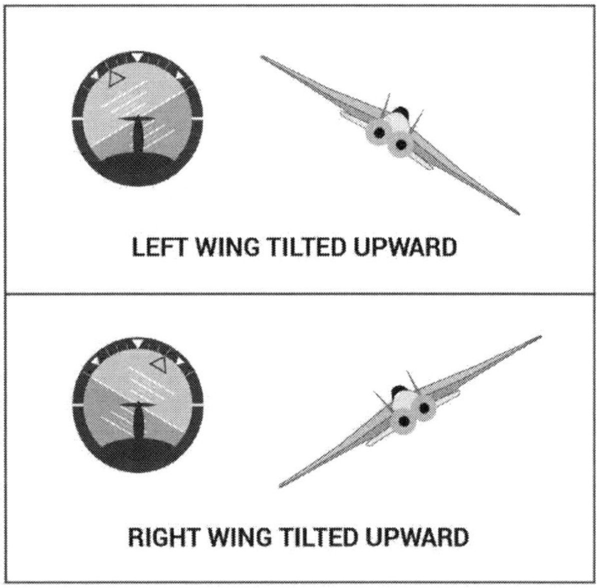

The questions in this section will provide compass and artificial-horizon indications instruments (see example below), and you will be required to determine the orientation of the aircraft using these two. Besides looking at the compass for direction, pay close attention to the artificial horizon to determine if the indication is that of a climbing or descending aircraft, or possibly an aircraft in level flight. Also it is important to verify the direction of banking. Once you have figured out the heading, the pitch, and the banking, you should be able to choose the correct answer from the simulated aircraft images provided.

For the purpose of these questions, the simulated aircraft will appear to be flying away from your view for north, facing you for south, facing with the nose to left of the page for west and to the right for east.

Example practice question: Looking at the instruments on the left, which choice depicts the orientation of the aircraft?

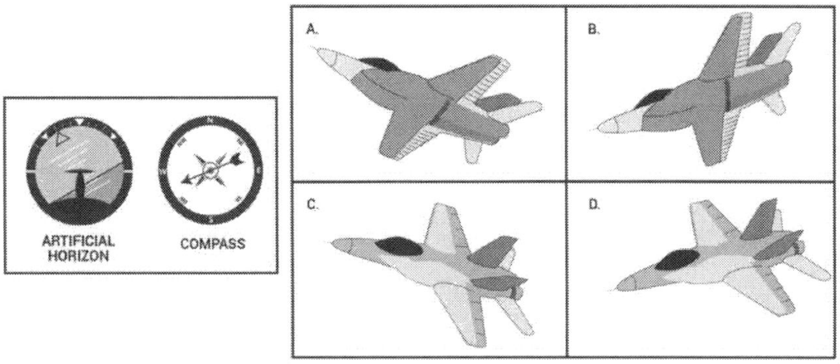

The correct answer to the example question is "A". The compass is showing a west-southwest heading. The artificial horizon shows the wings are above the horizon bar, indicating the aircraft is in a climb. Lastly, the artificial horizon shows the right wing is dipped, as the horizon bar is tilted opposite. This indicates the aircraft is banked to the right. Put it all together and you have an aircraft heading west-southwest (facing away and to the left), while it is in a climb and a right bank. The only choice that corresponds to this orientation is answer A.

Studying for the Compass and Artificial Horizon Portion of the Test

You may want to practice with a standard compass if you are not familiar with compass reading. Many smartphones have compass capabilities, or you can find one at a sporting-goods store. You probably will not be able to find an artificial horizon to practice with, so it is recommended that you prepare for this portion of the test using the following practice questions.

Block Counting

This section of the test measures your spatial reasoning and logic. You will be shown a three-dimensional (3-D) drawing of blocks. Some of these blocks may be touching, and, if so, you will be asked to determine the number of blocks that one particular block is touching. Keep in mind that some of the blocks may not be visible. There is no prior knowledge of block counting that is needed for this section of the test; just use logic and spatial reasoning.

In order for a block to "touch" another block, their faces must touch. If only two blocks' corners touch and not their faces, then they are not considered to be touching.

See the example problem below.

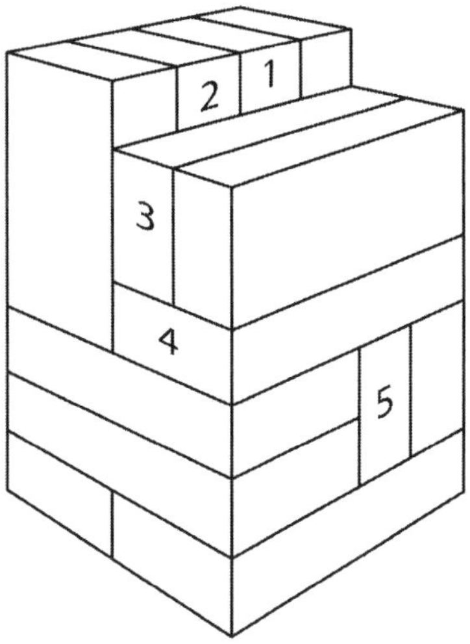

In this example, you know that Block 1 is touching 5 other blocks. Block 1 is touching Block 2 and 3, the block to the right of Block 1, Block 4, and Block 5.

Block 2 is also touching 5 blocks: Block 1, the block to the left of Block 2, Block 3, Block 4, and one of the horizontal blocks beside Block 5.

What about Block 4? Block 4 is touching an astonishing 9 blocks: Block 3, the block to the right of Block 3, Blocks 1 and 2 and the two on either side of them, Block 5 and the two blocks on the left of it, and the one block on the right of Block 5.

Sometimes you will have to infer how big a block is when only part of the block is shown.

Assembling Objects

The **Assembling Objects** (**AO**) section of the ASVAB exam tests a candidate's ability to think in three dimensions by having them follow a simple set of instructions and assemble an object from its component parts. This is an important skill because success in almost every technical field depends on being able to assemble complex systems from simpler parts or components. But relax! This is the same skill that's used to solve a jigsaw puzzle, fold origami, tie a knot, or take apart and reassemble simple machinery.

It's more important to become familiar with the test structure on the AO section than on any other part of the exam. Doing so will avoid wasting valuable time trying to understand the instructions when the AO section begins. To better understand this structure, think of a soldier reassembling a rifle or a technical specialist putting a pump back together. They start with the parts laid out to one side, then put the parts together according to the instructions. That's how the AO section is structured.

An example of a question similar to those found on the exam is shown below. Below the question are "bubbles" corresponding to the possible solutions shown in boxes 1 through 5. Choose the correct solution and fill in the "bubble" next to the letter that corresponds to it.

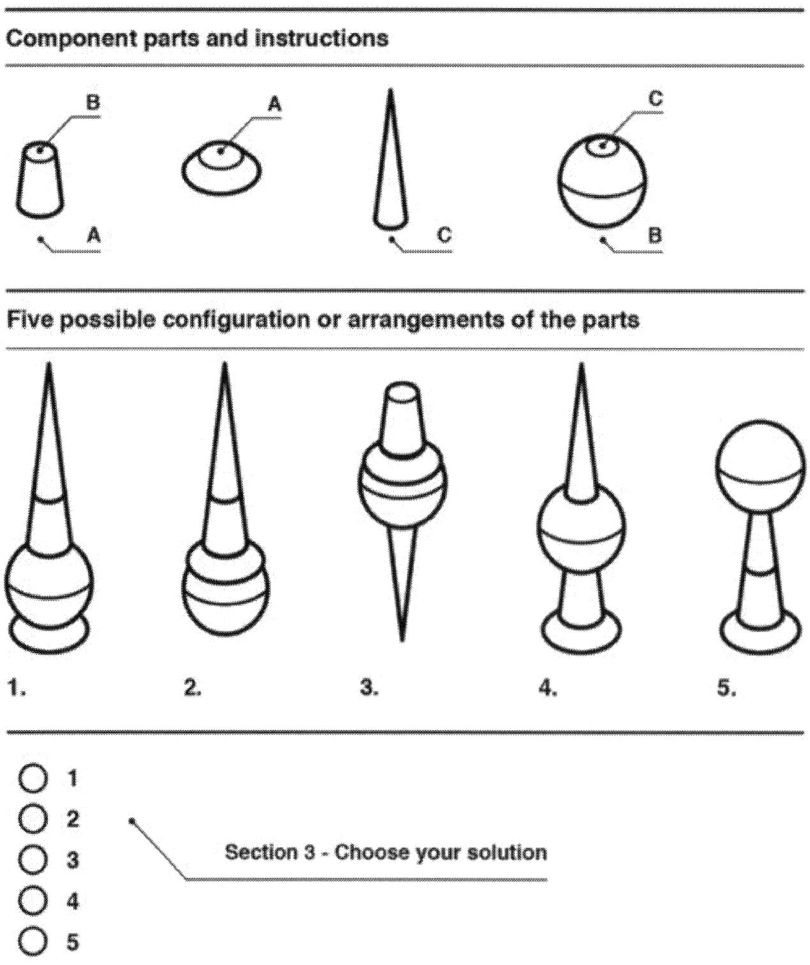

Understanding the Structure of an Assembling Objects (AO) Question

The most efficient way to solve AO questions is to systematically rule out the incorrect answers one at a time. Look at the entire system of parts first, and then work component by component.

In the example above, the system consists of four components: a truncated cone marked *A* on the bottom and *B* on the top face; a shorter, squatter truncated cone labeled *A* on the top face; a thin, tipped cone marked *C* on the base; and a sphere with a line around its "equator" marked *C* on its "north pole" and a *B* on its "south pole." This is a simple system with four components connected "in series," which means one after the other.

Look at Box 1. The thin, tipped cone fits neatly onto the taller of the two truncated cones and sits on top of the sphere. However, the instructions show that the top of the truncated cones must be joined to *B*, and the sharp conic section must be joined at its base to *C*, so these two pieces don't fit together. Therefore, Box 1 is not the solution.

Box 2 can be rejected immediately because it shows the same incorrect assembly.

Now look at Box 3. The two truncated cones are properly connected, with the squat one serving as the base. However, the base is shown sitting on top of the sphere when the surface of a part labeled *C* should be sitting there (which is the sharp cone). In addition, the surface of the squat base is not connected to any part, so Box 3 isn't the answer.

Now that three possible answers have been eliminated, it's easy to compare the last two configurations (Box 4 and Box 5) and see that the only one matching the problem's assembly requirements is Box 4.

Preparing for the Test

First, it's important to understand what a correct solution to an assembly problem is. As mentioned before, the unassembled parts shown in the left-hand box can be moved to different positions, rotated, or even flipped (turned through the axis of the page). They can be turned around so not all of the parts are seen, like the way a coffee mug can be turned so the handle isn't visible. The parts can also be turned so that only one face is visible, like how a cube looks like a square when viewed head on, or a disk looks like a thin rectangle when viewed from the edge. However, the parts won't be stretched or bent, so think of them as being made out of solid wood, rather than out of rubber or plastic.

It's also important to remember that the rotations must obey the laws of symmetry. A right-handed object can't be turned so that it becomes a left-handed object. Consider a pair of gloves; a right-hand glove can be turned around or over but, no matter how it's turned or rotated, it can't be turned into a left-hand glove without turning it inside out—and that's against the rules.

ASVAB Practice Test

Word Knowledge

Directions: Choose the word that most closely relates to the word in bold.

1. "I promise, I did not **instigate** the fight."
   a. begin
   b. ponder
   c. swim
   d. overwhelm

2. **Fortify** most nearly means
   a. foster
   b. barricade
   c. strengthen
   d. undermine

3. My girlfriend said, "Either you marry me, or I'm leaving you!" Not a very pleasant **ultimatum**.
   a. invitation
   b. journey
   c. greeting
   d. threat

4. **Wave** most nearly means
   a. flourish
   b. sink
   c. tide
   d. stagnant

5. Space is often referred to as the great **void**.
   a. around
   b. age
   c. empty
   d. diffuse

6. **Query** most nearly means
   a. bury
   b. wander
   c. ask
   d. praise

7. The thievery merited **severe** punishment.
   a. foul
   b. extreme
   c. cut
   d. shake

8. **Vexation** most nearly means
   a. boring
   b. pain
   c. revolving
   d. anger

9. The toddler, who had just learned to speak, seemed rather loquacious.
   a. verbose
   b. humorous
   c. silent
   d. cranky

10. **Grim** most nearly means
   a. frank
   b. dire
   c. corpse
   d. sharp

11. The bullies **disparaged** the younger boy, causing him to feel worthless.
   a. despaired
   b. belittled
   c. broke
   d. sparred

12. **Altitude** most nearly means
   a. behavior
   b. outlook
   c. haughtiness
   d. height

13. Though the valedictorian was very smart, he was too **egotistic** to have very many friends.
   a. conceited
   b. altruistic
   c. agrarian
   d. unconcerned

14. **Understand** most nearly means
   a. build
   b. fathom
   c. endow
   d. guilt

15. The car was jostled by the rocky **terrain**.
   a. firmament
   b. celestial
   c. arboreal
   d. ground

16. **Mitigate** most nearly means
  a. alleviate
  b. focus
  c. fiery
  d. conspire

17. The king's army was able to easily **encompass** his brother's army, and quickly crushed the rebellion.
  a. retreat
  b. brazen
  c. surround
  d. avoid

18. **Archetype** most nearly means
  a. ancestor
  b. literature
  c. policy
  d. model

19. After sleeping in his car for the past few months, the tiny hotel room seemed like a mansion by **contrast**.
  a. partisan
  b. variation
  c. revive
  d. improve

20. **Irate** most nearly means
  a. amiable
  b. innocent
  c. incensed
  d. tangible

21. Given his rude comments, her reaction seemed **plausible**.
  a. conceivable
  b. skeptical
  c. diurnal
  d. erudite

22. **Discourse** most nearly means
  a. praise
  b. disagreement
  c. speech
  d. path

23. The young boy seemed to be capable of nothing, other than his uncanny ability to **exasperate** his babysitter.
  a. annoy
  b. breathe
  c. disappoint
  d. stifle

24. **Bellicose** most nearly means

a. loud
b. angry
c. pugnacious
d. patriotic

25. Given the horrendous situation, the man's **equanimity** was appalling.

a. justice
b. hostility
c. equine
d. composure

26. **Preemptive** most nearly means

a. beforehand
b. prepare
c. hidden
d. initial

27. The rebels fought in order to **liberate** their brothers from the evil dictator.

a. agitate
b. instigate
c. fracture
d. release

28. **Mediocre** most nearly means

a. excellent
b. average
c. intrusive
d. inspiring

29. The jury was not impressed by the lazy defendant's **moot** argument.

a. factual
b. historical
c. debatable
d. exemplify

30. **Bestow** most nearly means

a. take
b. bequeath
c. energize
d. study

31. The starving man was disheartened when he reached the summit of the hill and realized that only a **barren** wasteland awaited him.

a. fruitful
b. infertile
c. sumptuous
d. lavish

32. **Refurbish** most nearly means
    a. renovate
    b. enlighten
    c. craven
    d. burnish

33. When she saw the crayon drawings on the wall, the mother had no choice but to **chastise** her sons.
    a. honor
    b. locate
    c. choose
    d. rebuke

34. **Sustain** most nearly means
    a. strength
    b. invigorate
    c. embolden
    d. expedite

35. When the boy saw how sincere the girl's apology was, he decided to **acquit** her of her faults.
    a. forgive
    b. stall
    c. acquire
    d. quit

Paragraph Comprehension

<u>Directions:</u> There are 15 questions in this portion of the test. Read each passage and question carefully and select the best answer.

1. When authors do not provide a clear explanation of events, what do readers often have to do instead of reading between the lines?
    a. Question
    b. Connect
    c. Infer
    d. Visualize

Use the passage below for questions 2 through 5:

Caribbean Island Destinations

> Do you want to vacation at a Caribbean island destination? Who wouldn't want a tropical vacation? Visit one of the many Caribbean islands where visitors can swim in crystal blue waters, swim with dolphins, or enjoy family-friendly or adult-only resorts and activities. Every island offers a unique and picturesque vacation destination. Choose from these islands: Aruba, St. Lucia, Barbados, Anguilla, St. John, and so many more. A Caribbean island destination will be the best and most refreshing vacation ever . . . no regrets!

2. What is the topic of the passage?
   a. Caribbean island destinations
   b. Tropical vacation
   c. Resorts
   d. Activities

3. What is/are the supporting detail(s) of this passage?
   a. Cruising to the Caribbean
   b. Local events
   c. Family or adult-only resorts and activities
   d. All of the above

4. Read the following sentence, and answer the question below.

   "A Caribbean island destination will be the best and most refreshing vacation ever ... no regrets!"

What is this sentence an example of?
   a. Fact
   b. Opinion
   c. Device
   d. Fallacy

5. What is the author's purpose of this passage?
   a. Entertain readers
   b. Persuade readers
   c. Inform readers
   d. None of the above

6. Read the following sentence.

   "Cats and dogs are domesticated animals that can learn fun tricks."

In this sentence, the author is using what literary technique regarding the two animals?
   a. Comparing
   b. Contrasting
   c. Describing
   d. Transitioning

7. Which of the following is NOT an example of a fictional text?
   a. Fairy tale
   b. Autobiography
   c. Myth
   d. Fable

8. Read the following passage, and then answer the question below.

   Rain, rain, go away, come again another day. Even though the rain can put a damper on the day, it can be helpful and fun, too. For one, the rain helps plants grow. Without rain, grass, flowers, and trees would be deprived of vital nutrients they need to develop. Not only does the rain help plants grow, on days where there are brief spurts or sunshine, rainbows can appear. The rain reflects and refracts the light, creating beautiful rainbows in the sky. Finally, puddle jumping is another fun activity that can be done in or after the rain. Therefore, the rain can be helpful and fun.

What is the *cause* in this passage?

a. Plants growing
b. Rainbows
c. Puddle jumping
d. Rain

9. In fiction or drama genres, who can express dialogue?

a. Main characters
b. Supporting characters
c. Narrators and characters
d. Supporting characters and narrators

10. Read the following sentence, and answer the question below:

"If I take my socks off, my feet will get cold. But if I put socks on, my feet will get hot."

What is this sentence an example of?

a. False analogy
b. Circular reasoning
c. False dichotomy
d. Slippery slope

Use the passage below for questions 11 and 12:

Lola: The Siberian Husky

Meet Lola . . . Lola is an overly friendly Siberian husky who loves her long walks, digs holes for days, and sheds unbelievably . . . like a typical Siberian husky. Lola has to be brushed and brushed and brushed—did I mention that she has to be brushed . . . all the time! On her long walks, Lola loves making friends with new dogs and kids. A robber could break into our house, and even though they may be intimidated by Lola's wolf-like appearance, the robber would be shocked to learn that Lola would most likely greet them with kisses and a tail wag . . . she makes friends with everyone! Out of all the dogs we've ever owned, Lola is certainly one of a kind in many ways.

11. Based on the passage, what does the author imply?

a. Siberian huskies are great pets but require a lot of time and energy.
b. Siberian huskies are easy to take care of.
c. Siberian huskies should not be around children.
d. Siberian huskies are good guard dogs.

12. Because of their own experience with Siberian huskies, the author of the passage may be described as which of the following?

a. Impartial
b. Hasty
c. Biased
d. Irrational

13. Which of the following is a text that is written by a reliable source and is objective and unbiased?
    a. Narrative
    b. Persuasive
    c. Informative
    d. Credible

14. Read the following passage and answer the question below.

    "Overall, we won the championship game! Max hit a winning home run, and we all cheered as he rounded home plate. Our team hoisted the championship trophy up into the air and celebrated with joy. It was such a great game ... I will never forget this day!"

What is this passage of a story most likely to be?
    a. An outline
    b. A summary
    c. An implication
    d. A forward

15. Choose the correct way to paraphrase the following statement.

    "When renovating a home, there are several ways to save money. In order to keep a project cost effective, "Do It Yourself," otherwise known as "DIY," projects help put money back into the homeowner's pocket. For example, instead of hiring a contractor to do the demo, rent a dumpster and do the demolition. Another way to keep a home renovation cost effective is to compare prices for goods and services. Many contractors or distributors will match prices from competitors. Finally, if renovating a kitchen or bathroom, leave the layout of the plumbing and electrical the same. Once the process of moving pipes and wires is started, dollars start adding up. Overall, home renovations can be a pricey investment, but there are many ways to keep project costs down."

    a. Home improvement projects can be pricey, but there are ways to keep costs down such as "Do It Yourself," or DIY; comparing prices of the materials and workers that will be used; and keeping the original floor plan for plumbing and electrical.
    b. Home renovations require a lot of work. Relocating plumbing and electrical wiring can be hazardous, which is why a contractor should be hired to complete the job.
    c. "Do It Yourself," otherwise known as DIY, projects are the most time- and cost-efficient way to complete home renovations. It is not necessary for homeowners to compare prices of contractors because they are their own best bet.
    d. Many contractors and distributors price-match competitors' pricing for goods and services. Home improvement companies often carry the same types of product, like flooring, plumbing, or lighting. So, if completing a home renovation, it is best for homeowners to shop around for exactly what they want.

Math Knowledge

1. $\frac{14}{15} + \frac{3}{5} - \frac{1}{30} =$

   a. $\frac{19}{15}$

   b. $\frac{43}{30}$

   c. $\frac{4}{3}$

   d. $\frac{3}{2}$

2. Solve for *x* and *y*, given $3x + 2y = 8, -x + 3y = 1$.

   a. $x = 2, y = 1$
   b. $x = 1, y = 2$
   c. $x = -1, y = 6$
   d. $x = 3, y = 1$

3. $\frac{1}{2}\sqrt{16} =$

   a. 0
   b. 1
   c. 2
   d. 4

4. The factors of $2x^2 - 8$ are:

   a. $2(x - 2)(x - 2)$
   b. $2(x^2 + 4)$
   c. $2(x + 2)(x + 2)$
   d. $2(x + 2)(x - 2)$

5. Two of the interior angles of a triangle are 35° and 70°. What is the measure of the last interior angle?

   a. 60°
   b. 75°
   c. 90°
   d. 100°

6. A square field has an area of 400 square feet. What is its perimeter?

   a. 100 feet
   b. 80 feet
   c. $40\sqrt{2}$ feet
   d. 40 feet

7. $\frac{5}{3} \times \frac{7}{6} =$

a. $\frac{35}{18}$

b. $\frac{18}{3}$

c. $\frac{45}{31}$

d. $\frac{17}{6}$

8. One apple costs \$2. One papaya costs \$3. If Samantha spends \$35 and gets 15 pieces of fruit, how many papayas did she buy?

a. 3
b. 4
c. 5
d. 6

9. If $x^2 - 6 = 30$, then one possible value for *x* is:

a. -6
b. -4
c. 3
d. 5

10. A cube has a side length of 6 inches. What is its volume?

a. 6 cubic inches
b. 36 cubic inches
c. 144 cubic inches
d. 216 cubic inches

11. A square has a side length of 4 inches. A triangle has a base of 2 inches and a height of 8 inches. What is the total area of the square and triangle?

a. 24 square inches
b. 28 square inches
c. 32 square inches
d. 36 square inches

12. $-\frac{1}{3}\sqrt{81} =$

a. -9
b. -3
c. 0
d. 3

13. Simplify $(2x - 3)(4x + 2)$

a. $8x^2 - 8x - 6$
b. $6x^2 + 8x - 5$
c. $-4x^2 - 8x - 1$
d. $4x^2 - 4x - 6$

14. $\frac{11}{6} - \frac{3}{8} =$

a. $\frac{5}{4}$

b. $\frac{51}{36}$

c. $\frac{35}{24}$

d. $\frac{3}{2}$

15. A triangle is to have a base 1/3 as long as its height. Its area must be 6 square feet. How long will its base be?

a. 1 foot
b. 1.5 feet
c. 2 feet
d. 2.5 feet

16. What are the zeros of the following function: $f(x) = x^3 + 4x^2 + 4x$?

a. -2
b. 0, -2
c. 2
d. 0, 2

17. What is the simplified quotient of $\frac{5x^3}{3x^2y} \div \frac{25}{3y^9}$?

a. $\frac{125x}{9y^{10}}$

b. $\frac{x}{5y^8}$

c. $\frac{5}{xy^8}$

d. $\frac{xy^8}{5}$

18. What is the solution for the following equation?

$$\frac{x^2 + x - 30}{x - 5} = 11$$

a. $x = -6$
b. There is no solution.
c. $x = 16$
d. $x = 5$

19. What is the inverse of the function $f(x) = 3x - 5$?

a. $f^{-1}(x) = \frac{x}{3} + 5$

b. $f^{-1}(x) = \frac{5x}{3}$

c. $f^{-1}(x) = 3x + 5$

d. $f^{-1}(x) = \frac{x+5}{3}$

20. Which equation is not a function?

a. $y = |x|$
b. $y = \sqrt{x}$
c. $x = 3$
d. $y = 4$

21. For the following similar triangles, what are the values of x and y (rounded to one decimal place)?

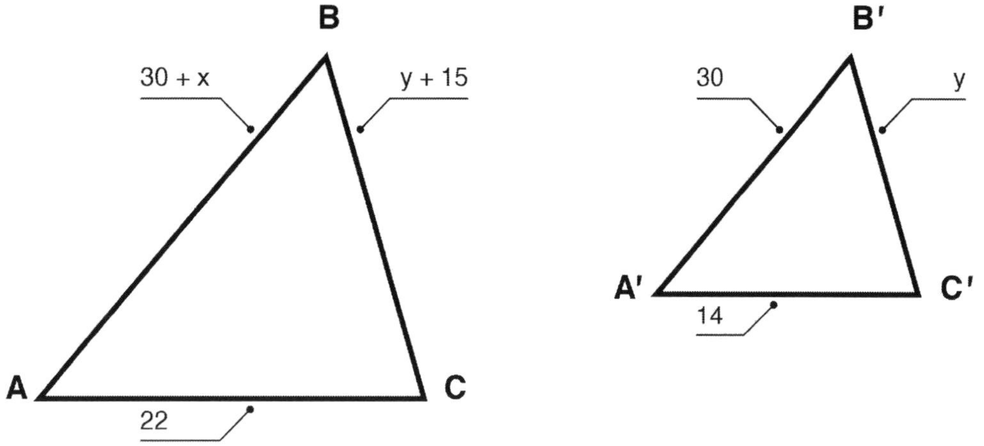

a. $x = 16.5, y = 25.1$
b. $x = 19.5, y = 24.1$
c. $x = 17.1, y = 26.3$
d. $x = 26.3, y = 17.1$

22. Which of the following correctly arranges the following numbers from the least to greatest value?

$$0.85, \frac{4}{5}, \frac{2}{3}, \frac{91}{100}$$

a. $0.85, \frac{4}{5}, \frac{2}{3}, \frac{91}{100}$

b. $\frac{4}{5}, 0.85, \frac{91}{100}, \frac{2}{3}$

c. $\frac{2}{3}, \frac{4}{5}, 0.85, \frac{91}{100}$

d. $0.85, \frac{91}{100}, \frac{4}{5}, \frac{2}{3}$

23. Simplify the following expression: $(3x + 5)(x - 8)$

a. $3x^2 - 19x - 40$
b. $4x - 19x - 13$
c. $3x^2 - 19x + 40$
d. $3x^2 + 5x - 3$

24. Simplify the following fraction:

$$\frac{\frac{5}{7}}{\frac{9}{11}}$$

a. $\frac{55}{63}$
b. $\frac{7}{1000}$
c. $\frac{13}{15}$
d. $\frac{5}{11}$

25. What is $\frac{420}{98}$ rounded to the nearest integer?

a. 3
b. 4
c. 5
d. 6

Electronics

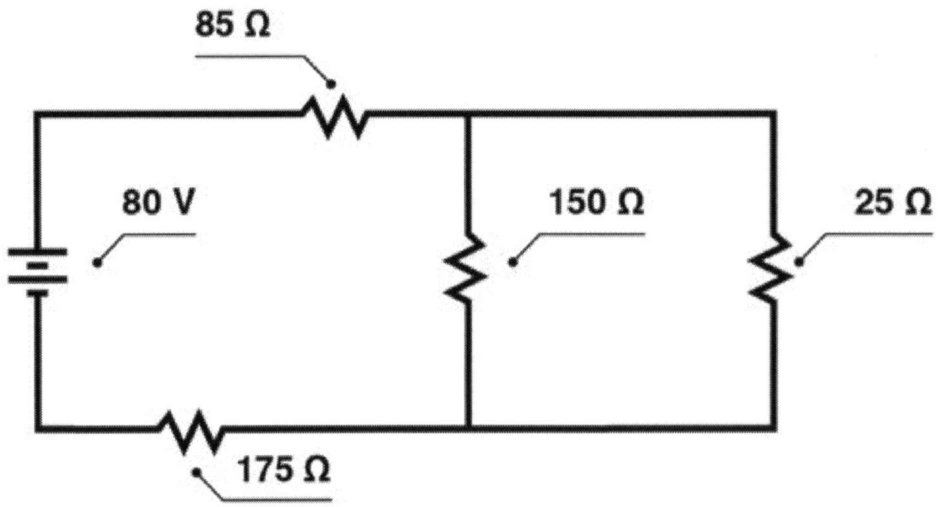

1. What is the total resistance in the circuit above?

a. 85 ohms
b. 435 ohms
c. 278.75 ohms
d. 260 ohms

2. What is the total current leaving the battery?
   a. 22,300 Amps
   b. 0.29 Amps
   c. 80 volts
   d. 80 Amps

3. What is the voltage lost at the 25-ohm resistor?
   a. 0.22 amps
   b. 0 amps
   c. 7.25 amps
   d. 5.4 volts

4. A 150-watt waffle iron is plugged into a 200-volt circuit at a diner. The waffle maker operates for 240 minutes. If the cost of energy is $.10 per kilowatt-hour, how much does it cost to use the waffle maker for the 240 minutes?
   a. $60
   b. $3.60
   c. $6.00
   d. $.60

5. The energy from electricity results from which of the following?
   a. The atomic structure of matter
   b. The ability to do work
   c. The neutrons in an atom
   d. Conductive materials like metals

6. Which of the following correctly lists the subatomic particles in an atom?
   a. Protons carry no charge in the nucleus, neutrons carry a negative charge in the nucleus, and electrons surround the nucleus in a cloud and carry a positive charge.
   b. Protons carry a positive charge in the nucleus, neutrons have no charge in the nucleus, and electrons have a negative charge and are found in a cloud surrounding the nucleus.
   c. Protons carry a positive charge in the nucleus, electrons have a negative charge in the nucleus, and neutrons have a negative charge and surround the nucleus in a cloud.
   d. Protons carry a positive charge, and they surround the nucleus in a cloud. The nucleus contains negatively charged electrons and neutrons, which carry no charge.

7. What property of metals lends them to be conductive materials?
   a. The protons in the outer shells are free to drift between atoms.
   b. The electrons in the outer shells are free to drift between atoms.
   c. The electrons in the outer shell are pulled in tightly by the nucleus so they do not drift away to surrounding atoms.
   d. The neutrons in the outer shell are pulled in tightly by the nucleus so they do not drift away to surrounding atoms.

8. Which of the following best describes the function of and symbol for a diode?

a. It is a type of variable resistor that controls voltage, and it is represented as: 

b. It is a type of variable resistor that controls voltage, and it is represented as: 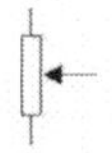

c. It ensures that current flows one way only, and it is represented as: 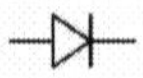

d. It ensures that current flows one way only, and it is represented as: 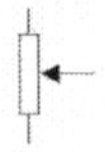

9. In the following circuit, what is the total resistance across the two terminals (A and B)?

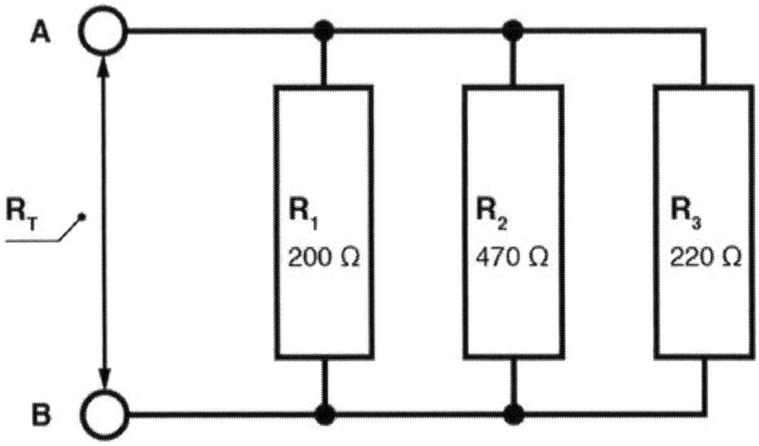

a. 85.67 ohms
b. 790 ohms
c. 0.0117 ohms
d. 200 ohms

10. Which of the following statements is true?
a. Conductors have high resistance because the electrons are easily detached from the atoms.
b. Conductors have high resistance because the electrons are not easily detached from the atoms.
c. Conductors have low resistance because the electrons are easily detached from the atoms.
d. Conductors have low resistance because the electrons are not easily detached from the atoms.

11. Which of the following statements are true regarding insulators?
a. Insulators provide more resistance than conductors; copper is a good insulator.
b. Insulators provide less resistance than conductors; copper is a good insulator.
c. Insulators provide more resistance than conductors; plastic is a good insulator.
d. Insulators provide less resistance than conductors; plastic is a good insulator.

12. Which of the following equations is not an accurate representation of Ohm's Law?
    a. $V = I \times R$
    b. $R = \frac{V}{I}$
    c. $I = \frac{V}{R}$
    d. $V = \frac{R}{I}$

13. Electric power can be measured in which of the following units?
    a. Volts
    b. Amperes
    c. Ohms
    d. Watts

14. How much energy is needed to run a 6000-watt air conditioner for 3 hours?
    a. 18 kilowatts
    b. 18 kilowatt-hours
    c. 18,000 kilowatt-hours
    d. 18,000 kilowatts

15. Which of the following is true regarding series circuits?
    a. The voltage drops across each resistor, but the current is the same in all of them.
    b. The voltage is the same across each resistor, but the current drops after each of them.
    c. The voltage drops across each resistor, and the current drops in each of them.
    d. The voltage and current are the same across each of them in the series.

16. Which of the following statements about parallel circuits is FALSE?
    a. If the resistance is different in each load, more current passes through the load with the lower resistance.
    b. If the resistance is different in each load, more current passes through the one with higher resistance.
    c. If the resistance is the same in both loads, then the same amount of current passes through each one.
    d. The voltage is the same across each resistor.

17. Which of the following is not a correct formula to determine electric power in watts?
    a. $W = V \times I$
    b. $W = I^2 \times R$
    c. $W = V^2/R$
    d. $W = I^2 \times V$

18. Which of the following statements about circuits is NOT true?
    a. The wiring on land-based, heavy machinery uses DC electricity.
    b. The voltage source for DC circuits has a constant value.
    c. AC electricity can be transmitted over long distances with much less loss of power than DC electricity.
    d. In the United States, AC electricity is generated at a frequency of 60 cycles per second with 120- or 240-volt service.

19. All EXCEPT which of the following statements are true regarding capacitors?
    a. It is a set of parallel plates separated by a non-conducting material.
    b. They don't stop ACs, but they do stop DCs.
    c. The electric charges built up on either side of the capacitor resist change equal to the voltage of the power source.
    d. The coils in the electric motors of AC equipment are examples of capacitors.

20. If a circuit has a 9-volt battery and a 3-ohm resistor, what is the power output of the battery?
    a. 27 watts
    b. 243 watts
    c. 81 watts
    d. 6 watts

Auto and Shop

1. What takes place during the upstroke of an engine's piston?
    a. Gas is cooled so the engine can achieve power.
    b. Coolant is injected so the engine doesn't overheat.
    c. Gas is compressed and exploded with a sparkplug.
    d. Oil is filtered around the exhaust.

2. What component generates electricity while the engine is on?
    a. Headlights
    b. Solenoid
    c. Coil
    d. Alternator

3. If a puddle of liquid is observed under a vehicle, what is the correct action?
    a. Mark the day on the calendar when the car should be serviced.
    b. Identify the liquid under the car and act accordingly.
    c. Taste the liquid. If the liquid tastes like oil, the oil pan needs replacing.
    d. Water from the air conditioner drains the coolant, indicating the radiator needs filling.

4. What component is the first in line from the engine in a vehicle's exhaust system?
    a. Muffler
    b. Exhaust Manifold
    c. Catalytic Converter
    d. Tailpipe

5. What are the most common types of brakes in a car?
    a. Disc brakes and drum brakes
    b. Air brakes and electric brakes
    c. Reverse brakes and forward brakes
    d. Induction brakes and engine brakes

6. Which suspension system component enables the rear wheels to move independently from each other?
   a. An axle
   b. A universal joint
   c. A damper
   d. A ball joint

7. Regarding a combustion engine, where is the oil pump usually located?
   a. In the oil pan
   b. Above the engine
   c. Next to the gas tank
   d. In the valve cover

8. Transmission fluid is typically what color?
   a. Green
   b. Purple
   c. Brown
   d. Black

9. Which vehicle component often needs to be replaced on a regular basis?
   a. Rack and pinions
   b. Brake pads
   c. Emergency brakes
   d. Window seals

10. A master cylinder is an important component in which vehicular system?
   a. Electrical
   b. Transmission
   c. Engine
   d. Brake

11. Which of the following liquid leaks needs to be stopped immediately?
   a. A clear liquid underneath the engine bay
   b. A purple liquid underneath the transmission
   c. A clear liquid coming out of the exhaust pipe
   d. None of the above

12. Which of the following is responsible for transferring power from the drive shaft to the axle?
   a. The differential
   b. The master cylinder
   c. The steering column
   d. The accelerator

13. How does the turning or pressing of a car's ignition key start the car?
   a. It provides the initial spark that the motor uses to create ignition.
   b. It opens up the fuel tank, allowing for the fuel delivery necessary for combustion.
   c. It completes the electrical connection needed to send the battery's electrical current to the ignition motor, which starts the motor.
   d. It turns on the battery, allowing for electric current to start the vehicle.

14. What are channel lock pliers?
    a. A fixed set of pliers that can tune the channel of a car's radio
    b. A funnel that channels oil into the engine of a car
    c. A type of adjustable pliers that have a right-angle positioned jaw
    d. A straight jaw pliers that are used to unlock car doors

15. When building a roof for a house, which procedure is the correct construction practice?
    a. Lay tar paper over the bare plywood
    b. Create space between the shingles so water flows into the side ducts
    c. Place bricks under each shingle for extra support
    d. Use short nails through the shingles to prevent damage

16. Which important part of a window frame must conform to building code?
    a. The sill
    b. The trimmer
    c. The stud
    d. The header

17. If a mechanic must cut off a car's exhaust tailpipe, what tool should the mechanic choose?
    a. A lathe
    b. A chop saw
    c. A Sawzall™
    d. An axe

18. What is the most important construction feature when building a brick wall?
    a. The bricks in the wall must be spaced evenly.
    b. The wall must have a deep four-foot foundation.
    c. The wall must be straight up and down and level.
    d. The wall must not have excess concrete.

19. What type of screw has a cross-slotted head?
    a. Allen
    b. Single slot
    c. Hexagonal
    d. Phillips

20. Which of the following is used as reinforcement in concrete?
    a. Lag bolts
    b. Rebar
    c. 2" × 4" boards
    d. Galvanized pipe

21. What is the purpose of a lathe?
    a. To grind down rough surfaces
    b. To drive long screws into wood
    c. To shave or shape a material such as wood or metal
    d. To bend metal to form the needed angle

22. Which of the following is necessary when welding?
   a. Air ventilation
   b. A hard hat
   c. Insulated clothing
   d. Safety glasses

23. How are shingles added to a roof?
   a. From left to right
   b. From right to left
   c. From bottom to top
   d. From top to bottom

24. Which of the following is used in brick laying?
   a. Cement
   b. Trommel
   c. Plaster
   d. Trowel

25. Which of the following is a feature of MIG welding?
   a. Use of a tungsten electrode
   b. Use of a continuously feeding wire
   c. Used on thinner gauge materials
   d. Used in an air-tight room

Mechanical Comprehension

1. A car is traveling at a constant velocity of 25 m/s. How long does it take the car to travel 45 kilometers in a straight line?
   a. 1 hour
   b. 3600 seconds
   c. 1800 seconds
   d. 900 seconds

2. A ship is traveling due east at a speed of 1 m/s against a current flowing due west at a speed of 0.5 m/s. How far has the ship travelled from its point of departure after two hours?
   a. 1.8 kilometers west of its point of departure
   b. 3.6 kilometers west of its point of departure
   c. 1.8 kilometers east of its point of departure
   d. 3.6 kilometers east of its point of departure

3. A car is driving along a straight stretch of highway at a constant speed of 60 km/hour when the driver slams the gas pedal to the floor, reaching a speed of 132 km/hour in 10 seconds. What's the average acceleration of the car after the engine is floored?
   a. 1 m/s^2
   b. 2 m/s^2
   c. 3 m/s^2
   d. 4 m/s^2

4. A spaceship with a mass of 100,000 kilograms is far away from any planet. To accelerate the craft at the rate of 0.5 m/sec^2, what is the rocket thrust?

a. 98.1 N
b. 25,000 N
c. 50,000 N
d. 75,000 N

5. The gravitational acceleration on Earth averages 9.81 m/s^2. An astronaut weighs 1962 N on Earth. The diameter of Earth is six times the diameter of its moon. What's the mass of the astronaut on Earth's moon?

a. 100 kilograms
b. 200 kilograms
c. 300 kilograms
d. 400 kilograms

6. A football is kicked so that it leaves the punter's toe at a horizontal angle of 45 degrees. Ignoring any spin or tumbling, at what point is the upward vertical velocity of the football at a maximum?

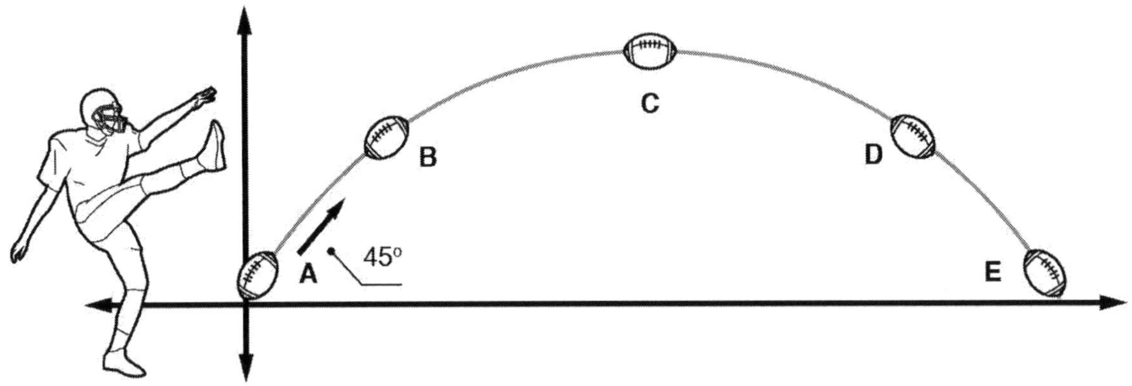

a. At Point A
b. At Point C
c. At Points B and D
d. At Points A and E

7. The skater is shown spinning in Figure (a), then bringing in her arms in Figure (b). Which sequence accurately describes what happens to her angular velocity?

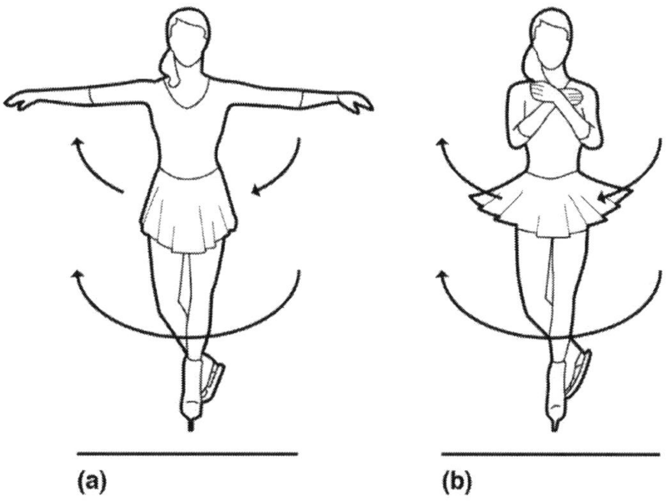

a. Her angular velocity decreases from (a) to (b)
b. Her angular velocity doesn't change from (a) to (b)
c. Her angular velocity increases from (a) to (b)
d. It's not possible to determine what happens to her angular velocity if her weight is unknown.

8. A cannonball is dropped from a height of 10 meters above sea level. What is its approximate velocity just before it hits the ground?

a. 9.81 m/s
b. 14 m/s
c. 32 m/s
d. It can't be determined without knowing the cannonball's mass

9. The pendulum is held at point A, and then released to swing to the right. At what point does the pendulum have the greatest kinetic energy?

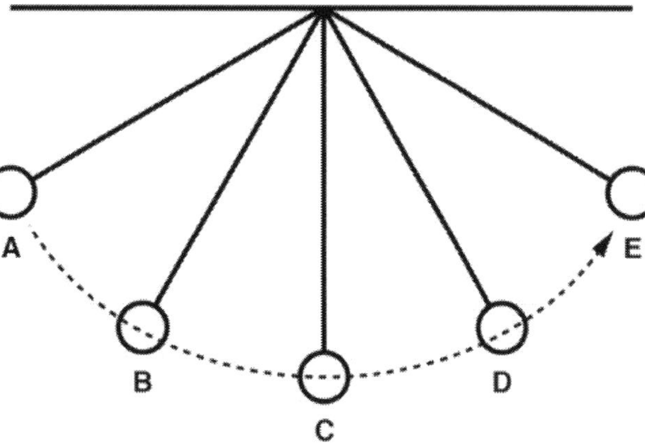

a. At Point B
b. At Point C
c. At Point D
d. At Point E

10. Which statement is true of the total energy of the pendulum?

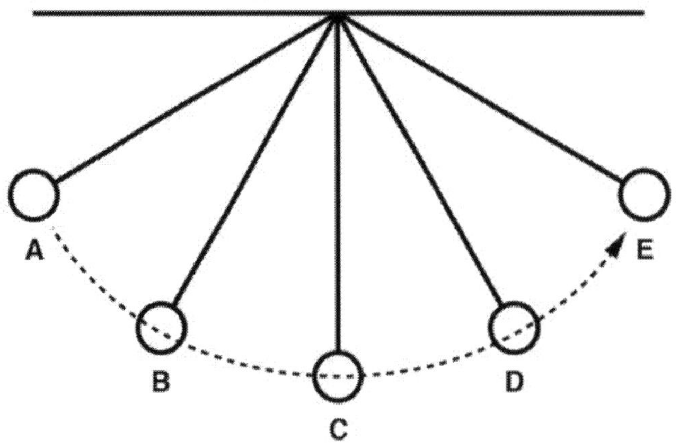

a. Its total energy is at a maximum and equal at Points A and E.
b. Its total energy is at a maximum at Point C.
c. Its total energy is the same at Points A, B, C, D, and E.
d. The total energy can't be determined without knowing the pendulum's mass.

11. How do you calculate the useful work performed in lifting a 10-kilogram weight from the ground to the top of a 2-meter ladder?

a. 10kg x 2m x 32 m/s^2
b. 10kg x $2m^2$ x 9.81 m/s
c. 10kg x 2m x $9.81m/s^2$
d. It can't be determined without knowing the ground elevation

12. A steel spring is loaded with a 10-newton weight and is stretched by 0.5 centimeters. What is the deflection if it's loaded with two 10-newton weights?

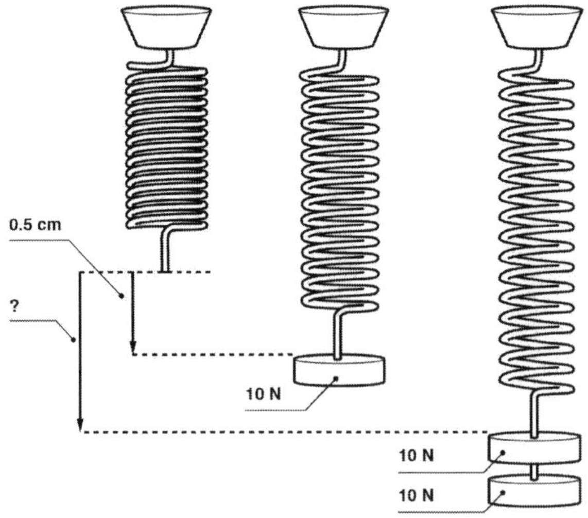

a. 0.5 centimeter
b. 1 centimeter
c. 2 centimeters
d. It can't be determined without knowing the Modulus of Elasticity of the steel.

13. A 1000-kilogram concrete block is resting on a wooden surface. Between these two materials, the coefficient of sliding friction is 0.4 and the coefficient of static friction is 0.5. How much more force is needed to get the block moving than to keep it moving?

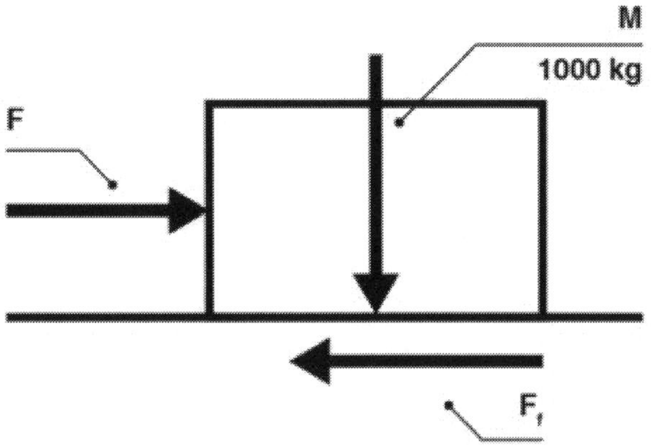

a. 981 N
b. 1962 N
c. 3924 N
d. 9810 N

14. The master cylinder (F1) of a hydraulic jack has a cross-sectional area of 0.1 m^2, and a force of 50 N is applied. What must the area of the drive cylinder (F2) be to support a weight of 800 N?

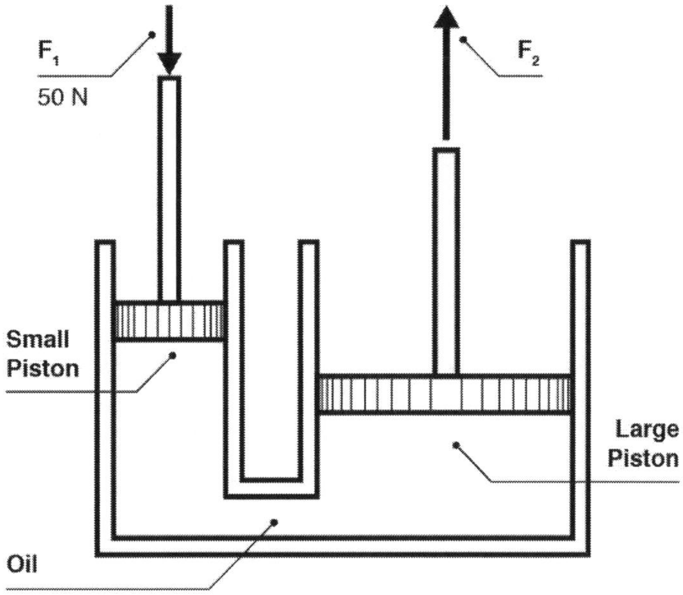

a. 0.4 m^2
b. 0.8 m^2
c. 1.6 m^2
d. 3.2 m^2

15. A gas with a volume V_1 is held down by a piston with a force of F newtons. The piston has an area of A. After heating the gas, it expands against the weight to a volume V_2. What was the work done?

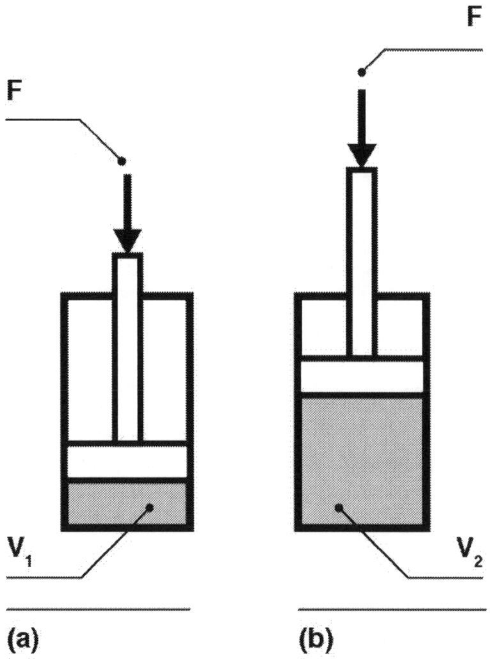

a. F/A
b. $(F/A) \times V_1$
c. $(F/A) \times V_2$
d. $(F/A) \times (V_2 - V_1)$

16. A 1000-kilogram weight is raised 30 meters in 10 minutes. What is the approximate power expended in the period?

a. 1000 Kg × m/s^2
b. 500 N·m
c. 500 J/s
d. 100 watts

17. A 2-meter high, concrete block is submerged in a body of water 12 meters deep (as shown). Assuming that the water has a unit weight of 1000 N/m^3, what is the pressure acting on the upper surface of the block?

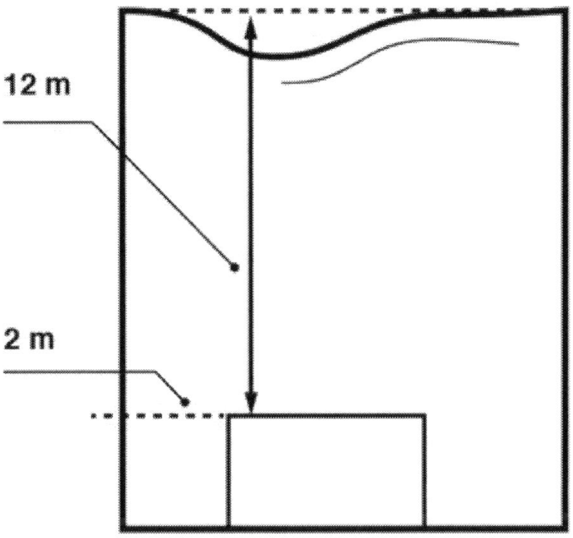

a. 10,000 Pa
b. 12,000 Pa
c. 14,000 Pa
d. It can't be calculated without knowing the top area of the block.

18. Closed Basins A and B each contain a 10,000-ton block of ice. The ice block in Basin A is floating in sea water. The ice block in Basin B is aground on a rock ledge (as shown). When all the ice melts, what happens to the water level in Basin A and Basin B?

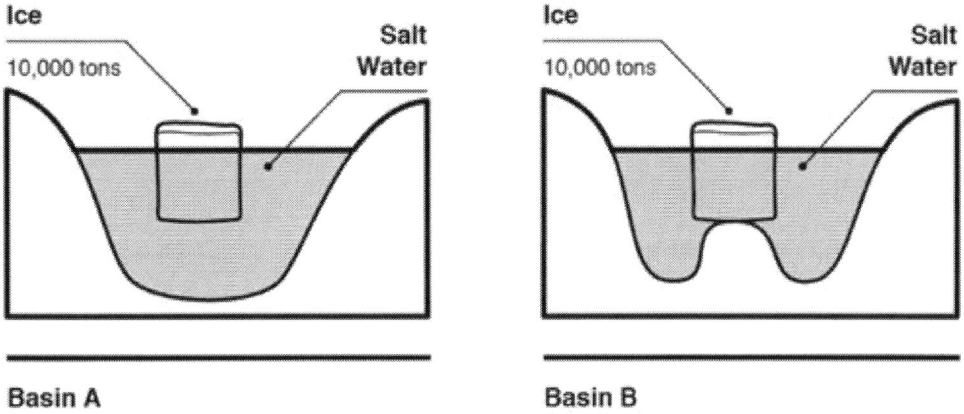

a. Water level rises in A but not in B
b. Water level rises in B but not in A
c. Water level rises in neither A nor B
d. Water level rises in both A and B

19. An official 10-lane Olympic pool is 50 meters wide by 25 meters long. How long does it take to fill the pool to the recommended depth of 3 meters using a pump with a 750 liter per second capacity?

a. 2500 seconds
b. 5000 seconds
c. 10,000 seconds
d. 100,000 seconds

20. Water is flowing in a rectangular canal 10 meters wide by 2 meters deep at a velocity of 3 m/s. The canal is half full. What is the flow rate?

a. 30 m^3/s
b. 60 m^3/s
c. 90 m^3/s
d. 120 m^3/s

21. A 150-kilogram mass is placed on the left side of the lever as shown. What force must be exerted on the right side (in the location shown by the arrow) to balance the weight of this mass?

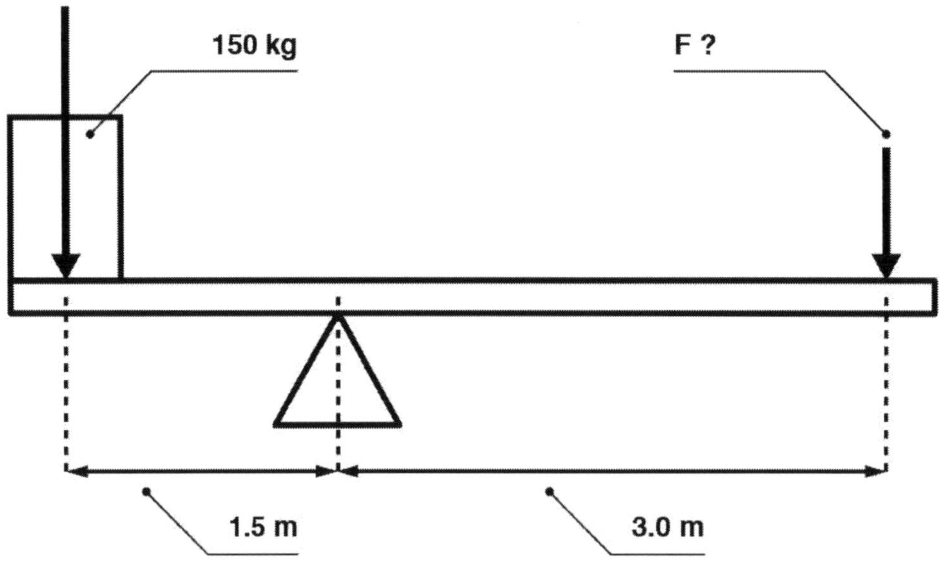

a. 675 kg.m
b. 737.75 N
c. 1471.5 N
d. 2207.25 N·m

22. For the wheel and axle assembly shown, the shaft radius is 20 millimeters and the wheel radius is 300 millimeters. What's the required effort to lift a 600 N load?

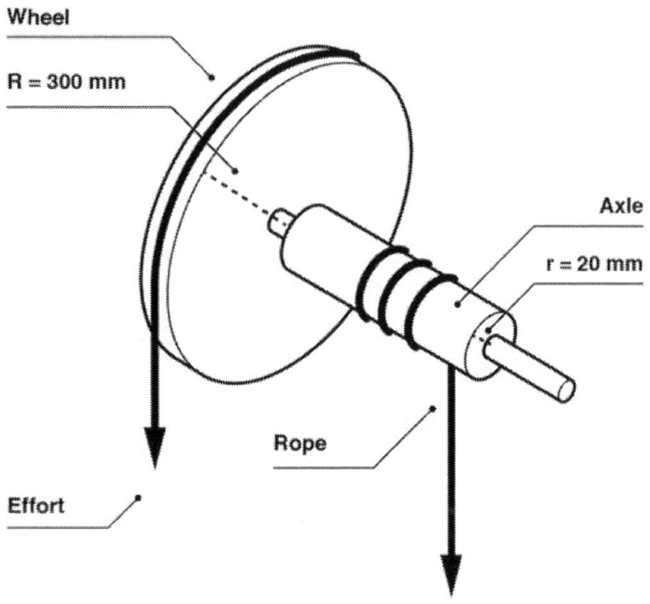

a. 10 N
b. 20 N
c. 30 N
d. 40 N

23. The driver gear (Gear A) turns clockwise at a rate of 60 RPM. In what direction does Gear B turn and at what rotational speed?

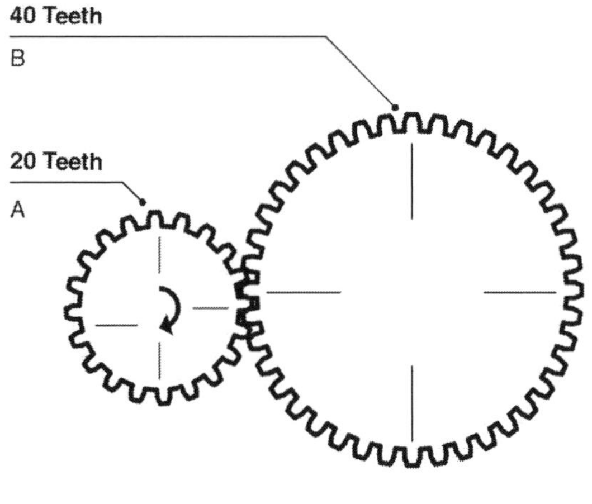

a. Clockwise at 120 RPM
b. Counterclockwise at 120 RPM
c. Clockwise at 30 RPM
d. Counterclockwise at 30 RPM

24. The three steel wheels shown are connected by rubber belts. The two wheels at the top have the same diameter, while the wheel below is twice their diameter. If the driver wheel at the upper left is turning clockwise at 60 RPM, at what speed and in which direction is the large bottom wheel turning?

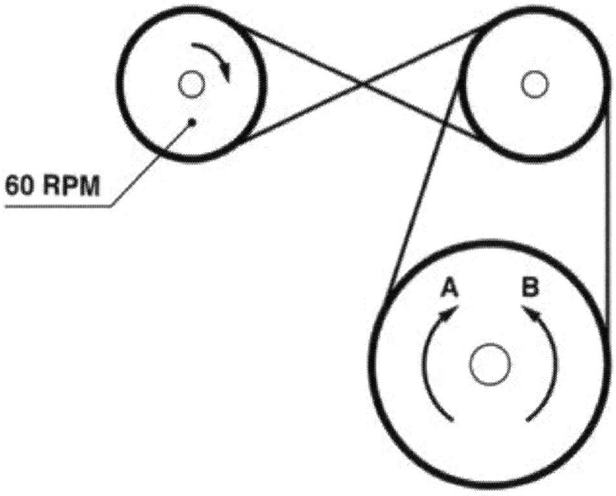

a. 30 RPM, clockwise (A)
b. 30 RPM, counterclockwise (B)
c. 120 RPM, clockwise (A)
d. 120 RPM, counterclockwise (B)

25. In case (a), both blocks are fixed. In case (b), the load is hung from a moveable block. Ignoring friction, what is the required force to move the blocks in both cases?

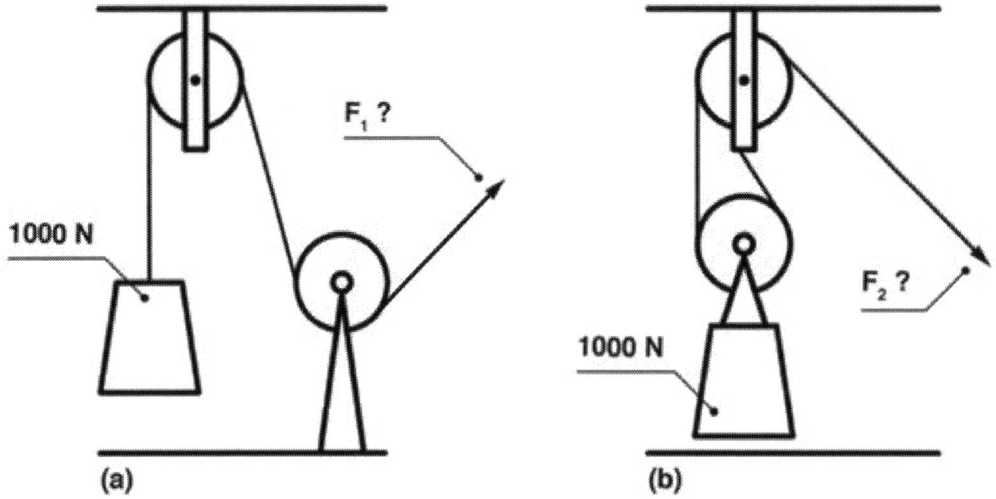

a. F_1 = 500 N; F_2 = 500 N
b. F_1 = 500 N; F_2 = 1000 N
c. F_1 = 1000 N; F_2 = 500 N
d. F_1 = 1000 N; F_2 = 1000 N

Assembling Objects

Section 1: For questions 1–12 below, which figure best shows how the objects in the left box will appear if they are fit together?

1.

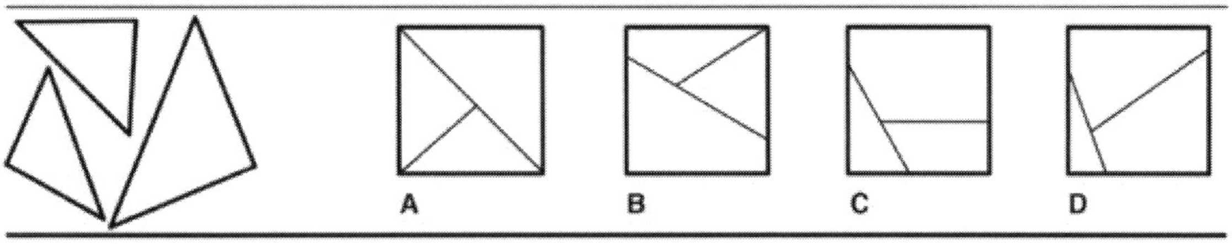

2.

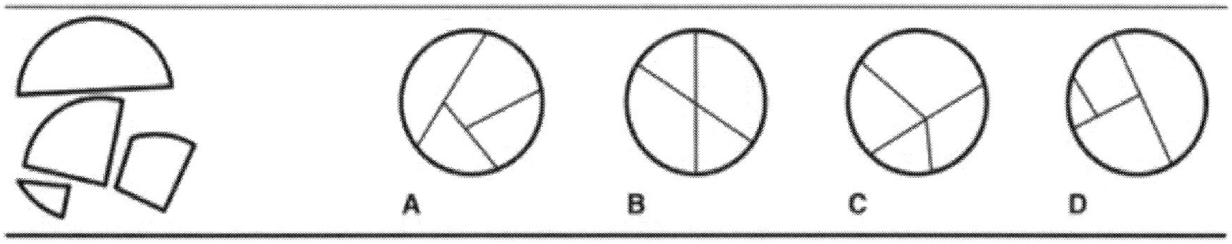

3.

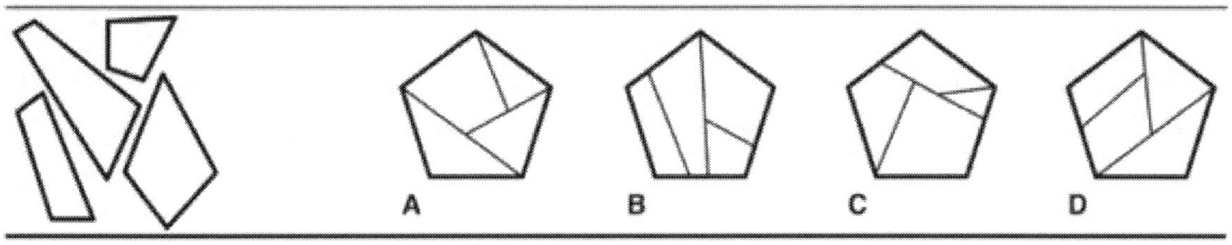

4.

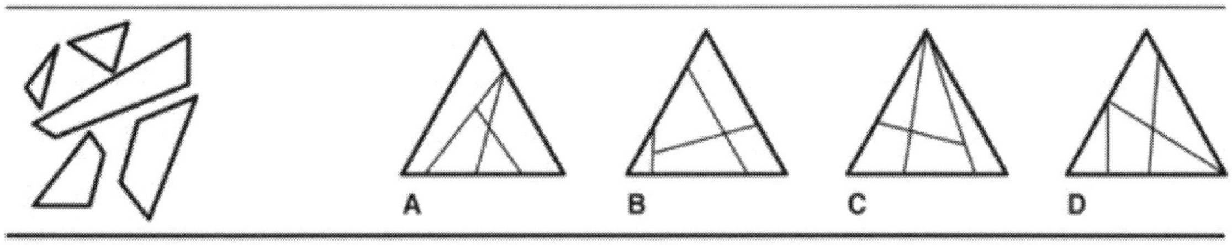

5.

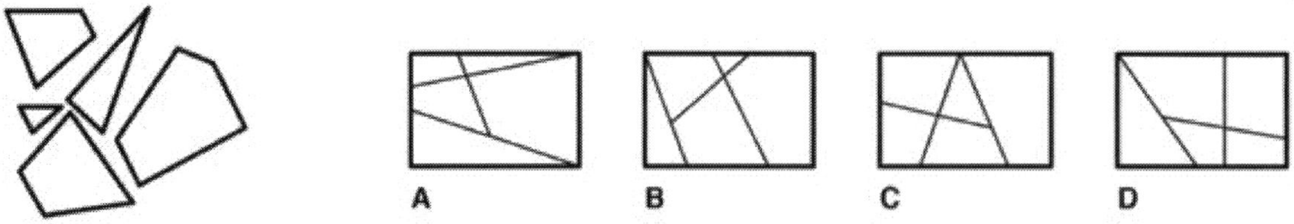

6.

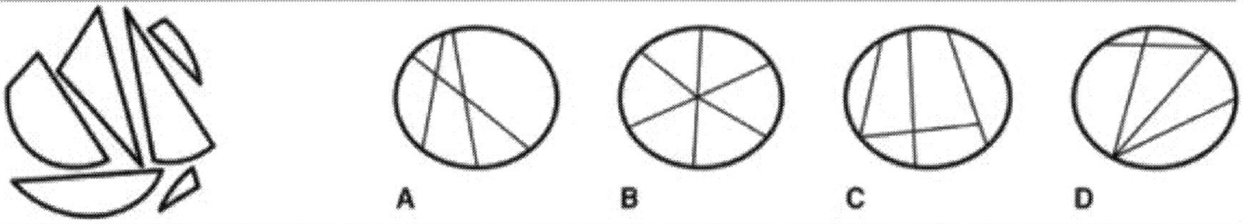

7.

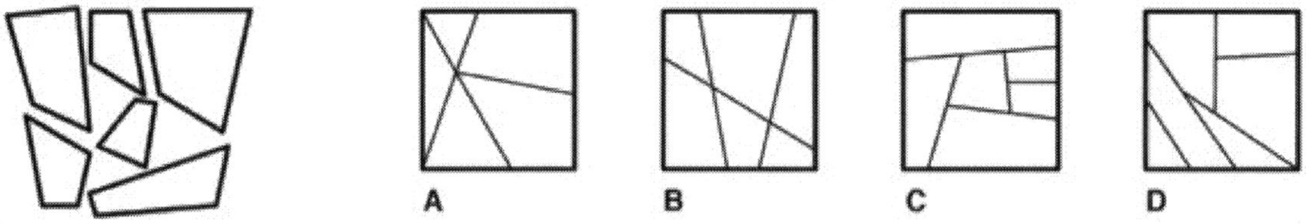

8.

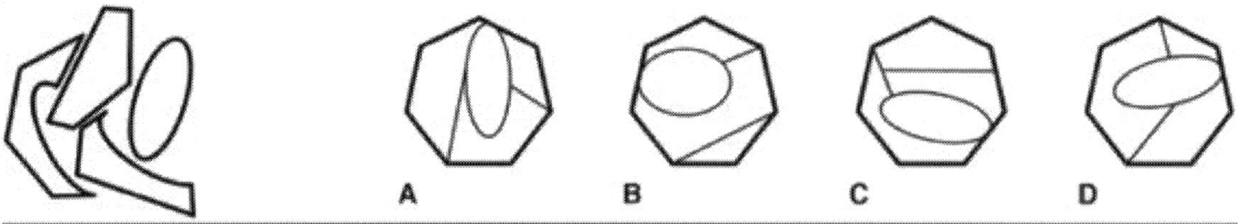

9.

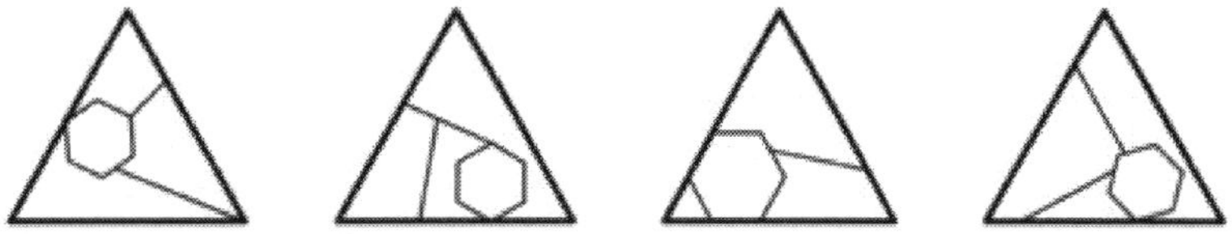

A B C D

10.

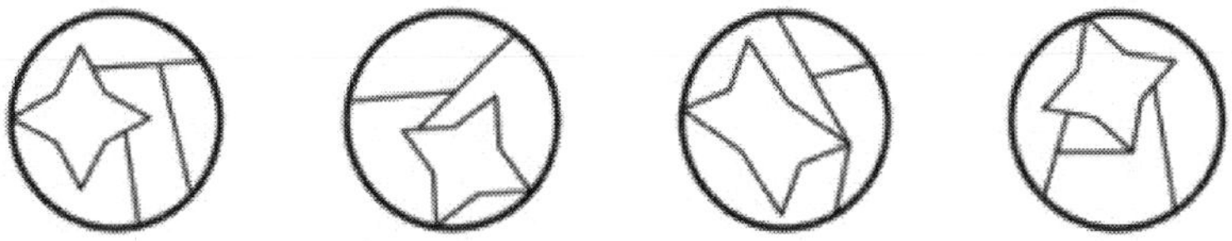

A B C D

11.

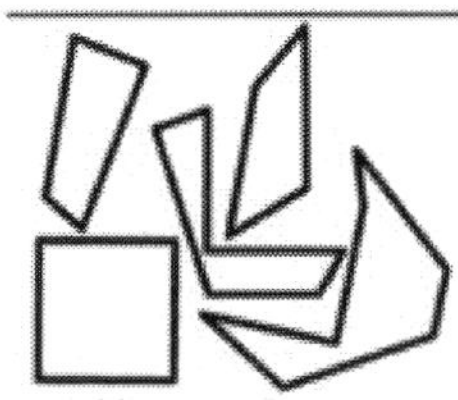

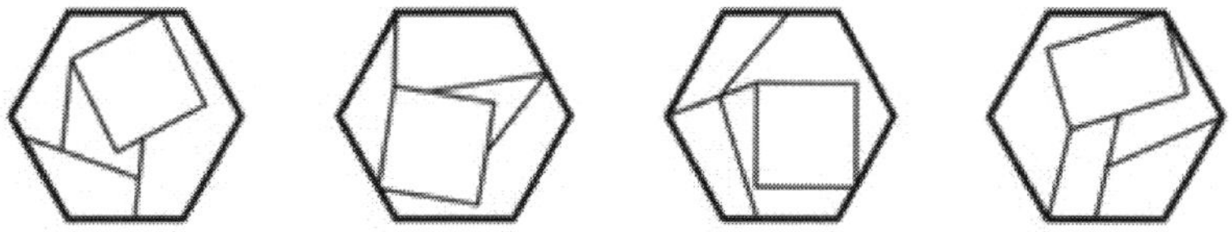

A B C D

12.

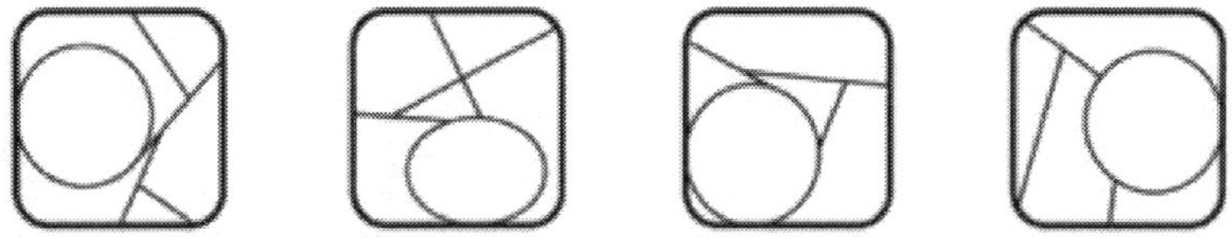

A B C D

Section 2: For questions 1–13 below, which figure best shows how the objects in the left box will touch if the letters for each object are matched?

1.

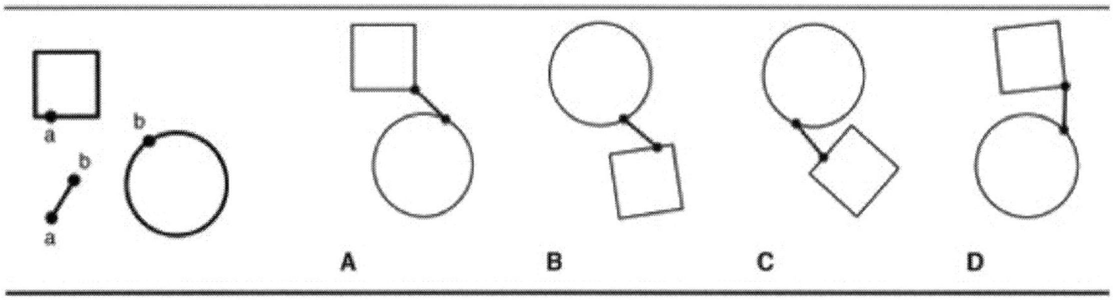

2.

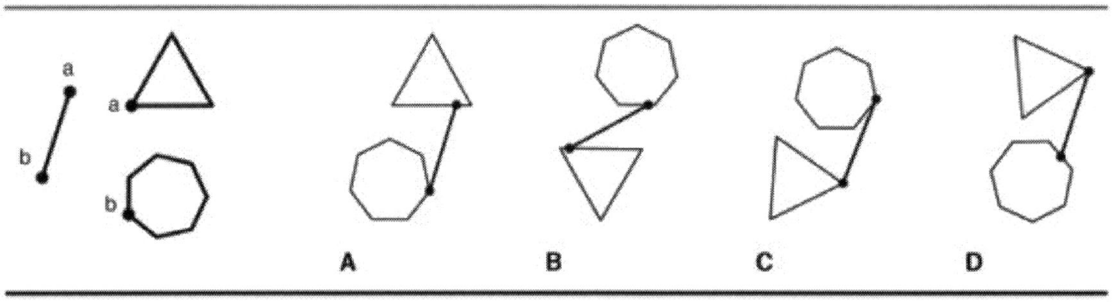

3.

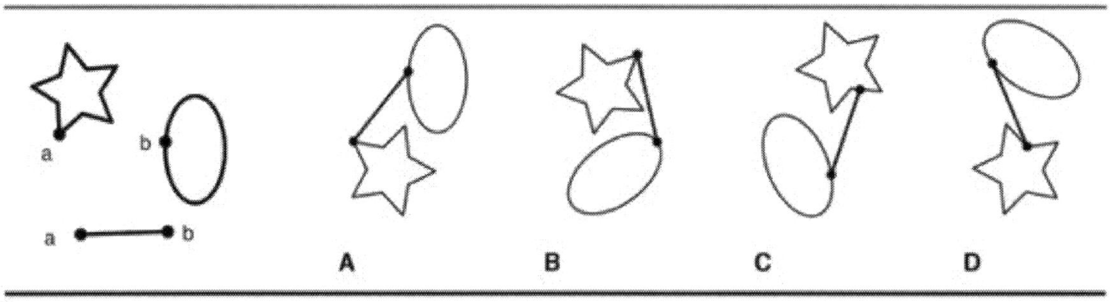

4.

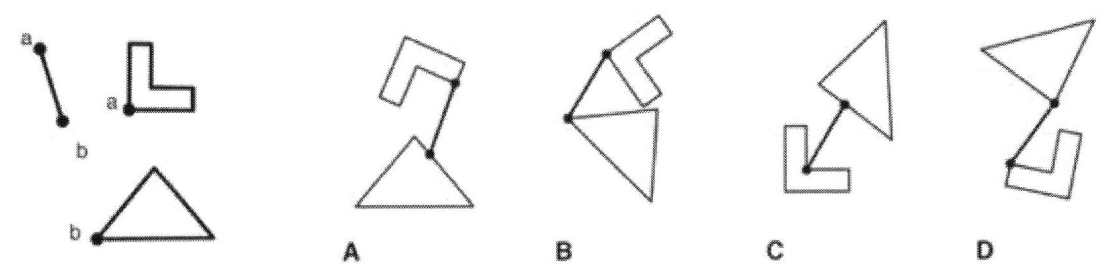

5.

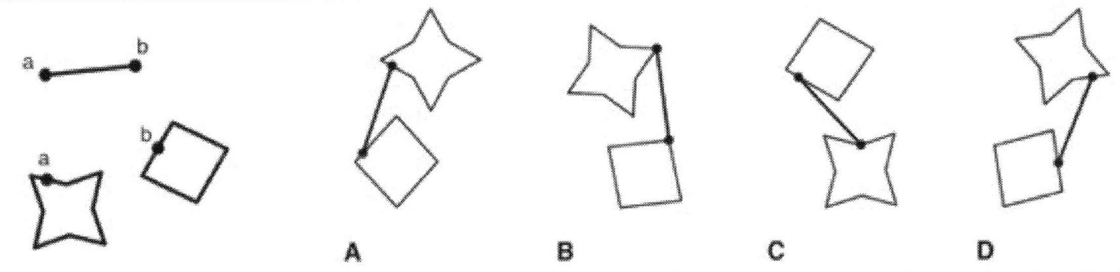

6.

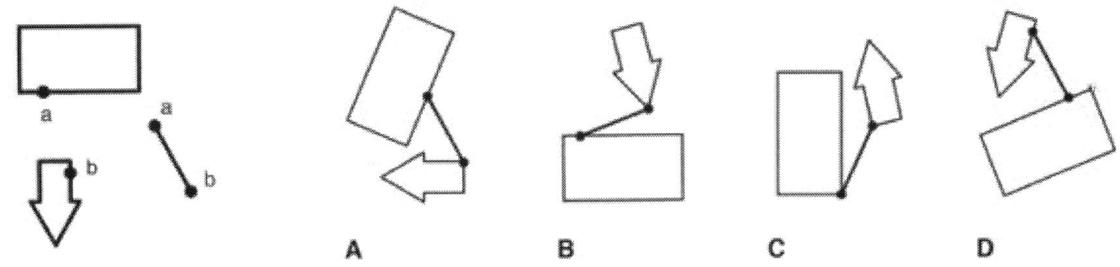

7.

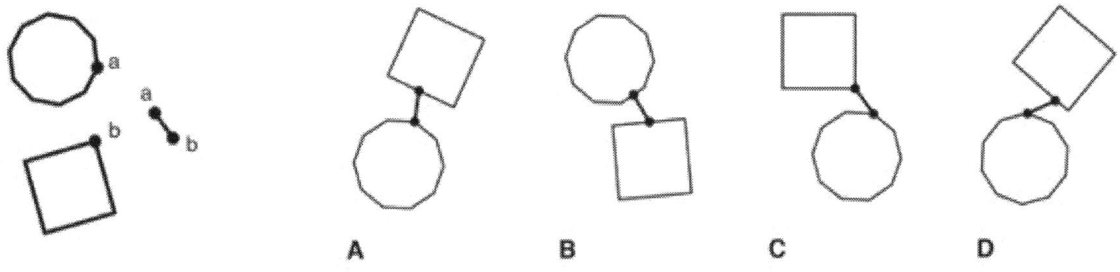

8.

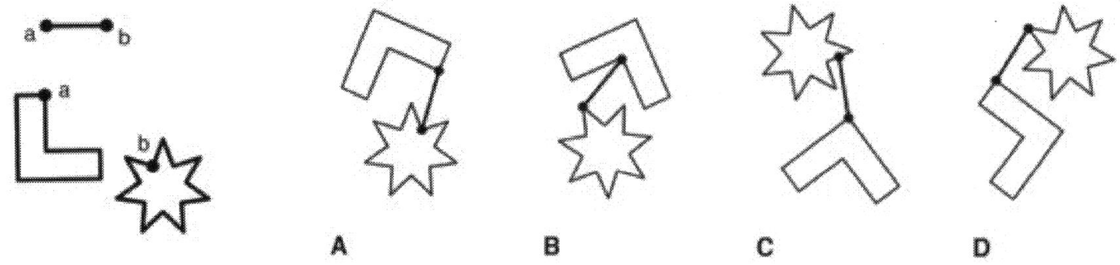

9.

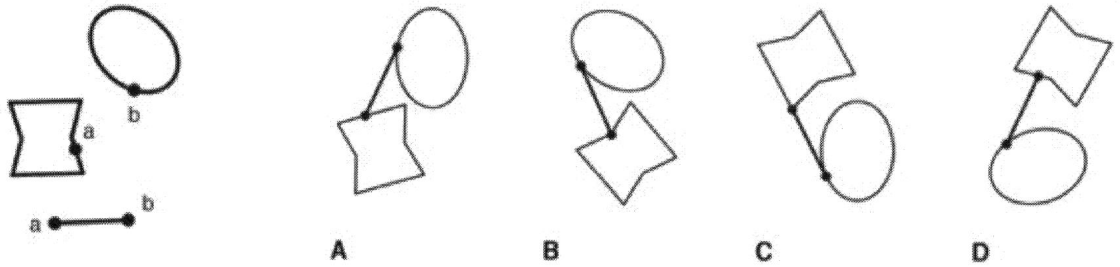

10.

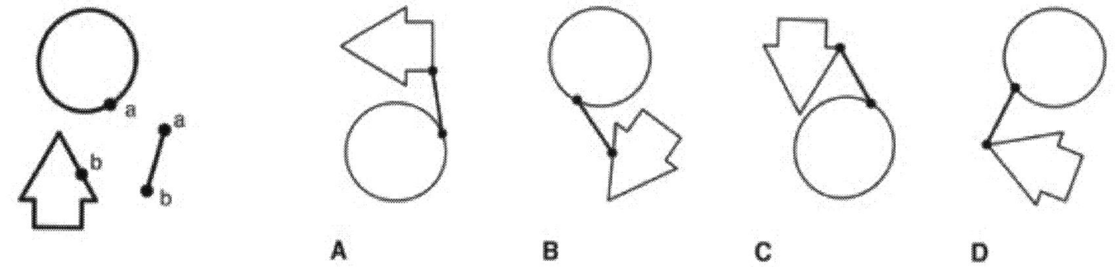

11.

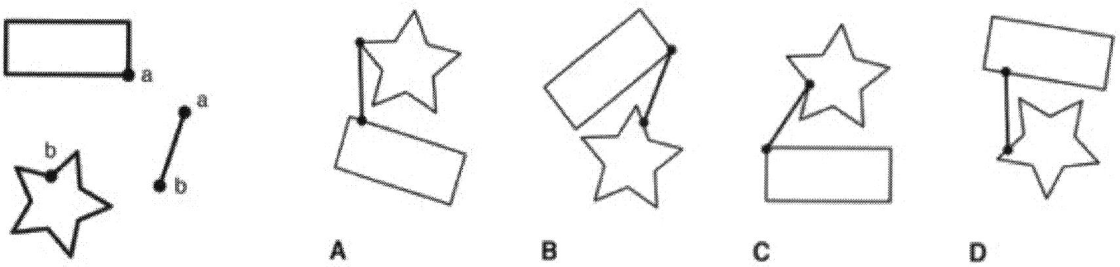

12.

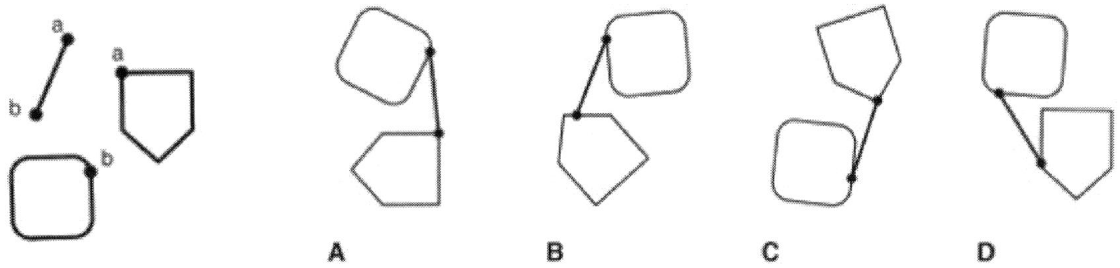

13.

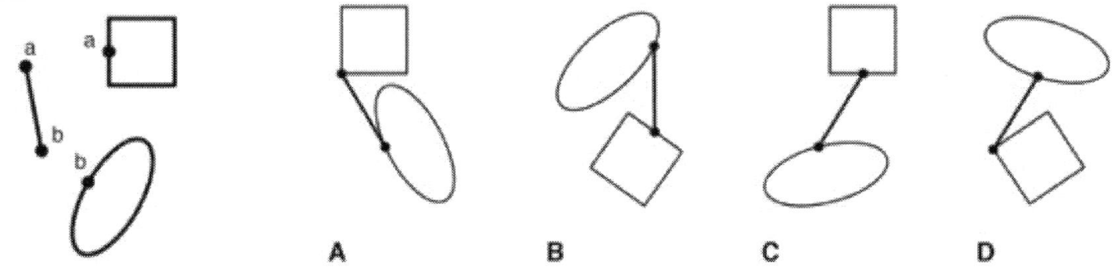

ASVAB Answer Explanations

Word Knowledge

1. A: Instigate refers to initiating or bringing about an action. While instigating something can be overwhelming, **overwhelm** describes the action, not what the action is. None of these choices match this except for **begin**, which is synonymous with instigate.

2. C: From the Latin root *fortis*, **fortify** literally means to make strong. **Foster** has nothing to do with the term at all. **Undermine** is to weaken, so this is the opposite. While a **barricade** can be used to fortify something, it is a means of protection, not the action of protection, unless used as a verb.

3. D: An **ultimatum** is a final demand or statement that carries a consequence if not met. The closest term presented is **threat** because, in context, an ultimatum carries some kind of punitive action or penalty if the terms are not met. Generally, it is usually used in a threatening or forceful context.

4. A: This was a tricky question because some choices connect **wave** to actions involved with water. **Sink** and **tide** are actions associated with the water, but are distinct from an ocean wave, which means wave is not used in context of an ocean wave, but as a verb to wave. To wave is to move around. **Stagnant** is to be still. **Flourish** describes a waving motion, making it the correct match.

5. C: It's easy to confuse void with **avoid**, which means keep away from. **Void** describes nothingness or emptiness. This means that **around** *(A)* is not the correct answer. Therefore, the best choice is **empty**, because this is the meaning of void.

6. C: Query comes from the Latin *querere*, which means to ask, so **query** means to ask a question. This Latin root also appears in the word **question**, which gives you a clue that the act of seeking answers is involved. **Ask** has the same meaning as query.

7. B: Severe reflects high intensity or very great. **Cut** and **shake** are verbs with actions that do not reflect severe. While something can be severely foul, **foul** is a broad description of something bad, but not necessarily of a high level of intensity. **Extreme** *(B)* describes something of the highest or most serious nature.

8. D: Vexation describes a state of irritation or annoyance. Think of the term vexed, meaning annoyed. The closest choice is **anger**, because vexation reflects annoyance, which, in most contexts, means a person is slightly angered or feels mild anger.

9. A: Loquacious reflects the tendency to talk a lot. While someone can be humorous and loquacious, **humorous** describes the kind of talk, not the fact that someone talks a lot. **Cranky** has nothing to do with the word, and **silent** is a clear opposite. This leaves **verbose**, meaning using an abundance of words; loquacious is a synonym.

10. B: Grim describes something of a dark or foreboding nature. **Frank** reflects sincerity, so does not relate. Neither does **corpse**, which is a body. **Sharp** describes a witty response or edged surface. This leaves **dire**, which is synonymous with grim. Both words reflect dark or unfruitful circumstances.

11. B: To **disparage** someone is to put them down. Although this may involve breaking a spirit and causing despair, **despair** is the result of disparage. To **spar** or fight may also be a result of disparage. **Belittle** means to bring someone down with words and is synonymous with disparage.

12. D: The other choices refer to **attitude**, a word spelled and pronounced similarly to altitude. Someone's attitude can reflect haughtiness, influence their outlook, and reflect their behavior. None of these terms describe **altitude**, which is the measure of height. **Height** is directly related to altitude.

13. A: Looking at the root word **ego**, egotistic must have something to do with the self—in this case, excessive self-interest. Such a person tends to be the opposite of **altruistic**, which means selfless. **Unconcerned** is also inappropriate, as egotistic people are concerned for themselves. **Agrarian** is an unrelated word concerning fields or farm lifestyle. **Conceited** is synonymous to egotistic.

14. B: Build and **guilt** can be ruled out because they are not related to **understand**. **Endow** is more difficult, because one can endow, or give, someone knowledge to understand, but endow involves the act of giving. **Fathom** is synonymous with understand; both terms reflect being able to grasp information.

15. D: Terrain, from the Latin *terra,* refers to the earth or physical landscape. **Celestial** and **firmament** both describe the sky. **Arboreal** describes things relating to trees. This leaves **ground**, another word for Earth or land, the same as terrain.

16. A: Mitigate refers to easing tension or making less severe. **Focus**, **fiery**, and **conspire** do not relate. **Alleviate** is synonymous, meaning to make less severe. Note the ending *-ate*, which also indicates function. Both terms reflect the function of easing difficult circumstances.

17. C: Encompass means to hold within or surround. **Avoid** and **retreat** are opposites. **Brazen** has no relation. **Surround**, meaning to **encircle**, is synonymous with **encompass**.

18. D: An **archetype** is an example of a person or thing, a recurrent symbol. An **ancestor** may be a good model of ideal behavior, but the term refers to someone who is related. **Archetypes** appear in literature, but these are different terms. **Policy** is unrelated. A **model** is a standard or representative, which is synonymous with archetype.

19. B: Contrast means to go against or to have a different perspective. **Revive** and **improve** are unrelated. **Partisan** can mean favoring one side, but variation is the best choice. **Variation** indicates clear difference, something that is not uniform and, therefore, contrasting.

20. C: Irate comes from the Latin *ira-*, which gives it the meaning of angry or irritable. **Amiable** means happy and friendly. **Innocent** and **tangible** have different and unrelated meanings. **Incensed** comes from the Latin *incedere*, which means to burn. Often this burning is a metaphor for extreme anger, the meaning of irate. Thus, incensed and irate are synonyms.

21. A: Plausible means likely to be possible or accepted, the opposite of **skeptical**. **Diurnal** relates to daytime, so is unrelated. **Erudite** means clever or intelligent, but not necessarily possible or correct. **Conceivable** means that something is able to be thought of or able to be done. Conceivable is the best match for plausible.

22. C: Discourse refers to spoken and written communication, or debate. **Path** doesn't have anything to do with discourse, unless used figuratively. While discourse may consist of praise or disagreement, all discourse—written or verbal—is a form of speech. Therefore, **speech** is the best term that encompasses the same meaning as discourse.

23. A: The Latin root, *asper*, means rough. **Exasperate**, then, means to make relations with someone rough or to rub them the wrong way. **Disappointment** can be the result an exasperating situation, but these are results of the term, not the same as exasperation itself. **Annoy** is a synonym, meaning to irritate and make someone slightly angry.

24. C: The Latin root *bell*, which comes from *bellum*, refers to war. Someone who is **pugnacious** is ready for a fight. One may be **angry**, **patriotic**, or **loud**, but none of these terms directly relate to warlike behavior like pugnacious.

25. D: Someone who displays **equanimity**, like the *equ*- prefix suggests, is level-headed and even-tempered. While equine and equanimity appear to share the *equ*- prefix, **equine** refers to horses. **Justice** and **hostility** don't relate at all. This leaves **composure**, which also describes one's ability to keep a calm and level-headed state.

26. A: Preemptive refers to an action taken before an anticipated result can occur, often as a preventive measure. **Prepare** is similar—it's defined as actions taken before an event—but it doesn't necessarily involve preventative measures as does preemptive. Preemptive measures can be hidden, but that describes the act. **Initial**—meaning first—is close because it can be the first action in a series, but again, it doesn't refer to an action that is preventative. **Beforehand** is an action done in advance, before something occurs.

27. D: Agitate means to annoy, which is not the same as the meaning in this sentence. **Instigate** can mean to start, which is not synonymous with **liberate**. **Fracture** is to crack or break something, which can metaphorically be attributed to liberation (breaking of chains), but is not directly related to the word liberate. From the Latin root *liber*, meaning free, liberate means to free or release. **Release** is synonymous.

28. B: Mediocre is from the Latin *medius*, meaning middle. It refers to something of only decent quality, not exceptional. This rules out **excellent** and **inspiring**, as both communicate ideas of surpassing quality. **Intrusive** is unrelated. **Average** means usual or nothing out of the ordinary, like mediocre.

29. C: Moot means uncertain or in dispute. We can eliminate **factual, historical,** and **exemplify** because these are common terms with no ties to moot. **Debatable** is defined as having uncertain circumstances, leading to discussion or dispute.

30. B: Bestow means to give or present. **Take** can be eliminated because to take is the opposite action of to give. **Study** and **energize** mean different things entirely. **Bequeath** means to give or leave to another person.

31. B: Barren means deserted, void, lifeless, or having little. A desert is barren because it produces little vegetation. **Fruitful**, **sumptuous** and **lavish** express richness and abundance, which contradict barren. **Infertile** means unable to produce life, which mirrors barren.

32. A: Refurbish is to restore, set things up again, or make repairs. **Enlighten**, **craven**, and **burnish** are unrelated to these ideas. Note instead the *re*- prefix in **renovate**, which means again. This gives refurbish and renovate a meaning of restoring again, or returning to a better state. In other words, renewal.

33. D: Chastise means to reprimand severely. **Honor**, **choose**, and **locate** are unrelated. **Rebuke** is defined as harshly disapproving someone. Both rebuke and chastise are verbs, making rebuke a match.

34. B: Sustain is to revitalize, or to give strength. **Strength** would be a good choice, but strength alone does not describe the re-strengthening that sustain embodies. The best choice is **invigorate**, which is a verb like sustain, meaning to strengthen. This makes invigorate the better choice. **Expedite** is unrelated. While **embolden** means to give someone courage, which is a form of strength, invigorate and sustain speak more toward physical circumstances.

35. A: Acquit means to free of blame or charge. While acquire and acquit appear similar, they are unrelated. **Stall** and **quit** are also unrelated. **Forgive** literally means to pardon of sins or offenses. While not appearing related by their spellings, their meanings are nearly a perfect match, and they are both verbs.

Paragraph Comprehension

1. C: When authors do not provide a clear explanation of events, readers need to infer. An inference is made when readers draw conclusions based off of facts or evidence. Readers have to infer when authors do not provide clear answers in the text. Inferring helps readers make predictions, draw conclusions, and reflect on what they read.

2. A: The topic of the passage is Caribbean island destinations. The topic of the passage can be described in a one- or two-word phrase. Remember, when paraphrasing a passage, it is important to include the topic. Paraphrasing is when one puts a passage into his or her own words.

3. C: Family or adult-only resorts and activities are supporting details in this passage. Supporting details are details that help readers better understand the main idea. They answer questions such as *who, what, where, when, why*, or *how*. In this question, cruises and local events are not discussed in the passage, whereas family and adult-only resorts and activities support the main idea.

4. B: This sentence is an opinion. An opinion is when the author states his or her judgment or thoughts on a subject. In this example, the author implies that the reader will not regret the vacation and that it may be the best and most relaxing vacation, when in fact that may not be true. Therefore, the statement is the author's opinion. A fallacy is a flawed argument of mistaken belief based on faulty reasoning.

5. B: The author of the passage is trying to persuade readers to vacation in a Caribbean island destination by providing enticing evidence and a variety of options. The passage even includes the author's opinion. Not only does the author provide many details to support his or her opinion, the author also implies that the reader would almost be "in the wrong" if he or she didn't want to visit a Caribbean island, hence, the author is trying to persuade the reader to visit a Caribbean island.

6. A: The author is comparing the two animals because they are showing how the animals are similar. If the author described the pets' differences, then they would be contrasting the animals.

7. B: Fiction is a story that is not true. An autobiography is an account of one's life written by that person, making it a true story, or nonfiction text. Fairy tales, myths, and fables are examples of fictional texts because they are made up stories.

8. D: Rain is the *cause* in this passage because it is why something happened. The effects are plants growing, rainbows, and puddle jumping.

9. C: Narrators and characters can express dialogue in fiction and drama genres. The narrator is the storyteller and can present the dialogue in either first or third person perspective. Characters play huge roles in the plot's development because they are the ones who move the storyline along.

10. B: Circular reasoning is when the reasoning is decided based upon the outcome or conclusion and then vice versa. Basically, readers can go in circles nonstop about which argument caused or had an effect on the other argument. In a false analogy, two objects or events are described as similar in a misleading or illogical way. False dichotomies, often presented as an either-or situation, are oversimplifications of arguments that neglect to address all of the possible options or sides in the argument. A slippery slope is when an author implies that something big will inevitably happen as a result of an initial smaller action.

11. A: The author implies that Siberian huskies are great pets but require a lot of time and energy. In the passage, the writer describes how huskies require lots of brushing and long walks and how they dig, making them not easy to care for. The author also describes how friendly Siberian huskies can be, even possibly greeting a robber at their own house, definitely not making them good guard dogs. Therefore, Siberian huskies are great pets but require a lot of time and energy.

12. C: The author may be biased because they show prejudice over one breed versus another in an unfair way. Impartial means fair and is essentially the opposite of biased. Hasty means quick to judge and irrational means unreasonable or illogical.

13. D: A credible text is trusted by readers, believable when the author is objective or unbiased, and written by a reliable source. Remember, text credibility is important when drawing conclusions because readers want reliable sources that support their decisions about authors' ideas.

14. B: The passage is most likely the summary of a story because it recaps the main idea, characters, what someone/something wanted, how the problem was solved, and what the result of the action was.

15. A: Paraphrasing should include the main idea and details are reworded to retell the passage. The option that best paraphrases the provided statement is: Home improvement projects can be pricey, but there are ways to keep costs down such as "Do It Yourself," or DIY; comparing prices of the materials and workers that will be used; and keeping the original floor plan for plumbing and electrical. The other options provided steer away from the topic or mention details that were not initially presented, making them incorrect.

Math Knowledge

1. D: The first step is to find a common denominator of 30:

$$\frac{14}{15} = \frac{28}{30}, \frac{3}{5} = \frac{18}{30}, \frac{1}{30} = \frac{1}{30}$$

Then, the numerators should be added and subtracted, resulting in:

$$\frac{28}{30} + \frac{18}{30} - \frac{1}{30} = \frac{28 + 18 - 1}{30} = \frac{45}{30}$$

In the last step, 15 is factored out from the numerator and denominator, yielding $\frac{3}{2}$.

2. A: From the second equation, the first step is to add *x* to both sides and subtract 1 from both sides: $-x+3y+x-1=1+x-1$, with the result of $3y-1=x$. Then, this is substituted into the first equation, yielding: $3(3y-1)+2y=8$, or $9y-3+2y=8, 11y=11, y=1$. Then, this value is plugged into $3y-1=x$, so $3(1)-1=x$ or *x* = 2, *y* = 1.

3. C: The square root of 16 is 4, so this expression simplifies to:

$$\frac{1}{2}\sqrt{16}=\frac{1}{2}(4)=2$$

4. D: The easiest way to approach this problem is to factor out a 2 from each term:

$$2x^2-8=2(x^2-4)$$

The formula $x^2-y^2=(x+y)(x-y)$ can be used to factor:

$$x^2-4=x^2-2^2=(x+2)(x-2)$$

$$2(x^2-4)=2(x+2)(x-2)$$

5. B: The total of the interior angles of a triangle must be 180°. The sum of the first two is 105°, so the remaining is 180° − 105° = 75°.

6. B: The length of the side will be $\sqrt{400}$. The calculation is performed a bit more easily by breaking this into the product of two square roots, $\sqrt{400}=\sqrt{4\times 100}=\sqrt{4}\times\sqrt{100}=2\times 10=20$ feet. However, there are 4 sides, so the total is $20\times 4=80$ feet.

7. A: To take the product of two fractions, the numerators and denominators are multiplied by their respective part in each fraction: $\frac{5}{3}\times\frac{7}{6}=\frac{5\times 7}{3\times 6}=\frac{35}{18}$. The resultant numerator and denominator have no common factors, so this is already simplified.

8. C: Let *a* be the number of apples purchased, and let *p* be the number of papayas purchased. There is a total of 15 pieces of fruit, so one equation is $a+p=15$. The total cost is $35, and in terms of the total apples and papayas purchased as $2a+3p=35$. If one multiplies the first equation by 2 on both sides, it becomes $2a+2p=30$. Then, this equation is subtracted from the second equation: $2a+3p-(2a+2p)=35-30, p=5$. So, five papayas were purchased.

9. A: This equation can be solved as follows: $x^2=36$, so $x=\pm\sqrt{36}=\pm 6$. Only -6 shows up in the list.

10. D: The volume of a cube is given by cubing the length of its side. $6^3=6\times 6\times 6=36\times 6=216$.

11. A: The area of the square is the square of its side length, so $4^2=16$ square inches. The area of a triangle is half the base times the height, so $\frac{1}{2}\times 2\times 8=8$ square inches. The total is $16+8=24$ square inches.

12. B:

$$-\frac{1}{3}\sqrt{81} = -\frac{1}{3}(9) = -3$$

13. A: To solve this problem, one has to multiply each of the terms in the first parentheses and then multiply each of the terms in the second parentheses:

$$(2x - 3)(4x + 2)$$

$$2x(4x) + 2x(2) - 3(4x) - 3(2)$$

$$8x^2 + 4x - 12x - 6$$

$$8x^2 - 8x - 6$$

14. C: To subtract fractions, they must have a common denominator. In this case, 24 can be used because it is the least common multiple of 6 and 8:

$$\frac{11}{6} - \frac{3}{8} = \frac{44}{24} - \frac{9}{24} = \frac{44 - 9}{24} = \frac{35}{24}$$

15. C: The formula for the area of a triangle with base *b* and height *h* is $\frac{1}{2}bh$. In this problem, the base is one-third the height, or $b = \frac{1}{3}h$ or equivalently $h = 3b$. Using the formula for a triangle, this becomes:

$$\frac{1}{2}b(3b) = \frac{3}{2}b^2$$

The problem states that this has to equal 6. So, $\frac{3}{2}b^2 = 6, b^2 = 4, b = \pm 2$. However, lengths are positive, so the base must be 2 feet long.

16. B: There are two zeros for the function $x = 0, -2$. The zeros can be found several ways, but this particular equation can be factored into:

$$f(x) = x(x^2 + 4x + 4) = x(x + 2)(x + 2)$$

By setting each factor equal to zero and solving for x, there are two solutions. On a graph, these zeros can be seen where the line crosses the x-axis.

17. D: Dividing rational expressions follows the same rule as dividing fractions. The division is changed to multiplication by the reciprocal of the second fraction. This turns the expression into $\frac{5x^3}{3x^2} * \frac{3y^9}{25}$. Multiplying across and simplifying, the final expression is $\frac{xy^8}{5}$.

18. B: The equation can be solved by factoring the numerator into $(x + 6)(x - 5)$. Since that same factor exists on top and bottom, that factor $(x - 5)$ cancels. This leaves the equation $x + 6 = 11$. Solving the equation gives the answer $x = 5$. When this value is plugged into the equation, it yields a zero in the denominator of the fraction. Since this is undefined, there is no solution.

19. D: This inverse of a function is found by switching the x and y in the equation and solving for y. In the given equation, solving for y is done by adding 5 to both sides, then dividing both sides by 3. This answer can be checked on the graph by verifying the lines are reflected over $y = x$.

20. C: The equation $x = 3$ is not a function because it does not pass the vertical line test. This test is made from the definition of a function, where each x-value must be mapped to one and only one y-value. This equation is a vertical line, so the x-value of 3 is mapped with an infinite number of y-values.

21. C: Because the triangles are similar, the lengths of the corresponding sides are proportional. Therefore:

$$\frac{30 + x}{30} = \frac{22}{14} = \frac{y + 15}{y}$$

This results in the equation $14(30 + x) = 22 \cdot 30$ which, when solved, gives $x = 17.1$. The proportion also results in the equation $14(y + 15) = 22y$ which, when solved, gives $y = 26.3$.

22. C: The first step is to depict each number using decimals. $\frac{91}{100}$ = 0.91

Multiplying both the numerator and denominator of $\frac{4}{5}$ by 20 makes it $\frac{80}{100}$ or 0.80; the closest approximation of $\frac{2}{3}$ would be $\frac{66}{100}$ or 0.66 recurring. Rearrange each expression in ascending order, as found in answer *C*.

23. A: When parentheses are around two expressions, they need to be *multiplied*. In this case, separate each expression into its parts (separated by addition and subtraction) and multiply by each of the parts in the other expression. Then, add the products together.

$$(3x)(x) + (3x)(-8) + (+5)(x) + (+5)(-8)$$

$$3x^2 - 24x + 5x - 40$$

Remember that when multiplying a positive integer by a negative integer, it will remain negative. Then add $-24x + 5x$ to get the simplified expression, answer *A*.

24. A: First simplify the larger fraction by separating it into two. When dividing one fraction by another, remember to *invert* the second fraction and multiply the two as follows:

$$\frac{5}{7} \times \frac{11}{9}$$

The resulting fraction $\frac{55}{63}$ cannot be simplified further, so this is the answer to the problem.

25. B: Dividing by 98 can be approximated by dividing by 100, which would mean shifting the decimal point of the numerator to the left by 2. The result is 4.2 which rounds to 4.

Electronics Information

1. C: Total resistance in a circuit that has both series and parallel elements is calculated by the following equations:

Total resistance = 85 ohms + 175 ohms + 1/(1/150 ohms + 1/25 ohms)

Total resistance = 260 ohms + 18.75 ohms

Total resistance = 278.75 ohms

2. B: The total resistance for the circuit was found in the previous problem (278.75 ohms), so this value is plugged into the equation as well as the voltage from the battery source (80 volts).

$I = V/R$ = 80 V/ 278.75 ohms = 0.29 amps

Current is measured in amps, not volts, so Choice *C* is incorrect. The other choices do not manipulate the equation appropriately.

3. A: Voltage lost is expressed in amps because it is referring to a reduction in current, so Choice *D,* 5.4 volts, is incorrect. Voltage will be lost at the 25-ohm resistor because this resistor is in a parallel circuit, so Choice *B,* 0 amps, is incorrect. Again, the voltage lost can be calculated by substituting known values into iterations of Ohm's Law.

$V = I \times R$ = (0.29 amps) × (18.75 ohms) = 5.4 volts. Then, this is substituted into the following equation:

$I = V/R$ = 5.4 V/25 ohms = 0.22 amps

4. D: The equation to determine the cost is cost = power (in kilowatt-hours) × time (in hours) × rate (in cents per kilowatt-hour). The important step is ensuring that all values are inserted in the equation with the correct units, so some conversions need to take place. Power is given as 150 watts, which equals 0.15 kilowatt-hours (150/1000). The time of 240 minutes is divided by 60 minutes/hour to yield 4 hours. Therefore:

cost = (0.15 kW) × (4 hr.) × (10 cents/kWh) = 6 cents/100 = $.06

Choice *A* did not convert the power into kilowatt hours but left it in watts. Choice *B* did not convert the time from minutes into hours. Choice *C* did not correctly convert the cost into dollars.

5. A: The physical structure of the atoms that compose matter lends itself to the production of electricity. The arrangement of the subatomic particles and the associated charges—mainly the negatively charged electrons in the cloud—are associated with the ability to create an electric current, which can be harnessed to do work.

6. B: The structure of atoms is as follows: The central nucleus contains protons and neutrons. Protons have a positive charge (+1), and neutrons are neutral, so they do not carry a charge. Around the nucleus is a cloud, which contains electrons in rings called orbitals. Electrons are negatively charged (–1), and those in the outermost ring—farthest from the nucleus—tend to be easier to remove from the atom.

7. B: Physical properties of atoms are influenced to some degree by the number and arrangement of electrons in the shells around the nucleus. The electrons in the outer shells in metals are free to drift between atoms. This movement potential allows them to jump between atoms, creating an electric current or flow, when subjected to an external force such as a magnetic field.

8. C: Diodes function in electrical circuit much like valves do with fluid dynamics or in veins. They prevent current from flowing in the unintended direction and instead only permit flow in one direction. The symbol is:

The arrow points in the direction of permitted current flow. Choices *A* and *B* described potentiometers, and Choice *D* showed the symbol for the potentiometer.

9. A:

$\frac{1}{R_{eq}} = \frac{1}{R_1} + \frac{1}{R_2} + \frac{1}{R_3}$ . .. so, in this circuit, $\frac{1}{R_{eq}} = \frac{1}{220} + \frac{1}{200} + \frac{1}{470}$

$$\frac{1}{R_{eq}} = \frac{1}{0.0117} \quad so \ R_{eq} = 85.67 \ ohms$$

Choice *B* added the resistances together as is done in a series circuit, but the given circuit is a parallel circuit. Choice *C* missed the final step that the resistance found is the inverse of R_{eq}. Choice *D* simply chose the lowest resistance of the given resistors, but this is not how to calculate the equivalent resistance in parallel circuits.

10. C: Electric conductors tend to be metals, such as silver, copper, and aluminum. They "conduct" electricity, which means that they help the electric current flow easily. This is largely because metals have low resistance because the electrons are easily detached from these atoms, so they are then free to jump from atom to atom and create a current. In contrast, insulators (such as wood, plastic, or rubber) have high resistance but low conductivity. Conductivity and resistance are opposite properties; a given single material cannot be highly conductive and highly resistant at the same time.

11. C: Insulators provide more resistance than conductors. As mentioned, conductors have little resistance. Insulators, such as plastic or rubber, in contrast, have high resistance. Essentially, they slow the flow of electric current much like friction deters mechanical motion.

12. D: Ohm's Law describes the relation between voltage and amperage, where voltage is a measure of electromotive potential much like potential energy of motion in kinetics. Amperage measures the electric current or the flow rate of 1 coulomb of electrons in a second. The basic law is *V* = *I* × *R*, but this can be manipulated in the following ways:

$$I = \frac{V}{R} \quad \text{or} \quad V = I \times R \quad \text{or} \quad R = \frac{V}{I}$$

13. D: The difference in potential between two separate points is a measure of volts. Amperes indicate the number of electrons that pass a specific point per second. Ohms measure the resistance to flow (essentially electrical friction). Watts are a measure of power or the rate at which electrical energy is used or converted into another type of energy. Watts are often converted to kilowatts or, when expressing power rates, kilowatt-hours.

14. B: The amount of energy needed to power a certain device is expressed in kilowatt-hours. Therefore, Choices *A* and *D* are incorrect. The amount of energy needed is the product of the power in kilowatts multiplied by the time in hours. The air conditioner is 6000 watts or 6 kilowatt-hours multiplied by 3 hours is 18 kilowatt-hours. Choice *C* did not properly convert the power from watts into kilowatts.

15. B: When devices are connected in a series circuit, the voltage is the same across each device (or resistor) in the loop, but the current drops after each device. Recall that for lightbulbs connected in series, this is observed by a decrease in the brightness of each successive bulb. This is one of the disadvantages of a series circuit. In contrast, the current increases with the addition of each resistor in parallel circuits.

16. B: In a parallel circuit, more charges will seek the path with least resistance. Because of this, more current passes through circuit paths with lower resistance. If the resistance is the same in both paths, then the same amount of current passes through each resistor. An important feature of parallel circuits is that the voltage is the same across each resistor; it does not drop as it does in series circuits. In series circuits, voltage drops after each resistor, and current is constant, and in parallel circuits, voltage stays the same after each resistor, and current increases. The total current can be calculated as the sum of the electric current in each branch of the parallel circuit.

17. D: Choice *A* depicts the basic equation for power, W, expressed in watts is $W = V \times I$, where V is the voltage in volts and I is the current in amps. Using Ohm's Law and substitution, $V = I \times R$ can replace the V so that $W = (I \times R) \times I$ or $I^2 \times R$, which was Choice *B*. Ohm's Law also holds that $I = V/R$, so substituting this equation for the I in the basic power equation yields $W = V \times (V/R)$ or $W = V^2/R$. Choice *D* is not a correct substitution and use of Ohm's Law and the power equation.

18. A: Most land-based, heavy machinery use AC electricity, not DC, because large amounts of electricity can be transmitted over long distances with AC while incurring significantly less loss of power than with DC electricity. DC circuits have voltage sources that provide a constant voltage, and the wiring on most ships, airplanes, and electronic circuits uses DC electricity.

19. D: The coils in the electric motors of AC equipment serve as inductors (not capacitors), which are typically coils of conducting wire in which a magnetic field is created by the electric current. Examples of capacitors are ceramic, Teflon, and air because these are non-conducting materials.

20. A: Electrical power is essentially the energy output over a given time. It is found by multiplying the current (in amps) from a voltage source by the voltage of that source. So, $P = IV$. Ohm's Law states that the voltage equals current in the circuit multiplied by the resistance ($V = IR$). Therefore, the power equation can be written two different ways, by substituting known relations from Ohm's Law:

$$P = I^2R \text{ or } P = \frac{V^2}{R} \qquad \text{So } Power = \frac{V^2}{R} = \frac{9^2}{3} = 27\ watts$$

Auto Shop

1. C: During the full cycle of an engine's piston, the piston's upstroke occurs as the piston travels up in the cylinder chamber, which decreases the space in the chamber, compressing the gas that has been injected in the chamber. When the piston has compressed the gas in the piston chamber, the gas will explode due to the hot electrical spark of the sparkplug that occurs during the apex of the upward motion of the cylinder head. The spark explodes the compressed gas, driving the piston downward from the force of the explosion in the piston chamber, which then mechanically transmits that power down to the transmission system of the vehicle. Choice *A* is incorrect because gas must be exploded by the spark of the sparkplug to achieve engine power. Cool gas does not produce power; only exploding gas produces power. Choice *B* is wrong because vehicle coolant has nothing to do with the piston. The power that the engine produces is derived from the explosion in the piston chamber. Coolant flows through channels in the engine block but the process has nothing to do with engine power. Choice *D* is also incorrect. If oil ever did leak onto an exhaust pipe, the oil would smoke, due to the extreme heat of the exhaust pipe caused by hot engine exhaust gases.

2. D: Electricity is created by the alternator's internal opposing magnets spinning past each other, creating a current. The alternator is turned by the power of the combustion engine and this also creates the motion. Choice *A* is incorrect because headlights use, rather than generate, power. Choice *B* is incorrect because the solenoid, which is in the starter system of the vehicle, controls electrical flow; it does not produce electricity. Choice *C* is wrong because the coil directs electrical flow; it does not produce electricity.

3. B: Identifying the type of liquid under a car can be the difference between driving away with no consequence or burning out the engine and causing an expensive repair. If the puddle is oil, then the engine may be in danger of burning out. If the puddle is just water from condensation produced by the vehicle's air conditioning system, then no action needs be taken because this water is normal. *A* is not the correct answer because the date marked on the calendar may be too late; damage might have already occurred. If the puddle is due to an oil leak, it can be an indication that the engine's oil pan has no oil, which can severely damage the engine. Some leaks, like an engine oil leak, must be addressed and repaired immediately before the vehicle is driven. Choice *C* is incorrect and dangerous. Contrary to what is shown in some movies, vehicle liquids should never be tasted. Vehicle liquids are toxic and tasting a liquid to identify it is not a sound option. Choice *D* is incorrect because the air conditioner does not drain the engine coolant system. Sometimes, water condenses due to the proper functioning of the vehicle's air conditioner, but this occurrence does not adversely affect any vehicle system.

4. B: The engine produces exhaust gases that must flow out from the engine. The exhaust manifold is the component that is placed next to the engine to capture the exhaust gases coming out of the engine. Due to the heat of the fresh exhaust exiting the engine, the exhaust manifold must be replaced every few years. The hot gases wear down the exhaust manifold component and engine vibrations erode the connection between the exhaust manifold and the engine. This causes the exhaust gases to escape directly from the engine, causing a very loud exhaust noise. *A* is incorrect because the muffler quiets the exhaust gases and is located more towards the rear of the vehicle, before the tailpipe. *C* is an incorrect choice because the catalytic converter lessens the engine's exhaust gases' effects on the environment, and is usually located somewhere midway under the vehicle, before the muffler. *D* is not correct because the tailpipe is the last component in the vehicle's exhaust system. The exhaust gases leave the vehicle through the tailpipe, which is located at the very rear of the vehicle.

5. A: Disc brakes and drum brakes are the most common type of brakes in a car. Most cars use the disc brake system on the front wheels. The rotor is a circular component of metal that is pressed by brake pads on both sides and this friction is what slows and stops a vehicle. Drum brakes also rely on friction; the drum brake shoes also slow and stop the vehicle using friction. *B* is incorrect because air brakes are mainly used on large trucks or buses. Electrical brakes are sometimes used on railroad systems. *C* is not the correct choice because reverse brakes are fictitious. Brakes always slow and stop forward and reverse motion of a vehicle. *D* is incorrect because induction brakes are sometimes used to stop certain electric motors. Engine braking is the act of using bigger, lower gears to slow the car down. This will slow down a car but does not actually utilize any form of braking systems.

6. B: The universal joint permits independent wheel suspension by splitting the axle, allowing the vehicle's occupants to experience a more stable, less bumpy ride. For example, if a right rear wheel travels over a big rock, the shock absorber will work independently just for that wheel. The left rear wheel will not be affected by the motion of the right wheel because the universal joint in the middle of the axle allows independent motion of the left and right rear wheels. Choice *A* is incorrect because an axle is a stiff, one-piece bar that the wheels are attached to, without any movable joints. Choice *C* is incorrect because a damper is a shock absorber that is positioned for each individual wheel and does not have anything to do with the wheels moving independently from one another. Choice *A* is not correct because a ball joint is integral within the vehicle's steering system and is not directly involved with the suspension system.

7. A: The oil pump is often located within the oil pan. The pump draws oil directly from the oil pan located below the engine. The placement of the oil pump within the oil pan enables the pump to easily pump oil directly to the engine located above. Choice *B* is incorrect because oil flows up from the bottom of the engine for a variety of reasons. Gravity is a primary reason; if the pump was located above the engine, then the oil would flow down from the top and then it would have to be pumped up to the top again, which would be a very inefficient design. When a car requires its oil changed to fresh oil, a mechanic simply loosens a nut on the oil pan underneath the engine and the oil flows out naturally. New oil is then poured in from the top of the engine. Choice *C* is wrong because gas tanks are usually located to the rear of the vehicle. It would be an illogical design to have the oil pumped to the front engine from the rear of the vehicle. Choice *D* is incorrect because the intake and exhaust valves over the pistons are located on top of the engine. The oil pan and pump are located towards the bottom part of the engine. This design also allows the mechanic to effectuate oil changes because the oil pan is easily accessible.

8. B: The color of transmission fluid is purple. If a leak deprives the transmission from an adequate amount of fluid, the entire transmission can burn out and lose all functionality. The transmission is typically the second-most expensive component in a vehicle to replace (after the engine). The Choice *A*, green, is incorrect. Green is often the color of anti-freeze, so if a green puddle is observed underneath the vehicle, it is most likely a coolant leak from the radiator, which is a serious problem. The engine can overheat and seize-up, totally disabling the vehicle. Any amount of leaking in the coolant system must be fixed immediately. Choice *C* in wrong. Transmission fluid can turn brown if it is old and needs to be replaced with new transmission fluid. Brake fluid can also turn brown if it is old and needs to be replaced. The color of transmission fluid should be regularly checked by using the transmission fluid dip stick. The color of transmission fluid should always be purple. If a brown color is observed, then the transmission fluid is old and needs to be changed. The number of miles between transmission fluid changes depends on the make, model, and year of manufacture of the vehicle. Choice *D* is incorrect because black fluid often denotes the color of oil. If a black puddle is observed underneath the vehicle, then service to the vehicle must be performed immediately, on the spot where the vehicle is parked. Severe damage to the engine can occur if the oil pan has an insufficient amount of oil.

9. B: Brake pads often wear out from normal driving and must be replaced. When brakes are applied, the pads contact the rotor, stopping the movement of the vehicle by employing friction on the brake disc of the wheel. The friction causes wear on the brake pad. Over time, the brake pads will totally wear down, causing the brake caliper to contact the brake disc, which leads to brake disc damage. Choice *A* is incorrect because rack and pinions are steering components that do not wear out quickly and have a useful life over a period of many years. Choice *C* is incorrect because the emergency brake is rarely used when the car is in motion. Most drivers use the emergency brake to lock the car into a stationary position, especially if the car is parked on a steep hill. The emergency break is intended to keep the vehicle from rolling while the vehicle is supposed to be in a stationary, parked position. Therefore, there is very little wear because the car is already stationary when the emergency break is employed and it is a system that usually locks the rear drum brake(s). Choice *D* is wrong because the rubber around the car's windows usually lasts for the duration of a vehicle's lifetime; they rarely need replacement.

10. D: The brake system is arguably the most important system in any vehicle. If a car cannot "go," it is usually not an immediate safety issue. However, if the brakes fail to stop a vehicle's motion, then physical damage and serious injury or death can result. The master cylinder holds brake fluid and pushes the fluid into the brake calipers when the brake pedal is depressed. If the brake fluid is not present in the master cylinder, then the brakes will not operate, as brakes depend on the principles of fluid dynamics to work. Choice *A* is incorrect because the electrical systems of a vehicle are not liquid-dependent systems. Choice *B* is also wrong. While transmissions use fluid dynamics to work, transmission systems do not have a component called the master cylinder. Choice *C* is incorrect because there is no component in the engine system that is called the master cylinder. The engine system of a car deals with gas and oil fluids; however, the term **master cylinder** is generally used only for a component attributed to the vehicle's brake system.

11. B: The purple liquid would be the transmission fluid. If this leak is not stopped and repaired, the entire transmission can be destroyed, causing costly repairs. Choice *A* would just be condensation from the air conditioner, which is a normal occurrence. Similarly, Choice *C* is also a regular occurrence, although the car should be driven more than a few miles so that the water is evaporated and the exhaust pipe does not rust.

12. A: The differential is the set of gears that transfers power from the drive shaft to the axle. Choice *B* is the cylinder that contains brake fluid. The steering column is a shaft that connects the steering wheel to the steering mechanism, so Choice *C* is incorrect. Choice *D*, the accelerator, is the far right pedal that controls the amount of gas that flows into the engine allowing for higher speeds.

13. C: It finishes the circuit that powers the ignition motor, or starter motor, which turns the crankshaft, which causes the cylinders to move up and down while valves above the cylinders inject fuel. Once the spark plugs ignite, the combustion process begins and the engine starts.

14. C: The jaws on these pliers are positioned at a horizontal right-angle, which enables the mechanic to grab onto a nut or bolt that would be hard to turn without the right-angle jaw feature of the channel lock pliers. The word *channel* in channel lock pliers denotes the tongue and groove adjustment feature on the pliers. Choice *A* is wrong because it describes pliers that are fixed. Choice *B* is incorrect because a funnel is not a type of pliers. Choice *D* describes a tool that has straight jaws but those on the channel lock pliers are at a right-angle for extra force and maneuverability.

15. A: Laying tar paper over the plywood on a roof protects the plywood, which would otherwise absorb water. The tar paper is essentially another layer of waterproofing under the shingles. After the tar paper is covering the surface of the plywood completely and stapled to it, the shingles are nailed to the tar paper. *B* is not correct because there should never be any space between the shingles because this would allow water to permeate between the shingles. Rain water and melting snow should flow over the shingles and then flow into gutters built around the perimeter of the roof. The gutters are designed to direct the water away from the foundation of a house. *C* is incorrect because the use of bricks for a roof is not a correct construction practice because bricks are too heavy for a roof and can collapse the roof into the house structure. *D* is incorrect because short nails are not of sufficient length to go through the shingle, the tar paper, and finally, the plywood of a roof. Only long nails should be used for securing shingles. Long nails hold the shingles securely to the tar paper and plywood.

16. D: The top of the window frame, the header, often must bear weight and is under the municipal umbrella of construction rules. This top part of the window frame is also the most complex, consisting of the most wooden boards or other material used. Choice *A* is incorrect because the sill, the bottom part of the window, while important, does not have to conform to municipal code building standards. *B* is not the correct choice because the trimmer extends down to the base, usually the floor, and due to its vertical nature, does not fall under a code statute. Also, the trimmer is a very strong, stable upright vertical component of the window frame as a result of its location and attachment next to the stud. Choice *C* is not correct because the stud is a board that extends vertically in the wall and is not part of the window's frame.

17. C: The battery powered Sawzall™ is a tool that can cut metal easily and also get into tight spaces. It is hand-operated and it gives the mechanic the flexibility to reach into tight spaces in the vehicle. Choice *A* is wrong because a lathe is a machine that skims and trims surfaces to desired dimensions. It is a large machine that is not suitable for cutting tasks while positioned under vehicles. Choice *B* is incorrect for several reasons. A chop saw is a circular saw with a hinged arm, used mainly for cutting wood with its large "teeth." Therefore, a chop saw blade is not suitable for cutting metal. Also, it is a large, heavy tool with a metal base that is very difficult to maneuver under a car. Choice *D* is incorrect because, while an axe might ultimately work in an emergency, it is not suitable for cutting off a metal tailpipe. The axe would mangle the steel and not produce a clean cut. Moreover, a stout striking surface must be placed behind the tailpipe when striking the tailpipe with the axe to protect other components behind the tailpipe from damage.

18. C: The most important factor in the construction of a brick wall is ensuring that the wall is straight and level. Gravity plays a crucial role in the construction process and the longevity and soundness of a wall. The force of gravity falls in vertical lines and can strengthen a wall that's built straight. The slightest tilt of the wall from vertical enables gravity to exert forces that can exacerbate the angle and bring the tilted wall down over time. Choice *A* is incorrect because brick spacing is not as important as straightness in the structural integrity of walls. Although even brick spacing is a proper construction procedure, a brick wall will stand satisfactorily if the bricks are not spaced evenly because the concrete in between the bricks will continue to support and offer load-bearing cohesion to the wall. Choice *B* is incorrect because a wall does not necessarily have to have a four-foot-deep foundation to be able to stand soundly. A foundation for a brick wall is a good building practice; however, if the wall is just a few feet tall, then the brick wall should stand satisfactorily with a foundation that is less than four feet. Choice *D* is incorrect because excess concrete, while not aesthetically pleasing, will not affect a wall adversely. The brick wall will remain standing even though the concrete was sloppily applied.

19. D: The Phillips-head screwdriver has a cross-cut head, in order to turn the top of the Phillips-head screw, which has cross-cut slots on the head. Choice *A* is incorrect because an Allen head base is usually an indentation with a hexagonal or octagonal depression on the head of the screw. Special Allen wrenches are required for these screws. Choice *B* is wrong because the single slot screw head is just a single line depression on the head of a screw and not a double depression. The single slot screw is the most recognized screw and although useful, the cross-cut Phillips-head screw is easier to use with a drill because the Phillips screw holds the bit of the Phillips screwdriver more securely, due to the increased surface area. Choice *C* is incorrect because hexagonal heads are similar to Allen screws; however, they often have a star-type pattern indented on the screw head.

20. B: Rebar is a long metal rod. These rods are used in foundations to provide reinforcement to the concrete. Choice *C* is wrong because concrete would not adhere to wood, so that wouldn't help. Also, Choice *A* is wrong because lag bolts can be used to secure other things to a slab but don't provide any type of reinforcement. Choice *D* is wrong because pipe would not be a good reinforcement due to the hollow design.

21. C: Lathes are used to turn down metal or wood. This means that as the object is rotated, some material is removed to either reshape or smooth the object. This is not the same as grinding because material is actually cut away, so Choice *A* is wrong. Even though it rotates, it is not used to drive screws, so Choice *B* is wrong. It also can't be used to bend angles, so Choice *D* is wrong.

22. A: Proper air ventilation is always needed when welding. An exhaust extraction system should also be used to help remove the excess fumes. Choice *B* is wrong because there is no need for a hard hat when welding. However, a proper welding mask should be worn. Insulated clothing may be worn while welding but it is not necessary. Finally, choice *D* is wrong because a welding mask should be worn instead of safety glasses. The mask will protect the eyes as well as the entire face.

23. C: Shingles should be added to the roof from the bottom to the top. This ensures that there are no gaps for water to trickle through as runs down the roof. Adding them from the top to the bottom would create multiple gaps for water to run through, so Choice *D* is wrong. Trying to add them from either side would also make it difficult to get them to overlap correctly, so Choices *A* and *B* are also wrong.

24. D: A trowel is used to smooth and wipe away extra mortar. Mortar is used to hold the bricks together, not cement or plaster, so Choices *A* and *C* are wrong. A trommel is a piece of machinery that is used to separate materials, such as minerals and solid waste, so that means Choice *B* is also wrong.

25. B: MIG welders use a continuously feeding wire, while TIG welders use a welding rod. TIG welders also use a tungsten electrode to transfer the current to the welding arc, which means that Choice *A* is wrong. Choice *C* is wrong because TIG welders are the ones used for welding thinner gauged metal. Finally, Choice *D* is wrong because the room should always be well-ventilated, and have an exhaust fan, when welding.

Mechanical Comprehension

1. C: The answer is 1800 seconds:

$$\left(45\;km \times \frac{1000\;m}{km}\right) \Big/ 25\frac{m}{s} = 1800\;seconds$$

2. D: The answer is 3.6 kilometers east of its point of departure. The ship is traveling faster than the current, so it will be east of the starting location. Its net forward velocity is 0.5 m/s which is 1.8 kilometers/hour, or 3.6 kilometers in two hours.

3. B: The answer is 2 m/s^2:

$$a = \frac{\Delta v}{\Delta t} = \frac{132\frac{km}{hr} - 60\frac{km}{hr}}{10\;seconds} = \frac{70\frac{km}{hr} \times 1000\frac{m}{km} \times \frac{hour}{3600\;sec}}{10\;seconds} = 2\;m/s^2$$

4. C: The answer is 50,000 N. The equation $F = ma$ should be memorized. All of the values are given in the correct units (kilogram-meter-second) so just plug them in.

5. B: The answer is 200 kilograms. This is actually a trick question. The mass of the astronaut is the same everywhere (it is the weight that varies from planet to planet). The astronaut's mass in kilograms is calculated by dividing his weight on Earth by the acceleration of gravity on Earth: 1962/9.81 = 200.

6. A: The answer is that the upward velocity is at a maximum when it leaves the punter's toe. The acceleration due to gravity reduces the upward velocity every moment thereafter. The speed is the same at points A and E, but the velocity is different. At point E, the velocity has a maximum *negative* value.

7. C: The answer is her angular velocity increases from (a) to (b) as she pulls her arms in close to her body and reduces her moment of inertia.

8. B: The answer is 14 m/s. Remember that the cannonball at rest "y" meters off the ground has a potential energy of $PE = mgy$. As it falls, the potential energy is converted to kinetic energy until (at ground level) the kinetic energy is equal to the total original potential energy:

$$\frac{1}{2}mv^2 = mgy \text{ or } v = \sqrt{2gy}$$

This makes sense because all objects fall at the same rate, so the velocity *must* be independent of the mass (which is why "D" is incorrect). Plugging the values into the equation, the result is 14 m/s. Remember, the way to figure this quickly is to have $g = 10$ rather than 9.81.

9. B: The answer is at Point C, the bottom of the arc.

10. C: This question isn't difficult, but it must be read carefully:

A is wrong. Even though the total energy is at a maximum at Points A and E, it isn't equal at only those points. The total energy is the same at *all* points. *B* is wrong. The kinetic energy is at a maximum at C, but not the *total* energy. The correct answer is *C*. The total energy is conserved, so it's the same at *all* points on the arc. *D* is wrong. The motion of a pendulum is independent of the mass. Just like how all objects fall at the same rate, all pendulum bobs swing at the same rate, dependent on the length of the cord.

11. C: The answer is 10kg x 2m x 9.81m/s^2. This is easy, but it must also be read carefully. Choice *D* is incorrect because it isn't necessary to know the ground elevation. The potential energy is measured *with respect* to the ground and the ground (or datum elevation) can be set to any arbitrary value.

12. B: The answer is 1 centimeter. Remember that the force (F) required to stretch a spring a certain amount (d) is given by the equation $F = kd$. Therefore, $k = F/d$ = 20N/0.5 cm = 20 N/cm. Doubling the weight to 20 N gives the deflection:

$$d = \frac{F}{k} = \frac{20N}{20N/cm} = 1\ centimeter$$

All of the calculations can be bypassed by remembering that the relation between force and deflection is linear. This means that doubling the force doubles the deflection, as long as the spring isn't loaded past its elastic limit.

13. A: The answer is 981 N. The start-up and sliding friction forces are calculated in the same way: normal force (or weight) times the friction coefficient. The difference between the two coefficients is 0.1, so the difference in forces is 0.1 x 1000 x 9.81 = 981 N.

14. C: The answer is 1.6 m^2. The pressure created by the load is 50N/0.1m^2 = 500 N/m^2. This pressure acts throughout the jack, including the large cylinder. Force is pressure times area, so the area equals pressure divided by force or 800N/500N/m^2 = 1.6m^2.

15. D: The answer is (F/A) x $(V_2 - V_1)$. Remember that the work for a piston expanding is pressure multiplied by change in volume. Pressure = F/A. Change in volume is $(V_2 - V_1)$.

16. C: The answer is 500 J/s. Choice *A* is incorrect because kg x m/s^2 is an expression of force, not power. Choice *B* is incorrect because N·m is an expression of work, not power. That leaves Choices *C* and *D*, both of which are expressed in units of power: watts or joules/second. Using an approximate calculation (as suggested):

$$1000\,kg \times 10\frac{m}{s^2} \times 30\,m = 300{,}000\,N \cdot m \quad \text{so} \quad \frac{300{,}000\,N \cdot m}{600\,seconds} = 500\,watts = 500\,J/s$$

17. B: The answer is 12,000 Pa. The top of the block is under 12 meters of water:

$$P = 1000\frac{N}{m^3} \times 12\,meters = 12{,}000\frac{N}{m^2} = 12{,}000\,Pa$$

There are two "red herrings" here: Choice *C* of 14,000 Pa is the pressure acting on the *bottom* of the block (perhaps through the sand on the bottom of the bay). Choice *D* (that it can't be calculated without knowing the top area of the block) is also incorrect. The top area is needed to calculate the total *force* acting on the top of the block, not the pressure.

18. B: The answer is that the water level rises in B but not in A. Why? Because ice is not as dense as water, so a given mass of water has more volume in a solid state than in a liquid state. Thus, it floats. As the mass of ice in Basin A melts, its volume (as a liquid) is reduced. In the end, the water level doesn't change. The ice in Basin B isn't floating. It's perched on high ground in the center of the basin. When it melts, water is added to the basin and the water level rises.

19. B: The answer is 5000 seconds. The volume is 3 x 25 x 50 = 3750 m^3. The volume divided by the flow rate gives the time. Since the pump capacity is given in liters per second, it's easier to convert the volume to liters. One thousand liters equals a cubic meter:

$$Time = \frac{3{,}750{,}000\ liters}{750\ liters/second} = 5000\,seconds = 1.39\,hours$$

20. A: The answer is 30 m^3/s. One of the few equations that must be memorized is $Q = vA$. The area of flow is 1m x 10m because only half the depth of the channel is full of water.

21. B: The answer is 737.75 N. This is a simple calculation:

$$\frac{9.81\,m}{s^2} \times 150\,kg \times 1.5\,m = 3\,m \times F \quad \text{so} \quad F = \frac{2207.25\,N \cdot m}{3\,meters}$$

22. D: The answer is 40 N. Use the equation $F = L \times r/R$. Note that for an axle with a given, set radius, the larger the radius of the wheel, the greater the mechanical advantage.

23. D: The answer is counterclockwise at 30 RPM. The driver gear is turning clockwise, and the gear meshed with it turns counter to it. Because of the 2:1 gear ratio, every revolution of the driver gear causes half a revolution of the follower.

24. B: The answer is 30 RPM, counterclockwise (B). While meshed gears rotate in different directions, wheels linked by a belt turn in the same direction. This is true unless the belt is twisted, in which case they rotate in opposite directions. So, the twisted link between the upper two wheels causes the right-hand wheel to turn counterclockwise, and the bigger wheel at the bottom also rotates counterclockwise. Since it's twice as large as the upper wheel, it rotates with half the RPMs.

25. C: The answer is F_1 = 1000 N; F_2 = 500 N. In case (a), the fixed wheels only serve to change direction. They offer no mechanical advantage because the lever arm on each side of the axle is the same. In case (b), the lower moveable block provides a 2:1 mechanical advantage. A quick method for calculating the mechanical advantage is to count the number of lines supporting the moving block (there are two in this question). Note that there are no moving blocks in case (a).

Assembling Objects

Section 1

1. A

2. D

3. B

4. A

5. B

6. D

7. B

8. C

9. A

10. D

11. C

12. A

Section 2

1. B

2. C

3. A

4. B

5. D

6. D

7. C

8. A

9. D

10. B

11. C

12. A

13. C

AFOQT Practice Test

Verbal Analogies

1. **Cat** is to **paws** as
    a. Giraffe is to neck.
    b. Elephant is to ears.
    c. Horse is to hooves.
    d. Snake is to skin.
    e. Turtle is to shell.

2. **Dancing** is to **rhythm** as **singing** is to
    a. Pitch.
    b. Mouth.
    c. Sound.
    d. Volume.
    e. Words.

3. **Towel** is to **dry** as **hat** is to
    a. Cold.
    b. Warm.
    c. Expose.
    d. Cover.
    e. Top.

4. **Sand** is to **glass** as
    a. Protons are to atoms.
    b. Ice is to snow.
    c. Seeds are to plants.
    d. Water is to steam.
    e. Air is to wind.

5. **Design** is to **create** as **allocate** is to
    a. Finish.
    b. Manage.
    c. Multiply.
    d. Find.
    e. Distribute.

6. **Books** are to **reading** as
    a. Movies are to making.
    b. Shows are to watching.
    c. Poetry is to writing.
    d. Scenes are to performing.
    e. Concerts are to music.

7. **Cool** is to **frigid** as **warm** is to
   a. Toasty.
   b. Summer.
   c. Sweltering.
   d. Hot.
   e. Mild.

8. **Buses** are to **rectangular prisms** as **globes** are to
   a. Circles.
   b. Maps.
   c. Wheels.
   d. Spheres.
   e. Movement.

9. **Backpacks** are to **textbooks** as
   a. Houses are to people.
   b. Fences are to trees.
   c. Plates are to food.
   d. Chalkboards are to chalk.
   e. Computers are to mice.

10. **Storm** is to **rainbow** as **sunset** is to
    a. Clouds.
    b. Sunrise.
    c. Breakfast.
    d. Bedtime.
    e. Stars.

11. **Falcon** is to **mice** as **giraffe** is to
    a. Leaves.
    b. Rocks.
    c. Antelope.
    d. Grasslands.
    e. Hamsters.

12. **Car** is to **motorcycle** as **speedboat** is to
    a. Raft.
    b. Jet-ski.
    c. Sailboat.
    d. Plane.
    e. Canoe.

13. **Arid** is to **damp** as **anxious** is to
    a. Happy.
    b. Petrified.
    c. Ireful.
    d. Confident.
    e. Sorrowful.

14. **Mechanic** is to **repair** as
    a. Mongoose is to cobra.
    b. Rider is to bicycle.
    c. Tree is to grow.
    d. Food is to eaten.
    e. Doctor is to heal.

15. **Whistle** is to **blow horn** as **painting** is to
    a. View.
    b. Criticize.
    c. Sculpture.
    d. Painter.
    e. Paintbrush.

16. **Paddle** is to **boat** as **keys** are to
    a. Unlock.
    b. Success.
    c. Illuminate.
    d. Piano.
    e. Keychain.

17. **Monotonous** is to **innovative** as
    a. Gorgeous is to beautiful.
    b. Ancient is to archaic.
    c. Loquacious is to silent.
    d. Sturdy is to fortified.
    e. Spectacular is to grandiose.

18. **Mountain** is to **peak** as **wave** is to
    a. Ocean.
    b. Surf.
    c. Fountain.
    d. Wavelength.
    e. Crest.

19. **Ambiguous** is to **indecisive** as **uncertain** is to
    a. Indefinite.
    b. Certain.
    c. Flippant.
    d. Fearful.
    e. Rounded.

20. **Fluent** is to **communication** as
    a. Crater is to catastrophe.
    b. Gourmet is to cooking.
    c. Ink is to pen.
    d. Crow is to raven.
    e. Whistle is to whistler.

21. **Validate** is to **truth** as **conquer** is to
    a. Withdraw.
    b. Subjugate.
    c. Expand.
    d. Surrender.
    e. Expose.

22. **Winter** is to **autumn** as **summer** is to
    a. Vacation.
    b. Fall.
    c. Spring.
    d. March.
    e. Weather.

23. **Penguin** is to **lemur** as **eagle** is to
    a. Howler monkey.
    b. Osprey.
    c. Warthog.
    d. Kestrel.
    e. Moose.

24. **Fiberglass** is to **surfboard** as
    a. Bamboo is to panda.
    b. Capital is to D.C.
    c. Copper is to penny.
    d. Flint is to mapping.
    e. Wind is to windmill.

25. **Myth** is to **explain** as **joke** is to
    a. Enlighten.
    b. Inspire.
    c. Collect.
    d. Laughter.
    e. Amuse.

Arithmetic Reasoning

1. If a car can go 300 miles in 4 hours, how far can it go in an hour and a half?
    a. 100 miles
    b. 112.5 miles
    c. 135.5 miles
    d. 150 miles
    e. 165.5 miles

2. At the store, Jan buys $90 of apples and oranges. Apples cost $1 each and oranges cost $2 each. If Jan buys the same number of apples as oranges, how many oranges did she buy?

a. 20
b. 25
c. 30
d. 35
e. 40

3. What is the volume of a box with rectangular sides 5 feet long, 6 feet wide, and 3 feet high?

a. 60 cubic feet
b. 75 cubic feet
c. 90 cubic feet
d. 100 cubic feet
e. 115 cubic feet

4. A train traveling 50 miles per hour takes a trip of 3 hours. If a map has a scale of 1 inch per 10 miles, how many inches apart are the train's starting point and ending point on the map?

a. 10
b. 12
c. 13
d. 14
e. 15

5. A traveler takes an hour to drive to a museum, spends 3 hours and 30 minutes there, and takes half an hour to drive home. What percentage of this time was spent driving?

a. 15%
b. 30%
c. 40%
d. 50%
e. 60%

6. A truck is carrying three cylindrical barrels. Their bases have a diameter of 2 feet and they have a height of 3 feet. What is the total volume of the three barrels in cubic feet?

a. 3π
b. 9π
c. 12π
d. 15π
e. 36π

7. Greg buys a $10 lunch with 5% sales tax. He leaves a $2 tip after his bill. How much money does he spend?

a. $12
b. $12.50
c. $13
d. $13.25
e. $16

8. Marty wishes to save $150 over a 4-day period. How much must Marty save each day on average?

a. $33.50
b. $35
c. $37.50
d. $40
e. $45.75

9. Bernard can make $80 per day. If he needs to make $300 and only works full days, how many days will this take?

a. 2
b. 3
c. 4
d. 5
e. 6

10. A couple buys a house for $150,000. They sell it for $165,000. What percentage did the house's value increase?

a. 10%
b. 13%
c. 15%
d. 17%
e. 19%

11. A school has 15 teachers and 20 teaching assistants. They have 200 students. What is the ratio of faculty to students?

a. 3:20
b. 4:17
c. 11:54
d. 3:2
e. 7:40

12. A map has a scale of 1 inch per 5 miles. A car can travel 60 miles per hour. If the distance from the start to the destination is 3 inches on the map, how long will it take the car to make the trip?

a. 12 minutes
b. 15 minutes
c. 17 minutes
d. 20 minutes
e. 25 minutes

13. Taylor works two jobs. The first pays $20,000 per year. The second pays $10,000 per year. She donates 15% of her income to charity. How much does she donate each year?

a. $4500
b. $5000
c. $5500
d. $6000
e. $6500

14. A box with rectangular sides is 24 inches wide, 18 inches deep, and 12 inches high. What is the volume of the box in cubic feet?

a. 2
b. 3
c. 4
d. 5
e. 6

15. Kristen purchases $100 worth of CDs and DVDs. The CDs cost $10 each and the DVDs cost $15. If she bought four DVDs, how many CDs did she buy?

a. One
b. Two
c. Three
d. Four
e. Five

16. Alan currently weighs 200 pounds, but he wants to lose weight to get down to 175 pounds. What is this difference in kilograms? (1 pound is approximately equal to 0.45 kilograms.)

a. 9 kg
b. 15.5 kg
c. 78.75 kg
d. 90 kg
e. 11.25 kg

17. Johnny earns $2334.50 from his job each month. He pays $1437 for monthly expenses. Johnny is planning a vacation in 3 months' time that he estimates will cost $1750 total. How much will Johnny have left over from three months' of saving once he pays for his vacation?

a. $948.50
b. $584.50
c. $852.50
d. $942.50
e. $984.50

18. The total perimeter of a rectangle is 36 cm. If the length of each side is 12 cm, what is the width?

a. 3 cm
b. 12 cm
c. 6 cm
d. 8 cm
e. 9 cm

19. Dwayne has received the following scores on his math tests: 78, 92, 83, 97. What score must Dwayne get on his next math test to have an overall average of at least 90?

a. 89
b. 98
c. 95
d. 100
e. 105

20. In Jim's school, there are 3 girls for every 2 boys. There are 650 students in total. Using this information, how many students are girls?

a. 260
b. 130
c. 65
d. 390
e. 90

21. Kimberley earns $10 an hour babysitting, and after 10 p.m., she earns $12 an hour, with the amount paid being rounded to the nearest hour accordingly. On her last job, she worked from 5:30 p.m. to 11 p.m. In total, how much did Kimberley earn on her last job?

a. $45
b. $57
c. $62
d. $42
e. $67

22. Keith's bakery had 252 customers go through its doors last week. This week, that number increased to 378. Express this increase as a percentage.

a. 26%
b. 50%
c. 35%
d. 12%
e. 42%

23. For a group of 20 men, the median weight is 180 pounds and the range is 30 pounds. If each man gains 10 pounds, which of the following would be true?

a. The median weight will increase, and the range will remain the same.
b. The median weight and range will both remain the same.
c. The median weight will stay the same, and the range will increase.
d. The median weight and range will both increase.
e. The median weight will decrease, and the range will remain the same.

24. Apples cost $2 each, while bananas cost $3 each. Maria purchased 10 fruits in total and spent $22. How many apples did she buy?

a. 5
b. 6
c. 7
d. 8
e. 9

25. Five students take a test. The scores of the first four students are 80, 85, 75, and 60. If the median score is 80, which of the following could NOT be the score of the fifth student?

a. 60
b. 80
c. 85
d. 100
e. 90

Word Knowledge

1. DEDUCE
    a. Explain
    b. Win
    c. Reason
    d. Gamble
    e. Undo

2. ELUCIDATE
    a. Learn
    b. Enlighten
    c. Plan
    d. Corroborate
    e. Conscious

3. VERIFY
    a. Criticize
    b. Change
    c. Teach
    d. Substantiate
    e. Resolve

4. INSPIRE
    a. Motivate
    b. Impale
    c. Exercise
    d. Patronize
    e. Collaborate

5. PERCEIVE
    a. Sustain
    b. Collect
    c. Prove
    d. Lead
    e. Comprehend

6. NOMAD
    a. Munching
    b. Propose
    c. Wanderer
    d. Conscientious
    e. Blissful

7. MALEVOLENT
   a. Evil
   b. Concerned
   c. Maximum
   d. Cautious
   e. Crazy

8. PERPLEXED
   a. Annoyed
   b. Vengeful
   c. Injured
   d. Confused
   e. Prepared

9. LYRICAL
   a. Whimsical
   b. Vague
   c. Fruitful
   d. Expressive
   e. Playful

10. BREVITY
   a. Dullness
   b. Dangerous
   c. Brief
   d. Ancient
   e. Calamity

11. IRATE
   a. Anger
   b. Knowledge
   c. Tired
   d. Confused
   e. Taciturn

12. LUXURIOUS
   a. Faded
   b. Bright
   c. Lavish
   d. Inconsiderate
   e. Overwhelming

13. IMMOBILE
   a. Fast
   b. Slow
   c. Eloquent
   d. Vivacious
   e. Sedentary

14. MENDACIOUS
    a. Earnest
    b. Bold
    c. Criminal
    d. Liar
    e. Humorous

15. CHIVALROUS
    a. Fierce
    b. Annoying
    c. Rude
    d. Dangerous
    e. Courteous

16. RETORT
    a. Conversation
    b. Jest
    c. Counter
    d. Flexible
    e. Erudite

17. SUBLIMINAL
    a. Subconscious
    b. Transportation
    c. Underground
    d. Substitute
    e. Penumbral

18. INCITE
    a. Understanding
    b. Illumination
    c. Rally
    d. Judgment
    e. Compose

19. MONIKER
    a. Name
    b. Mockery
    c. Umbrella
    d. Insult
    e. Burden

20. SERENDIPITOUS
    a. Creation
    b. Sympathy
    c. Unfortunate
    d. Calm
    e. Coincidental

21. OVERBEARING
    a. Neglect
    b. Overacting
    c. Clandestine
    d. Formidable
    e. Amicable

22. PREVENT
    a. Avert
    b. Rejoice
    c. Endow
    d. Fulfill
    e. Ensure

23. REPLENISH
    a. Falsify
    b. Hindsight
    c. Dwell
    d. Refresh
    e. Nominate

24. REGALE
    a. Remember
    b. Grow
    c. Outnumber
    d. Entertain
    e. Bore

25. ABATE
    a. Anger
    b. Forlorn
    c. Withdraw
    d. Excellent
    e. Crazed

Reading Comprehension

Aircraft propulsion must achieve two objectives: it has to balance the thrust and drag of a craft in cruising flight, and thrust must exceed drag in order to accelerate movement. Balancing the thrust and drag of a craft in cruising mode follows Sir Isaac Newton's first law of motion. This law states that an object in motion will remain so, in a straight line, with the absence of a net force to affect a change. In other words, if all external forces cancel each other, an object remains at a constant velocity. This is necessary to understand the idea of flight at a constant altitude. However, if a pilot affects a change to a craft's thrust, the balance between that thrust and the drag of a craft is disrupted. The net forces have been changed in a manner that will affect acceleration and propel the aircraft until there is a new balance between thrust and drag in velocity.

1. What is the topic of the paragraph?
    a. Aircraft propulsion is a difficult concept to understand.
    b. External forces must cancel each other out in order for an aircraft to fly.
    c. An aircraft that remains at a constant velocity will remain at a constant altitude as well.
    d. Aircraft propulsion involves two objectives involving the laws of motion.
    e. Thrust must exceed drag in order for an aircraft to accelerate.

2. Choose the option below that does NOT support the topic of this paragraph:

    One of the four forces that affects aerodynamics is weight. The total weight of an aircraft must be factored into the mechanics of flight. Lift also affects flight and must be considered. Weight must include the craft itself, accompanying gear, the fuel load, and any personnel. Carefully assessing weight will help a pilot calculate how to oppose the downward force of weight during flight.

    a. The sum weight of an aircraft is important to consider.
    b. Personnel should be calculated in overall weight.
    c. The mechanics of flight also includes lift.
    d. Weight is a downward force in aerodynamics.
    e. Fuel load cannot be eliminated in measuring weight.

3. Read the following paragraph, then select the topic:

    Standard weather briefings can be obtained from a variety of sources, including the FAA. Pilots can obtain abbreviated weather information from briefers to supplement available electronic information. Information that a pilot has previously obtained should be provided to the briefer in case conditions have changed. An outlook weather briefing is obtained six or more hours in advance of the flight. Lastly, it's important to obtain in-flight briefings to monitor ongoing weather conditions during the flight course itself.

    a. In-flight briefings monitor ongoing weather conditions during flight.
    b. Briefers are people who provide meteorological information to pilots.
    c. Standard weather briefings are the most comprehensive types.
    d. All briefings should be updated.
    e. There are a variety of weather briefing types.

4. Which of the options can be inferred by the passage below?

    Don't attempt to fly through thunderstorms. Try to safely and wisely circumnavigate them. Know your personal skills and limitations regarding weather flight before you gather forecast information. Keep in mind that a variety of conditions in-flight can change quickly. Don't fly into areas of rain where the air temperature is at or close to freezing. Always allow more margin of error for weather at night, and do not attempt to navigate through cloud "holes."

    a. Flying in inclement weather involves using sound judgment.
    b. Thunderstorms are not navigable.
    c. Changing conditions will lead to flight trouble.
    d. Freezing rain can be managed if the pilot knows what he is doing.
    e. Flying at night is tricky.

5. Read the following passage and select the best definition for the word in **bold**:

> Everyone had said his piloting **acumen** was not to be questioned. He had a knack for feeling the aircraft, as if it was an instinctual part of himself. He had a knowledge base he'd built up over years of study and thousands of flying hours; but moreover, he had the ability to think and act quickly in the most unexpected circumstances.

The word *acumen* means:

a. Ability to fly
b. Knowledge
c. Shrewdness and keen insight
d. Visual ability
e. Impressive number of flight hours

6. Read the following passage and select the best conclusion:

> Piloting is a consummate skill to obtain, but it isn't an impossible goal. A potential pilot must be versed in flight instruction, which consists of many classroom hours and even more flight hours. A potential pilot needs to have a logical mind, be armed with the right information for each flight, and be correctly trained in all piloting procedures. Anyone who lacks a crucial ingredient in training takes a serious risk when flying. With the right education and the right instruction, becoming a pilot is a rewarding venture.

a. Anyone can become a pilot.
b. Becoming a pilot is a risky proposition.
c. Innate ability is key in flight instruction.
d. Learning to fly, if taught and practiced correctly, is a fulfilling skill.
e. Piloting can be impossible to learn.

7. Read the following passage and identify the statement that best describes the author's position.

> Piloting is a consummate skill to obtain, and for many, it's a skill that remains unattainable. A potential pilot must be so well-versed in flight instruction that studying the requirements can seem overwhelming. In addition, thousands of flight hours must be logged in practice before a pilot can begin a career. The physical and mental demands made on many potential students can be prohibitive. It's a dedicated person who perseveres and becomes successful in the flight industry.

a. Piloting is a difficult goal requiring serious consideration.
b. Becoming a pilot is cost-prohibitive.
c. Piloting careers are few and far between.
d. The physical and mental demands on piloting students should be the main consideration when deciding on a career in flight.
e. Piloting involves a lot of luck and practice.

8. Carefully read the following passage, taking note of the letters that precede each sentence. Then select the option that best describes the text's correct sequence:

> Aviation's history expands over 2,000 years. A) Eventually, Leonardo da Vinci studied the flight of birds and began noting some basic principles of aerodynamics. B) It is said that kites were the first airborne, manmade "vehicles." They existed in China around the fifth century B.C. and were capable of carrying a person into the air. C) The first recorded attempt at flight was made by a Spanish citizen who covered his arms in feathers and

jumped. D) The late 18th century saw a major development in ballooning, and the steerable airship, or dirigible, was developed. E) Sir George Cayley significantly impacted aerodynamics in the early 19th century by contributing key ideas to flight physics. F) In 1903, Orville Wright flew 130 feet in twelve seconds.

a. The sequence is correct
b. B, D, C, A, F, E
c. A, C, F, D, E, B
d. C, B, A, D, E, F
e. D, F, E, B, C, A

9. Which of the following best states the author's purpose?

While many innovative aircraft have been developed throughout the history of flight, certain aircraft can be referred to as groundbreaking and revolutionary. Their existence has transformed flight and advanced the study of aviation. The Wright Brothers' 1905 plane, The Flyer, was the first to have three-axis control. It had innovative seating for its pilot and attained faster speeds due to increased power. The Monocoque, developed by Deperdussin manufacturers, introduced a new shell structure capable of handling the forces of stress. In 1919, Hugo Junkers introduced all-metal structures with thicker wings. The Douglas DC-1 bears the title of the first American, scientifically-designed structure.

a. The purpose is to inform by presenting examples of revolutionary aircraft inventions throughout flight history.
b. The purpose is to entertain the reader with stories about airplanes.
c. The purpose is to argue that Deperdussin's model, which handled the forces of stress, was the most revolutionary development in flight.
d. The purpose is to convince the reader that American, scientifically-designed structures were the best.
e. The purpose is to convince the reader that these examples are the only ones worth considering in the development of innovative flight.

10. Read the following passage, then select the option that best identifies cause and effect:

While it can be dangerous, turbulence during flight is common and manageable. Turbulence is a disruption in air flow. Think of it as a bump on the road while driving to work. It happens all the time and, when managed effectively, it's fairly benign. One type of turbulence is CAT (Clear Air Turbulence). It cannot be seen, and one way to avoid it is to fly at a higher, and likely smoother, altitude. Severe turbulence, a disturbance that results in an altitude deviation of 100 feet, is uncomfortable, but not dangerous.

a. Turbulence causes plane crashes.
b. Turbulence is caused by a disruption in air flow.
c. Turbulence is common and the effects are always dangerous.
d. Turbulence is uncommon and the effects are usually benign.
e. Turbulence is manageable by flying at a higher altitude.

11. Read the same, expanded passage below, then select the answer that best states the outcome:

> While it can be dangerous, turbulence during flight is common and manageable. Turbulence is a disruption in air flow. Think of it as a bump on the road while driving to work. It happens all the time and, when managed effectively, it's fairly benign. One type of turbulence is CAT (Clear Air Turbulence). It cannot be seen, and one way to avoid it is to fly at a higher, and likely smoother altitude. Severe turbulence, a disturbance that results in an altitude deviation of 100 feet, is uncomfortable, but not dangerous. A disruptive air flow that causes turbulence doesn't have to result in difficulty for the pilot. A well-trained pilot and crew can manage turbulence so that it isn't disruptive to passengers in flight.

a. If not managed, turbulence will result in disaster.
b. Weather maps predict CAT.
c. Flying at a higher altitude always solves the problem of turbulence.
d. A bump in the road is potentially more invasive than air turbulence.
e. Encountering turbulence is not a significant issue for pilots and will not likely result in air disaster.

12. Read the passage below and select the option that best states the author's purpose:

> The mechanics of flight are not difficult to understand, although the concepts often contain difficult terminology. Words such as yaw, pitch, and roll define aircraft axes, or dimensional center lines of gravity that intersect an airplane. Understanding these terms is crucial to understanding the mechanics of flight. Controls such as actuators generate forces that act on an aircraft. Rotational dynamics operate in tandem with translational ones to affect an aircraft's position and trajectory.

a. The purpose of the passage is to convince the reader that the mechanics of flight are easy to understand.
b. The purpose of the passage is to confuse the reader by using difficult terminology to explain a simple concept.
c. The purpose of the passage is to inform the reader about terminology in the mechanics of flight.
d. The purpose of the passage is to describe how axes and aircraft controls affect the mechanics of flight.
e. C and D.

13. Read the below paragraph and select the option that likely defines the word in **bold** within context:

> A helicopter pilot maneuvers many controls to maintain **equilibrium** in flight. These controls include the cyclic stick, anti-torque pedals, and the collective lever. The cyclic control maintains the pitch angle of the craft's rotating blades. The anti-torque pedals control the nose of the helicopter. The collective lever controls the pitch angle of the rotating blades together or independently as needed. All three controls help the pilot stay stable in flight.

a. Equilibrium means unsteady.
b. Equilibrium means pitchy.
c. Equilibrium means the collective pitch angle of a helicopter's blades.
d. Equilibrium means flight stability.
e. Equilibrium means the controls used to fly a helicopter.

14. Read the paragraph and select the option that best states cause and effect:

> The pilot looked to the left, and there it was: a tiny glimmer of white on the left wing. He was on the leading edge of it. He knew the temperature had dropped. He'd checked it repeatedly. He had been cleared at 9,000 feet but needed to go down. He needed to get to warmer air and get there quickly. He checked the terrain clearance and decided it was now or never. He popped out of the clouds and began his descent, chunks of ice flying off the fuselage.

a. Not checking a weather report ahead of time led to ice on the aircraft.
b. Flying too high resulted in icing.
c. The pilot didn't have the right clearance and encountered icing as a result.
d. A sudden, unexpected drop in temperature resulted in icing that the pilot had to account for.
e. Icing led to additional weight on the fuselage.

15. Read the paragraph and select the option that best defines the words in **bold**:

> Differential pitch control is a factor in helicopter flight. Differential pitch control affects the yaw axis and causes the helicopter to spin in the direction of its rotational, tilted rotors. **Coaxial** mounted helicopters, or crafts with dual rotors mounted above each other concentrically, require interaction between rotors. **Intermeshing** rotors, or helicopter rotors at a set angle to each other and turn in opposite directions, require increasing collective pitch on one blade set.

a. From the passage, it's impossible to tell what coaxial and intermeshing rotators are.
b. Coaxial rotors are dual and mounted above each other, while intermeshing rotors are angled apart from each other.
c. Coaxial means interaction and intermeshing means turning in an opposite direction.
d. Coaxial and intermeshing mean the same thing.
e. Coaxial and intermeshing rotors have nothing to do with differential pitch control.

16. Read the passage below and select the option that best identifies the main idea:

> The synchropter arrangement was first designed for use in Germany's anti-submarine war craft. Often referred to as intermeshing rotor configuration, this design sets two oppositional rotors at a slight angle from each other in a transverse manner so that they actually intermesh. The configuration allows a helicopter to function without a tail rotor in order to save power.

a. The development of the synchropter began during World War II.
b. Synchropter configuration is best understood as an intermeshing rotor configuration, oppositional in nature.
c. Oppositional rotors always intermesh.
d. Functioning without a tail rotor saves power for a helicopter.
e. Transverse rotors always intermesh.

17. Choose the option that best defines the word in **bold** below:

A helicopter pilot's use of control in a hover is critical to success. Correct use of the cyclic, the collective, and the anti-torque pedal controls help maintain balance. The cyclic is used to cut down on **drift** in the craft's horizontal plane. The collective helps maintain altitude, and the anti-torque control is used to direct the craft's nose direction.

a. Drift means unwanted movement within the helicopter's horizontal plane.
b. Drift refers to stable air around the helicopter.
c. Drift refers to the pilot's ability to control the cyclic.
d. Drift means hover.
e. Drift can be defined as unwanted movement within the helicopter's vertical plane.

18. Read the passage and select the answer that best states the logical conclusion:

A chain of events often defines incidents that lead to an accident. In aviation, this chain of events is often referred to as the "error chain." This term purports that it isn't one single event that leads to an air disaster but a chain of separate events. In other words, an accident is caused by more than one problem and most likely has more than one root cause. These events can be caused by human error or mechanical issues. A recent study indicates that pilot error is more likely to contribute to air disasters than mechanical problems.

a. Air disaster is unavoidable.
b. The error chain is specific to aviation.
c. A pilot's appropriate risk assessment before and during a flight will cut down on negative error chain events.
d. Mechanics aren't a consideration in the error chain.
e. Mechanics should be the primary consideration during flight.

19. Read the passage and select the correct answer to the question below:

Proper risk assessment for flight is critical for avoiding air disaster. As most events in the error chain can be addressed and controlled by the pilot, it's essential to consider all risks before and during flight. A pilot must perform all necessary informational checks prior to a scheduled flight. The flight path itself must be registered and approved. During the flight, a pilot must communicate regularly with others in the air and on the ground. Making sudden, unapproved changes during flight can lead to a negative chain of events. Being unprepared, uncommunicative, and unaware are all mistakes a pilot can make while on the job. Constant risk assessment is necessary to a successful and happily uneventful flight.

Which of the following statements provides the most encompassing overview with which the author would most likely agree?

a. Risk assessment includes mechanical checks and balances.
b. The pilot is the leading force in appropriate risk assessment.
c. Risk assessment is best conducted on the ground prior to flight.
d. Unapproved changes during a flight will always lead to problems.
e. Communication is the key factor in a successful flight.

20. Read the passage below and select the best meaning for the word in **bold**:

The United States attack helicopter came into its own during the 1990s. During Operation Desert Storm, the Apache fired against early warning radar sites to, in part, support ground troops. In addition, Apaches were able to destroy surface-to-air (SAM) sites via their Hellfire missile technology. The missiles **obliterated** many armored cars and tanks as well.

a. Obliterated can be defined as a type of Apache missile.
b. Obliterated means thoroughly destroyed.
c. Obliterated is defined as a military strategy.
d. Obliterated means flying low over armored cars and tanks.
e. Obliterated can be defined as an Apache flight technique, specific to Operation Desert Storm.

Situational Judgment

This section of the test measures your judgement when responding to interpersonal situations that are similar to those that you will face as an officer. Your response will be scored relative to a consensus judgement across experienced U.S. Air Force officers.

For each situation, you must pick the MOST EFFECTIVE and the LEAST EFFECTIVE way to respond to the situation.

The best approach to these questions is an analytical one. Try to take emotion out of the picture and judge what is the best logical approach to each situation. Choose the answer that will resolve the issue at hand as easily and quickly as possible. Your choice should also be one that will not lead to any further or new issues in the future. Although everyone will not view each situation exactly the same, the census response will help make up for this. This helps ensure that the truly most effective answer is chosen.

Situation 1

You have an innovative plan for your unit that, in your opinion, will improve performance. Not everyone in the unit is of the same opinion, and some downright oppose your plan. Even though the plan has not been put in motion, someone has already written a letter of complaint and sent it to your superior.

What would you do?

a. Don't worry about anyone else's opinion, and implement the plan.
b. Ignore the letter of complaint, and push forward with the plan.
c. Have a meeting with the unit, including the person who wrote the complaint to your superior, and explain to everyone again the chain-of-command and how it is to be used.
d. Discipline the person who wrote the letter of complaint so that no one else in the unit will break the chain-of-command in the future.
e. Give up your plan in the wake of opposition, and see what the unit would like to do.

1. Select the answer that contains the MOST EFFECTIVE way to respond to the situation.

2. Select the answer that contains the LEAST EFFECTIVE way to respond to the situation.

Situation 2

You have had a successful working relationship with an aide assigned to you. On a personal level, you dislike the assignee based on your opinion that they are arrogant and too critical of others. A senior officer is thinking of giving the aide a promotion, which would greatly benefit his/her future and put the aide on a fast track for future promotions.

What would you do?

a. Attempt to dissuade the senior officer by sharing your personal feelings about the aide.
b. You want the aide to just go away, so you give a recommendation for promotion.
c. You do not want the aide to be rewarded, so you recommend that the senior officer give it to someone else.
d. Other than expressing your opinion of the aide, you do not interfere with the selection process.
e. List your complaints about the aide in an anonymous letter to the senior officer.

3. Select the answer that contains the MOST EFFECTIVE way to respond to the situation.

4. Select the answer that contains the LEAST EFFECTIVE way to respond to the situation.

Situation 3

A coworker, who is another officer in your division, has to give an important speech in a few days. The officer has spent a great deal of time and effort on the report, but is still nervous about presenting it. After being asked by the officer to look over the report, you find some items that you feel need to be changed. You discuss these items with the other officer, who disagrees with you. You are positive that the changes you identified need to be made.

What would you do?

a. Mention the conversation to a senior officer prior to the speech as a way to make yourself look better, since you are right and the other officer wouldn't listen to you.
b. Do everything you can to convince the officer to review the report and supporting information and make the changes you have recommended.
c. Avoid going to the speech if at all possible.
d. Attempt to get a senior officer involved to order that the report be changed.
e. Do not say or do anything. You are not giving the speech.

5. Select the answer that contains the MOST EFFECTIVE way to respond to the situation.

6. Select the answer that contains the LEAST EFFECTIVE way to respond to the situation.

Situation 4

You have been teamed up with another officer on an important one-month assignment to draft a report. Unfortunately, early in the project your coworker has become ill and is required to be on leave. The illness keeps him/her out of the office much longer than expected. At the one-month mark on the report, your coworker is still ill and remains on leave. There is no way of knowing when your coworker will return to work and his/her expertise is needed to complete the assignment.

What would you do?

a. Order a subordinate onto the project in an attempt to complete the report.
b. To the best of your ability, put in as many hours as it takes to finish it yourself.
c. Don't give any details; just ask for the deadline to be extended.
d. Relay the situation to your superior and request help to finish the report.
e. Wait indefinitely for the coworker to return without regard to the timeline for the report.

7. Select the answer that contains the MOST EFFECTIVE way to respond to the situation.

8. Select the answer that contains the LEAST EFFECTIVE way to respond to the situation.

Situation 5

After a long day at work, you are at home and you realize you forgot to sign documents that need to go on to another unit for completion. The documents cannot move forward without your signature. While the documents are not urgent in nature, your oversight will cause another officer to be delayed and have to stay at work later than usual.

What would you do?

a. Go back to work and sign the papers.
b. The documents are not urgent, so you wait until the next day to sign them.
c. Show up to work early the next day to sign the documents, get them moving first thing in the morning, and hope the other officer won't have to stay late.
d. Get a subordinate at your office to sign your name on the documents so they can move forward.
e. Call the officer that this will impact and explain that the documents will be late in arriving.

9. Select the answer that contains the MOST EFFECTIVE way to respond to the situation.

10. Select the answer that contains the LEAST EFFECTIVE way to respond to the situation.

Situation 6

A week before you are about to be transferred to a new unit you receive a message from the officer in charge of that unit. The officer explains you are entering the unit at a critical time, as they are leading training exercises for highly skilled soldiers. The message goes on to indicate that you are expected to be a valuable contributor from the moment you arrive, with minimal assistance. However, your experience in this area is minimal.

What would you do?

a. Send a courteous thank you message in return and attempt to study for the new position.
b. Send no response to the email. You should have no problem taking on this new position.
c. Discreetly ask one of the officers in the new unit if he/she will be able to train you upon arrival.
d. You think you should remain with your current unit, so you request that your transfer be cancelled.
e. Respond to the senior officer's message with a request for a meeting, where you can discuss transition into the new position.

11. Select the answer that contains the MOST EFFECTIVE way to respond to the situation.

12. Select the answer that contains the LEAST EFFECTIVE way to respond to the situation.

Situation 7

A coworker, who is another officer, has lied about his/her time off. The officer had requested leave for a week to visit an ailing family member. The request for leave was granted. Through social media, you learned the officer was at the beach on vacation, hundreds of miles away from the ailing family member he/she was supposedly visiting.

What would you do?

a. Go see the commanding officer immediately to relay what you just discovered.
b. Anonymously send the social media evidence of the officer's actions to the commanding officer.
c. Since you now have a bargaining chip, you tell the officer you will keep this information to yourself in exchange for him taking on part of your weekly workload.
d. Tell the officer if he/she does anything unethical like that again you will have no choice but to report it.
e. You mind your own business and do nothing.

13. Select the answer that contains the MOST EFFECTIVE way to respond to the situation.

14. Select the answer that contains the LEAST EFFECTIVE way to respond to the situation.

Situation 8

After being in the same unit and performing the same job for two years, you are beginning to feel burned out. Even though you are successful in your current position, you wonder what other options may be available. You have been asking around to people in other units to gauge their experiences. Within a month the rumors in your unit have started that are you are looking for a transfer.

What would you do?

a. Address the concerns that are brought up and refocus on your current position.
b. Ask for a leave of absence so you can find a way to handle the situation.
c. Send a formal request for transfer to your senior officer, acknowledging the truth of the rumors.
d. Refocus on your position and ignore the rumors, even though they are true.
e. Continue looking for a new unit to transfer to, but deny the rumors that are circulating.

15. Select the answer that contains the MOST EFFECTIVE way to respond to the situation.

16. Select the answer that contains the LEAST EFFECTIVE way to respond to the situation.

Situation 9

Your current workload has you extremely busy, but you are managing to meet your deadlines and are producing quality work. A senior officer has asked if you would perform an additional assignment in conjunction with the work you are performing. While you would like to impress the senior officer and take on the additional work, you are already pushing yourself with your current workload. If you took on the extra work, the quality of work on both assignments would suffer.

What would you do?

a. Tell the senior officer that you would be glad to do the work, and then pass it on to a coworker to complete.
b. Apologize to the senior officer, and say you are too busy and that you cannot do the extra assignment.
c. Ask for a few days to think about it.
d. You can't say no so you take the assignment; you will just have to find a way to complete the work as quickly as possible.
e. Present an offer to pass the assignment to another qualified coworker, but inform the senior officer that unfortunately you are unable to complete the work yourself at this time.

17. Select the answer that contains the MOST EFFECTIVE way to respond to the situation.

18. Select the answer that contains the LEAST EFFECTIVE way to respond to the situation.

Situation 10

While assigned to a field office, you become aware that a coworker is extremely overworked with assignments being sent from other offices. The coworker's senior officers do not seem to notice that this person is overworked because your coworker does an excellent job, but they need to work extra hours to get the tasks completed.

What would you do?

a. You do nothing. That situation has nothing to do with you.
b. Sympathize with the coworker about his/her workload.
c. Assist the coworker and help with his/her workload as much as possible.
d. Request a meeting with the coworker's senior officer to inform the officer of the situation.
e. Task one of your subordinates to assist this person in the workload.

19. Select the answer that contains the MOST EFFECTIVE way to respond to the situation.

20. Select the answer that contains the LEAST EFFECTIVE way to respond to the situation.

Situation 11

You are in attendance at a meeting where two officers get in a heated dispute over policy changes. It is considered common knowledge around work that these two officers do not like each other on a personal level, but no one is sure why. Unable to come to an agreement on the policy, they ask you to settle the disagreement.

What would you do?

a. Resolve the dispute on the side of the officer that you favor.
b. Resolve the dispute on the side of the officer who can benefit your career the most in the future.
c. Put all personal feelings aside and choose what you believe is the best option.
d. Point out the officers' blatant issues with each other as the reason they cannot agree, and then remove yourself from the situation.
e. Disregard the request to settle the dispute on the policy; this is a good time to lecture these two on teamwork and cooperation in the military.

21. Select the answer that contains the MOST EFFECTIVE way to respond to the situation.

22. Select the answer that contains the LEAST EFFECTIVE way to respond to the situation.

Situation 12

You are working on reports for your senior officers with a coworker. The reports are used by the officers to track the training and readiness of soldiers for the most hazardous and difficult missions. You noticed your coworker appears to be manipulating these numbers, and they are not being entered correctly. If the soldiers are reported as having a higher amount of training than is required for these missions and then chosen, this could pose a huge risk to the missions and put lives in jeopardy.

What would you do?

a. Do nothing yet, but monitor the coworker to see what is going on.
b. Report this issue to your senior officer right away.
c. Review your coworker's numbers and correct them yourself.
d. Leave an anonymous note to your coworker to stop changing the numbers in the report and make sure what is turned in is accurate.
e. Wait for coworker to finish assignment, and then you will have proof of what is going on.

23. Select the answer that contains the MOST EFFECTIVE way to respond to the situation.

24. Select the answer that contains the LEAST EFFECTIVE way to respond to the situation.

Situation 13

A senior officer asks you in private how you feel about your supervisor. Your supervisor reports to this senior officer. You feel the officer in question overall does a good job, but could do better in a certain aspect of his/her job.

What would you do?

a. Express just that: They do a good job overall, but could use improvement in this one area.
b. Refuse to answer the question.
c. Give the supervisor a glowing review, without mentioning his/her weak area.
d. Discuss the solutions to improving the area where the officer is weak.
e. Write a note that explains your thoughts about the officer.

25. Select the answer that contains the MOST EFFECTIVE way to respond to the situation.

26. Select the answer that contains the LEAST EFFECTIVE way to respond to the situation.

Situation 14

You are serving on a board of three officers interviewing three candidates for promotion. Candidate 1 is a known family friend of your commanding officer, but is the most impressive of the three candidates through the interview process. Candidate 2 seems to be another good choice for the position. Candidate 3 did not do well in the interview process and does not seem like a good choice for promotion at this point. The other two officers on the board have voted, one for each of the first two candidates. You have the deciding vote.

What would you do?

a. You cast your vote for the second candidate, to avoid the appearance of favoritism.
b. You remove yourself from the board so that you do not have to vote.
c. You vote for Candidate 3, so you do not have to decide who gets the promotion.
d. You vote for Candidate 1, because that candidate is most qualified.
e. You refrain from the vote and ask for a new group of candidates.

27. Select the answer that contains the MOST EFFECTIVE way to respond to the situation.

28. Select the answer that contains the LEAST EFFECTIVE way to respond to the situation.

Situation 15

You are given an important assignment that involves working with an officer from a different unit. This officer appears to already have "one foot out the door," as retirement is near. The officer does not put much effort into the assignment, leaving you to do the bulk of the work.

What would you do?

a. Explain your feelings to your new coworker. Point out that the situation is not fair to you and that the work is very important and should be shared equally.
b. Put in a request for a new partner on the assignment.
c. Say nothing and do all the work necessary to successfully complete the assignment.
d. Just do the best you can with the realization the assignment will likely be unsuccessful due to lack of participation of your coworker.
e. Inform your senior officer of the situation.

29. Select the answer that contains the MOST EFFECTIVE way to respond to the situation.

30. Select the answer that contains the LEAST EFFECTIVE way to respond to the situation.

Situation 16

You have had a feeling that one of your subordinates may have an ambitious agenda and be deliberately undermining your work. Other officers have discussed that this subordinate wants to take your job.

What would you do?

a. Publicly attempt to humiliate the subordinate and reprimand him/her.
b. Do nothing and the situation may just go away.
c. Discuss the situation with the subordinate and explain that you expect his/her cooperation and support.
d. Ask for another officer to step in and discuss the problem with your subordinate.
e. File a report for insubordination to your senior officer.

31. Select the answer that contains the MOST EFFECTIVE way to respond to the situation.

32. Select the answer that contains the LEAST EFFECTIVE way to respond to the situation.

Situation 17

Recently it has come to your attention that office supplies are disappearing from the supply closet at a much faster rate than usual. There is no apparent reason that would account for the change in supply usage. Your gut is telling you that the officer that is last to leave the office may be taking items with him/her after everyone else has left. You do not have any evidence of your suspicion, but it does seem like things disappear on the shifts for which this officer is the last to leave.

What would you do?

a. Report your suspicions to a senior officer.
b. Secretly set up hidden cameras in an attempt to catch the thief.
c. Discuss your suspicions with the officer you suspect and ask for an explanation.
d. Discuss with fellow officers to see what they think is going on.
e. Don't do anything.

33. Select the answer that contains the MOST EFFECTIVE way to respond to the situation.

34. Select the answer that contains the LEAST EFFECTIVE way to respond to the situation.

Situation 18

Rumors have been circulating that your base is going to be shut down due to budgetary restraints. You are in attendance at a meeting between local community leaders and senior officers from your unit. The community leaders are willing to lobby to keep the base open in return for the support of the military leadership in some local initiatives, specifically disaster-relief coordination efforts. A community leader asks your opinion on the matter being discussed.

What would you do?

a. Answer the question honestly to the best of your ability, but explain you are not a senior officer.
b. Tell the leader you are not a senior officer and cannot give your opinion.
c. Defer the question to a senior officer without giving your opinion.
d. Give a thorough answer even though you have little knowledge on this topic.
e. Answer the question, but keep it positive; do not mention any possible negative result of what is being proposed.

35. Select the answer that contains the MOST EFFECTIVE way to respond to the situation.

36. Select the answer that contains the LEAST EFFECTIVE way to respond to the situation.

Situation 19

A subordinate in your unit has recently been showing signs of burnout and seems frustrated with his/her current position over the last month. You notice this coincides with a decline in the quality and quantity of his/her work. This negative attitude has been affecting the overall work environment with the fellow soldiers in the unit.

What would you do?

a. Report the situation to your senior officer.
b. Do nothing and hope the situation will improve on its own.
c. Point out this behavior and bad performance in a meeting with the entire unit.
d. Meet with the subordinate to discuss these issues, along with the effects on the unit, and present possible solutions.
e. Reassign the subordinate to alleviate the problem in your unit.

37. Select the answer that contains the MOST EFFECTIVE way to respond to the situation.

38. Select the answer that contains the LEAST EFFECTIVE way to respond to the situation.

Situation 20

In your current position, one of your many responsibilities is to brief a small team of some activities that are confidential in nature. You have accidentally sent an email containing some of this confidential information to an officer that is not on this team, and who does not have the security clearance to have access to the information you sent.

What would you do?

a. Immediately email this person and request they destroy the information you just sent. Then, immediately inform your supervisor of your mistake.
b. Tell your supervisor what happened and let him/her handle it.
c. Do nothing. Wait and see what happens.
d. Ask your senior officer if they can request that the individual be cleared for a higher security level since they have been presented with the material.
e. Send an email to the same person saying your email was hacked and to disregard any previous messages.

39. Select the answer that contains the MOST EFFECTIVE way to respond to the situation.

40. Select the answer that contains the LEAST EFFECTIVE way to respond to the situation.

Situation 21

Soldiers in your unit have been awaiting training at a nearby base. A request was made to be in the next training cycle, but soldiers from a different unit were chosen for the next block of training—even though they had not been waiting as long. You have no evidence, but you have a feeling your unit may not have been given the training block requested due to the training director disliking you on a personal level.

What would you do?

a. Ask the director if your soldiers can attend the same training along with the other soldiers selected.
b. Meet with the training director to determine the reason your soldiers were passed over and emphasize the importance of this training to your unit.
c. Do nothing; the decision has been made.
d. Send a critical letter to the director and your senior officer over this perceived injustice.
e. Discuss the situation with the other unit's senior officer to see if they would give up their training spots so your soldiers could have them.

41. Select the answer that contains the MOST EFFECTIVE way to respond to the situation.

42. Select the answer that contains the LEAST EFFECTIVE way to respond to the situation.

Situation 22

When you joined a new unit a couple of months ago, the leader of the unit was very helpful. You were given a great deal of training to carry out the duties and responsibilities of your new position. You are now feeling pretty confident in your abilities, but still have not been given the freedom to work your position independently.

What would you do?

a. Tell the unit leader's supervisor that they need to back off and give you the leeway to do your job.
b. Provide evidence and demonstrate your competence so the leader will leave you alone.
c. Meet with the leader, thank him for all the assistance and guidance, and discuss that you feel ready to work more independently.
d. Try to avoid the leader as much as possible and maybe the situation will correct itself.
e. Request another officer be assigned to your unit so that the leader will need to refocus attention on someone else.

43. Select the answer that contains the MOST EFFECTIVE way to respond to the situation.

44. Select the answer that contains the LEAST EFFECTIVE way to respond to the situation.

Situation 23

Almost two months ago you were assigned to a new unit. In that brief amount of time you have identified numerous deficiencies in existing operations and have developed solutions for these problems. The majority of the people you have discussed these issues with agree with your proposed solutions. However, the senior officer believes the solutions are too risky and may cause more harm than good.

What would you do?

a. Implement your proposed solutions, believing the senior officer will come around once he/she witnesses their success.
b. Accept the senior officer's decision and work within the current structure without making your changes.
c. Using the majority support of the unit, again confront the senior officer with your solutions.
d. In detail, create a comprehensive report on the benefits of implementing your proposed solutions. Deliver your report and subsequently accept your senior officer's decision either way.
e. Accept the senior officer's decision, then keep a log of the ways your solutions could have improved performance.

45. Select the answer that contains the MOST EFFECTIVE way to respond to the situation.

46. Select the answer that contains the LEAST EFFECTIVE way to respond to the situation.

Situation 24

You have always excelled in your work, and you received a promotion six months ago. Recent budget cuts have affected the quality of your work over the last few weeks. The budget cuts prevented you from having what you needed to perform your job efficiently and in the proper way. Your senior officer, however, is unaware of the budget effects and has expressed that you are the problem, your work is not up to par, and the performance drop is a result of poor management on your part.

What would you do?

a. Ask for advice or ideas from other officers who are dealing with the same issues resulting from budget problems.
b. Tell your senior officer the problem lies with your subordinates.
c. Get a list of complaints from your senior officer.
d. Ask for time off to get some perspective.
e. Defend your position and remind the senior officer of the budget cuts.

47. Select the answer that contains the MOST EFFECTIVE way to respond to the situation.

48. Select the answer that contains the LEAST EFFECTIVE way to respond to the situation.

Situation 25

Supply and delivery logistics are maintained in a base computer program. While you are coordinating a long line of deliveries, the computer system crashes. You are advised by computer support the problem may take an hour or more to fix. The delivery drivers are already getting impatient.

What would you do?

a. Request guidance from a senior officer.
b. Ask the drivers if they have any other deliveries they could make in the meantime and return later.
c. Try to avoid the drivers by going on a break.
d. Ask for assistance in advising all drivers of the issue and the possible wait time, and accommodate them in whatever way you can.
e. Receive the deliveries anyway.

49. Select the answer that contains the MOST EFFECTIVE way to respond to the situation.

50. Select the answer that contains the LEAST EFFECTIVE way to respond to the situation.

Self-Description Inventory

The self-description inventory is a personality test provided in the AFOQT. The self-description inventory is not included in the final score, so no one answer is better than another. Since these questions are helpful in assessing your personal characteristics, answer them as best you can and don't spend much time analyzing them. The purpose is to find an appropriate career match by comparing your answers to others who hold Air Force positions.

Physical Science

1. What is the total mechanical energy of a system?
   a. The total potential energy
   b. The total kinetic energy
   c. Kinetic energy plus potential energy
   d. Kinetic energy minus potential energy
   e. Potential energy divided by kinetic energy

2. What does the Lewis Dot structure of an element represent?
   a. The outer proton valence shell population
   b. The inner electron valence shell population
   c. The positioning of the element's protons
   d. The positioning of the element's neutrons
   e. The outer electron valence shell population

3. What is the name of the scale used in sound level meters to measure the intensity of sound waves?
   a. Doppler
   b. Electron
   c. Watt
   d. Decibel
   e. Seismograph

4. Which statement is true regarding electrostatic charges?
   a. Like charges attract.
   b. Like charges repel.
   c. Like charges are neutral.
   d. Like charges neither attract nor repel.
   e. Like charges attack each other.

5. What is the name of this compound: CO?
   a. Carbonite oxide
   b. Carbonic dioxide
   c. Carbonic oxide
   d. Carbon monoxide
   e. Carbonite dioxide

6. What is the molarity of a solution made by dissolving 4.0 grams of NaCl into enough water to make 120 mL of solution? The atomic mass of Na is 23.0 g/mol and Cl is 35.5 g/mol.
   a. 0.34 M
   b. 0.57 M
   c. 0.034 M
   d. 0.057 M
   e. 0.094 M

7. Considering a gas in a closed system, at a constant volume, what will happen to the temperature if the pressure is increased?
   a. The temperature will stay the same
   b. The temperature will decrease
   c. The temperature will increase
   d. It cannot be determined with the information given
   e. The temperature will increase and then slowly decrease.

8. What is the current when a 3.0 V battery is wired across a lightbulb that has a resistance of 6.0 ohms?
   a. 0.5 A
   b. 18.0 A
   c. 0.5 J
   d. 18.0 J
   e. 9.0 J

9. According to Newton's Three Laws of Motion, which of the following is true?
   a. Two objects cannot exert a force on each other without touching.
   b. An object at rest has no inertia.
   c. The weight of an object is the same as the mass of the object.
   d. Volume is equal to the change in momentum per change in time.
   e. The weight of an object is equal to the mass of an object multiplied by gravity.

10. What is the chemical reaction when a compound is broken down into its elemental components called?
   a. A synthesis reaction
   b. A decomposition reaction
   c. An organic reaction
   d. An oxidation reaction
   e. A composition reaction

11. What is ONE reason why speciation can occur?
   a. Geographic separation
   b. Seasons
   c. Daylight
   d. A virus
   e. Gravity

12. What is the broadest, or LEAST specialized, classification of the Linnean taxonomic system?
   a. Species
   b. Family
   c. Order
   d. Phylum
   e. Domain

13. How are fungi similar to plants?
    a. They have a cell wall
    b. They contain chloroplasts
    c. They perform photosynthesis
    d. They use carbon dioxide as a source of energy
    e. They use carbon monoxide as a source of energy

14. What important function are the roots of plants responsible for?
    a. Absorbing water from the surrounding environment
    b. Performing photosynthesis
    c. Conducting sugars downward through the leaves
    d. Supporting the plant body
    e. Seed development and reproduction

15. Which of the following would occur in response to a change in water concentration?
    a. Phototropism
    b. Thermotropism
    c. Gravitropism
    d. Hydrotropism
    e. Geotropism

16. What is the MAIN function of the respiratory system?
    a. To eliminate waste through the kidneys and bladder
    b. To exchange gas between the air and circulating blood
    c. To transform food and liquids into energy
    d. To excrete waste from the body
    e. To produce and secrete hormones

17. What type of vessel carries oxygen-rich blood from the heart to other tissues of the body?
    a. Veins
    b. Intestines
    c. Bronchioles
    d. Arteries
    e. Capillaries

18. Which system comprises the 206 bones of the body?
    a. Skeletal
    b. Muscular
    c. Endocrine
    d. Reproductive
    e. Lymphatic

19. Which factor is NOT a consideration in population dynamics?
    a. Size and age of population
    b. Immigration
    c. Hair color
    d. Number of births
    e. Number of deaths

20. Which type of diagram describes the cycling of energy and nutrients of an ecosystem?
    a. Food web
    b. Phylogenetic tree
    c. Fossil record
    d. Pedigree chart

Table Reading

This section of the test measures whether you can read a table accurately. The table below shows X- and Y-values in a grid format. The numbers on the horizontal, or top, part of the table are the X-values, and the numbers on the vertical, or side, part of the table are the Y-values. In other words, the X-values correspond to columns, and the Y-values correspond to rows. Each question will provide you with two coordinates, an X and a Y, and you must quickly interpret the table to determine the correct value. Each question will have five possible answers, and you should choose the correct one.

Using the example table below, here are some practice questions and explanations to better help you understand how to use these tables.

	-3	-2	-1	0	+1	+2	+3
+3	14	15	17	19	20	21	22
+2	15	17	19	21	22	23	24
+1	16	18	20	22	24	25	26
0	18	19	21	23	25	26	28
-1	20	22	23	25	27	28	30
-2	21	23	24	26	28	29	31
-3	22	24	25	27	29	30	32

Example Problem 1

X	Y	A	B	C	D	E
1	+1	22	25	20	19	16

The answer to this example question would be A, 22. To answer this problem, first go to the X-axis and find the 0 column. Then follow the 0 column down to the +1 row on the Y-axis. The number at that point is 22. Some corresponding coordinates for the incorrect answers in this example would be:

B = 25: +1, 0

C = 20: +1, +3

D = 19: 0, +3

E = 16: -3, +1

What are some helpful tips for answering these questions correctly?

- Take your time. The easiest way to make mistakes in this section is assuming that the questions are easy and subsequently making simple mistakes.
- Make sure to correctly read the X and Y headings. It is easy to select the second column when you have an X-value of 2, but that wouldn't be the right column.
- Start with the X coordinate and stay within that selected column. Do not mistakenly travel to another column when you are selecting the Y-value.
- After you have the X column selected, go down to the corresponding Y-value row. Remember, don't change columns!
- Use your fingers or a piece of paper to mark the columns and rows as it helps you keep track of where you are and not jump to a neighboring column or row.
- Practice these types of questions until you are comfortable answering them correctly and within a certain window of time. On test day, take the same amount of time as you had been with the practice questions.

The next five questions are based on the following table.

	-3	**-2**	**-1**	**0**	**1**	**2**	**3**
-3	20	21	24	27	23	26	25
-2	21	22	29	32	31	30	26
-1	23	25	26	27	24	21	20
0	25	26	30	31	32	29	22
1	31	28	29	22	20	24	27
2	28	33	20	30	21	23	25
3	30	28	26	24	22	20	32

1. (-3, 3)
    a. 30
    b. 20
    c. 32
    d. 23
    e. 24

2. (0, -2)
    a. 30
    b. 26
    c. 32
    d. 21
    e. 29

3. (+1, 0)
   a. 22
   b. 30
   c. 24
   d. 27
   e. 32

4. (-2, -3)
   a. 23
   b. 21
   c. 33
   d. 26
   e. 20

5. (-1, 0)
   a. 22
   b. 27
   c. 24
   d. 30
   e. 23

The next five questions are based on the following table.

	-3	**-2**	**-1**	**0**	**1**	**2**	**3**
-3	10	11	13	15	18	17	19
-2	17	20	19	16	14	12	10
-1	18	19	17	20	13	11	16
0	13	22	18	14	12	10	11
1	11	19	20	16	15	14	18
2	19	23	22	12	17	15	20
3	14	15	12	18	11	22	21

6. (3, 3)
   a. 10
   b. 21
   c. 16
   d. 12
   e. 19

7. (-2, 1)
   a. 14
   b. 11
   c. 20
   d. 17
   e. 19

8. (0, 0)
  a. 14
  b. 15
  c. 13
  d. 10
  e. 12

9. (1, -2)
  a. 19
  b. 17
  c. 22
  d. 14
  e. 11

10. (-1, 0)
  a. 20
  b. 12
  c. 15
  d. 13
  e. 18

The next five questions are based on the following table.

	-3	**-2**	**-1**	**0**	**1**	**2**	**3**
-3	30	31	32	33	34	35	36
-2	33	34	35	36	37	38	39
-1	34	40	41	39	38	37	36
0	35	33	31	32	30	40	41
1	31	35	37	33	39	41	43
2	37	36	33	34	35	39	38
3	32	30	31	35	36	34	31

11. (2, -2)
  a. 34
  b. 36
  c. 39
  d. 35
  e. 38

12. (1, -3)
  a. 31
  b. 38
  c. 34
  d. 33
  e. 36

13. (3, 2)
   a. 38
   b. 34
   c. 37
   d. 39
   e. 33

14. (0, -1)
   a. 39
   b. 31
   c. 33
   d. 32
   e. 34

15. (-2, -1)
   a. 41
   b. 40
   c. 35
   d. 37
   e. 31

The next five questions are based on the following table.

	-3	**-2**	**-1**	**0**	**1**	**2**	**3**
-3	50	51	52	53	54	55	56
-2	53	55	56	57	58	59	52
-1	54	60	57	58	52	61	53
0	55	53	58	59	60	52	54
1	56	59	54	60	51	53	55
2	57	54	55	61	59	57	56
3	51	52	53	54	55	56	57

16. (-3, 2)
   a. 55
   b. 52
   c. 53
   d. 57
   e. 56

17. (-2, 0)
   a. 57
   b. 52
   c. 61
   d. 53
   e. 51

18. (1, 1)
    a. 51
    b. 57
    c. 52
    d. 54
    e. 55

19. (2, -1)
    a. 56
    b. 60
    c. 61
    d. 53
    e. 59

20. (-1, 3)
    a. 55
    b. 53
    c. 52
    d. 54
    e. 57

The next five questions are based on the following table.

	-3	**-2**	**-1**	**0**	**1**	**2**	**3**
-3	40	41	42	43	44	45	46
-2	42	44	43	54	47	46	45
-1	44	46	45	52	53	48	43
0	46	48	47	50	49	44	51
1	48	50	49	48	51	52	47
2	50	52	51	46	47	42	49
3	52	54	53	44	45	50	41

21. (0, 2)
    a. 46
    b. 44
    c. 54
    d. 48
    e. 52

22. (3, -2)
    a. 54
    b. 50
    c. 45
    d. 49
    e. 42

23. (-1, 1)
    a. 53
    b. 45
    c. 51
    d. 49
    e. 42

24. (2, 3)
    a. 49
    b. 54
    c. 41
    d. 45
    e. 50

25. (-2, 1)
    a. 47
    b. 50
    c. 48
    d. 46
    e. 52

The next five questions are based on the following table.

	-3	**-2**	**-1**	**0**	**1**	**2**	**3**
-3	5	6	7	8	9	10	11
-2	6	7	8	9	10	11	12
-1	8	9	10	11	12	13	14
0	10	11	12	13	14	15	16
1	12	13	14	15	16	17	6
2	14	15	16	17	6	5	8
3	16	17	6	5	8	7	10

26. (3, 0)
    a. 5
    b. 10
    c. 8
    d. 11
    e. 16

27. (1, 2)
    a. 17
    b. 6
    c. 16
    d. 10
    e. 8

28. (-1, -1)
a. 16
b. 14
c. 10
d. 12
e. 7

29. (-3, -2)
a. 7
b. 12
c. 6
d. 14
e. 8

30. (3, -1)
a. 14
b. 7
c. 6
d. 12
e. 8

The next five questions are based on the following table.

	-3	**-2**	**-1**	**0**	**1**	**2**	**3**
-3	11	12	13	14	15	16	17
-2	12	13	14	15	16	17	18
-1	14	15	16	17	18	19	20
0	16	17	18	19	20	21	22
1	18	19	20	21	22	21	12
2	20	21	22	11	12	13	14
3	22	11	12	13	14	15	16

31. (-3, -1)
a. 14
b. 13
c. 20
d. 18
e. 12

32. (0, 1)
a. 20
b. 17
c. 21
d. 18
e. 14

33. (2, 1)
    a. 12
    b. 19
    c. 17
    d. 15
    e. 21

34. (3, -3)
    a. 22
    b. 17
    c. 16
    d. 11
    e. 20

35. (-1, 2)
    a. 19
    b. 16
    c. 14
    d. 22
    e. 12

The next five questions are based on the following table.

	-3	**-2**	**-1**	**0**	**1**	**2**	**3**
-3	20	21	22	23	24	25	26
-2	21	22	23	24	25	26	27
-1	23	24	25	26	27	28	29
0	25	26	27	28	29	30	31
1	27	28	29	30	31	20	21
2	29	30	31	20	21	22	23
3	31	20	21	22	23	24	25

36. (2, 2)
    a. 30
    b. 22
    c. 26
    d. 21
    e. 20

37. (1, -3)
    a. 27
    b. 23
    c. 24
    d. 29
    e. 22

38. (1, -1)
   a. 31
   b. 29
   c. 25
   d. 27
   e. 24

39. (2, -2)
   a. 26
   b. 30
   c. 22
   d. 20
   e. 21

40. (0, 3)
   a. 31
   b. 22
   c. 23
   d. 25
   e. 26

Instrument Comprehension

1. Looking at the instruments on the left, which choice depicts the orientation of the aircraft?

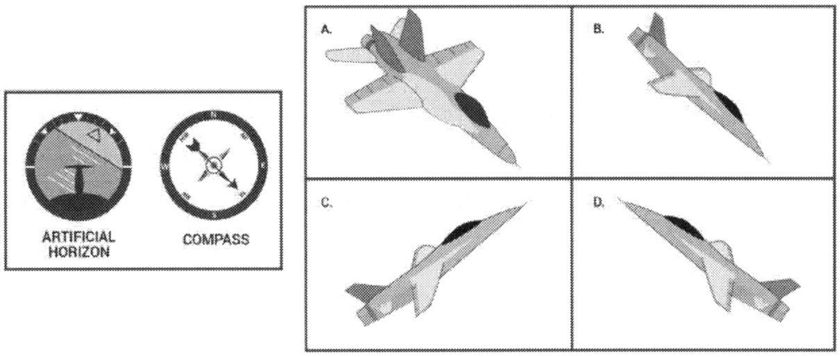

2. Looking at the instruments on the left, which choice depicts the orientation of the aircraft?

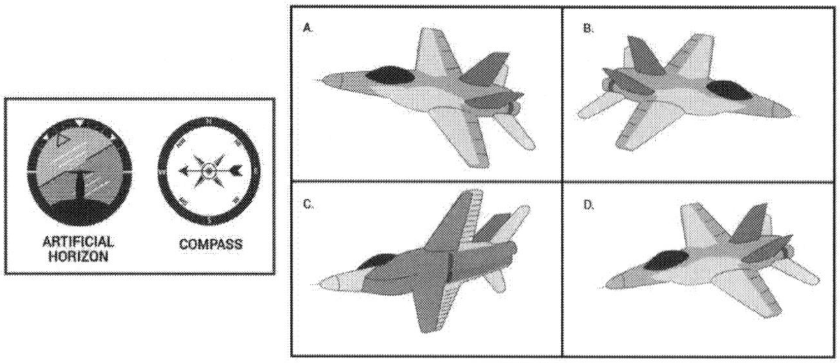

3. Looking at the instruments on the left, which choice depicts the orientation of the aircraft?

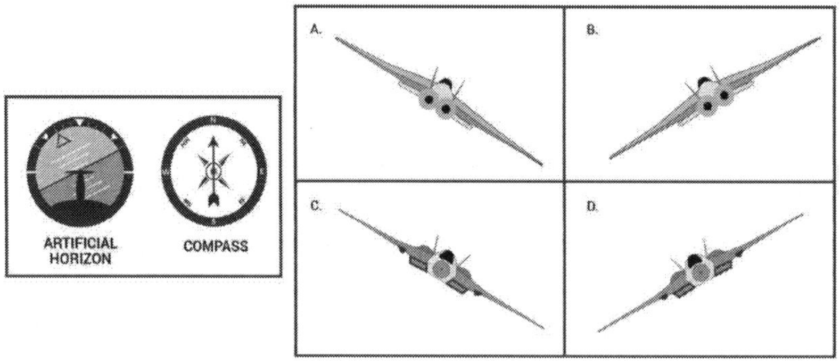

4. Looking at the instruments on the left, which choice depicts the orientation of the aircraft?

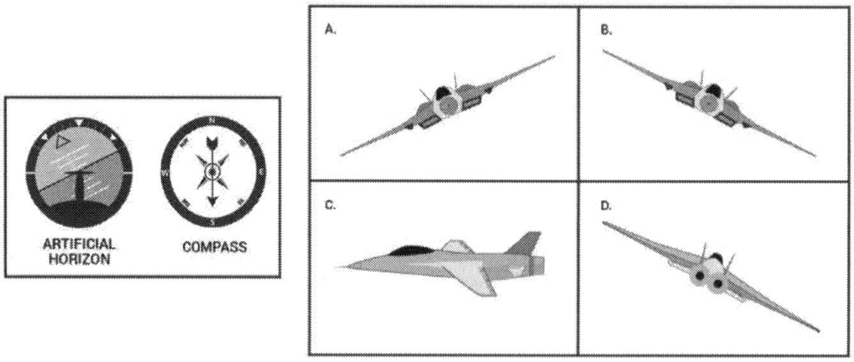

5. Looking at the instruments on the left, which choice depicts the orientation of the aircraft?

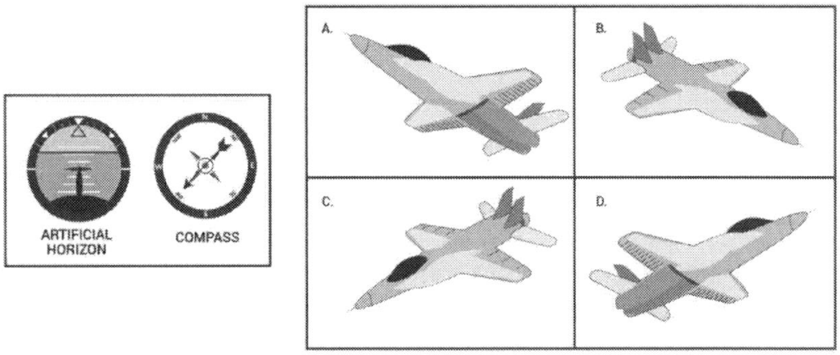

6. Looking at the instruments on the left, which choice depicts the orientation of the aircraft?

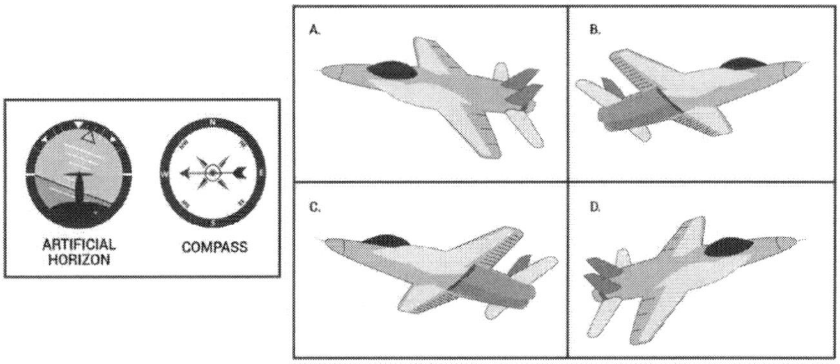

7. Looking at the instruments on the left, which choice depicts the orientation of the aircraft?

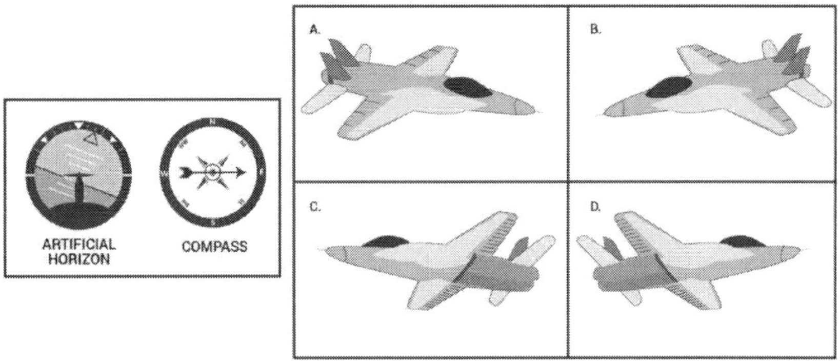

8. Looking at the instruments on the left, which choice depicts the orientation of the aircraft?

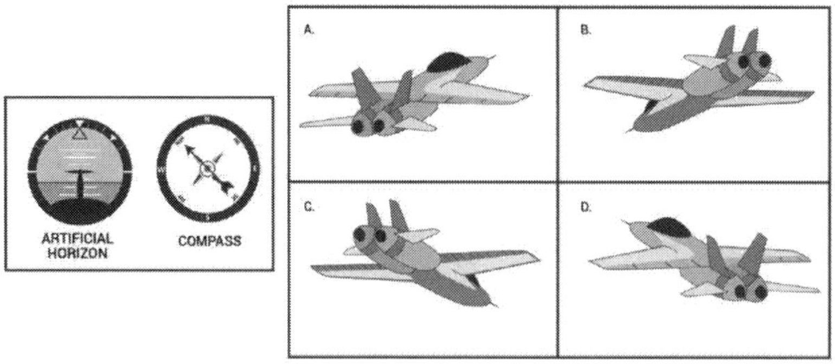

9. Looking at the instruments on the left, which choice depicts the orientation of the aircraft?

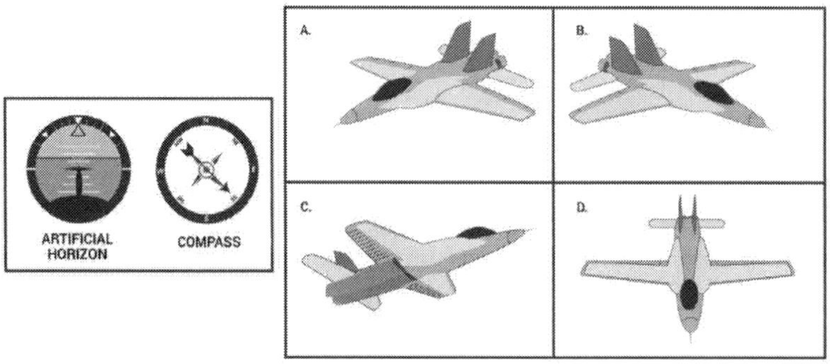

10. Looking at the instruments on the left, which choice depicts the orientation of the aircraft?

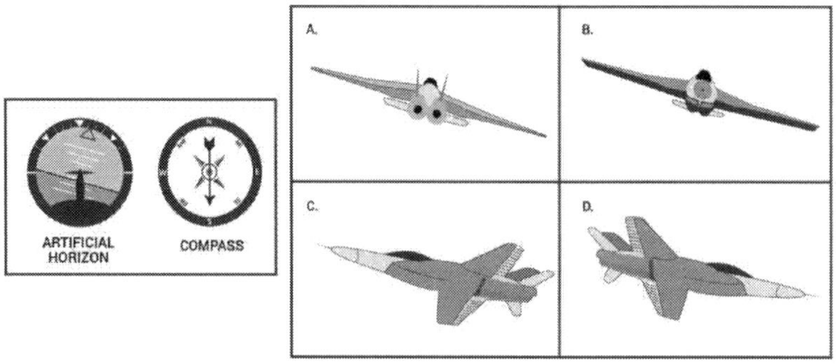

Block Counting

For questions 1-30, determine how many blocks the given block is touching.

Use the figure below for questions 1-5.

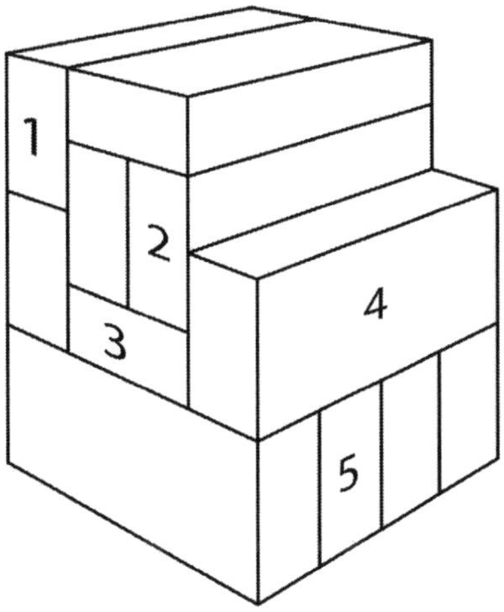

1. Block 1
    a. 1
    b. 2
    c. 3
    d. 4
    e. 5

2. Block 2
    a. 4
    b. 5
    c. 6
    d. 7
    e. 8

3. Block 3
    a. 5
    b. 6
    c. 7
    d. 8
    e. 9

4. Block 4
    a. 4
    b. 5
    c. 6
    d. 7
    e. 8

5. Block 5
    a. 2
    b. 3
    c. 4
    d. 5
    e. 6

Use the figure below for questions 6-10.

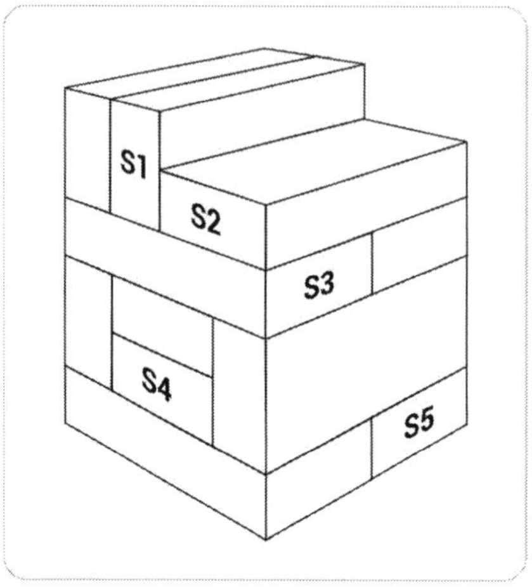

6. Block S1
    a. 1
    b. 2
    c. 3
    d. 4
    e. 5

7. Block S2
    a. 2
    b. 3
    c. 4
    d. 5
    e. 6

8. Block S3
    a. 5
    b. 6
    c. 7
    d. 8
    e. 9

9. Block S4
    a. 4
    b. 5
    c. 6
    d. 7
    e. 8

10. Block S5
   a. 3
   b. 4
   c. 5
   d. 6
   e. 7

Use the figure below for questions 11-17.

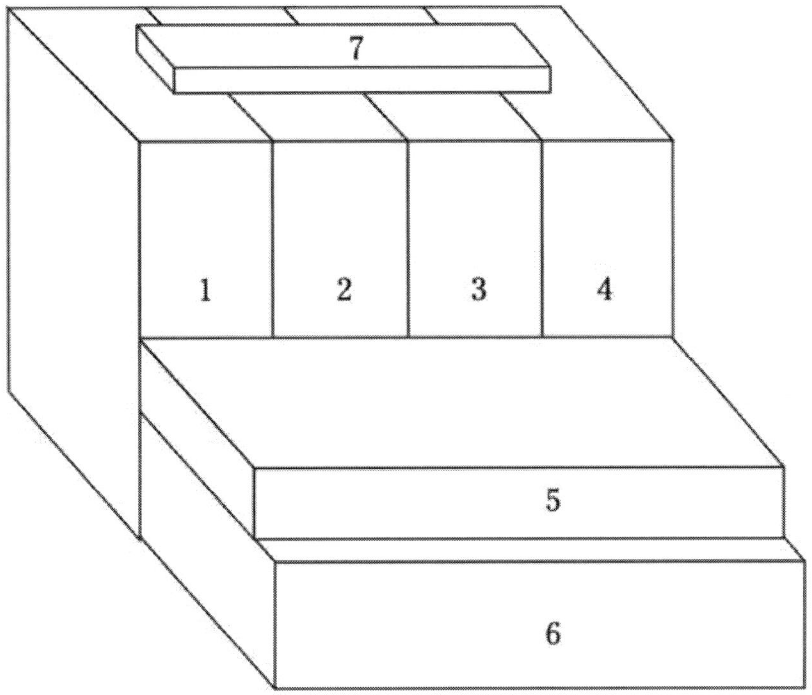

11. Block 1
   a. 1
   b. 2
   c. 3
   d. 4
   e. 5

12. Block 2
   a. 4
   b. 5
   c. 6
   d. 7
   e. 8

13. Block 3
    a. 5
    b. 6
    c. 7
    d. 2
    e. 1

14. Block 4
    a. 4
    b. 5
    c. 6
    d. 7
    e. 2

15. Block 5
    a. 2
    b. 3
    c. 4
    d. 5
    e. 6

16. Block 6
    a. 1
    b. 2
    c. 3
    d. 4
    e. 5

17. Block 7
    a. 3
    b. 4
    c. 5
    d. 6
    e. 7

Use the figure below for questions 18-22.

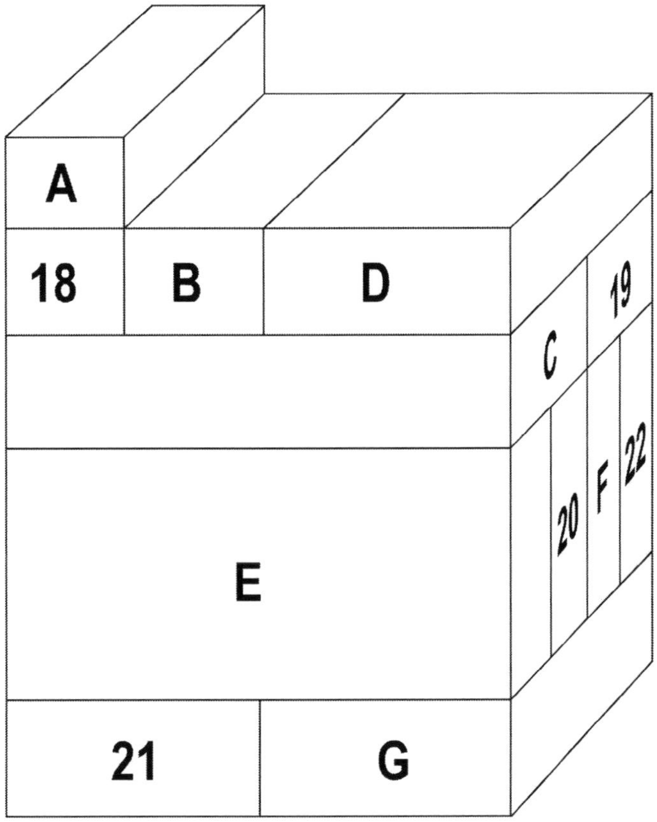

18. Block 18
    a. 1
    b. 2
    c. 3
    d. 4
    e. 5

19. Block 19
    a. 2
    b. 3
    c. 4
    d. 5
    e. 6

20. Block 20
    a. 1
    b. 2
    c. 3
    d. 4
    e. 5

21. Block 21
    a. 5
    b. 6
    c. 7
    d. 8
    e. 9

22. Block 22
    a. 4
    b. 5
    c. 6
    d. 7
    e. 8

Use the figure below for questions 23-26.

23. Block 1
    a. 1
    b. 2
    c. 3
    d. 4
    e. 5

24. Block 2
    a. 5
    b. 6
    c. 7
    d. 8
    e. 9

25. Block 3
    a. 4
    b. 5
    c. 6
    d. 7
    e. 8

26. Block 4
    a. 2
    b. 3
    c. 4
    d. 5
    e. 6

Use the figure below for questions 27-30.

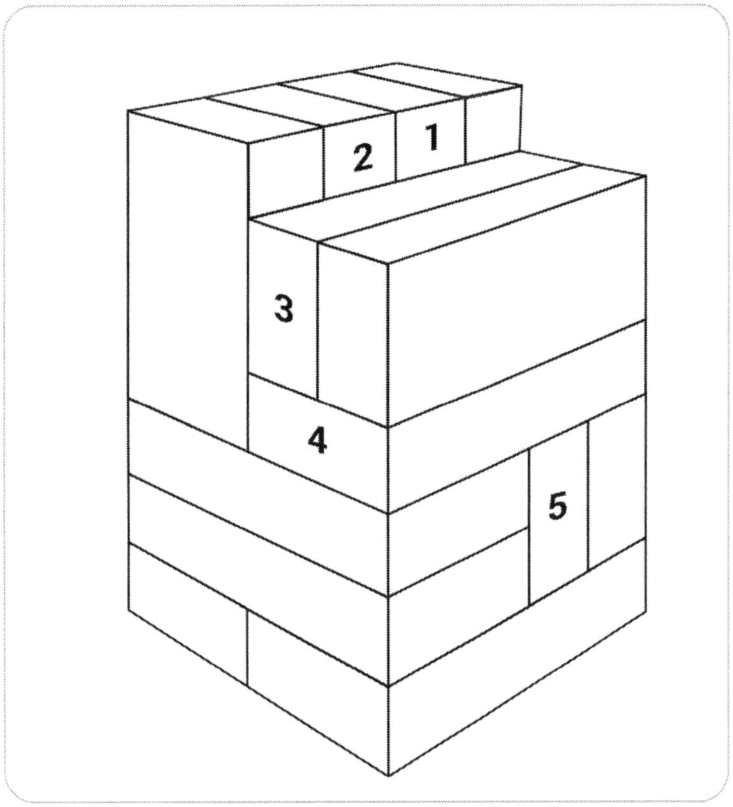

27. Block 1
    a. 1
    b. 2
    c. 3
    d. 4
    e. 5

28. Block 2
   a. 4
   b. 5
   c. 6
   d. 7
   e. 8

29. Block 3
   a. 2
   b. 3
   c. 4
   d. 5
   e. 6

30. Block 4
   a. 6
   b. 7
   c. 8
   d. 9
   e. 10

Aviation

1. Which of the following will create lift?
   a. Airflow against the tail section of the aircraft
   b. Faster flow of air over the wing than beneath it
   c. Raised ailerons
   d. Helium in the wings
   e. Thrust from the engine

2. Which of the following axes is controlled by ailerons?
   a. Lateral
   b. Longitudinal
   c. Vertical
   d. Equatorial
   e. Felling axes

3. Which of the following axes is controlled by elevators?
   a. Lateral
   b. Longitudinal
   c. Vertical
   d. Equatorial
   e. All of the above

4. Which of the following axes is controlled by a rudder?
   a. Lateral
   b. Longitudinal
   c. Vertical
   d. Equatorial
   e. None of the above

5. Which of the following is not a secondary or auxiliary flight control?
   a. Flap
   b. Spoiler
   c. Aileron
   d. Slat
   e. All of the above

6. What component is not part of an empennage?
   a. Stabilizer
   b. Rudder
   c. Elevator
   d. Truss
   e. Slats

7. Which of the following is not a type of landing gear?
   a. Ski
   b. Skate
   c. Skid
   d. Float
   e. Pontoon

8. Which is not a type of fuselage?
   a. Monocoque
   b. Semicoque
   c. Semi-Monocoque
   d. Truss
   e. None of the above

9. Who should be the most concerned about an aircraft's flight envelope?
   a. The pilot
   b. Air traffic controller
   c. Passengers
   d. Aircraft mechanic
   e. People on the ground

10. What is the minimum speed at which an aircraft can maintain level flight?
   a. Ceiling speed
   b. Cruising speed
   c. Stalling speed
   d. Mach 1
   e. Gliding speed

11. What is the maximum operating altitude for a design of an aircraft?
    a. Stratosphere roof
    b. Service ceiling
    c. Stratosphere ceiling
    d. Overhead ceiling
    e. Upper limit

12. Which of the following is another word for aerodynamic friction or wind resistance?
    a. Lift
    b. Gravity
    c. Thrust
    d. Drag
    e. Stall

13. What is the purpose of the horizontal stabilizer?
    a. Pushes the tail left or right in line with the aircraft
    b. Levels the aircraft in flight
    c. Controls the roll of an aircraft
    d. Decreases speed for landing
    e. Decreases speed in a turn

14. Where are ailerons located?
    a. The trailing edge of a rudder
    b. The outer leading edge of a wing
    c. The outer trailing edge of a wing
    d. The inner trailing edge of a wing
    e. The empennage

15. What occurs when the induced drag on an aircraft exceeds its lift?
    a. Roll
    b. Yaw
    c. Pitch
    d. Stall
    e. Gravity

16. Which is not considered to be one of the four fundamental flight maneuvers?
    a. Landing
    b. Straight and level
    c. Turns
    d. Descent
    e. Climbing

17. What force acting upon a helicopter attempts to turn the body of the helicopter in the opposite direction of the main rotor travel?
    a. Gyroscopic precession
    b. Centrifugal force
    c. Torque
    d. Coriolis effect
    e. Centripetal force

18. What is used to increase the pitch of the main rotor at the same time at all points of the rotor blade rotation?

a. Cyclic control
b. Collective control
c. Coriolis control
d. Symmetry control
e. Anti-torque control

19. Visual approach slope indicators are visible from what distance during clear, daylight hours?

a. 1-2 miles away
b. 3-5 miles away
c. 5-10 miles away
d. 10-20 miles away
e. 20-25 miles away

20. Non-precision instrument runways provide what kind of guidance?

a. Horizontal
b. Vertical
c. Locational
d. Directional
e. Multi-directional

AFOQT Answer Explanations

Verbal Analogies

1. C: This is a part/whole analogy. The common thread is what animals walk on. Choices *A*, *B*, and *E* all describe signature parts of animals, but paws are not the defining feature of cats. While snakes travel on their skins, they do not walk.

2. A: This is a characteristic analogy. The connection lies in what observers will judge a performance on. While the other choices are also important, an off-key singer is as unpleasant as a dancer with no rhythm.

3. D: This is a use/tool analogy. The analogy focuses on an item's use. While hats are worn when it's cold with the goal of making the top of your head warm, this is not always guaranteed—their primary use is to provide cover. There is also the fact that not all hats are used to keep warm, but all hats cover the head.

4. D: This is a source/comprised of analogy. The common thread is addition of fire. Protons contribute to atoms and seeds grow into plants, but these are simple matters of building and growing without necessarily involving fire. B and E relate objects that already have similar properties.

5. E: This is a synonym analogy. The determining factor is synonymous definition. Design and create are synonyms, as are allocate and distribute. Typically, items are found and allocated as part of management to finish a project, but these qualities are not innate in the word. Allocation generally refers to the division of commodities instead of multiplication.

6. B: This is a tool/use analogy. The common thread is audience response to an art form. *A*, *C*, and *D* deal with the creation of artwork instead of its consumption. Choice *E* describes a form of art instead of the audience engagement with such.

7. C: This is an intensity analogy. The common thread is degree of severity. While *A*, *D*, and *E* can all describe warmth, they don't convey the harshness of sweltering. *B* simply describes a time when people may be more likely to think of warmth.

8. D: This is a characteristic analogy and is based on matching objects to their geometric shapes. Choice *A* is not correct because globes are three-dimensional, whereas circles exist in two dimensions. While wheels are three-dimensional, they are not always solid or perfectly round.

9. A: This is a tool/use analogy. The key detail of this analogy is the idea of enclosing or sealing items/people. When plates are filled with food, there is no way to enclose the item. While trees can be inside a fence, they can also be specifically outside of one.

10. E: This is a sequence of events analogy. The common thread is celestial cause-and-effect. Not everyone has breakfast or goes to bed after sunset. Sunrise is not typically thought of as the next interesting celestial event after sunsets. While clouds can develop after sunsets, they are also present before and during this activity. Stars, however, can be seen after dark.

11. A: This is a provider/provision analogy. The theme of this analogy is pairing a specific animal to their food source. Falcons prey on mice. Giraffes are herbivores and only eat one of the choices: leaves. Grasslands describe a type of landscape, not a food source for animals.

12. B: This is a category analogy. The common thread is motorized vehicles. While Choices *A*, *C*, and *E* also describe vehicles that move on water, they are not motorized. Although relying on engines, planes are not a form of water transportation.

13. D: This is an antonym analogy. The prevailing connection is opposite meanings. While happy can be an opposite of anxious, it's also possible for someone to experience both emotions at once. *B*, *C*, and *E* are also concurrent with anxious, not opposite.

14. E: This is a provider/provision analogy. This analogy looks at professionals and what their job is. Just as a mechanic's job is to repair machinery, a doctor works to heal patients.

15. C: This is a category analogy. Both whistles and blow horns are devices used to project/produce sound. Therefore, the analogy is based on finding something of a categorical nature. While *A*, *B*, *D*, and *E* involve or describe painting, they do not pertain to a distinct discipline alongside painting. Sculpture, however, is another form of art and expression, just like painting.

16. D: This is a part/whole analogy. This analogy examines the relationship between two objects. Specifically, this analogy examines how one object connects to another object, with the first object(s) being the means by which people use the corresponding object to produce a result directly. People use a paddle to steer a boat, just as pressing keys on a piano produces music. *B* and *C* can be metaphorically linked to keys but are unrelated. *A* is related to keys but is a verb, not another object. Choice *E* is the trickiest alternative, but what's important to remember is that while keys are connected to key chains, there is no result just by having the key on a key chain.

17. C: This is an antonym analogy. The common thread is opposite meanings. Monotonous refers to being dull or being repetitive, while innovative means new and bringing in changes. All of the other choices reflect synonymous word pairs. However, loquacious, which means talkative, is the opposite of silent.

18. E: This is a part/whole analogy. This analogy focuses on natural formations and their highest points. The peak of a mountain is its highest point just as the crest is the highest rise in a wave.

19. A: This is a negative connotations analogy. Essentially all of the given words in the example express the same idea of uncertainty or not taking a definitive stance. Ambiguous means open to possibilities, which parallels to not being able to make a decision, which describes indecisive as well as uncertain. Uncertain also means not definite, which not only relates to the given words but also directly to indefinite.

20. B: This is an intensity analogy. Fluent refers to how well one can communicate, while gourmet describes a standard of cooking. The analogy draws on degrees of a concept.

21. B: This is a synonym analogy, which relies on matching terms that are most closely connected. Validate refers to finding truth. Therefore, finding the term that best fits conquer is a good strategy. While nations have conquered others to expand their territory, they are ultimately subjugating those lands and people to their will. Therefore, subjugate is the best-fitting answer.

22. C: This is a sequence of events analogy. This analogy pairs one season with the season that precedes it. Winter is paired with autumn because autumn actually comes before winter. Out of all the answers, only *B* and *C* are actual seasons. Fall is another name for autumn, which comes after summer, not before. Spring, of course, is the season that comes before summer, making it the right answer.

23. A: This is a pairs analogy. None of the given terms are really related. To find the analogy, the way that each term is paired should be analyzed. Penguin, a bird, is paired with lemur, which is a primate. When given eagle, the only logical analogy to be made is to find another primate to pair with a bird, which is howler monkey.

24. C: This is a source/comprised of analogy. This analogy focuses on pairing a raw material with an object that it's used to create. Fiberglass is used to build surfboards just as copper is used in the creation of pennies. While wind powers a windmill, there is no physical object produced, like with the fiberglass/surfboard pair.

25. E: This is an object/function analogy. The common thread between these words is that one word describes a kind of story and it is paired with the purpose of the story. Myth is/was told in order to explain fundamental beliefs and natural phenomena. While laughter can result from a joke, the purpose of telling a joke is to amuse the audience, thus making *E* the right choice.

Arithmetic Reasoning

1. B: 300 miles in 4 hours is 300/4 = 75 miles per hour. In 1.5 hours, it will go 1.5×75 miles, or 112.5 miles

2. C: One apple/orange pair costs $3 total. Jan therefore bought 90/3 = 30 total pairs, and hence 30 oranges.

3. C: The volume of a box with rectangular sides is the length times width times height, so $5 \times 6 \times 3 = 90$ cubic feet.

4. E: First, the train's journey in the real word is 3×50 = 150 miles. On the map, 1 inch corresponds to 10 miles, so there is 150/10 = 15 inches on the map.

5. B: The total trip time is $1 + 3.5 + 0.5$ = 5 hours. The total time driving is $1 + 0.5$ = 1.5 hours. So the fraction of time spent driving is 1.5/5 or 3/10. To get the percentage, convert this to a fraction out of 100. The numerator and denominator are multiplied by 10, with a result of 30/100. The percentage is the numerator in a fraction out of 100, so 30%.

6. B: The volume of a cylinder is $\pi r^2 h$, where *r* is the radius and *h* is the height. The diameter is twice the radius, so these barrels have a radius of 1 foot. That means each barrel has a volume of $\pi 1^2 3 = 3\pi$ cubic feet. Since there are three of them, the total is $3 \times 3\pi = 9$ cubic feet.

7. B: The tip is not taxed, so he pays 5% tax only on the $10. 5% of $10 is $0.05 \times 10 = \$0.50$. Add up $\$10 + \$2 + \$0.50$ to get $12.50.

8. C: The first step is to divide up $150 into four equal parts. 150/4 is 37.5, so she needs to save $37.50 per day on average.

9. C: 300/80 =30/8 = 15/4 =3.75. But Bernard is only working full days, so he will need to work 4 days, since 3 days is not sufficient.

10. A: The value went up by $165,000 – $150,000 = $15,000. Out of $150,000, this is $\frac{15,000}{150,000} = \frac{1}{10}$. Convert this to having a denominator of 100, the result is $\frac{10}{100}$ or 10%.

11. E: The total faculty is $15 + 20 = 35$. So, the ratio is 35:200. Then, divide both of these numbers by 5, since 5 is a common factor to both, with a result of 7:40.

12. B: The journey will be $5 \times 3 = 15$ miles. A car travelling at 60 miles per hour is travelling at 1 mile per minute. So, it will take 15/1 = 15 minutes to take the journey.

13. A: Taylor's total income is $20,000 + $10,000 = $30,000. 15% of this is $\frac{15}{100} = \frac{3}{20}$.

$$\frac{3}{20} \times \$30{,}000 = \frac{90{,}000}{20} = \frac{9000}{2} = \$4500$$

14. B: Since the answer will be in cubic feet rather than inches, start by converting from inches to feet for the dimensions of the box. There are 12 inches per foot, so the box is 24/12 = 2 feet wide, 18/12 = 1.5 feet deep, and 12/12 = 1 foot high. The volume is the product of these three together: $2 \times 1.5 \times 1 = 3$ cubic feet.

15. D: Kristen bought four DVDs, which would total a cost of $4 \times 15 = \$60$. She spent a total of $100, so she spent $100 – $60 = $40 on CDs. Since they cost $10 each, she must have purchased 40/10 = four CDs.

16. E: Using the conversion rate, multiply the projected weight loss of 25 lb by 0.45 $\frac{kg}{lb}$ to get the amount in kilograms (11.25 kg).

17. D: First, subtract $1437 from $2334.50 to find Johnny's monthly savings; this equals $897.50. Then, multiply this amount by 3 to find out how much he will have (in three months) before he pays for his vacation: this equals $2692.50. Finally, subtract the cost of the vacation ($1750) from this amount to find how much Johnny will have left: $942.50.

18. C: The formula for the perimeter of a rectangle is P=2L+2W, where P is the perimeter, L is the length, and W is the width. The first step is to substitute all of the data into the formula:

$$36 = 2(12) + 2W$$

Simplify by multiplying 2×12:

$$36 = 24 + 2W$$

Simplifying this further by subtracting 24 on each side, which gives:

$$36 - 24 = 24 - 24 + 2W$$
$$12 = 2W$$

Divide by 2:

$$6 = W$$

The width is 6 cm. Remember to test this answer by substituting this value into the original formula: $36 = 2(12) + 2(6)$.

19. D: To find the average of a set of values, add the values together and then divide by the total number of values. In this case, include the unknown value of what Dwayne needs to score on his next test, in order to solve it.

$$\frac{78 + 92 + 83 + 97 + x}{5} = 90$$

Add the unknown value to the new average total, which is 5. Then multiply each side by 5 to simplify the equation, resulting in:

$$78 + 92 + 83 + 97 + x = 450$$
$$350 + x = 450$$
$$x = 100$$

Dwayne would need to get a perfect score of 100 in order to get an average of at least 90.

Test this answer by substituting back into the original formula.

$$\frac{78 + 92 + 83 + 97 + 100}{5} = 90$$

20. D: Three girls for every two boys can be expressed as a ratio: 3:2. This can be visualized as splitting the school into 5 groups: 3 girl groups and 2 boy groups. The number of students that are in each group can be found by dividing the total number of students by 5:

650 divided by 5 equals 1 part, or 130 students per group

To find the total number of girls, multiply the number of students per group (130) by the number of girl groups in the school (3). This equals 390, which is answer D.

21. C: Kimberley worked 4.5 hours at the rate of \$10/h and 1 hour at the rate of \$12/h. The problem states that her pay is rounded to the nearest hour, so the 4.5 hours would round up to 5 hours at the rate of \$10/h. $(5h)(\$10/h) + (1h)(\$12/h) = \$50 + \$12 = \$62$.

22. B: First, calculate the difference between the larger value and the smaller value.

$$378 - 252 = 126$$

To calculate this difference as a percentage of the original value, and thus calculate the percentage *increase*, divide 126 by 252, then multiply by 100 to reach the percentage = 50%, answer *B*.

23. A: If each man gains 10 pounds, every original data point will increase by 10 pounds. Therefore, the man with the original median will still have the median value, but that value will increase by 10. The smallest value and largest value will also increase by 10 and, therefore, the difference between the two won't change. The range does not change in value and, thus, remains the same.

24. D: Let *a* be the number of apples and b the number of bananas. Then, the total cost is $2a + 3b = 22$, while it also known that $a + b = 10$. Using the knowledge of systems of equations, cancel the *b* variables by multiplying the second equation by -3. This makes the equation $-3a - 3b = -30$. Adding this to the first equation, the *b* values cancel to get $-a = -8$, which simplifies to *a* = 8.

25. A: Lining up the given scores provides the following list: 60, 75, 80, 85, and one unknown. Because the median needs to be 80, it means 80 must be the middle data point out of these five. Therefore, the unknown data point must be the fourth or fifth data point, meaning it must be greater than or equal to 80. The only answer that fails to meet this condition is 60.

Word Knowledge

1. C: To deduce something is to figure it out using reason. Although this might cause a win and prompt an explanation to further understanding, the art of deduction is logical reasoning.

2. B: To elucidate, a light is figuratively shined on a previously unknown or confusing subject. This Latin root, *lux* meaning *light*, prominently figures into the solution. Enlighten means to educate, or bring into the light.

3. D: Looking at the Latin word *veritas*, meaning *truth*, will yield a clue as to the meaning of verify. To verify is the act of finding or assessing the truthfulness of something. This usually means amassing evidence to substantiate a claim. Substantiate, of course, means to provide evidence to prove a point.

4. A: If someone is inspired, they are motivated to do something. Someone who is an inspiration motivates others to follow his or her example.

5. E: All the connotations of perceive involve the concept of seeing. Whether figuratively or literally, perceiving implies the act of understanding what is presented. Comprehending is synonymous with this understanding.

6. C: Nomadic tribes are those who, throughout history and even today, prefer to wander their lands instead of settling in any specific place. Wanderer best describes these people.

7. A: Malevolent literally means bad or evil-minded. The clue is also in the Latin root *mal-* that translates to bad.

8. D: Perplexed means baffled or puzzled, which are synonymous with confused.

9. D: Lyrical is used to refer to something being poetic or song-like, characterized by showing enormous imagination and description. While the context of lyrical can be playful or even whimsical, the best choice is expressive, since whatever emotion lyrical may be used to convey in context will be expressive in nature.

10. C: Brevity literally means brief or concise. Note the similar beginnings of brevity and brief—from the Latin *brevis*, meaning brief.

11. A: Irate means being in a state of anger. Clearly this is a negative word that can be paired with another word in kind. The closest word to match this is obviously anger. Research would also reveal that irate comes from the Latin *ira*, which means anger.

12. C: Lavish is a synonym for luxurious—both describe elaborate and/or elegant lifestyles and/or settings.

13. E: Immobile obviously means *not able to move*. The two best selections are *B* and *E*—but slow still implies some form of motion, whereas sedentary has the connotation of being seated and/or inactive for a significant portion of time and/or as a natural tendency.

14. D: Mendacious describes dishonesty or lying in several ways. This is another word of classical lineage. Mendacio in Latin means *liar*. While liar lacks the Latin root, the meanings fit.

15. E: Chivalrous reflects showing respect and courtesy toward others, particularly women.

16. C: Retort is a verb that means *to answer back*, usually in a sharp manner. This term embodies the idea of a response, emphasized by the *re-* prefix meaning *back, again*. While a retort is used in conversations and even as a jest, neither term embodies the idea of addressing someone again. Counter, however, means to respond in opposition when used as a verb.

17. A: Subliminal and subconscious share the Latin prefix *sub-*, meaning under or below, or more commonly used when talking about messages the sender doesn't want the receiver to consciously take note of. The word subliminal means beneath the consciousness. Thus, subconscious is the perfect match.

18. C: Although incite usually has negative connotations, leaders can incite their followers to benevolent actions as well. In both cases, people rally to support a cause.

19. A: While a moniker commonly refers to a title, this is technically a designated name. Monikers can be mockeries, insults, and/or burdens, but none of these are direct forms of a title or identification.

20. E: Events that occur through serendipity happen purely by chance. Serendipitous conveys the idea of something unplanned yet potentially desirable. Coincidental is defined as happening by chance.

21. B: Overbearing refers to domineering or being oppressive. This is emphasized in the *over* prefix, which emphasizes an excess in definitions. This prefix is also seen in overacting. Similar to overbearing, overacting reflects an excess of action.

22. A: The *pre* prefix describes something that occurs before an event. Prevent means to stop something before it happens. This leads to a word that relates to something occurring beforehand and, in a way, is preventive—wanting to stop something. Avert literally means to turn away or ward off an impending circumstance, making it the best fit.

23. D: Refresh is synonymous with replenish. Both words mean to restore or refill. Additionally, these terms do share the *re-* prefix as well.

24. D: Regale literally means to amuse someone with a story. This is a very positive word; the best way to eliminate choices is to look for a term that matches regale in both positive context/sound and definition. Entertain is both a positive word and a synonym of regale.

25. C: Abate is defined as something becoming less intense and fading. The only word that matches abate is withdraw, which means to go back or draw away from a particular position.

Reading Comprehension

1. D: Choice *A* can be eliminated, as this idea isn't stated in the selection. Choice *B* only represents a portion of the subject. Choice *C* is stated in the passage, but the paragraph isn't solely about constant velocity. Choice *E* is a supporting concept, not the main topic. Only Choice *D* answers the question.

2. C: Choices *A*, *B*, and *E* are stated in the passage. The sum weight of an aircraft is important to calculate, as are personnel and fuel load. Notice that Choice *E* states fuel load *cannot* be eliminated in measuring weight. Careful comprehension is important when reading Choice *E*. Choice *D* also supports the idea that weight affects aerodynamics. In Choice *C*, while it's true that the mechanics of flight includes lift, that detail doesn't support the overall topic of weight.

3. E: Choices *A*, *B*, and *D* are true, but they don't encompass all of the ideas presented in the passage. Choice *C* isn't stated and is incorrect. Choice *E* encapsulates all of the ideas presented in the passage.

4. A: From the provided paragraph, a reader may infer that a pilot should use sound judgment when flying. Choice *B* is not stated. Choice *C* is stated as fact but isn't true. Choices *D* and *E* are false as stated.

5. C: All of the options indicate some aspect of the pilot's acumen, but each is a contextual clue that, when put together, indicate the pilot has an overall shrewdness and keen insight when it comes to his flight talent. Choice *A* is incorrect as *acumen* isn't specific to flight. Choice *B* is insufficient, for knowledge alone doesn't encompass the other passage descriptors. The same can be said for Choice *D*; and, while Choice *E* is directly mentioned in the paragraph, an impressive number of flight hours is just one accomplishment of the pilot and too specific to encompass the pilot's other skills.

6. D: Choice *A* is incorrect; the passage doesn't state that anyone can become a pilot. The text implies that becoming a pilot carries some risk, but Choice *B* is not the correct answer, as the rest of the paragraph doesn't support that statement. Choices *C* and *E* are incorrect because they aren't stated. Only Choice *D* encompasses all of the text as the logical conclusion.

7. A: While the reader may disagree with the author's position, all of the statements in the passage indicate the author's position is that piloting is a difficult goal that requires serious consideration on the part of a potential flight student. Choices *B*, *C*, and *E* aren't stated. Choice *D* can be ruled out because the physical and mental toll on piloting students isn't the main position of the paragraph.

8. D: The text indicates a sequence throughout time. Sentence C relates the very first recorded attempt at flight. Sentence B indicates the first manmade vehicles in fifth century China. Sentence A addresses Leonardo da Vinci's famous work in flight during the Renaissance. Then, Sentences D, E, and F occur in the correct historical order.

9. A: The purpose is to inform the reader of certain facts by presenting examples of revolutionary aircraft throughout flight history. Choice *B* is incorrect. While the passage may be fun to read, its primary purpose is not entertainment. It doesn't tell a story. Choice *C* is incorrect. The main focus of the passage is not Deperdussin's model. Choice *D* is incorrect. The passage doesn't indicate that American structures were better than any other. Choice *E* is also incorrect. The reader would have to assume that the author intended to argue that these examples of aircraft development are the only ones worth considering. The first paragraph of the passage indicates they aren't.

10. B: Turbulence is caused by a disruption in air flow. Choices *A*, *C*, and *D* are incorrect as stated. Choice *E* is true, but it doesn't indicate a cause and effect relationship.

11. E: Choices *A*, *B*, and *D* are incorrect as stated. Choice *C* is likely correct but it isn't always correct as stated, and it doesn't encompass a conclusion or outcome. Only Choice *E* summarizes the best potential outcome to encountering turbulence.

12. E: The answer is Choice *E*, which encompasses the idea that the author's purposes are both to inform and describe. Choice *A* doesn't address the entire purpose. Yes, the author states the mechanics of flight are not difficult to understand, but that's not all the author does in the passage. Choice *B* is incorrect as stated.

13. D: Notice that the main idea of the passage—maintaining equilibrium in flight—is stated in the first sentence and re-stated in the last. The word *equilibrium* is re-defined for the reader as staying stable in flight. All other options are incorrect as stated.

14. D: The reader isn't given enough information to determine if Choice *A* is correct. Nowhere in the passage does the author indicate that 9,000 feet is too high, so Choice *B* is incorrect. The pilot had the correct clearance, so Choice *C* is incorrect as stated. Although icing led to additional weight on the fuselage, Choice *E* doesn't best address the cause and effect relationship depicted in the passage.

15. B: All other four options are incorrect as stated. Notice that after each bolded word, the author actually defines the words *coaxial* and *intermeshing*, as both are used to describe types of rotor configurations in helicopter design.

16. B: The main idea of the paragraph is best stated in Choice *B*. Choices *A* and *D* are true, but they don't reflect the entire main idea. Choices *C* and *E* are incorrect as stated. Notice that both options use the word *always*. Be wary of test options that use absolutes; rarely are such options correct.

17. A: Although the passage doesn't directly define drift, the reader can use previous knowledge in answering the question correctly. In addition, the reader can eliminate all other options as incorrect because none of them are true.

18. C: Choice *A* is untrue. Choice *B* doesn't state a conclusion applicable to the entire passage. Choice *D* is untrue as stated. Although mechanics should be considered during flight, Choice *E*, as it's written, doesn't state a conclusion applicable to the information in the passage.

19. B: Choice *A* is correct but doesn't encompass all of the main ideas in the passage. Choice *C* is untrue. Choice *D* is partially true but again, note the use of the word "always." In this case, making unapproved changes during flight (while highly inadvisable) doesn't always lead to problems. Choice *E* isn't true as stated. While communication is important to successful flight, it's not the key factor. As the author stated that most events in the error chain can be addressed and controlled by the pilot, Choice *B* is the best answer.

20. B: In this case, all other choices are incorrect. By using context around the word *obliterated*, the reader can infer that the meaning is "thoroughly destroyed."

Situational Judgment

1. C: (Most effective) Having an open meeting with everyone would reemphasize the important of the chain-of-command and resolve problems at the lowest possible level.

2. E: (Least effective) Giving up your position because of opposition would demonstrate weakness as a leader and lead to similar actions in future decisions.

3. D: (Most effective) This is a case of "integrity first." It is fine to voice your opinion to the aid, but better to refrain from interfering with the selection process based on personal feelings.

4. B or E: (Least effective) Giving a recommendation to make the aide go away would not uphold the core value of integrity. An honest opinion should always be given. The same could be said for an anonymous letter. Officers should always be forthright and honest when giving recommendations.

5. B: (Most effective) Part of being a good officer is to help peers. Try and point out what you would change in the speech and include why you would do it, and let the senior officer make the decision.

6. A: (Least effective) Never go to a superior with the intention of trying to make yourself look better by slandering a coworker. This is an integrity violation and will erode your credibility as an officer.

7. D: (Most effective) Situations come up in every unit that can impact the mission. In this situation, notify your supervisor immediately so they can get someone to replace the ill coworker and accomplish the mission.

8. B: (Least effective) Do not try to finish the project by yourself. Notify your supervisor immediately any time a situation arises that may impact completing the mission on time.

9. A: (Most effective) Be a professional and return to work. Sign the documents so that you are not causing another officer to work late due to your honest mistake.

10. D: (Least effective) Having a subordinate forge the documents puts your integrity and that of the subordinate at risk. Do not let a minor mistake like forgetting to sign a piece of paper ruin your credibility.

11. E: (Most effective) A response to the new commander's email would be the best solution to this scenario. Let him know that you are excited to take the new position and that you would like to set up a date and time to discuss the new role. This will help ensure a smooth transition.

12. B: (Least effective) Always take the opportunity to respond to an email from your new commander. It is the professional thing to do and will allow time to discuss what is expected of the new position, answer any questions, and learn how to excel.

13. D: (Most effective) This is an opportunity to teach, coach, and mentor a fellow officer by discussing the Air Force core values. By talking to the coworker and not telling his/her superior officer, you offer this person a chance to grow from the mistake without hurting his/her career.

14. C: (Least effective) Resorting to blackmail would make you just as guilty as your peer and would put your integrity on the line.

15. C: (Most effective) It is normal to reach a plateau in assignments. Let your senior officer know, and express that you are looking for a more challenging assignment to further your career and benefit the Air Force.

16. E: (Least effective) Remember, integrity first. Be honest in everything you do and no one can question your integrity.

17. E: (Most effective) Be honest with the officer and let him/her know that you are already dealing with a maximum workload. In addition, you have offered a solution to the problem by offering to distribute the work to another qualified coworker.

18. D: (Least effective) Taking on additional work without sufficient time will cause the quality of both projects to diminish.

19. D: (Most effective) Inform the senior officer of the situation and see if the projects can be redistributed to help alleviate stress for coworkers that are overwhelmed.

20. A: (Least effective) You were attentive to notice the situation; this is a good time to put service before self and offer a solution to the problem.

21. C: (Most effective) They asked you to resolve the dispute, so be the professional and make a decision.

22. E: (Least effective) Giving a lecture to both officers that asked you to settle the dispute would probably turn both of them against you. They must value your opinion, or they would not have asked for your assistance.

23. B: (Most effective) Safety issues need to be addressed immediately. It is your duty as an officer to notify the senior officer in charge if a coworker is manipulating numbers that could lead to an accident or incident.

24. A: (Least effective) It is your responsibility to speak up in this scenario. Again, integrity first. Anyone can prevent an accident.

25. A: (Most effective) If the senior officer asks the question, they want an answer. Be honest, and offer a candid assessment in the area in which he/she could improve.

26. B: (Least effective) Again, if a senior officer asks the question, he/she is looking for an answer. Refusing makes you and your supervisor look bad.

27. D: (Most effective) Make the correct decision and vote for the most qualified candidate.

28. C: (Least effective) By voting for Candidate 3, you are not being honest. Remember the honest decision is not always going to be the easiest. If you are always honest, no one will ever question your integrity.

29. A: (Most effective) Let your new coworker know that you want to do your best on this project, you value his/her help, and you think the work should be shared equally. In addition, offer congratulations on the coworker's upcoming retirement and encourage him/her to finish strong.

30. D: (Least effective) Do not have the frame of mind that the project is going to be mediocre or it will. Talk to your new coworker and come up with a plan to share the workload and develop a quality product.

31. C: (Most effective) Talk with the subordinate and let him/her know what you have heard and that you need his/her support in accomplishing the unit's mission.

32. B: (Least effective) Something has to be done in this scenario. If not, the situation is going to get worse.

33. C: (Most effective) The best action to take in this scenario would be to question the last officer to leave the supply room. This would allow him/her to explain the situation without directly accusing him/her of stealing, and it would be an initial step in the investigative process.

34. E: (Least effective) If no action is taken, supplies are going to keep disappearing, and the situation is not going to get any better.

35. A: (Most effective) Give an honest opinion on the subject, and explain you are not a subject-matter expert. In addition, refer to media and to the base public affairs office for further information.

36. B: (Least effective) Not answering the question could portray a negative opinion of the officer.

37. D: (Most effective) Meet with the unit and discuss the issue that has been presented. Offer a solution to the problem, stay positive, and make sure there is an opportunity for subordinates to take a break.

38. A: (Least effective) Always try and solve the problem before going to senior leadership. This would create distrust among subordinates and show senior officers a lack of leadership and inability to handle simple unit challenges.

39. A: (Most effective) Be honest and admit your mistake. The person receiving the email will be more than willing to delete the material. Your supervisor will appreciate the honesty and inform the chain-of-command.

40. E: (Least effective) Do not lie about the situation. All classified email chains are monitored, and covering up this mistake could lead to revocation of a security clearance.

41. B: (Most effective) Meeting with the training director may open up an opportunity for training in the near future. It also shows the commanding officer cares about the unit and people.

42. D: (Least effective) Sending out letters would be perceived as a false accusation, damage your reputation, and could have an effect on future requests for training.

43. C: (Most effective) The leader may not have realized they were creating this environment. Meeting with the superior will clear the air, and it should afford an opportunity to work more independently.

44. A: (Least effective) Telling the supervisor to back off would create animosity and make the situation worse.

45. D: (Most effective) Ultimately, the boss has the final decision. A well thought out plan with actions and contingencies may sway his/her decision.

46. A: (Least effective) This would be insubordination no matter how the plan worked out. Either way, the boss would feel disrespected.

47. A: (Most effective) Budget cuts will affect everyone in the unit. Talking to peers can offer solutions that may not have been previously discovered.

48. B: (Least effective) Do not blame subordinates. This will erode trust in the unit.

49. D: (Most effective) Keeping the drivers informed of the delay will help with them understand the situation. Accommodating them will help build rapport for future deliveries.

50. C: (Least effective) This would frustrate the drivers even more and may have an effect on future deliveries.

Physical Science

1. C: In any system, the total mechanical energy is the sum of the potential energy and the kinetic energy. Either value could be zero but it still must be included in the total. Choices *A* and *B* only give the total potential or kinetic energy, respectively. Choice *D* gives the difference in the kinetic and potential energy. Choice *E* gives the quotient of potential energy divided by kinetic energy, which is incorrect.

2. E: A Lewis Dot diagram shows the alignment of the valence (outer) shell electrons and how readily they can pair or bond with the valence shell electrons of other atoms to form a compound. Choice *B* is incorrect because the Lewis Dot structure aids in understanding how likely an atom is to bond or not bond with another atom, so the inner shell would add no relevance to understanding this likelihood. The positioning of protons and neutrons concerns the nucleus of the atom, which again would not lend information to the likelihood of bonding.

3. D: The decibel scale is used to measure the intensity of sound waves. The decibel scale is a ratio of a particular sound's intensity to a standard value. Since it is a logarithmic scale, it is measured by a factor of 10. Choice *A* is the name of the effect experienced by an observer of a moving wave; Choice *B* is a particle in an atom; Choice *C* is a unit for measuring power; and Choice *E* is a device used to measure an earthquake.

4. B: For charges*, like charges repel* each other and *opposite charges attract* each other. Negatives and positives will attract, while two positive charges or two negative charges will repel each other. Charges have an effect on each other, so Choices *C* and *D* are incorrect.

5. D: The naming of compounds focuses on the second element in a chemical compound. Elements from the non-metal category are written with an "ide" at the end. The compound CO has one carbon and one oxygen, so it is called carbon monoxide. Choices *B* and *E* represent that there are two oxygen atoms, and Choices *A*, *B,* and *E* incorrectly alter the name of the first element, which should remain as carbon.

6. B: To solve this, the number of moles of NaCl needs to be calculated:

First, to find the mass of NaCl, the mass of each of the molecule's atoms is added together as follows:

$$23.0\text{g (Na)} + 35.5\text{g (Cl)} = 58.8\text{g NaCl}$$

Next, the given mass of the substance is multiplied by one mole per total mass of the substance:

$$4.0\text{g NaCl} \times (1 \text{ mol NaCl}/58.5\text{g NaCl}) = 0.068 \text{ mol NaCl}$$

Finally, the moles are divided by the number of liters of the solution to find the molarity:

$$(0.068 \text{ mol NaCl})/(0.120\text{L}) = 0.57 \text{ M NaCl}$$

Choice *A* incorporates a miscalculation for the molar mass of NaCl, and Choices *C* and *D* both incorporate a miscalculation by not converting mL into liters (L), so they are incorrect by a factor of 10. Choice *E* is incorrect.

7. C: According to the *ideal gas law* ($PV = nRT$), if volume is constant, the temperature is directly related to the pressure in a system. Therefore, if the pressure increases, the temperature will increase in direct proportion. Choice *A* would not be possible, since the system is closed and a change is occurring, so the temperature will change. Choice *B* incorrectly exhibits an inverse relationship between pressure and temperature, or $P = 1/T$. Choice *D* is incorrect because even without actual values for the variables, the relationship and proportions can be determined. Choice *E* is incorrect; the temperature will slowly increase as the pressure increases.

8. A: According to Ohm's Law: $V = IR$, so using the given variables: $3.0 \text{ V} = \text{I} \times 6.0\ \Omega$

Solving for I: $\text{I} = 3.0 \text{ V}/6.0\ \Omega = 0.5 \text{ A}$

Choice *B* incorporates a miscalculation in the equation by multiplying 3.0 V by 6.0 Ω, rather than dividing these values. Choices *C*, *D* and *E* are labeled with the wrong units; Joules measure energy, not current.

9. E: The weight of an object is equal to the mass of the object multiplied by gravity. According to Newton's Second Law of Motion, $F = m \times a$. Weight is the force resulting from a given situation, so the mass of the object needs to be multiplied by the acceleration of gravity on Earth: $W = m \times g$. Choice *A* is incorrect because, according to Newton's first law, all objects exert some force on each other, based on their distance from each other and their masses. This is seen in planets, which affect each other's paths and those of their moons. Choice *B* is incorrect because an object in motion or at rest can have inertia; inertia is the resistance of a physical object to change its state of motion. Choice *C* is incorrect because the mass of an object is a measurement of how much substance of there is to the object, while the weight is gravity's effect of the mass. Choice *D* is incorrect; force is equal to the change in momentum per change in time, not volume.

10. B: A decomposition reaction breaks down a compound into its constituent elemental components. Choice *A* is incorrect because a synthesis reaction joins two or more elements into a single compound. Choice *C*, an organic reaction, is not possible, since it needs carbon and hydrogen for a reaction. Choice *D*, oxidation/reduction (redox or half) reaction, is incorrect because it involves the loss of electrons from one species (oxidation) and the gain of electrons to the other species (reduction). There is no notation of this occurring within the given reaction, so it is not correct. Choice *E* is incorrect; A composition reaction produces a single substance from multiple reactants, opposed to producing multiple products from a single reactant.

11. A: Speciation is the method by which one species splits into two or more species. In allopatric speciation, one population is divided into two subpopulations. If a drought occurs and a large lake becomes divided into two smaller lakes, each lake is left with its own population that cannot intermingle with the population of the other lake. When the genes of these two subpopulations are no longer mixing with each other, separate species that are variations of each other can arise.

12. E: In the Linnean system, organisms are classified as follows, moving from comprehensive and specific similarities to fewer and more general similarities: species, genus, family, order, class, phylum, kingdom, and domain. A popular mnemonic device to remember the Linnean system is "Dear King Philip came over for good soup."

13. A: Fungal cells have a cell wall, similar to plant cells; however, they use oxygen as a source of energy and cannot perform photosynthesis. Because they do not perform photosynthesis, fungal cells do not contain chloroplasts.

14. A: Roots are responsible for absorbing water and nutrients that will get transported up through the plant. They also anchor the plant to the ground. Photosynthesis occurs in leaves, stems transport materials through the plant and support the plant body, and phloem moves sugars downward to the leaves. Choice *E* is incorrect because flowers are responsible for seed development and reproduction, not the roots.

15. D: Tropism is a response to stimuli that causes the plant to grow toward or away from the stimuli. Hydrotropism is a response to a change in water concentration. Phototropism is a reaction to light that causes plants to grow toward the source of the light. Thermotropism is a response to changes in temperature. Gravitropism is a response to gravity that causes roots to follow the pull of gravity and grow downward, but also causes plant shoots to act against gravity and grow upward. Geotropism causes some plants to grow upward and some plants to grow toward the ground; it is the growth of plants with respect to gravity.

16. B: The respiratory system mediates the exchange of gas between the air and the circulating blood, mainly by the act of breathing. It filters, warms, and humidifies the air that gets breathed in and then passes it into the blood stream. The digestive system transforms food and liquids into energy and helps excrete waste from the body. Eliminating waste via the kidneys and bladder is a function of the urinary system. Glands that produce and secrete hormones are located in the endocrine system.

17. D: Arteries carry oxygen-rich blood from the heart to the other tissues of the body. Veins carry oxygen-poor blood back to the heart. Intestines carry digested food through the body. Bronchioles are passageways that carry air from the nose and mouth to the lungs. Capillaries exchange nutrients, waste, and oxygen with tissues at the cellular level.

18. A: The skeletal system consists of the 206 bones that make up the skeleton, as well as the cartilage, ligaments, and other connective tissues that stabilize the bones. The skeletal system provides structural support for the entire body, a framework for the soft tissues and organs to attach to, and acts as a protective barrier for some organs, such as the ribs protecting the heart and lungs, and the vertebrae protecting the spinal cord. The muscular system includes skeletal muscles, cardiac muscle, and the smooth muscles found on the inside of blood vessels. The endocrine system uses ductless glands to produce hormones that help maintain hemostasis, the reproductive system is responsible for the productions of egg and sperm cells, and the lymphatic system is a network of lymphatic vessels that carry a clear fluid called lymph towards the heart.

19. C: Population dynamics looks at the composition of populations, including size and age, and the biological and environmental processes that cause changes. These can include immigration, emigration, births, and deaths.

20. A: Ecosystems are maintained by cycling the energy and nutrients that they obtain from external sources. The process can be diagramed in a food web, which represents the feeding relationship between the species in a community. A phylogenetic tree shows proposed evolutionary relationships among species and is similar to the fossil record. A pedigree chart shows occurrences of phenotypes of a particular gene through the generations of an organism. A photosynthesis diagram shows a process by which plants make their own food.

Table Reading

1. A: Select -3 on the horizontal X axis of the table and move down to +3 on the vertical Y axis. This number is 30. (-3, -3) is 20, (3, 3) is 32, (1, -3) is 23, and (-1, -3) is 24.

2. C: The X axis is 0, while the Y axis is -2; this number is 32. (0, 2) is 30, (-2, 0) is 26, (-2, -3) is 21, and (2, 0) is 29.

3. E: The X axis is +1, while the Y axis is 0; this number is 32. (0, 1) is 22, (-1, 0) is 30, (-1, -3) is 24, and (0, -1) is 27.

4. B: The X value is -2 and the Y value is -3; this number is 21. (-3, -1) is 23, (-2, -2) is 33, (2, -3) is 26, and (3, -1) is 20.

5. D: The X value is -1 and the Y value is 0; this number is 30. (0, 1) is 22, (0, -1) is 27, (-1, -3) is 24, and (-3, -1) is 23.

6. B: The X value is 3 and the Y value is 3; this number is 21. (-3, -3) is 10, (3, -1) is 16, (-1, 3) is 12, and (3, -3) is 19.

7. E: The X value is -2 and the Y value is 1; this number is 19. (1, -2) is 14, (2, -1) is 11, (-2,-2) is 20, and (-1, -1) is 17.

8. A: The X value is 0 and the Y value is 0; this number is 14. (0, -3) is 15, (-3, 0) is 13, (-3, -3) is 10, and (1, 0) is 12.

9. D: The X value is 1 and the Y value is -2; this number is 14. (-2, 1) is 19, (1, 2) is 17, (-1, 2) is 22, and (2, -1) is 11.

10. E: The X value is -1 and the Y value is 0; this number is 18. (0, -1) is 20, (1, 0) is 12, (0, -3) is 15, (-1, -3) is 13, and (-1, 0) is 18.

11. E: The X value is 2 and the Y value is -2; this number is 38. (-2, -2) is 34, (-2, 2) is 36, (2, 2) is 39, and (2, -3) is 35.

12. C: The X value is 1 and the Y value is -3; this number is 34. (-3, 1) is 31, (1, -1) is 38, (-1, 2) is 33, and (1, 3) is 36.

13. A: The X value is 3 and the Y value is 2; this number is is 38. (2, 3) is 34, (-3, 2) is 37, (3, -2) is 39, and (-3, -2) is 33.

14. A: The X value is 0 and the Y value is -1; this number is 39. (-1, 0) is 31, (0, -3) is 33, (-1, -3) is 32, and (0,2) is 34.

15. B: The X value is -2 and the Y value is -1; this number is 40. (2, 1) is 41, (-2, 1) is 35, (2, -1) is 37, and (-2, -3) is 31.

16. D: The X value is -3 and the Y value is 2; this number is 57. (2, -3) is 55, (3, -2) is 52, (-3, -2) is 53, and (2, 3) is 56.

17. D: The X value is -2 and the Y value is 0; this number is is 53. (0, -2) is 57, (2, 0) is 52, (0, 2) is 61, and (-2, -3) is 51.

18. A: The X value is 1 and the Y value is 1; this number is is 51. (-1, -1) is 57, (1, -1) is 52, (-1, 1) is 54, and (1, 3) is 55.

19. C: The X value is 2 and the Y value is -1; this number is 61. (-1, 2) is 56, (-2, -1) is 60, (2, 1) = 53, and (-2, 1) is 59.

20. B: The X value is -1 and the Y value is 3; this number is 53. (3, 1) is 55, (1, -1) is 52, (1, -3) is 54, and (-1, -1) is 57.

21. A: The X value is 0 and the Y value is 2; this number is 46. (2, 0) is 44, (0, -2) is 54, (-2, 0) is 48, and (0, -1) is 52.

22. C: The X value is 3 and the Y value is -2; this number is 45. (-2, 3) is 54, (-3, 2) is 50, (3, 2) is 49, and (-3, -2) is 42.

23. D: The X value is -1 and the Y value is 1; this number is 49. (1, -1) is 53, (-1, -1) is 45, (1, 1) is 51, and (-1, -3) is 42.

24. E: The X value is 2 and the Y value is 3; this number is 50. (3, 2) is 49, (-2, 3) is 54, (-2, -3) is 41, and (2, -3) is 45.

25. B: The X value is -2 and the Y value is 1; this number is 50. (1, -2) is 47, (2, -1) is 48, (-2, -1) is 46, and (2, 1) is 52.

26. E: The X value is 3 and the Y value is 0; this number is 16. (0,3) is 5, (-3, 0) is 10, (0, -3) is 8, and (3, -3) is 11.

27. B: The X value is 1 and the Y value is 2; this number is 6. (2, 1) is 17, (-1, 2) is 16, (1, -2) is 10, and (-1, -2) is 8.

28. C: The X value is -1 and the Y value is -1; this number is 10. (1, 1) is 16, (-1, 1) is 14, (1, -1) is 12, and (-1, -3) is 7.

29. C: The X value is -3 and the Y value is -2; this number is 6. (-2, -2) is 7, (3, -2) is 12, (-3, 2) is 14, and (3, 2) is 8.

30. A: The X value is 3 and the Y value is -1; this number is 14. (-1, 3) is 7, (3, 1) is 6, (-3, 1) is 12, and (-3, -1) is 8.

31. A: The X value is -3 and the Y value is -1; this number is 14. (-1, -3) is 13, (3, -1) is 20, (-3, 1) is 18, and (3, 1) = 12.

32. C: The X value is 0 and the Y value is 1; this number is 21. (1, 0) is 20, (0, -1) is 17, (-1, 0) is 18, and (0, -3) is 14.

33. E: The X value is 2 and the Y value is 1; this number is 21. (1, 2) is 12, (-2, 1) is 19, (2, -2) is 17, and (-2, -1) is 15.

34. B: The X value is 3 and the Y value is -3; this number is 17. (-3, 3) is 22, (3, 3) is 16, (-3, -3) is 11, and (3, -1) is 20.

35. D: The X value is -1 and the Y value is 2; this number is 22. (2, -1) is 19, (1, -2) is 16, (-1, -2) is 14, and (1, 2) is 12.

36. B: The X value is 2 and the Y value is 2; this number is 22. (-2, 2) is 30, (2, -2) is 26, (-2, -3) is 21, and (2, 1) is 20.

37. C: The X value is 1 and the Y value is -3; this number is 24. (-3, 1) is 27, (1, 3) is 23, (3, -1) is 29, and (-1, -3) is 22.

38. D: The X value is 1 and the Y value is -1; this number is 27. (1, 1) is 31, (-1, 1) is 29, (-1, -1) is 25, and (1, -3) is 24.

39. A: The X value is 2 and the Y value is -2; this number is 26. (-2, 2) is 30, (-2, -2) is 22, (2, 1) is 20, and (-2, -3) is 21.

40. B: The X value is 0 and the Y value is 3; this number is 22. (3, 0) is 31, (0, -3) is 23, (-3, 0) is 25, and (0, -1) is 26.

Instrument Comprehension

1. B: The aircraft is heading southeast, descending, and banking left.

2. C: The aircraft is heading west, descending, and banking right.

3. A: The aircraft is heading north, in level flight, and banking right.

4. A: The aircraft is heading south, in level flight, and banking to the right.

5. C: The aircraft is heading southwest, descending, and without banking.

6. A: The aircraft is heading west, ascending, and banking left.

7. D: The aircraft is heading east, ascending, and banking left.

8. D: The aircraft is heading northwest, ascending, and without banking.

9. B: The aircraft is heading southeast, descending, and without banking.

10. B: The aircraft is heading south, ascending, and banking left.

Block Counting

1. C: Block 1 touches 3 blocks: block below Block 1 and 2 blocks on the right side.

2. A: Block 2 touches 4 blocks: block above Block 2, block on the left of Block 2, Block 3, and Block 4.

3. D: Block 3 touches 8 blocks: 4 blocks on the bottom (including Block 5), Block 4, Block 2, block on the left of Block 2, and block below Block 1.

4. C: Block 4 touches 6 blocks: 4 blocks below (including Block 5), Block 2, and Block 3.

5. D: Block 5 touches 5 blocks: block on the left of Block 5, block on the right of Block 5, Block 4, Block 3, and block below Block 1.

6. D: Block S1 touches 4 blocks: block on the left of Block S1, Block S2, Block S3, and block on the right of Block S3.

7. B: Block S2 touches 3 blocks: Block S1, Block S3, and block on the right of Block S3.

8. C: Block S3 touches 7 blocks: block on the left of Block S1, Block S1, Block S2, block on the right of Block S3, block above Block S4, block on the left of Block S4, and block on the right of Block S4.

9. B: Block S4 touches 5 blocks: Block S5, block on the left of Block S5, block on the left of Block S4, block on right of Block S4, and block above Block S4.

10. B: Block S5 touches 4 blocks: block on the left of Block S5, block above Block S5, Block S4, and block on the left of Block S4.

11. D: Block 1 touches 4 blocks: Blocks 2, 5, 6, and 7.

12. B: Block 2 touches 5 blocks: Blocks 1, 3, 5, 6, and 7.

13. A: Block 3 touches 5 blocks: Blocks 2, 4, 5, 6, and 7.

14. A: Block 4 touches 4 blocks: Blocks 3, 5, 6, and 7.

15. D: Block 5 touches 5 blocks: Blocks 1, 2, 3, 4, and 6.

16. E: Block 6 touches 5 blocks: Blocks 1, 2, 3, 4, and 5.

17. B: Block 7 touches 4 blocks: Blocks 1, 2, 3, and 4.

18. D: Block 18 touches 4 blocks: Blocks A, B, C, and 19.

19. E: Block 19 touches 6 blocks: Blocks D, C, B, 18, 22, and F.

20. E: Block 20 touches 5 blocks: Blocks C, E,F, G, and 21.

21. A: Block 21 touches 5 blocks: Blocks E, G, 20, F, and 22.

22. A: Block 22 touches 4 blocks: Blocks 19, F, G, and 21.

23. C: Block 1 touches 3 blocks: block above Block 1, Block 3, and block to the left of Block 3.

24. C: Block 2 touches 7 blocks: block to the left of Block 5, Block 5, block to the left of Block 3, Block 3, 2 blocks to the back and left of Block 2, and Block 4.

25. C: Block 3 touches 6 blocks: Block 1, block above Block 1, Block 2, Block 4, and 2 blocks to the back and left of Block 2.

26. D: Block 4 touches 5 blocks: block to the left of Block 5, Block 5, block to the left of Block 3, Block 3, and Block 2.

27. E: Block 1 touches 5 blocks: Block 2, block to the right of Block 1, Block 3, Block 4, and Block 5.

28. B: Block 2 touches 5 blocks: block to the left of Block 2, Block 1, Block 3, Block 4, and the block below Block 4 and to the left of Block 5.

29. E: Block 3 touches 6 blocks: block to the left of Block 2, Block 2, Block 1, block to the right of Block 1, block to the right of Block 3, and Block 4.

30. D: Block 4 touches 9 blocks: block to the left of Block 2, Block 2, Block 1, block to the right of Block 1, Block 3, block to the right of Block 3, block below Block 4 and to the left of Block 5, Block 5, and block to the right of Block 5.

Aviation

1. B: Faster flow of air over the wing than beneath it. The air moves over the curved surface of the wing at a higher rate of speed than the air moves under the lower flat surface, which creates lift due to the aircraft's forward airspeed and enables flight.

2. B: Longitudinal. The ailerons are mounted on the trailing edges of the wings, and they are used for controlling aircraft roll about the longitudinal axis.

3. A: Lateral. Elevators are mounted on the trailing edges of horizontal stabilizers and are used for controlling aircraft pitch about the lateral axis.

4. C: Vertical. The rudder is mounted on the trailing edge of the vertical fin and is used for controlling rotation (yaw) around the vertical axis.

5. C: Aileron. The aileron is a primary flight control.

6. E: Slats. Slats are part of the wing. The tail assembly of an aircraft is commonly referred to as the empennage. The empennage structure usually includes a tail cone, fixed stabilizers (horizontal and vertical), and moveable surfaces to assist in directional control. The moveable surfaces are the rudder, which is attached to the vertical stabilizer, and the elevators attached to the horizontal stabilizers.

7. B: Skate. Depending on what the aircraft is used for, it may have skis, skids, pontoons, or floats, instead of tires, for landing on ice or water.

8. B: Semicoque. There are two types of fuselage structures: truss and monocoque. The truss fuselage is typically made of steel tubing welded together, which enables the structure to handle tension and compression loads. In lighter aircraft, an aluminum alloy may be used along with cross-bracing. A single-shell fuselage is referred to as monocoque, which uses a stronger skin to handle the tension and compression loads. There is also a semi-monocoque fuselage, which is basically a combination of the truss and monocoque fuselage and is the most commonly used. The semi-monocoque structure includes the use of frame assemblies, bulkheads, formers, longerons, and stringers.

9. A: The pilot. To ensure an aircraft is being operated properly, a pilot needs to be familiar with the aircraft's flight envelope before flying.

10. C: Stalling speed. The stalling speed is the minimum speed at which an aircraft can maintain level flight. As the aircraft gains altitude, the stall speed increases, since the aircraft's weight can be better supported through speed.

11. B: Service ceiling. The maximum altitude of an aircraft is also referred to as the service ceiling. The ceiling is usually decided by the aircraft performance and the wings and is where an altitude at a given speed can no longer be increased at level flight.

12. D: Drag. Drag is the force generated when aircraft is moving through the air. Drag is air resistance that opposes thrust, basically aerodynamic friction or wind resistance. The amount of drag is dependent upon several factors, including the shape of the aircraft, the speed it is traveling, and the density of the air it is passing through.

13. B: Levels the aircraft in flight. The horizontal stabilizer provides for leveling of aircraft in flight. If the aircraft tilts up or down, air pressure increases on one side of the stabilizer and decreases on the other. This imbalance on the stabilizer will push the aircraft back into level flight. The horizontal stabilizer holds the tail down as well, since most aircraft designs induce the tendency of the nose to tilt downward because the center of gravity is forward of the center of lift in the wings.

14. C: The outer trailing edge of the wing. Ailerons are located on the outer trailing edges of the wings and control the roll of an aircraft.

15. D: Stall. An aircraft stall occurs at the critical AOA, where the induced drag exceeds the lift. During a stall, the wing is no longer able to create sufficient lift to oppose gravity. Stall angle is usually around 20°.

16. A: Landing. There are four fundamental maneuvers in flight: straight-and-level, turns, climbs, and descents. Every controlled flight usually includes a combination of these four fundamentals.

17. C: Torque. Torque from the engine turning the main rotor forces the body of the helicopter in the opposite direction. Most helicopters use a tail rotor, which counters this torque force by pushing or pulling against the tail.

18. B: Collective control. The collective control is used to increase the pitch of the main rotor simultaneously at all points of the rotor blade rotation. The collective increases or decreases total rotor thrust; the cyclic changes the direction of rotor thrust. In forward flight, the collective pitch changes the amount of thrust, which in turn can change the speed or altitude based on the use of the cyclic. During hovering, the collective pitch will alter the hover height.

19. B: 3-5 miles away. Visual approach slope indicator (VASI) is a light system designed to provide visual guidance during approach of a runway. The light indicators are visible 3-5 miles away during daylight hours and up to 20 miles away in darkness. The indicators are designed to be used once the aircraft is already visually aligned with the runway.

20. A: Horizontal. Non-precision instrument runways provide horizontal guidance only when there is an approved procedure for a straight-in non-precision instrument approach.

ASTB/OAR Practice Test

Math Skills (ASTB & OAR)

1. $\frac{14}{15} + \frac{3}{5} - \frac{1}{30} =$
   a. $\frac{19}{15}$
   b. $\frac{43}{30}$
   c. $\frac{4}{3}$
   d. $\frac{3}{2}$

2. Solve for *x* and *y*, given $3x + 2y = 8, -x + 3y = 1$.
   a. $x = 2, y = 1$
   b. $x = 1, y = 2$
   c. $x = -1, y = 6$
   d. $x = 3, y = 1$

3. $\frac{1}{2}\sqrt{16} =$
   a. 0
   b. 1
   c. 2
   d. 4

4. The factors of $2x^2 - 8$ are:
   a. $2(4x^2)$
   b. $2(x^2 + 4)$
   c. $2(x + 2)(x + 2)$
   d. $2(x + 2)(x - 2)$

5. Two of the interior angles of a triangle are 35° and 70°. What is the measure of the last interior angle?
   a. 60°
   b. 75°
   c. 90°
   d. 100°

6. A square field has an area of 400 square feet. What is its perimeter?
   a. 100 feet
   b. 80 feet
   c. $40\sqrt{2}$ feet
   d. 40 feet

7. $\frac{5}{3} \times \frac{7}{6} =$

a. $\frac{3}{5}$

b. $\frac{18}{3}$

c. $\frac{45}{31}$

d. $\frac{35}{18}$

8. One apple costs $2. One papaya costs $3. If Samantha spends $35 and gets 15 pieces of fruit, how many papayas did she buy?

a. Three
b. Four
c. Five
d. Six

9. If $x^2 - 6 = 30$, then one possible value for x is:

a. -6
b. -4
c. 3
d. 5

10. A cube has a side length of 6 inches. What is its volume?

a. 6 cubic inches
b. 36 cubic inches
c. 144 cubic inches
d. 216 cubic inches

11. A square has a side length of 4 inches. A triangle has a base of 2 inches and a height of 8 inches. What is the total area of the square and triangle?

a. 24 square inches
b. 28 square inches
c. 32 square inches
d. 36 square inches

12. $-\frac{1}{3}\sqrt{81} =$

a. -9
b. -3
c. 0
d. 3

13. Simplify $(2x - 3)(4x + 2)$

a. $8x^2 - 8x - 6$
b. $6x^2 + 8x - 5$
c. $-4x^2 - 8x - 1$
d. $4x^2 - 4x - 6$

14. $\frac{11}{6} - \frac{3}{8} =$

a. $\frac{5}{4}$

b. $\frac{51}{36}$

c. $\frac{35}{24}$

d. $\frac{3}{2}$

15. A triangle is to have a base $\frac{1}{3}$ as long as its height. Its area must be 6 square feet. How long will its base be?

a. 1 foot
b. 1.5 feet
c. 2 feet
d. 2.5 feet

16. Which is closest to 17.8×9.9?

a. 140
b. 180
c. 200
d. 350

17. 6 is 30% of what number?

a. 18
b. 22
c. 24
d. 20

18. $3\frac{2}{3} - 1\frac{4}{5} =$

a. $1\frac{13}{15}$

b. $\frac{14}{15}$

c. $2\frac{2}{3}$

d. $\frac{4}{5}$

19. What is $\frac{420}{98}$ rounded to the nearest integer?

a. 7
b. 3
c. 5
d. 4

20. Which of the following is largest?
   a. 0.45
   b. 0.096
   c. 0.3
   d. 0.313

21. What is the value of *b* in this equation?

$$5b - 4 = 2b + 17$$

   a. 13
   b. 24
   c. 7
   d. 21

22. Twenty is 40% of what number?
   a. 50
   b. 8
   c. 200
   d. 5000

23. Which of the following expressions is equivalent to this equation?

$$\frac{2xy^2 + 4x - 8y}{16xy}$$

   a. $\frac{y}{8} + \frac{1}{4y} - \frac{1}{2x}$
   b. $8xy + 4y - 2x$
   c. $xy^2 + \frac{x}{4y} - \frac{1}{2x}$
   d. $\frac{y}{8} + 4y - 8y$

24. Arrange the following numbers from least to greatest value:

$0.85, \frac{4}{5}, \frac{2}{3}, \frac{91}{100}$

   a. $0.85, \frac{4}{5}, \frac{2}{3}, \frac{91}{100}$
   b. $\frac{4}{5}, 0.85, \frac{91}{100}, \frac{2}{3}$
   c. $\frac{2}{3}, \frac{4}{5}, 0.85, \frac{91}{100}$
   d. $0.85, \frac{91}{100}, \frac{4}{5}, \frac{2}{3}$

25. Simplify the following expression:

$$(3x + 5)(x - 8)$$

a. $3x^2 - 19x - 40$
b. $4x - 19x - 13$
c. $3x^2 - 19x + 40$
d. $3x^2 + 5x - 3$

26. If $6t + 4 = 16$, what is *t*?
a. 1
b. 2
c. 3
d. 4

27. The variable *y* is directly proportional to *x*. If $y = 3$ when $x = 5$, then what is *y* when $x = 20$?
a. 10
b. 12
c. 14
d. 16

28. A line passes through the point (1, 2) and crosses the *y*-axis at *y* = 1. Which of the following is an equation for this line?
a. $y = 2x$
b. $y = x + 1$
c. $x + y = 1$
d. $y = \frac{x}{2} - 2$

29. There are $4x + 1$ treats in each party favor bag. If a total of $60x + 15$ treats are distributed, how many bags are given out?
a. 15
b. 16
c. 20
d. 22

30. Apples cost $2 each, while bananas cost $3 each. Maria purchased 10 fruits in total and spent $22. How many apples did she buy?
a. 5
b. 6
c. 7
d. 8

Reading Comprehension (ASTB & OAR)

Directions: Assume each passage below to be true. Then, pick the answer choice that can be inferred only from the passage itself. Some of the other answer choices might make sense, but only one of them can be derived solely from the passage.

1. Kate has to buy a camera for her trip. She is hiking the Appalachian trail, and it is a requirement that she must pack the lightest equipment possible. Kate has to choose between the compact system camera (CSC) and the digital single-lens reflex camera (DSLR).

   a. Kate has two issues: buying a camera and figuring out which equipment to pack.
   b. Kate will either buy the CSC or the DSLR, depending on which one is smaller.
   c. Kate won't buy the DSLR because it's way too expensive.
   d. Kate is worried that both cameras might be too large to fit in her pack.

2. He adopted a kitten before he went to work. He worried about her all morning. However, he wasn't too concerned when he got a call later that evening about his son being suspended.

   a. He was so worried about the two events he couldn't focus on his work.
   b. His son getting suspended didn't bother him because he was used to it.
   c. The two major events did not occur at the same time.
   d. He worried more about his son being suspended than the kitten.

3. Hard water occurs when rainwater mixes with minerals from rock and soil. Hard water has a high mineral count, including calcium and magnesium. The mineral deposits from hard water can stain hard surfaces in bathrooms and kitchens as well as clog pipes. Hard water can stain dishes, ruin clothes, and reduce the life of any appliances it touches, such as hot water heaters, washing machines, and humidifiers.

   a. Hard water has the ability to reduce the life of a dishwasher.
   b. Hard water is the worst thing to wash your clothes with.
   c. The mineral count in hard water isn't as hard as they say.
   d. Things other than hard water can clog pipes, such as hair and oil.

4. Coaches of kids' sports teams are increasingly concerned about the behavior of parents at games. Parents are screaming and cursing at coaches, officials, players, and other parents. Physical fights have even broken out at games. Parents need to be reminded that coaches are volunteers, giving up their time and energy to help kids develop in their chosen sport. The goal of kids' sports teams is to learn and develop skills, but it's also to have fun. When parents are out of control at games and practices, it takes the fun out of the sport.

   a. Physical fights break out at every single game.
   b. Parents are adding stress to the kids during the game.
   c. Forming a union would help coaches out in their position.
   d. Coaches help kids on sports teams develop their skills and have fun.

5. Tornadoes are dangerous funnel clouds that occur during a large thunderstorm. When warm, humid air near the ground meets cold, dry air from above, a column of the warm air can be drawn up into the clouds. Winds at different altitudes blowing at different speeds make the column of air rotate. As the spinning column of air picks up speed, a funnel cloud is formed. This funnel cloud moves rapidly and haphazardly. Rain and hail inside the cloud cause it to touch down, creating a tornado.

a. Tornadoes are formed from a mixture of cold and warm air.
b. Tornadoes are the most dangerous of extreme weather patterns.
c. Scientists still aren't exactly sure why tornadoes form.
d. Scientists continue to study tornadoes to improve radar detection and warning times.

6. Digestion begins in the mouth where teeth grind up food and saliva breaks it down, making it easier for the body to absorb. Next, the food moves to the esophagus, and it is pushed into the stomach. The stomach is where food is stored and broken down further by acids and digestive enzymes, preparing it for passage into the intestines.

a. Food waste is passed into the large intestine.
b. Nutrients pass into the blood stream while in the small intestine.
c. Food travels to the esophagus as soon as it is chewed.
d. Food travels to the esophagus after it is pushed into the stomach.

7. Jordan is the leader of the group, which means she must decide whether the topic for their presentation will be over climate change or food deserts. Jordan is also very diplomatic. Miguel is an expert in climate change while Kennedy has experience growing up in a food desert.

a. Jordan will pick climate change because it's a more important topic than food deserts.
b. Jordan has to decide whether personal experience is more important than research experience.
c. Jordan will flip a coin in order to decide which topic to present over.
d. Jordan probably likes Kennedy more since she is more relatable, so she will pick her topic.

8. Vacationers looking for a perfect experience should opt out of Disney parks and try a trip on Disney Cruise Lines. While a park offers rides, characters, and show experiences, it also includes long lines, often very hot weather, and enormous crowds.

a. Although Disney Cruise Lines is fun for the family, it has long lines, very hot weather, and enormous crowds.
b. Families with small children should not go to Disney parks because there are too many people and the weather is too hot.
c. At Disney parks, hot weather, lines, and crowds will be less extreme than at Disney Cruise Lines.
d. At Disney Cruise Lines, hot weather, lines, and crowds will be less extreme than at Disney parks.

9. As summer approaches, drowning incidents will increase. Drowning happens very quickly and silently. Most people assume that drowning is easy to spot, but a person who is drowning doesn't make noise or wave their arms.

a. Drowning happens silently and decreases as summer approaches.
b. Drowning happens silently and increases as summer approaches.
c. Each summer, more children drown than adults.
d. Many people in summertime wave their arms and make a lot of noise.

10. Last year was the warmest ever recorded in the last 134 years. During that time period, the ten warmest years have all occurred since 2000.

a. The hottest years in earth's history probably occurred during the dinosaurs' time.
b. The next 134 years will be hotter than the past ten years.
c. Out of the last 50 years, the ten warmest years have occurred since 2000.
d. Burning fossil fuels is what caused the ten warmest years since 2000.

11. A famous children's author recently published a historical fiction novel under a pseudonym; however, it did not sell as many copies as her children's books. In her earlier years, she had majored in history and earned a graduate degree in Antebellum American History, which is the time frame of her new novel.

a. The author's children's books are more popular than her historical fiction novel.
b. It's ironic that the author majored in history yet did not sell many copies of her novel.
c. The author did not sell many copies of her historical fiction novel because it was boring.
d. Most children's authors cannot cross literary genres without being criticized.

12. Hannah started smoking when she was nineteen years old. The day after Hannah finished a book called *Smoke Free*, she quit. She has been cigarette-free for over a decade.

a. Hannah will probably have respiratory problems as she gets older.
b. *Smoke Free* is the reason Hannah quit smoking.
c. Hannah is at least twenty-nine years old.
d. Everyone who smokes should read the book *Smoke Free*.

13. Heat loss is proportional to surface area exposed. An elephant loses a great deal more heat than an anteater, because it has a much greater surface area than an anteater.

a. Surface area causes heat loss.
b. Too much heat loss can be dangerous.
c. Elephants lose more heat than anteaters.
d. Anteaters lose more heat than elephants.

14. The landlord sent an interested tenant the following information about his three apartments for rent: A, B, and C. Apartment B was bigger than Apartment A. Apartment A was in front of Apartment C but above Apartment B. Apartment C was smaller than Apartment A.

a. Apartment B was above Apartment C.
b. Apartment B was smaller than Apartment C.
c. Apartment A was the biggest apartment.
d. Apartment B was in front of Apartment C.

15. People who argue that William Shakespeare is not responsible for the plays attributed to his name are known as anti-Stratfordians (from the name of Shakespeare's birthplace, Stratford-upon-Avon).

a. Dr. Porter believes that William Shakespeare is responsible for writing his own plays. He is known as an anti-Stratfordian.
b. Dr. Filigree believes that William Shakespeare is not responsible for writing his own plays. He is known as an anti-Stratfordian.
c. Dr. Casings believes that Shakespeare was born somewhere other than Stratford. He is known as an anti-Stratfordian.
d. Dr. Hendrix believes that Shakespeare died somewhere other than Stratford. He is known as an anti-Stratfordian.

16. Nina is allergic to dairy (which includes cheese and milk), and she doesn't eat any meat except for fish. At his barbecues, Oliver always invites Nina and consistently prepares her a meal that is suitable to her diet. Nina is planning on going to a barbecue later that Oliver is throwing.

a. Oliver prepares Nina a black bean burger with French fries.
b. Oliver prepares Nina grilled chicken with asparagus.
c. Oliver prepares Nina a cheese pizza with a side salad.
d. Oliver prepares Nina a veggie hot dog with a milkshake.

17. Samuel teaches at a high school in one of the biggest cities in the United States. His students come from diverse family backgrounds. Samuel observes that the best students in his class are from homes where parental supervision is minimal.

a. Samuel should write an academic paper based on his findings.
b. The parents of the bottom five students are probably the most involved.
c. In Samuel's observation, his best students have maximum interference from parents.
d. In Samuel's observation, his best students have minimal interference from parents.

18. Cynthia keeps to a strict vegetarian diet, which is part of her religion. She absolutely cannot have any meat or fish dishes. This is more than a preference; her body has never developed the enzymes to process meat or fish, so she becomes violently ill if she accidentally eats any of the offending foods.

a. Cynthia doesn't eat meat due to necessity.
b. Cynthia doesn't eat meat due to preference.
c. Cynthia doesn't eat meat due to preference as well as necessity.
d. Cynthia can develop a tolerance to meat by eating small pieces at a time.

19. Samantha wants to be a professional chef, so she started working at a nearby restaurant called *Chesapeake Cuisine*. Samantha also wants to go to college one day to study nutrition. Samantha's mom surprised her later that year by offering to send her to school, but she will only send her if Samantha goes to law school. Samantha cannot afford college on her own.

a. Samantha's mom is too controlling.
b. Samantha will never enjoy law school.
c. Samantha has to choose between going to law school and getting a degree in nutrition.
d. Samantha has to choose between working at *Chesapeake Cuisine* and going to law school.

20. Barbara had to have an exercise bike for $150 at a store, but soon found out there was a cheaper one online for $75. Barbara always went for cheaper machinery, but hardly ever returned items if she could help it.

a. Barbara bought both bikes but only used one of them.
b. Barbara returned the $150 bike and bought the $75 bike.
c. Barbara kept the $150 bike because she hated returning things.
d. Barbara did not want a bike that bad so she did not keep any of the bikes.

Mechanical Comprehension (ASTB & OAR)

1. A car is traveling at a constant velocity of 25 m/s. How long does it take the car to travel 45 kilometers in a straight line?
   a. 1 hour
   b. 3600 seconds
   c. 1800 seconds
   d. 900 seconds

2. A ship is traveling due east at a speed of 1 m/s against a current flowing due west at a speed of 0.5 m/s. How far has the ship travelled from its point of departure after two hours?
   a. 1.8 kilometers west of its point of departure
   b. 3.6 kilometers west of its point of departure
   c. 1.8 kilometers east of its point of departure
   d. 3.6 kilometers east of its point of departure

3. A car is driving along a straight stretch of highway at a constant speed of 60 km/hour when the driver slams the gas pedal to the floor, reaching a speed of 132 km/hour in 10 seconds. What's the average acceleration of the car after the engine is floored?
   a. 1 m/s^2
   b. 2 m/s^2
   c. 3 m/s^2
   d. 4 m/s^2

4. A spaceship with a mass of 100,000 kilograms is far away from any planet. To accelerate the craft at the rate of 0.5 m/sec^2, what is the rocket thrust?
   a. 98.1 N
   b. 25,000 N
   c. 50,000 N
   d. 75,000 N

5. The gravitational acceleration on Earth averages 9.81 m/s^2. An astronaut weighs 1962 N on Earth. The diameter of Earth is six times the diameter of its moon. What's the mass of the astronaut on Earth's moon?
   a. 100 kilograms
   b. 200 kilograms
   c. 300 kilograms
   d. 400 kilograms

6. A football is kicked so that it leaves the punter's toe at a horizontal angle of 45 degrees. Ignoring any spin or tumbling, at what point is the upward vertical velocity of the football at a maximum?

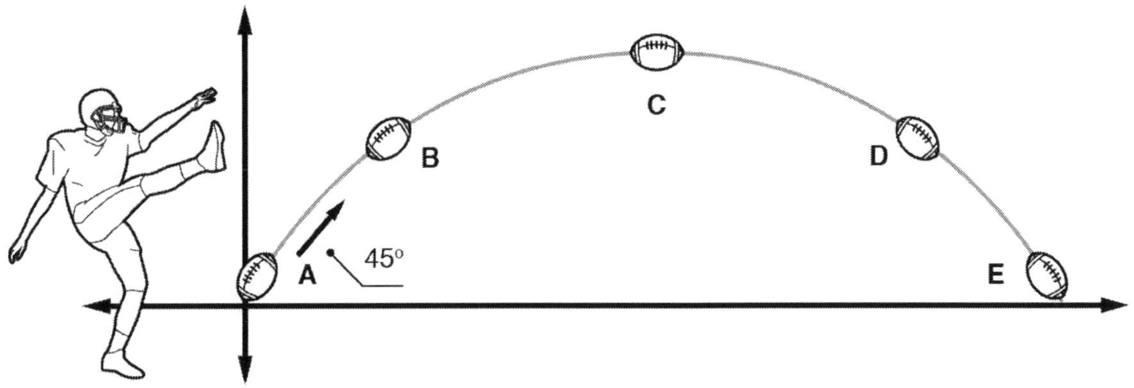

a. At Point A
b. At Point C
c. At Points B and D
d. At Points A and E

7. The skater is shown spinning in Figure (a), then bringing in her arms in Figure (b). Which sequence accurately describes what happens to her angular velocity?

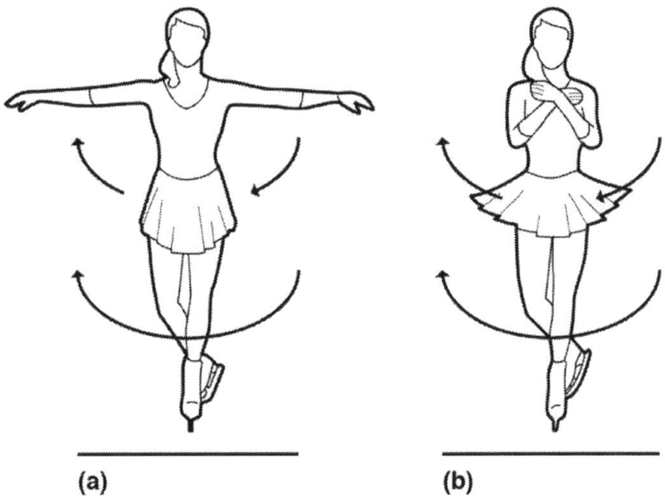

a. Her angular velocity decreases from (a) to (b)
b. Her angular velocity doesn't change from (a) to (b)
c. Her angular velocity increases from (a) to (b)
d. It's not possible to determine what happens to her angular velocity if her weight is unknown.

8. A cannonball is dropped from a height of 10 meters above sea level. What is its approximate velocity just before it hits the ground?

a. 9.81 m/s
b. 14 m/s
c. 32 m/s
d. It can't be determined without knowing the cannonball's mass

9. The pendulum is held at point A, and then released to swing to the right. At what point does the pendulum have the greatest kinetic energy?

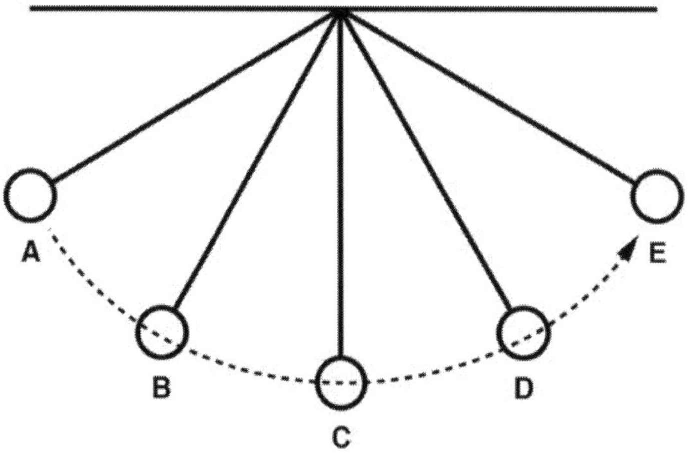

a. At Point B
b. At Point C
c. At Point D
d. At Point E

10. Which statement is true of the total energy of the pendulum?

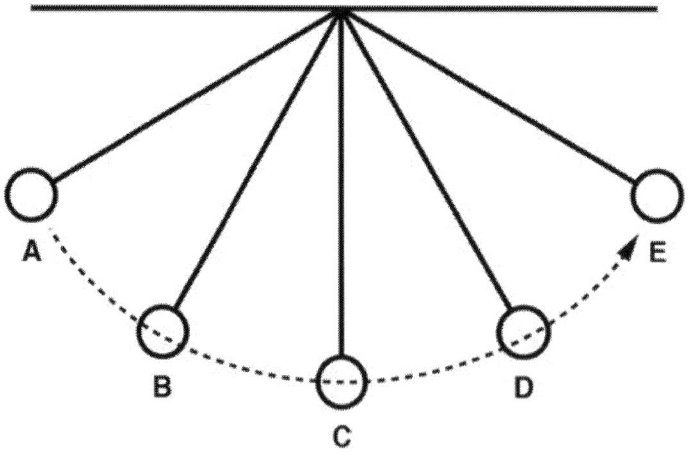

a. Its total energy is at a maximum and equal at Points A and E.
b. Its total energy is at a maximum at Point C.
c. Its total energy is the same at Points A, B, C, D, and E.
d. The total energy can't be determined without knowing the pendulum's mass.

11. How do you calculate the useful work performed in lifting a 10-kilogram weight from the ground to the top of a 2-meter ladder?

a. 10kg x 2m x 32 m/s^2
b. 10kg x $2m^2$ x 9.81 m/s
c. 10kg x 2m x 9.81m/s^2
d. It can't be determined without knowing the ground elevation

12. A steel spring is loaded with a 10-newton weight and is stretched by 0.5 centimeters. What is the deflection if it's loaded with two 10-newton weights?

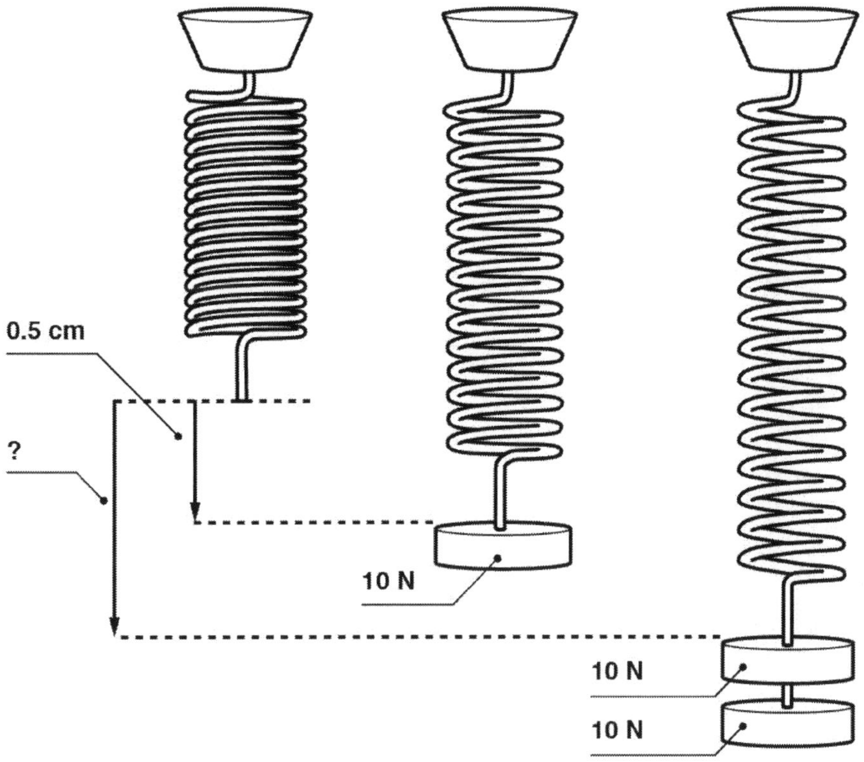

a. 0.5 centimeter
b. 1 centimeter
c. 2 centimeters
d. It can't be determined without knowing the Modulus of Elasticity of the steel.

13. A 1000-kilogram concrete block is resting on a wooden surface. Between these two materials, the coefficient of sliding friction is 0.4 and the coefficient of static friction is 0.5. How much more force is needed to get the block moving than to keep it moving?

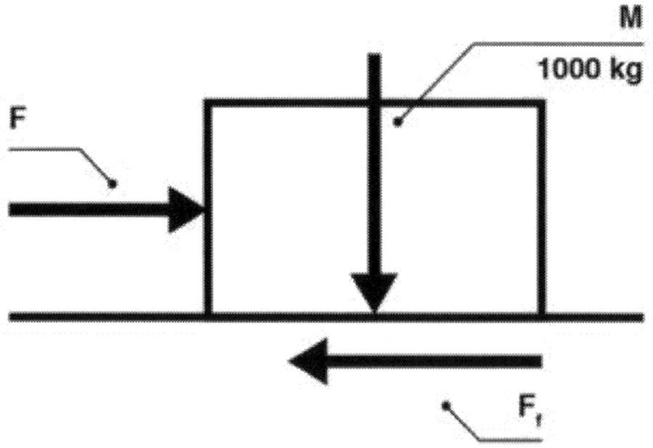

a. 981 N
b. 1962 N
c. 3924 N
d. 9810 N

14. The master cylinder (F1) of a hydraulic jack has a cross-sectional area of 0.1 m^2, and a force of 50 N is applied. What must the area of the drive cylinder (F2) be to support a weight of 800 N?

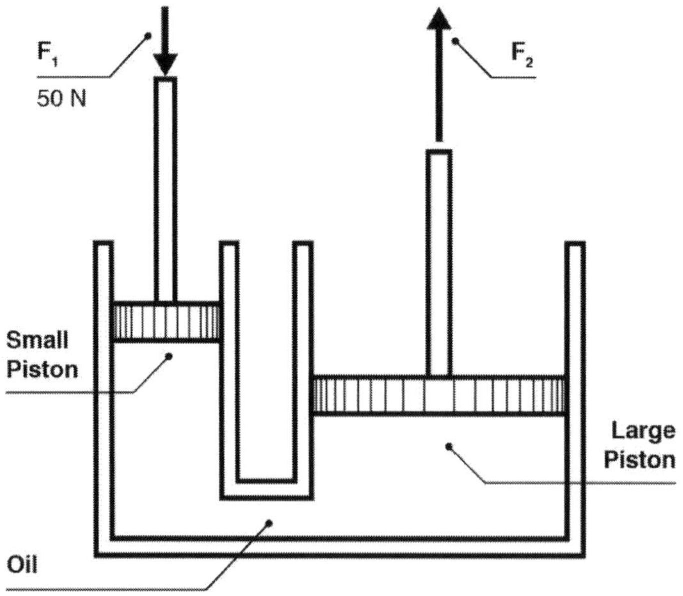

a. 0.4 m^2
b. 0.8 m^2
c. 1.6 m^2
d. 3.2 m^2

15. A gas with a volume V_1 is held down by a piston with a force of *F* newtons. The piston has an area of *A*. After heating the gas, it expands against the weight to a volume V_2. What was the work done?

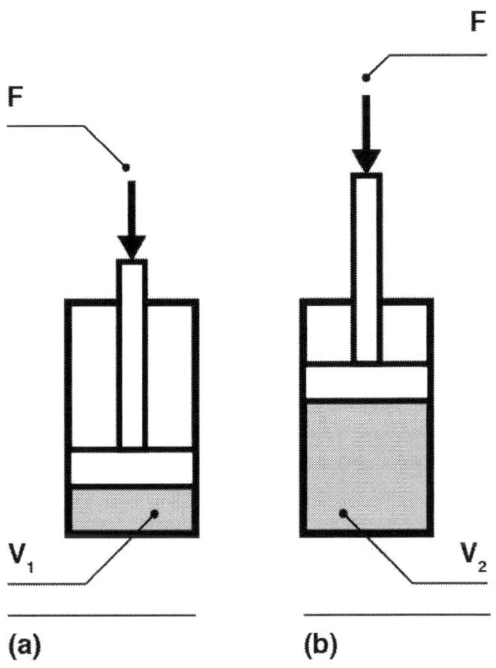

a. F/A
b. $(F/A) \times V_1$
c. $(F/A) \times V_2$
d. $(F/A) \times (V_2 - V_1)$

16. A 1000-kilogram weight is raised 30 meters in 10 minutes. What is the approximate power expended in the period?

a. 1000 Kg × m/s^2
b. 500 N·m
c. 500 J/s
d. 100 watts

17. A 2-meter high, concrete block is submerged in a body of water 12 meters deep (as shown). Assuming that the water has a unit weight of 1000 N/m^3, what is the pressure acting on the upper surface of the block?

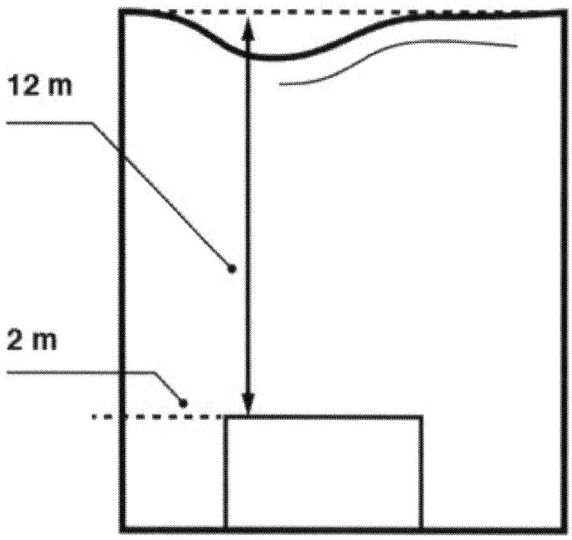

a. 10,000 Pa
b. 12,000 Pa
c. 14,000 Pa
d. It can't be calculated without knowing the top area of the block.

18. Closed Basins A and B each contain a 10,000-ton block of ice. The ice block in Basin A is floating in sea water. The ice block in Basin B is aground on a rock ledge (as shown). When all the ice melts, what happens to the water level in Basin A and Basin B?

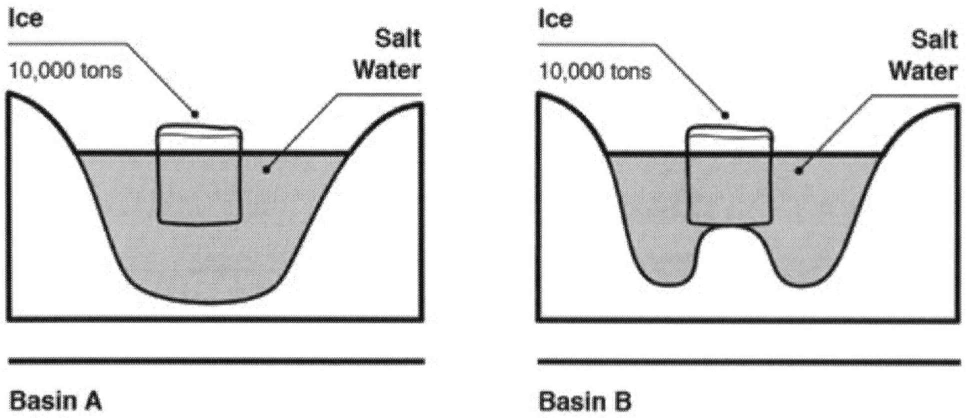

a. Water level rises in A but not in B
b. Water level rises in B but not in A
c. Water level rises in neither A nor B
d. Water level rises in both A and B

19. An official 10-lane Olympic pool is 50 meters wide by 25 meters long. How long does it take to fill the pool to the recommended depth of 3 meters using a pump with a 750 liter per second capacity?

a. 2500 seconds
b. 5000 seconds
c. 10,000 seconds
d. 100,000 seconds

20. Water is flowing in a rectangular canal 10 meters wide by 2 meters deep at a velocity of 3 m/s. The canal is half full. What is the flow rate?

a. 30 m^3/s
b. 60 m^3/s
c. 90 m^3/s
d. 120 m^3/s

21. A 150-kilogram mass is placed on the left side of the lever as shown. What force must be exerted on the right side (in the location shown by the arrow) to balance the weight of this mass?

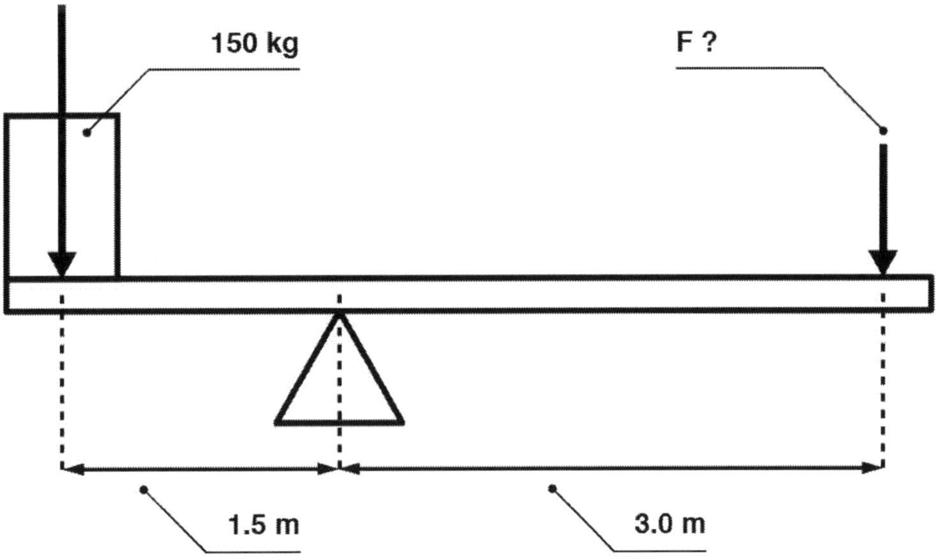

a. 675 kg.m
b. 737.75 N
c. 1471.5 N
d. 2207.25 N·m

22. For the wheel and axle assembly shown, the shaft radius is 20 millimeters and the wheel radius is 300 millimeters. What's the required effort to lift a 600 N load?

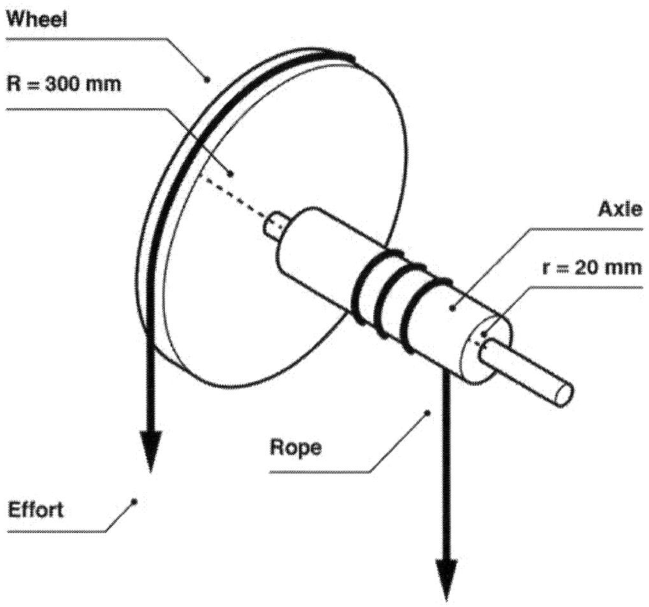

a. 10 N
b. 20 N
c. 30 N
d. 40 N

23. The driver gear (Gear A) turns clockwise at a rate of 60 RPM. In what direction does Gear B turn and at what rotational speed?

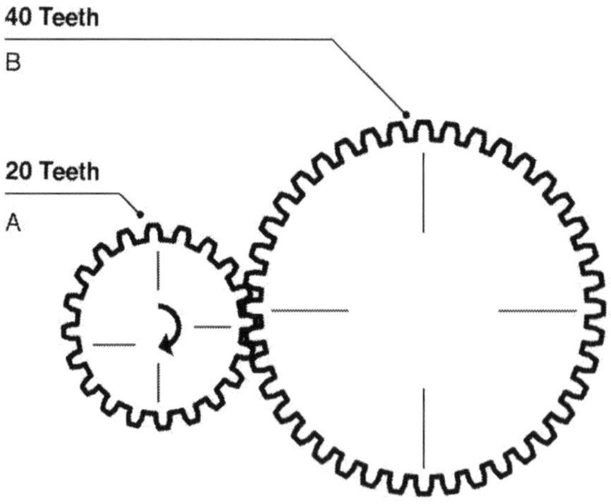

a. Clockwise at 120 RPM
b. Counterclockwise at 120 RPM
c. Clockwise at 30 RPM
d. Counterclockwise at 30 RPM

24. The three steel wheels shown are connected by rubber belts. The two wheels at the top have the same diameter, while the wheel below is twice their diameter. If the driver wheel at the upper left is turning clockwise at 60 RPM, at what speed and in which direction is the large bottom wheel turning?

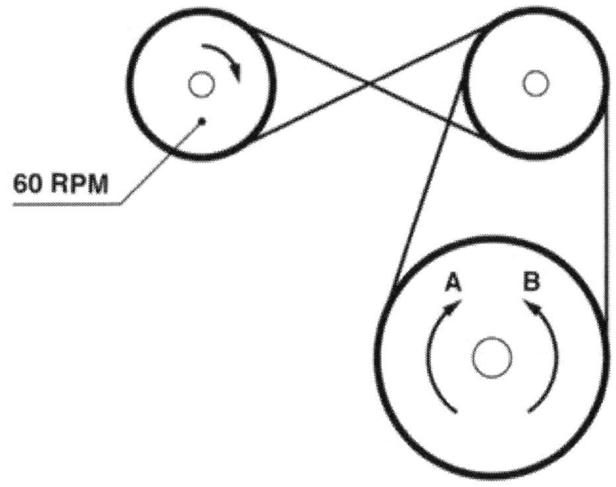

a. 30 RPM, clockwise (A)
b. 30 RPM, counterclockwise (B)
c. 120 RPM, clockwise (A)
d. 120 RPM, counterclockwise (B)

25. In case (a), both blocks are fixed. In case (b), the load is hung from a moveable block. Ignoring friction, what is the required force to move the blocks in both cases?

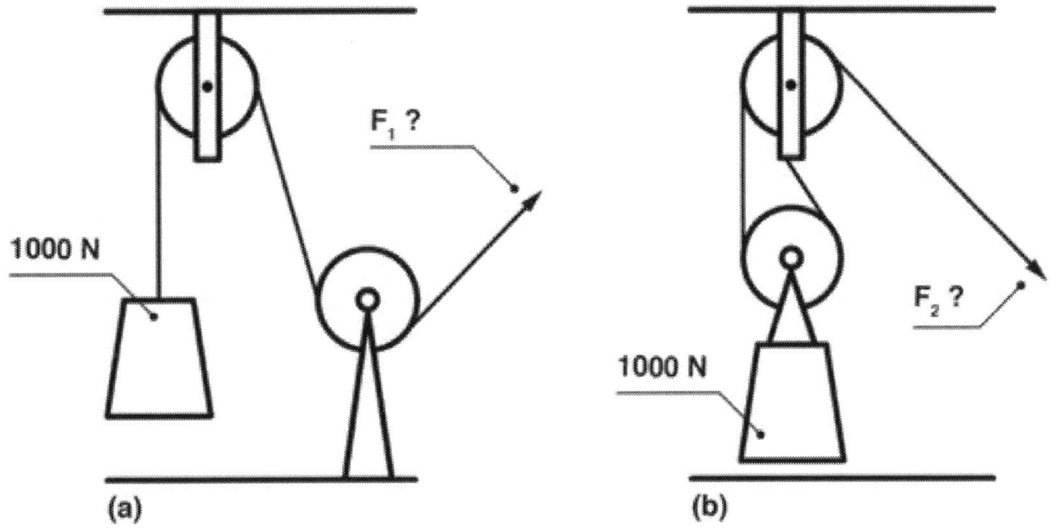

a. $F_1 = 500$ N; $F_2 = 500$ N
b. $F_1 = 500$ N; $F_2 = 1000$ N
c. $F_1 = 1000$ N; $F_2 = 500$ N
d. $F_1 = 1000$ N; $F_2 = 1000$ N

26. Considering a gas in a closed system, at a constant volume, what will happen to the temperature if the pressure is increased?

a. The temperature will stay the same
b. The temperature will decrease
c. The temperature will increase
d. The temperature will decrease then increase

27. What is the current when a 3.0 V battery is wired across a lightbulb that has a resistance of 6.0 ohms?

a. 0.5 A
b. 18.0 A
c. 0.5 J
d. 18.0 J

28. According to Newton's Three Laws of Motion, which of the following is true?

a. Two objects cannot exert a force on each other without touching.
b. An object at rest has no inertia.
c. The weight of an object is equal to the mass of an object multiplied by gravity.
d. For someone who is moving relative to a wave source, there occurs an effect of change in the frequency of the wave.

29. What is the total mechanical energy of a system?

a. The total potential energy
b. The total kinetic energy
c. Kinetic energy plus potential energy
d. Kinetic energy minus potential energy

30. What is the molarity of a solution made by dissolving 4.0 grams of NaCl into enough water to make 120 mL of solution? The atomic mass of Na is 23.0 g/mol and Cl is 35.5 g/mol.

a. 0.34 M
b. 0.57 M
c. 0.034 M
d. 0.62 M

Aviation and Nautical (ASTB)

1. When generating lift, what should the pressure below the airfoil be in relation to the pressure above the airfoil?

a. Greater than it
b. Less than it
c. Equal to it
d. The opposite of it

2. What is the load factor of a 2000-pound helicopter that is currently experiencing an effective load of 4000 pounds?

a. 0.25
b. 0.5
c. 1
d. 2

3. Which of the following type or types of drag increase as the speed increases?

I. Parasitic drag
II. Induced drag
III. Profile drag

a. I only
b. II and III
c. I and II
d. I and III

4. Which of the following decreases upon an increase to the collective pitch controller?

a. RPM
b. Altitude
c. Drag
d. Lift

5. Which of the following is FALSE about the governor?

a. It adjusts the throttle as needed.
b. It uses an electronic sensor.
c. It controls the pitch of the rotors.
d. It regulates the power to maintain RPM.

6. If the cyclic pitch control is pushed to the left, which way will the rotor disk tip and which way will the helicopter move?

a. Right; right
b. Right; left
c. Left; right
d. Left; left

7. Which direction(s) are the anti-torque pedals designed to move the nose?

a. Up and down
b. Left and right
c. Forward and backwards
d. The anti-torque pedals move the nose in all of the above directions.

8. Which of the following is NOT included in a helicopter's base empty weight?

a. The pilot
b. The engine
c. Optional equipment
d. Transmission oil

9. Which of the following are dangers of overloading a helicopter?

I. Decreased performance
II. Structural damage
III. Shifted center of gravity

a. II only
b. I, II, and III
c. I and II
d. I and III

10. If the helicopter is nose down while attempting to hover, and there are no winds, then it most likely has which of the following?
  a. Front-loaded center of gravity
  b. Aft-loaded center of gravity
  c. Balanced center of gravity
  d. A changing center of gravity

11. When performing a vertical takeoff to a hover, what should be done if the heading begins to change?
  a. Quickly adjust the cyclic pitch control
  b. Slowly adjust the cyclic pitch control
  c. Slowly adjust the anti-torque pedals
  d. Quickly adjust the anti-torque pedals

12. Which of the following would make a good reference point when attempting to hover?
  a. The tail rotor
  b. Another helicopter
  c. A building
  d. A moving car

13. Which of the following should not need to be maintained while performing a hovering turn?
  a. Altitude
  b. RPM
  c. Heading
  d. Position

14. Which of the following is a complication unique to sideward hovering flight, as opposed to forward and rearward flight?
  a. Increased clearance needed due to dipping of the tail during the maneuver
  b. Additional pressure needed on the anti-torque pedals to deal with the weathervane
  c. Drastically-reduced visibility
  d. Decreased RPM due to the increased pitch of the rotor blades

15. When performing an air taxi, which of the following should be avoided?
    I. Flying in the shaded area of the height-velocity diagram
    II. Flying over other aircraft, vehicles, and personnel
    III. Flying in crosswind conditions
  a. I only
  b. I and II
  c. I and III
  d. I, II and III

16. Which of the following does not need to be checked *before* beginning a normal takeoff from hover?
  a. Power
  b. Balance
  c. RPM
  d. Flight controls

17. In straight-and-level flight, which control is primarily used to increase airspeed?
   a. The collective pitch control
   b. The cyclic pitch control
   c. Anti-torque pedals
   d. The throttle

18. A helicopter pilot is attempting to take off when she notices that the helicopter's nose tilts down after leaving the ground. What is most likely the problem?
   a. Too much main rotor torque
   b. Imbalanced center of gravity
   c. Insufficient power
   d. Changing winds

19. A helicopter begins a descent at 300 feet above the ground, with the intent to lower to 200 feet above the ground. The pilot begins the descent at a steady rate of 400 FPM. At what altitude should he begin leveling out the helicopter?
   a. 200 feet
   b. 220 feet
   c. 240 feet
   d. 260 feet

20. Which of the following would NOT be included in the maximum internal weight?
   a. The pilot
   b. Cargo stored in the aft of the helicopter
   c. Useable fuel
   d. An object supported by a winch

21. A pilot wishes to reposition the helicopter while hovering to get to a designated runway for a surface takeoff. After performing a hovering turn to set her bearing properly, the pilot needs to move the helicopter forward. To do this, she should do which of the following?
   a. Increase the collective
   b. Briefly apply pressure to the cyclic, then release the cyclic
   c. Apply gentle and constant pressure to the cyclic
   d. Progressively increase the throttle

22. While performing a banking left turn, the pilot notices that the helicopter has begun to skid. What can he do to get out of this?
   a. Decrease pressure on the left anti-torque pedal or increase pressure on the right anti-torque pedal
   b. Decrease pressure on the right anti-torque pedal or increase pressure on the left anti-torque pedal
   c. Apply additional leftwards cyclic pressure
   d. Apply additional rightwards cyclic pressure

23. A pilot has successfully identified that the helicopter has an aft-loaded center of balance. Which of the following methods would correct this?

  a. Removing cargo from the back of the helicopter
  b. Applying additional forward cyclic
  c. Increasing the throttle
  d. Adding additional fuel

24. A helicopter performing a takeoff from hover has just entered effective translational lift and has begun to increase the collective. Which step of the takeoff is the helicopter currently in?

  a. Step one
  b. Step two
  c. Step three
  d. Step four

25. A pilot is performing a straight and level flight when he realizes that the helicopter has drifted to the left of the intended path. What should he do?

  a. Apply pressure to the right anti-torque pedal
  b. Apply rightward pressure to the cyclic
  c. Remove cargo from the back of the helicopter
  d. Speed up the helicopter to reach the destination before the helicopter drifts further

26. Which of the following would increase the torque on the helicopter?

    I. Applying pressure on the cyclic
    II. Decreasing the collective
    III. Increasing the throttle

  a. I
  b. II
  c. III
  d. II and III

27. Which of the following is true about induced drag?

  a. It is strongest when the helicopter is moving at higher speeds.
  b. It is created by the airfoil striking the air.
  c. It always pushes in a direction opposite of lift.
  d. All of the above are true.

28. If sufficient takeoff power is in doubt, what should the pilot do?

I. Delay the takeoff until the aircraft is lighter
II. Attempt the takeoff anyway to check power
III. Wait until the density altitude has decreased

a. I only
b. II and III
c. I and II
d. I and III

29. Which of the following is not one of the four fundamental maneuvers?

a. Turning
b. Straight and level flight
c. Climbing
d. Takeoff

30. A pilot notices that as the helicopter flies, the nose slowly drops. The cyclic is in its neutral position. What is most likely the cause of this?

a. The fuel in the rear of the helicopter is being used up, slowly shifting the center of balance forward.
b. The cyclic is improperly calibrated and tipping the helicopter even into the neutral position.
c. The helicopter is entering a higher density air front, pushing the nose down.
d. The helicopter's tail rotor is creating too much torque, pushing the tail up and the nose down.

31. Lowering the collective while the helicopter is flying straight and level will have what effect, assuming everything else remains constant?

a. It will cause the nose to pitch down, the helicopter's airspeed to increase, and it will produce left yaw.
b. It will cause the nose to pitch up, the helicopter's airspeed to decrease, and it will produce right yaw.
c. It will cause the nose to pitch down and the helicopter's airspeed will decrease.
d. It will have no appreciable effect on the airspeed of the helicopter.

32. While hovering, a pilot wishes to increase her altitude, so she uses the collective. Which control will the pilot NOT need to use while doing so, assuming ideal conditions?

a. The cyclic
b. The anti-torque pedals
c. The throttle
d. All the above are needed while raising the collective

33. After achieving the desired altitude, the pilot decides to perform a takeoff from a hover and applies forward pressure on the cyclic to begin forward movement. Which control will he NOT need to use while doing so, assuming ideal conditions?

I. The collective
II. The anti-torque pedals
III. The throttle

a. II only
b. I and II
c. I and III
d. I, II and III

34. Although both parasitic drag and profile drag increase as speed increases, which of the following correctly identifies the difference between the two?

a. Profile drag starts out as more significant than parasitic drag and remains more significant at all speeds.

b. Parasitic drag starts out as more significant than profile drag and remains more significant at all speeds.

c. Profile drag starts out as more significant, but parasitic drag becomes more significant at higher speeds.

d. Parasitic drag starts out as more significant, but profile drag becomes more significant at higher speeds.

35. When performing a hovering turn on a windy day, at what point is weathervane most likely to cause problems?

a. When the helicopter's heading is into the wind

b. When the helicopter's heading is with the wind

c. At the end of the turn

d. At the beginning of the turn

36. When climbing at cruising speed, in addition to raising the collective, the rate of climb can be increased by which of the following actions?

I. Applying rearward cyclic pressure to reduce airspeed

II. Increasing the throttle to increase power

III. Applying forward cyclic pressure to increase airspeed

a. I only

b. II only

c. III only

d. I and II

37. Which of the following maneuvers should be avoided when flying with a heavy load?

I. Large angle banking turns

II. High speed straight and level flight

III. Takeoff from hover

a. I

b. II only

c. III only

d. I, II and III

38. Which of the following influences the G load?

I. The weight of the helicopter

II. The weather

III. Air density

a. I only

b. I and II

c. I and III

d. II and III

39. At what pace should a helicopter in forward flight move?
    a. About as fast as a brisk walk
    b. No faster than jogging speed
    c. As fast as desired as long as control can be maintained
    d. Not faster than a run, and even slower if the area is uneven

40. Which control is a rate-controlled instrument?
    a. The collective
    b. The throttle
    c. The cyclic
    d. The anti-torque pedals

41. Which of the following will create lift?
    a. Airflow against the tail section of the aircraft
    b. Faster flow of air over the wing than beneath it
    c. Raised ailerons
    d. Helium in the wings

42. Which of the following axes is controlled by ailerons?
    a. Lateral
    b. Longitudinal
    c. Vertical
    d. Equatorial

43. Which of the following axes is controlled by elevators?
    a. Lateral
    b. Longitudinal
    c. Vertical
    d. Equatorial

44. Which of the following axes is controlled by a rudder?
    a. Lateral
    b. Longitudinal
    c. Vertical
    d. Equatorial

45. Which of the following is not a secondary or auxiliary flight control?
    a. Flap
    b. Spoiler
    c. Aileron
    d. Slat

46. What component is not part of an empennage?
    a. Stabilizer
    b. Rudder
    c. Elevator
    d. Slats

47. Which of the following is not a type of landing gear?
    a. Ski
    b. Skate
    c. Skid
    d. Float

48. Which is not a type of fuselage?
    a. Monocoque
    b. Semicoque
    c. Semi-Monocoque
    d. Truss

49. Who should be the most concerned about an aircraft's flight envelope?
    a. The pilot
    b. Air traffic controller
    c. Passengers
    d. Aircraft mechanic

50. What is the minimum speed at which an aircraft can maintain level flight?
    a. Ceiling speed
    b. Cruising speed
    c. Stalling speed
    d. Mach 1

51. What is the maximum operating altitude for a design of an aircraft?
    a. Stratosphere roof
    b. Service ceiling
    c. Stratosphere ceiling
    d. Overhead ceiling

52. Which of the following is another word for aerodynamic friction or wind resistance?
    a. Lift
    b. Gravity
    c. Thrust
    d. Drag

53. What is the purpose of the horizontal stabilizer?
    a. Pushes the tail left or right in line with the aircraft
    b. Levels the aircraft in flight
    c. Controls the roll of an aircraft
    d. Decreases speed for landing
    e. Decreases speed in a turn

54. Where are ailerons located?
    a. The trailing edge of a rudder
    b. The outer leading edge of a wing
    c. The outer trailing edge of a wing
    d. The inner trailing edge of a wing

55. What occurs when the induced drag on an aircraft exceeds its lift?
   a. Roll
   b. Yaw
   c. Pitch
   d. Stall

56. Which is not considered to be one of the four fundamental flight maneuvers?
   a. Landing
   b. Straight and level
   c. Turns
   d. Descent

57. What force acting upon a helicopter attempts to turn the body of the helicopter in the opposite direction of the main rotor travel?
   a. Gyroscopic precession
   b. Centrifugal force
   c. Torque
   d. Coriolis effect

58. What is used to increase the pitch of the main rotor at the same time at all points of the rotor blade rotation?
   a. Cyclic control
   b. Collective control
   c. Coriolis control
   d. Symmetry control

59. Visual approach slope indicators are visible from what distance during clear, daylight hours?
   a. 1 to 2 miles away
   b. 3 to 5 miles away
   c. 5 to 10 miles away
   d. 10 to 20 miles away

60. Non-precision instrument runways provide what kind of guidance?
   a. Horizontal
   b. Vertical
   c. Locational
   d. Directional

61. What was the *Great White Fleet*?
   a. The Rhode Island Navy
   b. German U-boats
   c. Sixteen Battleships
   d. British Navy Deserters

62. What is the term for a life-sized model ship for recruits to practice mooring, life handling, putting out to sea, and other aspects of basic seamanship?
   a. A marlinspike
   b. A crank
   c. A cumshaw
   d. A scuttlebutt

63. What is meant by the term *starboard*?
   a. The left side of the ship
   b. The right side of the ship
   c. The ship's rear
   d. The ship's front

64. Which U.S. Navy ship operates close to shore with the mission of detecting mines, diesel submarines, and crafts that move quickly along the surface?
   a. Submarines
   b. Cruisers
   c. Destroyers
   d. Littoral Combat Ships

65. Which of the following was introduced in the late 1990s to help determine a vessel's position with signals coming from satellites?
   a. ARPA
   b. Echo Sounder
   c. GPS
   d. LORAN

66. What does the acronym *NMOC* stand for?
   a. Naval Military Operations Center
   b. Naval Meteorology and Oceanography Command
   c. Naval Military Operations Command
   d. Naval Meteorology and Operations Center

67. What is the method of navigation employed by ships and aircraft that uses the vessel's last known position, its starting point, an awareness of its estimated drift, the distance covered, and its course record?
   a. Radar Navigation
   b. Latitude
   c. Satellite Navigation
   d. Dead Reckoning

68. You are in a vessel trailing behind another, and you wish to pass. Following proper protocol, you ask permission to pass by blasting two sounds of your vessel's horn. The give-way vessel responds with 5 blasts of its horn. What does this mean?
   a. Your vessel is NOT permitted to pass.
   b. Your vessel IS permitted to pass.
   c. Your vessel must wait 5 minutes before passing.
   d. Your vessel must pass on the right side of the give-way vessel.

69. What are Landing Platform Docks (LPDs)?
   a. Amphibious warfare vessels
   b. Cruisers
   c. Dry Docks
   d. Another term for helicopter pads

70. What does IMSAFE refer to?
   a. Impairment, Medication, Shock, Alcohol, Fatigue, Exercise
   b. Impairment, Misdiagnosis, Stress, Alcohol, and Emotion
   c. Illness, Medication, Stress, Alcohol, Fatigue, and Emotion
   d. Illness, Misdiagnosis, Shock, Alcohol, Fatigue, and Emergency

Naval Aviation Trait Facet Inventory (NATFI) (ASTB)

The Naval Aviation Trait Facet Inventory (NATFI) section is akin to a personality test. It is designed with the goal of specifically assessing a candidate's behavioral and personality suitability for success in an aviation program and service at the various career stages he or she will encounter.

On the NATFI section of the exam, test takers will encounter 88 statements presented in 44 pairs. Test takers must select the one statement from the pair that most accurately reflects the way they think, feel, or act, depending on the parameters provided in the possible responses. The statements in each pair are provided as complete sentences written in first-person perspective. Some of the 44 pairs will present two positive statements, addressing favorable personality traits. The following pair is an example of this type:

☐ I firmly believe that I am capable of being a strong leader.

☐ I am confident that I can excel in a wide variety of situations.

Other pairs will include two unflattering statements, such as the following:

☐ I tend to act impulsively.

☐ I am often disorganized.

Because the NATFI is a personality inventory, there are no "right" or "wrong" answers. Accordingly, it is unnecessary to study for this section. However, test takers can practice or prepare by reviewing the format of the section to ensure they understand what the NATFI entails.

A candidate's responses are evaluated for the specific personality traits the items are designed to measure. The evaluated traits are confidence, work motivation, warmth, unrestrained behavior, aggressiveness, and adaptability. The 88 statements address these aforementioned different personality traits that are then paired up in various combinations (and using different wording), so that the aggregate of the candidate's answers establishes a pattern for each of the traits. This pattern, determined by the set of all responses rather than by one single answer from the 44 pairs, helps to form a picture of the candidate's personality, behaviors, and ways of thinking and feeling. Admissions officers and administrators use this picture to determine what the candidate is like and if he or she is a good fit for the aviation program and career, based on prior research and consideration of what types of traits the most successful candidates embody. The personality picture painted can also help screen out candidates who lack the desired traits for program attrition and career success.

Performance Based Measures Battery (PBM) (ASTB)

The Performance Based Measures Battery (PBM) section of the ASTB measures a test taker's processing speed, divided-attention and multitasking ability, and manual dexterity through a variety of tracking tasks and dichotic listening exercises. The battery of exercises in this section evaluates the candidate's ability to accurately complete tracking tasks using a provided stick-and-throttle set, as well as his or her spatial orientation and dichotic listening aptitudes. The PBM exercises assess these skills in isolation as well as in simultaneous usage.

To minimize proctor involvement, the administration of the PBM employs picture screens accompanied by automated instructions. There are seven exercises in the PBM, the first of which evaluates the candidate's situational awareness. The remaining six items are intended to simultaneously measure elements of one's multitasking ability and dexterity in various forms. The candidate's multitasking aptitude is considered the strongest predictor of success in the aviation field. The following descriptions provide basic information about the seven exercises included in PBM:

1. Unmanned Aerial Vehicle (UAV) Test: evaluates spatial orientation and reasoning. The left side of the computer screen presents a North-up oriented tracker map with an aircraft symbol denoting the direction and position in which it is facing. The right side of the screen will show a map with a building and pictures of four adjacent parking lots (shown as gray blocks) that is intended to indicate the camera view relative solely to the aircraft heading. The panel will also include an aircraft symbol and a moveable crosshair. Using the map as a guide, the test taker's first task is to identify each parking lot's cardinal direction. Test takers are then instructed to move the crosshairs by using the joystick to target one of the specified parking lots. It is important to remember that the right panel, in which the test taker is guiding the aircraft, is shown relative to the aircraft heading. Test takers must mentally orient themselves as if they are positioned as the pilot in the aircraft so that they correctly move the crosshairs relative to the aircraft's heading.

It should be noted that test takers are afforded the option to practice this exercise in an unscored trial run prior to attempting it during the scored administration. It is recommended that test takers take advantage of this opportunity for a mock run, to familiarize themselves with the problem constraints as well as the provided equipment: a headset, joystick, and throttle.

2. Dichotic Listening Test (DLT): an audio test in which test takers will hear a series of numbers and letters in groupings through their headset, in one ear or the other. Test takers must listen carefully and will be directed to press one or two buttons on the joystick or throttle in response to the numbers, corresponding to whether an odd or even number (or particular letter sequence) is heard. For example, test takers may hear the following instructions: "Whenever you hear an odd number in your left ear, press the thumb button on the right throttle, and whenever you hear an even number in your left ear, depress the trigger on the joystick." Each audio series, called a string, will consist of seven numbers and/or letters. The DLT contains 40 strings. Speed and accuracy of responses are assessed; incorrect actions will penalize the test taker's score. This type of dichotic multitasking listening skill closely models the management of the many different radios coming into a cockpit. Research has demonstrated that people tend to process audio cues in the right ear faster than the left because the right ear is tied to left brain functions (which include language and speech processing). Audio cues that are isolated in the left ear are processed by the right side of the brain, which lacks the ability to completely process spoken language. Consequently, the information then has to get rerouted to the left side of the brain, causing the slower response time. It can be beneficial for test takers to dedicate additional practice time to left-ear listening.

3. Airplane Tracking Test (ATT): utilizes the right screen panel and the joystick in an exercise that involves tracking and guiding a moving image of a yellow-colored aircraft from the rear perspective. This aircraft moves in two-dimensions (horizontal and vertical) and test takers move red crosshairs in such a

way that demonstrates their ability to follow and anticipate the aircraft's movement. The crosshairs interact with the aircraft like magnets of the same polarity, such that moving the crosshairs toward the aircraft will repel or push the aircraft away. Because of this relationship, the test taker should anticipate the aircraft's movement in his or her tracking, as they attempt to move the aircraft to the desired target. It is important that test takers use finesse when using the throttle. Full-throttle deflections will aggressively intercept and repel the aircraft, which is often undesirable for the exercise. Test takers are informed if they have correctly locked onto the aircraft's trajectory and have leveled up by an information panel at the bottom of the screen. As the level of the exercise advances, the reactiveness of the aircraft increases.

4. Vertical Tracking Test (VTT): like the ATT, the VTT requires test takers to anticipate the aircraft's motion and attempt to "push" it with the crosshairs to the intended targets. The VTT uses the left throttle to control the airplane image presented on the narrower left panel of the screen.

5. Airplane Tracking and Horizontal Tracking Test (AHTT): a simultaneous combination of the ATT and VTT that assesses the test taker's ability to multitask and track both aircrafts at once. It is recommended that test takers practice with video games that incorporate targeting in at least two-dimensions.

6. Airplane Tracking, Vertical Tracking, and Dichotic Listening Test (AVDLT): assesses the candidate's speed, accuracy, and tracking skill when multitasking, combining the DLT and AHTT, utilizing both the right and left screen panels.

7. Emergency Scenario Test (EST): builds on the AHTT exercise by adding three light indicators representing potential emergency scenarios—engine, fire, and propeller—which appear at the bottom of the screen. These emergency indicators will illuminate red and an audio tone will sound to alert that action must be taken. Actions that manipulate the controls for power, fuel, and a reset must be memorized by the test taker because the required emergency procedure differ for each of the three potential dangers. The actions can be a series of buttons or sliders to engage on the throttle and/or joystick, which necessitate memorization skills, multitasking ability, and sustained concentration. The dichotic listening and two-panel tracking tests do enter a distress mode when an emergency sounds, which temporarily allows the speed and accuracy performance of those tasks to be suspended until the test taker has addressed the emergency situation. Instead, scoring during emergency procedures is based on the test taker's speed and accuracy in identifying and completing the appropriate actions, and his or her ability to prioritize this procedure while already multitasking. While this task may sound outrageously complicated, it's a realistic situation for aircraft officers, who often need to multitask, prioritize, and compartmentalize while on a mission. Successful officers must not only develop these multitasking skills cognitively but must also learn emotional control during stressful in-flight situations.

The PBM is the most hands-on, and in many ways, most practical section of the ASTB. As such, it provides valuable information to the test administrators and aviation program admissions officers about the candidate's potential understanding and skills related to the duties of a flight officer. Obtaining a high score on the PBM is important for overall ASTB exam success. While many test takers find this the most "fun" section of the ASTB, the included tasks are often some of the most unfamiliar or newest-learned. For this reason, test takers are encouraged to prepare for the Performance Based Measures Battery by practicing mental rotation problems (such as encountered in the first exercise with the parking lots) and familiarizing themselves with flight simulator software that uses a stick-and-throttle set, if possible.

Biographical Inventory with Response Verification (BI-RV) (ASTB)

The Biographical Inventory with Response Verification (BI-RV) is a self-paced, untimed section of the ASTB that gathers information about the candidate's relevant background experiences. These are applicable and potentially predictable of his or her success in the demanding and fast-paced aviation program and future career. Questions address factors such as high school and collegiate academic achievements and participation in extracurricular activities. The ASTB test developers believe that the BI-RV is a useful predictor of program attrition and aviation service success.

There are 110 questions on the BI-RV and it usually takes test takers between forty-five minutes and two hours and forty-five minutes to complete. Because the BI-RV section is untimed and addresses personal experiences with no universal "right" or "wrong" answers, test takers may complete it on any web-enabled computer, including the candidate's home computer, once an ASTB Examiner has provided them with a username and password. It can be completed either before or after any of the other ASTB sections and does not necessarily need to be completed in one sitting. Questions do not need to be answered in order, though test takers must address all unanswered questions to satisfactorily complete the section. Test takers who wish to take the BI-RV section prior to sitting for the remainder of the ASTB can contact their recruiter to receive the required credentials and instructions. Test takers have ninety days after receiving their login information to complete the BI-RV. It is generally recommended that test takers complete the BI-RV prior to attempting the written sections of the exam, because doing so will permit ASTB score release immediately after the scores for the remaining sections.

Some questions on the BI-RV will prompt test takers to provide further details and verification of their responses during the administration of the section. For example, if a test taker lists a leadership position for their collegiate newspaper, he or she will need to enter further details about this involvement including school name, position title, years of participation, and other salient information in the provided blank lines. It should be noted that the truthfulness of responses on the BI-RV (or any other section on the ASTB) is mandatory. Even if the test taker has already started or completed aviation training, any falsification of provided information is deemed sufficient grounds to disqualify and reject his or her candidacy and eligibility for the aviation program and service.

Because the BI-RV is simply a personal questionnaire addressing the test taker's academic, extracurricular, and aviation-related experiences and accomplishments, there is no way to study for the section. Honesty is the sole requirement. Candidates can prepare by reviewing their potentially-relevant experiences and making a list of positions held and accolades obtained so that this information is readily available when the questions prompt the test taker to verify his or her response with further details.

ASTB/OAR Answer Explanations

Math Skills (ASTB & OAR)

1. D: Start by taking a common denominator of 30. $\frac{14}{15} = \frac{28}{30}, \frac{3}{5} = \frac{18}{30}, \frac{1}{30} = \frac{1}{30}$.

Add and subtract the numerators for the next step:

$$\frac{28}{30} + \frac{18}{30} - \frac{1}{30} = \frac{28 + 18 - 1}{30} = \frac{45}{30} = \frac{3}{2}$$

where in the last step the 15 is factored out from the numerator and denominator.

2. A: From the second equation, add x to both sides and subtract 1 from both sides: $-x + 3y + x - 1 = 1 + x - 1$, with the result of $3y - 1 = x$. Substitute this into the first equation and get $3(3y - 1) + 2y = 8$, or $9y - 3 + 2y = 8, 11y = 11, y = 1$. Putting this into $3y - 1 = x$ gives $3(1) - 1 = x$ or $x = 2$, $y = 1$.

3. C: First, the square root of 16 is 4. So this simplifies to:

$$\frac{1}{2}\sqrt{16} = \frac{1}{2}(4) = 2$$

4. D: The easiest way to approach this problem is to factor out a 2 from each term.

$$2x^2 - 8 = 2(x^2 - 4)$$

Use the formula $x^2 - y^2 = (x + y)(x - y)$ to factor:

$$x^2 - 4 = x^2 - 2^2 = (x + 2)(x - 2)$$

$$2(x^2 - 4) = 2(x + 2)(x - 2)$$

5. B: The total of the interior angles of a triangle must be 180°. The sum of the first two is 105°, so the remaining is $180° - 105° = 75°$.

6. B: The length of the side will be $\sqrt{400}$. The calculation is performed a bit more easily by breaking this into the product of two square roots, $\sqrt{400} = \sqrt{4 \times 100} = \sqrt{4} \times \sqrt{100} = 2 \times 10 = 20$ feet. However, there are 4 sides, so the total is $20 \times 4 = 80$ feet.

7. D: To take the product of two fractions, just multiply the numerators and denominators.

$$\frac{5}{3} \times \frac{7}{6} = \frac{5 \times 7}{3 \times 6} = \frac{35}{18}$$

The numerator and denominator have no common factors, so this is simplified completely.

8. C: Let a be the number of apples purchased, and let p be the number of papayas purchased. There is a total of 15 pieces of fruit, so one equation is $a + p = 15$. The total cost is \$35, and in terms of the total apples and papayas purchased as $2a + 3p = 35$. If we multiply the first equation by 2 on both sides, it becomes $2a + 2p = 30$. We then subtract this equation from the second equation: $2a + 3p - (2a + 2p) = 35 - 30, p = 5$. So five papayas were purchased.

9. A: This equation can be solved as follows: $x^2 = 36$, so $x = \pm\sqrt{36} = \pm 6$. Only -6 shows up in the list.

10. D: The volume of a cube is given by cubing the length of its side.

$$6^3 = 6 \times 6 \times 6 = 36 \times 6 = 216$$

11. A: The area of the square is the square of its side length, so $4^2 = 16$ square inches. The area of a triangle is half the base times the height, so $\frac{1}{2} \times 2 \times 8 = 8$ square inches. The total is $16 + 8 = 24$ square inches.

12. B: $-\frac{1}{3}\sqrt{81} = -\frac{1}{3}(9) = -3$

13. A: Multiply each of the terms in the first parentheses and then multiply each of the terms in the second parentheses.

$$(2x - 3)(4x + 2)$$

$$2x(4x) + 2x(2) - 3(4x) - 3(2)$$

$$8x^2 + 4x - 12x - 6$$

$$8x^2 - 8x - 6$$

14. C: Use a common denominator of 24.

$$\frac{11}{6} - \frac{3}{8} = \frac{44}{24} - \frac{9}{24} = \frac{44 - 9}{24} = \frac{35}{24}$$

15. C: The formula for the area of a triangle with base *b* and height *h* is $\frac{1}{2}bh$, where the base is one-third the height, or $b = \frac{1}{3}h$ or equivalently $h = 3b$. Using the formula for a triangle, this becomes $\frac{1}{2}b(3b) = \frac{3}{2}b^2$. Now, this has to be equal to 6. So $\frac{3}{2}b^2 = 6, b^2 = 4, b = \pm 2$. However, lengths are positive, so the base must be 2 feet long.

16. B: Instead of multiplying these out, the product can be estimated by using $18 \times 10 = 180$. The error here should be lower than 15, since it is rounded to the nearest integer, and the numbers add to something less than 30.

17. D: 30% is $\frac{3}{10}$. The number itself must be $\frac{10}{3}$ of 6, or $\frac{10}{3} \times 6 = 10 \times 2 = 20$.

18. A: These numbers to improper fractions: $\frac{11}{3} - \frac{9}{5}$. Take 15 as a common denominator:

$$\frac{11}{3} - \frac{9}{5} =: \frac{55}{15} - \frac{27}{15} = \frac{28}{15} = 1\frac{13}{15}$$ (when rewritten to get rid of the partial fraction)

19. D: Dividing by 98 can be approximated by dividing by 100, which would mean shifting the decimal point of the numerator to the left by 2. The result is 4.2 and rounds to 4.

20. A: To figure out which is largest, look at the first non-zero digits. Answer *B's* first nonzero digit is in the hundredths place. The other three all have nonzero digits in the tenths place, so it must be *A*, *C*, or *D*. Of these, *A* has the largest first nonzero digit.

21. C: To solve for the value of b, both sides of the equation need to be equalized.

Start by cancelling out the lower value of -4 by adding 4 to both sides:

$$5b - 4 = 2b + 17$$
$$5b - 4 + 4 = 2b + 17 + 4$$
$$5b = 2b + 21$$

The variable *b* is the same on each side, so subtract the lower 2b from each side:

$$5b = 2b + 21$$
$$5b - 2b = 2b + 21 - 2b$$
$$3b = 21$$

Then divide both sides by 3 to get the value of *b*:

$$3b = 21$$
$$\frac{3b}{3} = \frac{21}{3}$$
$$b = 7$$

22. A: Setting up a proportion is the easiest way to represent this situation. The proportion becomes $\frac{20}{x} = \frac{40}{100}$, where cross-multiplication can be used to solve for x. The answer can also be found by observing the two fractions as equivalent, knowing that twenty is half of forty, and fifty is half of one-hundred.

23. A: First, separate each element of the numerator with the denominator as follows:

$$\frac{2xy^2}{16xy} + \frac{4x}{16xy} - \frac{8y}{16xy}$$

Simplify each expression accordingly, reaching answer *A*:

$$\frac{y}{8} + \frac{1}{4y} - \frac{1}{2x}$$

24. C: The first step is to depict each number using decimals. $\frac{91}{100}$ = 0.91

Multiplying both the numerator and denominator of $\frac{4}{5}$ by 20 makes it $\frac{80}{100}$ or 0.80; the closest approximation of $\frac{2}{3}$ would be $\frac{66}{100}$ or 0.66 recurring. Rearrange each expression in ascending order, as found in answer *C*.

25. A: When parentheses are around two expressions, they need to be *multiplied*. In this case, separate each expression into its parts (separated by addition and subtraction) and multiply by each of the parts in the other expression.

Then, add the products together.

$$(3x)(x) + (3x)(-8) + (+5)(x) + (+5)(-8)$$

$$3x^2 - 24x + 5x - 40$$

Remember that when multiplying a positive integer by a negative integer, it will remain negative. Then add $-24x + 5x$ to get the simplified expression, answer *A*.

26. B: First, subtract 4 from each side. This yields $6t = 12$. Now, divide both sides by 6 to obtain $t = 2$.

27. B: To be directly proportional means that $y = mx$. If *x* is changed from 5 to 20, the value of *x* is multiplied by 4. Applying the same rule to the y-value, also multiply the value of *y* by 4. Therefore, *y* = 12.

28. B: From the slope-intercept form, $y = mx + b$, it is known that *b* is the *y*-intercept, which is 1. Compute the slope as $\frac{2-1}{1-0} = 1$, so the equation should be $y = x + 1$.

29. A: Each bag contributes $4x + 1$ treats. The total treats will be in the form $4nx + n$ where *n* is the total number of bags. The total is in the form $60x + 15$, from which it is known $n = 15$.

30. D: Let *a* be the number of apples and *b* the number of bananas. Then, the total cost is $2a + 3b = 22$, while it also known that $a + b = 10$. Using the knowledge of systems of equations, cancel the *b* variables by multiplying the second equation by -3. This makes the equation $-3a - 3b = -30$. Adding this to the first equation, the *b* values cancel to get $-a = -8$, which simplifies to *a* = 8.

Reading Comprehension (ASTB & OAR)

1. B: Kate will either buy the CSC or the DSLR, depending on which one is smaller. We know that Kate "has to buy" a camera for her trip and that "it is a requirement that she must pack the lightest equipment possible." Choice *A* is incorrect. In the passage, we don't see Kate's issue of figuring out which equipment to pack, only which camera to buy. Choice *C* is incorrect. We don't have enough information on the price of the camera to make an educated guess. Choice *D* is incorrect; although we know the camera should be able to fit into Kate's pack, we don't know that Kate is worried about this.

2. C: The two major events did not occur at the same. We know that he worried about the kitten in the morning, and that he found out his son got suspended in the evening. Choice *A* and *D* are incorrect, as the passage states he wasn't too concerned about his son getting suspended. Choice *B* is incorrect; we don't have enough information to make an educated guess about why his son getting suspended didn't bother him.

3. A: Hard water has the ability to reduce the life of a dishwasher. Keep in mind that to make an inference means to make an educated guess based on the facts of the passage. The passage says "hard water can reduce the life of any appliances it touches." Since a dishwasher is an appliance, we can infer that hard water has the ability to reduce the life of a dishwasher. Choice *B* is an opinion and not based on fact. Choice *C* attempts to discredit the passage, and Choice *D* might be true, but we have no evidence of these things in the passage.

4. D: The passage essentially states that coaches help kids on sports teams develop their skills and have fun. Choice *A* is an absolute phrase and is not true in every situation. Choice *B* can be implied, but the passage does not mention the stress of the kids. Choice *C* gives advice beyond the statements in the passage.

5. A: The passage says "when warm, humid air near the ground meets cold, dry air from above, a column of the warm air can be drawn up into the clouds." Thus, we can say that tornadoes are formed from a mixture of cold and warm air. Choice *B* is not necessarily the opinion of the passage. Choices *C* and *D* might be true. However, they are not mentioned in the passage.

6. C: Food travels to the esophagus as soon as it is chewed. Choices *A* and *B* might be correct, but there is no evidence mentioned in the passage. Choice *D* is incorrect; food travels to the stomach after the esophagus, not the other way around.

7. B: Jordan has to decide whether personal experience is more important than research experience. Choice *A* is incorrect; while climate change is a hot topic, we don't know from the passage that it's considered more important than food deserts. Choice *C* is incorrect; although this could happen, it's not the *best* inference of the passage. Choice *D* is incorrect because we know that Jordan is very diplomatic and would not choose a topic in an unfair way. This leaves Choice *B*, which is the best choice because Jordan would be considering the evidence each partner has to offer for the best possible presentation.

8. D: At Disney Cruise Lines, hot weather, lines, and crowds will be less extreme than at Disney parks. Choices *A* and *C* are incorrect and state the opposite sentiment of the passage. Choice *B* might be true, but the passage does not state an opinion of this.

9. B: Drowning happens silently and increases as summer approaches. Choice *A* is incorrect, as this expresses the opposite sentiment. Choice *C* is not mentioned in the passage. Choice *D* uses some of the same language of the passage, but the statement itself is incorrect.

10. C: Out of the last 50 years, the ten warmest years have occurred since 2000. The last 50 years is part of the 134 years that the passage mentions, so this is correct. Choice *A* has no evidence in the passage; neither does Choice *B*. Choice *D* is not mentioned in the passage.

11. A: The author's children's books are more popular than her historical fiction novel. This is expressed by the following statements: "it did not sell as many copies as her children's books." Choices *B, C,* and *D* are not sentiments expressed by the passage.

12. C: Choice *A* may be true; however, it isn't supported by the text and therefore, it is not the best answer. Choice *C* is also true and relies on the passage for its information. Choice *B* is incorrect, as we have no way of knowing what the "deadliest" ingredients are in cigarettes. Finally, Choice *D* is incorrect; we do not know if "every single chemical" is deadly in a single cigarette, and the passage does not say this.

13. C: Elephants lose more heat than anteaters. The passage states directly that "an elephant loses a great deal more heat than an anteater" because an elephant is larger. We have no way of knowing if Choices *A* or *B* are true according to the passage. Choice *D* is opposite of the correct answer.

14. D: Apartment B was in front of Apartment C. We know this because it states that Apartment A was in front of Apartment C. We also know that Apartment A was on top of Apartment B, which automatically makes Apartment B in front of Apartment C. The rest of the answer choices are logically incorrect based on the information given.

15. B: People known as "anti-Stratfordians" are people who believe that Shakespeare was not responsible for writing his own plays. Choice *B* is the only answer choice that recognizes this fact in the passage. All the other answer choices are incorrect.

16. A: Oliver prepares Nina a black bean burger with French fries. This meal does not include dairy or meat, so this should be an example of Oliver "consistently preparing Nina food that is suitable to her diet." Choice *B* includes meat. Choices *C* and *D* include dairy, cheese pizza and a milkshake.

17. D: In Samuel's observation, his best students have minimal interference from parents. Choices *A* and *B* are suggestions, and not inferences from the text. Choice *C* is opposite of the correct answer.

18. C: Cynthia doesn't eat meat due to preference as well as necessity. Choices *A* and *B* are incorrect because they don't paint the full picture of Cynthia's situation. Choice *D* is incorrect, as this information is not mentioned in the passage.

19. D: The way Samantha's life is set up currently, she has to decide between working at the restaurant and going to law school. Choice *C* is tempting. However, since Samantha cannot afford college on her own, getting a degree in nutrition is simply not an option in this world. Choices *A* and *B* are opinions, and we cannot make an educated guess with the information provided.

20. B: Barbara returned the $150 bike and bought the $75 bike. Look at the language. In the world of the passage, Barbara "always" went for cheaper machinery but "hardly ever" returned items. Therefore, there was a possibility Barbara would return the bike, but there wasn't a possibility she would keep the more expensive bike. With Choices *A* and *D*, we do not have sufficient information to make an educated guess.

Mechanical Comprehension (ASTB & OAR)

1. C: The answer is 1800 seconds:

$$\left(45\,km \times \frac{1000\,m}{km}\right) \Big/ 25\frac{m}{s} = 1800\,seconds$$

2. D: The answer is 3.6 kilometers east of its point of departure. The ship is traveling faster than the current, so it will be east of the starting location. Its net forward velocity is 0.5 m/s which is 1.8 kilometers/hour, or 3.6 kilometers in two hours.

3. B: The answer is 2 m/s^2:

$$a = \frac{\Delta v}{\Delta t} = \frac{132\frac{km}{hr} - 60\frac{km}{hr}}{10\,seconds}$$

$$\frac{70\frac{km}{hr} \times 1000\frac{m}{km} \times \frac{hour}{3600\,sec}}{10\,seconds}$$

$$2\,m/s^2$$

4. C: The answer is 50,000 N. The equation *F* = *ma* should be memorized. All of the values are given in the correct units (kilogram-meter-second) so just plug them in.

5. B: The answer is 200 kilograms. This is actually a trick question. The mass of the astronaut is the same everywhere (it is the weight that varies from planet to planet). The astronaut's mass in kilograms is calculated by dividing his weight on Earth by the acceleration of gravity on Earth: 1962/9.81 = 200.

6. A: The answer is that the upward velocity is at a maximum when it leaves the punter's toe. The acceleration due to gravity reduces the upward velocity every moment thereafter. The speed is the same at points A and E, but the velocity is different. At point E, the velocity has a maximum *negative* value.

7. C: The answer is her angular velocity increases from (a) to (b) as she pulls her arms in close to her body and reduces her moment of inertia.

8. B: The answer is 14 m/s. Remember that the cannonball at rest "y" meters off the ground has a potential energy of $PE = mgy$. As it falls, the potential energy is converted to kinetic energy until (at ground level) the kinetic energy is equal to the total original potential energy:

$$\frac{1}{2}mv^2 = mgy \text{ or } v = \sqrt{2gy}$$

This makes sense because all objects fall at the same rate, so the velocity *must* be independent of the mass (which is why "D" is incorrect). Plugging the values into the equation, the result is 14 m/s. Remember, the way to figure this quickly is to have $g = 10$ rather than 9.81.

9. B: The answer is at Point C, the bottom of the arc.

10. C: This question isn't difficult, but it must be read carefully:

A is incorrect. Even though the total energy is at a maximum at Points A and E, it isn't equal at only those points. The total energy is the same at *all* points. *B* is incorrect. The kinetic energy is at a maximum at C, but not the *total* energy. The correct answer is *C*. The total energy is conserved, so it's the same at *all* points on the arc. *D* is incorrect. The motion of a pendulum is independent of the mass. Just like how all objects fall at the same rate, all pendulum bobs swing at the same rate, dependent on the length of the cord.

11. C: The answer is 10kg x 2m x 9.81m/s^2. This must also be read carefully. Choice *D* is incorrect because it isn't necessary to know the ground elevation. The potential energy is measured *with respect* to the ground and the ground (or datum elevation) can be set to any arbitrary value.

12. B: The answer is 1 centimeter. Remember that the force (*F*) required to stretch a spring a certain amount (*d*) is given by the equation $F = kd$. Therefore, $k = F/d$ = 20N/0.5 cm = 20 N/cm. Doubling the weight to 20 N gives the deflection:

$$d = \frac{F}{k} = \frac{20N}{20N/cm} = 1\ centimeter$$

All of the calculations can be bypassed by remembering that the relation between force and deflection is linear. This means that doubling the force doubles the deflection, as long as the spring isn't loaded past its elastic limit.

13. A: The answer is 981 N. The start-up and sliding friction forces are calculated in the same way: normal force (or weight) times the friction coefficient. The difference between the two coefficients is 0.1, so the difference in forces is $0.1 \times 1000 \times 9.81 = 981\ N$.

14. C: The answer is 1.6 m^2. The pressure created by the load is 50N/0.1m^2 = 500 N/m^2. This pressure acts throughout the jack, including the large cylinder. Force is pressure times area, so the area equals pressure divided by force or 800N/500N/m^2 = 1.6m^2.

15. D: The answer is *(F/A)* x (V_2 -V_1). Remember that the work for a piston expanding is pressure multiplied by change in volume. Pressure = *F/A*. Change in volume is (V_2 - V_1).

16. C: The answer is 500 J/s. Choice *A* is incorrect because kg x m/s^2 is an expression of force, not power. Choice *B* is incorrect because N·m is an expression of work, not power. That leaves Choices *C* and *D*, both of which are expressed in units of power: watts or joules/second. Using an approximate calculation (as suggested):

$$1000\,kg \times 10\frac{m}{s^2} \times 30\,m = 300{,}000\,N\cdot m \quad \text{so} \quad \frac{300{,}000\,N\cdot m}{600\,seconds} = 500\,watts = 500\,J/s$$

17. B: The answer is 12,000 Pa. The top of the block is under 12 meters of water:

$$P = 1000\frac{N}{m^3} \times 12\,meters = 12{,}000\frac{N}{m^2} = 12{,}000\,Pa$$

There are two "red herrings" here: Choice *C* of 14,000 Pa is the pressure acting on the *bottom* of the block (perhaps through the sand on the bottom of the bay). Choice *D* (that it can't be calculated without knowing the top area of the block) is also incorrect. The top area is needed to calculate the total *force* acting on the top of the block, not the pressure.

18. B: The answer is that the water level rises in B but not in A. Why? Because ice is not as dense as water, so a given mass of water has more volume in a solid state than in a liquid state. Thus, it floats. As the mass of ice in Basin A melts, its volume (as a liquid) is reduced. In the end, the water level doesn't change. The ice in Basin B isn't floating. It's perched on high ground in the center of the basin. When it melts, water is added to the basin and the water level rises.

19. B: The answer is 5000 seconds. The volume is $3 \times 25 \times 50 = 3750\,m^3$. The volume divided by the flow rate gives the time. Since the pump capacity is given in liters per second, it's easier to convert the volume to liters. One thousand liters equals a cubic meter:

$$Time = \frac{3{,}750{,}000\,liters}{750\,liters/second} = 5000\,seconds = 1.39\,hours$$

20. A: The answer is 30 m^3/s. One of the few equations that must be memorized is *Q* = *vA*. The area of flow is 1m×10m because only half the depth of the channel is full of water.

21. B: The answer is 737.75 N. This is a simple calculation:

$$\frac{9.81\,m}{s^2} \times 150\,kg \times 1.5\,m = 3\,m \times F \quad \text{so} \quad F = \frac{2207.25\,N\cdot m}{3\,meters}$$

22. D: The answer is 40 N. Use the equation *F* = *L* x *r/R*. Note that for an axle with a given, set radius, the larger the radius of the wheel, the greater the mechanical advantage.

23. D: The answer is counterclockwise at 30 RPM. The driver gear is turning clockwise, and the gear meshed with it turns counter to it. Because of the 2:1 gear ratio, every revolution of the driver gear causes half a revolution of the follower.

24. B: The answer is 30 RPM, counterclockwise (B). While meshed gears rotate in different directions, wheels linked by a belt turn in the same direction. This is true unless the belt is twisted, in which case they rotate in opposite directions. So, the twisted link between the upper two wheels causes the right-hand wheel to turn counterclockwise, and the bigger wheel at the bottom also rotates counterclockwise. Since it's twice as large as the upper wheel, it rotates with half the RPMs.

25. C: The answer is $F_1 = 1000$ N; $F_2 = 500$ N. In case (a), the fixed wheels only serve to change direction. They offer no mechanical advantage because the lever arm on each side of the axle is the same. In case (b), the lower moveable block provides a 2:1 mechanical advantage. A quick method for calculating the mechanical advantage is to count the number of lines supporting the moving block (there are two in this question). Note that there are no moving blocks in case (a).

26. C: According to the *ideal gas law* ($PV = nRT$), if volume is constant, the temperature is directly related to the pressure in a system. Therefore, if the pressure increases, the temperature will increase in direct proportion. Choice *A* would not be possible, since the system is closed and a change is occurring, so the temperature will change. Choice *B* incorrectly exhibits an inverse relationship between pressure and temperature, or $P = 1/T$.

27. A: According to Ohm's Law: $V = IR$, so using the given variables: 3.0 V = I × 6.0 Ω

Solving for I: I = 3.0 V/6.0 Ω = 0.5 A

Choice *B* incorporates a miscalculation in the equation by multiplying 3.0 V by 6.0 Ω, rather than dividing these values. Choices *C* and *D* are labeled with the wrong units; Joules measure energy, not current.

28. C: The weight of an object is equal to the mass of the object multiplied by gravity. According to Newton's Second Law of Motion, $F = m \times a$. Weight is the force resulting from a given situation, so the mass of the object needs to be multiplied by the acceleration of gravity on Earth: $W = m \times g$. Choice *A* is incorrect because, according to Newton's first law, all objects exert some force on each other, based on their distance from each other and their masses. This is seen in planets, which affect each other's paths and those of their moons. Choice *B* is incorrect because an object in motion or at rest can have inertia; inertia is the resistance of a physical object to change its state of motion. Choice *D* is the Doppler effect, so this is incorrect.

29. C: In any system, the total mechanical energy is the sum of the potential energy and the kinetic energy. Either value could be zero but it still must be included in the total. Choices *A* and *B* only give the total potential or kinetic energy, respectively.

30. B: To solve this, the number of moles of NaCl needs to be calculated:

First, to find the mass of NaCl, the mass of each of the molecule's atoms is added together as follows:

23.0g (Na) + 35.5g (Cl) = 58.8g NaCl

Next, the given mass of the substance is multiplied by one mole per total mass of the substance:

4.0g NaCl × (1 mol NaCl/58.5g NaCl) = 0.068 mol NaCl

Finally, the moles are divided by the number of liters of the solution to find the molarity:

(0.068 mol NaCl)/(0.120L) = 0.57 M NaCl

Choice *A* incorporates a miscalculation for the molar mass of NaCl, and Choice *C* incorporates a miscalculation by not converting mL into liters (L), so it is incorrect by a factor of 10. Choice *D* is incorrect.

Aviation and Nautical (ASTB)

1. A: The pressure below the airfoil needs to be greater to push upwards on the airfoil. If the pressures are equal, there will be no lift generated at all, and if the pressure above is greater, the pressure from above would actually push down on the airfoil, generating negative lift.

2. D: Since the effective load is double its normal weight, the load factor is 2. In this case, simple eyeballing of the numbers is likely enough to solve this problem. If the numbers were less convenient, the problem could still be solved by using the equation, $G=L_1/L_0$. Using 4000 as L_1 and 2000 as L_0, the result would be G=4000/2000, which equals 2.

3. D: Parasitic drag and profile drag both increase as airspeed increases. Induced drag decreases as airspeed increases. Both parasitic drag and profile drag are created by air resistance, which increases the faster the helicopter is going. However, induced drag is created by backwash from the main rotor and thus, it depends only on the angle of attack of the helicopter, which is typically lower in higher speed flight.

4. A: Raising the collective pitch control increases the pitch of the blades, which increases the angle of incidence. This generates lift, which results in increased altitude and drag, which then reduces the RPM, if the throttle is not simultaneously increased to compensate.

5. C: The governor utilizes an electronic sensor, which is fully-automated to maintain the RPM of the rotor blades. The governor does not, however, control the pitch of the rotors. That function is reserved for the collective pitch control and cyclic pitch control.

6. D: The tilt of the disk and the direction of horizontal movement are both directional with the cyclic pitch control. Therefore, both will go in the same direction that the cyclic pitch control is pushed, which, in this case, is left.

7. B: The anti-torque pedals allow the helicopter to alter its heading left and right. The pedals cannot move the nose up and down, nor can they create forward or backwards thrust. The cyclic is the instrument that controls the helicopter's attitude and is responsible for creating the thrust that moves the helicopter forwards and backwards.

8. A: All of the listed items are included in a basic empty weight except for the pilot. Had the question asked about the licensed empty weight, both *A* and *D* would have been correct, as the transmission oil is not included in that case.

9. C: While overloading a helicopter can cause a shifted center of gravity (if the helicopter is not properly managed), that is not a direct effect of overloading a helicopter. Structural damage and decreased performance, however, are both potential effects of overloading, regardless of how the weight is distributed.

10. A: A nose-down position means that there is more weight located near the front of the helicopter; thus, the helicopter is front-loaded. Had the helicopter been aft-loaded, the nose would have pointed up, and a centrally-balanced helicopter would be parallel with the ground.

11. C: If the heading is moving, the anti-torque pedals are used to compensate. The cyclic pitch control would be used to counteract a horizontal shift in position, rather than heading. Additionally, like all controls, the anti-torque pedals should be adjusted slowly to avoid over-controlling.

12. C: A moving object like a car would make a poor point of reference as it would be difficult—if not impossible—to figure out whether its shift relative to the current position is a result of its movement on the ground or the movement in the air. Likewise, using another helicopter as reference, even if that helicopter is also in hover, is ill-advised, as there is no guarantee its position is stable. Using one's own tail rotor is incorrect, given that this piece is attached solidly to the helicopter and will always appear stationary relative to the rest of the helicopter. A building, however, is fixed to the ground, which makes it an excellent point of reference.

13. C: Altitude, RPM, and position should ideally remain constant while performing a turn. Changing the heading, however, is the purpose of the maneuver.

14. B: Increased clearance is only necessary for rearward flight, and though there is some loss of visibility in making sideward motion versus forward motion, this is a more significant issue in rearward hovering flight. While RPM does decrease when adjusting the pitch of the blades, this is true of all maneuvers. Only the weathervane effect of the tail is truly unique to sideward hovering flight.

15. D: All three items should be avoided whenever possible, as they can all increase the risk of damage, either to the helicopter itself or to objects around it.

16. C: The power, balance, and flight controls must be checked before takeoff to ensure the helicopter can safely perform the maneuver. Fuel levels should also be sufficient for the planned mission. In contrast, the RPM should not be significantly changing during a hover, although it will need to be checked while performing the maneuver.

17. B: The cyclic pitch control is used to control airspeed. The anti-torque pedals are used to control heading, the throttle controls RPM, and the collective pitch controls altitude.

18. B: A nose-down helicopter is most often the result of a front-loaded center of gravity. Excessive torque results in the helicopter spinning, while insufficient power prevents the helicopter from successfully taking off.

19. C: By using the 10% rule, it is clear that leveling out at 240 feet before the target is ideal. If the helicopter does not begin leveling out until 220 or 200 feet, the helicopter will almost certainly overshoot the target, while stopping too early may result in ending short of the desired destination.

20. D: The pilot, cargo, and the fuel are all inside the helicopter and are counted towards the maximum internal weight. An object supported by a winch, however, is outside the helicopter and is instead applied to the maximum external weight.

21. B: The cyclic is an acceleration control and holding the cyclic down will cause the helicopter to continuously accelerate. Since the helicopter is in a hover, and high speeds should be avoided while performing forward flight, the correct method is to apply brief pressure, allowing the helicopter to accelerate to some speed and then release the cyclic to maintain that speed. Increasing the collective would only work to increase speed if the helicopter already had a forward attitude.

22. A: Skidding is caused when the rate of turn is too great for the angle of bank. Therefore, the solution to skidding is to decrease the rate of turn, which requires either less pressure on the pedal in the direction of the turn (in this case, left) or more pressure on the pedal in the opposite direction. While increasing the banking angle (by applying additional left pressure on the cyclic) would also stop the skidding, it would also make the banking angle greater, which would have numerous other effects. For this reason, correcting the anti-torque pedals is the preferred method.

23. A: Removing the offending weight is the simplest way to correct a bad center of balance. While applying forward cyclic would treat the symptoms of the problem, doing so would not do anything to resolve the root of the issue and would still result in reduced performance. The throttle has nothing to do with the center of balance and given that most fuel reserves are in the rear of the helicopter, adding fuel would likely exacerbate the problem.

24. C: Once effective translational lift has been reached, step two has officially ended, but since the pilot has only just entered ETL and applied the cyclic, the helicopter has not yet reached step four. Therefore, the helicopter is currently at step three.

25. B: Using the anti-torque pedals would help if the nose was drifting to the side, but if the helicopter itself is displaced from the flight path, the anti-torque pedals wouldn't help. Likewise, ignoring the problem or trying to hurry past the problem won't solve anything. Removing cargo will also not help in this situation. Using the cyclic to nudge the helicopter back solves the problem without creating any new ones and is the ideal answer.

26. C: Increasing the throttle will increase the power, which creates more torque. Decreasing the collective would actually decrease the torque, assuming that the throttle was appropriately controlled to keep RPM constant. The cyclic primarily rotates the rotor disk to convert lift to thrust and does not directly increase the torque of the helicopter.

27. C: Parasitic drag, not induced drag, is strongest at higher speeds, and profile drag is created by the airfoil striking the air. Induced drag actually generally gets less potent as airspeed increases. This is created by the vacuum left behind by the airfoils and the air rushing to fill that hole. Induced drag does, however, create the drag in the direction of lift, which is why induced drag's significance depends on the attitude of the helicopter.

28. D: If takeoff power is in question, the pilot should wait until the temperature cools off, and the density altitude will decrease. Also, departures should be planned either in the morning or later in the day. If possible, the load on the aircraft should be reduced or fuel burned off to reduce weight. If the takeoff is attempted and the aircraft does not have sufficient power, it could put the aircraft in an unsafe flight profile.

29. D: Takeoff, while a common maneuver, is not considered a fundamental maneuver, primarily because takeoff is at most performed once per flight, while turning, climbing, descending, and flying straight will be performed constantly.

30. A: While an improperly-calibrated cyclic is possible, something like that would most likely be noticed immediately, and the cyclic somehow getting more uncalibrated during flight would not explain why the pilot saw the helicopter slowly dropping. A higher air density would indeed have an impact on a helicopter's flight, but air density would change at such a slow gradient that the change would be imperceptible to the human eye. If the tail was producing too much torque, the tail would move horizontally, not vertically. Fuel, however, does have weight, and as the fuel is consumed, the weight of the remaining fuel would decrease.

31. A: The nose of the helicopter always follows the direction the collective is moved. For example, if the collective is increased, the nose of the helicopter pitches up. It does the opposite when lowered. Also, when the collective is raised, it takes the left pedal to counteract the torque effect and the right pedal when the collective is reduced.

32. A: When raising the collective, more power will be needed to keep RPM up, which will require raising the throttle in sync. More power to the rotor will result in more torque, which will require using the anti-torque pedals to compensate. The cyclic, however, should not be needed during this maneuver, except perhaps to negate any drift caused by wind. Were the helicopter in forward flight, the cyclic would need to have slight rearwards pressure applied to account for the additional lift creating additional thrust.

33. D: With the cyclic pushed forward, additional lift is created by the rotor disk tipping forward, but this comes at the expense of lift. Thus, the collective will need to be raised to keep altitude up, which will require additional power from the throttle and additional counter torque from the anti-torque pedals.

34. C: Profile drag is fairly consistent at most speeds, and although profile drag does increase somewhat with airspeed, parasitic drag rapidly catches and then surpasses profile drag in magnitude.

35. B: Weathervaning occurs when the wind blows at the helicopter and strikes the tail, which usually sticks out significantly from the rest of the body. This effect makes attempting to turn the helicopter into the wind (and thus, turning the tail with it) require less power, while attempting to turn the helicopter with the wind (and the tail into it) requires more power. While this makes turning at all points trickier, the effect becomes particularly challenging when the helicopter reaches a heading directly with the wind. At this point, the wind will go from resisting the turn to assisting with the turn, which can result in the helicopter turning much faster than expected. The opposite happens when the heading is into the wind, at which point the wind goes from assisting the turn to opposing it. This will often stall the turn, giving the pilot plenty of time to adjust the controls to accommodate the problem.

36. A: While the throttle will need to be increased as the collective increases to maintain RPM, the throttle should never be used to increase the rotor's RPM beyond the normal range. Applying additional forward cyclic will actually decrease the rate of climb as the greater angle of attack results in greater thrust, but reduced lift. Therefore, decreasing the angle of attack by applying rearward pressure will result in less thrust being generated, but more lift, thus increasing the rate of climb.

37. A: Straight-and-level flight is actually the best place for a heavily encumbered helicopter as the angle of attack is usually lowest there, allowing for less thrust and more lift. Similarly, there is no reason to avoid a takeoff from hover, if the helicopter has sufficient power to do so. The main reason most heavily-laden helicopters use a takeoff from surface instead is that they are too heavy to hover properly; thus, they are unable to perform the maneuver. However, performing a steep banking turn can be very dangerous in a heavy helicopter as the load factor can get rather high and potentially damage the helicopter or reach a point where the helicopter cannot produce enough power to maintain altitude, resulting in an undesired descent.

38. D: Both weather and air density can affect the efficiency of the air rotor and, thus, the G load. However, while the helicopter's weight does have an effect on the actual effective load on the helicopter, the G load is a multiplicative factor applied to—rather than derived from—the weight of the helicopter to determine the helicopter's effective weight.

39. A: Even in ideal conditions, unless the helicopter is preparing to takeoff or is already in straight and level flight, there is no reason for the helicopter to move faster than a brisk walk.

40. D: The cyclic is an acceleration-controlled instrument, while both the collective and throttle are position-controlled. Only the anti-torque pedals are rate-controlled.

41. B: Faster flow of air over the wing than beneath it. The air moves over the curved surface of the wing at a higher rate of speed than the air moves under the lower flat surface, which creates lift due to the aircraft's forward airspeed and enables flight.

42. B: Longitudinal. The ailerons are mounted on the trailing edges of the wings, and they are used for controlling aircraft roll about the longitudinal axis.

43. A: Lateral. Elevators are mounted on the trailing edges of horizontal stabilizers and are used for controlling aircraft pitch about the lateral axis.

44. C: Vertical. The rudder is mounted on the trailing edge of the vertical fin and is used for controlling rotation (yaw) around the vertical axis.

45. C: Aileron. The aileron is a primary flight control.

46. D: Slats. Slats are part of the wing. The tail assembly of an aircraft is commonly referred to as the empennage. The empennage structure usually includes a tail cone, fixed stabilizers (horizontal and vertical), and moveable surfaces to assist in directional control. The moveable surfaces are the rudder, which is attached to the vertical stabilizer, and the elevators attached to the horizontal stabilizers.

47. B: Skate. Depending on what the aircraft is used for, it may have skis, skids, or floats, instead of tires, for landing on ice or water.

48. B: Semicoque. There are two types of fuselage structures: truss and monocoque. The truss fuselage is typically made of steel tubing welded together, which enables the structure to handle tension and compression loads. In lighter aircraft, an aluminum alloy may be used along with cross-bracing. A single-shell fuselage is referred to as monocoque, which uses a stronger skin to handle the tension and compression loads. There is also a semi-monocoque fuselage, which is basically a combination of the truss and monocoque fuselage and is the most commonly used. The semi-monocoque structure includes the use of frame assemblies, bulkheads, formers, longerons, and stringers.

49. A: The pilot. To ensure an aircraft is being operated properly, a pilot needs to be familiar with the aircraft's flight envelope before flying.

50. C: Stalling speed. The stalling speed is the minimum speed at which an aircraft can maintain level flight. As the aircraft gains altitude, the stall speed increases, since the aircraft's weight can be better supported through speed.

51. B: Service ceiling. The maximum altitude of an aircraft is also referred to as the service ceiling. The ceiling is usually decided by the aircraft performance and the wings, and it is where an altitude at a given speed can no longer be increased at level flight.

52. D: Drag. Drag is the force generated when aircraft is moving through the air. Drag is air resistance that opposes thrust, basically aerodynamic friction or wind resistance. The amount of drag is dependent upon several factors, including the shape of the aircraft, the speed it is traveling, and the density of the air it is passing through.

53. B: Levels the aircraft in flight. The horizontal stabilizer provides for leveling of aircraft in flight. If the aircraft tilts up or down, air pressure increases on one side of the stabilizer and decreases on the other. This imbalance on the stabilizer will push the aircraft back into level flight. The horizontal stabilizer holds the tail down as well, since most aircraft designs induce the tendency of the nose to tilt downward because the center of gravity is forward of the center of lift in the wings.

54. C: The outer trailing edge of the wing. Ailerons are located on the outer trailing edges of the wings and control the roll of an aircraft.

55. D: Stall. An aircraft stall occurs at the critical AOA, where the induced drag exceeds the lift. During a stall, the wing is no longer able to create sufficient lift to oppose gravity. Stall angle is usually around 20°.

56. A: Landing. There are four fundamental maneuvers in flight: straight-and-level, turns, climbs, and descents. Every controlled flight usually includes a combination of these four fundamentals.

57. C: Torque. Torque from the engine turning the main rotor forces the body of the helicopter in the opposite direction. Most helicopters use a tail rotor, which counters this torque force by pushing or pulling against the tail.

58. B: Collective control. The collective control is used to increase the pitch of the main rotor simultaneously at all points of the rotor blade rotation. The collective increases or decreases total rotor thrust; the cyclic changes the direction of rotor thrust. In forward flight, the collective pitch changes the amount of thrust, which in turn can change the speed or altitude based on the use of the cyclic. During hovering, the collective pitch will alter the hover height.

59. B: 3 to 5 miles away. Visual approach slope indicator (VASI) is a light system designed to provide visual guidance during approach of a runway. The light indicators are visible 3 to 5 miles away during daylight hours and up to 20 miles away in darkness. The indicators are designed to be used once the aircraft is already visually aligned with the runway.

60. A: Horizontal. Non-precision instrument runways provide horizontal guidance only when there is an approved procedure for a straight-in non-precision instrument approach.

61. C: Sixteen Battleships. The Great White Fleet was introduced to the Navy by President Theodore Roosevelt in 1907 and quickly became part of the Navy's pride and joy, voyaging around the world from the end of 1907 to the beginning of 1909. Choice *A* refers to the first American Navy, Choice *B* refers to the German submarines during WWI, and Choice *D* refers to deserters of the British Royal Navy in the 1800s.

62. A: A marlinspike is a life-size model of a U.S, Navy ship, which allows new recruits to practice many skills, including line handling, mooring (securing a ship), and basic seamanship. Choice *B* refers to a mess deck worker, Choice *C* refers to an exchange of goods or services, and Choice *D* refers to a water fountain.

63. B: The right side of a ship is known as the starboard. It gets its name from old merchant sailing ships in which the steering board was on the right side. An old English term, *steobord,* refers to the steering side of a ship. Choice *A* refers to the port, Choice *C* refers to the stern, and Choice *D* refers to the bow or stem.

64. D: Littoral Combat Ships. *Littoral* refers to anything that is on or near a shoreline and is a term that dates back nearly 400 years. Choices *A*, *B*, and *C* are incorrect, as they all refer to vessels that head out to sea.

65. C: GPS, which stands for Global Positioning System, is a sophisticated and modern system of navigation that uses satellite signals to detect the nearly precise location of radio receivers on the Earth's surface. Choices *A*, *B*, and *D* are incorrect because not the ARPA, the Echo Sounders, nor the LORAN use satellites.

66. B: The Naval Meteorology and Oceanography Command (NMOC) is responsible for well over 2,000 military and civilian personnel found throughout the globe with one centralized focus—to strengthen naval operations via international partnerships and cooperation. Choices *A*, *C*, and *D* are all incorrect. None of these terms exist as operations or agencies within the U.S. Navy.

67. D: Dead Reckoning, or DR for short, refers to the ability to determine a vessel's or aircraft's location based on the vessel's or aircraft's course record, the distance covered, knowledge of its starting location, and knowledge of its approximate drift. Although not confirmed, the term may have originated from the *Dutchman's log*—an object capable of floating that was tossed into the water and labelled as *dead*. The vessel's operator could then approximate the vessel's speed relative to this dead and motionless object in the water. Choice *A* is incorrect because it refers to the transmission of microwave signals, Choice *B* is incorrect as it refers to the imaginary lines that run vertically around the Earth, and Choice *C* is incorrect as it refers to the use of satellite signals to determine an object's position.

68. A: The vessel is NOT permitted to pass. One of the widely-accepted rules regarding open water rights of way states that any time a give-way vessel signals five blasts of its horn, it is explicitly refusing the stand-on vessel's request to pass. Choice *B* is incorrect because two short blasts give permission to pass, and Choices *C* and *D* are incorrect, as they are not part of any navigation rules on the open water.

69. A: Landing Platform Docks (LPDs) are amphibious warfare vessels that not only transport forces onto enemy lands but can also house hundreds of troops and crew members. The U.S. Navy operates the largest fleet of LPDs in the world. Choice *B* is incorrect, as a Cruiser is NOT a dock, Choice *C* is incorrect because dry docks are not landing platform docks, and Choice *D* is incorrect because there is no dock that is synonymous with helicopter pads.

70. C: Illness, Medication, Stress, Alcohol, Fatigue, and Emotion. As part of its effort to ensure the safety and wellbeing of its entire personnel, the U.S. Navy has incorporated a personal safety and wellbeing checklist known as the IMSAFE. It encourages all enlisted personnel to monitor their personal health each and every day. Each member is responsible for monitoring his or her general state of health, use of medications, stress levels, alcohol consumption, level of fatigue, and emotional stability. Choices *A*, *B*, and *C* are all incorrect, as they are nonexistent in the U.S. Navy safety regulations.

Dear Officer Candidate Test Taker,

We would like to start by thanking you for purchasing this study guide for your exam. We hope that we exceeded your expectations.

Our goal in creating this study guide was to cover all of the topics that you will see on the test. We also strove to make our practice questions as similar as possible to what you will encounter on test day. With that being said, if you found something that you feel was not up to your standards, please send us an email and let us know.

We have study guides in a wide variety of fields. If you're interested in one, try searching for it on Amazon or send us an email.

Thanks Again and Happy Testing!
Product Development Team
info@studyguideteam.com

Interested in buying more than 10 copies of our product? Contact us about bulk discounts:

bulkorders@studyguideteam.com

FREE Test Taking Tips DVD Offer

To help us better serve you, we have developed a Test Taking Tips DVD that we would like to give you for FREE. **This DVD covers world-class test taking tips that you can use to be even more successful when you are taking your test.**

All that we ask is that you email us your feedback about your study guide. Please let us know what you thought about it – whether that is good, bad or indifferent.

To get your **FREE Test Taking Tips DVD**, email freedvd@studyguideteam.com with “FREE DVD” in the subject line and the following information in the body of the email:

a. The title of your study guide.

b. Your product rating on a scale of 1-5, with 5 being the highest rating.

c. Your feedback about the study guide. What did you think of it?

d. Your full name and shipping address to send your free DVD.

If you have any questions or concerns, please don’t hesitate to contact us at freedvd@studyguideteam.com.

Thanks again!

Made in the
USA
Middletown, DE

75699881R00289